W9-BRU-696

CRIME and PUNISHMENT
in *Early Massachusetts*

CRIME and PUNISHMENT in *Early Massachusetts* 1620 - 1692

A DOCUMENTARY HISTORY

By Edwin Powers

BEACON PRESS : BOSTON

Library of Congress catalogue card number 66-14490

Published simultaneously in Canada by Saunders of Toronto, Ltd.

Beacon Press books are published under the auspices
of the Unitarian Universalist Association

Printed in the United States of America

ACKNOWLEDGMENTS

MY greatest debt is to the men of seventeenth century Massachusetts whose words constitute the major part of this study and particularly to those who, with a sense of history, recorded in longhand their very personal feelings about the innate sinfulness of man and the need for his reformation and correction. I am indebted also, to the scholars who came after them, transcribed those handwritten documents (often almost illegible) and made them accessible to the world in scores of well-indexed historical and legal volumes. Although I have drawn largely from original documents, I have profited from the constantly increasing number of scholarly works on special phases of Colonial life, too numerous to mention here but acknowledged in appropriate footnote references.

The Social Law Library in the Suffolk County Court House and the Boston Public Library in Copley Square have been my chief sources of inspiration. The State Library at the Capitol also has been a constant source of information over the years. I would like particularly to express my deep appreciation to Mr. Edwin G. Sanford, reference assistant in the Public Library who, because of his extensive familiarity with Colonial history has reduced some of the inevitable frustrations of historical research; to Mr. Leo Flaherty in the office of the Massachusetts Archives who has been an able guide through the dark forests of original documents; to Karl Hill and Carl Seaburg, from Beacon Press, whose editorial encouragement and advice sustained me over the years; to Edward Darling, Director of the Department of Publications of the Unitarian Universalist Association who kept the fires lit beneath my chair; and finally to Hiller B. Zobel, co-editor of the *Legal Papers of John Adams* who read the entire manuscript and offered helpful suggestions.

CONTENTS

ILLUSTRATIONS

PREFACE

"IT may justly be marveled at," as William Bradford, the second governor of Plymouth Colony might have put it, that of the interminable array of books that tell the fascinating story of the founding of Massachusetts, its emergence into a body politic, and the gathering of Congregational churches by those who sought to follow the Gospel "in its puritie," none, to my knowledge, has taken as its focus a description of criminal behavior in seventeenth century Massachusetts and of the punishments inflicted upon the social offender. Yet, in the town of Plymouth, the seat of government of the little Colony of New Plymouth, and in the town of Boston of the Bay Colony, penology in America had its inception.

It is the purpose of this book to provide historical perspective to our present system of administering criminal justice in the Commonwealth. That is the formal justification, if one is needed, for offering one more contribution to the very extensive literature on that significant period of American history. Perhaps it would be more candid to say that the words of the chief actors in the drama as they came to life out of the venerable documents so intrigued me that, once launched on the task, there was no turning back—a task that has occupied much of my time and thoughts for more than a decade.

The nature of this book is simply a report of crime and punishment in the words of those who punished and those who suffered. To avoid the serious fault of taking their words completely out of context, I have attempted in some measure to relate them to the social, religious, and political temper of the times. Like all who write of events that occurred three centuries ago, I have tried always to keep in mind that I was not a participant-observer (although there were times when I was almost sure that I was); that I could not cross-examine my witnesses nor summon to the stand any of the vast throng of humble citizens who left no written record of their thoughts; that I was limited to a selected number of available letters, essays, sermons, diaries, and official documents; and that whatever came to my view was perceived through my own life experiences. I have therefore tried to avoid the role of judge and, if I have been critical of the Colonial people for doing that which today we could not condone or if I have been an apologist for their infliction of crude penalties upon those whose behavior or theological doctrines did not measure up to the strict Puritan standards of those formative years, it was not my original design. In short, this report is not an analytical or interpretive history of seventeenth century Massachusetts. It is my hope that the records will speak for themselves and that the reader will draw his own conclusions. If my own point of view shows through, as I presume it will, so be it.

This story of crime and punishment spans a period of 72 years, from the founding of Plymouth Colony in 1620 to the year 1692 when it merged with the Massachusetts Bay Colony to become a royal Province. Inquisitive readers who may ask what happened in succeeding centuries will find at the conclusion of most chapters an epilogue that in brief compass seeks to bring the story down to modern times.

Primary sources most frequently used were the official court records of Plymouth Colony, of the Massachusetts Bay Colony and of Suffolk and Essex Counties, the diaries of Bradford, Winthrop and Sewall, the many publications of the Massachusetts Historical Society and the Colonial Society of Massachusetts and the well-preserved documents of the Massachusetts Archives. These documents are more fully described in the "List of Abbreviations" on p. 564. Many other helpful sources of information are cited in the footnotes to each chapter.

Care has been taken to preserve the original orthography of all quoted passages, but I should mention a few minor changes. I have replaced the character "y" with "th" for which it stood, thus changing "y^{e}" to "the," "y^{t}" to "that," and "y^{n}" to "then;" while words shortened in the text have been spelled out, such as "common" for "com̄on," "letter" for "lẽr," "which" for "w^{ch}," and so on. The letter "v" has been changed to "u" and "i" to "j" where appropriate. Abbreviations for pound, shilling, and pence (li, s, and d) have also been spelled out. I have not attempted to relate these monetary values to present-day purchasing power because constant variations in the seventeenth century and modern inflationary trends would make the task a formidable one with little significance.

The plain literary style of the writers of that period was, for the most part, clear, straightforward, and colorful, needing no embellishment from me. I have tried to keep before me the ideal Bradford set for himself in his distinguished history "Of Plimoth Plantation," in describing the events leading up to the sailing of the *Mayflower,* which, he wrote:

> I shall endevor to manefest in a plaine stile, with singuler regard unto the simple trueth in all things, at least as near as my slender judgmente can attaine the same.

E.P.

Boston, Massachusetts
September 15, 1965

CRIME and PUNISHMENT
in *Early Massachusetts*

PROLOGUE

"A MOST EXCELLENT PLACE"

If the little Ant, and the sillie Bee seek by their diligence the good of their Commonwealth; much more ought Man.—*Capt. John Smith, 1616.*

WITH that clarion call to every Englishman to do his duty, Captain John Smith introduced his renowned publication, *A Description of New-England: or The Observations, and Discoveries, of Captain John Smith (Admirall of that Country) in the North of America, in the year of our Lord 1614. . . .*[1]

His courage, resourcefulness, and intelligence brought distinction to his name as a warrior, explorer, navigator, and mapmaker. But our present concern with this "Admirall of New-England" (a title conferred on him by his commercial backers, the Plymouth Company in London) is in his role as the most effective propagandist for New England, a name he himself gave to the eastern seaboard from Penobscot Bay to Cape Cod. His claim to fame rests no less on his daring enterprises than on his ability to tell about them in an enchanting and very personal manner, although, like successful propagandists of modern times, he may have overshot the truth in the interests of a highly exciting narrative. What later generations learned about this proud and stalwart character came largely from his eight publications (and their various revisions) printed in England during the years 1608 to 1631. His genuine enthusiasm for New England as he cruised along its coast and mapped its capes and harbors probably did much to put England into the plantation business, lending encouragement to those who sought to cast their lots with the Plymouth Colony or the Massachusetts Bay Colony, whose treatment of the social offender is the object of this documentary history.

Prior to his New England venture, Smith had already won a secure place for himself in the annals of American history for his part in the settlement of Jamestown, Virginia, in 1607, the first permanent settlement by Englishmen in North America. There his leadership, his talents as a shrewd Indian trader, and his skill in the arts of war, in which he was an old hand, saved that colony from early extinction. The best known incident in his two and a half years in the Chesapeake Bay area was his dramatic rescue from certain death (as he tells the story himself) at the hands of the Indian chief Powhatan when the Chief's young daughter, Pocahontas, who had come to know and admire the Captain, pleaded for him and "hazarded the beating out of her owne braines" to save his life.[2]

In his last publication (1631), reflecting on his adventuresome life in the service of kings and princes—and his commercial sponsors—he sketches the highlights of his career:

> Having beene a slave to the Turks,[3] prisoner amongst the most barbarous Salvages, [and] after my deliverance commonly discovering and ranging those large rivers [in the Chesapeake Bay country] and unknowne Nations [of Indians] with such a handfule of ignorant companions, that the wiser sort often gave mee [up] for lost, always in mutinies, wants and miseries [the disputes among the Virginia colonists as to who should be their president were bitter and never ending], blowne up with gunpowder [at Jamestown in 1609 he was seriously burned by an accidental explosion of gunpowder]; A long time prisoner among the French Pyrats [on his third attempt to cross the Atlantic from England, in 1615, pirates seized his ship through the treachery of his own crew] from whom escaping in a little boat by my selfe, and adrift, all such a stormy winter night when their ships were split, more than an hundred thousand pound lost, they had taken at sea, and most of them drowned upon the Ile of Ree [Ile de Ré, near LaRochelle, France, on the Bay of Biscay], not farre from whence I was driven on shore in my little boat, etc. And many a score of the worst of winter moneths lived in the fields; yet to have lived neere 37. yeares in the midst of wars, pestilence and famine; by which, many an hundred thousand have died about mee, and scarce five living of them went first with me to *Virginia*, and see the fruits of my labours thus well begin to prosper: though I have but my

labour for my paines, have I not much reason both privately and publickely to acknowledge it and give God thankes, whose omnipotent power onely delivered me, to doe the utmost of my best to make his name knowne in those remote parts of the world, and his loving mercy to such a miserable sinner. . . .[4]

The Captain represented the best type of English gentleman of that period, loyal to his church, his King, and his country. He was also a man of exemplary habits, if we may judge by a tribute paid him by one of his soldiers who fought with him in Transylvania in 1602:

"I never knew a Warryer yet, but thee,
From wine, Tobacco, debts, dice, oaths, so free.[5]

A portrait of Smith at the age of thirty-seven graces his map of New England, showing a man of strong features partially covered by an ample mustache and a full beard. Beneath the portrait are these lines:

These are the Lines that shew thy Face, but those
That shew thy Grace and Glory, brighter bee:
Thy Faire-Discoveries and Fowle-Overthrowes
Of Salvages, much Civilliz'd by thee
Best shew thy Spirit; and to it Glory Wyn;
So, thou art Brasse without, but Golde within.[6]

Smith showed a persistent devotion to duty and a compelling desire to promote the commercial interests of England in America. To those who were willing to take a chance, he held out new hope in a new land, promising that there, with a little effort, they would find more happiness than sitting by the fireside at home, oblivious of the vast undiscovered lands across the sea. In a note to the readers of his book on navigation he wrote:

. . . my greatest error . . . is but a desire to do good; which disease hath ever haunted mee since my child-hood; and all the miseries and ingratitudes I have indured cannot yet divert me from that resolution. . . .[7]

In April 1614, with two sailing vessels he arrived at the "Ile of Monahigan" [now Monhegan, an island about twenty-five miles southwest of Penobscot Bay in Maine] but with no intention of planting a colony.[8] His financial backers in London hoped he would "take Whales and make tryalls of a Myne of Gold and Copper." Whaling proved to be quite unprofitable. "We saw many," he reported, "and spent much time in chasing them; but could not kill any: they beeing a kinde of Jubartes [blackfish ?] and not the Whale that yeeldes Finnes and Oyle as wee expected. . . ." Nor was he any more successful in locating gold and copper, but he managed to return to England, after his eighty-day cruise along the New England coast, with a shipload of furs acquired in Indian trading and a quantity of fish. In the meantime he had mapped the coastline with remarkable accuracy, considering the navigational tools of that period. The coastal area from Penobscot to Cape Cod he quite naturally named "New-England," knowing that the King would approve. "At my humble sute," he wrote, "our most gracious King *Charles,* then Prince of *Wales,* was pleased to confirme it by that title, and did change the barbarous [Indian] names of the principall Harbours and habitations for such English, that posterity may say, King *Charles* was their Godfather; and in my opinion it should seeme an unmannerly presumption in any that doth alter them without his leave."[9] Alterations, however, were beyond the king's power to prevent. Only four of the many names proposed by Smith and entered on his map remain to this day: New England (formerly known by various names—Norumbega, North Virginia, Nuskoncus, Penaquida or Cannada); Cape Anna or Anne (formerly Cape Tragabigzanda, first proposed by Smith in honor of a Turkish lady who had befriended him in earlier years but, fortunately, changed by the King to Cape Anna and so entered on Smith's map); Charles River (formerly Massachusetts River, taking its name from the Indian tribe of that region); and Plymouth or New Plymouth or New Plimoth (formerly Accomack or Patuxet). Even "Smiths Iles," a group of small islands off what is now the New Hampshire coast, commemorating this distinguished explorer, now bear the name of the "Isles of Shoals." As for "Cape Codd," Smith recoiled from naming it after a mere fish and sought to dignify it by naming it "Cape James," after the British monarch, but the popular name given it by Gosnold a dozen years earlier prevailed.[10]

Upon his return to England, Smith immediately took pen in hand and produced his appealing *Description of New-England* in which he wrote:

Map of New England, 1620–1692

The Countrie of the Massachusets [that is, of the Massachusets Indians] which is the Paradise of all those parts. For, heere are many Ilse all planted with [Indian] corne; groves, mulberries, salvage gardens, and good harbours: the Coast is for the most part, high clayie sandie cliffs. ... Cape Cod ... is onely a headland of high hils of sand overgrowne with shrubbie pines, hurts [huckleberries], and such trash; but an excellent harbour for all weathers. This Cape is made by the maine Sea on the one side, and a great Bay on the other in forme of a sickle; on it doth inhabit the people [Indians] of Pawmet .... [11]

At the time of Smith's explorations the little plantation in Virginia had been all but wiped out by an Indian massacre but managed somehow to survive; the Dutch had "sat down" in the vicinity of the mouth of the Hudson River; the French had settled in the north country and along the St. Lawrence River but, strangely, "the New-England coast is yet still but unknowne and undiscovered." No Europeans had yet permanently settled in that beautiful and bountiful country that Smith believed was the "paradise of all those parts." He proudly gave the world his personal opinion:

Of all the foure parts of the world that I have yet seene not inhabited [and he had travelled, he said, in Europe, Asia, Africa, and America], could I have but meanes to transport a Colonie, I would rather live here then [than] any where.... [12]

Through his many writings published in London, Smith soon became renowned as the great advocate for New England. In 1616 he made a sound prediction that if "men of industrie, judgement and experience" should venture to plant a colony there "it might equalize [equal] any of those famous Kingdomes [of Europe, Asia and South America] in all commodities, pleasures and conditions ...."[13] His vivid descriptions of New England read like a release from a modern Chamber of Commerce:

The healthfulnesse of the aire, the richnesse of the soile, the goodnes of the woods, the abundance of fruits, fish, and fowle in their season.... [14]

I have sounded about five and twenty very good Harbors; in many whereof is Ancorage for five hundred good ships of any burthen, in some of them for a thousand, and more than three hundred Iles overgrowne with good timber ... and pure springs of most excellent water pleasantly distilling from their rockie foundations.... [15]

He wrote of the abundance of "bevers, otters, martins, blacke foxes" for the fur trade, as well as a variety of game for the hunter. He spoke of the "excellent soyle" for the farmer and the healthfulness of the climate and the "moderate temper of the ayre." Of his twenty-five men only two were sick—"but two that were many yeares diseased before they went." Reports of severe New England winters were dismissed with this statement:

> Some infirmed bodies, or tender educats, complaine of the piercing cold, especially in January and February, yet the French in Canada, the Russians, Swethlanders, Polanders, Germans, and our neighbour Hollanders, are much colder and farre more Northward; [and] for all that, rich Countreyes and live well. . . . New-England is in the heighth [latitude] of the North cape of Spaine, which is 10. degrees, 200. leagues, or 600. miles nearer the Sunne [the equator] than wee, . . .[16]

For those seeking profit, Smith had much to say. He believed (as most of his contemporaries did) that gold and silver and other precious metals would be found in New England, although he admitted that that discovery had not yet been made. "I am no alchymist," he said. But the fishing industry held out the promise of being incredibly lucrative:

> . . . honorable and worthy Countrymen let not the meannesse of the word *Fish* distaste you, for it will afford as good gold as the mines of Guiana or Tumbatu, with lesse hazard and charge, and more certaintie and facilitie. . . .[17]

Smith reported that his company had "taken by hookes and lines with fifteene or eighteene men at most, more than 60000. Cod in lesse than a moneth."[18] He is a bad fisherman who "cannot kill in one day with his hooke and line, one, two, or three hundred Cods."[19] There were not only a good supply of cod but there were "herring, ling, mullet and sturgion." Aside from the profit motive, there was fishing as a sport:

> . . . and what sport doth yeeld a more pleasing content, and lesse hurt or charge, then [than] angling with a hooke; and crossing the sweete ayre from Ile to Ile, over the silent streames of a calme Sea? wherein the most curious may finde pleasure, profit, and content. . . .[20]

And shellfish and lobsters!

> You shall scarce finde any bay, shallow shore or Cove of sand, where you many not take many clamps or Lobsters, or both at your pleasure, and in many places load your Boat if you please. . . . Worthy is that person to starve that here cannot live if [he] have strength and health, for there is no such penury of these blessings in any place but that one hundred men may in two or three houres make their provisions for a day, and he that hath experience to manage these affaires, with forty or thirty honest industrious men, might well undertake . . . to subject the Salvages, and feed daily two or three hundred men, with as good Corne, Fish, and Flesh as the earth hath of those kinds. . . .[21]

In short, New England "was a most excellent place, both for health and fertility. . . ."[22] Of course, there would be skeptics—who could believe these stories of such opulence?

> But if an Angell should tell you [that] any place yet unknowne can afford such fortunes; you would not beleeve him, no more then [than] *Columbus* was beleeved [that] there was any such land as is now the well knowne abounding *America*. . . .[23]

Yet Smith thought there should be a word of warning. Planting a colony, he wrote, was "not a worke for every one." It called for "all the best parts of art, judgement, courage, honestie, constancie, diligence and experience to do but neere well. . ."—traits and experience that Smith himself had in abundance.

How was it that a man so well equipped for leadership in a wilderness and so charmed by the richness of New England did not become the leader of the first permanent British colony in that area? Such fame was within his grasp. On his first trip to New England, though poorly equipped, he was tempted to stay; indeed, "had the fishing for Whale proved as we expected," he claimed, "I had stayed in the Country."[24] Standing on the high poop deck of his little sailing vessel as she slowly plowed her way back to England, he must have reflected on this enticing idea a thousand times. The very next year (1615) he stood ready to make another attempt. With the backing of some London merchants, he set out for America with great hopes and with a determined purpose "to beginne a Plantation." But his ships were no match for the fury of an Atlantic storm. "By extreme tempests that bore neare all my Masts by the boord," he wrote, "being more than two hundred leagues [six hundred miles] at Sea, was forced to returne to Plimoth [England] with a Jury-Mast."[25] The following year, four years before the *Mayflower* venture, he risked his life and his estate in another attempt, but English and French pirates intercepted his ships and he was cast up on the shores of France.[26] Were it not for these wicked pirates, history might have recorded the establishment of the Church of England at Plymouth and the ensuing chronicles of developments would have been totally different.

On his return to England, he made one more resolute effort to get merchants and adventurers together but found the task "more than a worke for *Hercules,* so violent is the folly of greedy covetousnesse."[27] He soon heard of the preparations of the "Brownists" (known to posterity as the Pilgrims) to set sail on the now famous *Mayflower.* His hopes revived. He promptly offered his knowledge and skill to the leaders if they would hire him as their navigator and captain. Again he met disappointment. "To save charges," he wrote, the Brownists "would try their owne conclusions, though with great losse and much miserie, till time had taught them to see their owne error; for such humorists [fanatics] will never beleeve well, till they bee beaten with their owne rod." He wryly commented later that the *Mayflower* adventurers endured "a wonderfull deale of misery, with an infinite patience; saying my books and maps were much better cheape to teach them, than my selfe."[28] If Smith had been hired as their Captain, instead of Miles Standish, their "wonderful deale of misery" might have been held to a minimum, yet Smith would probably not have proved a very congenial travelling companion on a long voyage, for he was an ardent Church of England man and would have found himself in a company where the leaders were fervent Separatists who loathed that Church and had been miserably treated by its bishops.

Smith was probably one of the best informed navigators of his day on the subject of American discoveries and explorations. He listed in his publications the names of those who preceded him: Columbus, the Cabots, Americus, Drake, Raleigh, Frobisher, Champlain, and many others. He read the noted works of Richard Hakluyt, English geographer and naval historian, whose *The Principall Navigations, Voyages, Traffiques and Discoveries of the English Nation* was a comprehensive compilation of all available manuscripts penned by the earliest English explorers.[29] Smith was, of course, familiar with the cruise of Batholomew Gosnold, an English navigator who established the first, though brief, English settlement in New England. In 1602 Gosnold and his men settled on the island of Cuttyhunk, one of the islands in a group that he called Elizabeth Isle, not far from what is now Woods Hole, but his stay was brief.[30] Before his return to England, Gosnold gave the name Cape Cod to that arm of sand stretching out into a sea full of codfish.

God had evidently prepared the land for his chosen people. He had effectively tamed the savages. When Smith arrived in New England he heard reports, later confirmed by many others, that a strange, swift, and virulent plague had sent most of the young and vigorous native warriors into early graves, thus depriving the tribes of the strength to drive the strange "white men" into the sea, as they might well have done. Smith, as well as the Pilgrims and the Puritans who followed in the next few decades, saw in this fatal epidemic the beneficent hand of God. His comments are representative of the popular belief of Christians of that period:

> . . . there is vast land enough for all the people in England, Scotland, and Ireland: and it seems God hath provided this Country for our Nation, destroying the natives by the plague, it not touching one Englishman, though many traded and were conversant amongst them; for they had three plagues in three years successively neere two hundred miles along the Sea coast, that in some places there scarce remained five of a hundred. . . .[31]

Smith saw here a ready solution to the problem of the unemployed and destitute that England was then struggling with. That solution was emigration to New England where—as succeeding generations proved—there was land enough to:

> . . . entertain all the poore artificers and laborers in *England,* and their families which are burthensome to their Parishes and Countries where they live, upon almes and benevolence for want of worke, which if they would but pay for their transportation, they should never be troubled with them more.[32]

In the last of his published works, Smith appealed to readers who might have still had some reservations about establishing or underwriting a plantation in New England, by four thoughtful arguments:[33]

1) *The Englishman's lawful right to possess those lands.*

> Many good religious devout men have made it a great question, as a

matter in conscience, by what warrant they might goe to possesse those Countries, which are none of theirs, but the poore Salvages. Which poore curiosity will answer it selfe; for God did make the world to be inhabited with mankind, and to have his name knowne to all Nations, and from generation to generation: as the people increased they dispersed themselves into such Countries as they found most convenient. And here in *Florida, Virginia, New-England,* and *Cannada,* is more land than all the people of Christendome can manure [cultivate], and yet more to spare than all the natives of those Countries can use and culturate. And shall we here [in England] keepe such a coyle [much ado] for land, and at such great rents and rates [taxes], when there is so much of the world uninhabited, and as much more in other places, and as good or rather better than any wee [English] possesse, were it manured and used accordingly. If this be not a reason sufficient to such tender consciences; for a copper knife and a few toyes, as beads and hatchets, they [the Indians] will sell you a whole Countrey; and for a small matter, their houses and the ground they dwell upon; but those of the *Massachusets* have resigned theirs freely . . . .

2) *Biblical precedent for it.*

. . . *Adam* and *Eve* did first begin this innocent worke to plant the earth to remaine to posterity, but not without labour, trouble, and industry: *Noah* and his family began againe the second plantation, and their seed as it still increased, hath still planted new Countries, and one Country another, and so the world to that estate it is; but not without much hazard, travell, mortalities, discontents, and many disasters: had those worthy Fathers and their memorable offspring not beene more diligent for us now in those ages, than wee are to plant that yet unplanted for after-livers; had the seed of Abraham, our Saviour Christ Jesus and his Apostles, exposed themselves to no more dangers to plant the Gospell wee so much professe, than we, even our selves had at this present beene as Salvages, and as miserable as the most barbarous Salvage, yet uncivilized.

3) *The great Princes of the world planted colonies and brought civilization to "barbarous and inhumane Nations."*

The Hebrewes, Lacedemonians, the Goths, Grecians, Romans, and the rest, what was it they would not undertake to inlarge their Territories, inrich their subjects, and resist their enemies. Those that were the founders of those great Monarchies and their vertues, were no silvered idle golden Pharisies, but industrious honest hearted Publicans ... riches was their servants, not their masters; they ruled as fathers, not as tyrants; their people as children, not as slaves; there was no disaster could discourage them . . . .

4) *Should not the English do as much as the Portugese and Spaniards?*

Lastly, the *Portugals* and *Spaniards* that first began plantations in this unknowne world of *America* till within this 140. yeares, whose everlasting actions before our eyes, will testifie our idlenesse and ingratitude to all posterity, and neglect of our duty and religion wee owe our God, our King, and Countrey ... why should English men despaire and not doe so much as any?

The "Admirall's" entrancing stories, appropriately adorned with the colorful rhetoric of that day, telling of hairbreadth escapes and brave encounters with warriors, Turks, and savages, unfortunately cannot be satisfactorily verified, for our knowledge of them comes almost wholly from his own pen, a fact that has caused many an historian to lift a skeptical eyebrow and frankly question his veracity. His copious narrations have inspired many biographies and critical essays, and, among those who have written about him, Smith has also had his staunch defenders. Nevertheless, his voyage to New England shores and his enthusiasm for the country were soon made known to interested and literate Englishmen. His voyage and his enthusiasm are the matters of chief interest to us here, and they have a ring of truth.

At the time Smith ranged the coast of New England, and in the years immediately following, there were others who loved New England and wrote of its charms, but the incomparable "Admirall," because of the vividness of his descriptions, his remarkable map, his genuine fondness for the land he surveyed, and the cogency of his arguments, became the most effective salesman for colonization at that time and had much to do with the early settlement and development of New England.[34]

† † †

One hour of earnest effort to plant a new Colony for Great Britain was worth more in the eyes of the King than a thousand words of description and fervent exhortation. When further English colonization westward became more than an idle dream, it was clearly evident that the American savages could no longer hold exclusive dominion over this "paradise." Emigration from England to America was inevitable. A Massachusetts Colony might become the equal, Smith predicted, of any of the known kingdoms of Europe, Asia, or South America "in all commodities, pleasures and conditions."

Six years after Smith's explorations of the land which he named "New England," the Mayflower Pilgrims, happily supplied with his map (although it was not their original intention of settling there), created in Plymouth the first permanent settlement in Massachusetts. In 1623 agents of the Dorchester (England) Company selected Cape Ann as a temporary, and as it turned out unprofitable, fishing post succeeded in 1628 by a small colony in Naumkeag (later called Salem) under Captain John Endecott who was sent over by the New England Company for a Plantation in Massachusetts Bay.

Between 1625 and 1630 a few individuals chose to establish themselves at Shawmut (later called Boston) and on some of the islands in the harbor and at a few scattered points to the east in territory now within the confines of the states of New Hampshire and Maine, without organizing a plantation in a formal political sense. In 1625, Captain Wollaston, "a man of pretie parts," and Thomas Morton with three or four eminent men and many servants, attempting to begin a plantation, "pitched themselves in a place within the Massachusets, which they called . . . Mount Wollaston" (later changing the name to "Merie-mounte," now part of Quincy). Morton, according to the story by Governor William Bradford of Plymouth Plantation, was a profane, licentious man, "having more craft than honestie." He "became lord of misrule, and maintained (as it were) a schoole of Athisme." He and his company "set up a May-pole, drinking and dancing aboute it many days togeather, inviting the Indean women, for their consorts, dancing and frisking togither, (like so many fairies, or furies rather,) and worse practises. As if they had anew revived & celebrated the feasts of the Roman Goddes Flora, or the beasly practieses of the madd Bacchinalians." Horrified at such ungodly revels, Captain Endecott caused the maypole to be cut down and rebuked them for their profanity and drunkenness but could not dampen their "joylity." When they sold guns to the Indians and taught them how to use them, the Pilgrims decided it was time to step in, not quibbling over their authority to take action against them. Having first admonished Morton and his "wicked & deboste crue" to forbear and having received only disdainful and threatening replies, a company of armed men recruited from the various English settlements thereabout, under the command of the short and stocky Captain Miles Standish (called by Morton, "Captain Shrimpe") advanced upon the revelers and overpowered them. It was an easy task, Bradford reported, because "they were so steeld with drinke as their peeces [guns] were to [too] heavie for them." They transported Morton back to Plymouth and shipped him off for England—the first forced return to his native land for moral turpitude of an emigrant to these shores. But he was irrepressible and soon reappeared in New England.

Finally, a year before his death, Smith may have learned of the founding of the highly successful Massachusetts Bay Colony in 1630 under the leadership of Governor Winthrop and his Puritan friends.

We shall now see how the Plymouth and Bay Colonies, were independently established and how each developed a code of criminal law and procedure that has left its imprint on the present administration of criminal justice in the Commonwealth of Massachusetts.

1. "OF PLIMOTH PLANTATION"

> All great & honourable actions are accompanied with great difficulties, and must be both enterprised and overcome with answerable courages. It was granted the dangers were great, but not desperate; the difficulties were many, but not invincible ... and all of them, through the help of God, by fortitude and patience, might either be borne, or overcome—*Governor William Bradford, 1620.*[1]

ON a wintry sixteenth of December in the year 1620 a perilously overcrowded sailing vessel of 180 tons burden, incongruously called the *Mayflower,*[2] with an original passenger list of 102 men, women, and children and a crew of some forty to fifty mariners,[3] dropped anchor in the protected harbor that Captain John Smith had named "Plimouth." Thus began the first permanent plantation in that part of America that Smith had called "the paradise of all those parts." William Bradford, one of that distinguished company, the second governor of Plymouth Colony and for thirty-seven years its most outstanding leader, left us a vivid history of that great adventure.[4]

The Bradfords, the Carvers, the Brewsters, the Winslows, and others whose names are now well known to students of history did not come from England to this "hideous & desolate wildernes, full of wild beasts & wild men" to foster the whaling industry or to search for mines of gold and silver or to seek a new passage to the South Sea (the Pacific Ocean). They did not share the motivations of Captain John Smith who looked upon New England not only as a "paradise" and one ideally suited for a permanent settlement but also as one that might prove of great commercial value to the Kingdom. Their springs of motivation lay deep in their religious experiences. Some years before their venture into the unknown they had decided to separate from the Church of England, cutting their ties cleanly and forever. They had made this break at a time when corruption, cruelty, and bigotry had brought the Church to a low point, just as the English of the previous century had followed the lead of Martin Luther (1483–1546) who had challenged the Pope and the Catholic hierarchy at a time when the "abuses" of Catholicism were most flagrant.

These deeply religious people were known as "Brownists" after Robert Browne (1550–1593), the first reform leader openly to advocate complete separation from the Church of England. They were more commonly called "Separatists," a literal denotation of their religious position. Although Bradford wrote "they knew they were pilgrimes" (referring to Hebrews 11:13), they were not known to the world as "Pilgrims" until long after the last of them had died. Originally, of course, they were all part of the great Reformation Movement of the sixteenth century, but as time went on they deemed the Protestant attempt to free itself from "popish trash" a feeble effort. They would go much further, desiring fervently to follow the Biblical ordinances in their simplicity, without "the mixture of men's inventions." Bradford believed that although England was the first nation to receive "the lighte of the gospell . . . after that grosse darknes of popery which had covered & overspred the Christian worled," Satan had infiltrated the ranks of the English ecclesiastics and induced them to hold fast against any reform from within. Any man who dared to cry out against the corruption of the Church of England or to seek to restore it to its original purity was in danger of his life. A number of the "Saints" (as Bradford called this little group of reformers of which he was a member) had already died on the block or scaffold, or suffered martyrdom by fire:

> . . . what warrs & opposissions ever since, Satan hath raised, maintained, and continued against the Saincts, from time to time, in one sorte or other. Some times by bloody death and cruell torments; other whiles imprisonments, banishments, & other hard usages; as [Satan] being loath his kingdom should goe downe, the trueth prevaile, and the churches of God reverte to their anciente puritie, and recover their primitive order, libertie, & bewtie. But when he could not prevaile . . . then [Satan] begane to sow errours, heresies, and

> wonderful dissentions amongst the professours them selves ... by which wofull effects followed; as not only bitter contentions, & hartburnings, schismes, with other horrible confusions, but Satan tooke occasion & advantage therby to foyst in a number of vile ceremoneys, with many unprofittable cannons & decrees, which have since been as snares to many poore & peaceable souls even to this day.

To Bradford and his colleagues, the "vile ceremoneys" were inventions of man, or the Devil, with no warrant in Scripture. Or they were borrowed from the Catholic Church, which was worse. Where, he asked, could one find Scriptural justification for archbishops, for a Prayer Book to be read by "dumb ministers" who are incapable of preaching, or for the numerous sacraments of the Church of England—other than baptism and the Lord's Supper? The cure for these "corrupt doctrines" seemed to lie in a return to the "anciente puritie" of worship with its "primitive order, libertie, & bewtie."

The issue, thought Bradford, was clear-cut. The Separatists were fighting for

> the right worship of God & discipline of Christ established in the church, according to the simplicitie of the gospell, without the mixture of mens inventions, and to have & to be ruled by the laws of Gods word, dispensed in those offices, & by those officers of Pastors, Teachers, & Elders, &c. according to the Scripturs. ...[5]

The Church of England, on the other hand

> under many colours & pretences, endevored to have the episcopall dignitie (affter the popish manner) with their large power & jurisdiction still retained; with all those courts, cannons, & ceremonies, togeather with all such livings, revenues, & subordinate officers ... [which] enabled them with lordly & tyranous power to persecute the poore servants of God ... even so farr as to charge (very unjustly, & ungodlily, yet prelatelike) some of their cheefe opposers, with rebellion & hightreason against the Emperour, & such other crimes.

The Separatists, a minor offshoot, were, as Morison put it, "the left-wingers of the Puritan movement."[6] They did not differ from the Puritans in their theological stand but saw a solution to their uncompromising position only in complete separation, while the Puritans retained some slight hope of purifying the established Church as it then existed, retaining substantial ties of loyalty to it.

The Separatists, forerunners of the Congregational church, had no formal ritual or creed, desiring merely to follow

> the infallible word of God, and pure Testamente of Christ, to be propounded and followed as the only rule and pattern for direction herein to all churches & Christians. And it is too great arrogancie for any man, or church to thinke that he or they have so sounded the word of God to the bottome, as precislie to sett downe the churches discipline, without error in substance or circumstance, as that no other without blame may digress or differ in any thing from the same. . . .

It became quite evident to a little group of devout men in the village of Scrooby, England, and others who were like-minded, that reform of the Church from within was a vain undertaking against the power of King James I, the "Defender of the Faith," just as it had been under the rule of Queen Elizabeth. To rebuke the officers of the Church was to defame the power of the state. There seemed to be no alternative but "to flee out of the land." In 1607 the Separatists decided to slip their necks out of the yoke, with no thought then that eventually they would plant a colony in New England.

Holland beckoned. It had already proven friendly to religious refugees who had had the audacity to defy the law forbidding them to leave England. Such defiance proved hazardous, but their desires were "sett on the ways of God . . . and they rested on his providence." After many tribulations, they managed to reach Amsterdam but the following year settled in the university city of Leyden, "a fair and bewtifull citie, and of a sweete situation," where they found opportunities for employment in the textile industry—a new vocation for those simple farmers. Such a decision took courage for

> to goe into a countrie they knew not (but by hearsay), wher they must learne a new language, and get their livings they knew not how, it being a dear [expensive] place, & subjecte to the misseries of warr [with the Spaniards], it was by many thought an adventure almost desperate, a case intolerable, & a misserie worse then [than] death . . . [and it] was not longe before they saw the grimme & grisly face of povertie coming upon them like an armed man . . . but they were armed with faith & patience against him . . . [and] by Gods assistance they prevailed and got the victorie.

There they continued for eleven or twelve years employed in "hard and continuall labor" but eventually managed to "raise a competente & comforteble living" and enjoyed "much sweete & delightefull societie & spirituall comforte togeather in the wayes of God, under the able ministrie, and prudente governmente of Mr. John Robinson [their minister], & Mr. William Brewster [elder of the church]."

"Not out of any newfanglednes, or other such like giddie humor . . . but for sundrie weightie & solid reasons," they decided to quit Holland and undertake a still more hazardous search for spiritual tranquility. Bradford lists four "weightie and solid reasons":

First, he noted that many of their own religious persuasion had remained in England, reluctant to "endure that great labour & hard fare, with other inconveniences" of a totally foreign environment. "Yea, some preferred & chose the prisons in England, rather then this libertie in Holland, with these afflictions. . . ." Thus there seemed to be little hope of building a larger and permanent congregation in Holland. Secondly, old age was stealing upon many of them, "and their great & continuall labours, with other crosses and sorrows, hastened it before the time." Furthermore, the danger of a Dutch-Spanish war became more probable. Thirdly, their children, because of their heavy burdens, "became decreped in their early youth; the vigor of nature being consumed in the very budd as it were." But "more lamentable" was the thought that many of their children, exposed to "the great licentiousnes of youth in that countrie, and the manifold temptations of the place, were drawne away by evill examples into extravagante & dangerous courses, getting the raines off their neks, & departing from their parents." If the strict control of the Puritan father over his sons were relaxed, "their posteritie would be in danger to degenerate & be corrupted." Lastly, "which was not the least," they were filled "with great hope & inward zeal" of advancing "the gospell of the kingdom of Christ in those remote parts of the world."

When discussions turned to a voyage across the mighty Atlantic, there were a few dissenters. Some feared the "many unconceivable perills & dangers," such as "the casulties of the seas (which none can be freed from)." Some thought "the length of the vioage was such, as the weake bodys of women and other persons worne out with age & traville could never be able to endure." But, if they should survive the ordeal by sea, they would face "famine, and nakedness," not to mention the "cruell, barbarous, & most treacherous" Indians or the possibility that "the chang of aire, diate, & drinking of water, would infecte their bodies with sore sickneses, and greevous diseases," for they were well acquainted with reports of the "ill success, & lamentable miseries befalne others in like designes."[7]

The answer to the doubting Thomases was the eloquent statement with which this chapter began. The leaders knew they could put their trust in God for "their ends were good & honourable; their calling lawfull, & urgente," and so they agreed they would proceed "by the best means they could."

After "humble praiers unto God for his direction & assistance . . . they consulted what perticuler place to pitch upon, & prepare for." Some urged Guiana in South America, a rich country "blessed with a perpetuall spring, and a florishing greenes" where food would be plentiful. Christopher Columbus had made note of that country in 1498 and in the following century Sir Walter Raleigh and, later, Dutch traders had visited there and made its advantages known to the world. But its disadvantages were also clear. In tropical countries one was subject to "greevuos diseases, and many noysome impediments" and a climate that "would not so well agree with our English bodys." Then, of course, there was always the "jealous Spaniard" who might overthrow them "as he did the French in Florida."

Virginia, settled in 1607, made known by the reports of Captain John Smith and others, offered an attractive possibility, but there was little likelihood that they could worship there as they pleased if they were neighbors to those who were loyal to the Church of England. Yet if they could obtain a patent for the *northerly* part of Virginia they could live as "a distincte body by them selves." The land under charter by the first Virginia Company (the London Company) extended as far north as forty-one degrees of latitude—just north of what is now Manhattan Island—and it had at that time no permanent settlement. Following months of negotiations with London merchants who were persuaded to underwrite the adventure in return for possible profits in trading and fishing, an agreement was reached with the Virginia Company and a patent was issued in 1620 in the name of John Peirce, granting them a right to settle near the mouth of Hudson's river—a river named by the Dutch by virtue of Henry Hudson's explorations in 1609.[8] Thomas Weston was one of the "adventurers," which was the name given to the financial backers of trading companies, who offered their own financial resources to support overseas projects. Weston insisted on harsh conditions to which the Separatists reluctantly agreed—"all profits & benifits that are gott by trade, traffick, trucking, working, fishing, or any other means . . . remaine still in the commone stock untill the divisions" at the end of seven years, at which time capital and profits would be equally divided between "adventurers" and planters. This was a hard bargain, but the time was late since many had settled their estates and "laid out their moneys" and there was no turning back.

Bradford related in great detail the many harassments and delays in getting the little band of Pilgrims out of Leyden (some of the Separatists came at a later date; some remained there until they died). From Leyden, they went back to England where two ships, the *Speedwell* and the much larger *Mayflower,* were made ready for the great ocean voyage. Twice the smaller ship, after setting its course for America, had to head back to port because of "the generall weaknes of the shipe," being "over masted, and too much pressed with sayles," the crew fearing "shee would not prove sufficiente for the voiage." Bradford later suspected that the *Speedwell's* captain had "ploted this strategem" to free himself from his agreement reluctantly made to take them across the Atlantic. On both occasions the *Mayflower* accompanied the *Speedwell* on her return but finally decided to go across alone, taking on some of the latter's passengers, risking the hazards of overcrowding.

Thus the *Mayflower,* under the command of Christopher Jones, set sail from Plymouth, England, on September 6, 1620, with a varied assortment of passengers and crew. The devout and godly—called by Bradford "the Saints"—constituted a relatively small but dominant group. There were in addition eighteen servants and many "strangers" who had boarded the ship at Southhampton or Plymouth and a large crew of hardy sailors who were not in the least interested in theological discourse or in spreading the gospel of Jesus Christ.

Sixty-five days at sea was an ordeal for the hardiest mariner and a sore trial for those unaccustomed to ocean travel. The Pilgrim Fathers were not old sea dogs or rugged explorers with the zest of a Drake, a Raleigh, or a Smith, nor were they impelled with a relish for the staking out of new territory in the name of the King. They were, for the most part, simple farmers. The only conquest they sought was a personal victory over evil, their only goal the establishment of a new order under God where they might show reverence to the ordinances of Christ.

"Many were afflicted with sea sicknes," while most of them were probably in a state of constant anxiety as the ship encountered "crosse winds, and mette with many feirce stormes." In mid-Atlantic a crisis of major proportions arose when one of the main crossbeams of the ship "bowed & craked, which put them in some fear that the shipe could not be able to performe the vioage." There was muttering among the crew who "were loath to hazard their lives too desperatly". The leaders called a conference, but "ther was great distraction & differences of opinion"—should they continue or turn back? At this turning point in history, the ship's carpenter produced "a great iron scrue" which they had brought with them from Holland. With this timely instrument they managed to raise the beam into its proper place and make everything secure "and so they commited them selves to the will of God, & resolved to proseede." What Bradford did not report when he wrote the story of the voyage ten years later were some of the hardships common to the sailing ships of that day which were taken for granted by all who committed themselves to the capriciousness of wind and wave. The diet was of dried peas and beans and also salt meats, with the absence of fresh vegetables or fruits or milk for the children, which must have proved unappetizing as well as unhealthful. Though the ship was supplied with beer, there was probably a scarcity of good drinking water and little else to be had to quench thirst. There were crowded and uncomfortable sleeping quarters, no fresh water for washing, no toilets, no privacy, no protection from wet weather, and, of course, no heating system and no refrigeration. "What could now sustaine them but the spirite of God & his grace?" What must have proved to be a greater heartache for Bradford and his friends was the utter lack of interest in religious matters on the part of many of the "strangers" and most of the professional mariners whose profanity was an occupational trademark. He recalled with some smug satisfaction the fate of one of the sailors—"a proud & very profane yonge man" who was constantly "contemning the poore people in their sicknes, & cursing them dayly with greevous execrations," saying he would "cast halfe of them overboard before they came to their jurneys end." But "the just hand of God" struck him down with a fatal disease, and he was the first to be thrown overboard. "Thus his curses light on his owne head."

On November 9, just over the *Mayflower's* horizon, appeared the sandy highlands of Cape Cod—many miles north of their objective which, as we have seen, was the land in the vicinity of what is now New York City:

> After longe beating at sea they fell with that land which is called Cape Cod; the which being made & certainly knowne to be it, they were not a litle joyfull. After some deliberation had amongst them selves & with the master of the ship, they tacked aboute and resolved to stande for the southward (the wind & weather being faire) tó finde some place aboute Hudsons river for their habitation. But after they had sailed that course aboute halfe the day, they fell amongst deangerous shoulds and roring breakers, and they were so farr intangled ther with as they conceived them selves in great danger; & the wind shrinking upon them withall, they resolved to bear up againe for the Cape, and thought them selves hapy to gett out of those dangers before night overtooke them, as by Gods providence they did. And the next day they gott into the Cape-harbor wher they ridd in saftie. . . .

With Captain John Smith's map of New England in their hands, they had no doubt that they had made a landfall on the long arm of the Cape, probably in the vicinity of the present Highland Light. The "deangerous shoulds and roring breakers" evidently marked the extension of the arm of the Cape southward into the sea where the water barely covers the sand. These shoals (off the present Monomoy Island) near what is now called Pollock Rip were even then known to be dangerous to shipping. This area, said Bradford, was called "Pointe Care, & Tuckers Terrour; but the French & Dutch to this day call it Malabarr, by reason of those perilous shoulds, and the losses they have suffered their." Since his time, hundreds of ships have been wrecked there, although the dangers have been well marked by buoys. Their decision to turn northward at this point and to make for Cape Cod Harbor (Provincetown) as rapidly as possible was a wise one. It is doubtful if many of the passengers who were deathly sick could have stood the long windward passage to the Hudson, where they would most likely have encountered hostile Indians. The sight of land after sixty-five days of gazing upon the endless expanse of the great Atlantic must have overcome all scruples about not following through to their original objective. Their desire for fresh water for drinking and for washing must have filled their thoughts with a yearning for the nearest harbor where they could anchor and put their feet at last on *terra firma*. Some fifty years later, Bradford's nephew, Nathaniel Morton, Secretary of the General Court of Plymouth Colony, alleged that Captain Christopher Jones, before leaving England, had been bribed by the Dutch to steer clear of their territory and hence had no intention of landing near Hudson's River, but there is no existing evidence to support this unlikely allegation.[9] At any rate, on November 11, the *Mayflower* sailed slowly into Cape Cod Harbor and there dropped her anchor.

> Being thus arrived in a good harbor and brought safe to land, they fell upon their knees & blessed the God of heaven, who had brought them over the vast & furious ocean, and delivered them from all the periles & miseries therof, againe to set their feete on the firme and stable earth, their proper elemente.

Though happy to set feet on solid ground, "their proper elemente," the weak and scurvey-ridden passengers were faced with a bleak outlook as winter approached:

> Being thus passed the vast ocean, and a sea of troubles before in their preparation . . . they now had no freinds to wellcome them, nor inns to entertaine or refresh their weatherbeaten bodys, no houses or much less townes to repaire too, to seeke for succoure. . . . And for the season it was winter, and they that know the winters of that cuntrie know them to be sharp & violent, & subjecte to cruell & feirce stormes, deangerous to travill to known places, much more to serch an unknown coast. Besids, what could they see but a hidious & desolate wildernes, full of wild beasts & willd men? and what multituds ther might be of them they knew not. . . . For summer being done, all things stand upon them with a wetherbeaten face; and the whole countrie, full of woods & thickets, represented a wild & savage heiw. If they looked behind them, ther was the mighty ocean which they

had passed, and was now as a maine barr & goulfe to seperate them from all the civill parts of the world. . . .

The *Mayflower* lay at anchor at the tip of the Cape for five weeks while exploring parties sought a suitable location for a permanent settlement. In their "first encounter" with the Indians, marked by flying arrows and musket shot, there were no casualties on either side, "though their arrows came close by them, & on every side [of] them." "Thus it pleased God to vanquish their enimies, and give them deliverance," and they were assured once more that their fate rested in God's hands. They finally came upon "a harbor fitt for shipping" with "diverse cornfeilds, and litle runing brooks" which presented an appeal in sharp contrast to the bleak sand dunes of Cape Cod Harbor. This was the harbor Captain Smith had named Plymouth, and this location was destined to be the seat of the government of Plymouth Colony until it merged with the Massachusetts Bay Colony in 1692. On December 15, the *Mayflower* weighed anchor and sailed westward across Cape Cod Bay, and, on December 16, "the winde came faire, and they arrived safe in this harbor . . . and the 25. day begane to erecte the first house for commone use to receive them and their goods."

Most of the passengers stayed on board the *Mayflower* as it lay at anchor in Plymouth Harbor, but the strong and ablebodied hurried ashore and fought against time to build their shelters before the coming of the winter snows. Although the *Mayflower* had hoped to return soon to England, for its supply of food and beer was running low, it dared not make the ocean passage in the dead of winter and lingered on until the middle of April, thus offering some protection from winds, storms, and Indians until the building crew had provided adequate living quarters made secure against Indian attacks.

Although the first winter proved to be relatively mild, many of that little band of pioneers were deathly sick with scurvey, a vitamin deficiency disease brought on by a diet completely lacking in fresh fruits and vegetables. Some others were too weak to resist whatever hostile germs were being circulated among them. Obviously, the Pilgrims were poorly prepared for survival in a strange land. Most of them were simple farmers, not explorers. They brought with them inadequate provisions; they lacked the tools for farming or fishing—two occupations upon which their survival depended. But they had the good fortune to meet with Indians who proved to be more helpful than hostile. By modern standards, the whole enterprise would have been considered foolhardy, but one cannot overlook the "faith of our Fathers," born of a trust in a God who would keep a watchful eye over them and who had said, "Man liveth not by bread alone. . . ." This faith was never lost, in spite of the tragic days that followed their landing:

> . . . in 2. or 3. moneths time halfe of their company dyed, espetialy in Jan: & February, being the depth of winter, and wanting houses & other comforts; being infected with the scurvie & other diseases, which this long vioage & their inacomodate condition had brought upon them; so as ther dyed some times 2. or 3. of a day, in the foresaid time; that of 100. & odd persons, scarce 50. remained. And of these in the time of most distres, ther was but 6. or 7. sound persons, who, to their great comendations be it spoken, spared no pains, night nor day, but with abundance of toyle and hazard of their owne health, fetched them woode, made them fires, drest them meat, made their beads, washed their lothsome cloaths, cloathed & uncloathed them; in a word, did all the homly & necessarie offices for them which dainty & quesie stomacks cannot endure to hear named; and all this willingly & cherfully, without any grudging in the least, shewing herein their true love unto their freinds & bretheren. A rare example & worthy to be remembred. . . .

Bradford himself was "near the point of death" and by the following April had "not yet recoverd of his ilnes." But when spring finally smiled on the Plymouth hillside,

> it pleased God the mortalitie begane to cease amongst them, and the sick and lame recovered apace, which put as it were new life into them; though they had borne their sadd affliction with much patience and contentednes, as I thinke any people could doe. But it was the Lord which upheld them, and had beforehand prepared them; many having long borne the yoake, yea from their youth.

And so it came about that the first permanent New England settlement was made without a formal charter authorizing the establishment of a civil government. What right, then, did the colonists have to set up an administration of criminal justice? Who had the right to punish another? Who would be the governors and who would be the governed?

As the *Mayflower* lay at anchor in Cape Cod Harbor and before anyone had gone ashore, the leaders of this group of restless men and women, who were eager to set foot on dry land and who were unfettered by any restrictive charter under the King's seal, sought to resolve these questions. They decided to draw up "a combination"—to which history has given the name "The Mayflower Compact." This decision was

> occasioned partly by the discontented & mutinous speeches that some of the strangers amongst them had let fall from them in the ship—That when they came a shore they would use their owne libertie; for none had power to command them, the patente they had being for Virginia, and not for New-england, which belonged to an other Government, with which the Virginia Company had nothing to doe. And partly that shuch an acte by them done (this their condition considered) might be as firme as any patent, and in some respects more sure. The forme was as followeth:
>
> In the name of God, Amen. We whose names are underwriten, the loyall subjects of our dread soveraigne, Lord, King James, by the grace of God, of Great Britaine, Franc, & Ireland king, defender of the faith, &c., haveing undertaken, for the glorie of God, and the advancemente of the Christian faith, and honour of our king & countrie, a voyage to plant the first colonie in the Northerne parts of Virginia, doe by these presents solemnly & mutualy in the presence of God, and one of another, covenant & combine our selves togeather into a civill body politick, for our better ordering & preservation & furtherance of the ends aforesaid; and by vertue hearof to enacte, constitute, and frame such just & equall lawes, ordinances, acts, constitutions, & offices, from time to time, as shall be thought most meete & convenient for the generall good of the Colonie, unto which we promise all due submission and obedience. In witness wherof we have hereunder subscribed our names at Cap-Codd the 11. of November, in the year of the raigne of our soveraigne lord, King James, of England, France, & Ireland the eighteenth, and of Scotland the fiftie fourth. Ano: Dom. 1620.

Not all of the passengers signed the combination. Only the men were invited to put their signatures to this now famous document. Probably some of the servants and some of the strangers were denied this opportunity, while others refused. But there were 41 signatures—enough to warrant the setting up of a government of a sort and to remove whatever scruples they might have had about inflicting penalties on those who disobeyed the laws they had proposed to enact.

For the early seventeenth century, not far removed from the era of feudalism and the absolute power of kings over the lives of their subjects, this document proved to be a giant step toward the ideal of representative government. Although it did not pretend to establish a democratic form, it laid a foundation for a "civill body politick" in the absence of a charter under the royal seal, and made possible a government of laws.[10]

Shortly after the signing ceremony, they chose as their first governor for one year John Carver, "a man godly & well approved amongst them." As soon as they had built shelters for their goods and habitations,

> they mette and consulted of lawes & orders, both for their civill & military Governmente, as the necessitie of their condition did require, still adding therunto as urgent occasion in severall times, and as cases did require. . . .

For the first few years they administered justice with considerable informality but with a relatively rare degree of humanity. There was little crime in those early years, as the necessity for fighting for their own survival—a fight that half of them lost—inspired sufficient community spirit to hold them together. Bradford reported "some discontents & murmurings" and a few "mutinous speeches & carriags," but "they were quelled & overcome by the wisdome, patience, and just & equall carrage of things by the Governor and better part, which clave faithfully togeather in the maine."

The following April Governor Carver, working in his fields, was stricken ill and died within a few days. His sudden death at the age of approximately 46 "caused great heavines amongst them. . . . He was buried in the best maner they could, with some vollies of shott by all that bore armes; and his wife, being a weak woman, dyed within 5. or 6. weeks after him. Shortly after, William Bradford was chosen Governor in his stead" and, until his death in 1657, he was reelected many times, guiding the Colony with a strong hand through many crises.[11]

In ye name of god Amen. We whose names are vnderwriten,
the loyall subiects of our dread soueraigne Lord King James
by ye grace of god, of great Britaine, franc, & Ireland king,
defender of ye faith, &c.
Haueing vndertaken, for ye glorie of god, and aduancemente
of ye christian faith and honour of our king & countrie, a voyage to
plant ye first Colonie in ye Northerne parts of Virginia. doe
by these presents solemnly & mutualy in ye presence of God, and
one of another, couenant, & combine our selues togeather into a
ciuill body politick; for our better ordering, & preseruation & fur-
therance of ye ends aforesaid; and by vertue hearof to enacte,
constitute, and frame shuch just & equall lawes, ordinances,
Acts, constitutions, & offices, from time to time, as shall be thought
most meete & conuenient for ye generall good of ye Colonie: vnto
which we promise all due submision and obedience. In witnes
wherof we haue hereunder subscribed our names at Cap-
Codd ye .11. of Nouember, in ye year of ye raigne of our soueraigne
Lord king James of England, france, & Ireland ye eighteenth
and of Scotland ye fiftie fourth. An: Dom. 1620.

Portion of a page from Governor Bradford's Diary, showing his copy of the original Mayflower Compact of 1620, which is now lost. Courtesy of the Massachusetts State Library.

2. THE MASSACHUSETTS BAY COLONY

> For wee must Consider that wee shall be as a Citty upon a Hill, the eies of all people are uppon us; soe that if wee shall deale falsely with our god in this worke wee have undertaken and soe cause him to withdrawe his present help from us, wee shall be made a story and a by-world through the world. . . .—*Governor John Winthrop, 1630.*[1]

AS the sailing ship *Arbella,* Captain Peter Milborne master, made its way slowly westward over the "stormye and boystrous" Atlantic in the spring of 1630, John Winthrop, lord of Groton Manor in Suffolk County, England, the first Governor of the Massachusetts Bay Colony,[2] read to his friends his "Modell of Christian Charity," of which the above quotation is a part. The *Arbella,* a ship of 350 tons, about twice the size of the Pilgrims' *Mayflower,* was "manned with 52 seamen, and 28: peeces of ordinance."[3] She was well stocked with "42 Tonnes of beere" (about 10,000 gallons) but had on board only "14 Tonnes of water caske" (about 3,500 gallons)[4] for her ten-weeks' cruise. Formerly bearing the name *Eagle,* she had been rechristened in honor of Lady Arbella Johnson, wife of Isaack Johnson, both of whom were passengers on this voyage. Other distinguished adventurers were Sir Richard Saltonstall, the only titled gentleman on board, an Assistant of the Bay Company and one of the nominees for the governorship when Winthrop was elected,[5] and Thomas Dudley and Simon Bradstreet, both of whom later became governors of the Bay Colony.

This sturdy craft was the flagship of an extraordinary fleet of eleven ships, all pointing their prows toward Massachusetts Bay, the largest assemblage of ships that had ever set out for New England's shores.[6] While four or five of the vessels were used almost exclusively for cattle and freight, some seven hundred men, women, and children were borne across the seas that spring to start a new community in the wilderness.

The *Arbella* left the Cowes near the Isle of Wight (an island a few miles off the English port of Southampton) on March 30, 1630, although almost two weeks passed before she left England behind and headed westward into the broad Atlantic.[7] The passage was relatively uneventful but Winthrop in a letter to his wife described it as "longe and troublesome"; however, he added, "the Lord made it safe and easye to us."[8] They sighted land on June 6 in the vicinity of Cape Sable at the southwestern extremity of Nova Scotia. Captain Milborne had carefully plotted a course farther north than that taken by the Pilgrims' *Mayflower,* fearing "the Southerne shoales. viz. of Cape Cod" that almost spelled disaster for the Pilgrims. As the ship lay in a calm sea within sight of what is now the coast of Maine, they sounded at thirty fathoms and threw over their fishing lines:

> . . . so we putt our shippe a stayes and tooke, in lesse than 2: howres, with a fewe hooks, 67: Coddfishe most of them, verye great fish some 1: yard and ½ long and a yard in Compass. This came verye seasonably for our salt fishe was now spent.

On June 8 as they cruised west southwest along the coast, Winthrop reported "we had now faire sunneshine weather, and so pleasant a sweet ayre, as did muche refreshe us, and there came a smell off the shore like the smell of a garden." On June 12 they passed between Bakers Island and Little Misery Island (about five miles east of Salem harbor) and "came to Anchor a little within the Ilands." That afternoon Captain John Endecott, who had arrived in that area in September of 1628 and had taken over the governorship of "The London Plantacion in Mattachusetts Bay in New England" the following April, went aboard the *Arbella* to extend his official and personal greetings to Winthrop who was to succeed him immediately as Governor of the entire Bay region. Endecott had gone to New England, with the title of Governor, to represent the Council for New England, to salvage what was left of the little settlement on the west side of Gloucester Harbor set up as a trading and fishing post by the "Dorchester [England] Adventurers" in 1623 but which moved to Naumkeag [Salem] in 1626.[9] Endecott invited Winthrop, Captain Milborne, and a few members of Winthrop's party to return with him to Naumkeag where they "supped with a good venyson pastrye, and good beere" while most of the other passengers went ashore to explore the southern edge of Cape Ann where they "gathered store of fine strawberries."

On June 14 the *Arbella* weighed anchor and moved slowly in toward shore, coming to rest "in the inward harbor"—probably the harbor now known as Beverly. The other ships of the fleet arrived within the next few weeks and on July 8 they "kept a daye of thanksgiving in all the plantations."

During the first few months of their struggle for survival and throughout the severe winter that followed, many of the "planters" died, including Isaack Johnson and his Lady, and Winthrop's own son who was lost in a drowning accident at Salem. Scurvy, the curse of sailors on long sea voyages, struck the Winthrop fleet as it had the *Mayflower* a decade earlier, although without such fatal consequences. By 1630 it was vaguely known by seafaring men that the cause of the disease was the lack of fresh vegetables and fruit. Speaking of that first dreadful winter, Winthrop recorded this comment in his diary:

> The poorer sort of people (who laye long in tents etc:) were much afflicted with the Sckirvye, and many dyed, especially at Boston and Charles towne, but when this shippe came [referring to the arrival of the *Lyon* at "Nataskat" on February 5, 1631], and brought store of Juice of Lemons, manye recovered speedyly.

In the face of heavy burdens, Winthrop himself never lost heart. In his first letter to his wife who had delayed her departure for New England, telling her of the loss of his son, Henry—"ah poore childe"—and of the "many sadd and discomfortable thinges" encountered, he gave her this assurance:

> Yet for all these thinges (I prayse my God) I am not discouraged, nor doe I see cause to repent, or dispaire of those good dayes heere, which will make amends for all.[10]

In a later letter, dated September 9, 1630, by which time some of the fainthearted had returned to England, Winthrop again testified to his faith in God that sustained him through all his tribulations:

> We doe hope, that our dayes of Affliction will soone have an ende.

. . . it is enough that we shall have heaven, though we passe through hell to it. we heer enjoy God and Jesus Christ, is not this enough? What would we have more? I thanke God, I like so well to be heer, as I doe not repent my comminge: and if I were to come againe, I would not have altered my course, though I had foreseene all these Afflictions.[11]

Although some dropped by the wayside, at least four hundred new settlers plodded on through the winter and formed the nucleus of a government that was later to merge with the Colony of New Plymouth to constitute the Province Government, and eventually the Commonwealth of Massachusetts. Before the year 1630 was out, the Bay Colony population grew to three times the size of the Plymouth Colony. Many of the first arrivals settled around Charlestown, Boston, Dorchester, Watertown, Roxbury, and Salem. During the next decade when the Anglican Church, under Archbishop Laud, bore down heavily on the Nonconformists many more vessels braved the Atlantic, transporting some 20,000 souls to the "New Canaan," a fact later referred to as "the great migration." Historians are in general agreement that the bulk of those who came to New England came from the middle and the more economically favored classes.[12]

On June 17, 1630, the leaders of the Company sought a suitable location for a permanent settlement: "We went to mattachusetts [meaning Massachusetts Bay or, more specifically, that part now known as Boston harbor and vicinity] to find out a place for our sitting downe. we went up mistick river about 6: miles."

Evidently Winthrop liked what he saw in that area for he later there laid out his farm—"Ten Hills" he called it—and built a summer home close to the Mystic River. The following year the General Court awarded him a grant of six hundred acres of land at "Misticke."[13] But Mishawum (the Indian name for Charlestown) seemed the most logical place for the seat of government. It was already the home of a few settlers who had come over in 1629 and had begun "to build a Towne there which wee doe call Cherton, or Charles Towne."[14] On the banks of the Charles River with easy access to the harbor and the sea, it appealed to Winthrop and Dudley who started to build their houses there. There the first Court of Assistants met on August 23, 1630. And there also on July 30 the Governor, the Deputy Governor Thomas Dudley, Isaack Johnson, and the Rev. John Wilson, their minister, drew up and signed a solemn covenant establishing their first church. They resolved to be joined "into one Congregation, or Church, under the Lord Jesus Christ our Head" which was later to be called the First Church and is now known as The First Church in Boston.[15]

Thus Charlestown might have become the permanent seat of government and eventually the capitol of the Commonwealth. But, at a time when there was a great deal of serious illness, its water supply presented a grave problem:

> The griefe of this people was further increased by the sore sicknesse which befell among them, so that almost in every Family Lamentation, Mourning, and woe was heard, and no fresh food to be had to cherish them, it would assuredly have moved the most lockt up affections to Teares no doubt, had they past from Hut to another, and beheld the piteous case these people were in, and that which added to their present distresse was *the want of fresh water,* for although the place did afford plenty, yet for the present they could finde but one Spring, and that not to be come at, but when the tide was downe, which caused many to passe over to the South-side of the River where they afterward erected some other Townes. . . .[16] (Italics added.)

There were at that time a few other small settlements not far from Charlestown that might have offered a solution to the problem of fresh water supply. There were a few families at Wessagusset (or Wessaguscus—now Weymouth); David Thomson was living on what is now called Thomson's Island in Boston harbor; Samuel Maverick had settled on Noddle's Island (now East Boston); and, as we have noted, early settlers had built a few houses at Salem. But none of these places held any special appeal for Winthrop or Dudley as a "place for our sitting downe." There was one early pioneer, however, who held the key to the perplexing question. William Blackstone, or Blaxton, lived alone on the west slope of a hill (later called Beacon Hill) in Shawmut (later Boston) which was then a sort of pear-shaped peninsula jutting into the harbor. The early records of the town of Charlestown tell us:

> Mr. Blackstone, dwelling on the other side of Charles River alone, at a place by the Indians called Shawmutt, . . . came and acquainted the Governor of an excellent Spring there; withal inviting him and soliciting him thither. Whereupon, after the death of Mr. Johnson

> [on September 30, 1630] and divers others, the Governor, with Mr. Wilson [the minister], and the greatest part of the church removed thither: whither also the frame of the Governor's house, in preparation at this town [Charlestown] was also (to the discontent of some) carried; where people began to build their houses against the winter; and this place was called Boston.[17]

Though the early Courts of Assistants met in Charlestown, the decision was soon made to hold a session across the river at Trimountain. This, for a brief period, was the name given to Blackstone's peninsula, for the residents of Charlestown could discern three hills looming across the water, and they preferred Trimountain to the Indian name Shawmut (or Mishawmut) which some authorities believed meant "a great spring." Meeting there for the first time on September 7, 1630, the Court of Assistants:

> Ordered, that Trimountaine shalbe called Boston; Mattapan, Dorchester; & the towne upon Charles Ryver, Waterton.[18]

The choice of Boston as a name seemed a most natural preference, for many of the chosen leaders of the Colony had lived in the town of Boston in Lincolnshire, England (old St. Botolph or Botolph's Town). The Rev. John Cotton who was soon to become a prominent New England minister (and in later years the father-in-law of Increase Mather) was then preaching in that ancient town. The following month the first General Court session to meet in Boston convened on October 19, 1630. On October 3, 1632, the Governor and Assistants made this pronouncement: "It is thought, by generall consent, that Boston is the fittest place for publique meeteings of any place in the Bay."[19]

The guiding spirits of the Puritan emigration were deeply religious men, willing to risk their lives and their estates, if need be, in "planting" a government of their own making where they could worship in a manner befitting their own understanding of God's Word. The Puritans were dissatisfied with the slow progress the Protestant churches had so far made in breaking away from "Popish" ritual, liturgy, and church government since the middle of the sixteenth century. It was their hope to restore the Church of England to the "purity" of the teachings of Christ without human embellishment, to envision a church expressive of a simple faith and a congregation comprising an independent body without dictation from either Anglicans or Romans. It was not deemed necessary, however, for a Puritan to make a complete break with the Church of England as the Separatists had done. He could remain loyal to both Church and King. But the attainment of these goals seemed to the Puritan intellectual leaders of that period a remote as well as hazardous undertaking so long as they remained under the domination of the Anglican bishops. When the opportunity came to draw up their own church covenants and settle their own ministers three thousand miles from London, they warmly embraced it. While the Pilgrims at Plymouth were, in a theological sense, Puritans, the Puritans who settled in and around Boston were Separatists in a physical sense and later in a spiritual sense, too, although stoutly maintaining they had not separated from the Church of England. Winthrop would have been shocked if any one had laid the charge of "Separatist" at his doorstep, for he would not turn his back on his brethren in the Church of England.[20] Once they were settled in America, there seemed to be little need for a quarrel with the mother church. The fight was virtually over for most of them. The present called for an act of creation—the building of a new church where authority resided in its members—the congregational order of religious worship.

In this creative act the Puritans did not feel that they were alone. Was not God with them in all of their undertakings? Was it not God's will that his gospel should be carried to foreign shores? Indeed God had made a solemn covenant with them—as he had done many times with the people of Israel—whereby they, on their part, would punish sin wherever they found it, and He would bless and prosper this great adventure. As Winthrop wrote:

> The Lord will be our God and delight to dwell among us, as his owne people and will command a blessing upon us in all our wayes, soe that wee shall see much more of his wisdome power goodnes and truthe then [than] formerly wee have beene acquainted with, wee shall finde that the God of Israell is among us, when tenn of us shall be able to resist a thousand of our enemies; when hee shall make us a prayse and glory, that men shall say of succeeding plantacions: the lord make it like that of NEW ENGLAND.[21]

What strength and courage one who was a true believer could derive from those words! And Winthrop never faltered in his belief. It seems beyond dispute that the leaders of the Bay Colony, as well as of the Colonies of New Plymouth, Connecticut, and New Haven "came into these parts of America with one and the same end and aime, namly, to advance the kingdome of our Lord Jesus Christ, & to injoye the liberties of the Gospell in puritie with peace."[22]

It is true that they were harassed in their homeland, prosecuted as Nonconformists, sometimes deprived of their pulpits and maligned, hated, and despitefully used, but the allegation that they left England because they were "persecuted" has probably been overdrawn. There is no evidence that Winthrop, Dudley, Endecott, or other leaders of the Puritan migration to America had actually suffered in a physical sense from persecution by the King or the Archbishop.[23]

But the pull of conscience was not the sole motivating force, at least for those who followed the "first planters." Crouse concluded that only about twenty percent of all who came to America in that first decade (1630–1640) were driven by a desire for religious freedom.[24] Most of them, in fact, never became members of the local churches after they had settled in Massachusetts. Thousands of people did not leave their farms and firesides merely to enjoy the privilege of worshipping as they pleased in a wilderness. There was, for example, the attractive possibility of becoming landowners rather than remaining tenants for life. There was the chance to escape from the economic distress that was plaguing England at that time and to start a new, and perhaps a more prosperous, life in a new country. The Rev. John White of Dorchester (England), writing in 1630, summed it up in a few words:

> As it were absurd to conceive they have all one minde, so were it more ridiculous to imagine they have all one scope. Necessitie may presse some; Noveltie draw on others; hopes of gaine in time to come may prevaile with a third sort: but that the most and most sincere and godly part have advancement of the *Gospel* for their maine scope I am confident. . . .[25]

Capitalizing on these motives, some very effective propaganda was being published and circulated in England based on manuscripts sent over by first-hand observers. We have already referred to Captain John Smith's colorful pleas for colonization and his characterization of New England as the "paradise of all those parts."[26] There were some adverse comments, it is true, but by and large the message was in effect that New England offered great opportunities for a healthy life in a new land where there was an abundance of game, fowl, and fish and a salubrious climate. The Rev. Francis Higginson's (or Higgeson) "Short and True Description of the Commodities and Discommodities of that Country" was an appealing account, not overlooking that marine crustacean now cherished by all New Englanders—the American lobster. "The least boy in the plantation," he wrote, "may both catch and eat what he will of them. For my owne part I was soone cloyed with them, they were so great, and fat, and lussious." As for the climate which seemed to be of great interest to Englishmen, for it was always mentioned in these "relations," he had nothing but praise:

> The Temper of the Aire of *New-England* is one speciall thing that commends this place. Experience doth manifest that there is hardly a more healthful place to be found in the World that agreeth better with our English Bodyes. Many that have beene weake and sickly in old *England,* by comming hither have beene thoroughly healed and growne healthfull and stronge. For here is an extraordinarie cleere and dry Aire that is of a most healing nature to all such as are of a Cold, Melancholy, Flegmatick, Reumaticke temper of Body. . . . [27]

On March 4, 1629, King Charles the First (1600–1649) in the fourth year of his reign (1625–1649) had affixed the Great Seal of England to a royal charter. He thereby gave to 26 English gentlemen the authority to establish "one bodie politique and corporate in deede, in fact and name," to be known as "The Governor and Company of the Mattachusettes Bay in Newe England."[28] This charter or "pattent" (as it was usually called) was the legal foundation of the government of the Bay Colony on which it rested for more than half a century. "Wee conceive the pattent (under God)," said the General Court 32 years later, "to be the first & maine foundation of our civil politye here, by a Governor & Company, according as is therein expressed."[29]

The Company created by the Charter was a joint stock company organized for profit (and required to return to the King one-fifth of all gold and silver found in Massachusetts) and authorized to operate in a foreign land, similar to other companies created in that era. Its officers—a Governor, a Deputy Governor, and eighteen Assistants—were to be elected annually by popular vote of its members, who were called "freemen." Ample authority was given to set

Charles By the grace of God

Portion of the Massachusetts Bay Colony Charter of 1629, granted to the "Governor and Company of the Mattachusettes Bay in Newe England," brought over by Governor John Winthrop in 1630. Courtesy of the Archives Museum of the Commonwealth of Massachusetts.

up a body politic on New England soil with executive, legislative, and judicial functions but without that clear separation of powers which would provide a system of checks and balances. The profit motive of the Company was soon subordinated to the political. Once settled in New England, its officers devoted their talents to setting up an orderly society under rules of the Puritans' own making. The only important restriction placed upon them was that their laws were not to be contrary to any existing English laws, but even this limitation was at times lightly regarded by the Colonists and not seriously challenged by the Crown until the Quaker episode several decades later. Time was to prove that for practical purposes the Colony became a workshop for the forging of its own special tools for the administration of justice. Winthrop himself had no thought of treating the Charter with that same literalness of mind that he so often displayed when discussing some passage of the Bible. Some ten years after the establishment of the government he made this realistic comment:

> ... how strictly the people would seem to stick to the Patent, where they think it makes for their advantage, but are content to decline it, where it will not warrant such liberties as they have taken up.[30]

The territory granted by the charter comprised a vast stretch of land extending clear across America from the Atlantic to the Pacific (called at that time the "South Sea"). On the south it extended as far as three miles south of the Charles River; on the north three miles north of the river "Monomack, alias Merrymack, or to the northward of any and every parte thereof," the two rivers being presumably roughly parallel to each other. This presumption was not in accord with the facts, as it was later discovered. This inaccuracy and the general vagueness of the description led to long and bitter boundary disputes in later years with the governments to the north and east—New Hampshire and Maine.[31] Little was then known about the immense body of land lying beyond the Hudson River, but in the year 1629 no one seemed particularly to care. That unusually well-informed explorer, Captain John Smith, who was familiar with the maps of that day, stated in 1614 that the distance from one sea to the other (that is, from the Atlantic to the Pacific) "is supposed by most Cosmographers at least more than two thousand miles."[32]

Differing from other trading company charters of that period, the Bay Company charter did not expressly state that the seat of government should remain in England. Whether this omission was deliberate or an oversight, or whether it was simply assumed at first that the Company would be ruled from London, is not now known.[33] Following the usual practice, the Virginia Company had been directed from its London office under the wary eye of the King and his ministers. The stockholders of the Bay Company, however, particularly those who were themselves to become planters, wanted no such yoke around their necks. They sought a government that would be as autonomous as possible but at the same time legal in form and loyal to the King. How else could one set up Puritan churches free of Anglican control? The question was put directly to the stockholders in 1629 at one of their London meetings. They were asked whether "for the advancement of the plantation, the inducing & encouraging persons of worth & qualitie [to] transport themselves and famyles thither, & for other weighty reasons" they should "transfer the government of the plantation to those that shall inhabite there, and not to continue the same in subordination to the Company heer, as now it is. . . ."[34] After weeks of deliberation and "long debate" (for the question had legal and political implications of considerable consequence) the General Court, meeting in London on August 29, 1629, decided the issue:

> As many of you as desire to have the pattent and the government of the plantation to bee transferred to New England, soe as it may bee done legally, hold up your hands: Soe many as will not, hold upp your hands. Where by erection of hands, it appeared by the generall consent of the Company, that the government & pattent should bee setled in New England, & accordingly an order to bee drawne upp.[35]

Pursuant to this order, Winthrop personally carried the Charter to New England, thus establishing a government on American soil, a government that could make its own decisions without continual subordination to a board of directors meeting in far-off England. The silence of the King in the face of this vote by which his direct control was weakened has never been explained. Many learned articles have been written on the enigma of the transfer and its legality without shedding a great deal of light on the subject.[36] Nevertheless, by placing the government of the Company wholly in New England the founders of the Bay Colony had an unequalled opportunity to develop a self-governing commonwealth. In effecting this innovation in trading company practices they showed a spirit of independence—a spirit that was to manifest itself over the years in ever increasing ways, finally culminating in a declaration of complete independence from England about a century and a half later.

Once the matter of the Charter had been settled and Mathew Cradock, Governor, had decided not to embark for New England, it became necessary to elect a man who would assume the reigns of government in the new Colony. A General Court meeting in London on October 20, 1629, noted that it had received "extraordinary great commendations of Mr. John Wynthrop, both for his integritie & sufficiencie, as being one every [very] well fitted & accomplished for the place of Governor . . . ." Three others were nominated with Winthrop: John Humfrey, Isaack Johnson, and Sir Richard Saltonstall. By a "generall vote and full consent" they elected Winthrop for the term of one year.[37] A few years later Winthrop, who had long been interested in the plan to establish a new government in America but had not been a member of the Bay Company and was not one of the 26 gentlemen mentioned in the Charter, modestly commented on his election:

> I was first chosen to be Governour, without my seeking or expectation,—there being then divers other gent. who, for their abilities every way, were far more fit.[38]

Puritan penology began hundreds of miles east of Boston. Sin and corruption could scarcely be concealed in the close living quarters of the *Arbella,* particularly with John Winthrop pacing the deck in mid-Atlantic and feeling a sense of responsibility for seeing that violations of God's ordinances were summarily punished. He observed that "manye yonge gentlemen in our shippe . . . behave themselves well, and are Conformable to all good orders," yet it was "a Common fault in our yonge people, that they gave themselves to drinke hott waters very imoderately."

One day two men from the ship's crew, deciding they did not wish to conform when the Governor declared a religious fast, "pierced a rundlet [a small barrel] of stronge water, and stole some of it." As the ship had no brig, stocks, or pillory, the offenders were placed "in bolts all night, and the next morning the principall was openly whipped, and kept with bread, and water that daye"—probably the first occasion when the bread-and-water diet was ordered by a Massachusetts official.

Two men who had been fighting were made to walk the deck until nightfall with their hands bound behind them, while another, for using "contemptuous speeches in our presence" was "layd in bolts till he submitted himselfe and promised open Confession." One of the enterprising servants bargained with one of the children, offering a box worth three pence in return for "3: bisketts a daye all the voyage" until he had accumulated about forty, which he sold to other servants. When the authorities discovered this little business deal they "caused his hands to be tyed up to a barr and hanged a baskett with stones about his necke and so he stood 2: howres." But when one of the ship's officers caused injury to one of the landsmen and the Captain had ordered him "to be tyed up by the hands, and a weight to be hanged about his necke," the Governor interceded for him "with some difficulty" and remitted his punishment. Here we see for the first time Winthrop's leniency in dealing with offenders—a leniency for which he was to be taken to task by his more austere associates on numerous occasions in the coming years.

These offenses, summarily judged by the Governor and other high officials on board the *Arbella* were of a relatively minor nature, although they would probably have been punishable offenses in England. They could not afford to let them go unpunished. On another ship, the *Talbot,* the Rev. Francis Higgeson, making the westward voyage in 1629, reported a much more heinous offense. Sodomy, for which a person over fourteen years of age might have been hanged in England, was to be declared a capital offense in the Bay Colony as soon as the lawmakers had found time to sit down to draw up their list of capital crimes. But what should one do on the high seas with "5 beastly Sodomiticall boyes" whose sins were so horrible that the Rev. Higgeson said they were "not to bee named"? No punishment on shipboard would suffice:

> The fact was so fowle wee reserved them to bee punished by the governor when he came to new England, who afterward sent them backe to the company to bee punished in ould England, as the crime deserved.[39]

In 1629 when Captain John Endecott was in Salem representing the "Company for a Plantation in Massachusetts Bay," a year before the arrival of the Winthrop fleet, Matthew Cradock and Thomas Goffe, Governor and Deputy Governor of the Company, sent from London several long letters of instruction to guide him in the administration of justice.[40]

> Bee unpartial in the administration of justice, and endeavour that noe man whatsoever, freeman, or servant to any, may have just cause of complaint herein . . . .

This insistence on justice for each person regardless of his station in life was later incorporated in the Colony laws.[41] This basic principle upon which the criminal law must rest if it is to survive was faithfully adhered to, although tempered at times by the prejudices of the period. The orders to Endecott were clear; namely, that he must "proceede without partialitie" to punish offenders "as the nature of their fault shall deserve," but he was to play no favorites—"the like course yow are to hold both with planters & their servants, for all must live under government & a like lawe."

There were some specific instructions too. Those who "doe any injurie (in the least kinde) to the heathen people [the American Indians] "must be punished. If the Indians "pretend right of inheritance" to any land in Massachusetts, then the Colonists must not take the land but "purchase their tytle, that wee may avoyde the least scruple of intrusion."

As for the choice between severity and leniency in the administration of punishment:

> Our desire is to use lenitie all that may bee, but, in the case of necessitie, not to neglect the other, knowing that correction is ordained for the Fooles backe . . . .

Finally, the London officials wisely advised that he publish his laws so that no one could claim ignorance, "and then feare not to putt good lawes, made upon good ground and warrant, in due execution."[42]

3. LAWMAKERS AND MAGISTRATES

> No mans life shall be taken away, no mans honour or good name shall be stayned, no mans person shall be arested, restrayned, banished, dismembred, nor any wayes punished, no man shall be deprived of his wife or children, no mans goods or estaite shall be taken away from him, nor any way indammaged under colour of law or Countenance of Authoritie, unlesse it be by vertue or equitie of some expresse law of the Country waranting the same, established by a generall Court and sufficiently published, or in case of the defect of a law in any parteculer case by the word of god. And in Capitall cases, or in cases concerning dismembring or banishment, according to that word to be judged by the Generall Court.—*The Body of Liberties, 1641.*[1]

TO keep their solemn covenant with God, the Puritan leaders of the Bay Colony were forever vigilant in suppressing sin and inflicting on evildoers "such punishment as their offences shall deserve," which the New England Company in London advised, "is to bee (as neere as may bee) according to the lawes of this kingdome [England]."[2] Sensitive to the demands of moral law, appreciative of the rights of Englishmen in the courts of their homeland, and endowed with some understanding of the common law, they endeavored to administer criminal justice "without partiality"–subject to the foibles of the human spirit.

At least a modicum of crime in New England was anticipated, in spite of the founders' lofty aims. Captain John Endecott, who ruled at Salem before the arrival of John Winthrop in 1630, was warned by the London office that he might expect "some libertines" (religious liberals) needing correction, some "swearers" (particularly among the servants), some who might make excessive use of "strong waters," and some who very likely would be addicted to "other sinns."[3] Soon after the establishment of the Bay Colony government under Winthrop and the gentlemen who had come with him from England—and in the Plymouth Colony a decade earlier[4]—an orderly procedure for the trial of offenders through judicial tribunals was set in motion. A relatively simple system of courts operating under legal procedures not differing greatly from those long established in England served the Colony well until a somewhat remodeled judiciary was made necessary by the revocation of the Charter in 1684. The basic structure of the judicial system owed its character to the Charter and hence was English in conception, but it was freely modified to fit the needs of the Colony, with little interference from the Crown.

The Charter had granted the Governor, Deputy Governor, Assistants, and Freemen power to:

> make, ordeine, and establishe all manner of wholesome and reasonable orders, lawes, statutes, and ordinances, directions, and instructions not contrarie to the lawes of this our realme of England . . . [and to impose] lawfull fynes, mulctes, imprisonment, or other lawfull correction . . . .[5]

The Charter empowered the founders to establish "one greate, generall, and solempe Assemblie" that was to meet four times a year, to be endowed with executive, legislative, and judicial functions and to be known as "The Great and Generall Courtes."[6] The elected Governor, with power to summon these courts, would presumably be the presiding officer, but the Charter gave him no special executive authority nor veto power, anticipating that the General Court itself would make all important decisions. It was not long after the first session of the General Court that Deputy Governor Thomas Dudley—ten years' Winthrop's senior—thought that the Governor had assumed too much authority. A bitter dispute arose over the Governor's right to take executive action when the Court was not in session. The kindly and honest Winthrop, always meticulous not to appear as an autocrat, denied that "he intended to make himself popular, that he might gain absolute power, and bring all assistants under his subjection." The Charter, he claimed,

Engraving of John Endecott, Governor of Massachusetts Bay Colony, made for the New England Historical Register from the original portrait hanging in the Council Chamber of the Massachusetts State House, Boston.

in "making him a governour, gave him whatsoever power belonged to a governour by common law or the statutes."[7] As the Court was in session relatively few days a year, it was necessary, particularly in a newly established government, for someone to make quick decisions. This Winthrop usually did, with the consent of the Assistants. Winthrop was at his best when under attack. He faced issues squarely and dealt with his public with forthright honesty and modesty. Probably one of the wisest men of this period, he was also a popular leader. He was elected to twelve one-year terms as Governor and during each of his nineteen years in New England he held the post of Governor or of Deputy Governor or of Assistant.

In early seventeenth century the practical politicians had not given much thought to the political theory—now so well accepted in America—that legislative, judicial, and executive functions should be embodied in separate institutions. The General Court empowered with all three was in a literal sense a "general" assembly, not unlike the English Parliament at that time which also had power to legislate and to conduct trials. Today the legislature of the Commonwealth of Massachusetts, though shorn of its judicial power except in cases of impeachment, is still popularly known as "The Great and General Court."[8]

The Governor saw no need for the General Court to meet quarterly, as contemplated by the Charter. From October 19, 1630, when it convened for the first time, until the end of the year 1634, there were only five sessions, although the Court of Assistants (comprising the same individuals, with a few variations, as those who sat on the General Court) was meeting at frequent intervals and taking care of a great deal of urgent business. In 1634, when the freemen had a voice in the matter, the Court voted to meet quarterly, but two years later it was obvious that two annual sessions would be sufficient and it was so decided: one in May "for elections & other affaires" and one in October "for makeing lawes & other publique occations of the commonwealthe, provided that the Governor may, upon urgent occation, call a General Courte att any other tyme."[9]

Having in mind the habit of Kings to dissolve Parliament when it suited their moods, a binding condition was placed on the law books, probably at the insistence of the freemen, that the General Court was not to be dissolved without a majority vote of its members.[10]

The General Court, the Charter stated, was to be comprised of the Governor, the Deputy Governor, and eighteen Assistants, each to be chosen annually by a General Court of Elections meeting in the spring and consisting of these officers and all others in the Colony who had the right of franchise and were called "freemen."[11] Clearly, there was no need of so many Assistants. Probably it would have been difficult in the early years to find eighteen men with the knowledge of governmental matters and the wisdom equal to those few who served the Colony so well at that time.[12] Actually, the first few sessions of the General Court comprised only four to six Assistants who sat with the Governor and the Deputy Governor, and even in later years no more than twelve or thirteen Assistants were ever elected at one time. This departure from the Charter brought no objection from London; in fact, some years later (1665) the King agreed that the number "shall not exceed eighteene, nor be lesse at any time then tenn."[13]

The Assistants were the key people in the Colonial government. They took their duties seriously and thought of themselves as responsible primarily to God, ever mindful of the dignity of the office. At a meeting in 1631 Assistants were given powers of magistracy and the terms "Magistrate" and "Assistant" became interchangeable.[14] Rules of conduct drawn up by some of the top officials at a joint meeting with the ministers in 1635 reflect the high standards hoped for. For example: "Magistrates should (as far as might be) ripen their consultations beforehand, that their vote in public might bear (as the voice of God) . . . and shall appear more solemnly in public, with attendance, apparel, and open notice of their entrance into the court."[15] Bickerings, petty jealousies, and accusations among the Assistants grieved the good Governor (Winthrop) who noted that "some alienation of affection among the magistrates and some other persons of quality" had developed. A rule was laid down that might well serve today as a standard of conduct for the lineal descendants of the Colonial Magistrates—the Senators of the Commonwealth government:

> The magistrates shall be more familiar and open each to other, and more frequent in visitations, and shall, in tenderness and love, ad-

monish one another, (without reserving any secret grudge,) and shall avoid all jealousies and suspicions, each seeking the honor of another, and all, of the court, not opening the nakedness of one another to private persons; in all things seeking the safety and credit of the gospel.[16]

Reluctant to place freemen in a position of power (on the theory that important affairs of state should be entrusted to men of greater sagacity and ability), the Governor, the Deputy, and Assistants at the first session of the General Court on October 19, 1630, ordered that these officials should be chosen by the Assistants out of their own group rather than "out of the freemen of the saide Company" as stated in the Charter. Although this decision "was fully assented unto by the generall vote of the people" it could not long endure.[17] As the population increased, the freeman demanded a greater voice in government. Eventually a broader, more democratic rule was adopted, placed in the Body of Liberties (1641) and incorporated in subsequent codes:

It is the constant libertie of the free men of this plantation to choose yearly at the Court of Election out of the freemen all the General officers of this jurisdiction ... Governor, Deputy Governor, Assistants, Treasurer, Generall of our warres. And our Admirall at Sea, and such as are or hereafter may be of the like genrall nature.[18]

The freemen of the Company who were, in a sense, its stockholders (when the Company was first organized in England) had a vested interest in the welfare of the Commonwealth and had a right (granted by the Charter) not only to elect those who should govern them but to share in the making of laws. But in the first year or two there were very few men in the Colony who had been elected as freemen of the Company in England who were not already serving as Governor, Deputy Governor, or Assistants. Hence no voice was heard at that time to protest the concentration of power in the hands of a few who, for the most part, were men of superior ability. But it was not long before these men had to yield to the demands of the common man for a vote in the making of laws by which all would be bound. The first step was the admittance "to the Freedome of this Common-wealth" on May 18, 1631, of a group of 116 men, most of whom were not members of any of the local churches, who took the freeman's oath on that day.

The conservative leaders feared a precedent in admitting men indiscriminately who might not be in sympathy with the high purposes of the Commonwealth and who might therefore vote men into office who might not preserve the theological doctrines upon which the Colony had been founded. Hence the Court ordered on that day: "for the time to come noe man shalbe admitted to the freedome of this body polliticke, but such as are members of some of the churches within the lymitts of the same."[19] This was an extraordinary order, quite lacking in any authorization from the Charter, but it continued in force, with strong objection raised by only a few dissident voices, until 1664. Thus only freemen could vote, and only church members (not simply churchgoers) could be freemen. "Most of the persons at New-England are not admitted of their Church, and therefore are not Freemen," wrote Thomas Lechford in 1641.[20] In the early years, therefore, the franchise was held by a small minority of the population. Morison believes that by 1652 at least, and possibly before that time, almost half of the male population had been accepted by the churches, although in the second half of the century church membership declined.[21] But in 1664 the church membership law was repealed. King Charles the Second, after the Restoration, wrote a letter to the General Court in 1662, directing that:

> All the freeholders of competent estates, not vitious in conversation and orthodoxe in religion, (though of different persuasions concerning church government) may have their votes in the election of all officers, both civill & military.[22]

Meeting in 1664, the General Court bowed to the King and repealed the 1631 law but proceeded immediately to set up other qualifications for those who from that time on wished to become freemen of the Colony: A certificate from a minister that they were "orthodox in religion, & not vitious in their lives" and another certificate from the selectmen that they were freeholders and taxpayers "or that they are in full communion with some church amongst us."[23] Hutchinson, writing a hundred years later, commented that the church membership law was thus "repealed in appearance only."[24] It was not difficult for the authorities to deny the franchise or to deprive a person of the franchise after it had already been granted, for it had long been the law that the Court in its discretion could order disfranchisement for any who "openly or willingly defame any court of justice" or any of the judges.[25] Later two other classes of persons could be "made uncapable of voting": a) Quakers or others who refused to attend church could lose their franchise "during theire obstinate persisting in such wicked waies & courses, & untill certifficate be given of theire reformation";[26] and b) those convicted of fornication, "a shamefull sin, much increasing among us" or "any other shamefull and vitious crime" might find disfranchisement added to their punishment.[27] Thus those who wished to become voting members of the "body politicke" must at least have come with clean hands.

An historic session of the General Court on May 14, 1634, marked the debut of representative government in the Bay Colony.[28] At the outset when the number of freemen was limited, all of them could join in making laws, but as their numbers increased "it was not possible," as Winthrop said, "for them to make or execute laws, but they must choose others for that purpose."[29] Winthrop had hoped that those chosen to represent others (who were called "Deputies") would come to the General Court to prefer their grievances but not to make any new laws, for that important matter, he believed, should be left to the Assistants, who, after all, were the elected representatives of all the people. But the Deputies came, three from each town—Newtowne (Cambridge), Watertown, Charlestown, Boston, Roxbury, Dorchester, Saugus (Lynn), and Salem—and took a major part in the enactment of new laws. Winthrop afterward acknowledged that "many good orders were made [at] this court."[30] He probably had in mind these important enactments:[31]

1. Only the General Court "hath power to chuse and admit Freemen";
2. Only the General Court "hath power to make and establishe lawes" or "to elect and appoynct officers";
3. Only the General Court "hath power to rayse moneyes & taxes, & to dispose of lands," etc.

Placing the taxing power in the hands of the General Court, which now fully represented the people, was a significant move, for the cry of "no taxation without representation" was heard in effect for the first time in 1631 when citizens of Watertown had objected to a tax assessment levied without their consent, basing their protest on "fear of bringing themselves and posterity into bondage."[32] In the next century the charge of taxation without representation was to be flung at the King and to become a rallying point for those who were to rebel and who were for this and other reasons to come to the decision that the American colonies "are, and of Right ought to be, Free and Independent States."

Two or three Deputies chosen by the freemen in each town were to have "the full power & voyces of all the said Freemen, deryved to them for the makeing & establishing of lawes . . ." although here again we find an important step taken without express authorization from the Charter. Later the number of Deputies was changed to two from each town of more than forty residents; smaller towns were to send only one, while towns of fewer than ten residents could join with the next town.[33]

The General Court then consisted of the Assistants (corresponding to the Senate of the present Commonwealth government) and the Deputies (corresponding to the House of Representatives) and sat as one body.

Any one could present himself for election as a Deputy provided he were a freeman of the Colony and could pass the strict test of orthodoxy. The law made it clear that no one could sit in the House of Deputies:

> that is unsound in judgment, concerning the maine points of Christian religion as they have binn held forth and acknowledged by the generalitie of the Prottestant Orthodoxe writers, or that is scandolus in his conversation, or that is unfaithfull to this Government.[34]

A further limitation was enacted in 1663: "No person who is an usuall & common atturney in any inferior Court, shall be admitted to sitt as a Deputy in this Court."[35]

To be chosen Deputy, one did not have to reside in the town he represented, for the freemen of any shire or town "have liberty to choose such Deputies for the Generall Court, either in their own shire Towne, or else where, as they judge fittest, so be it they be freemen, and Inhabiting this Jurisdiction."[36]

Although nonchurch members could not vote (prior to 1664), they had the right to petition the government and to have their requests or complaints heard:

> Every man whether Inhabitant or Forreiner, free or not free shall have libertie to come to any publique Court, Councel, or Towne meeting, and either by speech or writeing to move any lawfull, seasonable, and material question, or to present any necessary motion, complaint, petition, Bill or information, whereof that meeting hath proper congnizance, so it be done in convenient time, due order, and respective manner.[37]

Here we see the origin of that right to petition the General Court, held as a constitutional right by the present citizens of the Commonwealth of Massachusetts.[38]

Questions put before the General Court were, according to the Charter, to be decided by a majority vote of the whole body. But when the Assistants were outnumbered by the Deputies, then complete control of the deliberations of the Court could have been taken over by the Deputies. It was thus obvious to everyone that the number of Deputies—and hence their power—would increase as time went on. The Assistants, therefore, had jealously guarded their right to veto any motion of the Deputies, based on the logical assumption that the Assistants or Magistrates were men "precedinge in gifts & experience" and it would be dangerous, therefore, to allow the government to be dominated by Deputies "who cannot be counted in the same ranke with the magistrates."[39] The thought of taking away the "negative vote" from the Magistrates prompted this simile from the pen of Winthrop:

> I cannot liken it better to any thinge then [than] to the brake of a windmill: which hath no power, to move the runninge worke; but it is of speciall use, to stoppe any violent motion, which in some extraordinary tempest might otherwise endanger the wholl fabricke.[40]

What Winthrop and the other Magistrates wanted was a procedure that would assure them that no law would be enacted without their consent for, after all, they were a little closer to God, although the Deputies, on their part, might claim they were closer to the people. Gross errors of judgment in both legislative and judicial matters might be committed by Deputies unchecked by the wiser Magistrates. Here a fundamental principle of government was involved at a time when nowhere in the English-speaking world was a purely democratic form of government considered desirable. Governor Winthrop argued:

> If the Negative vote were taken awaye, our Government would be a meere Democratie wheras now it is mixt .... Where the Cheif Ordinary power and administration thereof is in the people, there is a Democracie: This I prove thus, If it be in the Deputyes it is in the people ... the Deputyes are the Democraticall parte of our Government.
>
> Now if we should change from a mixt Aristocratie to a meere Democratie: first we should have no warrant in Scripture for it: *there was no such Government in Israell.* We should heerby voluntaryly abase our selves, and deprive our selves of that dignity, which the providence of God hath putt upon us: which is a manifest breach of the 5th Commandment for *a Democratie is, among most Civill nations, accounted the meanest & worst of all formes of Government:* and therefore in writers, it is branded with Reproachfull Epithits as *Bellua mutorum capitum,* a Monster, etc. and Historyes doe recorde, that it hath been allwayes of least continuance and fullest of troubles.[41] (Italics added.)

Winthrop was sure that it was not in God's plan that the Colony should be ruled by *anyone* who happened to chose to run for election; one could not entrust the serious business of government to the common man. In this sense then, he was not a believer in democracy as we understand that term but, with the exception of the limited right of franchise, the Colony was gradually assuming the character of a representative democracy. And yet Winthrop would never have assented to the doctrine that all men are created equal. On the contrary, he believed that "God Almightie in his most holy and wise providence, hath soe disposed of the Condition of mankinde, as in all times some must be rich, some poore, some highe and eminent in power and dignitie; others meane and in subjection."[42] Such was the prevailing view of the Magistrates and Elders in the Colony at that time. The eminent minister, John Cotton, in a letter to England written in 1636, expressed this view: "Democracy, I do not conceyve that ever God did ordeyne as a fitt government eyther for church or commonwealth. If the people be governors, who shall be governed?"[43]

The dispute over the right of the Magistrates to negate the votes of the Deputies was brought to a head in 1642 by bitterly contested litigation over the ownership of a white sow. The plaintiff, Goody Sherman, a poor woman, took the case on petition to the General Court after a jury in the County Court two years earlier had rendered a verdict for the defendant Captain Robert Keayne, a gentleman of wealth and standing in the community and the chief promoter and first Captain of the Military Company of Massachusetts in 1639, later known as the Ancient and Honorable Artillery Company. A stray sow had been taken to Keayne who announced the find to the public and, as there were no claimants, placed it in a pen with one of his own. Later he killed one of the two pigs. Goody Sherman claimed he had killed her stray sow. Keayne replied that the sow he killed was his own—not the stray. The case then turned on the identification of the animal—"a Sowe all white, Save a black Spott under the eye of a biggnesse of a Shilling & a ragged Eare."[44] When the General Court put the matter to a vote after an extraordinary amount of testimony, the whole Court voted seventeen to fifteen for the poor woman. But the Magistrates had voted seven to two for the defendant, the Deputies fifteen to eight for the plaintiff (seven Deputies abstaining). As the Magistrates had the right to negate the vote of the Deputies, for a 1636 law stated that no law or sentence could be valid without the majority vote of both houses, the plaintiff could not prevail.[45] "There fell out a great business," wrote Winthrop, "upon a very small occasion." Should the Magistrates, it was asked, who were numerically in the minority, be able to thwart the will of the majority in legislative and judicial matters, contrary to the Charter?

After much debate the issue was resolved for a time, without complete satisfaction on either side, by an act passed in 1644 establishing for the first time a bicameral body that has survived to this day, both factions agreeing that when Magistrates and Deputies sat together, as they had up to this time, "diverse inconveniences" resulted. The act provided that "Henceforth the Magistrates sitt apart, & act all busines belonging to this Court by themselves . . . the Deputies in like manner sitting by themselves. . . ."[46]

This order further provided that acts passed by a majority of each house should then be "Ingrossed" and on the last day of each session "deliberately read over before the whole Court"—a practice substantially like that used today in the General Court.[47] "This order," said Winthrop in 1644, "determined the great contention about the negative voice."[48] Actually the contention continued, for this order merely confirmed the practice first established in 1636, but it did bring into being a legislature divided into two houses, following "the laudable practice of other states . . . in the issuing of busines of greatest & highest consequence."[49] In the ensuing years the Deputies made repeated efforts to return to a simple majority vote in the enactment of laws, but without success. The Magistrates hoped that in the decision of judicial matters at least they might have the sole voice, but even that hope was in vain, for in 1649 the Court agreed that judicial appeals would be decided by majority vote of the whole court.[50] But as time went on the General Court became almost exclusively a legislative body, and eventually the Court of Assistants became the highest judicial court. The dispute died down, but the bicameral character of the legislature remained, and the act of 1644, born of a white sow, stands as a landmark in Massachusetts history. Hutchinson, an eighteenth century Governor, turning back to the seventeenth century, observed:

> This I suppose was the second house of representatives in any of the colonies. There was . . . no express provision for it in the charter, they supposed the natural rights of Englishmen, reserved to them, implied it. In Virginia, a house of burgesses met first in May 1620. The government in every colony, like that of the colonies of old Rome, may be considered as the *effigies parva* of the mother state.[51]

As declared by the elders and assented to by the Magistrates and Deputies, the General Court was that "Chief Civil Power of this Commonwealth."[52] It was made clear to all that "the acts of this honoured Court, being the supreme authority, are not liable to quaestion by any. . . ."[53] There was no higher authority (such as the Supreme Judicial Court of the present Commonwealth) to interpret its acts. No appeals to England were permitted.[54] And yet the voting public held the controls, for no one, from Governor to Deputy, was put into office for a term of more than one year. The high officials of the government were, in fact, returned to office year after year by the electorate. It is probably true that the control of the affairs of state was, throughout the life of the Colony, in the hands of its most able, as well as its most respected, citizens.

The General Court was also the highest judicial body. It had both original and appellate jurisdiction in civil and criminal matters. During and after the second decade, however, it rarely tried cases although it retained its right to hear appeals from the lower courts and its right of impeachment. That "everie man shall have libertie to complaine to the Generall Court of any Injustice done in any Court of Assistants or other [court]" was a rule of law that was carried down to the end of the Bay Colony government.[55] Petitions or complaints presented directly to the General Court were frequently referred to the Court of Assistants for trial.

The first criminal case to come before the General Court was that of Walter Palmer. A coronor's Jury in 1630 had found that Austen Bratcher had died as a result of "strookes given by Walter Palmer" and that in their opinion Palmer's act constituted manslaughter. Upon receiving this report, the General Court (consisting of the Governor, Deputy Governor, and six Assistants) referred the case for trial to the Court of Assistants (consisting of the same authorities, with the replacement of one Assistant by another), where a jury was impaneled and found the defendant not guilty.[56]

Appeals to the General Court could always be made by a defendant in a capital case "if in the Court of Assistants, two of five, three of seaven, or such a proportion of Magistrates then present, shall actually dissent from the sentence of the Court."[57] But, in any event, there was always the possibility of a pardon. "The generall Court onely shall have power to pardon a condemned malefactor," and, if the Court were not in session, the Governor and the Deputy Governor ("Joyntly consenting") or any three Assistants (in joint agreement) could grant a reprieve.[58]

As its first speaker, the House of Deputies chose William Hathorne (sometimes spelled "Hawthorne," probably the more phonetic spelling) in 1644. A Deputy from Salem, where he was one of its most prominent citizens, he was chosen for this office again in the following year and in 1646, 1648, 1650, 1657, and 1660.[59] He was one of the ancestors of Nathaniel Hawthorne (1804–1864), noted American author.

As the number of settlements increased, the House of Deputies grew in numbers. Looking into the future, the Magistrates saw their own prestige and authority threatened and sought to put a definite limit on representation by the people. At that time (1645) thirty-five Deputies were the usual number. Reporting the action of the General Court, Winthrop wrote:

> The court, finding that the over number of deputies drew out the courts into great length, and put the country to excessive charges, so as some one court hath expended more [than] 200 pounds, etc., [similar to the complaint heard today concerning the size of the House of Representatives which was set at 240 by the Constitution of the Commonwealth[60]] did think fit to have fewer deputies, and so to have only five or six out of each shire . . . but upon trial, the greater number of towns refused it, so it was left for this time [and was not taken up again].[61]

It was suggested by the Magistrates that if both Houses were made equal in numbers then the Magistrates would be willing to give up the "negative vote," but the idea was not acceptable.

As the General Court became the chief legislative and administrative body, a question frequently debated was: Who or what body, when the Court was not in session, could assume the reins of government since the Governor alone had very little political power? This question, among others, was referred to the reverend elders who served as a sort of Supreme Court when interpretations of the Charter or of the acts of the General Court were needed and who advised that:

> The Magistrates are by patent [Charter] & election of the people, *the standing councell* of the commowealth, in the vacancy of the Generall Court, & accordingly may act, in all cases perteining to government, according to the patent, & laws made by the said Generall Court. . . .[62]

Although they had no power as a Council "to dispence justice," the Magistrates (which term always included the Governor and Deputy Governor) served an important function as the standing council but, like all Colonial officers, they had to stand for election each year.

The General Court in 1636 passed an unpopular and short-lived law providing for the election of a small number of Magistrates "for tearme of their lyves" and "not to be removed but upon due conviction of crime, insufficiency, or for some other waightie cause." The Governor, Sir Henry Vane, with John Winthrop and Thomas Dudley were duly elected to this Council for Life and in the following year were joined by John Endecott.[63] Three years later, when it was evident that a life tenure for any government official would not be tolerated by the people, the General Court declared that members of such a council would have no authority unless elected by the people as Magistrates at annual elections, and the Council for Life quietly went out of existence.[64] Other proposals were made to modify the composition of the standing council[65] but were equally unsuccessful, and the council remained as a sort of executive board for the management of the Colony.

The Court of Assistants was comprised of the Magistrates alone. At the outset, this court exercised both legislative and judicial powers but soon relinquished legislative functions to the General Court which met much less frequently in the early years. Commonly called "The Greate Quarter Courts," for presumably they were to convene once each quarter, they found after 1649 that two sessions annually would be sufficient, one in March and one in September, with authority in the Governor or, in his absence, the Deputy Governor to convene the Court for the trial of any person for a capital crime.[66] Until the lower courts were established in the counties, the Court of Assistants, meeting in Boston, was the chief court for criminal business (sharing this function with the General Court) but after 1636 limited its original jurisdiction to the more serious cases, "capital and criminal causes extending to life, member and banishment" and to divorce hearings. In 1649 it was decreed that this court would "take cognizance of no case or action tryable in any Countye Courte, unless it be by way of appeale."[67] One of the fundamental rights of "every man cast, condemned or sentenced in any Inferior Court" was "to make theire appeal to the Court of Assistants."[68] This court could also hear and determine all cases tried in the inferior courts where the bench and jury could not agree about their verdict so that neither could proceed "with peace of conscience."[69]

"Inferior Quarterly Courts" (to distinguish them from the Courts of Assistants, the "Great Quarter Courts") were evidently the workhorses of the judiciary, established in 1636 to "trie all civill causes, whereof the debt or damage shall not exceede 10 pounds, & all criminall causes not concerneing life, member, or banishment" with right of appeal to the next Court of Assistants, but those who "shall bringe any appeale without just cause [shall] be exemplaryly punished."[70]

When these courts were established, they were ordered to convene in four towns: Ipswich, Salem, New Towne (Cambridge), and Boston, with additional towns named after the counties were delineated. In 1643 the General Court created counties or "sheires": "The whole plantation within this jurisdiction is divided into four sheires, to wit: Essex, Middlesex, Suffolk, Norfolk."[71] Norfolk county was not the Norfolk county of the present Commonwealth government but included an area embracing the towns of "Salsberry," Hampton, Haverhill, "Excetter," Dover, and "Strawberry Banck," (Portsmouth). All but Salisbury and Haverhill now lie within the state of New Hampshire.

A few years after the counties had been established these courts were commonly, and later officially, called "county courts." Five Magistrates comprised a single court, but three constituted a quorum. If there were not a sufficient number of Magistrates to be drawn from the place where the court was to sit, the General Court could appoint from time to time associates who were not elected Magistrates—a striking innovation—but at least one of those on the bench had to be a Magistrate.[72]

These courts had a wide variety of judicial and administrative powers. Among them were the authority or duty:

to "take care that the Indians residing in the severall sheires shalbe civillized, . . . and instructed in the knowledge & worship of God";[73]

to "make Probate of any Will";[74]

to appoint "searchers" to see that money was not illegally transported out of the country;[75]

to punish those who charged for their labor above the wages fixed by law;[76]

to grant licenses to a "common victualler, keeper of a Cooks shop or House for commone Entertainment or publick Seller of wine, Ale, Beer, or Strong-waters by Retail";[77]

to maintain "an able & faithful" ministry and to purge from the ministry all who are "viscious or perniciously Hetrodox."[78]

A varied assortment of offenders appeared before these courts, from those who wore "Apparel exceeding the quality and condition of theire Persons or Estate" to those who beat their wives, as we shall see in later chapters.[79]

No administrative, legislative, or judicial decision could be made in the Colony without the assent of one or more Magistrates

—men of authority, prestige, and special privilege. To deny a Magistrate's lawful authority or to defame him in public was a serious offense. They and their familes were among those officials who were exempted from the restrictions on the wearing of "Gold or Silver lace, or Gold or Silver Buttons or any bone lace . . . silk hoods, or scarfs . . .," which was forbidden to "people of mean condition . . . [who] . . . take upon them the garb of Gentlemen . . . allowable to persons of greater Estates, or more liberal education yet . . . intollerable in persons of such like conditions."[80] They were exempted for many years (1645–1654) from personal (poll) taxes;[81] from ferry boat tolls;[82] from keeping arms;[83] from military training;[84] and from standing a constable's watch.[85]

They were entrusted with a multitude of minor governmental functions, such as the solemnizing of marriages (a ceremony not within the province of the clergy in those days);[86] the administration of the oath of fidelity;[87] serving on the Board of Overseers of Harvard College;[88] passing upon the requests of young men to court young maidens in the absence of their parents,[89] and performing other civic duties.

Sitting alone, a Magistrate had judicial authority to pass judgment and to deal out penalties of a minor nature on a great variety of social offenders who, if they believed they did not get a fair deal, could appeal to the County Court.[90] A Magistrate could also hear civil cases where the debt, trespass, or damage did not exceed twenty shillings (later changed to forty shillings).[91]

Sitting alone on the bench, a Magistrate had a wide vista of crime. A glance at a few of the areas of his jurisdiction will afford some idea of the kinds of behavior not considered particularly serious and yet worthy of punishment in seventeenth century Massachusetts.

Those who committed "small thefts" in "townes remote from any prison" where the fine was not over forty shillings.[92]

Children and servants who behaved "disobediently, & disorderly towards their parents, masters and governours; to the disturbance of families, and discouragement of such Parents and Governours."[93]

Those who catch "Mackrell . . . except for spending whilst fresh, before the first of July annually," for, the General Court observed, "the taking of Mackrel at unseasonable times do greatly diminish their increase."[94]

Those who play with cards or dice.[95]

Idle persons or stubborn persons . . .Runawayes, Common Drunkards, Pilferers, Common night-walkers and wanton persons, as tending to uncleanness in speeches or Actions, . . ."[96]

"Wandring Quakers."[97]

Suspicious persons; that is, Disorderly Persons "in case of Misdemeanour or vehement Suspition thereof."[98]

Those who failed to attend the public "Ministry of the Word" without just and necessary cause and "after due means of conviction used."[99]

Those who "gallop frequently" in the streets of Boston "to the great endaingering the bodies & lives of many persons, especially children, who are ordinarily abroad in the streetes, & not of age or discretion suddainly to escape such danger."[100]

Those who play "the Games of shufle-board and Bowling, in and about the Houses of Common entertainment, whereby much precious time is spent unprofitably, & much waste of Wine and Beer occasioned."[101]

Those who play any game for money or dance in the taverns.[102]

Those who spend their time "idlely or unprofitably," especially "common Coasters, unprofitable Fowlers, and Tobacco takers."[103]

Liars over the age of discretion (fourteen years). "All lying is contrary to truth," observed the General Court, "and some sort of lyes are not only sinfull (as all lyes are) but also pernicious to the Publick weal, and injurious to particular persons." Only this kind of lying was to be punished.[104]

Those who took another's "horse, mare, asses, or drawing beast" without authority of the owner.[105]

Those who "Swear rashly & vainly, by the Holy name of God, or other Oath."[106]

Those who, in a public place of entertainment are found "singing rudely or making a noise to the disturbance of the family or any other guests."[107]

Single women, or wives whose husbands are away, who "entertain or lodge any In-mate or Sojourner with the dislike of the Select men of the Town, or Magistrate, or Commissioners."[108]

"Loose, vaine, and corrupt persons . . . which insinuate themselves into the Fellowshipp of the younge people of this countrye, drawing them, both by night and by day, from their callings, studies, honest occupations, and lodging places, to the great dishonour of God, griefe of their parents, masters, teachers, tutors," etc. Such behavior today might be designated as "contributing to the delinquency of a minor." This law was evidently aimed at those who enticed the boys at Harvard College from their studies.[109]

Single Magistrates frequently had concurrent jurisdiction with the County courts. Two Magistrates sitting as one court might decide certain administrative matters. Any two Magistrates together with the Governor or Deputy Governor (or in their absence, any three Magistrates) could constitute a special court for strangers "who cannot without prejudice, stay to attend the ordinary Courts of Justice," with the same jurisdiction as a County Court and with a right of appeal to the Court of Assistants.[110]

A Court of Chancery, as a defense "against the rigour of the common law" made its appearance in 1685, comprised of Magistrates of each County Court.[111]

Selectmen in each town had important administrative functions granted to them by the General Court but had little to do with the administration of criminal justice. The Body of Liberties of 1641 stated that they had authority to make laws of a regulatory nature concerning the welfare of the town "provided they be not of a Criminall, but onely of a prudentiall nature, And that their penalties exceede not 20 sh. for one offence" and be "not repugnant to the publique laws and orders of the Countrie." The number of selectmen was limited to nine for each town.[112] They had authority to arrest drunkards and Quakers and performed quasi-judicial functions.[113]

In towns where no Magistrate resided, the General Court could appoint three Commissioners to try "small Causes" where the "debt, trespass or damage was not over 40 shillings" (originally 20 shillings) and provided it chose men "whose conversation is inoffensive, and whose fidelity to the Country is sufficiently known and approved of by the County Court of that Shire."[114] Commissioners could take recognizance and bind offenders over to the

County Court but could not commit to prison. Their jurisdiction in criminal matters did not equal that of a single Magistrate.[115]

By 1651 Boston had grown to such a large town that it was necessary to set up a court of seven Commissioners annually chosen by the freemen, to try civil actions where the damages were not over ten pounds and criminal actions to prevent "sinn and misdemeanors" where the fine would not exceed forty shillings. Defendants had a right of appeal to the Court of Assistants. The preamble to the law makes clear the need for this tribunal:

> Whereas by reason of the Concourse of people, and increase of trade in the Towne of Boston, Suites at Law are growne more frequent, whereby the County Courts are much prolonged, and for asmuch as many crimes are also committed in the said town, by strangers and others, which often escape unpunished; For the prevention whereof . . . .[116]

This law, enacted in 1651 "for triall for one whole yeare," was included in Colonial Laws of 1660 and 1672. The original jurisdiction of this body was Boston proper (the "Neck") and Noddles Island (East Boston), but the General Court extended it in 1674 to "the whole limit of Boston."[117]

These then were the legislative and judicial institutions that served the administration of the criminal law in the Bay Colony.[118] Fourteen years after the founding of the Bay Colony, Governor Winthrop in his "Discourse on Arbitrary Government" wrote:

> "England is in a State of long standing, yet we have had more positive and more wholesome Lawes enacted in our shorte tyme then [than] they had in many hundred years."[119]

† † †

As the seventeenth century neared its end, Puritan prestige in governmental affairs noticeably declined. The handwriting on the wall was clear.

The mother country had long been displeased with the growing independence of the Bay Colony, although it found little fault with the more conservative and compliant Colony founded ten years earlier in Plymouth. For long periods of time, seventeenth century England had been too engrossed with foreign wars and domestic problems to take drastic action. And yet, on more than one occasion, the King had threatened to revoke the Bay Colony charter to gain tighter control of affairs in his plantations far across the great Atlantic. During the fifty-five years of its existence, the Bay Colony, according to advices reaching London, had failed to conform strictly with the terms of the Charter by enacting laws repugnant to those of England and in other ways had disregarded its restrictions whenever it was inconvenient to abide by them; it had placed political power exclusively in the hands of members of the Congregational churches; it had denied the franchise to those who, by Puritan standards, were not "orthodox"; it had become overzealous in its punishment of Quakers and other heretics; it had relied too heavily on scriptural law in setting up a criminal code; it had definitely discriminated against members of the Church of England; it had demanded oaths of fidelity to the Colony, rather than to the King, and in its later years had used the terms "Commonwealth" and "State" instead of "Colony," connoting an unwarranted degree of independence; it had always refused to permit appeals to courts in England, boldly asserting that English writs did not extend beyond the seas; it had slighted English trade and navigation laws; it had for many years claimed jurisdiction over the eastern lands (now part of Maine and New Hampshire) originally claimed by Sir Ferdinando Gorges and John Mason; and it had commenced to coin its own money, an act that England considered a royal prerogative. In short, the Colonists, as viewed from the royal throne, had evidently assumed that they had evolved a strong body politic which, in law, was to be almost completely free of restrictions by either the Charter or the crown. Its spirit of independence was only too evident.

After witnessing half a century of Colonial self-government, English authorities saw the need of a stronger hand if they were ever to maintain sovereignty over this member of the fast-growing British Colonial Empire that showed promise of becoming an important factor in foreign trade. King Charles the Second had sent to Massachusetts a special commission as early as 1664 to demand some moderation in the Colonial drive toward independence, but it was greeted (in the language of the commissioners) by "a cloude of blacke reproaches & some seditious speeches," although it did effect the grudging repeal of a few of the Colonial laws that were particularly objectionable to the King. We shall not here dwell upon the long wrangle (from 1660 to 1684) between the Crown and the General Court, the insistence of the King's agent, Edward Randolph, that the King assert his authority, the visits to England of official representatives from both Colonies, or the lengthy correspondence carried back and forth across the Atlantic. Official replies from Boston showed the General Court alternating between abject surrender to the King's wishes and prevarications, evasions, or flat denials of his charges.

Finally, on October 13, 1684, a proceeding in the King's High Court of Chancery "cancelled, vacated and annihilated" the Charter of 1629, a document that had become practically a constitution for the Bay Colony. A copy of the Court's judgment reached Boston on July 2, 1685, and was officially read to the General Court on May 25, 1686.

For about seven years the Bay Colony passed through a period of tense uncertainty without a charter. In September 1685, the King asked Joseph Dudley (1647–1720), who was then in London, to serve temporarily as "President of the Territory and Dominion of New England" with authority over those who lived in the Bay Colony and the Provinces of New Hampshire and Maine and "the Narraganset County." Arriving in Boston the following May, he took over the reins of government from the General Court of the Bay Colony which, since the loss of the Charter, had been carrying on as usual. He was assisted by fourteen councillors, comprising some of the most prominent local leaders who were loyal to the King.[120] Dudley was a respected Massachusetts native, a Harvard graduate (class of 1665), a former member of the General Court, son of former Governor Thomas Dudley, and destined later to serve as royal Governor of the Province from 1702 to 1715. Able and affable, he seemed like a wise choice for the difficult position, but he ran into opposition from the General Court which could not acknowledge the legality of his appointment. There was an undercurrent of rebellion, for certain legal minds in Boston maintained that the judgment vacating the Charter was invalid because the Colony had no opportunity to be represented in the Court of Chancery on that historic occasion. When, in carrying out the King's wishes, Dudley permitted Episcopal church services to be held in the Town House (where the General Court usually met), he incurred further opposition.

Dudley met with the General Court on May 17, 1686, and frankly told them he could no longer address them as "Governor and Company" and made it clear that their Charter privileges had terminated. His official proclamation of his appointment and authority was read in open court on May 25, 1686, and "published by beat of Drumme and sound of Trumpet" and sent out to all the towns within his jurisdiction. He was now, he told them, "First President of his Majesties Council and Vice-Admirall of these Seas." Some of the deputies of the General Court would not accept his proclamation and sent in a document (called by Dudley and his Council "a libellious paper") claiming that New Englanders had been "abridged of their libertyes as Englishmen both in the matter of legislation and in the laying of taxes." There was, however, no threat of rebellion in this document, for the authors concluded with the statement that they would demean themselves "as true and loyall subjects to his Majesty" and would "in due time" ask for relief.

Without support from his Council of local citizens, Dudley probably could not have successfully bridged the gap between a self-governing Colony and a Province under direct control of the King. But he was never really put to the test. His term as President —the only President New England ever had—lasted just seven months.

The King appointed Sir Edmund Andros (1637–1714), a devout Episcopalian, to succeed Dudley. He arrived in Boston on December 20, 1686, accompanied by sixty "redcoats." He was addressed as "Sir Edmund Andros, Knight, Capt. General and Commander in Chiefe of his Majesties Territory and Dominion of New England." This royal Governor who had had administrative experience in presiding over the Province of New York (1674–1681) was impressive in appearance, splendid in attire, dignified, and capable but failed to win the affection of his subjects who found it difficult to express genuine loyalty to a Governor not chosen by popular election. With a Council of 28 men, Andros had complete power over the General Court. He soon had arrayed against himself not only the Puritan clergy, who were shocked at his insistence on holding Church of England services in the South Meeting House (the "Old South"), but also the general public who resented his tax levies, his refusal to recognize old land titles, and other administrative acts not derived from the consent of their elected representatives.

The changeover from a self-sufficient Colony to one under direct control from London through a Governor whose first loyalty was to the King—and a devout Catholic at that—was too abrupt for a freedom-loving people. However, there were some among them who rejoiced over the wane of Puritan power and the opportunity for greater freedom of worship. When word reached Boston in March 1689 that a revolt in England was in the making against a King who so openly espoused Catholicism and that William from the Netherlands, a Protestant, and his wife Mary, also a Protestant (and the daughter of King James) might ascend the throne, the repressed hostility of the people in and around Boston erupted in a bloodless revolution. On April 16, 1689, they deposed Andros and held him captive at Castle Island while various members of his Council, including Joseph Dudley, were thrown into jail. They later released him without harm and sent him to England on the ship *Mehetable*. Thus ended the "Dominion of New England."

William and Mary ascended the throne on May 26, 1689, and gave their approval to a new temporary governing authority called the Provincial Council, headed by Simon Bradstreet (1603–1697) as Governor from June 7, 1689, to May 16, 1692. He had been an elected Governor of the Bay Colony and was one of the last survivors of those who had come over on the *Arbella* with John Winthrop in 1630. He was assisted by a Council made up of two delegates from each town. As one of the original "planters," Bradstreet could not concede the legality of vacating the old Charter and petitioned the crown for its continuance. He revived the General Court and declared that all laws made by the Bay Colony, not repugnant to those of England, were still in force. He had hoped to set up "business as usual."

In the meantime, Increase Mather had hastened to London in April 1688 to seek the restoration of the beloved Charter or, failing in this quest, to preserve as much of the powers and privileges of a self-governing Colony as he could. After four years of effort "with inviolate Integrity, excellent Prudence, and unfailing Diligence," he was forced to concede that the old Charter would never be revived by King James or his successor King William. On October 7, 1691, a second Royal Charter created a new form of government, placing the Colonies more directly within the British empire and more surely under its control. Somewhat disappointed, Mather accepted it gracefully. "Although there are some things in this new Charter," he wrote, "which are not desirable, yet nothing that is intolerable."[121]

The Charter created "The Province of the Massachusetts Bay in New England," comprising both the Massachusetts Bay Colony and Plymouth Colony lands and the Province of Maine (but not New Hampshire) and "the Territory called Accadia or Nova Scotia" and all the land lying between them. In the two Massachusetts colonies, there were at that time about ninety towns and sixty thousand people.

From that time until 1774, the Province government was presided over by ten Royal Governors, four of whom were native New Englanders, appointed by the King for an unlimited tenure, thus ending the Colonial practice of electing their own Governors for one-year terms.[122] Other features of the Charter prescribed "henceforth and for ever" (not contemplating a revolution 84 years later) were these:

A Lieutenant Governor or Deputy Governor and the Secretary of the Province were also to be appointees of the King.

The Great and General Court was to consist of the Governor, Assistants and Freeholders. Twenty-eight Assistants or Councillors (corresponding to our present forty Senators who in the Constitution of 1780 were originally called "Counsellors and Senators") were to be chosen by the General Court, although the original 28 were chosen by the King to serve until May 1693. The freeholders (corresponding to our present Representatives) were to be elected by the towns.

Voting rights were to be available to all men whose freehold in land was valued at forty shillings per year or whose estate was valued at forty pounds sterling, thus removing all religious tests of "orthodoxy."

The General Court was given authority to enact laws not repugnant to those of England, but the Governor held the veto power which could not be overridden by the legislature. Each law passed by the General Court and signed by the Governor was to be immediately sent to England for approval, but it was to remain in force unless disallowed by the Privy Council within three years. The Governor therefore had considerable control over legislation, but the General Court held the purse-strings and could withhold his salary when pressure was needed to obtain his approval.

The General Court was also given all necessary power to establish courts, both civil and criminal, but had to permit appeals to England in civil cases where the matter in question exceeded three hundred pounds sterling in value.

The General Court was to meet annually on the last Wednesday in May (a practice that continued until 1831), but the Governor could call special sessions and could prorogue or dissolve the Court "as he shall Judge necessary."

The Governor could appoint "with the advice and consent of the Councill," and with seven days' notice (as is the practice today) all judges, justices of the peace, sheriffs, and others.

All present and future residents of the Province were to have all the rights of Englishmen "as if they . . . were borne within this Our Realme of England."

The General Court was to permit liberty of conscience "in the Worshipp of God to all Christians (Except Papists)" and was to teach the Indians knowledge of and obedience to "the onely true God and Saviour of Mankinde and the Christian Faith."

Still hopeful that New England might be rich in minerals, the architects of the Charter claimed for England "the Fifth part of all Gold and Silver Oar and pretious Stones" that might be discovered within the Province.

Meeting from time to time during the intercharter period, the General Court survived the vicissitudes of shifting sovereignty and convened again in 1692 under the new provincial government and continued into the eighteenth century. Reestablished by the Constitution of 1780, it has served as the legislative body of Massachusetts from Colonial beginnings to the present time, a period of 334 years. It is the oldest legislative assembly still in operation in the western hemisphere. Not until it had served for 300 years was any formal celebration held in recognition of its long history of usefulness to the people. (Perhaps only in relatively recent times have political leaders shown an interest in the founding and early beginning of New England's political institutions.) In 1930 in the administration of Governor Frank G. Allen, the General Court, in special session, celebrated its 300th anniversary and noted the progress of the state under nine generations of law makers.[123] The 300 years was computed from August 19, 1630, the first meeting of the General Court, to October 20, 1930, not taking into account the few earlier meetings held in England prior to the departure of Governor Winthrop and company for New England in March of 1630.

While in the latter part of the seventeenth century attorneys were disqualified from sitting as Deputies in the Bay Colony General Court, today we find approximately one-fourth of the 240-member House of Representatives comprised of members of the Massachusetts bar.

Rule by Royal Governors from the arrival of Sir William Phips in 1692 until the departure of General Thomas Gage in 1775 was never wholeheartedly accepted by the inhabitants of Massachusetts. It is not our purpose here to relate the story of the mounting causes for rebellion. The spirit of independence had repeatedly asserted itself down through the years and had eventually led to a definite break with England and an alliance with the other British colonies in America in a determination "to dissolve the political bands which have connected them with another, and to assume among the Powers of the earth, the separate and equal station to which the Laws of Nature and of Nature's God entitle them. . . ."

Control by the King ceased to exist when the Continental Congress met in Philadelphia in September 1774. Fighting commenced in April 1775, and the bitter struggle dragged on until 1781. During this difficult period, Massachusetts was without a Governor. Leadership, under the Province Charter, was borne by the elected Council of 28 men. After much spirited debate and a Constitutional Convention of 1779–1780, the people approved of a Constitution in 1780 that is still in force, its essential principles derived in part from the Charters of 1629 and 1692 and numerous declarations of the General Court of the Colonial period proclaiming the rights of a free people.

In the ensuing years three constitutional conventions (in 1820, in 1853, and in 1917) were called to reexamine the Constitution, to suggest revisions, and to propose amendments. Although a total of 81 articles of amendment have been approved and ratified by the people since the Constitution went into effect on October 25, 1780, when John Hancock was inaugurated as the first Governor of the Commonwealth, that remarkable document is still the form of government for the Commonwealth and is now the oldest written constitution in this hemisphere. It was in many respects a model for the Federal Constitution of 1787. It is a monument to the political sagacity of the founding fathers and particularly to the outstanding authority on constitutional law and political history of his time, John Adams (1735–1826) who in 1796 was elected the second President of the United States.

This "new Constitution of civil government" carried forward many of the features of the Colonial and Provincial governments and declared that:

> All the laws which have heretofore been adopted, used and approved in the Province, Colony or State of Massachusetts Bay, and usually practiced on in the courts of law, shall still remain and be in full force, until altered or repealed by the Legislature; such parts only excepted as are repugnant to the rights and liberties contained in this Constitution— (Part 2, ch. 6, sec. 6).

It set forth a "Declaration of Rights," similar in some respects to the Body of Liberties of 1641; it established a bicameral legislature with a senate and house of representatives "each of which shall have a negative vote on the other," as voted by the Bay Colony in 1644; it continued the Colonial practice of holding *annual* elections for Governor and other high officials, changing to biennial elections after 1918; it provided for annual meetings of the General Court on the last Wednesday in May, as required by the Charter of 1691, changing in 1831 to the first Wednesday in January; it granted power to the General Court to make "all manner of wholesome and reasonable" laws, adopting virtually the same phraseology as that used in the Charter of 1629 and repeated in the Charter of 1691; it established a "Council for advising the Governor" of nine persons (besides the Lieutenant Governor), later changed to eight, whose consent would be necessary on many gubernatorial appointments and on all pardons and commutations granted to those convicted of crime; it called for a legislature of Senators and Representatives to be elected by the people, similar to the Colonial General Court with its Assistants and Deputies, but demanded a property qualification for such officials, as well as for voters (removing that condition in 1892); it required that the Governor be a "Christian," but repealed that condition in 1821, reminiscent of the Colonial requirement of "orthodoxy"; it continued the right of the legislature to require towns to support a "Protestant" ministry if the towns did not do so voluntarily, but withdrew this right in 1833; it stipulated that judges be appointed "for good behavior" rather than having them serve, as in the Province government, at the pleasure of the governing authority; it preserved the powers and immunities granted to the President and Fellows of Harvard College, an institution established in the Bay Colony in 1636; it continued the right of free petition, first laid down in the Bay Colony in 1641 and guaranteed to the inhabitants other rights and liberties, many of which were derived from the Colonial governments; and wrote into this precious document many other wise provisions for the preservation of representative government in Massachusetts.

But of those features not drawn directly from the earlier Charters or previous enactments of the Colonial legislatures, the most noteworthy achievement of this Constitution was the clear separation of governmental powers—the legislative, the executive and the judicial—*"to the end it may be a government of laws and not of men."*

Courts dispensing justice in the Plymouth and Bay Colonies ceased to exist as such when the Province government came into being, and yet courts with different titles and similar jurisdiction were quickly put into operation and—with numerous changes—have been carried forward to the present time.[124] The Charters of 1629 and 1691 and the Constitution of 1780 had granted, in the same wording, "full power and authority to erect and constitute judicatories and courts of record, or other courts . . . ."

What are the courts today that carry on these traditional functions?

The Supreme Judicial Court, with the distinction of having the longest continuous existence of any court in the land, was derived from the Superior Court of Judicature of the Province period which, in turn, was the successor to the Colonial Courts of Assistants. The Province court was also called "The Superior Court of Judicature, Court of Assize and General Gaol Delivery" because of its practice at the end of each term to review the cases of all persons held in the gaol and reported to them by the Sheriff. The Supreme Judicial Court owes its present title to the Constitution of 1780 (the only court specifically mentioned therein) but is a continuation of the Province court established by the legislature in 1692 and is therefore 273 years old. (Some authorities place its birthday in the year 1699, for the act of 1692 was "disallowed" by the King's Privy Council, and it was not until 1699 that another act of the General Court, not objected to by the Privy Council, again gave it life.)

It originally consisted of three justices and exercised full judicial functions from the outset over civil and criminal matters and, like the original Court of Assistants, tried, with a jury, all capital cases. Since 1891 such cases have been tried in the Superior Court, while the Supreme Judicial Court has become almost exclusively an appellate court—the highest in the Commonwealth.

The Supreme Judicial Court is now comprised of a Chief Justice and six Associate Justices. It hears appeals on cases originally heard in the lower courts but has power to try certain cases on their merits. Convictions obtained in the Superior Court on first-degree murder indictments are almost invariably reviewed by this appellate court which may, after a review of the whole case, order a new trial or direct the entry of a verdict of a lesser degree of guilt or send the case back to the Superior Court for imposition of sentence if it is "satisfied that the verdict was against the law or the weight of the evidence, or because of newly discovered evidence, or for any other reason that justice may require."

The Superior Court, established in 1859, succeeding some of the earlier county courts, has original jurisdiction over all crimes and appellate jurisdiction over crimes tried in the district and municipal courts. All offenders indicted by a grand jury are tried in this court, where they are entitled to a jury trial to determine issues of fact and guilt or innocence. It is comprised of a Chief Justice who presides over this Court and assigns 41 Associate Justices to sit in the various counties on rotation.

Seventy-three District and Municipal Courts scattered throughout the Commonwealth provided with some 175 Justices, not all of whom are required to serve full time, dispose of about 95 percent of all criminal charges. An offender convicted in these courts in nonjury proceedings may appeal to the Superior Court and there demand a trial by his peers. Recently some counties have been experimenting with a procedure by which an offender convicted of a misdemeanor may ask for a trial by a six-member jury with the right of appeal on conviction directly to the Supreme Judicial Court, thus relieving the very heavy criminal calendar of the Superior Court. These courts deal mostly with minor violations of the law, including drunkenness, motor vehicle violations, and other misdemeanors, but they also have jurisdiction over felonies that are not punishable by a sentence to state prison of more than five years.

In each of the District Courts, except the Boston Municipal Court, the justices may hold juvenile sessions for disposing of complaints against boys and girls between the ages of seven and seventeen who have violated the law. These too, are nonjury sessions. The proceedings are considered noncriminal in nature and are not open to the public. The court is to approximate "as nearly as possible" the care, custody, and discipline the children should receive from their parents, for, as the law states, the children are not to be treated as criminals but "as far as practicable" as "children in need of aid, encouragement, and guidance."

The Boston Juvenile Court, established in 1906, is the only Court in the Commonwealth dedicated solely to the welfare of delinquent, neglected, and wayward children.

4. CIVIL RIGHTS AND LIBERTIES

The free fruition of such liberties Immunities and priveledges as humanitie, Civilitie, and Christianitie call for as due to every man in his place and proportion without impeachment and Infringement hath ever bene and ever will be the tranquillitie and Stabilitie of Churches and Commonwealths. And the deniall or deprivall thereof, the disturbance if not the ruine of both.

We hould it therefore our dutie and safetie whilst we are about the further establishing of this Government to collect and expresse all such freedomes as for present we foresee may concerne us, and our posteritie after us, And to ratify them with our sollemne consent.

We doe therefore this day religiously and unanimously decree and confirme these following Rites, liberties and priveledges concerneing our Churches, and Civill State to be respectively impartiallie and inviolably enjoyed and observed throughout our jurisdiction for ever.—*Preamble to the Body of Liberties, Boston, 1641.*[1]

A CITIZEN in the town of Boston in the sixteen thirties, brought before a Magistrate for the violation of one of the numerous Colonial laws, might very well have pleaded ignorance and won an acquittal on the ground that the law in question had not been "sufficiently published."[2] With no media of communication other than an occasional announcement "by beate of drum" or a public reading in the marketplace or a posting on the meeting-house door, he might not have heard that what he thought was an inoffensive pleasure had been proscribed by the small group of men who were then running the Colony. Thus three and a half centuries ago, ignorance of the law might have been an acceptable excuse unless the act was clearly contrary to the "immutable" natural law that all reasonable men inherently understood.[3]

In 1637, before the laws had been printed and published, three men "had been kept long in prison" for the crime of adultery—a capital offense. The Court was doubtful whether it had been made clear to the citizenry that this kind of behavior was of that order of seriousness and it was willing to resolve the doubt in favor of the accused, for there was little popular support for the taking of a life for a crime that did not involve violence. Asked their opinion, the elders said, "If the law had been sufficiently published, they ought to be put to death." Because of the uncertainty on this point, Governor Winthrop said, "it was thought safest, that these three persons should be [merely] whipped and banished."[4] Thereafter the law was confirmed and published as a capital offense.

Since 1630 the General Court and the Court of Assistants had been slowly building up a body of criminal law but, during the first decade, had not compiled a code nor made these laws available to the public. They remained in handwritten form in the possession of the Secretary. But "the people had long desired a body of laws, and thought their condition very unsafe, while so much power rested in the discretion of magistrates."[5] Although Magistrates were elected annually by those who had the franchise, the average citizen was jealous of their authority and sought to limit their power by the creation of some sort of a constitution or body of "fundamentals" that would guarantee civil rights and liberties to all men. They feared that wide discretionary power, not curbed by written laws, might lead to an arbitrary government. The Magistrates, placed on the defensive, slowly yielded to this insistent demand for "positive laws."[6]

The General Court as early as March 1635 had asked John Winthrop and Richard Bellingham (both of whom had had law training in England) to review all laws enacted since 1630 and to report to the next legislative session "which of them they judge meete to be altered, ebreviated, repealed, corrected, inlarged, or explained, etc."[7] This committee of two, like some legislative committees of the present day, filed no report, and nothing came of the matter that year. In 1636 a new committee was appointed including, among others, three ministers—John Cotton, Hugh Peter, and Thomas Shepard—"to make a draught of lawes agreeable to the word of God, which may be the Fundamentalls of this common-

Portrait of John Winthrop, Governor of Massachusetts Bay Colony. Courtesy of The American Antiquarian Society, Worcester, Massachusetts.

wealth, & to present the same to the nexte Generall Court. . . ." In the meantime the courts were ordered to continue to hear cases and make dispositions according to the laws already established and "where there is noe law, then as neere the lawe of God as they can."[8] Two years later, when no draft had been presented, the General Court complained that "the want of written lawes have put the Court into many doubts & much trouble," and again asked for a survey of existing laws. It called upon the freemen of every town to meet and collect the "heads of such necessary & fundamentall lawes as may bee sutable to the times & places whear God by his providence hath cast us," and to deliver their reports to the Governor so that he and the council and a new committee that included the Rev. Nathaniel Ward could make a "compendious abrigment" to present to the fall session of the General Court in 1638.[9]

Although the Magistrates and Deputies had the help of the freemen and the elders, this mighty effort to produce some sort of a model code "came to no effect; for, being committed to the care of many, whatsoever was done by some, was still disliked by others."[10] Not all of the Magistrates thought very highly of the idea of publication; many of them had mixed feelings about the whole business and were obviously using delaying tactics. Not only did they fear a design to restrict their discretionary power, but they saw the risk of a publication that would inevitably reach England where it would be found that the Colony had transgressed the limitations of the Charter in enacting laws repugnant to those of the realm. However, after repeated orders of the General Court to expedite matters, "at last it was referred to Mr. Cotton and Mr. Nathaniel Warde, etc., and each of them framed a model, which were presented [in 1639] to this general court. . . ."[11]

John Cotton, "a godly, grave and judicious divine," was one of the most beloved and influential ministers in the Colony. Formerly Vicar of St. Botolph's church in Boston, England, he had preached the farewell sermon to Winthrop and his party at Southhampton as they prepared to set sail for New England. Three years later he joined them in their new home. They chose him teacher of the First Church in Boston where he became the leader of the Congregational form of church discipline. Son of an attorney, he had some understanding of the law but was known more for his Biblical scholarship and his expositions of Puritan orthodoxy.[12]

Considering his training and his guardianship over Puritan morality, it was perhaps inevitable that his draft of the laws should draw heavily on Old Testament sources but at the same time manifest some knowledge of the common-law rights of Englishmen.

Winthrop called Cotton's production "A Model of Moses His Judicialls." It proved to be quite unacceptable to the General Court, though no reasons for it rejection appear in the Court records. Haskins speculates that Ward's list of twenty capital crimes was too severe and that his code was not sufficiently comprehensive.[13] Morison believes that one provision alone—providing for life tenure for counselors—would have aroused such opposition from the Deputies that the code would have had no chance of passing if a vote had been taken in the General Court.[14] Nevertheless, many of its provisions found their way into the Body of Liberties and into the codes of other Colonies. A copy of the "Judicialls" was promptly sent to England where it was published in 1641 and again in 1655 and for a number of years was there erroneously believed to be the official code of the Bay Colony.[15]

The Reverend Nathaniel Ward, a member of the newly appointed legislative committee was a graduate of Emmanuel College who came to New England in 1634 at the age of 56. He had studied law in England and had become a barrister there but decided, at the age of forty, to enter the ministry. "I have read almost all the Common Law of England, and some Statutes," he said. The town of Ipswich appointed him minister, where he served for two years and then resigned, returning to England in 1646. He is remembered today both for his individualistic style of satirical wit in his secular writings and for his formulation of the basic laws of the Colony.[16]

His "Body of Liberties" was not a compilation of all existing laws, but it was a comprehensive enumeration and exposition of one's civil rights and liberties incorporating many of the principles of the Common Law of England. It was a Bill of Rights—the forerunner of our present constitutional guarantees. It did not, however, have the binding force of a charter or a constitution. All or any part of it could be repealed at any session of the legislature, even though Ward had written into the last article his hope that:

> ... these rites and liberties, shall be Audably read and deliberately weighed at every Generall Court that shall be held, within three

> yeares next insueing, And such of them as shall not be altered or repealed they shall stand so ratified, That no man shall infringe them without due punishment.[17]

Although none of the 98 articles of Ward's code, other than no. 94 which dealt with capital crimes, provided for specific penalties, he intreated the legislature "to consider them as laws, and not to faile to inflict condigne and proportionable punishments upon every man impartiallie, that shall infringe or violate any of them."[18]

His "breviate of lawes," as it was sometimes called, was circulated among the towns, giving the freemen a chance to become acquainted with its terms before final consideration by the General Court. At its May 1640 session, the Court asked the elders and freemen "to ripen their thoughts & counsells about the same," but it took no action until December 1641.[19] Finally, in the handwriting of Winthrop (rather than that of the secretary, as was customary), appeared this note on the official record: "At this Court, the bodye of lawes formerly sent forth amonge the Freemen, etc., was voted to stand in force, etc."[20]

Considerable doubt exists as to whether the General Court ever officially adopted the Body of Liberties as such. The records (aside from Winthrop's note) do not specifically say so. Increase Nowel, for many years Secretary of the General Court and an Assistant when the matter was being deliberated, said later in his introduction to the Colonial Laws of 1648 that portions of the Body of Liberties were incorporated in those laws but "not as fundamentalls, for diverse of them have since been repealed, or altered, etc."[21]—a statement seemingly in contradiction of Winthrop's diary entry that "this session [the December 1641 session of the General Court] continued three weeks, and established 100 laws, which were called the Body of Liberties."[22] The question becomes academic when an examination of the record reveals that 89 of the 98 articles of Ward's code were incorporated verbatim, or with slight modification, into the Colonial Laws and became "the law of the country."[23] Many of the civil rights and liberties of the Colonial period survived and are now part of our organic law. They were based largely on English concepts of justice as found in the Common Law and in the Magna Carta of 1215—but with added contributions from the Mosaic Code in the drafting of the laws punishable by death. Before listing the articles of the Body of Liberties that were particularly pertinent to the administration of criminal justice, let us follow the story of the compilation of Colonial laws.

The desire persisted for a comprehensive code that would spell out all of the laws, civil and criminal, that would make the Colony a government of laws, not of men. The Charter of 1629 had assured the colonists and their posterity that they "shall have and enjoy all liberties and immunities of free and naturall subjects. . . as if they and everie of them were borne within the realme of England."[24] Was it not high time, the freemen asked, that such liberties and immunities were reduced to some permanent written form, lest the increasing influence of the clergy, the limitation of the franchise to church members, and the discretionary power of the Magistrates inhibit the free development of a government for and by the people?

Just as these questions were being most seriously considered, Robert Child (1613–1654), an intelligent and outspoken opponent of the government dominated by John Winthrop, Thomas Dudley, John Endecott, and a few others, arrived from England on his second trip to the Bay Colony. A wealthy bachelor of 32, Child had obtained from Padua a degree in "physick" (as medicine was called in those days). He was a man of many interests—agriculture, the planting of vineyards, alchemy (the early science of chemistry), lead mines, religion and politics. As a Presbyterian he had a natural distaste for the Congregational form of church organization that seemed to overshadow the religious life of the Colony at that time. He did not advocate complete freedom of worship. Religious tolerance for all was not his ideal. But he held strongly to the view that the Colony should be subject to the laws of England and that Parliament, then under Presbyterian influence, should be informed of the growing independence of the Colony, then under the domination of a few willful Congregationalists. And he dared say so. He was evidently familiar with the Charter. All true Englishmen, he maintained, whether Puritan or non-Puritan, church members or nonchurch members, should have an equal voice in government affairs. Members of the Church of England should be accepted into the New England churches or allowed to gather in their own churches "according to the best reformations of England and Scotland," by which he meant, Kittredge believed, that the Colony should permit the establishment of Presbyterianism in New England.[25] Such proposals, logical and proper as they might seem to us today, struck the Magistrates as insolent, defamatory, and dangerous. If Child had not been an educated gentleman entitled to some respect, he might have been whipped and banished, and that would have been the end of the matter.

He presented to the May 1646 session of the General Court a "Remonstrance and humble Petition," signed by himself and six friends, one of whom was David Yale, father of Elihu who was the first donor to Yale University.[26] The Court having deferred the matter until November, opportunity was afforded for warm disputes over the issues raised but, when the Court reconvened, the petition was flatly rejected.[27] It was feared that if Child should attract a greater following—which seemed not unlikely—the independence so far gained by the Colony was in real jeopardy and the cavalier manner in which the Colonial government had dealt with the Charter might come to the attention of an unfriendly Parliament. To some of the Magistrates this was a most serious challenge, but Richard Saltonstall (son of Sir Richard), Simon Bradstreet, and Richard Bellingham dissented from the condemnation of Child and the fine of fifty pounds assessed against him and the fines of lesser amounts against his co-petitioners. The following June, when incriminating documents were found in his trunk which was seized by the authorities as he was about to set sail for England, Child was again brought before the court and this time was fined two hundred pounds (an extraordinarily heavy fine) for sedition, for it was then obvious to the authorities that his design was to ask Parliament to revoke the Royal Charter.[28] He had threatened to appeal to Parliament—even before judgment was passed—but in this effort, too, he was completely frustrated. The Remonstrants were offered immunity if they should make "an ingenuous & publicke acknowledgment of their misdemeanours."[29] They declined the offer, and Child returned to England, leaving in his wake an aroused government activated to settle this matter of independence and to clarify the civil rights and liberties of its citizens.

Child's "humble" accusation that the Colonial leaders had breached the terms of the Charter and spurned their oaths of allegiance to England prompted Winthrop and his committee to pen the famous declaration of independence:

> Our allegiance binds us not to the laws of England any longer than while we live in England, for the laws of the parliament of England reach no further, nor do the king's writs under the great seal go any further. . . .[30]

Furthermore, they argued:

> We have no laws diametrically opposite to those of England, for then they must be contrary to the law of God and of right reason, which the learned in those laws have anciently and still do hold forth as the fundamental basis of their laws. . . .[31]

As the authorities saw it, Child had defamed the churches of Christ and the civil government by insinuating that the Colonial leaders intended "to exercise unwarranted dominion and an arbitrary government, such as is abominable to the parliament . . . thereby to make them slaves."[32] Such charges, the General Court believed, were so basically unsound and dangerous (for Child's audience would be the Parliament as well as the Bay Staters) that it requested Winthrop, Dudly, Bellingham, and the Auditor General to draw up a formal rebuttal—now known as "The Declaration of 1646."[33] It supplied an answer to every point raised in the "Remonstrance" and compared the "Fundamentalls" of the Colony with the Magna Carta and the Common Law of England, vigorously defending the Colony's right to set up its own tests of orthodoxy and to deny the franchise to the unorthodox in defiance of the terms of the Charter—or the wishes of Parliament. One is reminded of a statement Winthrop made some six years earlier:

> . . . if we should put ourselves under the protection of the parliament, we must then be subject to all such laws as they should make, or at least such as they might impose upon us; in which course though they should intend our good, yet it might prove very prejudicial to us.[34]

One is reminded also of a statement made by the General Court 32 years later when it resisted obedience to an act of Parliament relating to trade and navigation: "Wee humbly conceive, according to the usuall sayings of the learned in the lawe, that the lawes of England are bounded within the fower seas, and doe not reach Amerrica. . . ."[35]

The General Court, "unexpectedly prevented by multitude of other pressing occasions," had been unable from 1642 to 1646 to produce the code of laws it so much desired. But a few weeks after disposing of the "sedition" of Child, it ordered a complete compilation of

> all the liberties, lawes, & orders extant with us . . . whereby we may manifest our utter disaffection to arbitrary goverment [still smarting from the barbs of the Remonstrants], & so all relations be safely & sweetly directed & perfected in all their just rights and priviledges. . . .[36]

Two more years went by—"streights of time & other things intervening"—but at length in 1648 "The Book of the General Lawes and Libertys concerning the Inhabitants of the Massachusets" was printed in Cambridge and in a few months was ready for distribution, selling for "three shillings the booke." But each member of the General Court was to have a copy "without price."[37]

Haskins, in his concise and accurate analysis has caught the significance of this famous code of laws:

> In 1648 the colony laws were brought together into a comprehensive legal code which was an authoritative compilation not only of constitutional guarantees, provisions for the conduct of government, trade, military affairs, and the relations between church and state, but of the substantive law of crime, tort, property, and domestic relations. The Code was no mere collection of English laws and customs, but was a fresh and considered effort to order men's lives and conduct in accordance with the religious and political ideals of Puritanism. Traditional elements there were, but these were consciously reworked into a carefully thought-out and integrated pattern. Many of its provisions were notable improvements on the law of contemporary England in the sense that judicial procedure was simplified, criminal penalties mitigated, primogenitu e abolished, debtors accorded humane treatment, and rules of due process instituted to safeguard men's lives from the arbitrary exercise of governmental power. The first compilation of its kind in the English-speaking world, the Code of 1648 stands as a monument to the elements of tradition and design from which the early law of Massachusetts was fashioned.[38]

A second complete compilation and revision of the Colonial laws appeared in 1660—"The Book of the General Lawes and Libertyes"—carrying forward all earlier laws that had not been repealed.[39] A third revision was published in 1672—"The General

Laws and Liberties of the Massachusets Colony: Revised & Reprinted."[40]

The rights guaranteed a defendant in a criminal proceeding can be found clearly set forth in these Colonial laws. Most of them were taken directly from the Body of Liberties of 1641. Some were added later. These rights that are now part of the organic law of the Commonwealth of Massachusetts were first promulgated by the Puritan government seated in Boston:

1. *Due Process.* Both our State and our Federal Constitutions today afford an accused "due process of law" which, in effect, means that he may be punished only in accordance with "the law of the land." Article 1 of the Body of Liberties (quoted at the beginning of the previous chapter), which assures the accused that he will not be punished in any way except in accordance with the "expresse law of the Country" (unless, of course, his behavior is in violation of "the word of God"), was derived from the Magna Carta, a body of liberties that the English barons forced King John to agree to in the year 1215, which stated that:

   > No free man [thus excluding slaves] shall be taken or imprisoned or dispossessed, or outlawed, or banished, or in any way destroyed, nor will we go upon him, or send upon him, except by the legal judgment of his peers or by *the law of the land.*[41]

   There was nothing in this "liberty," however, to prevent the General Court from enacting a harsh or arbitrary law—as it did later to meet the threat of the Quakers.[42] The Court was restricted only in prosecuting a person when there was no law to warrant the prosecution. The government, therefore, would be a government of laws, not of men, but unreasonable men could make unreasonable laws.

2. *Equal Protection of the Law.* Article 2 of the Body of Liberties also drew upon the Magna Carta which read: "To no one will we sell, to no one will we deny, or delay right or justice."[43] Article 2 provided, "Every person within this Jurisdiction, whether Inhabitant or forreiner shall enjoy the same justice and law, that is generall for the plantation, which we constitute and execute one towards another without partialitie or

delay."[44] Notwithstanding this provision there were class distinctions that were indigenous to the culture and therefore taken for granted. For example, men of "meane condition, educations & callinges" could not "take uppon them the garbe of Gentlemen, by the wearinge of gold or silver lace, or buttons, or poyntes at their knees, to walke in greate bootes. . ."; nor could women of the same rank wear "silke or tiffany hoodes, or scarfes." The idea of "excesse in Apparrill" was considered "unbecoming a Wilderness condition." "The Rising Generation are in danger to be Corrputed and Effeminated," it was believed, and must therefore be warned, as their parents were, that all who wore apparel "exceeding the quality and condition of their Persons or Estate" would be fined.[45] As we shall see in a later chapter, no "true gentleman, nor any man equall to a gentleman" was to be publically whipped excepting under certain circumstances.[46] Hence, what the law meant was that all men *of the same rank* were to enjoy the same justice.

3. *No Discrimination Against Foreigners—if They Are Christians.*

   If any people of other Nations professing the true Christian Religion shall flee to us from the Tiranny or oppression of their persecutors, or from famyne, warres, or the like necessary and compulsarie cause, They shall be entertayned and succoured amongst us according to that power and prudence god shall give us.[47]

4. *No Torture to Extract Confessions.*

   No man shall be forced by Torture to confess any Crime against himselfe nor any other, unlesse it be in some Capitall case, where he is first fullie convicted by cleare and sufficient evidence to be guilty, After which if the case be of that nature, That it is very apparent there be other conspiratours, or confederates with him, Then he may be tortured, yet not with such Tortures as are Barbarous and inhumane.[48]

   One might say that such torture was outlawed completely in practice; at least there is little evidence of it in the court records, although there was a report of torture used to extract confessions in several cases in the Salem witchcraft prosecutions.

5. *The Right to Bail.*

   No mans person shall be restrained or imprisoned by any Authority whatsoever, before the Law hath sentenced him thereto, If he can put in sufficient securitie, bayle or mainprise, for his appearance, and good behaviour in the meane time, unlesse it be in Crimes Capital, and Contempts in open Court, and in such Cases where such expresse act of Court doth allow it.[49]

Later revisions of the law added four other classes of defendants who might have been denied bail: heretics, arsonists, Quakers, and those who refused to acknowledge and record mortgages.[50]

6. *Freedom from Double Jeopardy.* "No man shall be twise sentenced by Civill Justice for one and the same Crime, offence, or Trespasse."[51]

7. *Right to a Speedy Trial.* "Everie man that is to Answere for any Criminall cause, whether he be in prison or under bayle, his cause shall be heard and determined at the next Court that hath proper Cognizance thereof, and [if] it may be done without prejudice of Justice."[52] A later law required the prison keeper "from time to time to present a true list of all the Prisoners" to the courts to insure speedy justice for those awaiting trial.[53]

8. *Right to a Jury Trial.*

In all Actions at law it shall be the libertie of the plantife and defendant by mutual consent to choose whether they will be tryed by the Bench, or by a Jurie, lesse it be where the law upon just reason hath otherwise determined. The like libertie shall be granted to all persons in Criminall cases.[54]

A defendant might waive his right to a jury trial as Darby Bryan of Boston did in the Court of Assistants in 1677. On trial for adultery "being at the Barr & pleading not Guilty on the question whom he would be tried by, said by the Bench." The Court found him guilty and, although this was a capital offense, sentenced him to stand on the gallows with a rope around his neck for one hour, and then to be whipped with 39 stripes and after that to be imprisoned.[55]

A law had been enacted in 1634—and carried forward in all subsequent Colonial codes—that in trials where a man's life was at stake or where the penalty might be banishment, if the trial were held in an inferior Court, there must be "a special jury summoned for that purpose."[56]

9. *Right to Challenge the Jury.* In a criminal case a defendant could

> "challenge any of the Jurors. And if his challenge be found just and reasonable by the Bench, or the rest of the Jurie, as the challenger shall choose, it shall be allowed him, and *tales de circumstantibus* impaneled in their room [stead]."[57]

The right to be tried by one's peers was, of course, not unfamiliar to Englishmen. Again we turn to the Magna Carta, which stated that no one should be punished "except by the legal judgment of his peers or by the law of the land." This right, legal scholars tell us, was not the beginning of the jury system but a recognition of a preexisting system. But it was about this time (1215) that the practice was given up of subjecting offenders to ordeals of battle, of fire, and of water to determine guilt or innocence. The early trials used jurors as informers for the King. Later, jurors were usually witnesses to the facts in question or at least friends or neighbors of the defendant—certainly not impartial, as jurors are presumed to be today. The first important trial by jury recorded for posterity occurred in the sixteenth century—the trial of Sir Nicholas Throckmorton.[58]

Colonial jurors could bring in a special verdict ("non liquit") where evidence was obscure or defective, finding as to certain facts but leaving the judgment of the case to the bench; or if bench and jurors disagreed so "that either of them cannot proceede with peace of conscience," the case was referred to the General Court for final decision.[59] Jurors were not limited to the facts presented at the trial:

> Whensoever any Jurie of trialls or Jurours are not cleare in their Judgements or consciences conserneing any cause wherein they are to give their verdict, They shall have libertie in open Court to advise with any man they thinke fitt to resolve or direct them, before they give in their verdict.[60]

Thus jurymen could consult with any bystander in court if they thought he had information concerning the case. No one could be compelled to serve on a jury "above two Courts in a yeare, except grand Jurie men, who shall hould two Courts together at the least."[61] A juryman could not be forced to give his vote for or against, for "if he cannot see reason to give it positively . . . he shall have libertie to be silent, and not pressed to a determined vote."[62] Grand jurymen were paid "their necessary expences"; later laws allowed petit jurymen four shillings *per diem*, grand jurymen three shillings *per diem*.[63]

10. *In Capital Cases, Two Witnesses Were Necessary for a Conviction.* In the Fourth Book of Moses (Numbers 35:30) it was written: "Whoso killeth any person, the murderer shall be put to death by the mouth of witnesses: but one witness shall not testify against any person to cause him to die." Realizing the wisdom of this law and the danger of convicting a person on the biased testimony of one person, the Colonial law makers decreed: "No man shall be put to death, without the testimony of two or three witnesses or that which is equivalent thereunto."[64] Just what might constitute "that which is equivalent thereunto" was a crucial question in many cases. In 1646 the General Court decided that fleeing from justice might be considered equivalent; that is, after a person was indicted for a capital crime and failed to appear "after three proclamations publikely made in the towne where hee usually abides."[65] In a case heard in 1673, a confession made at the time of apprehension was deemed to constitute one witness.[66] "One clear witness," the elders said in 1641, "with concurrent and concluding circumstances are instead of two witnesses."[67] Thus one could not escape justice if only one individual could be found to testify against him provided there was other circumstantial evidence; nor could a person be unfairly convicted of a capital crime merely on the testimony of his enemy.

11. *No Imprisonment for Debt or Fine if One Had an Estate.* "If the Law can finde competent meanes of satisfaction," a person was not to be imprisoned for a debt or fine. In other words, imprisonment for nonpayment was a last resort. If a person had no means of satisfying a debt from his estate, a later law pro-

vided, he might be required to work it out in service but could not be placed in service excepting to persons "of the English nations."[68]

12. *Cruelty Outlawed.* "For bodilie punishments," read the Body of Liberties, "we allow amongst us none that are inhumane, Barbarous or cruell."[69] Whipping, provided it were not excessive, was not considered cruel at that time but a severe whipping without caution could prove fatal. Hence the Colonists adopted the limitations placed upon whipping by the Mosaic Code that prohibited more than forty stripes at one time.[70] Burning at the stake, cutting off of hands, or various forms of torture not uncommon in England at that time, would have been considered by the Puritans as "inhumane, Barbarous or cruell." No incident of such punishment appears in the Colonial records.

13. *No Hasty Executions.* To avoid executing the wrong person or possibly to permit the condemned time to make his peace with God:

    No man condemned to dye shall be put to death within fower dayes next after his condemnation, unles the Court see spetiall cause to the contrary, or in case of martiall law, nor shall the body of any man so put to death be unburied 12 howers, unlesse it be in case of Anatomie.[71]

14. *Reprieves and Pardons.*

    The Governor and Deputy Governor Joyntly consenting, or any three Assistants concurring in consent shall have power out of Court to reprive a condemned malefactour, till the next quarter or generall Court. The General Court onely shall have power to pardon a condemned malefactor.[72]

    It is interesting to note that the power to pardon a person condemned to death did not reside in the Governor. In the Colonial form of government, the Governor had very little power to act alone; his position gave him prestige and leadership in policy making but little else.

15. *The Right to Appeal.* Appeals were permitted from a lower court to a higher court and ultimately to the General Court, as we have seen in Chapter 3. Appeals to England were strictly

forbidden. When Thomas Knower threatened such an appeal at the very beginning of the Colonial government in Boston, he was "sett in the bilbowes" (an iron bar with sliding shackles locked around a person's legs, an instrument that served until the stocks were built).[73] Any appeal to England threatened the autonomy of the Colonial government, as demonstrated in the case of Dr. Child.[74] Appeals to a government on the other side of the Atlantic appeared to be more and more impracticable as time went on. Even appeals to a Commission sent to New England by the King were intolerable. John Porter in 1665 made an appeal from a Colonial Court to such a Commission. The General Court declared that "it would be an unsufferable burden" if a person duly sentenced by a Colonial Court should be able to appeal to a tribunal from England, for

> all sorts of persons formerly punished (though never so justly) now would hope for some reparation to be made to them, even such as suffered twenty, yea thirty yeares & more since, now resolving to trample upon the authority that sentenced them . . . .

The General Court logically concluded that, if such appeals had been permissible, then it would have been "impossible for his majesty to have a colony of people here. . . ." It reminded the King that the Colony had been lawfully set up in accordance with the rights granted under the Charter of 1629 and the planters of the Colony "had left theire deare relations, & parted with their inheritances in their native country, venturing the lives of themselves & families into this wildernesse, & here, without any expence of his Majestie, have raised up a colony of people. . . ." It was unbearable to them to "submit themselves, their lives, & estates, & their liberties, farr dearer then [than] them both, to another authority, whose rule is their owne discretion."[75]

16. *The Right to Counsel.* In the early seventeenth century lawyers had not achieved the recognition and status they later earned. There was an evident unwillingness to consider the practice of law an honorable and worthy profession. The following "liberty" therefore was at the time probably considered progressive:

Every man that findeth himselfe unfit to plead his owne cause in any Court shall have Libertie to imploy any man against whom the Court doth not except, to helpe him, Provided he give him noe fee or reward for his paines. This shall not exempt the partie him selfe from Answering such Questions in person as the Court shall thinke meete to demand of him.[76] (See Chapter 13)

17. *Not Everyone To Be Held Responsible for His Crimes.* "Children, Idiots, Distracted persons, and all that are strangers, or new commers to our plantation, shall have such allowances and dispensations in any Cause whether Criminall or other as religion and reason require."[77] (See Chapter 13)

18. *No Involuntary Servitude.*

There shall never be any bond slaverie, villinage [where a serf is held in subjection by his lord, as in the feudal system] or Captivitie amongst us unles it be lawfull Captives taken in just warres, and such strangers as willingly sell themselves or are sold to us. . . .

There were in the Colony a few Negro slaves, a few Indian captives of the wars, and in addition a few whom the Courts sentenced to slavery for the commission of crimes.[78] But even these "shall have all the liberties and Christian usages which the law of god established in Israell concerning such persons doeth morally require. . . ."[79]

19. *Protection of Servants.* Again taking their cue from the Bible (Exodus 21:26–27) the lawmakers declared that:

If any man smite out the eye or tooth of his man-servant, or maid servant, or otherwise mayme or much disfigure him, unlesse it be by meere casualtie [accident] he shall let them goe free from his service. And [the servant] shall have such further recompense as the Court shall allow him.[80]

The Colonial law was more liberal than the Mosaic in affording servants protection from physical injury by their masters.[81]

There were other rights and liberties of a later date not found in the Body of Liberties:

20. *Right to Defend Oneself.* The Bible had said (Exodus 22:2): "If a thief be found breaking up, and be smitten that he die, there shall no blood be shed for him." The Colonial law of 1647 (carried forward into the subsequent codes of laws) stated:

> If any person in the just and necessary defence of his life, or the life of any other, shall kill any person attempting to Rob or Murther in the Field or Highway, or to break into any dwelling house, if he conceive he cannot with safety of his own person otherwise take the Felon or Assailant, or bring him to Tryal, he shall be holden blameless.[82]

21. *The Presumption of Innocence.* The General Court in 1657 voted:

> Whereas in all civill cases depending in suit, the party affirmeth that the defendant hath done him wrong, & accordingly presents his case for judgment & satisfaction, it behoveth the Court & jury to see that the affirmation be proved by sufficient evidence, else the case must be found for the defendant; & so it is also in a criminall case, for in the eye of the law every man is honest & innocent unles it be proved legally to the contrary.[83]

22. *The Statute of Limitations.*

> No person shall be Indited, presented, informed against or Complained of, to any Court or Magistrate within this Jurisdiction, for the breach of any penall Law, or any other misdemeanour . . . unles the said Inditement or Complaint be made and exhibited *within one year* after the Offence be Committed . . . Provided alwayes, this law shall not extend to any Capitall Offences, nor any Crimes that may concerne loss of member or Banishment, or to any Treasonable Plotts or Conspiracies against the Commonwealth, nor to any fellonies above ten shillings. . . .[84]

Many legal scholars have debated the question as to whether —and to what extent—the Colonial legislators brought with them the Common Law of England, or whether they hammered out their own laws to suit their special needs in a "waste willdernesse" where they drew heavily upon "the law of God" as interpreted by the church elders.[85] To say that all Colonial law in seventeenth century New England was English Common Law is to overlook the official records, which speak for themselves. To say that the lawmakers relied exclusively on Scripture is equally erroneous. It is true that in the early days of the Colonies the word of God was always available to them if no express law of the country had been enacted to cover a given case, and the Congregational ministers were always ready to interpret the law (acting as a sort of Supreme Court), but, as time went on, the Colonies relied less and less on

Biblical ordinances. It is also true that a good deal of the Common Law was incorporated into the substantive law of crimes and that many Colonial procedural forms were taken directly from those in use in English courts. The Colonists cherished the Englishman's right to a trial by jury and to "due process." The spirit of the English law was implicit in their legal enactments. And yet there were few men in the Bay Colony or in Plymouth Colony who were legal scholars; there was no legal bar, and no law library. It is significant that, following the legal controversy with Dr. Child, the General Court in 1647 ordered a shipment of legal texts from England "to the end we may have the better light for making & proceeding about laws."[86] In short, one can say that they showed no necessary dependence on the Common Law, although they had considerable respect for it and turned to it more and more as the century wore on and as the influence of the ministers waned. Their law was their own law, of a mixture of Biblical and common-law origins, frequently more liberal and progressive than the law of England at that time.

Civil rights and liberties in the "Old Colony" did not differ greatly from those in its neighbor, the Bay Colony. Lawmakers in Plymouth, like those in Boston, struck off whatever laws they thought wise and necessary to preserve the kind of government they sought to establish in this "remote waste wilderness." As the years rolled on, the number of laws enacted by the General Court accumulated. Because they were not numbered, as they are today, nor classified by chapters nor printed for all to read, the people demanded a compilation, revision, and arrangement in alphabetical sequence. It was not until 1636 that the legislature gave formal recognition to this demand: "The ordnances of the colony & corporation being read, divers were fownd worthy the reforming, others the rejecting, & others fitt to be instituted & made."[87] The General Court thereupon appointed a committee consisting of the Governor, the Assistants, and four citizens of Plymouth, two from Scituate and two from "Duxburrow," to prepare a report for consideration by the next session of the legislature. Evidently this committee did not report to the next session; at least there is no record of it. In 1643 another committee was appointed to "peruse the lawes" and to report to the Court what laws should be repealed and what new laws should be enacted.[88] Finally, the people at a

Court of Election in 1658 approved a code that comprised all laws enacted during the period from 1623 to 1657 that were still in force.[89] This arrangement was published as the official law book, and copies were distributed to each town. Another edition appeared in 1672 comprising all laws in force as of 1671.[90] The last revision was issued in 1685, not differing materially from that which preceded.

The first law appearing in the early records (December 17, 1623) recognized the Englishman's right to a trial by his peers: ". . . all Criminall facts, and also all [matters] of trespasses and debts betweene man & man should [be decided] by the verdict of twelve Honest men to be Impanelled by Authority in forme of a Jury upon their oaths."[91]

The Plymotheans, like the Bostonians, were vitally concerned with the fundamental rights of a free citizen. Their document, called "The Generall Fundamentals," was composed between the years 1636 and 1671. How much of it was written in 1636 (by the committee appointed that year) and how much was the result of subsequent additions and revisions we cannot tell from the record; at least we can say that 1636 marked the beginning of the *first* "bill of rights" in America, although the completed document may not have appeared until after the Body of Liberties was published in Boston and distributed to the towns of the Bay Colony. The two documents had much in common.

The opening statement of the Fundamentals reflects their desire for an independent and republican form of government:

> Wee the Associates of New-Plimouth, comeing hither as Freeborn Subjects of the State of England, endowed with all and singular; the Priviledges belonging to such being: Assembled; Do in Act [enact], Ordain and Constitute; That no Act, Imposition, Law or Ordinance, be made or imposed upon us, at present or to come; but such as shall be made or imposed by consent of the Body of Freemen or Associates, or their Representatives legally Assembled: which is according to the free Liberties of the State of England.[92]

Other rights guaranteed by this document included the right of free annual elections of Governor and Assistants; equal justice for all; due process (no one to be punished "but by virtue or equity of some express Law of the General Court of this Colony, the known Law of God, or the good and equitable laws of our Nation");

jury trials "according to the commendable custome of England"; the right to challenge jurymen and, in capital cases, peremptory challenges "against six or eight of the Jury" (changed to twenty in 1685); the requirement of two witnesses in capital cases ("or that which is equivalent thereunto"); the right to make wills and dispose of property (if one is 21 years old); and finally the right of the churches for protection from the government (provided they were orthodox).[93]

† † †

We have witnessed the healthy devotion of Englishmen to their civil rights and liberties as exemplified in the Bay Colony's Body of Liberties of 1641 and the laws of both Colonies enacted by representatives in the General Courts. Such devotion, motivated by memories of overbearing treatment by bishops of the Church of England and by arbitrary acts of Kings, was never relaxed, although as we shall see in later chapters, there were periods of emotional stress when insistence on Puritan orthodoxy ran counter to fundamental rights carefully inscribed in their laws or guaranteed to all natural-born Englishmen by the Charter of 1629.

When, in the latter half of the eighteenth century, certain rights held dear by the American Colonies were curtailed by King and Parliament and "a long train of abuses and usurpations" by the mother country evidenced "a design to reduce them under absolute Despotism" and to establish "an absolute Tyranny" over them, freedom-loving Englishmen found it necessary "to dissolve the political bands" with Great Britain, as bravely proclaimed in their Declaration of Independence of July 4, 1776.

The Constitution of the Commonwealth of Massachusetts, accepted by the people in 1780, following a long-protracted war with his Majesty's forces, served as a model for the United States Constitution of 1787 and reflected many of the early civil rights and liberties of the Body of Liberties and the subsequent codes of law that incorporated almost all of its 98 articles which in turn were drawn, not only from the Christian Bible, but also from the Magna Carta and the traditional rights of Englishmen, which had frequently been modified and liberalized by the General Court.

It is interesting to note that many of the wise provisions of

Colonial lawmakers did not expire in 1684 with the "annihilation" of the Charter in 1684 but have continued down to this day and now constitute "the law of the land" in the Commonwealth of Massachusetts and in the United States. (See Appendix C).

Today citizens of the Commonwealth of Massachusetts enjoy rights that could not have been granted in the Puritan culture of the seventeenth century. It would, for example, have been "an abomination in the eyes of the Lord" to have permitted the kind of freedom of speech or of the press that is now guaranteed to every citizen by the first amendment to the Federal Constitution and by the sixteenth article of the Declaration of Rights of the Commonwealth Constitution (as rewritten by the 77th amendment). In the Bay Colony or the Plymouth Colony any person could speak his mind in any public assembly but what he said subjected him to a severe penalty if it were designed to malign or vilify any state or church official or defame authority or subvert the Christian faith. Likewise, printed publications that were found to be unorthodox, subversive, or treasonable would most likely be thrown into the fire and their authors fined or whipped or banished. The right of franchise, now stoutly defended for American citizens regardless of "race, color, or previous condition of servitude" was also strictly limited in the Colonies, for reasons set forth in Chapter 3.

We have witnessed in recent decades a notable extension of rights in the areas of religion, of public accomodations, of academic freedom, and of equal opportunities for women. Today, the rights guaranteed to the accused go far beyond the political philosophy of the most liberal of the seventeenth century Colonial leaders; for example, the extensive rights of a criminal at all stages of the proceedings against him, the restrictions on the process of search and seizure, with the rules of evidence and the criminal law strictly construed in favor of the accused, and more recently the federal Civil Rights Act of 1964. Yet, the open recognition of the rights of the individual in Colonial society as embodied in the Body of Liberties of 1641 and in subsequent Colonial laws, though limited by the culture of that period, was a most remarkable achievement.

5. CHURCH AND STATE

No earthly man can be
True subject to this State;
Who makes the Pope his Christ,
An Heretique his Mate.
—*Nathaniel Ward, 1645.*[1]

WHEN men of Boston or of Plymouth gathered in the public marketplace or outside the meetinghouse for an exchange of views on topics of the day, theological beliefs provided lively and heated material for disputation. Most people chose to stay well within the bounds of orthodoxy, but it was not an uncommon sight to see a person brought into court for some expressed heresy or for a few caustic comments on the long sermon of the previous Sabbath or simply for absenting himself once too often from public worship. Probably all literate members of the community knew their Bibles, while all had the opportunity of hearing the reverend elders on the Sabbath, or at the regular Thursday lecture, expound at some length the doctrine of the "covenant of grace" or the "salvation of the unregenerate" or the "indwelling of the Holy Ghost" or some other esoteric theological mystery.[2] Even the uneducated had some familiarity with current tenets and could usually distinguish between what was orthodox and what was not. If he could not make this distinction, it was safer for him to refrain from discussing religion in public.

That the state must work closely with the church was a proposition everyone took for granted. No one—unless it were Roger Williams—would have urged the General Court to "make no law respecting an establishment of religion, or prohibit the free exercise thereof," as their descendants did a century and a half later when they framed a constitution for the new union of independent states.[3] Did not England have its state church? Was not Catholicism the official religion of France? Did not everyone know that the Plymouth Colony had its birth in a little church in Scrooby, England, and that its planters had put their explicit trust in the loving hands of God? Was not the Bay Colony, too, a sort of divine protectorate that God had sustained through severe trials and afflictions?

In a culture where thinking men had few pastures in which to browse other than religion, it was natural that there was an intense preoccupation with that subject. Hence arose a constant vigilance over one's conscience and particularly over the conscience of one's neighbor, for the sins of a few might bring down God's wrath on all. John Winthrop, in his historic discourse on board the *Arbella* before setting out for New England's shores, had made it clear to all that the chief purpose of the new Bay Colony was "to improve [utilize] our lives to doe more service to the Lord . . . that ourselves and posterity may be the better preserved from the Common corruptions of this evill world, to serve the Lord and worke out our Salvation under the power and purity of his holy ordinances."[4]

The Lord's "holy ordinances" were clearly manifest in the Bible, made available in English in the King James Version of 1611. No Puritan doubted that this holy book was *revealed truth and the source of all reason and morality*. Inevitably, then, a government designed to perpetuate these truths and to give them vitality would form a close alliance with the church and would develop an administration of criminal justice that, in the early years at least, would derive its inspiration and much of its language from that honored book.

Increase Nowell, for about fourteen years the Secretary of the General Court in the Bay Colony and an Assistant in that Court for 25 years, expressed the church-state relationship in these words:

> This hath been no small priviledge, and advantage to us in New-England that our Churches, and civil State have been planted, and growne up (like two twinnes) together like that of Israel in the wildernes by which wee were put in minde (and had opportunitie put into our hands) not only to gather our Churches, and set up the Ordinances of Christ Jesus in them according to the Apostolick pat-

terne by such light as the Lord graciously afforded us; but also withall to frame our civil Politie, and lawes according to the rules of his most holy word whereby each do help and strengthen [the] other (the Churches the civil Authoritie, and the civil Authoritie the Churches) and so both prosper the better without such aemulation, and contention for priviledges or priority as have proved the misery (if not ruine) of both in some other places. . . .[5]

Perhaps Nowell had a hand in drawing up a statement published by the General Court in 1646 promulgating the theory that a community held together by religious ties is more apt to be law abiding:

In these countreys, where the churches of Christ are seated, the prosperity of the civill state is much advanced & blessed of God, when the ordinances of true religion & publike worship of God do find free passage in purity & peace. . . . the word [of God] is of generall & common behoofe to all sorts of people, as being the ordinary meanes to subdue the harts of hearers not onely to the faith, & obedience to the Lord Jesus, but also to *civill obedience,* & allegiance unto magistracy. . . .[6]

In Plymouth Colony a more peaceful relationship between these two institutions was seen through the eyes of its governor, William Bradford:

Oh, how great comfort was it now to see,
The churches to enjoy free liberty!

. . .

A prudent Magistracy here was placed,
By which the Churches defended were and graced;

. . .

Whilst things thus did flourish and were in their prime,
Men thought it happy and a blessed time,
To see how sweetly all things did agree;
Both in Church and State, there was an amity;
Each to the other mutual help did lend. . . .[7]

Those who held the power in the Bay Colony sincerely believed that "subjection to ecclesiasticall discipline is necessary for the well being of any Christian society."[8] And they held it to be their sworn duty to Christ to chastise those who disturbed the peace by openly denying this basic assumption or who reviled those who cherished it.

Such a close interdependance of church and state—a normal condition of affairs for that period of our cultural development—has led many historians to refer to these two colonies as "Bible Commonwealths" or "Puritan Oligarchies." Brooks Adams, the most severe critic of the Bay Colony of all the nineteenth century historians, characterized it as a "theocratic despotism."[9] Was it in fact a "theocracy"—a government responsible only to God whose laws were the laws of the realm, a government presided over by ministers who served as God's representatives? What does the record tell us?

There were obvious elements of a theocratic form of government built into the administration of the affairs of the Colonies, particularly in the Bay Colony:

1) Assistants, who had broad legislative and judicial powers, were, as we have seen, men of dignity and importance who looked upon their duties as divinely commissioned. They took an oath to perform these duties "according to the Laws of God and of this land, *for the advancement of the Gospel* and the good of the people of this Jurisdiction."[10]

2) When doubts arose as to how "the good of the people" could best be achieved, the civil authorities called in the ministers for advice that was always freely given. Opinions of the clergy were not binding on the courts or the legislative body, but no one could doubt their decisive importance. They were asked to advise on all manner of political questions, on matters of trade and foreign policy, on disputes between individuals and on interpretations of the criminal law, particularly as it concerned God's word as revealed in the Bible. The General Court on one occasion summoned some of "the reverend elders that are or may be in toune" to attend the next morning's session and "spend the forenoone in prayer."[11]

3) It was clearly "the duty of the Christian Magistrate," the law said, "to take care the People be fed with wholesome and sound Doctrine" pointing to the necessity of considering "the rich blessings of God, flowing from the good agreement of the Civil and Church-estate, and the horrible mischiefs and confusions that follow on the contrary."[12]

4) It was the clear duty of the courts to uphold the ordinances of God. The Body of Liberties of 1641 laid down a rule of law

that was carried forward in the subsequent legal codes: "Civill Authoritie hath power and libertie to see the peace, ordinances and Rules of Christ observed in every church according to his word. so it be done in a Civill and not in an Ecclesiastical Way."[13] The plain duty of a Plymouth Justice in respect to upholding the word of God was expounded by Nathaniel Morton, nephew of Governor Bradford and the clerk of the Plymouth General Court, in his "Address" introducing the revised laws of 1658:

> And although wee hold and doe afeirme that both Courts of Justice and Magistrates, whoe are the minnesters of the Lawe are essentially Civill; notwithstanding wee conceive, that as the Magistrate hath his power from God, soe undoubtedly hee is to improve [use] it for the honer of God, and that in the uphoalding of his worship and service, and against the contrary, with due respect also to bee had unto those that are really consienyous, though differing and decenting in som smaller matters; But if any really or in pretence of conscience shall professe that which eminently tendeth to the Inundation of Civill State, and violation of naturall Bonds, or the overthrow of the Churches of God or of his Worship, that heer prudence is to bee improved [used] in the Enacting and Execution of lawes.[14]

5) The state, as the guardian of the ministry, was vitally concerned with the supply and maintenance of orthodox ministers. At its first session in the Bay Colony, on August 23, 1630, the Court of Assistants turned its attention to the support of its two ministers, the Reverends Wilson and Phillips, and ordered that "houses should be built for them with convenient speede, att the publique charge" and that Phillips be paid in "meale, malte, Indean corne, oatemeale [and] salte fishe" in addition to a modest sum in English money, while Wilson would receive twenty pounds per year "till his wife come over."[15] In later years the General Court saw the need for establishing "a settled and incouraging maintenance of Ministers, in all Towns and Congregations within this Jurisdiction." Each town was to provide "some convenient house, for the use of the present Minister" and to be sure that "an honourable allowance be made" for which each inhabitant, whether church member or not, was assessed.[16] As time went on the ministers were not entirely satisfied with this plan, which caused some grumbling among the citizenry and never produced sufficient funds

to meet the ministers' total needs. The Rev. John Cotton of the Boston Church (later called the First Church) in a sermon reported by Winthrop said

> . . . when magistrates are forced to provide for the maintenance of ministers, etc., then the churches are in a declining condition. . . . ministers' maintenance should be by voluntary contribution, not by lands, or revenues, or tithes, etc.; for these have always been accompanied with pride, contention, and sloth, etc.[17]

6) The state soon became the fierce watchdog over the rise of new religious groups, establishing a rule that no residents of the Bay Colony could gather a new church fellowship without the approval of the General Court and such approval would not be given if the Magistrates and Elders of the churches in that neighborhood did not give their assent. If a church group were formed without this approval, its members would not be admitted to the freedom of the Commonwealth.[18] After the arrival of the Quakers —"that cursed Sect of Hereticks"—the state claimed the right to "purge" the town of any settled ministers who in the opinion of the General Court were "vitious in theire lives or pernitiously hethrodoxe in theire doctrines."[19]

7) Church membership was a prerequisite to the right to vote and to hold office, as we have already reported in a previous chapter. It must have seemed only basic commonsense to Winthrop and others to make certain by rigid laws that only the right sort of citizen should be permitted membership in an organization whose ideal was "to serve the Lord and worke out our Salvation under the power and purity of his holy ordinances."[20] Actually the denial of the right of franchise to the majority of the inhabitants (because they were not church members) caused no loud protests in the Bay Colony excepting from a few individuals. It was in fact necessary in 1647 for the General Court to threaten with a fine those who evaded the duties of citizenship by refusing to accept the status of freemen because it carried with it the obligation to serve as constables, jurymen, selectmen and so on.[21]

8) The ministers needed no legislative lobby to persuade the General Court to enact laws supporting the Puritan concept of the good life. (In a later section of this chapter we list the numerous criminal laws based on religious doctrines.) Members of the Gen-

eral Court were themselves members of the churches, and most of them were well grounded in Puritan orthodoxy and eager to see that what Winthrop called "a Christian common weale" was sustained by punitive legislation. But punishment did not always fall *immediately* upon the heretic. The hand of justice was usually stayed while the culprit was referred to a minister for "correction." The fate of Captain Partridge who arrived in Boston in 1645 to find himself forthwith involved in a touchy question of doctrine was a case in point. The Captain had served in Parliament and in respect to all other matters except religion was an acceptable "newcomer" and evidently greatly surprised at his reception in Boston. Winthrop tells us that on his voyage across the Atlantic, Partridge

> broached and zealously maintained divers points of antinomianism and familism, for which he was called before the magistrates [in Boston] and charged with the said opinions, to which he refused to give any answer. But before he departed, he was willing to confer with Mr. Cotton, which accordingly he did, and Mr. Cotton reported to the magistrates, that he found him corrupt in his judgment [on matters of doctrine], but ignorant of those points which he had maintained, so as he perceived he had been but lately taken with them, and that upon argument he was come off from some of the worst of them, and he had good hope to reclaim him wholly; but some of the magistrates requiring a present renouncing of all under his hand [that is, under his signature], he the said captain was not willing to [do] that before he were clearly convinced of his error in them. It was moved by some of the magistrates, in regard he had made so hopeful a beginning, and that winter was now at hand, and it would be very hard to expose his wife and family to such hardships, etc., to permit him to stay here till the spring, but the major part (by one or two) voting to the contrary, he was forced to depart, and so went to Rhode Island. . . .

The wise and gentle Winthrop, who was sometimes at odds with his peers who insisted on harsher penalties than he thought proper, found the decision of the court "offensive" and made this significant comment:

> But sure the rule of hospitality to strangers, and of seeking to pluck out of the fire such as there may be hope of to be reduced out of error and the snare of the devil, do seem to require more moderation

and indulgence of human infirmity where there appears not obstinancy against the clear truth.[22]

It was evident that the church and the state had "growne up like two twinnes," each upholding the other. The minister, as interpreter and expounder of the ordinances of God provided indispensable support to those who made the laws and judged their fellow men, while "the magistrate was bound by God to maintain the churches in purity and truth."[23] Did this close functional relationship between two distinct institutions make the Colonies theocracies? What facts can be adduced to show that the church and state were organically distinct?

1) The Royal Charter of 1629, from which the Bay Colony derived its powers, conferred no civil prerogatives upon the church nor did it include a single minister among those named as grantees. The government anticipated by the King and his advisors, although it turned out to be quite different from their expectations, was clearly not to be a theocracy dominated by critics of the Church of England.

2) Ministers did not attempt to gain control of the government by seeking political office. Probably they had no such ambition, prefering to exert their considerable influence from the pulpit. No express law forbade them from holding office but as early as 1632 "the congregation at Boston wrote to the elders and bretheren of the churches of Plimouth, Salem, etc., for their advice" as to "whether one person might be a civil magistrate and a ruling elder at the same time." All of them answered in the negative.[24] Both Colonies kept this sharp line of demarcation, although ministers were not averse to giving annual election-day sermons tinged with political innuendos. At a 1648 church synod held in Cambridge the clergy ruled: "As it is unlawful for the church-officers to meddle with the Sword of the Magistrates, so it is unlawful for the magistrate to meddle with the work proper to church officers."[25] The theoretical separation of church and state—not always meticulously honored in practice—was made clear by the Rev. John Cotton in 1636 in a letter written to London:

> ... magistrates are neyther chosen to office in the church, nor doe governe by directions from the church, but by civill lawes, and those

enacted in generall corts, and executed in corts of justice, by the governors and assistants. In all which, the church (as the church) hath nothing to doe. . . .[26]

3) Church members had no special immunity from the operation of the criminal law. The Body of Liberties of 1641 had declared that "Civill Authoritie hath power and libertie to deale with any Church member in a way of Civill Justice, notwithstanding any Church relation, office or interest."[27] On the other hand, although the church could censure civil authorities, "no church censure shall degrad or depose any man from any Civill dignitie, office, or Authoritie he shall have in the Common wealth."[28]

4) The civil government had granted the churches freedom to operate as they saw fit—subject to certain restrictions clearly set forth and probably drawn up with the aid of the churchmen themselves. For example, any "people of God" who had no church could "gather themselves into a Church Estaite" but they must be "orthodox in Judgement, and not scandalous in life" and must observe "the rules of Christ revealed in his word"; churches had liberty to "exercise all the ordinances of god, according to the rules of scripture"; they had free liberty of election and ordination, of admission and dismission; and no injunction could be placed upon them in point of doctrine.[29] They could celebrate days of fasting, prayer, and thanksgiving but between the years 1659 and 1681 could not celebrate Christmas in the Bay Colony because it was a pagan festival "superstitiously kept in other countrys."[30] The elders had free liberty to meet for conferences, and Christians "of all sortes" could hold private meetings. No restrictions were placed on church membership in respect to race or class. In this sense the churches were thoroughly democratic—barring only the unorthodox or scandalous. Winthrop reported in 1641:

> A negro maid, servant to Mr. Stoughton of Dorchester, being well approved by divers years experience, for sound knowledge and true godliness, was received into the church and baptized.[31]

Political and religious leaders, many of them self-righteous to the point of priggishness (as their opponents saw them), rejoiced in a government solidly grounded on the Word of God. Ministers claimed a monopoly on the art of making "true" interpretations of the Word, not because they thought of themselves as infallible but because they believed God's laws were so clear that their meaning should have been unmistakable to any student of the Bible—the source of all reason and morality. "You know," said Governor Winthrop to Anne Hutchinson, "there is no rule [in Scripture] that crosses another."[32] But the affairs of government and the judging of others had to be left to fallible humans subject to the biases of their culture and their own natural weaknesses—which was the root of much of their troubles. Certainly, they gave no quarter to religious liberals.

The Charter of 1629 had been silent on the subject of religious liberty, but King Charles the Second (1630-1685) in a letter to the Bay Colony General Court in 1662, following the Quaker episode, declared that "the principall end & foundation of the charter was & is the freedome & liberty of conscience."[33] The General Court replied that "the professed & reall end of the first adventurers," as his Majesty said, was indeed "that wee & ours [but certainly not anyone who happened to come to New England] might enjoy a greater liberty in the worship of God then [than] was at that time allowed to us, (when wee left our deare native country). . . ."[34] One of the duties of allegiance to the King, the General Court had said a few years earlier, was "in propogating the gospell, defending & upholding the true Christian or Prottestant religion according to the faith given by our Lord Christ in his word; our dread soveraigne being stiled 'defender of the faith'. . . ."[35]

If the Colonies had remained small compact units comprised solely of the religious zealots who "planted" them with a common purpose "to advance the kingdome of our Lord Jesus Christ, and to injoye the liberties of the Gospell in puritie with peace," they might have developed into harmonious societies, agreeing "sweetly in all things." But during the first decade of the Bay Colony's existence, thousands of men, women, and children landed uninvited on the shores of the Bay, many of whom did *not* share the Puritans' consuming interest in theology and chafed at shaping their daily lives to conform to *their* standards. The Puritans were unwilling to face the fact that New England was becoming a refuge for many different religious sects. To insist on religious conformity among the new arrivals or, at the least, to see that they did not disturb "church peace" or interfere with the Congregational way of worship was, they believed, to do only what Christ would have done had he presided over the town of Boston. To condone heresy was to condone sin. Even "for a governour to suffer any within his gates to prophane the sabbath" was, as the Rev. Mr. Cotton saw it, "a sinne against the 4th commandment, both in the private householder and in the magistrate." To the objection that the compulsory church attendance law in the Bay Colony made men hypocrites, he replied that it were better for people to be hypocrites than profane persons. "Hypocrites give God part of his due, the outward man, but the prophane person [that is, one who did not attend church services] giveth God neither outward nor inward man."[36]

Certain that they had the comforting backing of the Lord, those in power resolved that any man who dared hinder the advancement of "the kingdom of our Lord Jesus Christ" in New England would be properly humbled by penal laws willingly enacted by a sympathetic General Court. Inscribed on the title page of the code of laws of 1648, of 1660, and of 1672 were the words of the Apostle Paul in his Epistle to the Romans (13:2): "Whosoever therefore resisteth the power, resisteth the ordinance of God: and they that resist shall receive to themselves damnation."

The ordinary citizen who offended against these laws could be dealt with in court by an admonition or by a small fine or, in aggravated cases, by a whipping or some punishment of humiliation. But what could be done with the articulate and influential offenders from respected English families—men and women of the stature of Roger Williams and Anne Hutchinson?

Roger Williams, his wife, and two small children, had come uninvited to the Bay Colony shortly after its establishment, setting foot on New England soil for the first time in February 1631.[37] This young English Puritan minister was bright, likeable, courageous, a vigorous controversialist, and, above all, an avowed Separatist. In England he had taken a strong dislike to the Book of Common Prayer and the ritual of the Church of England, as had all Puritans, but he was not one to take a passive stand on important issues. He believed all faithful Puritans should make a clean and public break with the Mother Church, a step the leaders of the Bay Colony had always feared to take. They had not separated from the Church itself "but only from the corruptions and disorders which had sprung up in that church of recent years."[38] They had hoped that the New England churches would be a purified form of the Church of England and yet independent of its control. Governor Winthrop, particularly, would not accept the view that members of the English church were beyond redemption and he resented slurs cast upon them. "Whores and drunkards they are not," he said, "weake Christians they are indeed, and the weaker for want of that tender Care, that should be had of them"—but such weakness did not warrant open separation.[39]

Williams refused a call from the Rev. John Cotton's church in Boston because its congregation would not openly stand for complete separation nor humbly confess their sin in having had communion with such a corrupt church while they were in England. The Salem church, over Winthrop's protest, called Williams as its "teacher," but after a short stay there he left for Plymouth where he expected to find a warmer climate for separatism. There he was graciously received and encouraged to express his liberal views that were not entirely acceptable to some of Plymouth's older citizens. William Brewster, for example, then in his 69th year, Governor Bradford's "dear and loving friend" who had "suffered much for the Lord Jesus and the gospells sake," was dismayed and alarmed over the sermons of this young radical. And yet Williams had a winning personality, and Bradford spoke kindly of him:

> Mr. Roger Williams (a man godly & zealous, having many precious parts, but very unsettled in judgmente) came over first to the Massachusets, but upon some discontente left that place, and came hither (wher he was friendly entertained, according to their [the Plymotheans] poore abilitie,) and exercised his gifts amongst them, & after some time was admitted a member of the church; and his teaching well approoved, for the benefit wherof I still blese God, and am thankfull to him, even for his sharpest admonitions & reproufs, so farr as they agreed with truth. He this year begane to fall into some strange opinions, and from opinion to practise; which caused some controversie betweene the church & him, and in the end some discontente on his parte, by occasion wherof he left them some thing [somewhat] abruptly. . . . But he is to be pitied, and prayed for, and so I shall leave the matter, and desire the Lord to shew him his errors, and reduce him into the way of truth, and give him a setled judgment and constancie in the same; for I hope he belongs to the Lord, and that he will shew him mercie.[40]

Salem again called him and in 1633 Williams accepted the call as assistant pastor, and in 1635, upon the death of its minister, he was chosen minister of the Salem church. At the age of 31, Williams had acquired a reputation in New England as an influential young preacher who would not, in spite of sage advice, refrain from injecting controversy into his preaching and declaring his mind on issues he thought the churches should face. Encouraged by the support he received from his parishioners, he boldly urged his congregation to renounce all the other Bay Colony churches "as full of anti-Christian pollution."[41] It was immediately evident that he had overshot his mark, for only a minority of church members in Salem would go along with this radical proposal.

Williams was not fighting for religious toleration as such. He had little respect for the views of those who were not Puritans. Yet he believed in the right of a person to worship as he pleased without government interference, so long as that person did not disturb the peace. He saw no religious values in the Mohammedan or Roman Catholic faiths and in later years he wrote of "the grandest Seigniories of the Turkish and Popish Empires, the two so mighty apposers of the Son of God" and predicted that God would break their proud necks.[42] Of the Quakers who came into New England in the late 1650s he wrote of their "uncleane spirit" and "their insufferably proud and contemptuous behavior," saying he was "as zealous for my Lord Jesus as they are for Sathan." He referred to George Fox, the founder of the Society of Friends, as "G. Fox & his Fantasticks" and entitled his book attacking Fox and George Burroughs, the Quaker preacher, "George Fox digg'd out of his Burrowes" which surely did not reflect a completely tolerant mind. And yet he sedulously maintained, almost singlehandedly, that no matter how much one disagreed with another's views on religious matters, the right to freedom of conscience should be inviolate:

> I confess in this plea for freedom to all Consciences in matters (merely) of worship, I have impartially pleaded for the freedom of the consciences of the Papists themselves, the greatest enemies and persecutors (in Europe) of the Saints and Truths of Jesus.[43]

This breadth of vision was antithetical to that of the New England Puritan of that day. The Rev. John Cotton, spokesman of Puritanism, engaged with Williams (after he left Massachusetts) in a friendly exchange of views. Cotton took the position that he would punish only the one whose conscience was sinful, absolving one who unwittingly and in good conscience fell into error. He believed that there were certain fundamental truths "so cleare" that one "cannot but bee convinced in Conscience of the dangerous Errour" of rejecting them, especially after one had been instructed and twice admonished. Could a reasonable person, for example, deny "Jesus Christ is the Redeemer & only Mediatour & the Scriptures are the Word of God"?[44] Had not Paul the Apostle said, "A man that is an heretick after the first and second admonition reject; knowing that he that is such is subverted, and sinneth, being condemned of himself"?[45] Persistence in "error" after hearing the "truth" expounded by Puritan ministers was not, according to Cotton, "out of Conscience, but against Conscience." Such a person is "not persecuted for Cause of Conscience, but for sinning against his Owne Conscience." It was proper, therefore, to punish the sinner. Cotton believed the state should take over the function of punishment. On the other hand, although Williams did not deny the "fundamentall truths"—after all, he was a good Puritan—he deplored the method of correction:

> To batter downe Idolatry, false worship, heresie, schisme, blindnesse, hardnesse, out of the soule and spirit, it is vaine, improper, and unsutable to bring those weapons which are used by persecuters, stocks, whips, prisons, swords, gibbets, stakes, & c . . . but against these spirituall strong holds in the soules of men, Spirituall Artillery and weapons are proper. . . . civill weapons are improper in this businesse, and never able to effect ought in the soule. . . .[46]

If the New England Puritans had adopted "Spirituall Artillery and weapons" only against the heretic and the blasphemer and confined the administration of criminal justice to crimes against the person or against property or against the peace and security of the state, as Williams had advocated, historians would have had no occasion to call the Bay Colony a "theocratic despotism." But the times were not ripe for a Roger Williams' philosophy of government.

The Rev. John Cotton, the prophet and apostle of Christ in New England, held that it was not what the Magistrate thought was right or wrong but what God had clearly ordered. "The times are evill indeed," he said, "when the pressing of obedience to the rule [of God] shall be counted persecution." He found ample authority in both the Old and the New Testaments for the punishment of those who openly advocated heretical and "schismatical tennents." For "the obstinate foole, a whip is fitter (sayeth Solomon) for such a backe."[47]

In a letter written after his banishment, Williams made clear his understanding of "liberty of conscience" in a classic hypothetical illustration:

> There goes many a ship to sea, with many hundred souls in one ship, whose weal and woe is common, and is a true picture of a commonwealth, or a human combination or society. It hath fallen out sometimes, that both papists and protestants, Jews and Turks, may be embarked in one ship; upon which supposal I affirm, that all the liberty of conscience, that ever I pleaded for, turns upon these two hinges—that none of the papists, protestants, Jews, or Turks, be forced to come to the ship's prayers or worship, nor compelled from their own particular prayers or worship, if they practice any. I further add, that I never denied, that notwithstanding this liberty, the commander of this ship ought to command that justice, peace and sobriety, be kept and practiced, both among the seamen and all the passengers. If any of the seamen refuse to perform their services, or passengers to pay their freight; if any refuse to help, in person or purse, towards the common charges or defence; if any refuse to obey the common laws and orders of the ship, concerning their common peace or preservation; if any shall mutiny and rise up against their commanders and officers; if any should preach or write that there ought to be no commanders or officers, because all are equal in Christ, therefore no masters nor officers, no laws nor orders, nor corrections nor punishments;—I say, I never denied, but in such cases, whatever is pretended, the commander or commanders may judge, resist, compel and punish such transgressors, according to their deserts and merits. . . .[48]

Concerning the Puritan's "Declaration of the Liberties the Lord Jesus hath given to the Churches" and other rights expressed in the Bay Colony's Book of Laws, Williams had a few caustic comments:

> New Englands Lawes . . . tell us how free it shall be for people to

> gather themselves into Church-estate? how free to choose their owne Ministers? how free to enjoy all the Ordinances of Christ Jesus, &c.? But yet, provided . . . that the Civill State must judge of the Spirituall, to wit, Whether persons be fit for Church-estate, Whether the Gathering be right, Whether the peoples choice be right, Doctrines right, and what is this in truth, but to sweare that blasphemous Oath of Supremacie againe, to the Kings and Queenes and Magistrates of this and other Nations in stead of the Pope, &c.?[49]

In the brief span of time in which he preached and lectured and made his influence felt in Boston, in Plymouth, and in Salem, Williams had advanced four unpopular propositions:

1) New England churches should separate openly and completely from the Church of England and acknowledge their sin in having formerly had communion with it.

2) The church should not punish men for what they believe as a matter of conscience so long as they do not disturb the civil peace. Williams drew a very apt quotation from history (unfortunately after he had left Massachusetts), citing the statement of the Roman Emperor Maximilian the Second (1527-1576) who had granted religious liberty to the Lutherans: "There is no sin ordinarily greater against God, said he, then [than] to use violence against the Consciences of men."[50] The state, Williams insisted, should not use its authority to enforce the first four of the Ten Commandments—a doctrine that gained wide acceptance 140 years later but in the 1630s was considered rank heresy. The state then would have been powerless to punish those who did not worship the "true" God or who used the name of the Lord in vain; nor could it have required church attendance or demanded obedience to the many laws restricting activities on the Sabbath.

3) The King, Williams maintained, had no right to grant land to the English, for this land belonged to the Indians. The great Charter, in Williams' view, was mere parchment. Although some of the settlers had bought their land from the Indians, Williams' claim, if established, would have thrown a cloud over many land titles. Some of the tracts needed by the settlers had been purchased from the Indians, some were taken as spoils of war, and some were not used or claimed as Indian settlements and were open to whoever first cultivated them. It is not clear now to what extent the first planters heeded the advice or directive of the Bay

Company sent to Endecott in 1629 before the Winthrop fleet left England:

> If any of the salvages pretend right of inheritance to all or any part of the lands granted in our pattent, wee pray yow endeavour to purchase their tytle, that we may avoyde the least scruple of intrusion.[51]

Williams, at any rate, four or five years later, indicted the Bay Colony leaders for this very "intrusion." As though he wished to make matters more embarassing for the Colonial leaders who were becoming increasingly annoyed over his "dangerous opinions," he wrote a little book that was clearly antiroyalist. He claimed the late King James "had told a solemn public lie" in saying that he was "the first Christian prince that had discovered this land." He charged the late king with "blasphemy for calling Europe Christendom" and made some derogatory remarks about the then reigning King Charles. When rebuked for these seditious and startling pronouncements he replied that he had meant them only for the Governor's private edification and offered his book, or any part of it, to be burned. "At the next court," Winthrop wrote, "he appeared penitently, and gave satisfaction of his intention and loyalty. So it was left, and nothing done in it."[52]

4) On a matter of doctrine, Williams had insisted that an oath was a form of worship and hence could not be administered to an "unregenerate" person—a doctrine that would have greatly handicapped the administration of criminal justice had it prevailed. Expanding on this point, Williams held that a regenerate person could not pray in the presence of those who were "unregenerate" even if they were members of his own family.

It became obvious to every thoughtful person in the Colonies that either the government must change its political philosophy and the churches their rigid doctrinal position or that they must ask Williams to leave the jurisdiction. What else could be done? Many attempts had been made by the other Congregational ministers to dislodge him from his "dangerous and erronious views." He had been before the courts and had been fully warned. He would not recant. An admonition or a fine would surely not silence his tongue. Bodily punishments or any form of humiliating correction such as the stocks or pillory, would have been inappropriate for a man of his social standing.[53] Its patience at an end, the General Court in 1635, made its decision:

> Whereas Mr. Roger Williams, one of the elders of the church of Salem, hath broached & dyvulged dyvers newe & dangerous opinions, against the aucthoritie of magistrates, as also writt letters of defamation, both of the magistrates & churches here, & that before any conviction, & yet mainetaineth the same without retraction, it is therefore ordered, that the said Mr. Williams shall departe out of this jurisdiction within sixe weeks nowe nexte ensueing, which if hee neglect to performe, it shall be lawfull for the Governor & two of the magistrates to send him to some place out of this jurisdiction, not to returne any more without licence from the Court.[54]

The ministers, too, approved of this sentence of the court "and his own church had him under question also for the same cause."[55] But Winthrop reports, without revealing his identity, that one minister did not approve. The Rev. Mr. Cotton, in a letter sent to Williams after his departure, told him that the court's decision "was neither done by my counsell nor consent, although I dare not deny the sentence passed to be righteous in the eyes of God."[56]

No one questioned the court's authority to banish, and Williams accepted the verdict without threat of appeal. The Charter had given the Bay Colony the right:

> for their speciall defence and safety, to incounter, *expulse,* repell, and resist by force of armes . . . all such person and persons as shall at any tyme hereafter attempt or enterprise the destruction, invasion, detriment, or annoyaunce to the said plantation or inhabitants. . . .[57]

That Williams had been an "annoyaunce" to the plantation had been fully proven.

As cold weather was approaching, making a journey out of the jurisdiction hazardous, his time was extended, but when the magistrates heard that during this interim Williams was still boldly speaking out, a secret plan was made to seize him and forthwith ship him back to England. The secret was poorly kept, and Williams, who was not in confinement or under restraint, managed to elude the authorities and undertook a perilous trek southward. He reached Narragansett Bay and there, thanks to the "merciful providence of God," gave the name "Providence" to a settlement that served for many years for those "distressed for conscience." In 1644 he obtained from the King a charter for Providence, Newport, and Portsmouth but in a new charter of 1663 the official designation of a wider area was "Rhode Island and Providence Plantations"—a name officially used today by the State of Rhode Island.

Williams harbored no ill feelings against his many friends in the Massachusetts Colonies. Until his death he kept up a warm correspondence with Winthrop and Winthrop's son and many others whom he loved and respected. Because of his friendliness with the Indians, whose language he had mastered, he rendered valiant service in preventing an alliance between the Pequot and Narragansett tribes who were bent on the destruction of the English.[58]

His restless and imaginative mind continued its courageous search for new religious truths in an era of religious conservatism. He became for a short time a Baptist and founded what is considered to be the first Baptist church in America. Soon thereafter, he became a Seeker—a member of a sect despised by the Puritans (for it had little respect for orthodoxy) but, like modern Unitarianism, a sect that inspired its members to seek religious truth wherever they could find it.

Forty years after Williams' clandestine departure, the Council of the Bay Colony tendered him a conditional invitation to return but, then in his seventies, he decided to decline the offer and to remain with his friends and family in Providence, which he did until his death seven years later. The Council order signed by the secretary, Edward Rawson, and dated March 31, 1676, read:

> Whereas Mr. Roger Williams stands at present under a sentence of Restraint from coming into this Colony yet considering how readyly & freely at all tymes he hath served the English Interest in this time of warre with the Indians & manifested his particular respects to the Authority of this colony in several services desired of him, & further understanding, how by the last assault of the Indians upon Providence his House is burned & himself in his old age reduced to an uncomfortable & disabled state Out of Compassion to him in this condition The Council doe Order and Declare that if the sayd Mr. Williams shall see cause & desire it he shall have liberty to repayre into any of our Towns for his security & comfortable abode during these Public Troubles, He behaving himself peaceably & inoffensively &

> not disseminating & venting any of his different opinions in matters of Religion to the dissatisfaction of any.[59]

The scene, of course, had changed. Winthrop, Endecott, Hooker, Cotton, Wilson, Shepard and many others had gone to their rewards. But if Williams had returned it is doubtful if he could have met the condition of the invitation—not to vent "any of his different opinions in matters of Religion to the dissatisfaction of any."

Williams was not hailed as "the apostle of religious liberty" or the "earliest champion of democratic government" until many years after his death. Even as late as 1876, a petition presented to the General Court of the Commonwealth asking for a revocation of the sentence of banishment failed of passage, the reason being, according to Burrage, partly because of the possible aspersion it might cast upon the reputation of the early Colonial leaders and partly because people of that period were not convinced that the banishment was not fully deserved.[60] A similar petition presented in 1899 and 1900 likewise failed of passage.[61] In 1901 a petition to erect a memorial statue in the State House, or on its grounds, in honor of Williams was submitted and considered each year until 1905 when it evidently died in committee.[62] Again in 1906 another petition was filed in Williams' honor to seek approval of the General Court of the advice given by Governor Winthrop (who, in spite of his sharp disagreement with Williams' religious and political views, never lost his respect and fondness for him) asking the council in 1637 to consider recalling the man they had forced out of the Colony.[63] This petition also failed to win the approval of the Commonwealth General Court.

However, in 1936, just three hundred years after Williams had hastily left Massachusetts to avoid deportation to England, Governor James Michael Curley approved a resolve of the General Court that stated:

> Resolved, that, in so far as it is constitutionally competent for the general court to revoke the sentence of expulsion passed against Roger Williams by the general court of the Massachusetts Bay Colony in the year sixteen hundred and thirty-five, the same is hereby revoked.[64]

Anne Hutchinson, another resolute and articulate dissenter, sought a home in New England where she could worship with her spiritual leader whom she had known in England, the brilliant Puritan scholar and teacher of the Boston Church, the Rev. John Cotton. He, too, had left England for religious reasons when the prelates of the Church had silenced his eloquent voice in St. Botolph's pulpit.[65] Of gentle birth, Anne was the daughter of an English deacon who more than once had borne the yoke of imprisonment for his criticism of the bishops. In the words of John Winthrop who came to know her well, Anne was "a woman of ready wit and bold spirit."[66] Her devoted husband William, to use again Winthrop's characterization, was "a man of a very mild temper and weak parts, and wholly guided by his wife."[67] He accompanied Anne and their children who reached Boston on September 18, 1634, after a long summer voyage on the *Griffin,* one year and one month before the court ordered the banishment of Roger Williams.

Her quarrel with New England orthodoxy developed shortly after the Hutchinsons settled themselves comfortably in their home in the very center of activities, not far from Beacon Hill.[68] There she welcomed the women of the neighborhood and encouraged free discussion of their social and religious lives, an opportunity not previously afforded to Puritan women, who took no direct part in either civil or church government and had no vote at the annual elections. She was "well beloved, and all the faithful embrassed her conference and blessed God for her faithful discourses."[69] Women flocked to her house, eagerly sought her counsel, and admired their hostess, whose charm, gentleness, and facility of expression were like a spring tonic. An informal gathering of women meeting regularly grew into a sort of women's club—the first of its kind in America. Occasionally some of the prominent men of Boston dropped in to listen to this unusual woman, among them the young and handsome Henry Vane (1613-1662), who was Governor for a year (1636-1637) and one of her admirers. At the outset Anne merely reviewed the sermon of the previous Sabbath for those women who, because of household cares, were unable to attend. But, like most reviewers, she soon became a critic. We have a report of an "eye and eare-witnesse of the carriage of matters there" that, although partisan, probably reflected the view of the Governor and most of the clergy:

> Mistris Hutchinsons double weekely lecture which she kept under a pretence of repeating Sermons, to which resorted sundry of Boston,

> and other Townes about, to the number of Fifty, sixty, or eighty at once; where, after she had repeated the Sermon, she would make her comment upon it, vent her mischievous opinions as she pleased, and wreathed the Scriptures to her owne purpose; where the custome was for her Scholars to propound questions, and she (gravely sitting in the chaire) did make answers thereto. The great respect she had at first in the hearts of all, and her profitable and sober carriage of matters, for a time, made this her practise lesse suspected by the godly Magistrates, and Elders of the Church there, so that it was winked at, for a time . . . but it held so long, untill she had spread her leavin [leaven] so farre, that had not providence prevented, it had proved the Canker of our Peace, and ruine of our comforts.[70]

Admonished for her "dangerous opinions," all the more resented because she was a woman, Anne was convinced she had a mission to fulfill. With the boldness of Roger Williams, she resolved to continue—come what might. Never before had her audience seen a woman so able to hold her own in discussions of intricate theological doctrine and to quote appropriate verses from Scripture. Winthrop later told her such conduct was "not tolerable nor comely in the sight of God or fitting for your sex."[71] Her views struck him as more dangerous than those of Roger Williams whose position was so far to the left that few of the influential people in the Colony would concur in his political philosophy. Every day brought more adherents to the Hutchinson tenets, threatening an eventual uprising against the citadel of orthodoxy. Anne had not planned her strategy or intended to unseat any of the civil or church leaders in order to advance her own brand of religious thinking. In retrospect, however, it is clear that she had become a threat to the conservative Puritan preachers of that day by advancing certain doctrines.

In the first place, she held that the person of the Holy Ghost might dwell in a "justified" person, (that is, one who was assured of salvation) and that inner grace, intuitively sensed, was of greater import than "deeds of the law" or "works of righteousness" expressed by "the outward man." To know, in a sort of mystical way, that the Spirit of the Lord dwelt within marked one as a truly religious person, while church attendance, the saying of prayers, and performing good deeds alone might be mere shallow symbols of piety. The inherent danger in such a view, according to her critics (chiefly John Winthrop, the Rev. John Wilson of the Boston Church, the Rev. Thomas Weld of Roxbury, and several of the Magistrates), was that if one's outward behavior were of little consequence he could, if he possessed inner grace, behave as he pleased. Carried to extremes this doctrine gave license to a "justified" person to disobey all civil law and thus laid one open to the charge of antinomianism (literally against the word or against the law).[72] The Puritans were acquainted with history and recalled stories of the Anabaptist uprising in Münster, Germany, in 1534 and 1535 —just a hundred years earlier—when a radical wing of the Protestant Reformation, capitalizing on the doctrine of divine inspiration and inner grace, swung so far from the Roman Catholic teachings that they justified whatever the "outward man" did. What did conduct and obedience to law matter if one had inner grace? That religious movement in Germany led to a horrible outbreak of licentiousness, polygamy, and murder. Were New England church members, under the influence of Anne Hutchinson, to follow the example of Münster? Anne and her followers flatly denied that they were antinomians, but the fear persisted. Although their outward behavior was above reproach, who could tell when the tide would turn?

Secondly, Anne seemed to be carrying the revolt of the Puritans against the absolute authority of the English bishops one step further. Why, she said in effect, should *anyone* stand between herself and her God? Need one depend for divine inspiration on the learned divines who were self-appointed interpreters of the Holy Word?—a question that tended to lower the esteem and prestige of the clergy. What was most disconcerting and alarming was that Anne professed to have had revelations directly from God. Not even the best of the Puritan ministers had been so favored. God's revelations could be found in the Bible, and they would stand for all eternity. God was not, at this late date, to throw religious scholars into confusion by any *new* revelations to man—and certainly not to a mere lay woman![73] To a growing coterie of admirers, Anne's discourses provided more inspiration and religious rapture than the long and learned expositions from the Puritan pulpits. "This Master-piece of Womens wit," as Edward Johnson called her in his book published in London in 1654, was destined to arouse the animosity of most of the religious leaders of the Bay Colony.

Johnson gives us a sort of composite opinion that might have been expressed at the time by an average church member:

> Come along with me, and I'll bring you to a woman that preaches better Gospell than any of your black-coats that have been at the Ninnyversity, a woman of another kind of spirit, who hath had many revelations of things to come, and for my part, I had rather hear such a one that speaks from the meere motion of the spirit, without any study at all, than any of your learned Scollers, although they may be fuller of the Scripture.[74]

Thirdly, Anne underscored the contrast between a "covenant of grace" and a "covenant of works," accusing the ministers, when they cross-questioned her, of preaching only the latter, but making exceptions of her dear friend John Cotton and her brother-in-law John Wheelwright. She clearly implied that ministers Hugh Peter, Thomas Shepard, Thomas Weld, George Phillips, John Wilson (Cotton's associate), and others were not able ministers of the New Testament and had not the "seal of the spirit."[75] As the arguments grew to white heat, Winthrop remarked that "it began to be as common here to distinguish between men, by being under a covenant of grace or a covenant of works, as in other countries between Protestants and Papists."[76] Anne was thus reluctantly drawn into a virtual condemnation of New England preaching as stiff, legalistic, and lacking in that love and grace taught by Jesus. Inevitably the forces of orthodoxy were mobilized against her, and they proved to be too powerful for her to withstand.

When it became evident that Anne was gathering around her a group of influential citizens, the Colonial leaders became alarmed. Quoting again from our eyewitness reporter, we find among her adherents:

> Some of the Magistrates, some Gentlemen, some Scholars, and men of learning, some Burgesses of our Generall Court, some of our Captaines and Souldiers, some chiefe men in Townes, and some men eminent for Religion.[77]

Ministers who opposed Anne's teaching were sensitive to comments that were heard around the town of Boston that they were "proud," "grossely Popish," "under a Covenant of Workes." Magistrates who suggested that criminal proceedings be commenced against Anne were hearing themselves referred to as "Ahabs, Amaziahs, Scribes and Pharisees, enemies to Christ, led by Satan, that old enemy of Free Grace." And so it was said:

> . . . the faithfull ministers of Christ must have dung cast on their faces and be no better then Legall Preachers, Baals Priests, Popish Factors, Scribes, Pharisees, and opposers of Christ himself.[78]

The orthodox ministers were aware of the popular appeal of the antinomians, fearing that their congregations would consider the "Law [of God], and the Preaching of it . . . of no use at all, to drive a man to Christ" and that they would disregard the letter of the Scripture and hence have no sorrow or repentance for sin but just "stand still and waite for Christ to doe all" for them. One could "abide in the height of comfort, though he falls into the grossest sinnes that he can. . . ."[79]

Again orthodoxy was faced by a challenge that it had to meet by patient and tolerant understanding or by calling upon the courts for immediate suppression of such "dangerous errors." To the Puritan mind there was only one path open to them; there was only one rule to walk by, and they were compelled to act as they thought Christ would have acted—with courage and decisiveness, no matter how unpopular the choice. These were troubled times and some wondered whether the Colony, then only six years old, could survive the mounting criticism. A general fast day was called for in all the churches, the occasion being, in Winthrop's words:

> the miserable estate of the churches in Germany; the calamities upon our native country, the [English] bishops making havock in the churches, putting down the faithful [Puritan] ministers, and advancing popish ceremonies and doctrines, the plague raging exceedingly, and famine and sword threatening them; the dangers of those at Connecticut, and of ourselves also, by the Indians; and *the dissensions in our churches.*[80]

Before court action was initiated, John Wheelwright (1592-1679), her brother-in-law, whom she greatly admired and who had come to Boston in May 1636 and was chosen minister at Wollaston, spoke his mind in support of Anne. It was not long before he grew into disfavor for preaching a sermon on the subject of "justification by sanctification" and, like Anne, was accused of saying that the settled ministers of Boston were preaching a "covenant of works" and that some were "Antichrist." It was also believed that he was dangerously close to the doctrine of direct inspiration. All of this smelled like sedition in the nostrils of John Winthrop. Were it not that Wheelwright was adding coals to the Hutchinsonian fires, his single odious sermon might have been passed by. But to preach as he did at that particular time was "without excuse," the Governor said, for he had intended to disturb the peace and in fact had done so. Thus his acts amounted to sedition.

Wheelwright flatly denied he had disturbed the peace or that he had said all that he was accused of saying in that famous sermon and refused to retract one word of it. Although no disturbance in a physical sense could be proved, the General Court, having lost patience with the so-called antinomians, found him guilty of "contempt and sedition and justifying himselfe & his former practise" and ordered him disfranchised and banished.[81] This decision was made over the protest of Vane and a few others in the General Court and was generally unpopular. More than sixty church members had put their names to a petition to the Court asking for an acquittal, saying he preached "no other but the very expressions of the Holy Ghost himselfe, and therefore cannot justly be branded with sedition."[82] The petition itself was branded as "a seditious libell" by the Court and many of the signers were disfranchised or dismissed from membership in the General Court or banished from the Colony, although some who were willing to admit their sin in signing this fateful petition had their sentences remitted.[83] Thus one who openly supported Wheelwright was in grave danger. One Steven Greensmyth, for example, had said that in his opinion "all the ministers (except Mr. Cotton, Mr. Wheelwright, and hee thought Mr. Hooker) did teach a covenant of works." For choosing a most inopportune time to express publicly an opinion that ran counter to the irascible mood of the General Court, Greensmyth was heavily fined (forty pounds) and ordered to make a public acknowledgement "to the satisfaction of every congregation."[84]

Wheelwright's "answer was, that if he *had* committed sedition, then he ought to be put to death." He threatened to appeal the decision of the Court to English authorities but was informed that "an appeal did not lie; for by the king's grant [the Charter] we had power to hear and determine without any reservation."[85] To meet the popular unrest over the harsh sentence of the Court, Winthrop spent considerable time in speaking and writing in its defense. His point was that the civil and church peace had been disturbed by such dangerous tenets; that Wheelwright's sermon had divided the churches and tended to "make the people looke at their magistrates, ministers, and brethren as enemyes to Christ. . . ."[86] To Winthrop it was clear that it was sinful of those in authority to tolerate such views, "the evill fruite" of which was quite apparent.

Wheelwright, denied a chance to appeal to England, complied with the order of banishment of November 4, 1637, said farewell to his friends and family, and set out for a small English settlement on the Piscataqua in territory now in the state of New Hampshire, his family joining him the following spring. There he laid the foundations of the town of Exeter. He made his peace with the Colony and in 1644 "the court released his banishment."[87] Finally he settled in Salisbury. At the time of his death, he was the oldest minister in the Bay Colony, having passed his 79th birthday.

As an aftermath of the antinomian affair and because the Colony feared that new arrivals from England might also be infected with these dangerous and divisive tenets, the General Court enacted a temporary immigration law "to keep out all such persons as might be dangerous to the commonwealth," providing a fine for those who entertained such persons for more than three weeks.[88] The purpose of this law, as the secretary of the General Court, Edward Rawson, saw it, was "to keepe out such whose Lives were publickely prophane and scandalous" and "those whose judgements were Corrupt."[89] Again there was strong popular objection to this order of the General Court. Henry Vane claimed that the Colony had no right to deny admission to people merely on suspicion that they might prove dangerous, but only when they are "*shown* to be dissolute or prophane persons"; besides, he wrote, there will be more trouble brewing when this law gets "noysed abroad, than the entertainment of those people against whom this law is made." The law indeed was "most wicked and sinnefull and may make us more cruell and tyranicall over Gods children than Pagans, yea than Sodomites. . . ."[90] Already authorities in England were becoming concerned over restrictions on religious worship in New England and the young liberal Henry Vane was deeply disturbed over the rising tide of intolerance. But Winthrop strongly supported this new enactment. "The intent of the law," he wrote, "is to preserve the welfare of the body; and for this ende to have none received into any fellowship with it who are likely to disturbe the same, and this intent (I am sure) is lawful and good." Drawing an appealing analogy, he argued that "a family is a little common wealth, and a common wealth is a greate family. Now as a family is not bound to entertaine all comers, no not every good man (otherwise than by way of hospitality) no more is a common wealth. . . . We are not bound to exercise mercye to others to the ruine of ourselves."[91]

After disposing of the Rev. Mr. Wheelwright, "the court also sent for Mrs. Hutchinson, and charged her with divers matters. . . ."[92] The court proceedings could hardly be called a trial. There was no jury, no lawyer for the defense, and her accusers were her judges. Standing before Governor John Winthrop, Deputy Governor Dudley, Magistrates and Deputies, and many of the ministers whom she had accused of preaching a "covenant of works," in the court at Newtowne (Cambridge) in November 1637, Anne Hutchinson listened to the charge presented by Winthrop:

> Mrs. Hutchinson, you are called here as one of those that have troubled the peace of the common-wealth and the churches here; you are known to be a woman that hath had a great share in the promoting and divulging of those opinions that are causes of this trouble, and to be nearly joined not only in affinity and affection with some of those the court had taken notice of and passed censure upon [referring to Wheelwright and his friends] but you have spoken divers things as we have been informed very prejudicial to the honour of the churches and ministers thereof, and you have maintained a meeting and an assembly in your house that hath been condemned by the general assembly as a thing not tolerable nor comely in the sight of God nor fitting for your sex, and notwithstanding that was cried down you have continued the same, therefore we have thought good to send for you to understand how things are, that if you be in an erroneous way we may reduce you that so you may become a profitable member here among us, otherwise if you be obstinate in your course that then the court may take such course that you may trouble us no further, therefore I would intreat you to express whether you do not assent and hold in practice to those opinions and factions that have been handled in court already, that is to say, whether you do not justify Mr. Wheelwright's sermon and the petition.

Mrs. Hutchinson replied: "I am called here to answer before you but I hear no things laid to my charge."[93]

In the long two-day examination the accused countered almost every charge brought against her: her public meetings, her disrespect of authority (a violation of the Fifth Commandment), her reproach of the ministers who preached "a covenant of works" and did not have the "seal of the spirit," her moral support of Wheelwright, and her disturbance of the peace of the churches and commonwealth. Her defense was able and full of Scriptural citations, although Winthrop—certainly not an unbiased reporter—said the charges "were clearly proved against her, though she sought to shift it off."[94] It is probable that she might have had the support of the majority of the court had she refrained from claiming revelations from God. Her decision not only to assert this claim but to say that God would deliver her from the condemnation of the court and that any action taken against her would bring a curse upon the Colony and its posterity played directly into their hands. Such revelations surely must have come from the Devil!

The presiding officer at her "trial," Governor Winthrop, called for a vote:

> The Court hath already declared themselves satisfied concerning the things you hear, and concerning the troublesomeness of her spirit, and the danger of her course amongst us, which is not to be suffered. Therefore if it is the mind of the Court that Mrs. Hutchinson for these things that appear before us, is unfit for our society—and if it be the mind of the Court that she shall be banished out of our liberties, and imprisoned until she be sent away, let them hold up their hands.[95]

"If you do condemn me for speaking what is in my conscience," the proud prisoner at the bar replied, "I must commit myself to the Lord."[96]

After all but three held up their hands, the Court entered the official order of banishment:

> Mistress Hutchinson, (the wife of Mr William Hutchinson,) being convented for traduceing the ministers & their ministery in this country, shee declared volentarily her revelations for her ground, & that shee should bee delivered & the Court ruined, with their posterity, & thereupon was banished, & the meane while was committed to Mr. Joseph Weld untill the Court shall dispose of her.[97]

Mr. Joseph Weld was the brother of the Rev. Thomas Weld of Roxbury who had called her "this great imposter, an instrument of Satan . . . the American Jesabel."[98] In this camp of the enemy, removed from her friends, she had a most unhappy time, awaiting the day of her departure. There she was visited by the ministers she had opposed who sought to draw her from her many "errors." She made some retractions and admitted that speaking against the magistrates at the court was "rash and ungrounded" in respect to her "revelations" and yet she maintained her fundamental position. "Much time and many arguments . . . spent to bring her to see her sin. . .[were] all in vain."[99] By that time she was so distraught and confused as to what she had retracted and what she had maintained in the theological maze through which she had been made to travel that she was called a liar and a blasphemer and all hope of her "repentence" was abandoned.

Her most humiliating experiences followed the court action. Her own church summoned her to stand trial before the Governor and the leading ministers of the town, with Cotton, Shepard, Wilson, Peter, and Davenport in the role of prosecutors.[100] She was made to stand before the congregation for two long sessions and affirm or deny that she had made heretical pronouncements on some two dozen theological doctrines touching such subjects as the distinction between spirit and soul, immortality by redemption or immortality by creation, and the resurrection of the physical body. Anne admitted some of her tenets were erroneous, but she was not able to clear herself of other charges. Her views on resurrection (that the physical body did not rise) would mean, said Cotton, no resurrection at all, and we would die like beasts and this view would be an open door to "all Epicurisme & Libertinisme. . . . Your opinions frett like a Gangrene, & spread like a Leprosie . . . & will eate out the very Bowells of Religion." Anne humbly replied, "I spoke rashly and unadvisedly," but no matter what she said by way of explanation, frequently citing chapter and verse from the Bible as she was put through a theological cross-examination, she was unconvincing.

The Rev. Hugh Peter made it clear, as Winthrop had previously reminded her, that the ministers could not tolerate such opinions coming from a person of her sex:

> Yow have stept owt of your place, yow have rather bine a Husband than a Wife, & a preacher than a Hearer, & a Magistrate than a Subject, & soe yow have to carry all Thinges in Church & Common Wealthe as you would, & have not bine humbled for this.[101]

The ministers showed little compassion but they were deadly serious; they feared the ruin of the churches if they did not put an end to her unorthodox preaching. Wilson, who had smarted from her accusations, told the assembled congregation that he looked on her "as a dayngerus Instrument of the Divell raysed up by Sathan amongst us. . . . We should sine against God if we should not put away from us soe Evell a Woman, guiltie of such fowle Evells." Cotton, who had been her friend and who had tried on many occasions to lead her out of her errors, told her "I have often feared the highth of your Spirit & being puft up with your owne parts, & therefore it is just with God thus to abase you." The congregation, with very few dissenting, agreed that she must be abased and humbled. Anne asked for their prayers but her "repentence" was not considered "cordial & sincere." She is, said Shepard, "a notorious Imposter. . .she never had any trew Grace in her hart." Wilson delivered the solemn words of excommunication:

> In the name of the Lord Jesus Christ & in the name of the Church I doe not only pronownce yow worthy to be cast owt, but I doe cast yow out and in the name of Christ I doe deliver you up to Sathan, that yow may learne no more to blaspheme, to seduce & to lye, and I doe account yow from this time forth to be a Hethen & a Publican & soe to be held of all the Bretheren & Sisters, of this Congregation, & of others: therefore I command yow in the name of Christ Jesus & of this Church as a Leper to withdraw your self owt of the congregation.[102]

"After she was excommunicated," Winthrop wrote, "her spirits, which seemed before to be somewhat dejected, revived again, and she gloried in her sufferings, saying, that it was the greatest happiness, next to Christ, that ever befel her."[103]

Following the sentencing of Anne, the General Court found "just cause of suspition" that those who had been "seduced and led into dangerous errors" by her and her brother-in-law John Wheelwright, might some day rise up like the men of Münster and might

> upon some revelation, make some suddaine irruption upon those that differ from them in judgment, for prevention whereof it is ordered, that all those whose names are underwritten shall . . . deliver at Mr. Canes [Captain Robert Keayne?] house, at Boston, all such guns, pistols, swords, powder, shot, & match as they shalbee owners of, or have in their custody. . . .[104]

Some 59 individuals in Boston were required to surrender their arms, the Court asking other towns to make similar orders. Those who had acknowledged their sin in signing the petition in favor of Wheelwright were excused from the order. This decision of the General Court was as unpopular as it was unnecessary, although possibly grounded on genuine fear. No disturbance resulted, and the weapons were returned to their owners two years later.[105]

The General Court, "being sensible of the great disorders growing in this common welth" then enacted a law providing for a fine, imprisonment, disfranchisement or banishment "as the quality & measure of the offence shall deserve" for any one convicted of defaming the courts or the justices or the sentences thereof.[106] With the bitter religious controversy at an end, precedents established for the swift punishment of the brave dissenters and penal laws enacted for the suppression of defamation of the courts, the Bay Colony must have felt secure from further attacks on its orthodoxy. But all of this was done at the tragic cost of free debate and discussion of religious doctrine.

In the spring of 1638 the Hutchinson family set out on the long and difficult journey to Rhode Island, settling on the island of Aquidneck. Anne's husband died in 1642. Anne, with some of the younger members of her family, sought the quiet of a new life in the Dutch settlement near New Amsterdam. They chose an isolated farm near what is now Pelham in Westchester County on Long Island Sound.[107]

In the Puritan mind there was little doubt that God took a very personal interest in New England affairs. Through natural phenomena and strange happenings He had a way of communicating approval or disapproval so unmistakably that His will could be interpreted without much sophistication. In the Hutchinson affair, for example, three tragic events gave the Puritan leaders that comfortable feeling that they had acted in accordance with

His will. Was Anne in truth the "New England Jezebel"—a Biblical term that connoted all that was evil in womanhood?[108]

1) Mary Dyer and her husband William, a milliner, were members of the Boston church. Much younger than Anne, Mary was her companion and admirer and was, we are told, "notoriously infected with Mrs. Hutchinson's errors." She was "a very proper and fair woman" but, Winthrop could not help adding, "very censorious and troublesome, (she being of a very proud spirit, and much addicted to revelations,). . . "[109] Just before Anne's excommunication from the church, Mary had been delivered of a stillborn child, badly malformed, two months before full term. Anne and Jane Hawkins, the midwife (who had been under suspicion for witchcraft), and one other woman were the only witnesses. On the advice of the Rev. Mr. Cotton who saw in it "a providence of God," the body was secretly buried and the matter closed. But "some rumor began to spread that the child was a monster"—and therefore quite probably a sign of God's great displeasure over Mary's pro-Hutchinson sympathies. The Governor therefore felt it his duty to enter the case and called for an investigation. He summoned the midwife and got from her a lurid description of the body, completely confirming the "monster" rumor:

> . . . it had a face, but no head, and the ears stood upon the shoulders and were like an ape's; it had no forehead, but over the eyes four horns, hard and sharp; two of them were above one inch long, the other two shorter; the eyes standing out, and the mouth also; the nose hooked upward; all over the breast and back full of sharp pricks and scales, like a thornback; the navel and all the belly, with the distinction of the sex, were where the back should be, and the back and hips before, where the belly should have been; behind, between the shoulders, it had two mouths . . . instead of toes, it had on each foot three claws, like a young fowl, with sharp talons.[110]

Thinking that Hawkins, whose credibility was in question as she had been under suspicion as a witch, might have drawn an exaggerated picture, the Governor, with the advice of some of the other magistrates and elders—for the whole town was now interested in this sign from God—had the body disinterred and confirmed the description substantially as given. "Most of those things were to be seen," wrote Winthrop, "as the horns and claws, the scales, etc." He made this observation:

> ... the father of this monster, coming home at this very time, was, the next Lord's day, by an unexpected providence [that is, before it was known that he was the father of a "monster"], questioned in the church for divers *monstrous* errors, as for denying all inherent righteousness, etc., which he maintained, and was for the same admonished.[111]

2) Anne Hutchinson too, after she had arrived in Naragansett Bay "was delivered of a monstrous birth." This story spread rapidly through the Bay Colony and was discussed by the Rev. Mr. Cotton on a lecture day who concluded that "it might signify her error in denying inherent righteousness" and in asserting certain unorthodox opinions.[112]

Anne's most bitter critic, commenting on the Dyer and Hutchinson "monsters," was sure he had caught God's message. The Rev. Thomas Welde, minister of Roxbury made this observation:

> Then God himself was pleased to step in with his casting vote and suffrage from Heaven, by testifying his displeasure against their opinions and practices, as clearly as if he had pointed with his finger, in causing the two fomenting women, in the time of the height of the opinions, to produce out of their wombs, as before they had out of their brains, such monstrous births, as no chronicle (I think) hardly ever recorded the like. ... He that runs may read their sin in these judgments.[113]

The story of the "monstrous births" spread far and wide and must have been a topic of general conversation throughout the Colony. Roger Williams heard the reports in Rhode Island and wrote to friends in the Colony making some inquiries about these strange events. Governor William Bradford of Plymouth wrote to Governor Winthrop. He said he had heard "of a monsterous, and prodigious birth which she [Anne] should discover [reveal] amongst you. . . . I should be much behoulden unto you, to certiffie me in a word or tow, of the trueth and forme of that monster."[114]

To the orthodox, God had made manifest his final decision: "And see how the wisdome of God fitted this judgement to her sinne every way, for looke as she had vented misshapen opinions, so she must bring forth deformed monsters . . this is now come to be knowne and famous over all these Churches, and a great part of the world. . . ."[115]

3) One more of God's "providences" struck Anne and her family after they had settled in what is now Westchester County, New York. There they had hoped to live out their lives peacefully beyond the reach of bishop or magistrate. But in 1643, the year after their arrival, a band of Indians bent on rooting out the English who had settled in their territory, descended upon the Hutchinson household and slew the entire family save one daughter who was captured but lived to tell the story. The Boston ministers who had opposed her probably saw in this tragic event, as did the Rev. Thomas Welde, the hand of God. Welde wrote that he had never before heard of such an outrage committed by Indians in those parts "and therefore God's hand is the more apparently seen herein, to pick this woful woman, to make her, and those belonging to her, an unheard of heavy example of their cruelty above others."[116]

Wheelwright had made his peace with the Bay Colony and was permitted to return, taking a pastorate in Salisbury, where he served for seventeen years until his death in 1679. Roger Williams, as we have noted, was invited back to Massachusetts in 1676 (although he refused the invitation), but three centuries passed before his expulsion was "revoked" by the General Court of the Commonwealth. And so it was with Anne Hutchinson—"the American Jesabel." The Commonwealth, 278 years after the event, honoured her memory with a statue placed on the lawn of the Capitol. Dated 1915, it is inscribed:

> In Memory of Anne Marbury Hutchinson—Baptized at Alford—Lincolnshire England 20 July 1591—Killed by the Indians at East Chester New York 1643—A Courageous Exponent of Civil Liberty and Religious Toleration.

The Bay Colony survived the Williams and Hutchinson assaults upon the Puritan fortress by asking these brave dissenters "to be gone as fast as they can, the sooner the better," as the Rev. Nathaniel Ward said the Colony should advise all tolerationists and liberals.[117] But it was soon threatened with another group of "troublers of churches," the forerunners of the modern Baptist faith, a devout group of men and women who were ready to defend with their lives the position that the baptism of infants was not part of God's plan. In spite of the Puritan's insistence that such a view was doctrinally erroneous, the "obstinate and wilfull" adversaries could correctly maintain that the New Testament reported no instance of Christ baptizing an infant or of condoning such baptism. It logically followed that, as the Gospels reported only the baptism of adults, all adults who had been baptized as infants would have to be rebaptized. Those who held this view were called Anabaptists, from the Greek *ana,* meaning "over again."

Superficially, one might see no cause for alarm in this departure from New England orthodoxy. The Anabaptists were not revolutionaries, used no violence, had no political ambitions or desire to overthrow the Congregational churches. But the very word "Anabaptist" immediately raised Puritan blood pressure because of its historical association with the original Anabaptists of sixteenth century Germany whose heresies spread beyond this single doctrine and to whose evil conduct we have already referred.[118] This new sect might also justify all kinds of sinful deeds by revelations from Heaven and, like the antinomians, might prefer a personal and intuitive union with the Holy Ghost to the leadership of a Godly, Puritan minister who, because of his extensive scholarship and familiarity with the Bible, was the *true* interpreter of God's word. When it became known that these new sectaries wished to establish their own "Church of Christ," independent of the Congregational churches, the issues were clearly drawn.

The Puritans could not allow the Baptists to prevail. If infant baptism is "a nullitie," then, the General Court said, all adults in the Colony would be "unbaptized persons, & so consequently [there would be] no regular churches, ministry, or ordinances."[119] A new criminal law was called for, and the rigid and unpopular Anabaptist law was enacted in 1644:

> Forasmuch as experience hath plentifully & often proved that since the first arising of the Anabaptists, about a hundred years since, they have bene the incendiaries of common wealths, & the infectors of persons in maine matters of religion, & the troublers of churches in all places where they have bene, & that they who have held the baptizing of infants unlawfull have usually held other errors or heresies together therewith, though they have (as other hereticks use to do) concealed the same . . . & whereas divers of this kind have . . . denied the ordinance of magistracy, & the lawfulness of making warr, & others the lawfulnes of magistrats, & their inspection into any breach of

> the first table [the first four of the Ten Commandments] which opinions, if they should be connived at by us, are like to be increased amongst us, & so must necessarily bring guilt upon us, infection & trouble to the churches, & hazard to the whole common wealth . . . .

If the Court found such persons "wilfully & obstinately to continue" to hold to such a course after efforts had been made to correct them, they were to be banished.[120]

To a large sector of the population this law seemed excessively severe. When news of it reached England and Puritans there heard of the Colonists' treatment of the Anabaptists, they did not hesitate to express their views. "Heere is great complaint against us," wrote Puritan Stephen Winthrop from London to his brother John Winthrop, Jr., in Boston on March 1, 1645, "for our severetye against Anabaptists."[121] "The law of banishing for conscience," wrote Sir George Downing, formerly a resident of the Bay Colony and a graduate of Harvard in its first class (1642), in a letter from London in the same year, "makes us stinke every wheare."[122] Evidently John Winthrop was unmoved by this news from Downing, his young nephew.

"Divers merchants and others" in Boston asked for a suspension of the law, and many members of the General Court were favorable to the suggestion, but the church's influence over the legislature was overpowering.[123] Winthrop, then Deputy Governor, revealed the political strength of the clergy in his report:

> But many of the elders, hearing of it [the protest against this new law], went first to the deputies and after to the magistrates, and laying before them what advantage it would give to the anabaptists, (who began to increase very fast through the country here, and much more in England, where they had gathered divers churches and taught openly, and had published a confession of their faith,) entreated that the law might continue still in force, and the execution of it not suspended, though they disliked not that all lenity and patience should be used for convincing and reclaiming such erroneous persons. Whereupon the court [the General Court] refused to make any further order about the petition.[124]

Thus the law was put into execution, and two years later the public condemnation of infant baptism or leaving the meetinghouse while the ceremony was being performed was written into the law of "damnable Heresies" and carried on down to the end of the

Bay Colony's existence.[125] The first person to feel the full force of this law was:

> A poor man of Hingham, one Painter, who had lived at New Haven and at Rowley and Charlestown, and been scandalous and burdensome by his idle and troublesome behaviour to them all, was now on the sudden turned anabaptist, and having a child born, he would not suffer his wife to bring it to the ordinance of baptism, for she was a member of the church, though himself were not. Being presented [in court] for this, and enjoined to suffer the child to be baptized, he still refusing, and disturbing the church, he was again brought to the court not only for his former contempt, but also for saying that our baptism was antichristian; and in the open court he affirmed the same. Whereupon after much patience and clear conviction of his error, etc., because he was very poor, so as no other but corporal punishment could be fastened upon him, he was ordered to be whipped, not for his opinion, but for reproaching the Lord's ordinance, and for his bold and evil behavior both at home and in the court. He endured his punishment with much obstinancy, and when he was loosed, he said boastingly, that God had marvellously assisted him. Whereupon two or three honest men, his neighbors, affirmed before all the company, that he was of very loose behavior at home, and given much to lying and idleness, etc. . . .[126]

Public protests against this law mounted, but the General Court voted in 1645 that the laws "should not be altered at all, nor explained."[127] But strong support came from Dorchester and "Roxberry" the following year when 78 petitioners urged the General Court not to abrogate or weaken the laws against Anabaptists —a request that was quickly granted.[128] In 1649 the General Court, hearing that the number of Anabaptists was rapidly increasing in "Sea Cuncke" in Plymouth Colony where thirteen or fourteen adults were rebaptized, wrote a letter to that Colony urging them to take care "of the suppressing of errors," stating: "The infection of such diseases, being so neere us, are likely to spread into our jurisdiction," and reminding them that both Colonies must render an account to God who had entrusted them "with the keeping of both tables [of the Ten Commandments]."[129]

Prosecutions of Anabaptists continued for many years. The following cases in the county courts were typical:

> William Winter of Lynn presented for saying that they who stay

> while a child is baptized worship the devil, . . . they who stayed took the name of the Father, Son and Holy Ghost in vain, and broke the Sabboth . . . . To make confession next Lords day at Lynn in the open congregation and to answer at next General Court. [130]

> Thomas Patience, by a common fame, and upon vehement suspicion, not only of holding, but also of fomenting the error that baptism of infants is no ordinance of God, & hindering his child from baptism. [Evidently he was not punished, for the record read, "Gone away."][131]

> Mrs. Kinge and James Hubberd, for not believing in infant baptism, the latter for his arguments in public" [were brought into court in Lynn].[132]

> Goodman Joseph Redknape for not suffering a child of his to be baptized. His wife to see it done next Lords day. If her husband object the constable of Lynn to take him to Boston to the prison. [In court Redknape said:] "The Covenant of Grace is farr otherwise than the Jewes had."[133]

About this time (1645) Edward Winslow, Governor of Plyouth Colony in 1633, 1636, and 1644, wrote a letter to his friend, John Winthrop of Boston with the consoling thought that "all the troubles of New England are not at the Massachusets [Bay Colony]." A resolution for complete religious toleration had been introduced in the Plymouth Court of Assistants. The gist of it, wrote Winslow, was this:

> To allow and maintain full and free tollerance of religion to all men that would preserve the civill peace and submit unto government; and there was no limitation or exception against Turke, Jew, Papist, Arian, Socinian, Nicholaytan, Familist, or any other, etc.

This was a startling proposal, out of keeping with the spirit of the times. Complete tolerance for "Papists" in Massachusetts was not to come for more than two centuries. Winslow "utterly abhorred" the idea. Governor Bradford, Thomas Prence and other magistrates were sure it would lead to "sad consequences" and did not allow it to come to vote for they feared that if it were adopted "it would eate out the power of godlines." It would indeed, Winslow added, "make us odious to all christian common weales." And yet it must have had considerable support. "You would have ad-

Portrait of Edward Winslow, Governor of Plymouth Colony in 1633, 1636, and 1644. Courtesy of the Pilgrim Hall, Plymouth, Massachusetts.

mired [been amazed]", he commented, "to have seen how sweet this carrion relished to the pallate of most of our deputies!"[134]

The Reverend Samuel Willard, writing later in 1681 and looking back on the church's struggle with the Anabaptists, makes clear the intensity of feeling toward these disturbers of the peace:

> Experience tells us that such a rough thing as a New-England Anabaptist is not to be handled over tenderly . . . if we must tarry till all men are agreed about what is truth, before we oppose Error, we shall stay till there is no need of it . . . if they could get head among us, they would certainly undermine the churches, ruine order, destroy piety, and introduce prophaness.[135]

Among those more severely dealt with were Obadiah Holmes and his friends John Crandell and John Clarke who had come from Rhode Island in 1651. The latter, calling himself "Physician of Rode Island in America" published a full account of the "persecution" of the Anabaptists.[136] Fines, whippings, and imprisonment for long periods of time were suffered by them in martyr-like fashion. Governor John Endecott, the sternest of the Puritans, had succeeded the more kindly Winthrop as Governor and denied these men a fair trial, telling them they deserved death although they had committed no capital offense and had reminded the Governor of the fundamental law of the land as set forth in the Body of Liberties. From the Rev. John Wilson, chief foe of the Hutchinsonians, they could expect no greater Christian charity. One of the Anabaptists, as reported by Clarke said:

> I blesse God I am counted worthy to suffer for the name of Jesus; whereupon John Wilson (their Pastor as they call him) strook me before the Judgment Seat, and cursed me, saying, the Curse of God, or Jesus goe with thee.[137]

The offenders took their punishment manfully. Like present-day Christian Scientists, they claimed that, supported by the indwelling spirit of the Lord, they could feel no physical pain. In this respect, a first-hand account of one of the Anabaptists whipped by order of the court is of interest:

> And as the man began to lay the stroaks upon my back, I said to the people, though my Flesh should fail, and my Spirit should fail, yet God would not fail; so it pleased the Lord to come in, and so to fill

my heart and tongue as a vessell full, and with an audible voyce I brake forth, praying unto the Lord not to lay this Sin to their charge, and telling the people, That now I found he did not fail me, and therefore now I should trust him for ever who failed me not; for in truth, as the stroaks fell upon me, I had such a spirituall manifestation of Gods presence, as the like thereunto I never had, nor felt, nor can with fleshly tongue expresse, and the outward pain was so removed from me, that indeed I am not able to declare it to you, it was so easie to me, that I could well bear it, yea and in a manner felt it not, although it was grievous, as the Spectators said, the Man striking with all his strength (yea spitting on his hand three times, as many affirmed) with a three-coarded whip, giving me therewith thirty stroaks; when he had loosed me from the Post, having joyfulnesse in my heart, and cheerfulnesse in my countenance, as the Spectators observed, I told the Magistrates, you have struck me as with Roses. . . .

In later years (1665-1668) Thomas Gold (or Gould) and four of his friends found the Bay Colony authorities still adamant in their attitude toward "obstinate and turbulent Annabaptists." These men had attempted to set up their own "Church of Christ." Appealing from a judgment of the Court of Assistants to the General Court, they were found: "justly convicted of high presumption against the Lord & his holy appointments, as also the peace of this government . . . contemning the authority and lawes here established."[138]

Fines, imprisonment, and eventual banishment was the lot of Gold and his friends. Refusing to have their children christened was bad enough, but to attempt to set up their own church where they could prescribe their own church discipline and condemn the Puritan orthodox churches as "bad and corrupt" was more than the General Court could stand, for this was tantamount to:

setting up a free schoole for seduction into wayes of error, & casting off the government of Christ Jesus . . . to the disturbance not only of our eclesiasticall enjoyments, but also contempt of our civil order & the authority here established doeth manifestly threaten the dissolution & ruine both of the peace & order of the churches & the authority of this government.[139]

Again a public protest was in vain. When certain residents of Boston and Charlestown (Gold had been a citizen of the latter) petitioned the court for merciful consideration of Gold and his friends who had been confined in the prison for many months prior to the order of banishment, their petition was deemed a rebuke of the court and the promoters of this gesture of Christian compassion were admonished and fined.[140]

A sharp protest came from Sir Richard Saltonstall, then in England: "It doth not a little grieve my spirit to heare what sadd things are reported dayly of your tyranny and persecutions in New-England, as that you fyne, whip and imprison men for their consciences. . . ."[141]

The Puritan ministers were never at a loss for a good sound defence of their position. Never admitting "persecution," they found ample justification for proceeding sternly against those who they believed had come into New England to destroy the church or state. The Rev. John Cotton, replying to Saltonstall, said that Obadiah Holmes had come into the Bay Colony from Plymouth where he had been excommunicated and began to rebaptize elder persons—knowing that such conduct was against God's law and against the law of the Colony. As for his whipping, it was "voluntarily chosen," for if he had paid a thirty-pound fine or accepted the offer of his friends to pay it for him, he would not have been whipped.[142] As for Thomas Gold (or Gould), the Rev. Samuel Willard wrote that he was not punished merely because he refused to have his child baptized but because he spoke "contemptuously and irreligiously of the emptiness & nullity" of the law "and used unbecoming gestures.... [There is] a vast difference between doubting about an ordinance, and professedly vilifying of it by unhandsome words and carriages."[143]

No matter how dissident the Protestant chord, comprised of numerous competing sects, each claiming to be the true interpreter of God's Word, there was an obvious community of feeling that the priests from Rome represented the antichrist, that archenemy of the Saviour, the Pope himself. Had a group of Roman Catholics come upon the New England scene to propagate the faith, the seventeenth century General Court would have swung into action to cut off a threat more serious to the Puritans than that of Roger Williams or Anne Hutchinson. But the threat did not materialize. The Catholics who came to America in that century wisely chose to settle elsewhere. The few visiting Catholics who came for brief visits to Boston, or the occasional servant, proved to be harmless and were politely tolerated.[144]

Of all Roman Catholics, the Jesuits (those militantly devout members of The Society of Jesus that was founded in the previous century) were particularly feared and despised. John Winthrop the Younger, son of the Governor, had received a letter from England in 1632 with this startling intelligence: "I heare the french have this summer transported a company of priests and Jesuits and such vermine to Canada; but how longe they will staye there, it is a question. I conceive the land to [too] cold for theire hott natures."[145]

When the Governor heard the French were planning a settlement near Cape Sable (at the southern tip of Nova Scotia) with "divers priests and Jesuits among them," he recalled the history of the activities of those soldiers of Christ whose reputation in Europe was—as Protestants discerned it—appalling and fearful. With unnecessary but genuine alarm, he immediately summoned to a joint meeting the Assistants "and the ministers and captains, and some other chief men, to advise what was fit to be done for our safety, in regard the French were like to prove ill neighbours (being Papists)."[146] The upshot of the meeting was a resolve to strengthen the Bay Colony's fortifications. The fear of an armed invasion by the French proved to be unfounded.

In 1647 the General Court decided to take precautionary measures against the Jesuits. It enacted a law, similar in effect to one then on the statute books of England and the only law relating to Jesuits in the Bay Colony.[147] Although the law was unnecessary and probably never invoked, it expressed the Puritan's sympathy with fellow Protestants in Europe who saw the spread of the Catholic faith in areas once dominated by Protestants:

> This Court taking into consideration the great Wars, Combustions and Divisions which are this day [1647] in Europe and that the same are observed to be raised and fomented, chiefly by the secret underminings, and solicitations of those of the Jesuitical Order, Men brought up and Devoted to the Religion and Court of Room [Rome], which hath occasioned divers States to expel them [from] their Territories, for prevention whereof among our selves; . . . No Jesuite or

Spiritual or Ecclesiastical person (as they are termed) Ordained by the Authority of the Pope or See of Room [Rome], shall henceforth at any time repair to or come within this Jurisdiction.[148]

The penalty for disregarding this ban on immigration was "banishment or otherwise as the Court shall see cause," and for returning to the Colony uninvited after banishment the penalty was *death*. Exceptions were to be allowed for those who might come to the Massachusetts shores "by Ship-Wrack or other Accident" or those who might come on friendly ships, so long as they made a rapid departure. No execution or even a banishment of any Jesuit can be found in the official records, diaries, or reports that are now extant.

There were a few Catholic servants in the Colony, probably more toward the end of the century than in the early days when intolerance was at its height. If the Irish maid in Essex County is typical, it is evident that Catholics could find little religious solace in the Congregational meetinghouse. Sarah Linseay "aged about thirty years" testified that:

she asked the Irish maid about going to the public meeting and she replied that 'it was a develish place for thay did not goe to mast and what suld she doe there for shee was resolved to stay out her time with her master and misteris and then goe whome to her one [own] contry againe wher see mit goe to mast.'[149]

John Endecott acted out his hostility to the Roman Catholic Church which immediately got him into hot water with his fellow magistrates. One day in 1635 he whipped out his sword and cut the cross out of the English flag. To Puritans the cross was a distasteful symbol of popish idolatry, but Winthrop feared this treasonable act might give "occasion to the state of England to think ill of us." For such a serious offense a humble citizen might have been given a severe whipping. Endecott was "sadly admonished" by the General Court "and also disinabled for beareing any office in the common wealth, for the space of a yeare nexte ensueing." The sentence was no heavier, Winthrop wrote, "because they were persuaded he did it out of tenderness of conscience, and not of any evil intent."[150]

Before the drive to root out the Anabaptists had fully spent itself, the Colonies were aroused to their greatest pitch of intolerance and cruelty toward those who would not conform to Puritan orthodoxy, when missionaries from the Society of Friends "invaded" New England and stirred the Puritans to an unholy wrath. We have reserved a special chapter for that disenchanting story.

Eloquent and well documented sermons and Thursday lectures were not sufficient to preserve the pure and uncorrupted worship of God and to confine social behavior within norms acceptable to Him, as the Puritans interpreted His ordinances. The inspired words of prophets and priests of another race and another land recorded some three thousand years before the founding of Boston furnished ample warrant for punishing the blasphemer, the heretic, and the lesser offender who dared chart an independent path to salvation. Inevitably a code of criminal laws grew up to stabilize and strengthen a culture so vulnerable to erosion by numerous nonconformists, fanatics, profane persons, and liberals.

Laws grounded on religious doctrine calling for the penalty of death are described in Chapter 9. We report here the most prominent Bay Colony penal laws meriting a penalty less than death for acts deemed offensive to the Lord, many of which survived beyond the seventeenth century:

1) A fine up to fifty pounds or a severe whipping for one who professed the Christian religion and was over the age of sixteen and yet "wittingly and willingly" denied that any one or more of the books of the Old and the New Testaments (the name of each book being spelled out in the law) were "the written and infallible Word of God"—unless when accused he publicly recanted. On a second conviction, one ran the risk of banishment or death if he maintained his "wicked opinion . . . obstinately and pertinaciously."[151]

2) Public reproval for any Christian who interrupted the preacher or charged him with error or cast reproach upon him or made "Gods wayes contemptible & ridiculos." On second conviction one was liable to a fine of five pounds or to be required to:

> stand two houres openly upon a Block or Stool, four feet high, on a Lecture day, with a paper fixed on his breast, written in Capital Letters: AN OPEN AND OBSTINATE CONTEMNER OF GODS HOLY ORDINANCES that others may hear and be ashamed of breaking out into like wickedness.[152]

3) Those who "go about to destroy or disturbe the order of the churches" by renouncing them:

> either upon pretence that the churches were not planted by any new apostles, or that ordinances are for carnall Christians, or babes in Christ, & not for spirituall or illuminated persons, or upon any other such like groundles conceite

were made subject to a fine of forty shillings for each month they continued in such "obstinacy."[153] This law was evidently designed to curb the religious liberals—usually referred to as "libertines."

4) As it was written in the book of Exodus: "Thou shalt not revile the gods, nor curse the ruler of thy people," so the General Court decreed, after the Hutchinson affair, a severe whipping or fine for those who reviled the office of magistrate.[154] After the Quaker episode, the legislators added the words "or Ministers, as is usuall with the Quakers."[155]

5) A seizure of one's property if he refused to pay the tax assessed to support the church and the minister.[156]

6) A fine of five shillings or imprisonment for absence from church services without just and necessary cause.[157] Later amended to a fine only and to include absences from publick fast days and days of Thanksgiving.[158]

7) Punishment, at the judge's discretion, for profaning the Sabbath by doing "servile worke . . . such as are not workes of piety, of charity, or of necessity" or for travelling on the Lord's day "either on horsebacke or on foote, or by boats from or out of their oune towne to any unlawfull assembly or meeting." Later the penalty was prescribed of a ten shilling fine for the first offense to be doubled for subsequent offenses, and, if the offender acted with "high handed Presumption," the judge had power to augment the penalty at his discretion.[159] Judging from the number of offenders who appeared before the courts this law was difficult to enforce. New arrivals from England were not used to keeping the Sabbath after the manner of the Hebrews.

In later years when the churches were beginning to lose their hold upon the new generation and people could not easily be restrained from engaging in activities that were not pious, charitable, or necessary, the General Court devised two new weapons in the fight to keep the Sabbath from being profaned. It decreed in 1677 1) that twice a year (in March and September) the minister read from the pulpit all of the Lord's Day laws and caution the people to take heed thereof; and 2) that selectmen of each town appoint "tything men" (one man for each ten families) to inspect all homes in his neighborhood and, in the absence of the constable, to arrest "all Saboath breakers & disorderly tiplers," licensed tavvern keepers, and those who permitted violations of the Sabbath laws in their homes.[160]

We do not know how effective this new law was in preventing violations, but it is probably safe to assume that spying on one's neighbors was not a happy pastime. We note this record from the Essex County Court in 1679:

> Jonathan Ager and Isack Foott, tything men, upon complaint against Mary Meds for constantly neglecting the public worship of God on the Lord's day, went to her house, knocked at the door "and caled and at lenth waked her dafter [daughter] and with severall calings she wakened her mother and so let us in, and being asked the reson of the above said neglect and she said with angrie words we had more neede to look after Rude boys: and bid us goe out of her hous: and said she cold not nor wold not goe to metting for noe of them all." Also they had told Isack Whitecer, servant to Francis Skerry, at several times when they met him, to go into meeting, threatening to report him to authority, but he did not mind their words.[161]

Possibly the first tithingmen lacked the necessary tact to carry out their unpopular tasks. At any rate, two years after the original enactment, the General Court (in 1679) ordered the selectmen of each town to "take care that Tything men be Annually chosen . . . of their *most prudent and discreet Inhabitants,*" and enlarged their powers and duties. Not only were they to seek out and report Sabbath breakers, but they were to ferret out those who sold liquor without licenses and to search men's cellars wherever they might suspect "wines, strong beer, Ale, Cider, Perry, Matheglin, Rhum, Brandy, etc" were lodged. They were required to give the names to the Magistrate of:

> all single persons that live from under Family Government, stubborn and disorderly Children and Servants, night-walkers, Typlers, Sabbath breakers, by night or by day, and such as absent themselves from the publick Worship of God on the Lords dayes, or whatever else course or practice of any person or persons whatsoever tending

to debauchery, Irreligion, prophaness, and Atheism amongst us. . . .[162]

8) Young Puritans born in New England evidently did not take kindly to the advice of their elders that they be good Sabbatarians. The General Court found it necessary to remind them that any "prophaness of the Sabbath" made them "great provokers of the high displeasure of the Almighty God," by:

> playing in the streetes, and other places . . . uncivily walking the streetes and feilds, travailing from toune to toune, going on shipboard, frequenting common howses [taverns] and other places to drincke, sport and otherwise to mispend that precious time. . . .

This law applied only to those over the age of seven—"not that wee aproove younger children in evill"—but if the offenders were between the ages of seven and fourteen the punishment would fall upon their parents, who would first be admonished, but on the second offense would be fined five shillings and on the third offense ten shillings. Subsequent convictions would entail further punishments in the discretion of the court. Youths fourteen years of age and over would be similarly fined or, if they did not pay the fine, they would be whipped.[163]

9) The above law was to regulate conduct only "during the Day Light of the Lord's Day." Another law was needed to prevent "prophaness" on Saturday evening, for the Hebrew Sabbath began at sunset on the previous day. "Sporting" or drinking or simply being present in any house of entertainment on Saturday evening was prohibited, for such behavior "tends, not only to the hindering of due preparation for the Saboath, but . . . renders the ordinance of God unprofitable, & threatnes rooting out of the power of godlines, and procuring the wrath & judgments of God upon us & our posterity."[164]

10) About twenty years later, another law was needed to prevent people from seeking their Saturday evening pleasures outside of the town of Boston. The General Court ordered in 1679 that a Ward be established consisting of a selectman or constable and "two or more meete persons" to prevent "any cart to passe out of the toune after sun sett, nor any footeman or horseman" unless they could show that such a trip was necessary.[165] Other towns were given authority to do likewise.

11) Before special laws were enacted to punish Quakers for uttering heretical doctrines, the General Court in 1646 listed a number of "damnable heresies" that tended to "the subversion of the Christian Faith & destruction of the soules of men" and carried them on the law books down to the end of the Bay Colony government:

"Denying the immortality of the soule, or the resurrection of the body" or that there was "any sinn to be repented of in the regenerate, or any evil done by the outward man to be accounted sinn" or that "Christ gave himselfe a ransome for our sinns";

affirming that we are not "justified by his death & righteousnes, but by the perfection of our owne workes";

denying "the Morality of the fourth Commandement";

opposing the baptizing of infants or leaving the meetinghouse while infants were being baptized (a heresy added to the list after the Anabaptist controversy);

denying that the government had a right "to punish the outward breaches of the first Table" that is, the first four of the Ten Commandments (a heresy also added to the list some years after Roger Williams and a few others had challenged the government's right).

Anyone found guilty of any of these heresies or of inducing others to utter them was subject to a heavy fine but, after 1648 one who continued to hold such opinions obstinately after means had been taken to convince him of his error, was subject to banishment.[166]

12) Swearing, as distinct from blasphemy, was a very common offense and usually punished by a fine. Blasphemy, by cursing God or denying his existence, went to the very heart of religious belief and was, as we shall see in Chapter 9, a capital offense. Swearing "rashly & vainely, either by the holy name of God, or any other oath," might bring one into court where the maximum penalty was a ten-shilling fine or a one-to-three-hour spell in the stocks. Should one who uttered a series of oaths pay a fine for each one? An amendment to resolve this question provided for a twenty-shilling fine for more than one oath on a single occasion before one left the room or place where he was swearing and a whipping or imprisonment for failure to pay the fine. "Prophane or wicked Cursing" of an animal was similarly punishable.[167]

13) As the Indians must have been ignorant of "the true God," it was deemed necessary to see that they did not profane the Lord's day or continue their "worship to their false gods, or to the devill." Indian "powaws" were therefore forbidden, violators to be fined five pounds, and each person present, if over the age of discretion, to be fined twenty shillings.[168]

The laws of Plymouth Colony calling for conformity to Puritan orthodoxy and to the strict observance of the Sabbath were substantially similar to those of the Bay Colony, although less severely administered.[169]

We cannot say how many men, women, and children were deterred from the commission of acts in violation of these laws by the contemplation of a fine, a public whipping, or banishment from the Colonies. We do know that the official records report a large number of offenses calling for appearances in court, but the reports are incomplete and do not allow of a representative sample of cases. We shall reproduce here from the official records a few interesting illustrations taken at random:

It is ordered, that Roberte Shawe shalbe severly whipt, for wicked curseing; sweareing, justifyeing the same, & gloryeing in it, as hath been proved by oath.[170]

John Hogges, for swearing Gods foote, & cursing his servant, wishing a poxe of God take you, was fined 5 pounds.[171]

[Hugh Buets (or Bewett or Burts) was found guilty of heresy by a jury in the Court of Assistants and his] errors [were considered] dangeros for infection of others.[172] [According to Governor Winthrop, his heresy consisted in] holding publicly and maintaining that he was free from original sin and from actual also for half a year before, and that all true Christians after [word omitted, possibly "conversion"] are enabled to live without committing actual sin. [Buets was banished and was told not to return] upon paine of being hanged. [He went to Providence where he was well received.][173]

[Edward Tomlins, a former Deputy in the General Court], retracting his opinions against singing in the churches, was discharged.[174]

Roger Scott of Lynn presented for common sleeping at public exercise on the Lord's day, and for striking him who awaked him.[175]

Wm Hewes and son John fined 50 shillings each and to confess "for deriding such as Sing in the Congregacon tearming them fooles" and

Wm for saying that Mr. Whiting preached confusedly, and John for charging Mr. Cobbitt with falsehood in his doctrine.[176]

The wife of Thomas Olever, for saying that all ministers in the country were blood-thirsty men, to be tied to the whipping post with a slit stick on her tongue. . . .[177]

Mr. Hennie Walton of Lynn was presented for saying that "he had as Leeve to hear a Dogg Barke as to heare Mr. Cobbett Preach."[178]

[Richard Rowland of Marblehead was admonished by the court for sleeping in church.] He confessed that he slept sometimes.[179]

[Philip Veren who had been before the court on numerous occasions for not attending church services and who had spoken out against the execution of Quakers] was ordered to be set by the heels in the stocks one hour for disowning the country's power, in open court, about forcing any to come to the public worship.[180]

Allester Grimes, for working at the hoe on the Lord's day was fined or to be whipped. [Two boys had witnessed this violation of law.][181]

Andrew Newcomb presented for hoyseing his Sailes to dry them on the Sabbath day, which hee Owned in Court but pleaded necessity there haveing been such a long Season of wet weather foregoing, upon due consideration of the case the Court Sentenced him to bee admonished in open Court & pay Fees of Court. . . .[182]

Henry Sherlot a frenchman that is newly come into this toune [Boston] as he saith a Dancing master etc. [also a fencer] a person very Insolent & of ill fame that Raves & scoffes at Religion of a Turbulent spirit no way fit to be tollerated to live in this place [was banished by the Court of Assistants in 1681].[183]

† † †

Toward the close of the seventeenth century a number of factors emerged, both in England and in the Colonies, that caused a relaxing of Puritan control over the affairs of men and forever precluded a return to the low point of tolerance reached during the Quaker prosecutions in the Bay Colony in the years 1656 to 1669.[184] These factors that decreased Puritan control in government were the growing acceptance of the idea of religious freedom;[185] the removal of the religious qualification for the franchise and the substitution of a property test as set forth in the Charter of 1692; the

"Act of Toleration" decreed by Parliament in 1689; the rise of strong dissenting sects opposed to and in competition with the original Puritan-Calvinistic-Congregational ecclesiastical power; the commerical growth of the Colonies and the advent of a more heterogeneous population, not particularly concerned with theological hairsplitting; the growth of rationalism and scientific inquiry in England and America; and, finally, the coming to power in Massachusetts of a new generation of men who had never personally experienced the deep religious motivations of their Puritan forebears.

Strong undercurrents of hostility and bigotry toward Roman Catholics, so characteristic of Puritan thinking in the seventeenth century, persisted for many years beyond the Reformation and the revolt of the Puritans against the "popish" ceremonies of the Church of England. Even Locke had not sanctioned full toleration of Roman Catholics in England, on the ground that they owed allegience to a foreign power. The Toleration Act of 1689 which suspended operation of penal laws against those who worshipped outside of the established church of England specifically denied its protection to Roman Catholics or to anyone who refused to disavow the Catholic doctrine of transubstantiation—a doctrine that for many years had prompted thousands of words of acrimonious debate. Besides Roman Catholics, it refused protection also to anyone who renounced the doctrine of the Trinity.

The Province Charter of 1692 took a giant step toward liberality in religious matters by granting "a liberty of Conscience" in the worship of God *but* made it very clear that that liberty applied "to all Christians (*Except Papists*)."[186] Protestants, then, were to be tolerant toward each other but needed to go no further.[187] This exception made it possible for the Province government to enact a new law in 1700 (not unlike the Bay Colony law of 1647) aimed directly at the Jesuits or any representative of the "pope or see of Rome."[188] It ordered such persons to leave the jurisdiction within two and a half months after publication of the law. Failure to comply made one subject to a sentence to life imprisonment as "an incendiary and disturber of the publick peace and safety and an enemy of the true Christian religion" and to the death penalty if he escaped from prison. This law seemed just as unnecessary as the Colonial legislation, for the only Jesuits in the Province at that time where two missionaries to the Indians in territory now part of the state of Maine. The traditional abhorrence of the Society of Jesus on religious grounds, combined with fear of its political influence in cementing French and Indian alliances against the English, probably motivated this legislation.

The Province government enacted no further laws directed against Jesuits or representatives of the Pope, but anti-Catholic sentiments, drawn from the dark well of bigotry, assailed the eighteenth and nineteenth centuries and have not wholly disappeared to this day although half the population of the Commonwealth is now of this faith.[189] Antipathy in the eighteenth century took the form of sermons on the evils of "popery," anti-Catholic catechisms, biased school texts, and more subtle forms of propaganda by Protestants who rejected the "idolatry," the "superstition," and the "human inventions not warranted by Scripture" attributed to Roman Catholics whose Pope, it was said, was the Biblical antichrist.[190] It was not until November 2, 1788, that a glimmer of tolerance was observed when the first Catholic mass was celebrated in the town of Boston.[191]

Public schools in New England in the following century continued to foster this prejudice which even pervaded the state prison where the Protestant chaplain would permit no Catholic services nor allow prisoners access to Catholic literature from its opening in 1805 until 1875 when the General Court, at the urging of Catholic authorities, ordered that an inmate must "not be denied the free exercise of his religious belief and the liberty of worshipping God according to the dictates of his conscience in the place where he is confined."[192] The first Catholic service in the state prison at Charlestown was conducted on June 6, 1875, by Father Byrne of that city. Forty-two years later, the people approved the 46th amendment to the Massachusetts Constitution that stated, in part, that no inmate of a publicly controlled reformatory, penal, or charitable institution shall be deprived "of the opportunity of religious exercises therein of his own faith."

Denied by the Province Charter—and by public opinion—of their power to enforce compliance with their own notions of orthodoxy, Puritan ministers took a dismal view of their declining influence and the prevalent growth of impiety. In a memorial to the Governor and the General Court, they wrote in 1694:

> Wee being very solemnly & sadly, sensible of the declining, decaying, (if not) dying state of Religion, . . . the totall degeneracy & apostacy (if not) of the present, yet of, ye rising, & succeeding, generations . . . Worldlyness . . . in all the lusts . . . is the originall, radicall, capitall sin, of New England. . . .

By "lusts" they referred to certain criminal acts which they believed were no longer strictly controlled, such as polygamy, adultery, incest, profaneness, sensuality, and, particularly, drinking and "company keeping, in taverns and alehouses." They implored the government to unsheath the civil sword to put an end to this ungodliness.[193]

Governor Jonathan Belcher on September 22, 1730, confirmed this opinion of moral decline that was not checked until "The Great Awakening" of the 1740s when a wave of evangelism initiated by the Rev. Jonathan Edwards was given great impetus by evangelist George Whitefield who preached to enormous crowds in Congregational churches and on Boston Common and toured New England, winning thousands of converts, much in the manner of a modern Billy Graham.[194] Such "awakening" was evidently needed, for Governor Belcher in a strongly worded proclamation to the people deplored the then current "Blasphemy, Prophane Cursing and swearing, Prophaning of the Lord's Day, excessive Drinking, Lewdness, or other dissolute and disorderly Practices."[195]

As the eighteenth century emerged out of the Puritan-dominated seventeenth, the faint dawn of religious toleration brought significant changes in the penal laws. No longer could courts try men for bringing "damnable heresies"[196] into Massachusetts or for crossing swords with Puritans over involved theological issues or for refusing to yield to the Congregational form of church discipline. The Province government permitted the Baptists and the Quakers to conduct their church services unmolested. The Episcopal Church had first celebrated the Lord's Supper in Boston on August 2, 1686, and in the following year worshipped in its newly built edifice on the corner of the Old Burying Ground.[197] There was toleration for all Protestant religions, but the General Court was reluctant to give up all control. It took the position that for the state to maintain an established church was not inconsistent with the Charter's "liberty of conscience," a view sharply disputed by the Baptists, who took their grievances to the crown and who were later joined by the Quakers and other "dissenters."[198]

The government early in its history (1692) had ordered each town to select an "able, learned orthodox minister or ministers," men "of good conversation," the costs to be borne out of taxes assessed on all townspeople regardless of their religious affiliations.[199] From time to time this law was strengthened by providing penalties for towns that failed to comply and by giving courts authority to fine or imprison selectmen or to make distraint upon their goods for willful disobedience. Individuals who refused to pay the tax to support *the* church of the Province were similarly punished.[200] The Baptists (officially called Anabaptists or Antipedobaptists) had, by the first quarter of the eighteenth century, grown into a powerful force, drawing many of their members from the Congregational churches. A few preferred prison to compliance. The Quakers, too, were quietly gathering strength during that period of sectarian diversification. They were no longer the "ranting" disturbers of Congregationalism like the original Quakers who came to Massachusetts in 1656, although they were still despised by many Congregationalists—and by Episcopalians too.

The "dissenters," by appeals to their sympathetic counterparts in England and to the Crown and by winning some popular support in New England, insisted on the *disestablishment* of the church. If they had achieved a complete victory, Massachusetts might have witnessed a swift and effective separation of church and state as early as the second or third decade of the eighteenth century—an achievement that was not to come for another one hundred years. But in 1727 the General Court reached a compromise solution in the direction, at least, of freedom of worship. It enacted a series of "exemption laws," requiring "dissenters" to pay a tax but assuring them that it would be applied only to the support of their own religious group, provided their refusal to support the established church was based on "scruples of conscience" and they could show that they "usually" attended their own religious services in a meetinghouse not more than five miles from their homes.[201] These laws, carried down to the end of the Province period, were accepted with little enthusiasm and led to strife and dissension and fraud, but the government was able to resist successfully the increasing demands for disestablishment. It is not within the province of this report to relate the story of the long interdenominational struggle for church independence so thoroughly reported by church historians.[202]

The fight for complete religious freedom was taken up with renewed vigor by the first Continental Congress in 1774, the Baptists taking a leading role, but fell short of victory. A formidable task therefore confronted the authors of the "Declaration of Rights" (in 1778—1780) that became Part 1 of the Constitution of Massachusetts. Could they draw up an article that would assure the perpetuation of the worship of God and at the same time give proper consideration to conflicting religious ideologies in a government that had explicitly acknowledged "the goodness of the Great Legislator of the Universe" and the equality of all men? Could they meet the consistent demands of the Baptists, still the most powerful opponents of the establishment, that there be no established church at all and that the government recognize completely and forever "the sacred rights of conscience," and yet win the approval of the Congregationalists whose impoverished ministers (outside of Boston) were calling for a continuation of tax support? Evidently, the answer was "No." Article Three of the "Declaration," as finally written, did not receive universal support. It recognized the power of the state to keep alive a church establishment. To many, this power seemed perfectly logical in a government whose very preservation (according to the Constitution) depended on "piety, religion, and morality."

Adopted by the voters in 1780 and destined to last for 53 years, Article Three declared in effect that the government has the right to require each town to make suitable provisions for religious worship and that *Protestant* teachers (reflecting a continuance of anti-Catholic sentiment) of piety, religion, and morality should be supported by taxes paid by citizens of the towns (excepting in towns like Boston where churches were usually supported by voluntary contributions). Following the Province "exemption laws," Article Three allowed a taxpayer to indicate to which church he wished his taxes to be alloted. The towns, not the churches, were to choose the local minister—a provision that led to some confusion and litigation. It also established the principle, long in operation in the Colonies, that the legislature could "enjoin" citizens to attend religious services if they could "conscientiously and conveniently attend"—a provision that was more liberal than the early Puritans would have approved. To avoid charges of favoritism, the article concluded that "every denomination of christians, demeaning themselves peaceably, and as good Subjects of the Commonwealth, shall be equally under the protection of the Law: And no subordination of any one sect or denomination to another shall ever be established by law." Objection later was made to limiting this equal protection clause to those of the Christian faith. The Eleventh Amendment of 1833 changed "every denomination of christians" to "all religious sects and denominations."

Thus the state exercised its powers over the towns in order to preserve a religious Commonwealth, and the fight for disestablishment then led by the Baptists, Methodists, and Universalists, but not the young Unitarians who were on the side of establishment, continued into the nineteenth century.[203] A constitutional convention in 1820 struggled with the question of how to insure adequate religious instruction in Massachusetts without governmental coercion but, after long debates and discussions, failed to find the answer. It was believed at that time by many thoughtful people who stood for liberty of conscience that if all New England churches had to depend on voluntary contributions the religious foundations of the Commonwealth would be severely shaken. Finally, after 53 years of governmental oversight of religious teaching, the Commonwealth in 1833 did what the other states had done before them—it gave up direct governmental control over all religious institutions. The Eleventh Article of Amendments to the Massachusetts Constitution was approved by the people in that year on November 11th—an armistice day in interdenominational warfare. Wiping out the objectionable Article Three, this new amendment gave to the churches the right to elect their own pastors and teachers and ended permanently the requirement that citizens of the towns must be taxed to support the local churches.

It is interesting to note that many years before this time, on September 17, 1787, the Federal Constitution was adopted by the states and its first ten amendments (The Bill of Rights) were ratified by the required number of states on December 15, 1791.[204] The first article of the Amendments provided, in part, that "Congress shall make no law respecting an establishment of religion, or prohibiting the free exercise thereof. . . ." It was not until many years later, however, that, by reason of the Fourteenth Amendment adopted and ratified in 1868, Article One was deemed to apply to the states, rather than to the Federal government alone. And it was not until 1917 that the voters of Massachusetts approved of Article 46 of the Amendments to the Constitution of the Commonwealth, Section 1 of which stated: "No law shall be passed prohibiting the free exercise of religion."

To make it unconstitutional in Massachusetts to apply public funds to religious schools, Article 18 of the Amendments was approved in 1855. Article 46 of the Amendments, approved in 1917, replaced the former article in the Massachusetts Constitution but retained with more explicit elaborations the prohibitions against the use of public funds to support institutions "wherein any denominational doctrine is inculcated."

We shall here take notice of two kinds of human behavior prohibited by laws based upon Scripture and derived from the laws of the Puritan Colonies that have caused some concern to the Commonwealth government and that are still—with some modifications—punishable by Massachusetts courts.

Blasphemy. The Massachusetts Bay Colony, in its Body of Liberties of 1641 made blaspheming of "god, the father, Sonne or Holie ghost, with direct, expresse, presumptuous or high handed blasphemie" or the cursing of God "in like manner" a crime punishable by death.[205] The compiled laws of 1648, 1660, and 1672 republished this law with further elaborations. The Province government, unable to get the King's approval for making this a capital law, nevertheless reenacted it, with less serious penalties.[206] The Commonwealth government has continued this law down to the present day. A comparison of the 1648 law (identical with the 1660 and the 1672 enactments) with the present law shows that we have not departed entirely from Puritan thinking in our criminal code:

The Colonial Law of 1648	*The Law of the Commonwealth Today*
[Derived from the Law of 1641 which, in turn, was derived from Scripture: Leviticus 24:15, 16.]	[Based on the Colonial Law, the Province Law, the Commonwealth Law of 1782, and carried down to the General Laws, chap. 272, sec. 36.]

If any person within this Jurisdiction whether Christian or Pagan shall wittingly and willingly presume to BLASPHEME the holy Name of God, Father, Son or Holy-Ghost, with direct, expresse, presumptuous, or high-handed blasphemy, either by wilfull or obstinate denying the true God, or his Creation, or Government of the world: or shall curse God in like manner, or reproach the holy Religion of God as if it were but a politick device to keep ignorant men in awe; or shall utter any other kinde of Blasphemy of the like nature & degree they shall be put to death.

Whoever wilfully blasphemes the holy name of God by denying, cursing or contumeliously reproaching God, his creation, government or final judging of the world, or by cursing or contumeliously reproaching Jesus Christ or the Holy Ghost, or by cursing or contumeliously reproaching or exposing to contempt and ridicule, the holy word of God contained in the holy scriptures shall be punished by imprisonment in jail for not more than one year or by a fine of not more than three hundred dollars, and may also be bound to good behavior.

To sentence a man to jail today for a violation of this law would probably meet with public disapproval, particularly if he were charged only with denying "the final judging of the world." The last recorded criminal trial where a conviction of blasphemy was appealed to the Supreme Judicial Court of the Commonwealth, and upheld, was the famous case of Abner Kneeland (1774–1844) in 1838 that stirred the city of Boston and brought many liberals to his defense. The court held that the law was not repugnant to the Constitution of the Commonwealth in seeking "to punish a denial of God, made with a bad intent, and in a manner calculated to give just offense." Kneeland, a former Universalist minister, as editor of the newspaper *The Boston Investigator,* wrote and published an article critical of the theological beliefs of the Universalists. At his trial Kneeland claimed he was not an atheist but a pantheist and that God and nature were synonymous. He wrote that he did not believe in the Universalists' God. It was, he said, "a mere chimera of their imagination"; their story of Christ was "as much a fable and fiction as that of the God Prometheus"; their "miracles" were due to natural causes or tricks and impostures and their belief in immortality was incredible. Then the storm broke. He was tried and convicted in the Boston Municipal Court in 1834 and sentenced to three months in jail. After many delays, appeals, and retrials, the case finally came before the full bench of the Supreme Judicial Court in 1838. Chief Justice Lemuel Shaw, upholding the lower court in a 14-page opinion, sentenced the blasphemer to sixty days in jail which he was required to serve. Justice Marcus Morton wrote an interesting 21-page dissenting opinion.[207]

"Remember the Sabbath day, To Keep it Holy." To force obedience to the Fourth Commandment, to reserve the Lord's Day exclusively for worship and to bar all secular activities on that day was a duty imposed upon the government and willingly accepted by all Puritan groups. These strict Puritan regulations survived the seventeenth century and, with some modifications, were carried forward on the statute books of the Province and Commonwealth governments.

In 1692 the Province government commanded every one to apply himself "to duties of religion and piety publickly and privately" from sundown on Saturday through Sunday evening. It prohibited all business, games, sports, recreation, travel (making allowance for emergency situations), swimming, unnecessary walking, or riding; in short, any activity that could not be explained as a work of necessity or charity. Taverns were to be closed to all inhabitants but might serve strangers or travelers with necessary refreshment.[208]

This law was reenacted a number of times by the Province government, each reenactment usually adding to the list of forbidden activities. Penalties provided for a period of time (up to three hours) in the stocks or public cage or as much as five days in the prison. But church-attendance laws were far more liberal than those in the Colonial period. A law of 1760 made it criminal to be absent from public worship continuously for one month unless one had "good and sufficient excuse." Probably few people obeyed this law. To enforce observance of the Sabbath, the General Court in 1760 asked each town to appoint wardens to go about the streets and wharfs to command obedience. When children were fined for playing on the Lord's Day, their parents had the choice of paying the fines or going to prison.[209]

Down through the centuries, laws regulating behavior on Sunday have always been on the statute books of Massachusetts, although those of the twentieth century have been far less restrictive. In recent years many modifications have been accepted by the General Court, which has exempted more and more business enterprises whose open doors on Sunday have been deemed in the public interest. But there are still acts that one cannot perform with impunity on Sunday. The question has been raised whether such laws, long upheld by the courts, are now considered unconstitutional. Can a state impose upon a non-Christian, criminal sanctions for activities performed on a day that is not his holy day of worship? No one can dispute the fact that our Lord's Day prohibitions were derived from a belief in the Bible as the Word of God—a belief not shared by everyone. As we have seen, they were laws designed to support the orthodox Puritan faith.

Appellate courts are now reversing earlier decisions. These laws are now considered "social laws," desirable not for the perpetuation of religious worship but for the advancement of the health and welfare of all citizens. Although there is probably a growing number of people who are demanding total repeal of all Sunday laws, there is some popular support for court opinions that uphold the enactment of reasonable restrictions on Sunday on other than sectarian grounds. On matters of religion the government is taking a neutral position. We can, if we wish, "remember the Sabbath day, to keep it holy" but, in the spirit of Roger Williams, we are not compelling by the sword obedience to any of the first four of the Ten Commandments.[210]

The words of Justice William Douglas of the United States Supreme Court written in 1952: "We are a religious people whose institutions presuppose a Supreme Being"[211] aptly describe the Commonwealth of Massachusetts. Its Constitution tells us that "the public worship of God and instructions in piety, religion and morality, promote the happiness and prosperity of a people and the security of a Republican Government."[212] Its Constitution exhorts us to worship God. It is not only the right of a citizen of the Commonwealth to "worship the Supreme Being, the great Creator and preserver of the Universe," but it is "the *Duty* of all men in society, publickly, and at stated seasons" to worship him.[213]

A religious test as a qualification for public office was a routine matter in a government under Puritan control. The Constitution of 1780 could not suddenly create a purely secular Commonwealth. During the first 41 years of the life of this Commonwealth (that is, up to 1821), no Jew, nor any other person outside the Christian faith, nor atheist could take office as Governor, Lieutenant Governor, Councillor, or member of the General Court. These elected officials were required to take a solemn oath: "I believe the Christian religion, and have a firm persuasion of its truth. . . ."[214]

Our churches are still tax exempt; tax supported chaplains of different faiths serve the inmates of our prisons and charitable institutions; we still require an oath terminating in "So help me, God"; we still open our courts with a terminal prayer "God save the Commonwealth!"; a church flag flies above our state or national emblem; and in many other ways we officially acknowledge our dependence on and our gratitude toward a Supreme Being.

Governor John Winthrop of the Bay Colony would not, we presume, wholly disapprove, if he were here today, of this kind of reverence. But the striking difference between his government and that of today is that a person is now immune from punishment by the state for publicly declaring his own interpretation or denial of God or the written Word (provided his declaration does not amount to blasphemy) or for attending or absenting himself from religious services (providing he does not disturb the worship of others) or for refusing to contribute toward the support of a religious institution.

The "wall of separation" spoken of by Thomas Jefferson is not a solid or insurmountable one. We have rather, as Stokes put it, a "benevolent separation" between church and state, a friendly, cooperative relationship without coercion or sectarian preferences. But new problems now arise, such as some tax support for church-related schools, religious education in the schools, church-motivated censorship, government support of birth-control education, to mention a few of the controversial issues.

And yet, from the stern penalties for heresy suffered by seventeenth century liberals, we have come a long way to the statement of our political philosophy by the United States Supreme Court in 1871 which is sound law today:

> The law knows no heresy, and is committed to the support of no dogma, the establishment of no sect.[215]

6. "BODILIE PUNISHMENTS"

> Strict discipline, both in criminal offences and in martial affairs, was more needful in plantations than in a settled state, as tending to the honor and safety of the gospel. . . .—*Governor Winthrop, 1635.*[1]

IN the town of Boston on the 29th day of October, 1672, Mary Plumb stood humbly before the court to answer a charge of "Lascivious carriage by being seene in bed with a man."[2] On the bench that day, Governor Bellingham presided.[3] He was then in his eightieth year, an incorruptible Puritan, trained in the law in England where he had been a court recorder and at one time a member of Parliament. Assisting him were John Leverett, Esq., the Deputy Governor, destined to be elected Governor the following year on the death of Bellingham, and grandfather of John who served as president of Harvard College from 1707 to 1724; Edward Ting (or Tyng), Esq., a well-to-do merchant and prominent citizen with long experience in legal affairs; and William Stoughton, Esq., a graduate of Harvard and bearer of an M.A. degree from Oxford, trained in both theology and law. Elected the first Deputy Governor in the Province period, Stoughton is best remembered as the presiding judge in the witchcraft trials in Salem in 1692.[4]

There was nothing particularly unusual about the case of the Bay Colony against Mary Plumb. As she faced these austere gentlemen she put up no defense, asked for no mercy. In her thoughts must have been the painful image of her appearance before these same jurists just four months earlier on the charge of having been "in the Chamber of Timmothy Connell late at night . . . in Suspitious manner."[5] On that occasion too she had admitted the charge. In fact, she had then "acknowledged in Court she was there naked to her Shift [chemise] where were two men in Bed" and had bravely accepted the consequences—"to be whip't with twenty Stripes." As she faced this Suffolk County Court for the second time she knew that a public whipping was the most likely penalty for one who defied the strict sex code of Boston or Plymouth, and she listened with no surprise to the sentence of the court that she be "whip't severely with fifteen stripes & to pay fees of Court & prison & to stand committed to the house of correction till the Select men of Dorchester provide a meete service for her." We can imagine that presiding Justice Bellingham underscored the word "severely." It was no doubt his prayer that the physical and psychological pain that Mary was about to endure would be a sharp deterrent to such lewd practices. But Mary was not so easily weaned from her lascivious habits. Just twelve months later she was to be brought before the same court on another charge: "haveing a Childe it not appearing Shee was ever married."[6] A third and more severe whipping with a possible sentence to the House of Correction awaited her, but "the Constable made return hee could not finde her" and she drifted off into dark obscurity.

When Mary Plumb felt the sting of the lash on her bare back, witnessed by the curious and the morbid standing about in the marketplace, she was not experiencing a sadistic invention of the Puritans. Down through the ages, whipping had been the most common form of punishment for serious crimes that were not capital offenses, adopted by governments from time immemorial, by the military, by parents in curbing childish transgressions, and by reform schools and prisons in maintaining discipline. It was a common penalty under the laws of Moses; it was practiced in old England; it was the accepted discipline of the seventeenth century houses of correction and the approved form of chastisement of Harvard College scholars who were dealt with "in the hall, openly."[7]

Carried to extremes a whipping could cause death, an eventuality the Colonists wished to avoid. Bay Colony lawmakers had protected the rights of an offender who, after all, had not committed a crime that warranted the death penalty by posting definite limits to the powers of government. In the first place, they decreed that no one should be punished at all:

> unlesse it be by vertue or equitie of some expresse law of the Country waranting the same, established by a generall Court and sufficiently published, or in case of the defect of a law in any parteculer case by the word of God. . . .[8]

No arbitrary whipping at the whim of some martinet was permissible. At the very outset, before the General Court had met or any laws had been enacted, the Court of Assistants at its first meeting in the Bay Colony on August 23, 1630, had forbidden any Justice of the Peace to take the law into his own hands by inflicting "any corporall punishment without the presence & consent of some of the Assistants."[9] Curiously, the first to disregard this order was Sir Richard Saltonstall, one of the few titled gentlemen to venture to New England with Winthrop and a prominent member of the Court until his return to England the following year. He was fined five pounds "for whipping 2 severall persons without the presence of another Assistant contrary to an act of Court formerly made."[10] Eight years later, for reasons not stated in the records, he was "discharged of the said 5 pounds.[11]

Secondly, they ruled out *cruelty* in the official administration of Colonial justice. Parents could whip their children, teachers their pupils, masters their servants, but not to excess. A provision of the Body of Liberties of 1641 carried down to the end of the Colonial period made this prohibition clear: "For bodilie punishments we allow amongst us none that are inhumane Barbarous or cruel."[12]

Thirdly, they sought to protect servants and slaves from overbearing masters or from those who thought they had the prerogatives of feudal lords. Many a master was reprimanded or punished by the courts for cruel treatment of his domestics.[13] The Bay Colony had borrowed a curious law from the Book of Exodus. The Colony law read:

> If any man smite out the eye or tooth of his man-servant, or maid servant, or otherwise mayme or much disfigure him, unlesse it be by meere casualtie, he shall let them goe free from his service. And shall have such further recompence as the Court shall allow him.[14]

Furthermore, abused servants could leave their masters without being charged with being runaways: "If any servants shall flee from the Tiranny and crueltie of their masters to the howse of any freeman of the same Towne, they shall be there protected and susteyned till due order be taken for their relife. . . ."[15]

Fourthly, the law sought the prevention of cruelty to children or domestic animals:

> If any parents shall wilfullie and unreasonably deny any childe timely or convenient mariage, or shall exercise any unnaturall severitie towards them, such childeren shall have free libertie to complaine to Authoritie for redresse.[16]
>
> No man shall exercise any Tirrany or Crueltie towards any bruite Creature which are usuallie kept for mans use.[17]

Fifthly, they provided penalties for wife beating or husband beating:

> Everie marryed woeman shall be free from bodilie correction or stripes by her husband, unlesse it be in his defence upon her assalt. If there be any just cause of correction complaint shall be made to Authoritie assembled in some Court, from which onely she shall receive it.[18]
>
> No man shall strike his Wife, nor any Woman her Husband, on penalty of such fine not exceeding ten pounds for one offence, or such Corporal punishment as the County Court shall determine.[19]

Sixthly, they set an upper limit on the number of stripes a constable might inflict, for the unpleasant task of whipping fell to the lot of the constables "unless they can get another to do it."[20] Ordinarily, a whipping was not considered cruel treatment, but, at the hands of some vindictive fellow who might derive sadistic pleasure from the task, an excessive number of stripes could prove to be inhumane, barbarous, or cruel. Where should one draw the line? Again the authorities turned to the Word of God where it was written in the Book of Deuteronomy: "Forty stripes he may give him, and not to exceed: lest, if he should exceed, and beat him above these many stripes, then thy brother should seem vile unto thee."[21]

Accordingly, the Colonies adopted a rule that "no man shall be beaten with above 40 stripes."[22] No case appears in the official reports of any court decreeing or of any constable inflicting above 40 stripes at any one time. The usual number "laid on" was

15 or 20, the greatest number, when the offense was considered particularly detestable, was 39. They adopted the Hebrew practice of stopping on or before the 39th stripe. Had not the Apostle Paul said in his Second Letter to the Corinthians, "Of the Jews five times received I forty stripes save one"?[23]

But the law did not say that a person whose behavior was unusually vile could not be whipped on two separate occasions for a total of more than forty stripes. The law was, in fact, amended to read: "No Man shall be beaten with above forty stripes for one Fact at one time. . . ."[24] There was always the possibility then that the court, by spacing the whippings, could see that more than forty were administered. Mary Hawkins barely escaped this fate when she was convicted by the Suffolk County Court in 1675 of "bold whorish carriages & having a bastard Childe & impudent & pernicious Lying."[25] That was not her first appearance. At a previous session of this same court she had brought charges against Ezekiel Fogg "for committing Fornication with her & begetting her with Childe." On her second appearance the court's sentence was that she:

> . . . bee whip't at a Carts tayle up from the dwelling house of John Hall in Boston formerly Ezekiel Foggs Lodgeing into the Town round about the Town house & soe to the prison with twenty five Stripes severely, & within one month following to bee whip't again severely with twenty Five stripes. . . .

Mulling over her fate as she sat in the Boston prison awaiting the second whipping, Mary wrote "a humble petition" to the Court of Assistants:

> That where as your pore petitioner hath through her very great sin & wickednes many ways agrivated, brought herselfe under the just sentence of the Countie Court, one part of which hath bene already inflicted upon me & though I can not but owne that I deserve not onely the other part to be inflicted, but by reason of my sin being so agrevated as It was, never to have any countenans or favour [shown] to me either from god or [man] yet considering gods wonderful mercy to humble peniten[ts] (though very hainous) calls upon them to turne from the wickednes & live, & that the same spirit of Compashon he works in his people, imboldens me humbly to Supplicate your honours that you will be pleased to remitt that other part of the punishment that is not yet inflicted, desireing the lord to worke still more

& more in my soule a greater sence of my sin & give me truly to repent & turne to him & to loath my selfe & sin which I hope in weaker measure I doe, thus leaveing my condition in the lords & your hands praying for your honours I subscribe myselfe

your Honours pore afflicted prisoner
mary hokahans.[26]

The judges were no doubt impressed with this most moving appeal, skillfully drawn to touch them where they were most vulnerable. Could the high court show less "compashon" than God himself toward this poor, repentant sinner? The court handed down this decision: "to Grant hir request & Remitts hir second punishment ordering the keep[er] of the prison to Dissmiss hir from the prison & set hir at liberty."[27]

Seventhly, in sentencing an offender to be whipped, courts considered the person's position on the social scale. It would have been debasing for proud English gentlemen who held high office in church or state, particularly those who had a right to place an "Esq." after their names, to be whipped in the marketplace before the rude gaze of their peers, their inferiors, and especially their own servants. It was understood therefore that men and women of the upper classes who could well afford to pay a fine should not, under ordinary circumstances, be subjected to a whipping. The Body of Liberties had made this distinction clear by prohibiting the whipping of "any true gentleman" or "any man equall to a gentleman" with one important exception: "unles his crime be very shamefull, and his course of life vitious and profligate."[28] In other respects the English were subject to their own criminal laws equally with Indians or foreigners. As God had said to Moses: "Ye shall have one manner of law, as well for the stranger, as for one of your own country: for I am the Lord your God,"[29] so the Body of Liberties had commanded that:

> Every person within this Jurisdiction, whether Inhabitant or forreiner shall enjoy the same justice and law, that is generall for the plantation, which we constitute and execute one towards another without partialitie or delay. . . .[30]

Judges had such wide discretion in administering the criminal law that it is impossible to list all offenses that might have led to the whipping post. The penalties were sometimes stated in the law

Portrait of Sir John Leverett, Governor of Massachusetts Bay Colony. Courtesy of the Essex Institute, Salem, Massachusetts.

in general terms, such as the offender "shall suffer Corporal punishment as Authority shall determine," or he shall suffer imprisonment or a fine or a whipping at the judge's discretion. The statutes did spell out, however, a large number of specific offenses for which whipping was made one of the appropriate penalties. By 1672 in the Bay Colony the culprits mentioned below might have been whipped if the court believed they merited that form of "bodilie punishment," although most of them in actual practice were given the alternative of a fine. This list gives us a picture of the kinds of transgressors the Colony thought wicked enough to chasten by the infliction of physical sufferings, or at least to warn of that possibility:

Those who were convicted the second time of burglary or robbery from the person "in the field or high-wayes."[31]

Children or servants who stole fruit from orchards, unless their parents or masters paid treble damages.[32]

Those who took other men's horses, without authority to do so, to ride them "at their pleasure."[33]

Children and servants who "behave themselves disobediently and disorderly towards their Parents, Masters and Governours; to the disturbance of families, and discouragement of such Parents and Governours."[34]

Those who "openly or willingly defame any Court of Justice, or the Sentences and Proceedings of the same, or any of the Magistrates, or other Judges. . . ."[35]

Those who "revile the Office or person of Magistrates or Ministers, as is usual with the Quakers."[36]

Those who set fires in certain seasons in the woods or commons so as to endanger the corn fields.[37]

Those who engaged in "the great sin of Gaming" by dice or cards, a crime which by 1670 had shown an increase.[38]

Those above the age of sixteen who professed the Christian religion and yet denied that one or more of the books of the Old or New Testaments were "the written and infallible Word of God."[39]

"Vagabond Quakers" who "besides their Absurd and Blasphemous Doctrines, do like Rogues and Vagabonds come in upon us."[40]

Men who commit fornication with any single woman.[41]

Persons over the age of fourteen who for the second time were guilty of telling "pernicious lies."[42]

Disorderly or unruly sailors on board their ships.[43]

Husbands who struck their wives or wives their husbands.[44]

Those who "prophane Gods Holy Sabbaths and contemn the publick Worship of his House."[45]

Those found drinking in taverns on the Sabbath (which began at sunset Saturday) or "young people and others [who] take liberty to walk and sport themselves in the streets or fields" on that day.[46]

"Youths and Maids above fourteen years old, and all elder persons whatsoever . . . for Playing, uncivil Walking, Drinking, Travailing from Town to Town, going on Ship board, Sporting, or any way mispending that precious time . . ." on the Sabbath; but such offenders were to be whipped only if they failed to pay the fine assessed and only if the offense occurred "during the Day light of the Lords day."[47]

He who swore "rashly or vainly by the Holy Name of God, or other Oath," provided he swore "more Oaths then one at a time, before he remove out of the Room or Company where he so Swears" and provided he refused or was unable to pay a fine. This restriction on swearing included profane or wicked cursing of his horses, cattle, or swine.[48] It was evidently difficult to enforce this law. It was thought necessary in 1675 to strengthen the government's hand by an additional law on swearing that made one liable to the same penalty if he heard an oath and did not immediately report it to authority.[49] It is doubtful if anyone was brought into court on this charge.

Vagabonds who "wander from their Families, Relations and Dwelling Places from Town to Town, thereby drawing away Children, Servants, and other persons, both younger and elder, from their lawful Callings and Imployments, and hardning the hearts of one another against all Subjection to the Rules of Gods Holy Word, and the Established Laws of this Colony" if they could not "give a good and satisfactory account of such their Wandring up and down."[50]

Such were the laws of the Bay Colony setting forth the crimes for which a whipping would be in order up to 1672. Subsequently the authorities saw fit to add a few more to the list:

Any "Baud, Whore, or vile Person," male or female, who kept a "Whore-House or Brothel House" (1673).[51]

Disorderly or rude children in the meetinghouse (during the church services) who, after the first offense were found to be "Delinquent" and declared "Incorrigible" (1675).[52]

Youths who—like many youths of later centuries—in "a woful Breach of the Fifth Commandment" went out at night and met "with Corrupt Company without leave, and against the mind, and to the great grief of their Superiours, which evil practice is of a very perillous Nature, and the Root of much Disorder" were to be whipped or fined on the second or subsequent conviction (1675).[53]

A review of the Colonial court records gives one the impression that one who held the sex mores of the times in light esteem would sooner or later have an engagement with the constable at the whipping post. This impression is confirmed by a sampling of Bay Colony cases during the later years of the Colonial government when the power of the Puritan churches was on the wane after the founding fathers had passed to their reward and the population was increasing—and sin along with it.[54] Of the 215 persons whom the Suffolk County Court sentenced to a whipping for a wide variety of offenses in an eight-and-a-half year period (1671–1680), almost half (46 percent) had been convicted of sex behavior that fell far enough below current standards to warrant this form of "bodilie punishment." Of this 46 percent, three-fourths had been found guilty of fornication. Of the sex offenders not guilty of fornication, sixteen were found to be lewd, lascivious or wanton; three were guilty of adultery or suspicion of adultery; two of attempted rape; and two of bigamy. Not all who were sentenced to a whipping were actually whipped, for many of them were offered, and probably accepted, the alternative of a fine.

Fornication, then, seemed to have been a relatively common crime at that time (1665)—"a shameful Sin, much increasing amongst us, to the great dishonour of God, and our profession of his Holy Name."[55] Unmarried couples committing this crime might have been subject to various penalties: enjoyning marriage, a fine, or corporal punishment or any or all of these. The first was derived from the Hebrew law that a man in such cases "shall surely endow her [his partner in the crime] to be his wife."[56] Usually, however, a fine or a whipping seemed to be the court's choice. Premarital affairs were evidently not uncommon and were similarly punished. If a child were born to a married couple prior to the expiration of the expected number of weeks from the date of marriage, such birth was conclusive evidence that they had sinned.[57] In such cases a whipping of fifteen or twenty stripes was in order, but in most cases the court permitted the payment of a rather heavy fine. The Jones case was fairly typical:

> John Jones & Sarah his wife convicted by theire own confession in Court of committing Fornication before marriage: The Court Sentenced them both to bee whip't the said John with Fifteen Stripes & Sarah with ten Stripes or to pay Forty Shillings in mony fine to the County & fees of Court Standing committee, etc.[58]

Unless the secret sin were made manifest some months later by a bawling infant, or unless the couple confessed, as they sometimes did when accused, one wonders how the courts managed to charge so many young people with the crime of fornication, a crime that was certainly not committed under the constable's nose. Perhaps the case of John Pearce and the widow who later became his wife might afford a clue. The court had sentenced them to be whipped or fined "for uncleanness before marriage." Damaging evidence had been submitted by a neighbor, Clement Coldam, "aged about fifty," who had sworn:

> . . . hearing that John Pearce was accustomed to take widow Stanard to his house at night and she was seen to go away in the morning, [he] went to Pearce's house and looked in at the window, etc. He called Anthony Dey and Deacon Steevens, and they saw enough to warrant a complaint against the said Pearce. . . .[59]

Usually when a couple were convicted of fornication the woman received a lighter penalty, but this practice was not adhered to if the major responsibility for the sin could be placed upon her, as in the case of Palmer and his alluring partner:

> George Palmer having committed folly with Margery Rugs, through her allurement, because hee confessed volentarily, hee was onely set in the stocks, & so dismissed. Margery Rugs, for intiseing & allureing George Palmer, was censured to bee severely whiped [Boston, 1640].[60]

A few selected court cases presented in chronological order might fairly represent the kinds of sex behavior the Colonial leaders tried to curb by a public whipping:

John Bickerstaffe was censured to bee severely whiped for committing fornication with Ales Burwoode . . . Ales Burwoode was censured to bee whiped for yelding [yielding] to Bickerstaffe without crying out, & concealing it 9 or 10 dayes [Boston, 1638].[61]

John Kempe [a servant] for filthy uncleane attemps with 3 yong girles was censured to bee whipt both heare, at Roxberry & at Salem very severly & was committed for a slave to Lt. Davenport [Boston, 1639].[62]

Dorothy Temple, for uncleanes and bringing forth a male bastard, is censured to be whipt twice; but shee faynting in the execution of the first, the other was not executed [Plymouth, 1639].[63]

John Pope, for his unchaste attempt upon a girle, & dalliance with maydes, & rebellios or stubborne carriage against his master, was censured to bee severly whiped [Boston, 1640].[64]

John Hobell shall be well whipt by the Constable for two misdemenors first for proceeding to get promises of Marriage from Abigail Burt, after that both he and she had been prohibited by her Father severall tymes, and also for offeringe and attemptinge to doe the act of fornication with her as they both confesse though as far as we can discerne by any proofe of Justice the act was not done [Springfield, 1641].[65]

Robt Cocker bethrothed himself too securely to one maiden, and then contracted with another woman. To be severely whipped, and to pay to Thomas Kinge, who subsequently married the first maiden, five pounds [Salem, 1642].[66]

Cornelious Hulett to be whipped ten Stripes on some lecture day in seasonable weather, for fornication with Elisabeth Due, having confessed before Rev. Edward Norice and others [Salem, 1654].[67]

Thomas Bird, for committing of severall adulterouse practices and attempts, soe farr as strength of nature would permitt, with Hannah Bumpas, as hee himselfe did acknowlidge, was sentanced by the Court to bee whipt two severall times, viz, the first time att the present Court, and the second time betwixt this and the fifteenth day of July next. And the said Hannah Bumpas, for yeilding to him, and not makeing such resistance against him as shee ought, is sentenced to bee publickly whipt, which accordingly was performed [Plymouth, 1662].[68]

> Archuball Forrest convicted of being in bed with Julian wife of Richard Knight, Sentenced to bee severely whip't with thirty stripes and to pay fees of Court . . . Julian Knight for being found in bed with Archubal Forrest Sentenced to bee severely whip't with twenty stripes and to pay fees of Court.[69] [Boston, 1679. Nine months later Julian was convicted by the same court of drunkenness] and entertaining of Archuball Forrest in the absence of her husband [and was] forbidden giving any further entertainment to said Forrest. [She was also sentenced to a whipping of ten stripes or a fine of ten shillings, Boston, 1680].[70]

> [Richard Benitt was not only sentenced to a whipping] for telling of sundry lyes, and for his lacivious and light behaviour with Deborah Woodcocke [but also was required to pay 21 pence a week] for the space of three yeers from the date heerof, for and towards the keeping of the child borne of the said Deborah, [for she had claimed Benitt was its father, Plymouth, 1681].[71]

The court meeting at Ipswich ordered James Creeke to be severely whipped or to pay a fine for heinous, lascivious, and adulterous behavior with Elizabeth Perkins, Luke Perkins' wife. He denied the most serious charges but damaged his case when he admitted in court that he had in fact kissed Elizabeth and he told the astonished magistrates that "he accounted his kissing her to be good manners and as other men did." At any rate, to deny the kissing would have been futile, confronted as he was with numerous witnesses. In a town like Ipswich—or Salem or Boston, for that matter—how could one escape the searching eyes of one's neighbors who were eager and ready to report any sign of "uncivill behaviour." Mary Brown, for example, a nineteen-year-old girl had testified that:

> she had seen Creeke kiss Perkins's wife several times and had seen her go into his shop when he was at work, pull up his hat, look into his face, tickle him and bring him drink, making a great deal more of him that she ever saw her make of her own husband. She had seen them kiss on the street which made deponent much ashamed to be seen in their company.

John Brown, "aged about forty-five years," also gave his testimony in the Creeke case. Returning from his pasture one day, he told the court, he had seen James and Elizabeth "tickling one another about the ribs." He swore that "he was so ashamed that he went into his own house. . . ." John Brown and Mary, his wife, both testified that

> the second or third Sabbath day after Master Hubbard [the Rev. William Hubbard, Ipswich minister] had preached upon the text "Wherewithal shall a young man cleanse his way", they saw soon after meeting, Creek go down into the orchard with Elizabeth Perkins. Mary said she had heard about the actions and now she might catch them if it were possible, so standing at the end window next to their orchard she could see them handling linen with their heads close together. Presently her daughter came in and said she saw them kissing [Ipswich, 1682].[72]

To be sure, the greatest severity seemed to have been accorded those who deviated from the strict code of behavior in sexual matters, yet there were many others guilty of a wide variety of offenses who were similarly chastised. Of all classes of offenders, those most harshly treated were probably the Quakers, whose story we have reserved for a separate chapter. We shall present here a few court cases to show the diversity of crimes for which the traditional whipping seemed suitable.

> John Baker shalbe whipped for shooteing att fowle on the Sabboth day Etc [Boston, 1630].[73]

> Roberte Shawe shalbe severely whipt, for wicked curseing; sweareing, justifyeing the same, & gloryeing in it, as hath been proved by oath [Boston, 1632].[74]

> John Lee shalbe whipt & Fined for calling Master Ludlowe [a Justice of the Peace] false-hearted knave & hard-hearted knave heavy Friend etc. [Boston, 1634].[75] [Lee was soon in trouble again:]

> John Lee shalbe whipt & Fyned 40 pounds for speakeing reproachfully of the Gouvenor sayeing hee was but a Lawer's clerke, & what understanding hadd hee more then himselfe, also taxeing the Court for makeing lawes to picke mens purses, as also for abuseing a mayde of the Governours pretending love in the way of marriage, when himselfe professes hee intended none, as also for intiseing her to goe with him into the cornfeild etc. [Boston, 1634].[76]

> John Pease shalbe whipt, & bound to his good behaviour, for strikeing his mother, Mistress Weston, & derydeing of her, & for dyvers other misdemenours, & other evill carriages [Boston, 1635].[77]

> William Shepheard servant to William Summer shalbe whipt for

stealeing victualls from his master & beanes from the Indians [Boston, 1636].[78]

Master Woods servant Isaack Robinson whipped for running away from his master very often and enticing others to run away [Salem, 1637].[79]

George Barlow for his idlenes was censured to bee whiped [Boston, 1637].[80]

Dorothy Talbie was one of the unfortunate characters of the seventeenth century whose mental aberations were little understood by her contemporaries. She was evidently obsessed with the idea of inflicting injury upon her own family. She came before the Salem court in 1637 charged with "laying hands on her husband to the danger of his life, and contemning authority of the court." The court noted that she had made "frequent" and apparently unwarranted attacks on her husband and ordered that she be "chained to a post, being allowed only to come to the place of gods worships" and to be held there until she repented.[81] Upon release she again attacked her husband. The court ordered a whipping which proved to be totally ineffective.[82] Dorothy next appeared in the Court of Assistants, this time charged with the murder of her own child. The Court saw the futility of further correction and condemned her to death.[83]

James Till, for lying, & allureing John Bryan to drinking, and slandering his dame Emerson, saying he would go whome [home] & lye with her, is censured to be whipt [Plymouth, 1639].[84]

Thom: Gray, for being drunke, prophaning of the name of God, keeping a tipling house, & drawing his knife in the Courte, was censured to bee severely whiped & fined 5 pounds.[85] [Boston, 1639–1640]. [Nine months later Gray was again in court for drunkenness and was] severely whiped. [John Endecott, then an Assistant, later Governor, administered the whipping himself.][86]

Mary Osborne, for her grosse miscarriage [misbehavior] in giveing her husband quick silver, & other abuses, was censured to be severely whiped [Boston, 1641].[87]

Hugh Browne's wife, for breaking his head and threatening that she would kill him, so that he is ever weary of his life, throwing stones at him, causing his face to bleed, calling him beast, and wishing him hanged and that he might never come home, to be severely whipped

[Salem, 1641].[88]

Peter Hambrow, for stealeinge a shirt of John Presburies, is censured to be whipt at the post, which was accordingly done [Plymouth, 1644].[89]

Ursula the wife of Henry Edwards presented for striking her husband & abusive Carriage & Language the presentment was Owned [confessed] & she was Sentanced to be whipt with ten Stripes or pay twenty Shillings fine . . . [Boston, 1672].[90]

Thomas Davis of Medfeild convicted in Court by his own confession of Stealing a pair of blew drawers Etc from Hannah Manning widdow, and having formerly been convicted of the like and other Crimes.[91] [Boston, 1679. Davis had been declared by the Court of Assistants as one of a pair of "Incorrigible Theeves."[92] He was sentenced to be whipped with fifteen stripes, to pay treble damages to the widow, and, on release from prison, to depart the town of Boston.]

[Luke Perkins was whipped for saying] base words [of the Ipswich minister, Master Thomas Cobbet—that he] was more fit to be in a hogsty than in a pulpit, and that he had been a vile man in his former days [Ipswich, 1681].[93]

It was not customary to whip a very young child at the public whipping post. It is not possible to say at just what tender age the authorities drew a line. Rarely does the age of the offender appear in the records. Sometimes parents were ordered by the court to perform the whipping at home when the offender was a child, as in the cases of the Chandler children or of Bezaliel Leveret who was a grandson of John Leveret who was then Governor:

John Chandler & Elisabeth Chandler Son & daughter of John Chandler senior of Roxbury being presented to this Court for wanton uncivill & unseemely carriages. The Court . . . doe Sentence the said John & Elisabeth to bee severely whip't by theire Father & mother in theire own house in the presence of the Constable & John Stebbins The Father to correct his Son & the mother her daughter with such a Number of Stripes as the Constable & said Stebbins shall judge meete not exceeding fifteen Stripes apeice & that the said Children bee put asunder & not suffered to dwell together till the Court take further Order [Boston, 1674].[94]

Bezaliel Leveret a Childe [had found some] yardes of ribbon [belonging to Asaph Eliott and sold it.] The Court Orders his Father Master

Hudson Leverett to correct him in the presence of a Constable [Boston, 1674].[95]

The courts subjected two classes of offenders to a particularly painful and humiliating penalty. Quakers and "bauds," or prostitutes, were sometimes stripped to the waist, tied to the tail end of a cart, and, as the cart moved slowly through the town or sometimes from town to town, the constable applied the lash.

Sarah Ensigne, for commiting whordome agrevated with divers cercumstances, was centanced by the Court to bee whipt att the carts-taile; and that it be left to the descretion of such of the majestrates as shall see the said punishment inflicted for the number of stripes, but not to exceed twenty, which accordingly was inflicted this Court [Plymouth, 1665].[96]

Prostitution had evidently made some insidious advances into the Bay Colony also. In 1672 the notorious Alice Thomas (mentioned in Chapter 8) was found guilty not only of being an accessory in the burglary of warehouses and vessels in the nighttime, selling liquor without a license, profaning the Lord's Day by selling drink, and entertaining idle persons, but of the more serious crime of:

giving frequent secret and unseasonable Entertainment in her house to Lewd Lascivious & notorious persons of both Sexes, giving them oppertunity to commit carnall wickedness, & that by common fame she is a common Baud [Boston, 1672].[97]

After making restitution for the stolen goods, paying a heavy fine, and standing on the gallows with a rope about her neck, Alice was condemned to the hated cart's-tail whipping. The court ordered that she:

bee carried from the prison to her one [own] house and brought out of the gate or foredoore strip't to the waste, & there tyed to a Cart's Taile, and soe to be whip't through the Streete to the prison with not under thirty nine Stripes, & there in prison to remaine during the pleasure of this court.

This case jolted the legislature into action. Sterner measures were needed to curb prostitution. The General Court, meeting in Boston on the 8th of October, 1672, declared:

Whereas by sad experience; It is too obvious to all our people and

> others, that the sin of Whoredome and Uncleanness grows amongst us, notwithstanding all the wholsome Laws made for the punishing and suppressing such land Defiling Evils; And whereas there is of late, too just ground to suspect a greater Evil growing upon us, by the bold and audacious Presumption of some, to erect a Stews, Whore-House, or Brothel-House; for the nourishing such wickedness, the encrease of which Evil, if not timely prevented, many tend to the debauching of multitudes of persons, and tend to the utter ruine of their Estates, Soul and Body. It is therefore Ordered by this Court, and the Authority thereof; That if any Person, Male, or Female, shall presume to set up or keep any such House, wherein such wicked lusts may be nourished, and Whoredome committed, every such Baud, Whore, or vile Person . . . shall be severely whipt at the Carts-tayle, through the Streets, where such Offence, or Offences hath been committed, with *Thirty Stripes,* and thence to be committed to the House of Correction, and by the Master of the said House to be kept with hard fare, and hard labour, by dayly Task, and in defect of their duty to be severely whipt every night with *Ten Stripes;* and once at least in every Week, the said Baud and his Complices in such vile and sinful Courses, the Baud to be their Leader, and the other two and two in hair Frocks and blew Caps by the Executioner to be fastned to a hand Cart, and forced along to draw all the filth laid up in the Cart, through the Streets, to the Sea side going to the Gallows in Suffolk, and in all other Counties where the Court of each Shire shall appoint, and so returned to the House of Correction, to be alike kept with hard Fare and Labour, according to the Custome of the House during the Courts pleasure, there to remaine.[98]

Notorious thieves and burglars were very likely to feel the hot branding iron upon their foreheads—a fate that could befall runaway servants, too, although they were more apt to satisfy the law at the whipping post. Branding was not a common penalty but, if the crime were considered serious and threatened the peace and security of the government, it was available to the courts. Breaking into a dwelling house, for example, was "apt to be injurious to the Goods and Lives of others" and could not be considered an ordinary misdemeanor. Hence on the very first conviction of burglary or of robbing any person "in the field or high-wayes," one could be branded on the forehead with the letter *B*.[99] In later years, "vagabond Quakers" who defied orders of banishment might have been branded on their shoulders with the letter *R* (presumably for "Ranter").[100]

A permanent scar would surely warn all who henceforth might have dealings with the culprits but this trademark was not necessarily of long duration, for constables might, at times, have followed the practice sometimes resorted to in England of using a light touch or an iron not heated sufficiently to destroy the tissue. This penalty was usually reserved for men, although there is a report of at least one woman, Hanna Huchens, branded in Salem in 1674.[101]

Criminal justice in Plymouth Colony traced a distinctive pattern. There, serious crimes were less common than in the Bay Colony and the constable's whip less in evidence. The General Court did not enact laws for the branding of burglars and robbers but did authorize the branding with "a Roman F" (presumably for "Forger") those found guilty of forging deeds or defacing or stealing public records. Plymouth also permitted in rare instances, a burning on the hand, face, or shoulder, rather than the branding of a letter.[102] A few court cases will illustrate the enforcement of these laws:

> Richard Hopkins shalbe severely whipt, & branded with a hott iron on one of his cheekes, for selling peeces [guns] & powder & shott to the indeans. Hereupon it was propounded if this offence should not be punished hereafter by death [Boston, 1632].[103]

> [In considering the case of Roberts Scarlett] a knowen theife, whoe since his comeing hither hath committed dyvers fellonyes [the court ordered that he be] severely whipt & branded in the forehead with a T, & after sent to his said maister [Benjamyn Felton], whome the Court enjoynes to send the said Scarlett out of this jurisdiction[104] [Boston, 1635. In spite of his branding, Scarlett did not want to leave Boston. A year later he was still in town, for the General Court had decided that] haveing hope of amendment hee is admited to stay.[105]

> Edward Shaw was indicted for the felonious takeing of XV shillings from the person of William Corvannell, and was found guilty, and had his censure to be severely whipt, and burnt in the shoulder with a hot iron; which was accordingly executed upon him [Plymouth, 1638].[106]

> Nicolas Vauden, for running away from his master Robert Crose, having been convicted formerly divers times, and stealing 7 pounds 9 shillings from his master, also loss of time in pursuing him and bringing him back, was ordered to pay 40 pounds [an extra-ordinary fine for a servant to pay] to his master, to be branded on the fore-

head with the letter R [for Runaway] and to be severely whipped. [Ipswich, 1670].[107]

John Smith, convicted for breaking open Thomas Grosses his house & stealing money & Rings the Court Sentenced him to bee branded with the Letter B in the forehead [Boston, 1672].[108]

Phillip Keyn, alias Oake, . . . for breaking open the house of Roger Rose & picking the lock of a box & taking out mony thence; which he confessed in Court & judged it to bee thirty five shillings. The Court Sentences him to bee branded in the Forehead with the letter B [and to make three-fold restitution—Boston, 1672].[109]

George Major, for burglary and stealing pork and beef from John Knight, was fined and ordered to be branded on the forehead with the letter B and bound to good behavior [Ipswich, 1677].[110]

[George Fairfax, a servant already convicted of two burglaries, one of them on the Sabbath, was found guilty of stealing silver clasps and buckles and money from his master, Timothy Dwight. He was branded on the forehead with a "B" but this penalty seemed inadequate to the court. Thus, in addition to the branding, he was ordered to be severely whipped, sold to a new master, and to make three-fold restitution—Boston, 1681].[111]

The only mode of "dismembring" used as punishment was the cutting off of one or both ears, an unusual form of retribution adopted in a few scattered instances as a stern warning to those who might pose a serious threat to the government, such as Quakers or "open villifiers" of the law or those who had the presumption to commit their burglaries or robberies on the Lord's Day (for which, in addition to a branding, they might lose one ear for the first offense; two for the second).

Phillip Ratcliff was the first offender in Boston to lose an ear through judicial process, having met this fate shortly after the government was established. A servant of Master Craddock, Ratcliff had been convicted of "most foul, scandalous invectives against our churches and government," stated Governor Winthrop.[112] At this time (1631) power was concentrated in the Governor and Assistants who were extremely jealous of their prerogatives and could not tolerate abuse at this early stage in the formation of a strong government. The court decreed:

Phillip Ratliffe shalbe whipped, have his eares cutt of [off], fyned 40 pounds, & banished out of the lymitts of this jurisdiction, for uttering mallitious & scandulous speeches against the government & the church of Salem, etc.[113]

Ratcliff himself was probably surprised at the severity of this treatment merely for making certain "speeches." Embittered, he returned to England where he joined others in an attempt to convince the King that the Colonial leaders were acting beyond their authority.[114] Indeed, this penalty was probably more harsh than any given in future years for a like offense—with the exception of the castigation of the Quakers.

"James Luxford, for his forgery, lying, & other foule offences, was censured to bee bound to the whiping poast till the lecture from the first bell, & after the lecture to have his eares cut of [off]; & so hee had liberty to depart out of our jurisdiction" (Boston, 1640).[115] Luxford was not a first offender. Five months prior to this sentence, he had been fined one hundred pounds (an almost impossible fine) and placed in the stocks for "haveing two wifes." He was ordered to return to England by the first opportunity.[116] Perhaps one of the reasons for the severe treatment of Luxford was that he had been Governor Winthrop's steward and had mismanaged his estate, causing the Governor a great financial loss.

Thomas West, a young lad, lost an ear for burglary and stealing on the Sabbath (Salem, 1657).[117]

Maurice Bretts was an old offender who had been tried for murder and found not guilty[118] and in the same year tried for adultery and found "not legally guilty" but "guilty of very filthy carriage, etc."[119] For such a verdict he thought the sentence was unusually severe, for the court had ordered him to stand on the gallows for a time, to be severely whipped, and then banished. He protested as he stood before the court for sentence. The record does not reveal his words but for "his Contemptuous Carriage" the court added that he should stand in the pillory on the morrow: "at one of the clock his eare nayld to the pillory & after an howrs standing there to be cut of [off] & to pay twenty shillings for his swearing or to be whipt with ten stripes."[120] Bretts evidently took this sentence in silence but later filed with the court a "humble petition," asking for mercy. The court then remitted "the nayling and cutting of [off] his eare" (Boston, 1675).[121]

A few years after the Bretts case a Frenchman, Peeter Lorphelin, tried for "clipping" government coins and lying about it, was not so fortunate. He lost both ears (Boston, 1679).[122]

Uriah Cleoments who "lately Came from England in the Pynke Adventure" also lost two ears for two separate burglaries. He was required to make restitution or, if he could not do so, he was to be "sold to any of the English plantations" (Boston, 1685).[123]

Disfiguring a person by slitting his nostrils was an old English custom that found little support in the Colonies. The only case reported in the records available to us was that of Fairfield whose crime and punishment are described in Chapter 9 on capital punishment.[124]

No reports of the piercing of the tongue with a hot iron appear in the Plymouth Colony records or in the early records of the Bay Colony. But in the "Lawes and Ordinances of Warre" we find that a soldier could suffer this penalty for blaspheming "the Holy & Blessed Trinity, God the Father, God the Son, & God the Holy Ghost."[125] We have no evidence as to whether or not this penalty was actually applied.

One person at least, in the later years of the Bay Colony was sentenced to be taken to the pillory "to have his head & hands put in & have his toung drawne forth out of his mouth & peirct through with a hott iron."[126] Joseph Gatchell's tongue thus paid the penalty for uttering blasphemous words. Gatchell had his own ideas about "Gennerall Salvation" which differed from the orthodox view, and he had the courage to say so publicly on a number of occasions. What he said was:

> that all men should be saved, being Answered that our Saviour christ sent forth his disciples & Gave them Commission to preach the Gospell (i e) that whosoever Repents & believes shall be saved; to which Joseph Gatchell Answered if it be so, he was an Imperfect Saviour & a foole. . . . [He had also said]. . . . ther was no God, divill or hell. . . .

Such blasphemy was, of course, a capital offense and Gatchell could have been more severely punished than he was.

There were milder ways of controlling a wagging tongue. A

cleft stick placed on the tongue effectively prevented talking. George Dill for being drunk was made to "stand att the meeting hous doar next Lecture day, with a Clefte stick upon his Tong, & a pap[er] upon his hatt subscribed [']for gross Lyinge[']" (Salem, 1639).[127] There was the instance when "Robert Shorthose, for swearing by the bloud of God, was sentenced to have his tongue put into a cleft stick, & to stand so by the space of haulfe an houre" (Boston, 1636).[128] Ten years later there was the sentence of the "Wife of Thomas Olever (also Ollyver), for saying that all ministers in the country were bloodthirsty men, to be tied to the whipping post with a slit stick on her tongue" (Salem, 1646).[129]

The ducking stool as a form of punishment for "scolds" might be considered almost an afterthought in Colonial penology in spite of the prominence it has acquired in fiction, for it was not until 1672 that the Bay Colony placed it on the law books, although it was known for many years in England. We can find no report of its use in the court records of Suffolk or Essex counties or in the reports of the Court of Assistants. It may have been ordered once or twice in the Springfield courts. It is possible that magistrates sitting alone decreed its use in towns where the records have not been preserved. The law establishing the penalty read:

> Whereas there is no express punishment (by any Law hitherto established) affixed to the evil practise of sundry persons by Exorbitancy of the Tongue, in Railing and Scolding; It is therefore Ordered; That all such persons convicted before any Court or Magistrate, that hath proper cognizance of the case, shall be Gagged, or set in a Ducking stool, and dipt over Head and Ears three times in some convenient place of fresh or salt water. . . .[130]

A ducking stool was not the most practical device for punishing "exorbitancy of the Tongue," although it may have had a dramatic and symbolic appeal. It was necessarily a more complicated structure to build than the stocks, pillory, or whipping post, and its operation involved considerable care and preparation. It was of no value unless erected near a body of water, making it impossible to set it up at the marketplace, and the water must have had sufficient depth to enable the operator to immerse the hapless victim "over Head and Ears." There was no legal requirement that the towns had to provide themselves with such an instrument. Possibly for these reasons, it was not a common form of punishment when other "cures" were readily available.

As an alternative, the law allowed the constable to gag the owner of the offending tongue, a much less cumbersome way of dealing with it. Nevertheless we can find scarcely any report of gagging. There is the case of Bridget Oliver who, for calling her husband "opprobrious names", such as "old rogue" and "old Devil," and that on the Lord's day, was required to stand gagged for about an hour in the public marketplace of Salem in 1678.[131]

† † †

The power and influence of the Puritans who governed the Plymouth and Bay Colonies for so many years had obviously declined as the eighteenth century came into being. The population of the Province in 1700, estimated at 55,941,[132] was not so homogeneous as it had been. Although the Congregational church was still the "established" church, the Episcopalians, the Baptists, the Quakers, and other dissenters were becoming a power to be reckoned with in governmental deliberations. It was no longer necessary, under the Charter of 1692, for members of the General Court, or for candidates for any other political office, to qualify first as members of one of the Congregational churches. But to assume that in new hands the legislature would show a more merciful attitude toward the social offender and resort less to "bodilie punishments" is to take an unwarranted view of the temper of the times. Unfortunately, data is not available for adequate comparisons in terms of criminal prosecutions between the seventeenth and eighteenth centuries, but it seems reasonable to conclude from a study of the Province laws that crimes of piracy, robbery, counterfeiting, profane cursing and swearing, and violations of the Lord's Day statutes were on the increase and were of great concern to the government, and that punishments were more severe.

In the eighteenth century pirates on the high seas were creating "great disorders, wicked practices and depredations" and, when convicted, nothing less than hanging satisfied the government. "Ill-minded wicked ruffians" were robbing travelers on "the common roads or highways." "Many persons . . . so hardy and wicked, for base lucre and gain to themselves" were forging and uttering counterfeit bills of credit. Men were profanely cursing and swearing—"a horrible, impious and execrable vice . . . so highly displeasing to Almighty God, and offensive to every Christian" and likely to "justly provoke the divine vengeance to increase the many calamities this people now [1746] labour under"; while many were dishonoring God by not keeping the Sabbath holy "to the grief and disturbance of all pious and religiously disposed persons."

A brief review of legal sanctions employed by Massachusetts' courts after 1692 shows that "bodilie punishments" were carried on the law books throughout the Province period and taken up again by the General Court of the Commonwealth during its early years. The "punishments of humiliation" and lesser penalties of the Colonial period, to be described in the following chapter, were also still in favor. For the convenience of the reader we shall in this epilogue include both categories of punishment as we review some of the more common crimes that were not deemed serious enough to warrant the death penalty after 1692.

In the Province Period, 1692–1780

Adultery, no longer a capital offense, was still a crime that touched off a punitive attitude. In addition to a whipping of up to forty stripes (the maximum allowed at one time), offenders were required to sit on the gallows for one hour, the law in such cases always reading: "with a rope about their neck, and the other end cast over the gallows," to give them a feeling of the deadly seriousness of the crime. As a punishment of "humiliation," the adulterer or adulteress was required to wear "ever after" a "capital A, of two inches long and proportionable bigness, cut out in cloth of a contrary colour to their cloathes, and sewed upon their upper garments, on the outside of their arm, or on their back, in open view." A whipping of up to fifteen stripes awaited offenders on each occasion they were found without their letters.[133]

What the Bay Colony might have called *"suspicion of adultery"*—always difficult to prove—was made quite clear: "If any man be found in bed with another man's wife," unless it could be shown that "one party was surprized and did not consent" (in which case that party would be excused), he or she would be severely whipped up to thirty stripes.[134] After 1763 one convicted of this crime could have avoided the whipping by paying a fine of up to one hundred pounds, if he could afford it, but if he could not he was subject to imprisonment of not more than six months or a whipping of up to thirty stripes.[135]

An *incestuous marriage* called for the same penalty as adultery, but the wearing of a capital I was to replace the wearing of a capital A.[136]

The *wearing of women's clothes by men,* or vice versa, entailed a fine up to five pounds or "corporal punishment," as the court saw fit.[137]

For *fornication* with a single woman (not amounting to adultery) each offender could be whipped up to ten stripes or fined up to five pounds, a less severe penalty than provided for in the Colonial laws.[138] In a later law "to prevent spurious and mixt issue," fornication involving a Negro or "molatto" with an English person or person of any other Christian nation called for more severity. Both would be severely whipped (in the court's discretion), the Negro or "molatto" to be sold and sent out of the Province.[139]

Assaulting, or offering violence or insolence to women on the street or lanes or despoiling them or defacing their attire or attempting to do so (not amounting to rape, which was a capital offense) made one liable to a whipping of up to ten stripes or a thirty-day sentence to the house of correction, but on a second conviction one might have suffered "a burning in the hand."[140]

The penalty for *obscenity,* composing or publishing any "filthy, obscene or prophane song, pamphlet, libel or mock-sermon," was a fine up to twenty pounds or a requirement that the offender stand in the pillory "once, or oftener, with an inscription of his crime, in capital letters, affixed over his head.[141]

Blasphemy, formerly a capital crime, and, as we have pointed out at the end of Chapter 5, still a crime in the Commonwealth of Massachusetts, called for one or two of these penalties, in the court's discretion: imprisonment up to six months and, until the prisoner find sureties for his good behavior, whipping, standing in the pillory, sitting on the gallows, "boreing through the tongue with a red hot iron."[142]

The penalty for *lying* provided that a person fourteen years of age, or older, who "wittingly and willingly" told a lie or libel to any one's defamation or intentionally spread a false report could be fined up to twenty shillings or, if he could not pay the fine, could be whipped or made to sit in the stocks for three hours in the court's discretion.[143]

Drunkards were subject to a fine of five shillings but if they could not pay they were placed in the stocks up to three hours. On the second offense they were required to find sureties for their good behavior or be sent to the common gaol until they produced them. If the drunkard were an Indian, he was subject to a whipping up to ten stripes if he could not pay his fine.[144] Retailers of wine and liquors were to be fined if they sold drinks to "reputed drunkards or common tiplers" whose names were posted in their taverns.[145]

For *willful perjury* in a court of record one might have been fined twenty pounds and if he could not pay this heavy fine he would have been sent to the pillory for one hour and there have his ears nailed to the boards. He could also be sent to the prison for six months and be forever "disabled" as a witness in any court unless his judgment was reversed.[146]

Counterfeiting was not a difficult crime to commit if one had some familiarity with the simple printing presses of that day. Producing counterfeit notes or bills of credit threatened the financial structure of the government and had to be severely punished. Hence in 1704, people who "for base lucre and gain to themselves" were found guilty of counterfeiting the Province bills of credit could have been: branded on the right cheek with the letter F, forced to pay double damages to anyone defrauded by their evil doings, set on the pillory to have one ear cut off, and then sent off to prison for one year without bail. If he could not pay his prison charges, his goods and chattels would be forfeited in an amount treble the face value of the counterfeit bills.[147] Counterfeiting any of her majesty's coins (Queen Anne was then on the throne) or clipping, filing, or debasing them called for the death penalty, but if they were coins of the Province one might satisfy the law by standing on the pillory with one ear nailed thereto and submitting to a whipping of up to forty stripes.[148] During the perilous days of the war with England, counterfeiting government bills of credit entailed any or all of the following penalties: sitting on the gallows for one hour, a fine of up to thirty pounds; prison up to six months and a whipping of up to thirty-nine stripes. Upon release from prison the offender had to pay treble damages to any one aggrieved by his crime, working off his debt in service if he could not pay.[149] The following year this crime merited the death penalty.[150]

For counterfeiting the state's lottery tickets in the years 1778 and 1779 (a lottery authorized for the benefit of soldiers of the Continental army) any or all of the following penalties were possible: sitting on the gallows for one hour, a whipping of up to thirty-nine stripes, imprisonment for a term of three to twelve months and an enormous fine of up to one thousand pounds.[151] But for counterfeiting the first bills of credit of the United States of America in those same years one could have been fined up to five thousand pounds in lieu of the gallows or prison penalties.[152]

One could lose one ear, in addition to having to serve one year in prison and to pay double damages for *forgery* of a deed, a will, or other sealed writing.[153]

Loss of one ear was also prescribed for sending letters of *extortion,* making threats against the receiver of the letter unless he met the writer's demands for money. In addition, the law called for one hour on the gallows and a prison term for three years at "hard work," the prisoner to be taken out of the prison every three months for a whipping of twenty stripes. We cannot say whether this severe penalty was ever imposed. The law had only a three years' duration.[154]

The common crime of *theft* was punished in the early years of the Province by a fine of up to five pounds or a whipping of no more than twenty stripes and a payment of treble damages to the victim in money or in service.[155] But in later years this crime increased, and the penalties for a second offender were made more severe if the object stolen was valued at forty shillings: treble damages and the gallows for one hour and a whipping up to thirty stripes. But for the third offender, if the object stolen was valued at three pounds or more, the penalty was death.[156]

For *burglary* of a dwelling house, shop, barn, malt house, etc., the court could order the offender branded with letter B on his forehead, but, on the second offense, he could be whipped up to thirty-nine stripes and made to sit on the gallows for one hour. On his third offense he was to be considered incorrigible and suffer the penalty of death.[157] In spite of these stern penalties, the crime of burglary increased. The General Court decided in its 1769–1770 session to make burglary a capital offense if the offender had broken into a dwelling house in the nighttime with intent to commit a felony therein or had entered without breaking in the day or night but with such intent and had broken out at night.[158]

The crime of *robbery* in the field or highway also called for the branding of the letter B on one's forehead; the gallows for one hour and a severe whipping of up to thirty-nine stripes on the second offense and death on the third conviction.[159] Like burglary, this crime also increased in the early eighteenth century. A six-month's prison sentence was added to the penalty of burning in the forehead or hand and the forfeiture of treble damages, with death on second (rather than third) conviction.[160] Finally, in its 1761–1762 session, the General Court decided that something would have to be done to stop the increasing number of robberies and made that crime a capital offense on first conviction.[161]

Duelling was not uncommon in the eighteenth century but had never been legally approved. A person who challenged another to a duel or fought, aided, or abetted a duel (provided no death ensued) could be fined up to one hundred pounds or sent to prison for six months or whipped or required to put up sureties for his good behavior. The court, in its discretion, could order any one or all of these penalties.[162] Sometime prior to 1728 several duels had been fought—"to the great dishonour of Almighty God, in defiance of the laws of nature and nations." Repealing the old law, the General Court provided new penalties: the offender to be carried in a cart to the gallows (just as a condemned person might have been carried in full view of the public) where he would sit for one hour and then be taken to the common gaol for twelve months, without bail. Upon release from gaol he would be required to furnish sureties for his good behavior for another twelve months.[163]

"Rogues, vagabonds, common beggars and other lewd, idle and disorderely persons" were usually, upon conviction, commited to the house of correction. An old law directing each county to provide a house of correction was never fully carried out. By 1769 it proved to be a hardship to send men and women from distant parts of the Province to the nearest institution. An alternate penalty was provided for this class of offender: a whipping of up to ten stripes or the stocks for three hours.[164]

There were many laws enacted to punish *those who profaned the Lord's Day*. Most of the penalties called for a fine, but the stocks for two hours, imprisonment for twelve hours, or sitting in a cage were the most common penalties for those who did not pay the fine. The government acknowledged in 1760 that these laws had not been very effective in keeping people, particularly the younger generation, from playing or travelling on that holy day, which commenced at sundown of the preceding day. The General Court proclaimed that it was "the duty of all persons, upon the Lord's Day, carefully to apply themselves, publickly and privately, to religion and piety . . .", a principle that was written later into Article 2 of the Declaration of Rights of the Constitution of the Commonwealth,[165] and is today the law of the land.

A *general law* of 1693 provided that sitting in the stocks or cage or imprisonment for no more than twenty-four hours or a whipping of no more than ten stripes might be appropriate penalties for one who broke the peace or profaned the Sabbath or was a drunkard or "unlawful gamester" or was guilty of profane cursing and swearing if he could not or would not pay a fine. Judges usually had a good deal of discretion.[166]

In the Commonwealth Period, 1780–1836

The General Court of the Commonwealth in framing its criminal laws gave its endorsement to the traditional "bodilie punishments" and "punishments of humiliation" of Colonial and Province days. In the first decade of the Commonwealth's existence, for example, an offender might be publicly whipped with forty stripes or find himself sitting on the gallows or standing in the pillory for several hours, or he might be branded on the forehead or, if he were "a cheat and a fraud," he might even lose an ear.[167] However, the practice of causing the convicted criminal to wear letters signifying his crime or having his hands burned or his tongue bored through with a red hot iron had evidently fallen into disuse.

But a new era in penology was dawning. John Hancock, the first Governor of the Commonwealth, in a message to the legislature during his second term in 1793, said:

> It may be well worthy of your attention to investigate the question whether the infamous punishments of cropping [ears] and branding,

> as well as that of the public whipping post, so frequently administered in this Government, are the best means to prevent the commission of crimes, or absolutely necessary to the good order of Government or to the security of the people. It is an indignity to human nature, and can have but little tendency to reclaim the sufferer. Crimes have generally idleness for their source, and where offences are not prevented by education, a sentence to hard labour will perhaps have a more salutary effect than mutilating or lacerating the human body. . . .[168]

John Hancock's philosophy reflected the spirit of the times. In the years immediately following, fines and imprisonment became the predominate penalties. The Commonwealth sent its first prisoner in December 1805 to the new, massive, granite State Prison in Charlestown. Eight years later Governor Caleb Strong approved a statute that authorized judges in sentencing men and women whose offenses still called for a public whipping or standing in the pillory or sitting on the gallows or imprisonment in the common gaol to commit them instead to the State Prison for a term of no more than five years *at hard labour,* preceded by solitary confinement for no more than three months.[169]

In 1819 Governor John Brooks extolled the salutory benefits to be derived from imprisonment. The opportunities offered at the State Prison to the "unhappy convicts" who would be taught to read and write and would be offered religious and moral instruction "seem to be well calculated," he wrote in his report to the legislature, "to operate on ingenuous minds and lead them to permanent reformation."[170] To which the senate replied:

> It is certainly worthy of the philanthropist and statesman, to dispense, as far as possible, with the use of severe and sanguinary laws. . . . Our criminal code has never been cruel. But it will be a triumph of humanity, if the penitentiary system can be so improved, as to accomplish more effectually than corporal punishment, the prevention of crimes, and at the same time promote the reformation of the guilty.[171]

Thus imprisonment for serious crimes that did not warrant the death penalty soon replaced other forms of punishment. The General Court outlawed whipping as a legal penalty in 1826.[172] The Revised Statutes of 1836 showed no traces of the once common "bodilie punishments" and "punishments of humiliation" so familiar to the courts of the Colonial period, the Province period, and the early Commonwealth period in Massachusetts. Penology had taken a new turn. It put its faith in the penitentiary as the most effective method of crime control and of reformation of the social offender.

7. "PUNISHMENTS OF HUMILIATION" AND OTHER PENALTIES

A Reproofe entereth more into a wise man, then [than] 100 stripes into a foole.—*Governor Winthrop, 1644.*[1]

ALTHOUGH the Puritans spoke of "bodilie punishments" and "punishments of humiliation," there was no clear distinction between these two general methods of dealing with the public offender. The former entailed acute physical suffering for a relatively short period of time but were also associated with some degree of humiliation, for the accused was forced to bear his pain in the presence of his fellow men. "Punishments of humiliation" substituted psychological for physical pain, constituted an assault on one's pride, and probably acted as a strong deterrent to a sensitive soul. Respected citizens of the upper social strata, however, were not so treated. If they were called to account for some violation of the law—and they not infrequently were—the courts were satisfied with the assessment of a fine, unless, of course, their offenses were particularly heinous. The town drunkards, on the other hand, usually unable to pay a fine each time they were found drunk, were suitable candidates for the stocks.

Whom did the courts wish to shame? What kinds of crimes seemed to call for this kind of justice? Let the record speak for itself:

Stocks and Pillory

For petty thieves, drunkards, and liars who could not or would not pay a fine, the Bay Colony specifically prescribed sitting in the stocks with hands and feet held fast between wooden planks, while forgers and those who destroyed public records might be ordered to stand in the pillory with head and hands firmly clamped between boards.[2] But magistrates had such broad discretion they could send a man to the stocks or pillory for many other offenses if they thought it might shame him into conformity or satisfy the magistrates' need to express their own or the community's moral indignation.

The pillory, evidently, was considered the more arduous ordeal and the more humiliating too, for one's head was held immovably exposed to public view, but it was less often used. Plymouth Colony records make no mention of a pillory, but their laws required each township to build a pair of stocks. Both of these forms of punishment had been carried over from old England and were well known to all seventeenth century citizens.

> John Hews & Jone his wife adjuged to sitt in the stockes because the said Jone conceived with childe by him before they were publickely married, though in the time of contract [Plymouth, 1633].[3]

> John Wedgewood, for being in the company of drunkards, was to bee set in the stocks at Ipswich [1639].[4]

> John Stacey junior for being distempered with drinke was set in the stocks [Boston, 1639].[5]

> Edward Palmer, for his extortion, takeing 1 pound 13 shillings 7 pence for the plank & woodwork of Boston stocks, is fined 5 pounds, & censured to bee set an houre in the stocks [Boston, 1639. Palmer's fine was later reduced to ten shillings, but he was made to sit in the stocks for which he had furnished the material and for which he had charged too much].[6]

> Richard Willis, for rebaldry speeches by him spoken, was sentanced to site in the stockes, which accordingly was performed [Plymouth, 1664].[7]

Alice, wife of Richard Berry of Yarmouth, evidently had a covetous nature, not tamed by brief spells in the local stocks. She had been charged with "stealing of an neckcloth from William Pearce, his wife" and the very next month she was in court again:

> . . . for goeing into the house of Samuell Arnold, and taking bacon and eggs when there was noe body att home. Sentanced, for this and other doeings of like nature . . . to sit in the stockes for the space of an houre att Yarmouth in som publick place [Plymouth, 1653].[8]

The following year Alice was busy again, the court finding her guilty of "... goeing into the home of Benjamine Hammond, when noe body was att home, and felloniously tooke away a womans shift, that was new made, but without sleeves, and a peece of porke" (Plymouth, 1654).[9] In 1655 she was required to pay a fine or sit in the stocks for one hour "... for theivish milking the cow of Thomas Phelps, of Yarmouth" (Plymouth, 1655).[10]

Elizabeth Legg was also a familiar figure in the local courts. Essex county magistrates haled her into court in 1647 for reviling the minister, the Reverend Walton, who promptly brought a civil suit against her.[11] In 1651 she appeared for "scandalous falling out on a Lords day,"[12] and in 1654 for again slandering the reviled Reverend. She was then required to sit in the stocks for an hour and to confess in open court that she:

> did evell & Sinfull in Speakeing Slitely and scornefull of Master Walton, & in perticuler in Saying I could have a boy from the Colledg [Harvard] that would preach better then Master Walton for half the wages [Salem, 1654].[13]

In 1656 we find her charged with selling "strong beer,"[14] and eleven years later her name is in the court docket for "making a disturbance in the meeting house."[15]

> Philip Veren was ordered to be set by the heels in the stocks one hour for disowning the country's power, in open court, about forcing any to come to the public worship [Salem, 1663].[16]

> ... Robert Crosman ... for cursing the celect men of Taunton, and for expressing himselfe in his passion as if he would make himselfe away, hee was centanced by the Court to be sett in the stockes on a publicke training day att Taunton [Plymouth, 1671].[17]

Mary Bedwell was ordered to sit in the stocks for two hours (rather than the more usual one hour) for "... keeping company & being too familiar with Walter Hickson" and, in addition to this humiliation, was to be whipped and fined and warned that she should not be in the company of Hickson without other company, for she was a married woman. Walter was similarly dealt with (Boston, 1674).[18]

John Holleday, for lying and falsifying a deed, had to "stand in the pillory in Boston upon three several Lecture dayes following immediately after the Lecture for the space of one hour at each time . . ." (Boston, 1677).[19] For forging a note, Benjamin Barker suffered the same fate (Boston, 1678).[20]

Symbols and Signs

To dramatize his sin and intensify his mortification, the courts sometimes required an offender to wear on his outer garment the initial letter or letters of his crime. Relatively few were subjected to this form of humiliation.

Robert Coles, town drunkard, was required to wear for nine weeks a red letter D "sett upon white" on his outward garment whenever he appeared in company (Boston, 1634).[21] Richard Wilson, a servant, for stealing from his master "money & diverse small things" wore a T (for thief) "set upon his upmost garment" (Boston, 1639).[22]For six months, John Davies wore the letter V (for venery?) "upon his breast upon his uppermost garment" after being whipped both in Boston and in Ipswich, following a conviction of "grosse offences in attempting lewdness with divers woemen . . ." (Boston, 1639).[23]

Katheren Aines, a married woman,

> for her unclean and laciviouse behavior with . . . William Paule, and for the blasphemos words that shee hath spoken, is centanced by the Court to bee forthwith publickly whipt heer att Plymouth, and afterwards att Taunton, on a publicke training day, and to were [wear] a Roman B [for bawd ?] cutt out of ridd [red] cloth and sowed to her uper garment on her right arme; and if shee shalbee ever found without it soe worne whil shee is in the government, to bee forthwith publickly whipt. . . .

Alexander, Katheren's husband, was not without guilt and was required to witness his wife's whipping. The court stated,

> for his leaving his family, and exposing his wife to such temptations, and being as baud [procurer] to her therin, is centanced by the Court for the present to sitt in the stockes the time the said Paul and Katheren Ainis are whipt, which was performed; and the said Alexander Anis is to pay the charges of his wifes imprisonment and punishment, which said charge, in regard the said Anis is very poor, is to pay it by twelve pence per weeke untill it is all payed . . . [Plymouth, 1657].[24]

Thomas Bray of Yarmouth, a single person, and Anne, wife of Francis Linceford, ". . . have committed the act of adultery and uncleanesse, and have divers tymes layne in one bed together in the absence of her husband, which hath beene confessed by both parties in the publike Court . . . ." They were required, after a severe whipping at the public post, to "weare (whilst they remayne in the government) two letters, viz; an AD for Adulterers, daily, upon the outeside of their uppermost garment, in a most emenent place thereof . . ." with the understanding that if they failed to do so they would be whipped again and their letters immediately put on again (Plymouth, 1641).[25]

Another relatively rare penalty (though more common than the wearing of letters sewed onto one's garment) was the requirement that an offender stand for a few hours in some public place bearing a paper on which was written in large letters a brief description of the crime for which he was found guilty. This penalty was not limited to any particular crime. Its choice probably depended largely on the imagination of the magistrate, but a law of 1646 made it especially appropriate for those who reviled the church. One who did not pay a five pound fine on second conviction of showing contempt for God's Word—"the desolating sin of Civil State and Churches"—could be made to

> stand two hours openly upon a Block or Stool, four foot high, on a Lecture day, with a paper fixed on his breast, written in Capital Letters, AN OPEN AND OBSTINATE CONTEMNER OF GODS HOLY ORDINANCES, that others may hear and be ashamed of breaking out into the like wickedness. . . .[26]

How the courts hoped to shame men and women from "breaking out" into varieties of sinful behavior can be shown by a few cases from the official records:

> Thomas Scot, & his wife for committing fornication before marriage, were enjoyned to stand an houre . . . in the market place, with each of them a paper with great letters, on their hatts . . . [Boston, 1642].[27]

Elizabeth Due, a married woman, convicted of slandering one of the Salem Endecotts by claiming that he was the father of her child, was whipped with twenty stripes and then required to stand on a lecture day before the public with a paper on her forehead reading "A SLANDERER OF MR. ZEROBABELL ENDICOTT" (Salem, 1654).[28]

Susannah Buswell, wife of Isaac, was convicted of burglary and lying and had pinned upon her head as she sat in the meetinghouse during lecture "about the middle of the alley" a placard reading "FOR BURGLARY & LYING" (Salem, 1677).[29]

Sarah Scott for "Reviling and strikeing her Mother" was made to

> . . . stand upon a Block or Stoole of two foote high in the Markett place in Boston upon a thursday immediately after lecture with an inscription upon her breast in a faire character ["] For undutifull abusive & reviling speeches & carriages to her naturall mother ["] . . . [Boston, 1673].[30]

Hannah Gray, according to one of her neighbors, was "a lying little devil." Another neighbor said she had seen Hannah in the company of Andrew Davis, acting in a lascivious manner. A seventeen-year old girl testified that her brother had told her how Hannah used to entice "the scoller boys" (from Harvard, presumably) and use "baudly language." The court ordered her to stand at the meetinghouse at Salem and later at Beverly with a paper on her head on which was written in capital letters; "I STAND HEERE FOR MY LACIVIOUS & WANTON CARIAGES" (Salem, 1674).[31]

John Veering was not only drunk and abusive to his wife, calling her "whore," but dared to speak out against the minister, the Reverend James Allen, whom he called "a black hypocriticall Rogue." In addition to "thirty Stripes severely laide on," he was to stand

> in the open market place in Boston, exalted upon a Stoole for an houres time on a thursday after Lecture; with a paper fastned to his breast, with this inscription in a lardge character A PROPHANE & WICKED SLANDERER & IMPIOUS REVILER OF A MINISTER OF THE GOSPLE & Church-members . . . .

Perhaps the court took into consideration the fact that Veering was drunk when he made his verbal attack on the minister. At any rate, after "humble acknowledgment made in open Court," his sentence was reduced to a fine and the posting of bonds for his good behavior (Boston, 1674).[32]

Joseph Severans was ordered to stand at the meetinghouse door in Hampton for a half hour preceding the lecture. Upon his breast was pinned this inscription, "THIS PERSON IS CONVICTED FOR SPEAKING WORDS IN A BOASTING MANNER OF HIS LASCIVIOUS & UNCLEANE PRACTICES" (Salem, 1675).[33]

Thomas Jay had a reputation "for Lascivious carriages towards some young persons of the Female kinde." The court gave him a choice of paying twenty shillings fine or of standing "upon a block or stoole in the market place in Boston with a paper upon his breast written in a Large character FOR LASCIVIOUS CARRIAGES TOWARDS YOUNG WOMEN . . . (Boston, 1676).[34]

Sitting on the Gallows

To sit or stand on the gallows for an hour with a rope thrown loosely about one's neck must have given an offender an opportunity to contemplate the wages of sin. This penalty was used sparingly and reserved chiefly for those who had offended against the code of sex morality:

> Thomas Owen, for his adulteros practises, was censured to bee sent to the gallos with a roape about his neck, & to sit upon the lather [ladder] an houre, the roapes end throwen over the gallos, [and] so to returne to prison . . . [Boston, 1641].[35]

Maurice Brett, for adultery with Mary Gibbs, might have been sentenced to death but the jury found him "not legally Guilty but Guilty of very filthy carriage, etc." In addition to whipping and banishment, the court ordered him "to be Carried to the Gallows & there with a Roape about his necke to stand half an hower . . ." (Boston, 1675).[36]

Darby Bryan, in a jury-waived trial in the Court of Assistants, was found guilty, the court stating "in the night being found in Bed with Abigaile Johnson [he did] Comitt the Act of Adultery. . . ." The court ordered that he be taken "from the prison to the Gallowes presently after the lecture in Boston & there . . . to stand with a Roape about his necke & fastned thereto one hower . . ." The court also ordered that he be whipped with thirty-nine stripes and that Abigaile receive the same penalty (Boston, 1677).[37]

Phillip Darland of Beverly, indicted for adultery, was found guilty of "vile filthy and abominably libidinous Actions with mary knights, wife of John knights of Jeffrey Creeke" and forced to stand for one hour on the gallows with a rope around his neck, after which he was to receive a severe whipping (Boston, 1683).[38]

Public Confessions

A humble and sincere confession of sin or error made in the presence of one's fellow men was believed to be good for the soul and was sometimes deemed a satisfactory penance by the courts. In the case of Sara, the wife of Hugh Norman of Yarmouth, for example, the court said:

> . . . for misdemenior and lude behavior with Mary Hammon uppon a bed, with divers lasivious speeches by her allso spoken, . . . the said Court have therefore sentanced her . . . for her wild behavior . . . to make a publick acknowlidgment, so fare as conveniently may bee [the details might have been embarassing in this case of homosexuality] of her unchast behavior, and have allso warned her to take heed of such cariages for the future, lest her former cariage come in remembrance against her to make her punishment the greater [Plymouth, 1650].[39]

Thomas Wheeler who had been fined "for profane and foolish dancing, singing and wanton speeches, probably being drunk," was also found guilty of reviling the Reverend Mr. Cobbett and was ordered to make public confession at time of worship in Lynn by reading this confession:

> Whereas I Thomas Wheeler of Lin have been convicted at the last court at Salem for speakinge sinfull and reprochfull speechis against Master Cobbett caluminatinge the doctrine by him delivered . . . doe acknowledge my greate sin and offence in soe speakinge humblie intreatinge those whom it doth concerne to passe it by . . . p[ro]misinge for the time to come god helpinge me to be more watchful over my words and speechis. . . . [Salem, 1653].[40]

Evidently the Reverend Mr. Cobbett was a controversial preacher, for the record shows several presentments brought by the courts against men and women who were openly critical of his preaching or his theological views. Wheeler, not long after his first plea for forgiveness, was again in court for criticizing the minister, whom he compared to Korah who, according to the story in the Book of Numbers, had led a revolt against Moses. Again he acknowledged his " . . . evell to the glory & praise of god & to my owne shame & hope for time to come shalle be more Carefull" (Salem, 1654).[41]

Some years earlier William Winter of Lynn asked the minister's forgiveness for having accused him of speaking against the ordinance of infant baptism[42] and that same year Henrie Walton was brought to court for saying "he had as Leeve to hear a Dogg Barke as to heare Master Cobbett Preach" (Salem, 1643)[43]

William Middleton and Elizabeth, his wife, confessed to fornication before marriage. After paying a sizable fine, they were given the choice of a public whipping or a public confession by making ". . . a satisfactory acknowledgment in the publique congregation where they usually hear, & thereof to bring a certificate under the hands of the Church officers of that Congregation" (Boston, 1672).[44]

Anthony Crosbie was a physician in Ipswich who found himself in court on a charge of drunkenness. He claimed that he was not drunk but simply weary because in his capacity as a physician he had "sate upe foure nights together with a strainger beinge in eminent Danger . . . and [he] dranke no maner of stronge drinke or very little. . . ." Nevertheless, he admitted he had been drunk on numerous other occasions and wished to make this humble acknowledgement of his sin:

> I have Horiblie and abundantlie very often provoked god [,] greved his people ocasioned others by my exa[m]ple:abused my selfe spent my time and a greate part of my estate. Hazerded the lives and healths of those patients who have Relyed uppon me for Cure by neglecting seasonable attendance as Rules of art Require. I speake not [t]his for favours sake: But Concienciously accountinge my selfe bound openly and unfeinedly to Confese and acknowlige that great and grosse sine which I have Beene gultie of and lived in so many years formerly to the great dishoner of god and greife of others & wronge to my selfe & estate: for which I desire from the Botome of my heart forgiveness & serius Repentance of god whome I have cheefely ofended & also of all his people & all others whome I have any way occasioned to be gultie of this great sin which I desire the prayers of all to god for me that I may uterlie forsake & never Returne to it as the dog to his vomit [Ipswich, 1672].[45]

There were a number of other legal penalties in addition to those which have been considered.

Fines

Magistrates were usually content with the payment of a fine of a few shillings or pounds unless the crime was particularly serious or shocking. A fine was the most common penalty in the seventeenth century—just as it is today. It was common practice to make a fine an alternative to a whipping or other penalty or to combine it with one or more other forms of punishment. Selecting a few out of the hundreds of court cases where fines were imposed we can see the great variety of offenses meriting this "censure":

Captain John Stone, a stranger from Virginia, for calling Justice Roger Ludlowe "a just as [ass]" and "abuseing" him "both in words and behaviour," was fined in 1633 the enormous sum of one hundred pounds and "prohibited comeing within this pattent without leave from the Government, under penalty of death." Merely for a play upon words this penalty would have been extraordinary, but Justice Ludlowe was a Justice of the Peace, an Assistant (and later a Deputy Governor), and a brother-in-law of John Endecott, while Stone, according to Governor Winthrop, had "carried himself very dissolutely in drawing company to drink" and was "found upon the bed in the night with one Bancroft's wife." When called to account, he made "threatening speeches against Ludlowe," who had him placed in irons and brought his case before the grand jury on the capital charge of adultery, but the jury could not find a true bill. Stone left immediately for Virginia without paying his fine. Upon reaching Connecticut he fell in with some Pequot Indians who murdered him and his party. Subsequently the General Court cancelled the fine.[46]

> Master Ambros Marten, for calling the church covenant a stinking carryon & a humane [human] invention, & saying hee wondered at Gods patience, feared it would end in the sharpe, & saide the ministers did dethrone Christ, & set up themselves: hee was fined 10 pounds, & counselled to go to Master [Richard] Mather to bee instructed by him [Boston, 1639].[47]

John Stone of "Gloster" was fined fifty shillings for critical comments concerning the Reverend Mr. Blinman's sermons, saying, ". . . if an angell from Heaven should preach the same he would not beleeve it . . . that Blinman had falcelie interprited scripture . . . in Nehemiah & Ezra" (Salem, 1644).[48]

The Essex County Court fined Edmund Ingolls "for bringing home sticks in both his arms on the Sabboth" (Salem, 1646).[49] The same court fined Edward Colcott for being drunk the second time, the record stating that he was so "verrie far gone with drinke" that he had forgotten he was before the court the day before (Salem, 1648).[50] Francis Usselton was fined for cursing a swine belonging to Henry Haggett, for it was just as criminal to profanely and wickedly curse a creature as it was to curse a person. Francis had said to the swine, "A pox of god upon her & the divill take her" (Salem, 1657).[51]

There was dissension in the Barlow family, not only between George and his wife but between him and his daughters-in-law, which broke out in violence and led to a variety of penalties: fine or whipping, stocks, and admonition:

> Anna Bessey, for her crewell and unaturall practice towards her father in law, Gorge Barlow, in choping of him in the backe, not withstanding the odiousnes of her fact, the Court, considering of some sercomstances, viz, her ingeniouse confession, together with her present condition, being with child, and some other particulares, have sentanced her to pay fine of ten pounds, or to bee publickly whipt at some convenient time when her condition will admitt therof.
>
> Dorcas Bessey and Mary Bessey, for carriages of like nature towards theire said father in law, though not in soe high a degree, were both sentanced to sit in the stockes during the pleasure of the Court; which accordingly was performed. The younger, viz, Mary Bessey, was sharply reproved by the Court, as being by her disobeydience the occationers of the evill abovemencioned.
>
> George Barlow and his wife were both severly reproved for theire most ungodly liveing in contension one with the other, and admonished to live otherwise [Plymouth, 1662].[52]

Richard Berry and his friends, William Griffin and Richard Michell and their wives, decided to play a game with cards, defying a law made eight years previously forbidding any one "to play att Cards or Dice," even in one's own home. That sort of thing was apt to lead "to the corup[t]ing of youth with other sad consequences."[53] Each of them had to pay a forty shilling fine (Plymouth, 1655).[54]

Zebeon Letherland had to pay a thirty shilling fine for "excessive drinking" although he denied the charge. When the court was informed that "hee was drunk that day Mistress Whittingham was buried" he was assessed another fine of twenty shillings (Boston, 1672).[55]

"Roger Rose, for sailing out of a harbor on a Lord's day, at Gloster, was fined" (Salem, 1679).[56] "Eliphal Streeton convict in Court for doing Servile worke on the Sabbath day by working with her needle Sentenced to pay ten shillings in mony fine." (Boston, 1677).[57] Perhaps the court would have let this pass with an admonition, but Eliphal had been previously convicted several times for not attending public worship on the Sabbath.

Admonitions

In the less serious cases and sometimes in cases where for lack of evidence only a "suspicion of guilt" was found, magistrates might dismiss the charge with a go-and-sin-no-more gesture:

> Thomas Williams, the servant of widow Warren, was accused for speaking profane and blasphemous speeches against the majestie of God, which wer these: ther being some discention betweene him & his dame, shee, after other things, exhorted him to fear God & doe his duty; he answered, he neither feared God, nor the divell, this was proved by witneses, and confesed by himselfe. This, because the Courte judged it to be spoken in passion & distemper, with reprove did let him pass, upon humble acknowledgmente of his offence; though the Governor [Bradford] would have had him punished with bodly punishmente as the case seemed to require [Plymouth, 1635].[58]

"Master Thomas Makepeace, because of his novile disposition, was informed wee were weary of him unlesse hee reforme . . . ." In the margin of the record was written, "Mr. Makepeace advised to reforme" (Boston, 1639).[59]

> Arther Howland, of the towne of Marshfeild, for not frequenting the publicke assemblyes on the Lords daies. Referred to conferance and further admonished to labore to walk inofensively [Plymouth, 1651].[60]

> Richard Hollingworth admonished for much sleeping in time of

public ordinances, and frequent absence therefrom on Lord's day afternoons. He pleaded in defence, illness and bodily infirmity [Salem, 1649].[61]

Samuell Eaton and Goodwife Halle, of the towne of Duxburrow, for mixed daunsing. Released, with admonition [Plymouth, 1651].[62]

Edward Holman, and Martha, the wife of Thomas Shrive, warned by the Court to keep out of the companie of each other, on perill of suffering corporall punishment by whipping [Plymouth, 1653].[63]

Whereas Jonathan Hatch hath bine convicted of unnessesarie frequenting the house of Thomas Crippin, and therby hath given occation of suspision of dishonest behavior towards Francis, the wife of the said Crippin, the Court hath admonished him and warned him for the future not to give such occation of suspicion as aforesaid by his soe frequently resorting to the said house or by coming in the companie of the said woman, as hee will answare it att his perill [Plymouth, 1666].[64]

Peregrin White, born on the *Mayflower* as it lay at anchor in Massachusetts Bay, the first white child born in New England, attained the age of 84 and outlived the entire Mayflower company. Brought into court in 1649 for fighting with William Halloway he was "cleared, with admonission to take heed for the future" (Plymouth, 1649).[65] Peregrin became a prominent member of the Colony. At the age of seventeen he volunteered to engage in the fight against the Pequot Indians; a few years later he joined Captain Miles Standish in another Indian encounter, being the standard bearer of the company; in 1649 he and his wife were fined for fornication before marriage or contract; and in 1651 he was chosen "survayor of the Hiewaies" in the town of Marshfield.[66]

Benjamine Hurd, convicted for advising William Read in prison not to confess the burning of the Barne & nothing else could hurt him with severall such like expressions tending to encouradge him in denying his crimes, he confessed what was alledged, & the Court sentenced him to be admonished & pay fees of Court [Boston, 1672].[67]

Mary Thorne presented for Abusing and Striking her husband the presentment not being fully proved The Court Sentanced her to bee cautioned [Boston, 1672].[68]

Edmund Gatch Servant to Robert Sanford bound over to this Court to Answer for his overrunning of a Childe with his Cart, which hee owned in Court. The Court Sentances him to bee admonished & to pay Fees of Court [Boston, 1673].[69]

Elizabeth Wheeler & Joanna Peirce being Summoned to appeare before the Court to answer for theire disorderly carriage in the house of Thomas Watts being married women & founde sitting in other mens Laps with theire Armes about theire Necks The Court upon theire acknowledgment of theire fault & promiss to avoide such Offences for time to come admonished them ordered them to pay Fees of Court & soe discharged them [Boston, 1674].[70]

Thomas Platts Butcher being presented for keeping open his Shop & selling meate after it's darke upon Saturdays in the Evening [the Sabbath commenced when the sun set on Saturday] thereby profaning the Sabbath, it being the first conviction The Court admonish't him, ordered him to pay Fees of Court & so discharged him [Boston, 1675].[71]

Nicholas Paige was admonished "for travelling from Waymoth to Boston on the Sabbath which hee owned . . ." (Boston, 1676).[72] Edward Evered confessed that he had killed a sheep late on a Saturday night (that is, on the Sabbath) "but excused it with his being a stranger and unacquainted with the customs of the Country and promising to reform was admonish't and ordered to pay fees" (Boston, 1677).[73] "Elizabeth Eggen presented for entertaining of Strangers in her husbands absence was admonish't not to give entertainment to Lodgers" (Boston, 1678).[74]

Disfranchised

A person might be deprived of his right to vote—temporarily or permanently—for verbal attacks on any part of the administration of criminal justice.[75] John Gosse, for example, was fined and disfranchised for "common railing" against the government in 1639 (Boston).[76]

Sold into Slavery

Slavery was sanctioned in the Colonies up to the time of the adoption of the Constitution of the Commonwealth of Massachusetts in 1780. The slave population was made up largely of Indians captured in the wars, a few imported Negro slaves, and a few condemned to slavery for crimes committed in the Colonies. No one of standing in the community was condemned to slavery; usually those so dealt with were Indians or lowly servants.

An Indian by the name of Wappatucke (or Wampetucke) had been breaking into houses and stealing. The Plymouth court convicted him of burglary and ordered

> that he bee sold for a perpetuall servant; and it is left to the honored Governor and the Worship[full] Mr. Barnabas Laythorpe [Barnabas Lothrop, an Assistant] to dispose or make sale of the said Indian, and give a bill of sale for them that buy him, and to proportion the money made of him to them that have received damage by him ... [Plymouth, 1685].[77]

Wappatucke's Indian friends immediately got busy and sold some of their land "for their redemption of their countryman, Tom Wampetucke, from his being sold out of the country for his misdemeanor" (Plymouth, 1685).[78]

Unusual Penalties

Judges had wide discretion in fitting the punishment to the crime; thus it is quite impossible to mention every variety of penalty decreed by the many magistrates who sat in both jurisdictions. We find, for example, in Plymouth, one of the penalties ordered in the case of Robert Latham who so maltreated his servant that the latter died was that "all his goods are confiscate unto his highnes the Lord Protector [Cromwell]" (Plymouth, 1655).[79] Joane Miller of Taunton got off lightly with an order to be "punished att home" for "beating and reviling her husband, and egging her children to healp her, biding them knock him in the head, and wishing his victials might choake him" (Plymouth, 1655).[80]

Abraham Pottle and four others were "presented for disorderly liveing, & therefore to be required to give an account of how they live" (Plymouth, 1637).[81] The court ordered that Captain James Johnson, who had been accused of "giving entertainment to persons at unseasonable houres of the night & other misdemeanors," should "breake up housekeeping & to dispose of himselfe into some good orderly Family within one Fortnight next following or that then the Selectmen of Boston take care to dispose of him as abovesaid" (Boston, 1675).[82]

Cowesett, an Indian, entered John Bennet's home, demanded

a drink, and pulled Bennet's hair. On conviction he was sentenced to lose his own hair which was to be "cut round close of [off] from his head" (Boston, 1672).[83] The Indian was also whipped and ordered to leave Boston.

John Godfrey of Ipswich, for subborning witnesses, was "utterly disabled as a witness in any case in the future" unless "restored by authority" (Salem, 1669).[84] John Synderlands, Sr., for defrauding Major Clarke's band (of which he was treasurer) of a considerable sum of money, was to be "disabled from bearing any office for the space of three yeares" (Boston, 1675).[85]

Jonathan Atherton for wounding an Indian with his sword, although he claimed provocation, was ordered to "defray all the charges about the cure of saide Indian if it bee not already done & disinable him for wearing a Sword during his continuance in this Colony, or till this Court take further order . . ." (Boston, 1672).[86]

Banishment

We have already cited a number of cases of banishment of persons thought to be harmful, or simply undesirable, citizens. This penalty was fairly common and is still used occasionally by the courts. In recent times the federal government has deported aliens found guilty of crimes of "moral turpitude."

Multiple Penalties

Magistrates quite commonly sentenced a person to suffer more than one penalty. For example, a person might pay a fine and be whipped; or a whipping and standing on the gallows would be his lot for a single offense. Henry Spencer, a servant, had committed numerous offenses: running away and stealing from his master a coat, a piece of serge, two Bibles, a rapier and belt, a pewter bottle, and a piece of linen cloth. He then broke into another house and stole a horse and saddle, and off he went. A hue and cry was raised, and he was soon caught and thrown into the Ipswich prison. He broke out of prison and was recaptured and brought into court on multiple charges to face multiple penalties:

A severe whipping
A branding on the forehead with the letter B
A fine of five pounds to the court

A payment to his master of treble damages (thirteen pounds)
A payment to his master for loss of time (forty shillings) and
Removal from the Ipswich prison to the Boston prison where he would be confined until his master could dispose of him into service with a new master (Salem, 1665).[87]

No Punishment

There were a few occasions when a person was brought into court, confessed his crime, and was dismissed by the magistrates without censure or penalty of any kind. Mary Powell was a case in point. She was the servant of William Swift, who was "the survayor for the Highwaies" in the town of "Sandwidge" and later the constable in that town. She had confessed to the crime of fornication with one David Ogillior, an Irish servant of Edward Sturgis. Her story touched the hearts of the magistrates:

> Shee saith shee was alured therunto by him goeing for water one evening, hopeing to have married him, beeing shee was in a sadd and miserable condition by hard service, wanting clothes and living discontentedly; and expressing great sorrow for her evell, she was cleared for the present, and ordered to goe home againe [Plymouth, 1655].[88]

† † †

A brief review of the laws enacted after 1692 showing how these penalties were carried on down through the Province and early Commonwealth periods has been combined with an account of the "bodilie punishments" during that era and can be found at the end of Chapter 6.

8. "IN DURANCE VILE"

> A Prison is the Grave of the Living, where they are shut up from the World and their Friends, and the Worms that gnaw upon them are their own Thoughts and the Jayler. 'Tis a House of meagre Looks, and ill smells: for Lice, Drink, and Tobacco, are the Compound: Or, if you will, 'tis the Subburbs of Hell; and the Persons much the same as there .... *John Dunton, 1686.*[1]

COLONIAL prisons, or gaols as they were sometimes called, were familiar symbols of law and order to Englishmen. As long as there had been a Kingdom, some kind of dungeon, cage, or prison had been used to keep in close confinement those held for trial or awaiting the performance of some order of authority as well as those who were sentenced merely to suffer "in durance vile." All who had come from England were acquainted, some from first-hand experience, with these traditional institutions. Prisons as we know them today—massive structures designed for the confinement of large numbers of offenders for relatively long periods of penal servitude—were unknown at that time.

To build on American soil institutions known from time immemorial called for no special ingenuity. Everyone knew that prisons were a necessary adjunct to orderly government. There was no need for the Colonial people to justify their motives for imprisoning offenders nor to elaborate any rationale to satisfy the sociologists of coming generations who might ask whether they sought vindictiveness, social protection, or the rehabilitation of the offender. It was taken for granted that the hand of the sinner must be stayed lest God be dishonored and that punishment in itself carried out in the full view of everyone would put the fear of God and of the law into the hearts of the ungodly. It was essential, then, that the prison building be placed close to the meetinghouse where the laws of man were made and the laws of God obeyed.

The erection of a prison in the town of Boston was a matter of immediate concern to the first settlers. At their first meeting on August 23, 1630, the Court of Assistants ordered that "any justice of the peace may *imprison* an offender,"[2] just as he might have done in England. And yet there was no prison. The following year when the building of a prison had been contemplated but not yet commenced, Nicholas Knopp was taken to task by the court and given a choice of penalties:

> Nicholas Knopp, is fyned five pounds for takeing upon him to cure the scurvey by a water of noe worth nor value, which he solde att a very deare rate, to be *imprisoned* till he pay his Fine, *or* give securitye for it, *or* els to be whipped, & shalbe lyable to any mans action of whome hee hath receaved money for the said water.[3]

Fortunately for Knopp, two friends promised to pay the fine for him, thus saving him from the inevitable whipping.

In the fall of 1632, the General Court decided that "there shalbe a howse of correction & a house for the beadle [keeper] built att Boston, with what speede conveniently may be."[4] (Here the court probably used the term "house of correction" synonymously with "prison" but, as we shall see, the former term later took on a special meaning, for that institution served a quite different purpose.) The General Court found however—as it finds today—that a prison cannot be built as speedily as desired. Two years later (1634) Master Brenton, the builder, was ordered to oversee the work, and in 1635 he was directed to finish it at the public charge.[5] We assume, then, that the Boston prison was not ready for occupancy until five years after the first session of the Court of Assistants. In 1641 the General Court thoughtfully added: "The prison should be made warme & safe."[6]

From later reports we learn that the prison was seldom warm during the long winter months and was notoriously insecure, being a wooden structure with barred windows, easily broken out of by the "escape artists" of that day unless they were heavily shackled or thrown into an inner room for "close confinement." There was some evidence that Colonial prisons, like their counterparts today, were equipped with special security rooms. When writing about Hackett, condemned to die on the gallows and sweating out his last few days on this earth, Winthrop reported that he was "shut up in an inner room within the prison."[7] It was no doubt "a house of meagre Looks, and ill smells," as Dunton reported when he made a personal inspection of the place at the time of his interview with James Morgan, the condemned murderer. It stood in the very center of activity near what is now the City Hall Annex on the south side of Court Street, which was then called Prison Lane and, in the Province period, Queen Street. Like all Colonial prisons, it was poorly adapted to withstand erosion from without and the digging, sawing, and burrowing from within by those who sought and not infrequently made their escape. After thirteen years of constant use, it was declared unfit. A committee of inspection appointed by the General Court found "a great part of the groundsils & the tenants of the studs are very rotten" and partitions between the rooms "very weake to keepe prisoners a part," while "much of the planke that covers the house is very rotten."[8] Orders were immediately issued for substantial repairs: "the house to be covered with shingles, which done, the upper roomes may be of great use to the country in severall respects."[9] To help meet the costs of construction the government solicited private loans, offering about ten per cent interest.[10] Workmen could not always be paid in currency but evidently did not object to the rather common practice of collecting part of their wages "in the best sorte of corne."[11] Over and over again throughout the Colónial period, workmen were hired to make the prison strong,[12] but the desideratum of all prisons—an escape-proof institution—was never achieved.

The Boston prison standing squarely in the midst of the bustling activities of the little town attracted a good deal of attention, but the prison yard was enclosed by a fence to keep the public at a distance. By 1674 the committee of inspection found "the pales [fence] which compas in the prison will in probability soone fall, if there be not spedy course taken to new post them."[13] In later years the fence may have disappeared since it was reported that prisoners could peer through the barred windows and accept food and money from their friends, but, in 1659 when Quakers spent many miserable weeks packed in the small prison rooms like cattle in pens, the General Court decided to put a stop to unrestricted communication with the outside and ordered that

> there shall be a sufficient fence erected about the common prison, in Boston, & house of correction, such as may debarre persons from conversing with the prisoners, & the charge thereof to [be] borne half by the county of Suffolke & the other halfe by the countrie. . . .[14]

The fence was probably retained thereafter as a permanent feature of the prison. The Suffolk County Court ordered in 1675 that "there bee a strong & substantial Fence made up about the prison yard towards the Streete,"[15] and five years later the General Court decided that "the prison houses in Boston and fences about the same, be forthwith repaired or rebuilt."[16]

For eighteen years the Boston prison served the entire Bay Colony. It became, therefore, a sort of "state prison," supported partly by the central government and partly by Suffolk County. By 1652 the need for additional local prisons in outlying counties was brought into focus by the transportation problem, the General Court stating:

> Whereas there is but one prison in all this jurisdiction, and very inconvenient to send persons from all partes of the countrye when there is occasion to the same, itt is therefore ordered, that there shall be another prison erected and built at Ipswich. . . .[17]

Mary Oliver, for example, who had been brought into the Salem court many times for her habit of saying what she thought about the elders and the Governor—and her thoughts concerning the public figures of her day were usually bold and caustic—was "sentenced to prison at Boston indefinitely for her speeches at the arrival of some new comers." Here then was a typical transportation problem. The year was 1639. The distance to Boston was some fifteen miles over poor roads. But there was no local prison, and so the Court ordered that she "be taken by constables of Salem and Lynn to the prison at Boston."[18]

The Ipswich prison[19] was probably constructed promptly, for references to it appear in 1654. In June of that year the records of the Salem court report Jane Collins "lying ten weeks and upwards in prison," having been called a witch by a neighbor.[20] Like all Colonial prisons, the Ipswich building was vulnerable to the clever prisoner who wished to match his wits with the keeper. In 1659 the court authorized the keeper to buy locks and whatever else he needed "to make the dores and prisson strong."[21]

The Bay Colony had gradually pushed its claims eastward into new territory (an area that later became part of the state of Maine) and established the county of "Yorke" in 1653.[22] By 1658 it had annexed all that part of Maine then settled by white men and by 1672 had claimed jurisdiction as far east as Penobscot Bay. In 1654 the General Court ordered that the inhabitants of "Kettery," Saco, Cape "Porpus," "Yorke," and Wells get together on the matter of supporting the building and maintenance of a prison in that region.[23] It is believed that the old York prison was built pursuant to that order, but the exact date of construction is not known. It is the only one of the old Colonial prisons that has survived destruction. After some three hundred years, it stands as an historical museum in the town of York, Maine.[24]

By 1660 the rapidly developing western part of the plantation needed a prison to serve its own courts. The General Court ordered that year that "Springfield County Court be & is heereby impowred to erect & improove a prison & house of correction, as other countys have. . . ,"[25] and the following year Springfield and Northampton were allowed their taxes "for this yeare ensuing, for & towards the erecting of a prison or house of correction at Springfeild . . . and be finished by the next Court of Election."[26]

The Ipswich prison was available to the Salem court, but the population increase in that region warranted another prison in the town of Salem itself. Accordingly, in 1668 a prison was placed in the center of the old town of Salem, near the first meetinghouse.[27] The following year Benjamin Felton was appointed keeper[28] but met with the usual vexations in trying to keep men confined when they were determined to break out. A more secure prison was built in 1684. It was that prison that housed so many of the poor wretches who were crammed into a small space awaiting trial on charges of witchcraft in the summer of 1692.

The Salem prison was probably much like the others in respect to accomodations or the lack of them. Without adequate food, light, heat, ventilation, or sanitary facilities, these Colonial institutions must have really appeared to those within as "the Subburbs of Hell." It would seem from the records of the Suffolk and Essex County Courts that nearly everyone confined for more than a few days either attempted a prison break or wrote appealing letters to the courts for mercy. For example, Job Tookie, a servant, was thrown into the Salem prison for disobedience in 1682 on orders of his master. He wrote many highly articulate letters to his master asking for mercy but without avail. "No one alive knows or is able to Expresse what I have suffered since I came into this place," he wrote, "and still dayly doe. . . ." He had no medical attention, although complaining of "an Extraordinary payne in my side" when committed to the prison. After *ten weeks* of close confinement in a small room with no sanitary facilities, he was "almost poysoned with the stincke" and claimed that he had never "so much as a minutes tyme to take the Air Since I came into this Dolesome place."[29] After fourteen weeks of close confinement in the Salem prison, he petitioned the court for release, asking it to take into consideration "this sad Miserable and deplorable Condition I am now in. . . ."[30] The Court possibly did so but the record is silent at this point.

As time went on, local prisons in other parts of the country were built to take their places in the penological scheme.

In the early days of the settlement of Plymouth, the construction of dwellings, fortifications, and meetinghouses took priority over the building of a prison. The prison ordered to be built in 1638 was probably Plymouth's first. Prior to that time, they had ample facilities for dealing with the lawbreaker. If it were necessary that he be held until some punishment could be carried out, he could be confined in a cage. "In every constablerick," the General Court directed in 1636, there was to be "a Cage which shall be of competent strength to detain a prisoner."[31] It had probably been the custom to use cages even before that date. After a prison had been built, the law concerning cages was dropped, but when Quakers came into the Colony in 1658 and were, it was said, "threatening to pull downe all churches and ordinances of God to thrust us out of the wayes of God,"[32] the use of cages was revived. The General Court ordered that each town should have a cage "especially att Sandwich Duxburrow Marshfeild and Scitteate" (which were the usual meeting places of the Quakers who came into Plymouth Colony). In 1667 when the prosecution of this religious group had abated, the law was repealed. Cages were not substitutes for prisons. They were used occasionally and only for brief periods of confinement. The constable's authority in 1660 in dealing with the Quakers was limited: "If hee put them into the stockes they shall not continew there above two houres if in the winter nor above four houres if in the summer; and if hee put them Into the Cage they shall not continew there longer then untill night if in the winter; and not longer then the next morning in the summer. . . ."[33] This law was repealed the following year.

In 1667 the Bay Colony, too, ordered the building of cages in the marketplaces of Boston and other towns for the temporary detention of violators of the Sabbath laws, who could be held until the courts could deal with them. Probably little use was made of these cages, but the authorities at that time felt compelled to tighten the enforcement of laws concerning "the profanation of the Sabboath," for King Philip's War (1675-1677) had taught them that God had seen fit to inflict them with that horrible war for their backsliding in their observance of the Lord's Day.

The first official order to build a prison in Plymouth did not appear until 1638, eighteen years after the founding of the Colony.[34] They decided it should be twenty-two feet in length, sixteen in breadth, and two stories high "and to be erected upon the wast ground betwixt Mrs. Fuller and Mr. Hicks."[35] It was evidently completed in 1641 at a little higher cost than originally planned, for the builder, John Mynard, was allowed "3 pounds more . . . besides his dyett, for his worke donn about the prison over & above the bargaine."[36]

When some of the most hostile of the Indian tribes launched a prolonged and vicious attack on the Colony in 1675 (known as King Philip's War), fear was expressed that the friendly Indians from Natick, of the Massachusetts tribe, might break forth in a treacherous assault on the English in spite of their loyalty to the Rev. John Eliot who had taught them to pray to the white man's God. In a war that might well have wiped out the entire Colony had not some of the Indians been loyal to the English, opinion was divided on what measures to take toward these "praying Indians." The Bay Colony decided it would be the safer course for the duration of the war to order that some 350 of them—men, women, and children—be rounded up, disarmed, and "disposed of to Deare Island [in Boston harbor], as the place appointed for their present aboade."[37] This order was carried out in October 1675.

The heavily wooded island was not a fortress, and escape from its confines was not at all difficult. The General Court thereupon ordered that any Indians found "stragling off the said places of theire confinement" could be lawfully "destroyed" by any Englishman who happened to see them. Furthermore, any person convicted of stealing or carrying away any of these Indians from the island would be dealt with under the capital law against manstealing.[38]

Without experience in managing a penal colony, the authorities soon found their burden too great. They had no intention of starving their charges to death, and yet, involved in a desperate war for survival, they were not in a position to supply them with adequate food and shelter or even to guard them. The Indians had to shift for themselves, living mostly on shellfish or whatever else they might find in the woods, but the winter of 1675-1676 was cold and bleak.[39] It soon became obvious that they were "ready to perish for want of bread, & incapacitated to make provission for the future." The General Court thereupon ordered that "there be a man with a boate provided, who, with some of the Indians, shallbe imployed in catching of fish for theire supply." When spring came, the English would have been greatly relieved if they could have abandoned the whole project. The General Court reasoned that the population could, at least, be rapidly reduced if the nearby towns would take some of the friendly Indians from the island and "imploy them in scouting, labouring, or otherwise, with some of their owne men, (the said townes bearing the charge)." Those who remained could be engaged in planting crops on the island.[40]

After the termination of hostilities (King Philip was killed in the summer of 1676 but the war dragged on for another year), the remaining exiles were returned to "the place of hills" which was their native Natick. Friendly relations were soon resumed, and in 1679 an agreement was made for an exchange of land between the town of Sherborne and the Natick Indians, setting aside forty acres for a "Free schoole, for teaching the English & Indian children there the English tongue & other sciences."[41]

A small island close to the shore, commanding the entrance to Boston Harbor, had been selected at the very beginning of the settlement as the most appropriate location for a fort. The decision had been made in 1634 to build a fort "40 Foote longe & 21 Foote wide, for defence of this colony."[42] Private subscriptions from public-spirited citizens financed the first costs.[43] Here cannons were mounted and a garrison stationed.[44] No ship could enter the harbor in daylight without being noticed by the soldiers stationed on the island who, if the occasion warranted, could fire a cannon at intruders. That their fire could be deadly is evidenced by a story told by Governor Winthrop:

> Three ships arrived here from Ipswich, with three hundred and sixty passengers. The last being loath to come to an anchor at Castle Island, though hailed by the Castle boat, and required, etc., the gunner made a shot, intending to shoot before her for a warning, but the powder in the touchhole being wet, and the ship having fresh way with wind and tide, the shot took place in the shrouds, and killed a passenger, an honest man. The next day the governor charged an inquest, and sent them aboard with two of the magistrates (one of them being deputed coroner), to take view of the dead body, and who, having all the evidence, etc., found that he came to his death by the providence of God.[45]

"The Castle" or "The Island," as it was sometimes called, was almost continuously garrisoned, though for a short period in 1643 it was abandoned as a fort, for the government was getting "weary of the charge of maintaining" it.[46] However, for most of the Colonial period, it was equipped with cannon and manned by soldiers under command of a captain. Early in its history the Bay Colony saw the wisdom of using the Castle for special cases or for criminals who would not conform to the rules of the common prison. This fortified island became on a small scale a sort of Boston "Alcatraz," serving in the seventeenth and eighteenth centuries a purpose similar to that of that fortified island in San Francisco harbor where the federal government until recently confined its most difficult prisoners. Many years later (1785), it became the Commonwealth's state prison.

Chausop, an Indian from Block Island, was the first prisoner of record to be sent to the Island. He was taken out of the Boston prison in 1636 and brought before the court (we do not know on what charge) "& for the present was adjudged to bee sent to the iland, & there to bee kept as a slave for life to worke, unles wee see further cause."[47] It is unlikely that he stayed there for life, but his future course does not appear in the records.

The following year, Richard Osborn, who evidently was just

an idler, was requested to give a weekly account to the constable of "how hee doth improve his time; & if hee neglect, further order to bee taken, by puting him to the Castle."[48]

Nicholas Upshall (or Upsall), a highly respected Boston resident, and reputed to have been the first "convert" to the Quaker faith, had dared to befriend these despised people and to stand up before the magistrates in their defense. He was thrown into the Boston prison in 1656 and then fined and banished at the age of sixty under penalty of imprisonment if he returned, which he evidently did about three years later.[49] Again they sent him to prison for an indefinite period (which proved to be at least one year). There he was the "occasion of drawing many Quakers & others affected to that sect thither,"[50] much to the chagrin of the Governor and the Assistants. Upshall held no office in the government but he was a popular and influential Bostonian. He was one of the earliest settlers, having come over with the Winthrop fleet, a freeman, a selectman when he lived in Dorchester, a church member (one of the founders of the Old North), a charter member of the Military Company (known to later generations as the Ancient and Honorable Artillery Company), and the host of the famous Red Lyon Inn in the town of Boston.[51] Governor Endecott, the most bitter antagonist of the Quakers, knew that he had a formidable opponent in Upshall who, in his quiet way, could easily become a martyr symbol, winning more converts to "heretical doctrines" should he be allowed to communicate with his friends and neighbors. Under Endecott's influence, the General Court ordered that

> Nicholas Upshall be forthwith sent to the Castle Island, there to remaine upon his oune charge, & that none be suffered to come unto him to speake or conferr with him, except such of his oune family which may come to bring him necessary supplyes, & this order to continue till the Court take further order. The Capt of the Castle is to see to the due observation of this order.[52]

On the petition of Upshall's wife, Dorothy, the General Court modified its order. It decided that he should not go directly to the Castle but be confined for four months in the house of Lieutenant John Capen, a Deputy from Dorchester, with the stern warning that should he "corrupt any with his pernitious opinions" or communicate with Quakers, he would be sent to the Island.[53] We do not know in what way Upshall defied the Court's orders, but the following year (1662) it reminded him that he had been sentenced to "perpetual imprisonment" and had "greatly abused" his reprieve. The authorities once more confined him to Capen's house with the admonition that disobedience would again lead to prison.[54] There is no evidence that he ever saw the inside of the Castle after all. He died in 1666, having spent most of his last ten years in banishment or in prison or in the custody of Capen.

In the reign of King Edward the Sixth (1547-1553), a radical departure from the traditional methods of dealing with lawbreakers was put to the test. Instead of the infliction of physical pain or bodily mutilation or the sudden snuffing out of life on the gallows, a new method was designed to deal with the growing number of the ragged unemployed cast adrift as the industrial economy spread over England and the Continent. Many of these men and women became petty thieves, rogues, beggars, prostitutes, and drunkards, who wandered aimlessly about, threatening the King's peace. In 1553 the King established in a district of London called Bridewell (from the presence there of a well of St. Bride or St. Bridget) an institution called, appropriately, a House of Correction. Here beggars, vagabonds, and "loose women" were committed by the courts. The distinctive feature of this institution was that the prisoners would not lie about in fetters but would be engaged in manual labor, enforced by the whip if necessary, and be exposed to some moral and religious instruction. The best antidote for idleness, it was believed, was forced labor and the teaching of a trade. Here was a remarkable milestone in the history of penology. Unfortunately, the high standards established at the outset deteriorated in the course of time. When the great prison reformer John Howard made his inspection of the jails and prisons of England and Europe (1773-1777), few of these houses could claim any honest efforts at "correction" or be distinguished from a miserable prison.

Nevertheless, the first Bridewell and those that soon followed proved to be a success. In the reign of Queen Elizabeth I (1558-1603), Parliament decreed in 1575-1576 that:

> In everye Countye . . . one Two or more Abyding Howses . . . shalbe provided, and called the Howse or Howses of Correction for setting on worcke and punishinge . . . of such as . . . shalbee taken as Roges. . . .[55]

Other Houses of Correction were built, not only in England but on the continent.[56] In Amsterdam similar institutions began operations in 1596 with the same basic idea of providing work for petty offenders, most of whom had no trade or means of livelihood. Some writers believe that the Hollanders were pioneers in this innovation, not deriving their ideas directly from the English, in spite of the similarity of purpose and design.[57]

When the English planted their Colonies in New England, houses of correction (commonly called "Bridewells") were thus well known.[58] In fact, before Winthrop left England in 1630, the London corporation had sent a letter of advice to John Endecott who was then (1629) in Salem, declaring among other things,

> for the better governing and ordering of our people, espetiallie such as shalbe negligent and remiss in performance of their dutyes, or otherwise exorbitant, our desire is, that a *house of correction* bee erected and set upp, both for the punishment of such offendours, and to deterr others by their example of such irregular course.[59]

Not forgetful of the advice to Endecott, the Bay Colony authorities no doubt had intended for some time to establish "Bridewells" in the Colony, but it was not until 1655 that the General Court ordered that "there shall be a howse of correction provided in each county at the counties charge, to be setled, ordered, and improoved as the magistrates in each County Court or Court of Assistants shall agree. . . ."[60]

This order could not be fully carried out. It was quite impractical for each county to raise the needed funds at that time. Realizing this fact, the Court directed the following year that "it shall be in the power of every County Court to make use of such prison as is at present erected in theire county for a howse of Correction, till the howses of correction be finished."[61]

Plymouth Colony was concerned not only with the large number of idle and vagrant persons in or traveling through its jurisdiction in the middle of the seventeenth century but, after 1656, the influx of Quakers had posed for them, as for the Bay Colony, a special problem. These religious people had refused to take the oath of fidelity or to turn out for military training or to show any respect to officials of church and state.[62] As in the Bay Colony, Quakers were frequently referred to in Plymouth as "vagrants," a term of reproach used generally for those who followed "noe lawfull calling to earne their owne bread." The General Court in 1658 decided that a house of correction was an immediate need:

> Att this Court, Captaine Josias Winslow and Constant Southworth are requested and appoined by the Court, together with the Tresurer, . . . to take order with workeman and to cause provision to bee made reddy for the erection of a building to bee joyned to the prison att Plymouth, to bee a house of correction; the same to bee of equal heighth with the said prison, and to bee fourteen foot in length, & bee aded to it, and a chimny to it.[63]

The Plymouth revised laws of 1658 made clear the kind of offender they deemed most suitable for house of correction treatment:

> . . . with all convenient Speed a worke house or house of Correction bee erected that all such vagrants as wander up and downe without any lawfull calling and alsoe all Idle persons or rebelliouse children or servants that are stuborne and will not worke to earn theire owne bread and yett have not wherwith to maintaine themselves may bee put to this house of Correction and there bee Imployed in such worke as shalbee there provided for them and to have noe other Supply for theire sustainance then what they shall earne by theire labour all the while that they continew there and alsoe that some faithfull man bee appointed by the Court to bee overseer of this house of correction. . . .[64]

As it turned out, the building was not erected with great speed. Two years later the court found it necessary to repeat the order with a directive to the Treasurer "to take some speedy course for the doeing of it; and that a fitt person bee chosen by the magistrates to bee the overseer therof."[65]

Both in the Bay Colony and in the Plymouth Colony it was customary to build the house of correction next to the prison—a practice that was carried down through the centuries to the present time. In Plymouth, for example, the house of correction was to be "an *addition* . . . fourteen foot long of equall hight with the prison att the one end therof; with two chimneyes in it; one in the lower rome and the other in the uper rome with a yard before it fenced with a fence of eight foot high made of boards."[66]

In 1679 the Bay Colony decided to separate the prisons from the houses of correction:

> Complaints being made, that through the misgovernment of the prison in this towne [Boston], & the confusion of bridewell with the prison howse, the execution of justice & restraint of disorderly & rude persons is greatly obstructed, this Court doeth order, that provission be made that they be in distinct places, at farther distance then [than] now they be one from another. . . .

(The Court thereupon appointed a committee of three to make an inspection and to report back to the Court.[67])

How was the House conducted? The General Court of the Bay Colony decreed in 1656:

> That at the first coming into the howse, the master of the correction howse himself, . . . shal whip the delinquent not exceeding tenn stripes, and after that he shall imploy him or her by dayly stint; and if he or shee be stubborne, disorderly, or idle, and not performe theire taske, and that in good condition, it shall be in the masters power to abridg them of part of theire usuall food, or give them meete correction, as the case shall requier from time to time. . . .[68]

In 1656 the first law in the Bay Colony, setting up what we might call a pioneer prison industry, was experimental—"not to be in force after one year" but the following year it was continued indefinitely:

> That the selectmen of the towne, where such howse is appointed, shall have liberty & power to procure, in a voluntary & prudent way, some competent stocke of hemp & flax, or other materialls, &, uppon account, to committ the same into the hands of the master of the howse, to be imploied at his discretion by the labours of such delinquents as shall from time to time be committed unto him from authoritie. That the stock being in value or kinde, preserved to such as put in the same, & all the bennefit attained by the labor of the persons committed shallbe to the use of the master, allowing only so much as will keepe the delinquent with necessary bread & water, or other meane foode out of the same, as fower penc out of the shilling earned by his or her labor. [Later changed to six pence out of the shilling.][69]

Who should be sent to these houses, instead of to the common prison? In general, the candidates for this special treatment were the social misfits, the poor, the unemployed, and the drunkards, together with a few who committed petty or annoying offenses against the peace and dignity of the government. By and large, these men and women were products of the society in which they lived, caught up in an increasingly difficult economic struggle for existence. They were not "public enemies" to be feared and hated for aggressive attacks on the law-abiding public. The authorities could afford, then, a bit of compassion toward them, as exemplified in their efforts to teach them a trade, while, at the same time, retaining the whip hand. Here then was a promising first step in the rehabilitation of the imprisoned individual offender. "Correction" had made its bow in the arena of penology.

Judges still had considerable discretion as to whether to send a person to the prison or to the house of correction, but the latter institution was designed primarily for the following classes of offenders: a) "Idle persons" who "will not worke to earn theire own bread"; b) "Stubborn persons against such as have Authority over them" (meaning children, servants, slaves, or apprentices); c) "Runawayes"; d) "Common Drunkards"; e) "Pilferers"; f) "Common nightwalkers" (both male and female); g) "Wanton persons, as tending to uncleanness in speeches or Actions," or the lewd and lascivious.

As time went on, the Bay Colony enacted additional laws, widening the scope of commitments to the houses of correction:

a) Quakers (after 1656).[70]

b) "Common coasters" (that is, those who wandered idly up and down the coast), "vagrants," and those who led "a vagabond life." It was believed that such people were "drawing away children, servants, & other persons, both younger & elder, from their lawfull callings & imployments, & heardning the hearts of one another against all subjection to the rules of Gods holy word & the established lawes of this collony. . ." (after 1662). Constables had power, with or without a warrant, to arrest anyone who could not "give a good & sattisfactory account of such their wandering up & downe" and to bring him before the next magistrate who could order him whipped and sent home. If the "rogue" or "vagabond" would not reveal his home or refused to get out of the jurisdiction, he could then be sent to the house of correction to remain there until the next session of the county court.[71]

c) "Common Bauds, Whores or vile Persons" (after 1673).[72]

d) Youths, who in the time of worship in the meetinghouse, "commit disorder and Rudeness" could be found delinquent by the court and, on the second offense, declared incorrigible and committed to the house of correction (after 1675).[73]

e) "Idle persons" whose names were sent in by the selectmen of the town after their inspection of families (after 1675). At the time of King Philip's War, many new regulatory laws were enacted, for it was believed that through this war God was punishing the Colony for its backsliding. Idleness had always been abhorrent to the Puritans. At this most crucial time, the General Court declared that "the sin of Idleness (which is a Sin of Sodom) doth greatly Increase" and must be immediately ferreted out and punished, the town selectmen being required to report all idle persons.[74]

f) Those who refused to take the Oath of Allegiance as required by King Charles the Second (the English sovereign from 1660 to 1685) might have been sent to the prison or house of correction for three months (after 1678).[75]

g) Indians who refused to live in reservations specifically set aside for them might be sent to the prison or house of correction until they were willing to comply (after 1681).[76]

The General Court appointed Richard Brackett keeper of the Boston prison in 1637.[77] In later years appointments were usually made by the County courts.[78] Keepers were required to live in houses built and furnished by the government and placed close to the prison, but they had no prescribed hours of work. Prisoners, once they were locked in, were probably unattended much of the time, particularly at night. Judging from the number of escapes, probably most prisons were understaffed. Usually the keeper was depended on to do all of the work, but he could hire assistants when needed and seek reimbursement from the General Court. It was not until ten years after his appointment that Brackett asked that regular prison guards be recruited to assist him in his duties. The General Court authorized him in 1647 to

> huire 2 able men, such as may be trusted with a matter of so great moment, & if he cannot huire any such, then upon sight hereof the cunstables of Boston, or any of them, shall from time to time impresse 2 such men, who shall assist the keeper in guarding the prisoners day & night, & when they go to publike meetings, & they shalbe alowed 3 shillings per day & night, each of them, out of the fines of the prisoners.[79]

Brackett's salary was established at thirteen pounds, six shillings and eight pence per year, plus full maintenance.[80] A few years after his appointment, he successfully petitioned for an increase to twenty pounds.[81] Salaries differed from town to town. As keepers had ways of augmenting their income, it is impossible to say what the average might have been. Keepers of the Boston prison sometimes had the concession of selling beer to their charges.[82] Theophilus Willson, keeper of the Ipswich prison, submitted bills for special services, which seemed to be the common practice. For example, for putting fetters on and taking them off, he was paid two shillings; for "turning the key" (that is, locking in or releasing one inmate) five shillings.[83] Eventually prison guards were called "turnkeys," a term that lasted well into the twentieth century in Massachusetts.

One of the duties of the keepers—and still an obligation on the part of superintendents of today's correctional institutions—was to keep "a true list" of all prisoners in his charge and "not to discharge any theire custody but by the authority of the lawe."[84]

It was evidently the policy of the government to keep prison costs at a minimum. This objective could be achieved by making the prisoner pay his way, starting from the time of his conviction. If he had to be transported to the prison, he was required to pay the cost, if he were able.[85] For his stay in a Bay Colony prison he was required to pay two shillings, six pence per week;[86] in Plymouth Colony, two pence a day up until 1646, three pence up to 1660, and thereafter four pence.[87] If he could not pay, the keeper had to petition the General Court for reimbursement for food that he himself had furnished. Even those who were discharged from the prison (where they had been awaiting trial) after a finding of not guilty, had to pay their prison fees.[88] Any prisoner unfortunate enough to be confined in the Ipswich prison in 1657 and unable to pay the fees had to live on bread and water.[89] The coarse prison diet could usually, with the keeper's permission, be supplemented by food brought in by friends or relatives.

The official records abound with reports of men who had "broken prison." One might speculate as to the reasons for the frequency with which prisoners outwitted keepers: 1) There was a lack of sufficient personnel to keep the prisons under close surveillance at all times; 2) old wooden structures challenged the ingenuity of the "escape artist"; 3) evidently prisoners were not always chained or fettered; 4) there were, occasionally, accomplices from the outside—"evill disposed persons that supply them with instruments"; 5) the penalty for escaping or aiding in an escape was not particularly severe; 6) once a prisoner had "broken prison" and sneaked out of the town where he might have been recognized, he had a fair chance of freedom, for no system of identification had been developed; 7) the living conditions and food in the prison were such that every prisoner who was confined for more than a few days must have been highly motivated to attempt escape.

The government, of course, was much concerned over this problem for "to have justice now deluded by an escape would reflect much dishonour upon the Courte." As the responsibility was primarily the keeper's, the law provided that:

> if the escape of any Prisoner appeare to be through the fault or neglect of the jaylor, he shall then bee lyable to such penalties as the prisoner was, according as the Court which hath cognisance thereof shall determine.[90]

This idea of reversing the roles of keeper and prisoner is still the law in Massachusetts but enforced no more strictly than in the Colonial period.[91] The Bay Colony records reveal no cases where a keeper was made to suffer the same punishment for which the escaper was liable. Ordinarily, if neglect could be shown, the keeper was merely fined.

When an escape occurred, the keeper was usually on safe ground in pleading the weak condition of the prison. For example, in an escape from the Boston prison in 1678, the keeper claimed the escapers got free by "Breaking up the Lower floare . . . & Workeing themselves out under the Ground Sill . . . which they more Easyly did and with the Less noyes for that the floare of the said prison is much Rotten & Decayed. . . ."[92] When one John Haskens escaped from the Ipswich prison, the keeper, Theophillus Willson, (appointed keeper in 1653 but at the time of the escape in 1680 was "aged about 79 years") testified to the mysterious break. He had locked Haskens "into the strongest room in Ipswich prison," he said, but "in thirty-six hours, he had broken prison without any apparent help by man or implement."[93] Two other men who inspected the Ipswich prison testified "they found not one room there that was sufficient to keep in a man who had the dexterity of an ordinary man." Josiah Gatchell added his testimony, saying that "the keeper locked in two men, who came out without the door being unlocked. He saw one man pull up one of the boards overhead in the prison with his hand, going into the chamber of the prison, and others went out under the groundsill and some went out next the worke house [House of Correction]." As for the Salem prison, Gatchell said "any man having no instrument except his own hands could come out as he pleased."[94] From the number of escapes noted in the records of the county courts, we assume that the lack of strong detention facilities was typical of the prisons of that period.

When an escape was noted, it was the duty of the constable to sound "a hue and cry" and give a description of the escaper, a description usually so vague that it was of little help unless the offender were known in the town in which he was hiding. For example, Constable Clifford described James Booth, "whoe broake prison this last night [in 1675] at Salem & made an escape," in the following language: "He is of a midle stature, brownish haire & complection, a blemish [in] one of his eyes, of a drawning speech, a taylor by trade."[95]

No doubt some escapes were due to the policy of letting prisoners out for brief periods of time on special occasions. It was testified, for example, that Benjamin Felton, keeper of the Salem prison in 1672 "had often been known to take prisoners out of the prison to help him about his own occasions, and some times men have run away in the meantime."[96] Probably, in most cases, the prisoners did not break faith with the keeper. The court granted William Lytherland permission to leave the Boston prison to attend "the Ordinances of christ" and to visit his sick wife with his keeper.[97] Ordinary prisoners were usually released on request to attend church services, for the idea of employing chaplains in the prison had not yet been adopted. Jeffery Moyle was given "liberty to walke in the Town by day with a Keeper."[98] Even the notorious Alice Thomas was given "Liberty to bee abroade from Eight of the clocke in the morning till Six a clocke at night. She giving Sufficient Security to the Keeper to Return to Prison every night at the hour Appointed & to be a true prisoner & this Liberty to continue till the first day of the next Court of this County."[99] This special concession to Alice was noteworthy for it established the possibility of a sort of "day work program" (as it might be called today) for a person who had been called by the court " a common Baud."[100] She had evidently been in the Boston prison six months when this favor was granted. She had frequently been before the courts and found guilty of a number of crimes—accessory to burglary, selling liquor without a license, profanation of the Sabbath, and entertaining children in her tavern where liquor was sold. Her most blatant offense was that she had opened her tavern to "Lewd Lascivious & notorious persons of both Sexes, giving them opportunity to commit carnall wickedness."[101] Shortly after her conviction, the General Court enacted a law in 1673 providing severe penalties for "the sin of Whoredome and Uncleanness."[102]

From the extensive collection of locks and other restraint equipment listed in an inventory made at the Boston prison in 1646 and turned over to the new keeper, George Munnings, one might assume that no prisoner could possibly get away. Evidently these devices were used only for special cases or when the court ordered "close confinement." Among these items were many large padlocks for doors, padlocks "to put upon mens leges," a "footlocke with a chain fastened to it," handlocks with a "bowlt in them," "large irons or Bilboes, greate & small," four "necke irons,"and so on.[103]

Outside accomplices, those "evill disposed persons that supply them with instruments," were occasionally successful. Upon conviction, such persons were "liable to the same corporal punishment which the Prisoner was liable unto, and also [may] incurre such further penalty by Fine, Imprisonment, or Corporal punishment" as the court shall appoint.[104] But again we find such accomplices lightly punished. Isaac Read, for example, convicted of "conveying a file & Gimblett to the prisoners. . .whereby to practice theire Escape whereby the prison was broken & Jeffery Richardson ran away," was sentenced merely to a whipping or a fine.[105] Robert Dendy on another occasion received the same punishment as Read for freeing prisoner Richard Cooly by supplying him with a "Gimblett."[106] Jacob Rowell for assisting Henry Salter to break out of Ipswich prison was merely fined.[107] Aiding or concealing an escaped prisoner was also lightly punished. After two men were convicted for concealing an escaped prisoner and were merely admonished by the court (for the prisoner had been recaptured), the court laid down a rule that no one would be allowed within the prison yard at Ipswich or within twenty feet of the prison on the side where there was no fence, without the keeper's permission "upon paine & penalltye to be proceeded against as contemnors of authoritye and abbettours of malifactors."[108]

Not all escapers were men. Mary Punnell, a runaway servant guilty of fornication, escaped from the Boston prison in 1674.[109]

The court, after sentencing an offender in a criminal case, usually ordered him "to stand committed [to the common prison] untill sentence bee performed" or "till hee give security to performe the Sentence." This use of the prison was by far the most common. If the sentence involved a sizable fine, the court committed the offender to the prison until the fine was paid, unless, of course, he was able to pay it immediately. If the fine were small, he was often placed on his honor to pay at a later date but some took advantage of this liberality. To the Puritan mind, such neglect was not a trivial matter. In 1646 the Court declared that "delayes in executing justice is dangeros to any state." If the fine were not paid, or the offender did not put up security "speedily to do it," he was to be "imprisoned or kept to worke till it be paid," because the Court reasoned if a fine were not "duely levied, . . . then sinn is unpunished, & the name of God may thereby suffer."[110]

A person might also be held in prison awaiting trial, but the magistrates were opposed to holding such persons for long periods of time—as they are sometimes held today. Colonial courts would readily have subscribed to the modern dictum that justice delayed is justice denied. The Body of Liberties (1641) had provided that "Everie man that is to Answere for any criminall cause, whether he be in prison or under bayle, his cause shall be heard and determined at the next Court that hath proper Cognizance thereof, And may be done without prejudice of Justice."[111] This law was carried on the statute books down to the end of the Colonial period and was probably reasonably well enforced. It was common practice to release a person on bail if he could not be tried at once, for everyone was entitled to bail excepting "in Crimes Capitall, and Contempts in open Court, and in such cases where some expresse act of Court doth allow it."[112] Another exception was later made when the prosecution of that "pernicious Sect, commonly called Quakers" reached white heat, for, in dealing with these people who continuously defied the law, the General Court decided that, if committed to prison, they would have to "remaine without bayle untill the next Court of Asistants."[113]

Following the practice in England, the Colony permitted plaintiffs in civil suits to cause their adversaries to be thrown into the common prison on their failure or refusal to pay the debt or damages awarded by the courts. This practice became increasingly common. The courts were crowded with civil suits. Nearly everyone seemed to delight in suing his neighbor, often on some trivial charge of slander. Thousands of debtors suffered imprisonment, not only in the Colonial and Province periods, but in the Commonwealth government as well, for this practice did not completely terminate until 1843.[114]

Those who had to go to prison because they could not pay a small debt were most likely also unable to pay the keeper his prison fees. To protect the keeper, the law made the plaintiff liable for the prisoner's "Food, & phisicke [medicine], & other necessaries."[115] On the plaintiff's failure to pay, the debtor was released. No debtor could be imprisoned, however, if the law could satisfy the debt out of his estate;[116] nor could a debtor be held in confinement if he swore that he was not worth five pounds.[117] A keeper who released a prisoner held for debt without permission of the court or the creditor stood liable to the creditor for the debt.[118]

In spite of laws designed to protect debtors from overzealous creditors, a debtor could sometimes be held in prison for a very long time. Thomas Broughton, for example, indebted to John Checkly, was imprisoned in Boston in May 1664. In August he petitioned the Court for permission to attend "the publicke ordinances on the Lords days & at other times." Permission was granted with the creditor's consent and with the attendance of the keeper. There is evidence that he was still in prison in October of that year. In May 1667, he was granted permission to go to court, accompanied by his keeper, to sue Checkly and to return to prison. In October 1668, he told the court he "hath been long in prison" and had nothing to satisfy the judgment and had not concealed his assets. In May 1669, the court appointed commissioners to examine his assets. It would seem then that Broughton was in prison during most or all of a five-year period.[119]

Most historians of the Colonial period had given the impression that the prisons of that day were used *only* for the confinement of persons awaiting trial or the execution of their sentences or of debtors or of religious and political prisoners. It is true that those were the major functions of the prisons. There is ample evidence to show, however, that in addition to those traditional purposes the prisons were in fact frequently used as punishment for the violators of the criminal statutes, as they are today. Imprisonment as punishment was chosen relatively less often than fines or whippings, for the prisons were small and could hold but a few at one time. Furthermore, unless the prisoner could pay for his own maintenance, he became a charge on the government, a burden the Colonial people wished to avoid.

A number of criminal laws, in fact, specifically provided for imprisonment as a penalty. In Plymouth, for example, a man or woman could be imprisoned (but not for more than three days) for sexual intercourse before the marriage ceremony.[120] Those who created a public disturbance or defamed the courts or attempted to corrupt an official keeper of the public records could be imprisoned for an indefinite period.[121] There were many laws, too numerous to list here, providing for either a fine or imprisonment for violators. Nonpayment of fines in a criminal case was, of course, a common ground for imprisonment—an option voluntarily chosen by Quakers and others who preferred to challenge the authority of the government. Likewise, anyone requested by the court in a criminal case to put up sureties for his good behavior could be imprisoned if he refused to comply. Kenelme Winslowe, for example, served four weeks in the Plymouth prison rather than comply with such an order after he was convicted of "approbrious words against the church of Marshfield, saying they were all lyers."[122] Judges, however, had such broad discretionary powers in criminal cases that it was not necessary in most cases that a sentence to prison be based on a specific statutory authorization.

Rarely was a person sentenced for a long period of time. Most sentences were for an indefinite period. One might be sentenced, for example, "for a time," or "dureing the pleasure of the Court," or "till Saturday morning next," or "until the last day of the week at night."[123] The sentence of Edward Woodley, a servant, "for attempting a rape, swearing, & breaking into a house" was an example of a kind rarely found in the records. After a severe whipping, he was sentenced in 1636 to *"a yeares imprisonment,* & kept to hard labour, with course dyot, & to weare a collor of yron."[124] The Boston prison was not equipped to keep men confined for long periods of time, and the house of correction had not yet been built. Furthermore, the imprisonment of this servant proved "prejudicial" to his master. He was, therefore, released after serving six months, on condition that the victim of the attempted rape "shall professe her freedome from feare."[125]

We present a few selected cases to show the variety of crimes for which the magistrates chose imprisonment as punishment:

Thomas Millerd (or Miller), pilot and mate on the good ship Hector, was committed to prison in June 1636, "for certeine seditious & opprobrious speaches, saying wee are all rebells & traytors, & hee would justify it to the Governors face. . . ."[126] He was evidently in prison until the following September, when he was released after submitting a humble apology in writing, stating that his remarks "did proceed from the rashness & distemper of my owne braine, without any just ground or cause. . . ."[127]

"Webb Adey for his licentious and disorderly manner of liveing. Committed to prison [in Plymouth]."[128] "Master Gray committed to prison [in Plymouth] for sweareing."[129] "William Willoughby for beeing distempered with wine, & mispending his time & neglecting both publique, & private Ordinances, was committed to Prison [in Boston] to bee kept to worke there."[130]

Gyles Ricard, Senior, "for swearing by the wounds of God, was sentanced to bee committed to prison, and there to bee in durance the space of twenty foure houres."[131] ("Wounds of God" was a sacrilegious reference to Christ's wounds which later became contracted to "zounds.") This brief stay in the Plymouth prison evidently did not reform him. The following year, for swearing the second time, he was committed to prison for 12 hours. The court explained that the lighter sentence was due to "some materiall cercomstance about the case respecting the witnesses, which occationed the mittigation of the punishment."[132]

William Steevens of Gloucester, a ship's carpenter, went to Salem prison for one month for uttering some disloyal remarks concerning King Charles the Second. He was also disfranchised and declared ineligible to hold office, but stated after the sentence that he had no desire to hold office anyway.[133] "Joseph Armatag, presented for common Barratry" by the Salem Quarterly Court was found guilty and committed to prison for 24 hours.[134] Thomas Smith, Sr., evidently spent about two years in confinement, but it is not clear whether he spent this time in the Boston prison or in the house of correction. His crime was "drunkeness & madness" and "putting his wife and children in fear of their lives."[135]

Joseph Gatchell went to prison (in Salem) accused of being the father of two children by his brother's wife. He shortened his stay there by breaking out and escaping. One can hardly blame him for wanting to escape. He described that "noysom place" as "not fitt for a christian man to breath in." It was, he said, "impossible that any humane [human] creature should endure to live in so pestiferous a stinke."[136] On being recaptured, he was given a fine and one more week in the prison. Unfortunately for Gatchell, the following year he was sentenced to spend another week in the place he despised—this time for "reviling and reproachful speeches against the magistrates and ministry." He couldn't bear the thought of another sentence and, on his humble petition to the court, the sentence was respited. His petition showed that he had "neither house nor home. . . ." His wife was "a very weake woman" and "should he be now imprisoned for the weeke his wife & poore babe must perish. . . ." The court relented.[137]

John Baker went to prison in Salem for one week accused of "threatening children and others that he would kill them, and other approbrious speeches and bad language."[138]

† † †

One can scarcely do justice in brief compass to the long and fascinating story of the growth and development since 1692 of the penal and correctional institutions of the Commonwealth and the evolution of a correctional philsophy. Such an undertaking merits a separate volume, one that could draw upon the abundant documentary material available to the researcher. Nineteenth and early twentieth century penologists were a talkative lot and left no doubt about their thoughts on incarceration as a method of reformation and punishment. Nor did they leave any doubt about the rationale for the particular kind of "prison discipline" they thought would best serve the community. In a brief survey of Massachusetts penology of the past two and three-quarter centuries we can do little more than to note:

1) Down to the present day, the practice has continued of holding the less serious offenders in the local jails and houses of correction.[139]

2) A "state prison" was established for the entire Commonwealth for the more serious offenders, first at Castle Island in Boston Harbor (1785), then in Charlestown (1805), and finally in Walpole (1956).[140]

3) A new state prison was built in Concord (1878) to replace the old prison in Charlestown, which was thereupon temporarily abandoned.[141]

4) The state prison at Concord was converted into the Massachusetts Reformatory, now known as the Massachusetts Correctional Instiution, Concord, for the less experienced male offenders over the age of 15 (1884). The older and more "hardened" criminals were returned to the old State Prison in Charlestown.[142]

5) The Women's Reformatory Prison at Sherborn (1877) as a separate institution for female adult offenders (now known as the Massachusetts Correctional Institution, Framingham) followed closely on the heels of the establishment of a separate institution for women and girls in Indiana, which was the first of its kind in the United States.[143]

6) A special institution for male juvenile offenders was built in Westboro (1848), the State Reform School now known as the Lyman School for Boys and its branch, the Massachusetts Nautical School (1859—1872), was followed in 1855 by the opening of a State Reform School for Girls at Lancaster, now known as the Industrial School for Girls, designed for "the instruction, employment and reformation of exposed, helpless, evil disposed and vicious girls." An Industrial School for Boys was opened in 1909 at Shirley, and subsequently numerous other institutions were developed to care for delinquent and wayward children under the supervision and control of the present Division of Youth Service of the Department of Education.[144]

7) An almshouse was opened in Bridgewater in 1855, which,

after 1872, served as the State Workhouse and in 1887 became the State Farm. Since 1955, it has been known as the Massachusetts Correctional Institution, Bridgewater, and now cares for four kinds of inmates: men sentenced solely for drunkenness, the male defective delinquent, the male criminal insane, and men who have been adjudicated "sexually dangerous persons."[145]

8) A Temporary Industrial Camp at Rutland for the purpose of reclaiming and improving waste land and furnishing healthy outdoor employment for men transferred from the jails and houses of correction (and later from the state institutions) was opened in 1904 and was combined the following year with a hospital for prisoners afflicted with tuberculosis transferred from the state and county institutions, under the title "Prison Camp and Hospital" which served until 1933–1934.[146]

9) The first "community prison" in the United States was built at Norfolk for the more promising adult male offenders. Officially opened in 1931 as the State Prison Colony, it is now known as the Massachusetts Correctional Institution, Norfolk.[147]

10) Three forestry camps were constructed on state reservations for adult male offenders in 1952, 1955, and 1965.[148]

11) Concepts of "prison discipline" have changed over the past 150 years. Spirited debates occurred between the defenders of "the Pennsylvania system" of silent and completely solitary imprisonment and those who advocated a modified plan of solitary imprisonment at night but congregate work in the shops under a rule of silence during the day, known as "the Auburn system," which was adopted and fiercely defended by Massachusetts penologists. Large-scale prison industries were developed, followed by the emergence of what has been called, with questionable accuracy, "the new penology" and the "treatment-centered correctional institution" of today. It might not be inappropriaate, within the limits of this treatment, to discuss three common misconceptions that have developed out of an inadequate appreciation of penological history in Massachusetts.

First, there is the misunderstanding of the uses which were made of prisons in the early days. One will frequently find in penological literature the statement that prisons were *not* used as places for the punishment of those who violated criminal laws in Massachusetts until *after* the commencement of the Commonwealth government in 1780 and that the earlier prisons were used merely to hold persons awaiting trial or pending the execution of their sentences to corporal punishment or death or to detain debtors or political or religious undesirables.[149] But, as we were able to show in this chapter, Colonial prisons *were* in fact used for the confinement of common criminals, as they are used today, although with less frequency and for relatively shorter terms.

In the Province government (1692–1775) prisons and houses of correction served with increasing frequency as places of punishment for those who breached the criminal laws. A few selected criminal laws of that period (omitting those dealing with the observance of the Sabbath) will make it clear that the General Court saw those institutions as practical tools in the general administration of criminal justice (without giving up corporal punishment altogether) although it is highly unlikely that many of the prisoners were confined for the maximum term provided by law:

Twenty days in prison, without bail, (or three hours in the cage or stocks) for one who did not pay his fine for selling "wine and strong liquors" without a license.[150]

Thirty days in the house of correction (or a whipping) for " assaulting, or offering any insolence or violence to any women or womankind, in the fields, streets or lanes."[151]

One month in prison (or a fine) on a second conviction of carrying wood from the Common or from another's land.[152]

Three months in prison (or a fine) for selling to or exchanging with any Indian "strong beer, cyder, wine, rum, brandy or any other strong liquors, clothing or any other thing . . ." without a license.[153]

Three months in prison (in addition to a fine) for buying, or knowingly receiving clippings or filings from coins.[154]

Six months in prison (without bail) for willful perjury in a court of record.[155]

Six months in prison, later changed to twelve, (or other penalties at the court's discretion) for duelling with a dangerous weapon.[156]

Six months in prison (or a fine) for customs officers who accepted bribes.[157]

Six months in prison (in addition to a fine) for making or passing counterfeit coins or for stamping out "pieces of brass or tin at the rate of a penny each."[158]

Six months in prison (in addition to other penalties) for highway robbery.[159]

Six months in prison (or a fine, not exceeding one hundred pounds or a whipping not exceeding thirty stripes) "if any man be found in bed with another man's wife," the penalty to apply to both.[160]

"One whole year" in prison, without bail, (in addition to other penalties) for forgery.[161]

Three years in a house of correction "at hard labour" for forging or counterfeiting money or coin.[162]

Three years in prison (in addition to other penalties) for "sending any incendiary or menacing letters in order to extort sums of money." In this case imprisonment was made particularly rigorous, for "every three months [the prisoner was to] be brought out and whipt 20 stripes on the naked back, at the publick whipping post."[163]

Twenty years in a house of correction on the second conviction of forgery or counterfeiting money or coins "and there to be kept at hard labour."[164]

"Perpetual Imprisonment" (presumably a life sentence) for Jesuits or seminary priests or other ecclesiastical persons deriving their authority from the Pope or see of Rome, teaching others to say "popish prayers" or celebrating mass or conducting any "Romish ceremonies" in the Province after September 10, 1700. (The law was published on June 29 of that year.)[165]

Another quite common erroneous belief is that the first penal institution in the United States to which the more serious offenders could be committed from all parts of the state for a term of years at hard labor was the reconstructed Walnut Street Jail in Philadelphia. It is true that this jail, in accordance with an act of the Pennsylvania Legislature passed on March 27, 1789, and with another act passed the following year stipulating solitary confinement for the more "hardened and atrocious offenders," can be properly referred to as "the first *penitentiary* in the world for the housing of convicted felons."[166] Yet the first institution in the United States serving an entire state as "a place for the reception and secure confinement of all such persons as shall be sentenced to confinement and hard labour for the term of their natural lives, or for any shorter space of time" was the fortress on Castle Island in the Harbor of Boston, so designated by an act of the General Court of Massachusetts on March 14, 1785.[167]

We have already related in this chapter the early history of Castle Island which, in the seventeenth century, was used as a sort of Boston "Alcatraz" for the confinement, under military discipline, of certain offenders whom the jails had difficulty in holding. In the eighteenth century the practice continued of sending to the Island an occasional dangerous criminal or one who had escaped from a local jail or of using it in time of war as a prison camp. It served as the State Prison from 1785 until 1798 when the United States government purchased it from Massachusetts as part of the federal plan of harbor fortifications. During its thirteen years' service as a state prison, a total of 278 men were committed there under varying sentences. In its first year, inmates of the local jails and houses of correction serving a sentence of one year or more were transferred to the Island, but the courts committed men there directly on sentences "to hard labour." The most frequent sentence was for a term of three years, although sentences usually ranged from nine months to ten years, with five men receiving a life sentence.

Two prison industries—the making of nails and the picking of oakum—kept inmates busy, but plans for escape were soon hatched, for communication among its inmates was not restricted. Governor James Bowdoin, familiar with the common failing of all Colonial and Province prisons, made, at the very outset (1785) a most accurate prophecy in a message to the General Court:

> . . . criminals of almost every species, and from every part of the Commonwealth, are adjudicable to hard labour at *Castle Island.* It may be expected, therefore, that in a short time there will be a great number of them sent thither; who being of the most flagitious and abandoned charcters, will attempt any desperate measure to procure their liberty . . . . Would it not be proper, Gentlemen, that the barrack should be palisadoed [fenced in], and in other respects made sufficiently strong to prevent their escape. . . . ?"[168]

Special security measures were taken in response to the Governor's suggestions, but the old problem of escape persisted. In the thirteen years of its existence, the prison was unable to prevent forty-five prisoners from "procuring their liberty" without leave, about sixteen percent of all commitments, including three men serving life sentences.

Judged by modern standards of security, Castle Island proved to be a failure as a state prison. Authorities were convinced, however, that this first venture in confinement at hard labor for relatively long terms was a better method of reclaiming offenders than corporal punishment or confinement in idleness in the local jails. Two Governors gave their endorsements. Governor Samuel Adams in 1794 said:

> This mode of punishment has been found by experience to be of great utility, in the preservation of good order and in the producing of safety in the Commonwealth, and has a manifest tendency to render unnecessary those sanguinary punishments which are too frequently inflicted in other Governments.[169]

Another endorsement came from Governor Increase Sumner in 1799, after the experiment had terminated:

> And here permit me to ask, whether any punishment hitherto devised, for offences not Capital, has been found more effectual for reclaiming Offenders, by its tendency to establish habits of Industry, affording time for reflection, & the apparent dread which that mode of punishment excites in the minds of the more dissolute part of the Community? I believe it will not be doubted, that the Commonwealth, since the institution of that mode of punishment, has been abundantly more free from high-handed Offences, than at any former period.[170]

Strangely enough, we find no mention in the official reports of Massachusetts Governors or legislators of the experiment then going on in the Walnut Street Jail in Philadelphia (which was in its "heyday" from 1790–1799) with its block of cells for the segregation of hardened offenders in solitary confinement where, it has been said, the prison system as we know it today, had its origin. The Boston venture in penology, which preceded the Philadelphia experiment by five years, was the beginning of the Massachusetts prison system.

The third common misconception is that students of modern penology frequently assume that the attempt to reform (or rehabilitate) the criminal in an authoritative setting, such as in a state prison, was an imaginative and unique idea introduced sometime in the twentieth century. This assumption is not borne out by the official reports of Massachusetts prisons.

Three hundred years ago in the prisons of the Massachusetts Bay Colony, the saving of a prisoner's soul was sought through the visitations of the clergy who, on many occasions, endeavored to divert him from his evil course and hoped, through prayer and recitations from the Bible, to set him again on the path of righteousness. In the Province government, too, when prisons were used more extensively, the reclamation of a prisoner was not lost sight of.

How was this ideal of reformation applied behind the merciless walls of the massive stone prison in Charlestown which opened its doors to receive its first prisoners on December 12, 1805? After Castle Island was ceded to the United States, the Commonwealth was determined to build a prison where men could be employed at hard labor and yet held *securely* for the duration of their sentences. The new "penitentiary prison of the Commonwealth" was declared to be "one of the strongest and best built prisons in the world." Its purpose was clear: "*Reformation* as well as punishment of the convict."[171] But the means for achieving this purpose were unknown. As Governor John Brooks commented in 1820, the change from corporal punishment to imprisonment was "a device of modern times . . . the commencement of a great and complicated experiment in jurisprudence and morals."[172] Large congregate prisons were beginning to appear in other states,[173] but there were few precedents and no standards of prison discipline. Overshadowing the experiment was the fear of prison riots and the real possibility of escapes. The first Board of Visitors believed that reformation might be brought about by affording a prisoner ample opportunity for reflection and penitence (an idea promoted by Quakers in Philadelphia, from which the word "penitentiary" was derived) while, at the same time, denying him all the amenities of living and forcing him to submit to a regime that would make him "clay in the hands of the potter." The result was that he lost all self-esteem and ambition and became fired with only one hope—that of a pardon or escape.

Reformation, still the ideal, thus got off to a bad start. It could scarcely be fostered in a prison that was primarily "a place of terror." The rules of the Board laid down in the early years of the prison foreshadowed failure:

a) The prisoner's diet "though wholesome and sufficient to support the calls of nature, [was] to be the coarsest kind," following the precedent of Colonial prisons where "a course diet" was considered part of the punishment. The day's rations provided in the first few years would today be considered a dietician's nightmare:

Sunday. One pound of bread, of the cheapest materials, and one pound of coarse meat, made into broth.

Monday. One pound of bread and one quart of potatoes.

Tuesday. One pint of Indian meal, made into hasty pudding, half a gill of molasses, and a quart of soup made of ox heads and offal.

Wednesday. Same as Monday.

Thursday. One quart of Indian meal, made into hasty pudding.

Friday. Same as Tuesday.

Saturday. Half a pound of bread, four ounces of salt pork, and a quart of pea or bean porridge.[174]

The diet improved as time went on but for many years prisoners were allowed no drinks of any kind (excepting water) or fresh fruit or vegetables or the use of tobacco in any form.

b) Prisoners' clothes "while calculated to keep him warm, ought to be arranged as to be considered as a means of punishment." All clothes worn by prisoners were half red and half blue. After 1812, when it became apparent that the prison had discharged many men unreformed and that "second-comers" and "third-comers" were being admitted with increasing frequency, the rules stated that the former should wear garments colored red and blue with a yellow stripe and that the latter should wear garments of four colors—red, blue, yellow, and black.[175]

c) The usual discipline for infractions of the rules was a whipping or solitary confinement on bread and water. An 1818 law ordered that time spent in solitary confinement was not to count as time served on a man's sentence. Men who attempted to escape were to wear "an iron ring on their left leg, to which a clog, attached, shall be suspended during the continuance at the prison, unless restored to favor by the Board."[176]

Prisoner Burke, in 1813, for plotting to destroy the workshops by fire was chained to a ringbolt for 24 hours and placed in solitary confinement "with the heaviest chain which can be procured."

George Lynds, for attempting to escape was forced to wear "an iron jacket" for eight days, to stand in the aisle of the chapel for two Sundays, sleep in solitary for ninety days, and wear a clog and chain for 82 days.

Taking a clue from the Puritan punishments of humiliation, the Board ordered erected in the prison yard a gallows upon which refractory prisoners could be placed with a rope around their necks for one hour each week for three weeks. They might also be required to wear an iron collar and chain for sixty days and eat by themselves (at that time prisoners ate in a dining hall) and "wear a yellow cap, with ass's ears, for sixty days." Occasionally a prisoner might be made to wear a placard with letters spelling out his offense, as in Puritan days. One prisoner, for example, was required to stand on an elevated platform with "a label on his breast: 'for stabbing two fellow-convicts.' "[177]

d) Hard labor was the prisoner's lot, with no pay for his pains. It was hoped that the prison would be self-supporting through the sale of inmate-made products. There were many years in the nineteenth century when the sale of goods did in fact exceed all costs, showing at times a considerable profit for the state. During this early period, prison industries were varied: stone hammering (with stone supplied from the banks of the Merrimac), shoemaking, weaving, brush making, coopering, cabinetmaking, and the manufacturing of spikes and nails. Women convicts, of whom there were about seventy committed to the prison beginning in 1807, were returned to the jails in 1825 when it became evident that Charlestown was not a proper place for them. They had been employed in spinning, knitting socks, and mending and assisting in making shirts. The old and feeble prisoners were engaged in oakum picking—"the last poor resort when there is nothing better to do."[178]

e) Seven years were automatically added to the sentence of a second offender, according to the 1818 law, while a man returning to prison on a new sentence after having served a second commitment was to serve a life sentence, plunging him into the depths of despair. Before releasing a second offender, the authorities tattoed "Mass. S.P." and the date of discharge, on the inner surface of his upper left arm, for purposes of easy identification on any subsequent arrest or return to prison. This law was repealed after a few years' trial.

The Board stated in unequivocal language the philosophy of "treatment" underlying these early rules:[179]

A prisoner's mind "ought to be reduced to a state of humiliation and discipline."

Communication with each other, "and more especially with the world, ought to be suppressed, except on the most urgent occasions."

"The interference of friends ought not to be allowed."

Only the Bible or "moral books" should be available to the inmate.

"Luxuries of all kinds ought to be withheld."

"Newspapers, songs, or books of diversion ought never to be permitted to enter within the walls . . . the prison should be considered as a world by itself, and its inhabitants know nothing of what is passing without its orbit."

"The smallest deviation from duty [ought to be] punished with severity."

The officers of the prison "should bear in mind that, as a body, the convicts are depraved characters, constantly plotting mischief . . . . They should consider the prison as a volcano, containing lava, which, if not kept in subjection, will destroy friends and foes; and therefore they should ever be on their guard against an eruption."

The end results of this kind of prison discipline were soon apparent—many insurrections, frequent assaults, the forging of deadly weapons in the shops, escapes and many attempts to escape, and a general feeling of hopelessness and degradation. A Senate study commission reported:

> The frequent recommitments and the very few and those doubtful, cases of reformation among the discharged convicts, were discouraged [sic] to the benevolent advocates of a mild system of criminal law. The people were becoming discontented with the taxes levied to support institutions so inefficacious, and little apparently remained to be done but to relinquish the humane experiment and resort to the former punishments of whipping, branding and hanging."[180]

When, in the eleventh year of the "experiment," the 280 inmates "made insurrection in the yard," sixteen managed to get over the walls, although one was fatally injured and all but one were eventually recaptured. A commission appointed by the legislature "to consider at large the subject of the State Prison" and to study "the mode of governing the Penitentiary of Pennsylvania, and others of a similar nature" pondered the question whether the prison should be "*abandoned as useless, or bad in its tendency.*" The Commission recommended the prison not be abandoned "till the system shall have been fairly tried, till experience shall have proved its inefficiency or demonstrated its superiority."[181]

After an investigation by the legislature a few years later, the House concluded that "the charitable attempt to reclaim criminals at the same time that we punish them, ought not lightly to be abandoned, nor hastily to be pronounced ineffectual. . . ."[182] But in 1826, after 21 years of this "great and complicated experiment," Governor Levi Lincoln stated that, although the prison industries were bringing into the state treasury more than the total costs of the institution, *as a penitentiary, the system is utterly ineffectual, to purposes of reform or amendment.*"[183]

There was general agreement as to the cause of failure. "The hopelessness of moral reform" in the opinion of the Governor, arose from "the manner of their confinement, and the consequent opportunities allowed them for association and evil communications with each other."[184] The cure: Rigid enforcement of the rule of silence. As the prison had not been built with a sufficient number of cells for each inmate to live alone, many of them lived together (sometimes as many as sixteen) in large rooms or dormitories—"committee rooms of mischief." The decision was made therefore to build within the walls a new prison (later known as the "North Wing") with a cell for each prisoner, following the plan adopted by the Auburn Prison in New York State.[185] This new addition was finished and occupied on October 3, 1829, thus marking a new milestone in Massachusetts penology. Three hundred and four cells, 7 feet long, 7 feet high but only 3½ feet wide, with doors of wrought iron, poorly ventilated and lighted and sparsely furnished and with no toilet facilities other than a bucket, became the living quarters for the prisoners 17 hours out of each 24. A man was allowed out of his cell only to march to the shops or to chapel or to the kitchen where he picked up his food and returned to eat it alone and in silence. At no time, except in dire need or emergencies, could a prisoner talk with a fellow inmate.[186]

Within a year or two the officers of the prison reported a "highly improved condition . . . it is now made, eminently, what a Penitentiary should become, a place of just yet merciful correction and of the means of moral reform."[187] The secret of success (from the point of view of the administration) was solitude and silence, similar to the Pennsylvania system of prison discipline with the important exception that men worked side by side during the day in congregate shops, thus learning a trade and producing an income for the state:

> The solitary cell alone can withdraw the depraved offender from a hardening correspondence with kindred vice, and, by cutting off the sources of extraneous excitement, leave his mind to the occupation of reflection, to the reprovings of an awakened conscience, and to the successful application of means for his reformation and moral improvement."[188]

It was believed that the prison had "been converted into a School of salutary instruction and reform. . . ."[189] Five or six years after the new system had been put into operation, authorities were convinced they had found the secret of reformation of the criminal. Governor John Davis in 1835 said:

> Experience proves that this solitary life is the most efficient corrective of vice, that has ever been employed in the prison. Nothing subdues the hardened offender like withdrawing the ailment upon which his mind has been nursed—like removing the exciting causes which nourish vice by intercommunicaton—like silencing the merry song—the ribald jest—the narrative of past exploits and the hopes excited by plans of future adventure—like leaving the culprit to himself, to dwell upon his agonizing reflections—to taste the bitterness of remorse, and to feel the sting of his own accusing conscience.[190]

But did this kind of treatment, supplemented by moral instruction, education, and industry, actually effect reformation of the prisoners? No research on this point is available, but Governor George N. Briggs seventeen years after the "new prison" was opened claimed that it did. "Generally, those who leave the prison, leave it with a respect for the laws . . . and with kind feelings toward their officers. They go again into the world, many of them with the purpose and hope, by a correct course of conduct, of restoring themselves to their friends, instead of breathing out threatenings and vengeance against their fellow men."[191] Warden Frederick Robinson reported in 1847, "No death, no escape, no outbreak, no resistence of authority, and but few violations of the regulations . . . order, industry, good and kind feelings, have been the rule. . . ."[192]

Another milestone in prison discipline at Charlestown was reached in 1858. On April 1 of that year, Gideon Haynes, a former state representative, became the fourteenth and most enlightened and progressive warden the prison had had since its opening. He entered upon his duties with no previous experience in prison administration, finding the prison in "a disorganized and confused condition" for it had been served by five wardens in the previous six years. In December of 1856 Deputy Warden Charles W. Walker and Warden Solon H. Tenney had been murdered by inmates and thirteen years previously Warden Charles Lincoln, Jr., had been fatally stabbed by an inmate later declared insane.

Warden Haynes abolished all forms of corporal punishment, used solitary confinement only for the desperate and unmanageable inmate, improved living conditions, and in many other ways placed his emphasis on the reformation of those in his charge. A few of his statements clarify his position on prison discipline:

> The theory that prisons should be places of restraint coupled with deep and intense misery is obsolete.[193]

> [There is not a prisoner,] no matter how low or degraded, how hardened or steeped in crime, who had not a spot in his heart that could be reached with proper management.[194]

> Reformation is the first and most important consideration of the warden . . . the primary object of all imprisonment for crime.[195]

> The prison is *a moral hospital,* the inmates the morally diseased. It is the duty of the prison to cure.[196]

Contrary to the early rule of the prison that officers should consider the prisoners as "depraved characters," Haynes looked upon the officers one hundred years ago as a progressive warden might consider them today:

> Prison officers should be selected with reference to the reformation of the prisoners, and all who have forgotten, or have never heard, that human nature within and without a prison is essentially the same, that reformation is always possible, and that the mercy of God is not suspended by a sentence of the court, should at once be discharged.[197]

A good officer, he said in an earlier report, is one "who is even tempered, firm and straight-forward in his intercourse with them,—who knows something of human nature,—who studies the characters of the different men he has in charge,—who, in short, is a gentleman, and never forgets it." Such an officer "will manage these men without trouble."[198]

Did Haynes' administration succeed? According to his own statements, it did. It was "without doubt the best prison in the world . . . its success exceeds expectations." He believed that eighty percent of the inmates had been "reclaimed," a conclusion based on the decreasing number of recommitments. After fourteen years as Warden, he concluded that the problem of "how the discipline of a prison can be enforced, I think has been satisfactorily solved in Massachusetts."[199] A committee of the Prison Association of New York, after visiting various prisons in the United States and Canada, reported in 1867 that it

> had no hesitation in pronouncing the State Penitentiary at Charlestown the banner prison in the country. In its construction, its ventilation, its staff of officers, its discipline, and all its appointments, it seems to us fairly entitled to this pre-eminence.[200]

Treatment was so mild and "beneficent" that Warden Haynes was told that he was treating prisoners so well that persons would commit crimes in order to be sent there![201]

How much credence can be given to such glowing reports of reformation, in the absence of adequate data, is difficult to determine, especially in view of the fact that about this time many penologists had about concluded that reformation was almost impossible in the prisons of that era.

We cannot review here the uneven course of reformation during the next one hundred years. At times it fell upon wretched and evil days; at other times it seemed to advance with fresh enthusiasm as new inducements to reform were introduced. Our purpose here is simply to show that the *ideal* of reformation was not a product of the "new penology" but was carried on down through the centuries from the time when prisons were designed as "places of terror" for the serious social offender.

Today the goal of returning prisoners to the community as useful citizens is still the obligation of the prison administrator, but the techniques are vastly different. The psychologist, the psychiatrist, the sociologist have penetrated the traditional aloofness of the prison. Religion, large-scale prison industries, academic and vocational education, social work, recreation, health services, supplemented by practical assistance from public-spirited individuals and social agencies, the guidance of parole officers, and the shafts of light from the researcher's desk have combined to meet this obligation. The era of complete silence has long since disappeared; the dignity and rights of the individual are respected.

But the prison as an institution of reform has lately fallen under severe criticism. It has not become, as Warden Haynes hoped it would one hundred years ago, "a moral hospital." Penology is approaching another turning point. We have witnessed in recent years the demand for the development of many substitutes for imprisonment, such as the wider use of probation, a more flexible parole system, more minimum-security institutions, and the placing of the drunkard and the sex deviant in hospitals or clinics, rather than in prisons. We shall see in the next few decades the gradual disuse of the huge, fortresslike structures that now hold securely a heterogeneous group of offenders, many of whom do not need and do not profit by incarceration in a maximum-security institution. In its place will be substituted the "clinical" institutions for the few enemies of society who cannot be otherwise controlled.

In short, today's penologists are again pondering the question, as their predecessors did in 1817, whether the state prison as an instrument of punishment *and* reform should be "*abandoned as useless or bad in its tendency*."

9. "THEY SHALL SURELY BE PUT TO DEATH"

> As I Remember it is noted concerning the blessed Martyr, that if he did hear of any that were condemned or accused on the account of Witchcraft, Murder, Roberries or any other Impiety, He would smite upon his breast and say, *In this breast of mine, is that which would have caused mee, to have been guilty of the same evill, if the Grace of God had not prevented mee.—Rev. Increase Mather, 1674.*[1]

THE Puritans resolved to rule the Bay Colony with a strong hand but with a Christian heart. In their serious deliberations over the perennially controversial question as to what kinds of behavior merited the extreme penalty, no voice was raised suggesting an easy solution, such as the adoption of the criminal code of England which at that time was sending men and youths to the gallows for the stealing of a shilling. The Puritans had early demonstrated an independent spirit in matters of government, as well as a high regard for the sanctity of life. They were destined to establish a code of laws in line with their own ideas of justice and, of course, in accordance with "the word of God."

Their charter had not commanded them to follow English law. It had merely directed their attention to a single restriction, incidentally, that they most liberally interpreted: Enact no laws "contrarie to the Lawes of this our Realme of England."[2]

Although free to choose their own capital laws, these God-fearing people could not in good conscience order the taking of a human life if there were no justification for it in Scripture. Indeed, they would go one step further. In spite of clear Biblical precedent, they would not hang a man if they did not in their own hearts believe he merited that fate.

Hazarding their lives and estates by fleeing from the wrath of English Lords and Bishops into "this vaste wildernes," they saw in their own life experiences many colorful parallels to the vicissitudes of the Israelites who escaped Egyptian bondage by flight, under God's protection, to the land of Canaan. God had given the Hebrews, through Moses, a code of laws that might well serve New England, but no Puritan believed that the entire Mosaic Code should be transposed bodily to the new Canaan. The Puritans were realists, after all. If most of the capital laws of the Hebrews were totally unsuitable as guides of conduct for seventeenth century Englishmen in America, then they could be disregarded.[3] If some of the laws selected from the Bible for inclusion in the Massachusetts code proved to be impracticable, then they need not be enforced to the hilt. They could well remain on the statute books as reminders of the standard of conduct expected of Godly people. The Puritans, it is true, were more literal in their interpretation of the Bible than their Anglican cousins, but in this grave business of taking a human life to balance the scales of justice they would surely temper the word of God with their own homespun code of ethics. No Puritan would deny that:

> The Holy Scriptures of the Old and New Testament [were] . . . written by the prophetts, apostles, and holy men of God, inspired by the Holy Ghost, conteyning in them the infallible and whole will of God, which he purposed to make knoune to mankinde. . . .[4]

Nevertheless, they held strongly to the belief that the rule of reason and the law of nature permitted them to make necessary adaptations on the basis of knowledge gained from new experiences. Governor Winthrop had pointed the way to a liberal interpretation when he said (italics added):

> The Fundamentalls which God gave, to the Comw [Commonwealth] of Israell, were a sufficient Rule to them, to guide all their Affaires: We havinge the same, with all the *Additions, explanations and deductions, which have followed:* it is not possible, we should want a Rule in any Case: if God give wisdome to discerne it.[5]

Parts of the Hebraic code had quite possibly been adapted or at least derived from an earlier Semitic code promulgated by King Hammurabi of the Babylonian and Assyrian Empires. The King also had received his code, too, directly from God; not the Jahweh of the Hebrews but Shamash, the sun God, some 2270 years before Christ and about 700 years before Moses.[6]

Scholars are divided as to the extent that the earlier code influenced the later. There is no evidence that the Hebraic code in any single instance borrowed directly from the Babylonian, yet there are a number of almost exact parallels and many laws in both that show an identity of principle, such as the laws dealing with witchcraft, false testimony in capital cases, man-stealing, highway robbery, rape, and adultery. The "eye for an eye and tooth for a tooth" doctrine also appears in both codes. Speculation as to a likely relationship between these two ancient bodies of law did not, of course, disturb Puritan thinking, for this oldest code of civil and criminal law known to man was not discovered by later civilizations until 1901–1902. Puritan faith was wedded to the thirty-nine books of the Old Testament and to the twenty-seven books of the New.[7]

When the Rev. Nathaniel Ward, who, more than anyone else, was responsible for the final draft of the Body of Liberties, selected twelve capital laws for inclusion in that historic document, he took them directly from the books of Exodus, Leviticus, Numbers, and Deuteronomy. He placed after each law (except the twelfth) a Biblical annotation showing its specific derivation from "the word of God." In some he made slight changes for better adaptation to the new government or to allow for certain common-law principles, but throughout he retained the basic thought of the Hebrews. The result of the acceptance of this code by the Colony in 1641 was that a citizen of Boston was, at least in theory and in respect to these twelve laws, under the same peril of death at the hands of the government as a citizen of Israel had been some thirty-two centuries earlier in a land some five thousand miles away.

Ward's selection would not have pleased those Londoners who feared the Colonists' growing independence, but the approval of the Londoners was not asked for. Not more than half of the capital crimes in Ward's list would have merited the death penalty in England, where the hangman plied a busy trade, while most of the capital crimes drawn from the Common Law, or decreed by Parliament, such as burglary, robbery, larceny, and many other crimes against the person and against property did not appear at all as death-penalty crimes in this early Massachusetts code. Nor was his choice wholly satisfactory to the Colonists themselves. But it was a bold beginning, quite independent of the royal seal and with no limitation on the number of additional penalties that might later be enacted.

The crimes for which a person "shall be put to death," or, to use the Biblical expression found in four of the Colonial laws, "shall surely be put to death," are here reproduced with their most relevant Scriptural counterparts in a parallel column. The laws quoted are taken from the 1672 compilation of the Bay Colony Laws, the italicized words indicating departures from the original as printed in the Body of Liberties.

1. *Idolatry*

Colonial Law: If any man after Legal Conviction shall HAVE or WORSHIP any other God but the LORD God, he shall be put to death, Exod. 22:20; Deut. 13:6,10; Deut. 17:2,6.

Biblical Counterpart: He that sacrificeth unto any God, save unto the Lord only, he shall be utterly destroyed—Exod. 22:20. Thou shalt have no other gods before me. Thou shalt not make unto thee any graven image, or any likeness of any thing that is in heaven above, or that is in the earth beneath, or that is in the water under the earth. Thou shalt not bow down thyself to them, nor serve them: for I the Lord thy God am a jealous God. . . .—(Exod. 20:3–5).

Idolatry was a real temptation for some of the tribes of Israel, surrounded as they were by worshippers of other faiths who might easily induce them to bow down to "graven images" or pagan gods. It was believed necessary at that time, in order to build a unified religion under their own God, Jahweh, to warn those who strayed from the Hebrew faith by prescribing the penalty of death. *But it was not an issue in New England.* No prosecutions for the violation of this law appear in the court records. (Those who denied God altogether were prosecuted under another law—that of Blasphemy.) We can imagine the difficulty in any court of law to prove that an offender who worshipped God did not worship "*the* Lord God." The only unhappy violators against whom a verdict might have been obtained were the Indians who, as judged by Puritan standards, worshipped a pagan God or gods.[8] But none was ever hanged on this account. The General Court did its best to put a stop to Indian "powwows" within the Bay Colony but always showed a tolerant attitude toward those natives who were slow to accept the white man's God. A few years after this law first appeared, the General Court ordered a mere fine as a penalty for any Indians who shall "at any time pawwaw, [spelled also powwow and powaw] or performe outward worship to their false gods, or to the devill. . . ."[9] Indeed, as we have seen, the Puritans on so many occasions declared that one of the chief purposes of the Plantation in New England was to convert the savages to Christianity, not to kill them for their ignorance. The Rev. John Eliot, ordained as a teacher in the church of Roxbury in 1632, studied the Indian language and in 1646 set out to reveal to the natives the gospel of God in Christ Jesus, devoting his whole life from that date on to serving their spiritual needs.[10] His group of "praying Indians" at Natick, his conversion of many of the "pagans" to orthodox Protestantism, and his heroic achievement in translating the entire Bible into the Indian tongue testified to his devotion to this ideal. But he was dedicating his life to saving them from eternal damnation—not from the hangman's noose.

2. *Witchcraft*

Colonial Law: If any Man or Woman be a WITCH, that is, Hath or Consulteth with a familiar Spirit they shall be put to death, Exod. 22:18; Levit. 20:27; Deut. 18:10,11.

Biblical Counterpart: Thou shalt not suffer a witch to live—Exod. 22:18. A man also or woman that hath a familiar spirit, or that is a wizard, shall surely be put to death: they shall stone them with stones: their blood shall be upon them—Levit. 20:27. There shall not be found among you any one that maketh his son or his daughter to pass through the fire, or that useth divination, or an observer of times, or an enchanter, or a witch, or a charmer, or a consulter with familiar spirits, or a wizard, or a necromancer—Deut. 18:10,11.

Witchcraft by its very nature implied a denial of God and an allegiance with the Devil. It was punishable by death under both the code of Hammurabi and that of Moses.[11] It was also a crime calling for hanging or burning in England and in most European countries in the first half of the seventeenth century.

3. *Blasphemy*

Colonial Law: If any Person *within this Jurisdiction, whether Christian or Pagan,* shall *wittingly and willingly presume to* BLASPHEME the *holy* name of God, FATHER, SON, or HOLY-GHOST, with direct, expresse, presumptuous, or high-handed Blasphemy, *either by wilfull or obstinate denying the true God, or his Creation, or Government of the World,* or shall curse God in like manner, *or reproach the holy Religion of God, as if it were but a politick devise; to keep ignorant men in awe; or shall utter any other kind of Blasphemy of the like nature and degree,* they shall be put to death, Levit. 24:15, 16.

Biblical Counterpart: And thou shalt speak unto the children of Israel, saying, Whosoever curseth his God shall bear his sin. And he that blasphemeth the name of the LORD, he shall surely be put to death, and all the congregation shall certainly stone him: as well the stranger, as he that is born in the land, when he blasphemeth the name of the Lord, shall be put to death—Levit. 24:15,16.

The simple statement of this law as it first appeared in the Body of Liberties went through several alterations. It was later decided that no one should be punished for blasphemy who did not "wittingly and willingly" blaspheme, and these words were added. In 1646 the lawmakers added the phrase "whether Christian or pagan" to make it definitely apply to the Indians, in case there had been any doubt on that point. Although the Puritans were reluctant to punish anyone for this crime who had not had the advantages of a Christian upbringing, nevertheless they were equally reluctant to place the entire Colony in jeopardy of God's wrath. The General Court thus justified the inclusion of Indians within the scope of this capital law, although its records reveal no case where an Indian was hanged or even indicted for this crime. Its ingenious "justification" no doubt gave the Court some reassurance that God would understand:

> Albeit faith be not wrought by the sword, but by the word, & therefore such pagan Indians as have submited themselves to our government, though we would not neglect any due helps to bring them on to grace, & to the meanes of it, yet we compell them not to the Christian faith, nor to the profession of it, either by force of armes or by poenall laws; nevertheles, seing the blaspheming of the true God cannot be excused by any ignorance or infirmity of humane nature, the eternall power & Godhead being knowne by the light of nature & the creation of the world, & common reason requireth every state & society of men to be more carefull of preventing the dishonour & contempt of the most high God (in whom we all consist) than of any mortall princes & magistrates, it is therefore ordered & decreed, by this Courte, for the honor of the eternall God, whom onely we worship & serve, that no person within this jurisdiction, whether Christian or pagan, etc.[12]

The second change (enacted at the same time and incorporated in all subsequently enacted codes) was aimed directly at atheists or possibly the "liberals" of that day who maintained that religion was "but a politick device, to keep ignorant men in awe," a phrase that brings to mind Karl Marx's famous characterization of religion two centuries later, as "the opium of the people."

This Puritan tradition still survives in Boston. No citizen of Massachusetts today can willfully and maliciously deny God's "final judging of the world" or ridicule "the holy word of God contained in the holy scriptures" without risking a sentence to a jail or house of correction for a maximum period of one year.[13]

4. *Murder*

Colonial Law: If any person shall commit any wilfull MURTHER upon premeditate malice, hatred or cruelty, not in a mans necessary and just defence, nor by meer casualty against his will, he shall be put to death, Exod. 21:12,13; Numb. 35:31.

Biblical Counterpart: He that smiteth a man, so that he die, shall be surely put to death—Exod. 21: 12. Moreover ye shall take no satisfaction for the life of a murderer, which is guilty of death: but he shall be surely put to death—Numb. 35:31. Whoso sheddeth man's blood, by man shall his blood be shed: for in the image of God made he man—Gen. 9:16. Thou shalt not kill—Exod. 20:13.

Murder is a crime punishable by death in all ancient and most modern law codes. The distinction between a homicide in which the perpetrator might be blamed for his act, and thus "deserve" to die, and one in which he might be held blameless was not made clear in the particular annotations chosen by Ward who therefore borrowed from the Common Law of England the elements of premeditation, malice, cruelty, self defense, and accidental homicide. Jewish law had not neglected these elements (as we shall see when discussing manslaughter) but the Scripture cited by Ward or the blunt words of the Ten Commandments left the whole subject of homicide in some confusion—a confusion that the Common Law sought to resolve. Elsewhere in the Book of Exodus (22:2) the idea of justifiable homicide was recognized: "If a thief be found breaking up [a home], and be smitten that he die, there shall no blood be shed for him." The General Court, following this authority, decreed in 1647:

> If any person, in the just and necessary defence of his life or goods, or the life of any other, shall kill any person attempting to rob or murther in the field or high way, or to breake into any dwelling house, if he conceive he cannot, with safety of his owne person, otherwise take the felon or assaylant, or bring him to triall, he shalbe holden blameles, Exod. 22:2.[14]

5. *Manslaughter*

Colonial Law: If any person slayeth another suddenly, in his ANGER or CRUELTY of passion, he shall be put to death, Levit. 24:17; Numb. 35: 20,21.

Biblical Counterpart: And he that killeth any man shall surely be put to death—Levit. 24:17. But if he thrust him of hatred, or hurl at him by laying of wait, that he die; Or in enmity smite him with his hand, that he die: he that smote him shall surely be put to death; for he is a murderer: the revenger of blood shall slay the murderer, when he meeteth him—Numb. 35: 20,21. See also Numb. 35:22–25.

Jewish law used the term "manslayer" but not the substantive legal term "manslaughter." Nevertheless, it permitted a "manslayer" who slew without enmity, hatred, or design to flee to a designated "city of refuge" where "the revenger of blood" could no longer pursue him and where he had a chance, at least, of survival. A hypothetical case of manslaughter where the killer "was not worthy of death" was described in the Book of Deuteronomy (19: 4–6). A woodsman had killed his neighbor when, in the act of hewing wood, the axhead accidentally slipped from the handle and struck his friend a mortal blow. The New England lawmakers likewise would not have considered that act a homicide "worthy of death"; nor would have the administrators of the Hammurabic code which provided that an unintentional killing in a quarrel called for a fine, not death, if it were "without malice."[15] The Colonial law of manslaughter that warranted a hanging, however, involved the elements of "anger or cruelty of passion." Today such a homicide would more likely be considered manslaughter (punishable by no more than imprisonment for twenty years) and yet a *cruel* homicide, even without premeditation, may call for the death penalty, for the law of Massachusetts still carries this tradition and states that murder "committed with extreme atrocity or cruelty" is murder in the first degree.[16]

6. *Poisoning*

Colonial Law: If any person shall slay another through guile, either by POYSONING or other such Devilish practise, he shall be put to death, Exod. 21:14.[17]

Biblical Counterpart: But if a man come presumptuously upon his neighbour, to slay him with guile; thou shalt take him from mine altar, that he may die—Exod. 21:14.

7. *Bestiality*

Colonial Law: If any Man or Woman shall LYE with any BEAST or Bruit Creature, by carnal Copulation, they shall surely be put to death, and the Beast shall

Biblical Counterpart: And if a man lie with a beast, he shall surely be put to death: and ye shall slay the beast. And if a woman approach unto any beast, and lie

be slain and buried, and not eaten, Levit. 20:15,16.

down thereto, thou shalt kill the woman, and the beast: they shall surely be put to death; their blood shall be upon them—Levit. 20: 15,16.

8. *Sodomy*

Colonial Law: If any Man LYETH with MANKINDE as he lyeth with a Woman, both of them have committed Abomination, they both shall surely be put to death, *unless the one party were forced, or be under fourteen years of age, in which case he shall be severely punished,* Levit. 20:13.[18]

Biblical Counterpart: If a man also lie with mankind, as he lieth with a woman, both of them have committed an abomination: they shall surely be put to death; their blood shall be upon them—Levit. 20:13.

9. *Adultery*

Colonial Law: If any Person COMMIT ADULTERY with a Married or Espoused Wife, the Adulterer and Adulteress shall surely be put to death, Levit. 20:19; 18:20; Deut. 22:23,27.

Biblical Counterpart: And the man that committeth adultery with another man's wife, even he that committeth adultery with his neighbour's wife, the adulterer and the adulteress shall surely be put to death—Levit. 20:10. Moreover thou shalt not lie carnally with thy neighbour's wife, to defile thyself with her—Levit. 18:20. If a man be found lying with a woman married to an husband, then they shall both of them die, both the man that lay with the woman, and the woman: so shalt thou put away evil from Israel—Deut. 22:22. Thou Shalt not commit adultery—Exod. 20: 14. [See also Deut. 22:23–30.]

The Hammurabic code stated that "if a man's wife be caught lying with another man, both shall be bound and thrown into the water, unless the husband of that woman desire to pardon his wife, or the king his servant."[19] It is interesting to note that in the Hammurabic code an unmarried woman, and in the Hebrew code an unmarried woman or woman not betrothed, were not punishable for adultery with a married man. The Colonial law preserved this distinction, which has been carried down into the laws of the Commonwealth of Massachusetts.[20]

In Puritan eyes, adultery struck at the foundations of family life and deserved severe punishment, yet it was not a capital offense in England prior to 1650, although many attempts had been made there to make it so.[21] Ten years before the Body of Liberties was drawn, a decision as to the proper punishment for this crime was forced upon the Court of Assistants by one John Dawe, the Court stating in that case:

> John Dawe shalbe severely whipped for intiseing an Indian woman to lye with him. Upon this occation it is propounded wither [whether] adultery, either with English or Indian, shall not be punished with death. Referred to the nexte Court to be considered of.[22]

As no law on adultery had yet been enacted or published (for the government had been in existence for only one year), the next Court of Assistants decided that it could not take Dawe's life, but ordered for the future: "If any man shall have carnall copulation with another mans wife, they both shalbe punished by death."[23]

Another flagrant case of adultery soon challenged the courts. John Hathaway, Robert Allen, and Margaret, wife of Edward Seale, confessed to this crime and were found guilty by a Quarter Court in Boston in 1637.[24] Under a more rigid Governor these three might have met their fate at the end of a rope, but Winthrop, evidently sensitive to a healthy popular aversion to hanging adulterers, consulted the elders who assured him that if the law had been sufficiently published "they ought to be put to death." The Court conceded some doubt on that point, for the law was originally made by the Court of Assistants "by *allowance* of the General Court." It decided, therefore, that some other punishment would be "safest." Accordingly, the Court ordered these three offenders to be "severely whiped, & banished, never to returne againe, upon paine of deathe," and for the future, in cases of this kind, the General Court, confirming the order of the Court of Assistants, declared "that whosoever lyeth with another mans wife, both shalbe punished by death; & this is to bee promulgated," and two years later, lest there be any misunderstanding, the General Court reaffirmed its order, stating that it is "to stand in force."[25]

10. *Man-stealing*

Colonial Law: If any man STEALETH A MAN or Man-Kinde, he shall surely be put to death, Exod. 21:16.

Biblical Counterpart: And he that stealeth a man, and selleth him, or if he be found in his hand, he shall surely be put to death—Exod. 21: 16. [See also Deut. 24:7.]

Stealing a child for ransom is a modern crime known as "kidnapping"—a slang term for "man-stealing."[26] Jewish law was designed to prevent the stealing of a slave or servant for the purpose of making "merchandise of him."[27] As it turned out, there was little need for this law in the Bay Colony.

11. *False Witness in Capital Cases*

Colonial Law: If any Man rise up by FALSE-WITNESSE wittingly, and of purpose to take away a mans Life, he shall be put to death, Deut. 19:16; 18:16.

Biblical Counterpart: If a false witness rise up against any man to testify against him that which is wrong; Then both men, between whom the controversy is, shall stand before the LORD, before the priests and the judges, which shall be in those days; And the judges shall make diligent inquisition: and, behold, if the witness be a false witness, and hath testified against his brother; Then shall ye do unto him, as he had thought to have done unto his brother . . .—Deut. 19:16–19.

If one gives false testimony intentionally in a capital case whereby a jury is impelled to bring in a verdict of guilty, one has committed a crime that might be considered a subtle form of murder. Even in the Hammurabic code, "if that case be a capital suit, that man shall be put to death."[28] This crime is still considered one of our most serious, though infrequent, offenses.[29]

12. *Conspiracy and Rebellion*

Colonial Law: If any man CONSPIRE and ATTEMPT any INVASION, INSURRECTION or

Biblical Counterpart: [In the Book of Numbers the author recites the story of the rebels led by Korah,

publick REBELLION against our Commonwealth: or shall endeavour to surprise any Town or Towns, Fort or Forts therein; or shall Treacherously and perfideously attempt the Alteration and Subversion of our frame of Polity or Government fundamentally, he shall be put to death, Numb. 16; 2 Sam. 3; 2 Sam. 18; 2 Sam. 20. [In the Body of Liberties there were no Biblical annotations to this law, but they were added in subsequent compilations.]

who] gathered themselves together against Moses and against Aaron. . . . And it came to pass that the ground clave asunder that was under them; And the earth opened her mouth, and swallowed them up, and their houses, and all the men that appertained unto Korah, and all their goods. They, and all that appertained to them, went down alive into the pit, and the earth closed upon them: and they perished from among the congregation—Numb. 16:31–33.

In 1682 a change was made in this law by replacing the phrase "against the commonwealth" by the phrase "against the kings majesty," for King Charles the Second had objected to the Colonial use of the word "commonwealth" wherever it appeared, possibly because of its connotation of independence or because it was a reminder of the Commonwealth period (1649–1660) of Oliver Cromwell's rule in England.[30]

Thus the Bay State authorities securely anchored their first twelve capital laws in "the word of God," giving a warning to all who lived within its jurisdiction that defiance of the new Hebraic-Puritan code of social behavior would be severely dealt with. Lest any child might be brought up in ignorance of these laws, the General Court in 1642 ordered the Selectmen of each town to see that none of the heads of families

> suffer so much Barbarism in any of their families, as not to endeavour to teach, by themselves or others, their Children and Apprentices, so much learning, as many enable them perfectly to read the English tongue, and knowledge of the Capital Lawes. . . .[31]

13. *Rape*

As time went on after the acceptance of the Body of Liberties with its twelve capital laws, the range of offenses "meriting" death proved to be too limited. The crime of rape, for example, Ward had omitted from the capital list, presumably because there was no warrant for it in Scripture.[32] And yet all who had come over from

England knew it was a capital crime there and an offense particularly revolting to Godly people.

"As people increased, so sin abounded, and especially the sin of uncleanness, and still the providence of God found them out. . . ."[33] Governor Winthrop penned these lines at the conclusion of the notorious Fairfield case that shocked the good people of Boston into a decision. "This year," he wrote in his Diary in 1641, "there was discovered a very foul sin."[34] Daniel Fairfield, "an half Dutchman," about forty years old, lived with his wife, a "lusty young woman," near the Salem farm of John Humfrey, one of the Magistrates. Humfrey "much neglected" three of his daughters, all under the age of ten, entrusting their care to "a company of rude servants." Over a period of two years, Fairfield visited the Humfrey farm and carried on sexual "dalliance" with these young girls. During part of this period he was joined by two male servants. The girls proved to be willing participants in sex play; indeed the eldest (who was nine years old at the time of discovery), the Governor tells us, had "grown capable of man's fellowship, and took pleasure in it." Magistrate Humfrey, evidently unaware of what was going on, left the Colony for England in 1641. The eldest of these three girls confessed to an older sister who brought her before the Governor to whom she related the whole sordid episode.

From the citizenry of Salem and Boston came angry murmurings that the gallows alone could be sufficient atonement for this crime. The simple contrition and repentance of the offenders was not enough. With great patience and honesty the authorities launched a thorough investigation of both the facts and the law, concluding that, as the girl was not "of the age of understanding," her consent was immaterial. If the crime were rape—and there was some doubt even as to this fact—the offenders must be punished, but the Colony could not send anyone to his death if it had not published a law to this effect, unless there could be found in the "word of God" some justification for a hanging. Governor Bellingham consulted "all the elders of the country, both our own, and Plimouth, and Connecticut, New Haven, etc. They took it into consideration divers months, and at last returned different answers." Most of them agreed that it was indeed rape but that there was no express law in the Bible authorizing a death sentence. Some argued that such a "presumptuous sin" (citing Deut. 17:12) warranted death, but the General Court "after much dispute" concluded, with many dissenting, that they could not demand the lives of the offenders but they could at least punish them severely.

The Court thereupon sentenced Fairfield, the prime target of outraged feelings, to some of the most severe penalties short of death that it ever meted out to any offender (with the possible exception of penalties inflicted on some of the Quakers) in the whole history of the Bay Colony. He was to be

> severely whipped at Boston and at Salem, and confined to Boston neck, upon pain of death, if he went out, etc., he should have one nostril slit and seared at Boston, and the other at Salem, and to wear an halter about his neck visibly all his life, or to be whipped every time he were seen abroad without it, and to die, if he attempted the like upon any person, and 40 pounds to Mr. Humfrey.[35]

The Court let the other two defendants off with fines and double whippings (one in Boston, one in Salem) and required one of them to wear a halter during the pleasure of the Court and to be confined to Lynn. "The parties received their punishments very patiently, without any striving or complaining, (though they had near 40 stripes), and acknowledged their sins to be greater than their punishment, etc."[36] The Court, two years later, modified its restrictions on Fairfield's mobility, permitting him to work in any part of "Boston lymits" and "also at Roxberry," so long as he did not go "above five miles from Boston meeting house."[37]

In 1652 the General Court granted the petition of Fairfield's wife that her husband be permitted to take off the rope he had been required to wear about his neck for ten years![38] However, there was little chance for the disfigured Fairfield to live down his disgrace. Twice he petitioned for leave to get away from the Colony altogether and in 1656 he was granted liberty "to goe in one of theise shipps to England as he desiers; provided, if he ever come againe, he shall forthwith retourne to the same condition as now he is in, & be forthwith committed to prison."[39]

Immediately after sentencing Fairfield, the General Court enacted laws providing death for rape of a child under ten years of age, "whether it were with or without the girles consent," and for rape of "any mayde or woman that is lawfully married or contracted."[40] For some reason, possibly because there was still some hesitancy about the lack of warrant for it in "the word of

God," neither of these laws was incorporated in the compiled laws of 1648 or 1660, and thus after 1648 they ceased to be operative.

The Court also enacted a law making rape of "any mayde or single woman" above the age of ten punishable by death or, in the discretion of the Court, by some "other greivous punishment."[41] This law was incorporated in all subsequent codes.[42] Although not in conformity with the Mosaic law, it did provide a way out through an alternative punishment.

After 1648 the law remained in an unsettled state, as to the crime of rape of a child under ten. In 1654 the General Court of Elections, acknowledging the need for

> more full provission . . . by lawe . . . then is already [provided] for the suppressing the most odious & abominable sinne of blasphemy, as also the uncleane and wicked practizes of abusing young girles under tenn years of age, and forcing or ravishing of damosells above that age,

appointed Massachusetts' *first* legislative committee to study sex offenses, by ordering that

> Mr. Nowell [Secretary of the General Court], Captain Atherton, Captain Thomas Clarke, Captain Eliazer Lusher, and Mr. Edward Jackson, be a committee to advise with some of the reverend elders . . . to prepare, drawe up, and present to the next Gennerall Court what they judge meete to be passed as lawes for the reformation of the evills above said.[43]

There is nothing in the record to indicate that any new laws were enacted as a result of the study by this recess committee of the legislature.

It took another shocking case to jar the General Court into action and to overcome its apparent reluctance to make capital a crime that had not been a capital offense in Israel. Following the severe penalties suffered by Fairfield in 1641, there was no similar case reported to the Court of Assistants until 1669—long after he had returned to England and his case had grown dim in the memory of Bostonians. Patrick Jeanison was charged with rape of an eight-year-old child.[44] "For want of law," the Magistrates referred the case to the General Court, stating that it "seemeth not to be a lesse offence with one of 8 yeares then with one above tenne yeares, which the lawe provides for," and yet there was still no positive law to cover such a case. The matter, therefore, had to be referred to the General Court. The Deputies thought some "grevious punishment" would suffice, but the General Court ordered *death* for this crime: "Forasmuch as carnall copulation with a woman child under the age of tenn yeares is a more heynous sin then with one of more yeares, as being more inhumaine & unnaturall in itself, & more perrillous to the life & well being of the child. . . ."[45]

14. *Cursing or Smiting Parents*

Colonial Law: If any Childe or Children above Sixteen years old, and of sufficient understanding, shall CURSE or SMITE their natural FATHER or MOTHER, he or they shall be put to death, unless it can be sufficiently testified, that the Parents have been very unchristianly negligent in the education of such Children, or so provoked them by extreme and cruel Correction, that they have been forced thereunto to preserve themselves from Death or Maiming, Exod. 21:17; Levit. 20:9; Exod. 21: 15 (1646).[46]

Biblical Counterpart: And he that curseth his father, or his mother, shall surely be put to death—Exod. 21:17. For every one that curseth his father or his mother shall be surely put to death: he hath cursed his father or his mother; his blood shall be upon him—Lev. 20:9. And he that smiteth his father, or his mother, shall be surely put to death—Exod. 21:15.

The English modification of the unequivocal statement of the Hebrew law made the penalty applicable only to a child over the age of sixteen and allowed the child certain reasonable defenses.

15. *Stubborn or rebellious sons*

Colonial Law: If a Man have a STUBBORN or REBELLIOUS SON of sufficient years of understanding (viz.) sixteen years of age, which will not obey the voice of his Father, or the voice of his Mother, and that when they had chastened him, will not hearken unto them, then shall his Father and Mother, being his natural

Biblical Counterpart: If a man have a stubborn and rebellious son, which will not obey the voice of his father, or the voice of his mother, and that, when they have chastened him, will not hearken unto them: Then shall his father and his mother lay hold on him, and bring him out unto the elders of his city, and unto the gate of his

Parents lay hold on him, and bring him to the Magistrates assembled in Court, and testifie unto them, that their Son is stubborn and rebellious, and will not obey their voice and chastisement, but lives in sundry and notorious Crimes: such a son shall be put to death, Deut. 22:20,21.[47]

place; And they shall say unto the elders of his city, This our son is stubborn and rebellious, he will not obey our voice; he is a glutton, and a drunkard. And all the men of his city shall stone him with stones, that he shall die: so shalt thou put evil away from among you; and all Israel shall hear, and fear—Deut. 21:18,19,20,21. [This reference was probably the one intended.]

This law followed closely the Hebrew version, although it likewise was not applicable to a child under sixteen. As in Hebrew law, a conviction required the testimony of both parents. The General Court repealed this law in 1681,[48] although Massachusetts has to this day retained a "stubborn-child" law.[49]

16. *Burglary*

In the early days of the Bay Colony, burglary was not a crime that called for much attention, but as men of all classes poured out of England in "the great migration," many of them with no thought of following the Bible "in its puritie," this crime increased and soon took its place in the list of serious crimes with which crowded and prosperous towns are usually afflicted.

In 1644, when the law simply provided that burglary should be "severely punished," leaving the manner of punishment to the judges' discretion,[50] the towns of Cambridge and Boston were buzzing with a story that a break into two dwellings in the nighttime and a theft of fifteen pounds in currency had been solved by the arrest of two most unusual burglars. Not only were the culprits students at Harvard College, but both were sons of ministers. One was James Ward, son of Nathaniel Ward of Ipswich who had written into the Body of Liberties twelve capital laws. Ward, Senior, had providentially omitted burglary, presumably because it was not a capital law in Israel, although it was in England at that time. The other offender was Thomas Welde, son of the Rev. Thomas Welde of Roxbury, a prominent elder and an overseer of the College.[51] Winthrop tells this story:

"being found out, they were ordered by the governours of the college to be there whipped, which was performed by the president himself [Rev. Henry Dunster]—yet they were about 20 years of age; and after they were brought into court and ordered to two fold satisfaction, or to serve so long for it. . . .[52]

By 1647 the General Court decided it was time to provide specific penalties for burglary of a dwelling house. It was ordered that for a first offense the letter B would be branded on the culprit's forehead; for the second offense he would be severely whipped in addition to a branding, but on the third offense the government would declare him "incorrigible" and sentence him to *death*. If any man was so bold as to commit this crime on the Lord's Day, taking mean advantage of those who were required to go to meeting, he would pay more dearly for it: for the first offense, branding and the loss of an ear; second offense, branding and the loss of the other ear; third offense, *death*.[53]

Many years later (1672) similar penalties were ordered for breaking into any "ware house, shop, mill, malt house, barne, or out house, etc., any vessell on any shoare, or in any cove, creeke, or upon the water. . . ."[54]

17. *Robbery*

The crime of robbery of "any person in the field or highwayes" was punishable by the same law and in like manner as that which provided for the crime of burglary of a dwelling house.[55]

18. *Defiance by Jesuits*

Any Jesuit, or official representative of the Pope or See of Rome, who was banished from the Colony and then returned in defiance of the order of banishment fell under the threat of *death*. Actually, few Jesuits entered the Colony. This law was largely a reflection of hostility toward anyone or anything affiliated with the Roman Catholic Church.[56]

19. *Heresy*

Although at the outset heresy was never considered so serious an offense as blasphemy, it was nevertheless a "hainous crime," for it tended to "the overthrow of all true Religion, and Salvation."[57] Just what was heretical and what was not frequently admitted of diverse interpretations, even among the elders. It was decided in 1646 to spell out the heresies that would be specifically forbidden, such as the denial of immortality, of resurrection, of redemption, and others of a more subtle nature.[58] But at this time the usual penalty was a mere fine, although notorious heretics could be banished under a general right reserved by the government to banish whomever they wished and for whatever reason they thought meet. In 1648 a few more heresies were included in the list, such as the opposing of infant baptism (as the Anabaptists had done) or denying that the Magistrates had any authority to enforce the first four of the Ten Commandments and asserting that this should be left to church discipline (one of the heresies of Roger Williams some years earlier). One who persisted, after having ample opportunity to recant, was definitely a candidate for banishment.[59]

But these laws did not put an end to public expression of heretical views. By 1652 it was believed that the law needed further amplification and strengthening to curb those who were over the age of sixteen (thus presumably having sufficient understanding to know better) and who professed the Christian religion and yet dared deny, either by word or writing, that any of the books of the Bible were the "written and infallible word of God." Each of the sixty-six books of the Bible was named in the law, and one who "wittingly and willingly" made this denial was to be fined or whipped. However, *death* or banishment (as the Court shall judge) awaited an offender who "after his recantation, sentence, or execution [of the sentence] shall the second time publish, and obstinately and pertinaciously maintaine the said wicked opinion. . . ."[60]

20. *Arson*

"The dainger of such a wicked enterprise [as arson], especially in townes where the howses are neere adjoyning" was fully realized, and yet, strangely enough, up until 1652 no specific punishment for arsonists was decreed. However, in that year a law was enacted punishing by a whipping and the necessity of paying double indemnification anyone over the age of sixteen who wittingly and willingly set on fire a barn, stable, or mill. But, if such a person in like manner set on fire a dwelling house, meetinghouse, or storehouse (or any other object that caused these buildings to burn), he was to be, on due conviction, "put to *death,* and to forfeite so much of his lands, goods, or chattels as shall make full satisfaction to the party or parties damnified. . . ."[61]

21. *Defiance by Quakers*

On the law books for a number of years (1658–1681) was a law designed to force Quakers to stay out of the jurisdiction, placing their lives in peril if they dared defy an official order of banishment—as some of them did. (See Chapter 10.)

22. *Soldiers in Military Camps*

In 1675, when the Colony was in a state of war [King Philip's War], an English soldier was made subject to the *death* penalty under special "Lawes and Ordinances of warr" for striking an officer, departing from his charge without license, drawing his sword against his officer, resisting an officer, uttering words of sedition or mutiny, or committing "Rapes, Ravishments or Unnatural Abuses or Adultery," or murder, or selling, spoiling, or carrying away ammunition.[62]

23. *Piracy and Mutiny*

Although there were scattered instances of piracy all through the seventeenth century, it seemed to become an acute problem only in the later years of the Colony. In 1673 the General Court decided it must put a stop to "the wicked and unrighteous practises of evill men . . . piractically seizing of shipps, ketches, etc." It ordered that anyone who "shall piractically or Feloniously seize any ship or other vessell, whither in the harbour or on the seas, or shall rise up in rebellion against the master, officers, merchant, or owners of any such ship . . . shall be put to *death.*"[63]

24. *Treason against the King*

Following some correspondence with King Charles the Second shortly after the rumor in London in 1678 that Catholics plotted to kill the King and seize the government—known as the

"Popish Plot"—the General Court made treason against the King punishable by *death* for any one who upon due conviction "on the Oathes of two lawfull and credible witnesses"

> shall compasse, imagine, or intend the death or destruction of our soveraigne lord, the king, (whom Almighty God preserve with a long and prosperous reigne) or to deprive or depose him from the style, honour, or kingly name of the imperiall crowne of England, or of any other his majesties dominions. . . .[64]

25. *Military Service with Certain Foreign States*

The last capital law of the Bay Colony was enacted in 1684 when conditions both locally and abroad were very unsettled. The Charter was about to be revoked, and the Catholic King James was destined to ascend the throne the following year on the death of King Charles the Second. This law decreed *death* for anyone in the Bay Colony who served in the armies of foreign countries against any of the King's allies.[65]

Thus the Bay Colony enacted twenty-five capital laws in the years 1630 to 1684. Twenty-one of these laws prescribed no penalty but death. Two made the penalty death only on second or third conviction, while two others prescribed death only as an alternative sentence. In attempting to curb five of the listed crimes (burglary, robbery, heresy, arson, and those relating to Quakers), the General Court did not write "death" into the law until milder penalties had proved ineffective.

Governor Winthrop had consistently adhered to the theory that a judge should be free to censure an offender by a penalty somewhat less severe than that prescribed by law if circumstances warranted the exercise of that discretion. If all penalties were fixed in advance, he argued, there would be little need for learned or merciful judges:

> Judges are Gods upon earthe: therefore, in their Administrations, they are to holde forthe the wisdome & mercye of God, (which are his Attributes) as well as his Justice: as occasion shall require. . . .
>
> . . . if Judges be tyed to a prescript punishment, & no libertye lefte for dispensation or mitigation in any case, heer is no place lefte for wisdome or mercye: whereas Solomon saythe Prov: 20:28: mercye & truth preserve the Kinge; & his throne is upholden by mercye. . . .

A judge therefore could quite properly and invariably did take into consideration "the qualitye of the person" appearing before him for sentence and his "evident repentance." Winthrop had found support for this viewpoint in Hebrew law and had marshalled his evidence well to support it:

> Adultery & incest deserved deathe by the Lawe, in Jacobs tyme (as appears by Juda his sentence, in the case of Thamar): yet *Ruben* was punished onely with losse of his Birthright, because he was a Patriark.
>
> *David* his life was not taken awaye for his Adulterye & murder, (but he was otherwise punished) in respect of public interest and advantage, he was valued at 10000: common men.
>
> *Bathsheba* was not putt to deathe for her Adulterye, because the Kings desire had with her the force of a Lawe.
>
> *Abiathar* was not putt to death for his Treason, because of his former good service, and faithfulnesse.
>
> *Shemei* was Reprived for a tyme, & had his pardon in his owne power, because of his profession of Repentence in such a season.
>
> *Those which brake the Sabbaothe* in Nehemiah his tyme, were not putt to deathe, but first admonished, because the state was not setled, etc.
>
> *Joab* was not putt to deathe for his murders, in Davids tyme, for avoydinge imminent public danger, the sonnes of Zeruiah had the advantage of David, by their interest in the men of Warre: and the Commonwealth could not yet spare them. . . .[66]

Long after Winthrop's time, historical scholarship confirmed the correctness of his observations. The stern law of the Hebrews was often mollified by Rabbinical interpretations reflecting the humanity of the priesthood. Horowitz calls the mitigation of punishment through interpretation "one of the most striking examples in human history of social evolution, of a development from the rude and savage to the refined and humane."[67] The "eye for an eye, tooth for a tooth" doctrine was, he believes, more metaphorical than actual. Youths who cursed and smote parents or were "stubborn and rebellious sons" were not actually killed for those transgressions, for rabbis limited the application of these capital laws by setting up certain antecedent conditions. This same sort of practical modification of austere law took place in England in the early nineteenth century when juries refused to convict offenders of "petty" crimes that might have led the offenders to the gallows. And the same force is, of course, operative today in Massachusetts when statutory penalties outrun the conscience of the people.

Many individuals were indicted and tried for capital crimes in the Bay Colony. Most of them, on conviction, were administered a "grievous" penalty, but their lives were spared. Even in the later half of the Colony's life, when the number of hangings increased, any capital offender had a very good chance of escaping the hangman's noose, unless he were found guilty of murder, withchcraft or piracy—and even in such cases an execution was not inevitable.

We shall select, by way of illustration, only a few of the many recorded cases showing the amelioration of the law by judge and jury in the practical administration of criminal justice. In dozens of cases the court might legally have ordered that the offender "shall be hanged by the neck untill he be dead"—but chose a less severe penalty.

As to the crime of *blasphemy,* Benjamin Saucer, a soldier of the King, was one of the relatively few indicted for this capital crime, which, of course, was far more serious than simple "prophaness" or swearing, for in denying God or His Kingdom one struck at something very deep in the Puritan soul. Saucer was clearly guilty of "uttering most prophane and unheard of blasphemy, saying, that Jehovah was the divill, that he [Saucer] knew no God but his sword . . . ."[68]

Here was a direct challenge to the authorities. In June 1654, he was tried as a capital offender and might have been the first (and only one) to suffer death for his blasphemy. The jury evidently did not think he should die for it and brought in "theire verdict not making the blasphemye Capitall." The Magistrates could not see how the penalty could be avoided and "receiveth not their verdict" for both the law and the facts were undisputed. The case was then taken to the General Court for final disposition, but, as that body was not to meet for several months, the defendant lay "in chaines and fetters" in the Boston prison where he found ample time to draw up a long petition to the General Court, alleging in most humble terms:

. . . I am a true borne subject of England: a subject to his Highnesse Oliver [Cromwell] Lord Protector: of England: Scottland: and Ireland: and to the States of England: for whose sakes I have not thought my life to deare, often to venture it in their cause and quarrell, as tendinge and mindinge the good of the English nation in generall: in prosecution of my employments as a souldier: I was moved to take a voyage to New England: to serve his Highnesse in some service that might tend to the good of this country: which service I cheerfully undertooke: in the prosecution whereof I meet with many difficulties distresses, and perills, and dangers at Sea: but in God's time I arrived here joyfull that I was in a capacity to serve my nation in these remote Corners of the world. It soe fell out that being occasionally a shoare (havinge beene before a long time on Shipboard) and meetinge with divers of our fellow souldiers, wee were to [too] free in our mirth and drinke, by reason whereof some takinge notice thereof as it seemeth, fell a discoursinge with mee, and as they say beinge hasty and proud, returned unseemely, and ungodly, and as they say divelish language.

It is most certainly true I am shamefully ignorant of God, and you may wonder it should bee soe, but soe it is though I have had some meanes of knowinge more than I doe, and I thanke God I now know more of God then I did when hether I first came, and I dare not speake or thinke evelly of the name of God soe farre as I know him. . . .

But thus I am a free borne subject of England, and was sent out as a servant employed in the service of his Hignesse, and the State of England: I am noe inhabitant of this place, therefore give mee liberty without offence: in the presence of God and this assembly, to appeale unto the State and Government, to whom I doe belonge: and I do hereby appeale to his Highnesse, and the State of England.

If I have wronged any mans estate, or done injustice to any, I am ready to answer it, to satisfaction. where I have offended God I hope hee will abundantly pardon. Thus begginge the blessinge of God amongst you, in your proceedings: I rest

Your poore prisoner
Benjamin Sacer

Dat: Octob. the 25th 1654.[69]

Unfortunately, we are deprived of a final decision by the General Court for, as the record states:

. . . the bench & jury [in the Court of Assistants] differing in the verdict whither the crime was capitall or not, the case came to the [Gen-

> eral] Court in course to be determined; the said Saucer appeared before the Court, and pleaded not guilty; the evidences were heard against him; but before the Court came to a sentenc, the said Saucer made an escape out of prison.[70]

That blasphemy was considered a serious crime there could be little doubt, though probably few at that time believed it merited death. The relatively mild punishment of a Harvard College student for this crime twenty years later (1674) was reported by Judge Samuel Sewall. The student had dared publicly utter "blasphemous" words concerning the "HG," as Sewall recorded it in his Diary. Everyone knew that implicit belief in the "Holy Ghost" was a cardinal tenet of Puritan theology which not even an inquiring mind at Harvard could question with impunity. However, no one thought he deserved death. The community was satisfied with a lesser penalty: A public whipping before all the scholars; a suspension "as to his taking his degree of Bachelour"; a requirement that he sit alone at mealtime during the pleasure of the President and Fellows and that he be "in all things obedient, doing what excercise was appointed him by the President" under threat of expulsion. President Leonard Hoar prayed before and after the whipping.[71]

As to the crime of *murder,* one who committed his crime with evident malice and premeditation was very likely to end his days on the gallows. But there was always room for compassion. In the case of the Negro servant, Anne, for example, although the grand jury found that she did "maliciously & willfully murder an Infant child then borne of hir owne body" and the trial jury found her guilty of "having a Bastard child & [having] privately conveyed it away," she was released with a whipping, a month in prison, and the humiliation of standing on the gallows with a rope around her neck for one hour.[72]

As to the crime of *manslaughter,* the distinction between murder and manslaughter, as we have seen, was somewhat vague, for both crimes could lead to the gallows. The task of trying to distinguish these two crimes becomes then somewhat academic. A jury could, of course, bring in a verdict of manslaughter on an indictment for murder. In that case usually the life of the offender was spared. John Newhall, III, and a friend, in the town of Lynn were indicted for murder for:

> of their malice forethought upon the body of Ralph King, Jr., . . . with force and Arms a violent assault did make and with their hands Feet and Knees did strike kick, stamp and crush the said Ralph King, Jr. thereby giveing him many grievous and mortall wounds and brusies of which wounds and brusies he did grievously Languish untill the 22nd day of the said November [7 days later] and then of the aforesaid mortall wounds and bruises dyed. . . .

The jury found Newhall guilty of manslaughter and his friend guilty of accessory to manslaughter, but both were released after payment of a heavy fine.[73]

John Betts' life was also spared. He had fatally beaten his servant with "a greate plough Staffe" and other crude implements. The Court ordered that he be severely whipped, humiliated, and fined but stated that it did

> not finde John Betts legally guilty of the murdering of his late servant . . . but strong presumptions and great probabilities of his guilt of so bloody a fact, and that he hath exercised and multiplied inhumaine cruelties upon the said Knight. . . .[74]

Leonard Pomeroy was found guilty of manslaughter, but he also was not turned over to the hangman, his punishment consisting of a branding of his hand and the forfeiture of all his goods. The Court of Assistants described the crime:

> . . . in the house of Ruth Harding [he] did maliciously wickedly & Feleoniously quarrelling so with Thomas Pinnock murther him by throwing him downe on the Floore from a chaire where he satt giving him a cruell blow on the upper part of his breast neere his throate & kicking him with his Foote of which wound & blow he presently sickned voided much blood in clodds & so continued till he died of said blowes. . . .[75]

The case of Franklin, then, stands out as an exception. Here, evidently, the Court's sympathies were directed to the victim, a child who had just come over from London without his family, to serve as an apprentice in the Colony. He was an "illdisposed" child and suffered from the scurvy and was, Winthrop said, "withal very noisome." Franklin, his master, treated him with "continual rigor and unmerciful correction," exposing him to cold and wet in the winter season, and once hung him in the chimney. One day Franklin tied him to a horse in such a way that the boy "was sometimes sitting and sometimes hanging down" and brought him to Boston, a distance of five miles. The boy in great distress repeatedly called for water, but Franklin turned a deaf ear. Within a few hours after his arrival in the town, the boy died. Franklin was charged with murder. His defense was that he intended, by stern correction, to reform the boy, not to harm him. "Though *prima intentio,"* Winthrop argued, "might be to reform him, yet sure *proxima intentio* was evil because it arose from distemper of passion." The continual acts of cruelty, he believed, brought the boy to his death by degrees, the last act being simply the consummation of it. Scriptural authority for demanding the death penalty was sought in the Books of Exodus and Deuteronomy. All the magistrates seemed satisfied with the conclusion that Franklin ought to die for this crime. (He had been found guilty in the Court of Assistants but as there seemed some doubt as to whether the crime was capital, he was reprieved while the magistrates debated the issue.) Franklin protested the verdict to no avail, justified his conduct, and professed assurance of salvation. "Only a little before he was turned off the ladder, he seemed to apprehend some hardness of heart, that he could not see himself guilty of that which others did."[76]

As to the crime of *adultery,* without much popular support the legislature made adultery a capital crime and yet, time after time, juries refused to bring in verdicts that might have led to the scaffold. The infliction of the extreme penalty was avoided by such verdicts as: "not guilty according to Indictment but found him Guilty of vile, filthy and abominably libidinous Actions. . . ."[77] ". . . guilty of adulteros practises."[78] ". . . Guilty of very suspitious acts leading to Adultery. . . ."[79] ". . . Not legally Guilty according to Indictment but doe find hir Guilty of Prostituting hir body to him to Committ Adultery."[80]

Possibly one reason for cautiousness on the part of juries and judges in adultery cases was that, by the very nature of the case, it was difficult to get clear evidence. Two witnesses were required as evidence in all capital cases—or one witness and circumstances that might be considered "equivelent" to another.[81] The jury in the Elizabeth Hudson case found her "guilty of lieing in bed with Peter Turpin" but felt constrained to bring in a "special verdict": "If by law, Elizabeth Hudsons lieinge in Bed with Peter Turpin be A[d]ultery we find her Guilty—If by law, Elizabeth Hudsons lieinge in Bed with Peter Turpin be not adultery we find her not guilty." With this doubt in the case, the court found her not guilty of a capital offense but punished her severely nevertheless.[82]

In the case of Henry Dawson, the jury could find only a "suspicion of adultery." Dawson admitted that he was living in the same house with a married woman whose husband was in England and that in time he "grew over familiar" with her "so as she would be with him oft in his chamber, etc., and one night two of the servants, being up, perceived him to go up into their dame's chamber, . . ." The servants reported what they saw, and Dawson "confessed not only that he was in the chamber with her in such a suspicious manner, but also that he was in bed with her, but both denied any carnal knowledge. . . ." The jury found them not guilty of adultery but "guilty of adulterous behavior." Winthrop concluded that the jury "judged it safest in case of life to find as they did . . . neither God's law nor ours doth make suspicion of adultery (though never so strong) to be death."

A verdict of mere suspicion, however, did not mean immunity in Colonial law. Both parties were made to stand on the gallows for an hour with a halter around their necks, and were ordered to be whipped or to pay a fine of twenty pounds. (Dawson was also tossed out of the First Church.) The testimony of the woman was that

> he did indeed come into bed to her, which so soon as she perceived, she used the best arguments she could to dissuade him from so foul a sin, so as he lay still, and did not touch her, but went away again as he came; and the reason why she did not cry out, was because he had been very faithful and helpful to her in her husband's absence, which made her very unwilling to bring him punishment or disgrace. . . .

The touching epilogue is told by Winthrop:

> The husband [on his return] (although he condemned his wife's immodest behavior, yet) was so confident of her innocency in point of adultery, as he would have paid the 20 pounds [fine] rather than she should have been whipped; but their estate being but mean, she chose rather to submit to the rest of her punishment than that her husband should suffer so much for her folly. So he received her again, and they lived lovingly together. . . .[83]

When the excitement over this case had subsided, the General Court, probably instigated by Winthrop who had followed this case with great interest as judged by his copious Diary notes, decided something had to be done to minimize opportunities for this sort of behavior. In 1647, observing that

> divers married persons, both men and weomen . . . whose wifes & husbands are in England or elsewhere, by meanes whereof they live under great temptations & some of them commit lewdnes & filthines here . . . & others make love to weomen, & attempt marriage, & have attained it, [and] some of them live under suspition of uncleannes, . . .

it ordered that such married persons who lived in the Colony while their spouses were in England return "by the first oportunity of shiping" unless they could show cause why they should remain.[84]

As to the crime of *false witness,* in capital cases, trials for this crime were rare. Perhaps the case of Reuben Cuppie was borderline. Cuppie had accused Richard Pitfold of the capital crime of "Bestiallitie," but the Court said he failed in "making the same to appeare, which had it been true would have indangered the said Pitfolds Life." Perhaps Cuppie had not actually testified falsely. At any rate, he was let off with a whipping and payment of the Constable's charge.[85]

As to the crime of *rape,* usually rapists were not executed. The most common penalty was a severe whipping and the humiliation of standing on the gallows with a rope around one's neck for an hour or so. In aggravated cases, one might have to wear "a roape about his necke, hanging downe two foote long, to continew during the Courts pleasure" and to be whipped after every neglect to wear it in public. Negroes and Indians were more likely to be reduced to slavery. An Indian called "Twenty-rod," for rape of "an Indian Girle about 9 yeares of age" was sentenced "to bee sold for his life to some of the Cariba Islands & if he returne into this Jurisdiction againe to be put to death . . . ."[86]

The lives of others convicted of rape of children under ten were also usually spared. Daniel Fairfield, whose case we previously related, owed his life to the unsettled state of the law. Robert Wyar and John Garland, servants accused of "ravishing two yong girles" at about the same time (1643), were let off with whippings and fines probably because they were young boys. The jury found them "not guilty, with reference to the Capitall Law," and yet they confessed their "filthy dalliance."[87]

The case of Edward Saunders of Watertown (charged in 1654 with the rape of Ruth Parsons) was heard in the General Court because the judge and jury in the lower court could not agree. Evidently the General Court did not want to take Saunders' life, declaring that it did:

> not finde him guilty of death, but justly deserving a high and severe censure, and doe therefore order, that he shall be severely whipt, first, in Boston, the next lecture day, after the lecture; 2nd, in Water Toune, after some lecture or other publicke meeting . . . not exceeding thirty stripes at a time; and also, that he shall henceforth weare a rope about his necke, hanging downe two foote long, to continew during the Courts pleasure; and if he be found above forty rodd from his house without such a roape . . . then, for every such offence or neglect, to be whipt againe . . . in the same manner . . . by the present constable.[88]

Many years later in Salem, William Nellson, for rape upon a child under ten years of age, was released after a severe whipping.[89]

As to the crime of *cursing and smiting parents,* young Beleiffe Gridley was clearly guilty of this crime, if the testimony can be credited, but he probably aroused mixed feelings of pathos and anger and was scarcely a comfortable subject for a hanging. At any rate, they did not march Beleiffe, or anyone else to the gallows for this crime. The jury's verdict in the Suffolk County Court (1664) read:

> Wee find him Guiltie of many diabolicall expressions and Cursing him self in a high nature as allso reviling and unnaturally reproching his father by Calling of him lyer and drunkerd and drunken sot as allso Lifting upp his fist against him with horible wishes Against him self if hee did not burne his fathers house about his ears: allso reproching the name of god by profaine swering as allso unnatturall kicking his sister upon the belly to her great hazzard and dainger: Unherd of wickednesses in this place but according to the Indictment and evidences wee doe not find him Guiltie of the breach of any Capitall Law and wee Leave him to the farther sentenc of the honoured bench.

The sentence was a whipping of 35 stripes "severely to be layd on" and:

to stand on the pillory on the next lecture day presently after lecture for one whole hower with a paper fixt on his breast by the Marshall Generall his hands bound down to [the] pillory with this Inscription in Capitol letters:

"This is for Reviling & unnaturall reproaching of his naturall father & most desperate Cursing of himself"[90]

As to the crime of *being a stubborn and rebellious son,* John Porter, Jr., a thirty-year-old bachelor living with his parents in Salem, was the Colony's most notorious prodigal son and (so far as we can determine) the only one brought before the Court of Assistants on this capital charge. He had taken a journey into a far country and there wasted his substance with riotous living. On his return his father received him with love and affection, but here the story departs radically from the Biblical parable as reported by St. Luke (15:11–32).

He cursed and abused both his parents and ill-treated his father's servants. Brought into court, he was tried as a capital offender and might have been the first and only person to be hanged as a "stubborn and rebellious son" had not his mother refused to join her husband in pressing charges against her own son.

Spread upon the minutes of the Great and General Court is a case "narrative" so rich in human feeling, and so revealing of the Colony's attitude toward those who did not respect their parents as God had commanded them to do, that it is here reproduced in full:

Boston, the 30th of May, 1665

A narrative of the case of John Porter, Junior

John Porter, Junior, the sonne of John Porter, Salem, in the county of Essex, in New England, yeoman, being about thirty yeares of age, & of sufficient capacity to understand his duty unto his superiours, according to the fifth comandment, but he, being instigated by the divill, & his currupt heart destitute of the feare of God, did not only prodigally wast & riotuously expend about fower hundred pounds of money & goods committed to him by his Father, for his improvement [use] in two voyages to the Berbadoes, & so for England, where by his evill courses he ran himself further into debt, (& was there imprisoned, from whence being relieved by the charritable asistance of some Friends of his Father,) all which debts his father did voluntarily discharge. After this, returning to New England, his parents entertained him with love & tenderness as their eldest sonne, & provided for him [what] was expedient & necessary. All these theings have been clearely demonstrated to the Court; but notwithstanding the said John Porter, Junior, did carry himself very perversly, stubbornely, & rebelliously towards his naturall parents, who are persons of good repute for piety, honesty, & estate.

He called his father theife, lyar, & simple ape, shittabed. Frequently he threatned to burne his fathers house, to cutt downe his house & barne, to kill his catle & horses, & did with an axe cutt downe his fence severall times, & did set fire of a pyle of wood neere the dwelling house, greatly endangering it, being neere thirty roads [rods].

He called his mother Rambeggur, Gammar Shithouse, Gammar Pissehouse, Gammar Two Shoes, & told hir her tongue went like a peare monger, & sayd she was the rankest sow in the towne; & these abusive names he used frequently.

He reviled Master Hawthorne, one of the magistrates, calling him base, corrupt fellow, & said he cared not a tird for him.

He reviled, & abused, & beate his fathers servants, to the endangering of the life of one [of] them.

He was prooved to be a vile, prophane, & common swearer & drunkard; he attempted to stab one of his naturell brethren. All which things are prooved by the oathes of sufficient wittnesses upon record.

In this vile & unsufferable course he continued severall yeares, but more especially the two last yeares, sixty two & sixty three [1662 and 1663]. At length, his father, in the sence of his sonnes wickedness & incorrigiblenes, & the dayly danger of himself, his estate, & family, by his meanes, sought releife from authority, first more privately, which was ineffectuall, & afterwards more publickly, before the County Court held at Salem [March 4, 1663], & by that Court was committed to the house of correction at Ipswich, where he was kept some time; & afterward, being set at liberty, did persist in his former wicked course, & being againe complained of by his father to the said Salem Court the fowar and twentieth of the ninth moneth [November], 1663, where his offences being found to be of a high nature, he was committed to prison at Boston, there to remaine for a triall at the Court of Asistants, where he was called to answer upon the fowerth of March, 1663. [1664]

The complaints against him, the said Porter, were produced, the wittnesses brought face to face, & his charge prooved; also, his owne naturall father openly complained of the stubbornes & rebellion of this his sonne, & craved justice & releife against him, being over pressed thereunto by his unheard of & unparrelled outrages before named. Unto which complaints the said John Porter, Junior, had liberty to answer for himselfe. He impudently denied some things, others he excused by vaine pretences, & some he ouned, but gave no signe of true repentance; whereupon the said Court proceeded to give sentence against him, the summe whereof is, to stand upon the ladder at the gallowes, with a roape about his neck, for one hower, & afterwards to be severely whipt, & so committed to the house of correction, to be kept closely to worke, with the diet of that house, & not thence to be releast without speciall order from the Court of Asistants or the General Court, & to pay to the country as a fine two hundred pounds.

If the mother of the said Porter had not been overmooved by hir tender & motherly affections to forebeare, but had joyned with his father in complaining & craving justice, the Court must necessarily have proceeded with him as a capitall offendor, according to our law, being grounded upon & expressed in the Word of God, in Deut. 22:20, 21. See Capital Lawes, p. 9, sec. 14.

This notorious offendour, John Porter, before his sentence was fully executed, found meanes to make an escape out of the prison in Boston, & presented himself before three of his majesties honorable commissioners then at Warwicke, with complaints of injustice, unto whom they granted a warrant, under their hands, for a hearing of his case at Boston, before themselves, the eighth of May, sixty five, & in the interim granted him protection against all authority, officers, & people, as by the copie of the said warrant may more fully appeare.[91]

Just before Porter's case was heard, the King had sent over to the Colony a Royal Commission of four persons empowered to hear all complaints and appeals of the residents of Massachusetts in all matters—criminal, civil, and military.[92] This move, the General Court believed, was an unwarranted interference with Colonial self-government, "greatly infringing the priviledges of our charter, & derogatory to his majesties authority here established."[93] Nevertheless, in spite of the General Court's very strong objections presented officially and repeatedly to the Commission and to the King, the Commission proceeded to hear Porter's appeal from the Court of Assistants and granted him immunity and protection. The General Court complained—but without avail—that such action "tendeth much to the emboldning & encourging such notorious malefactors, & weakening the hands of lawfull authoritie."[94] The Court was probably right but it was powerless to carry out any further sanctions against Porter who had evidently convinced the Commissioners he had been unfairly treated. The Commissioners certainly knew there was no such capital law in England.

As to *treason* or conspiracy against the Commonwealth, "In the time of warr with the Indians" (King Philip's War) Walter Gendall confessed that he had betrayed the English by counselling with the Indians. The Court spared his life but ordered that he be made to: "Runn the Gantelop (gantlet) through the military Companyes in Boston . . . with a Roape about his necke . . ." and to forfeit his lands to the government, pay costs and charges of the proceedings, and then to leave the jurisdiction under threat of life imprisonment if he returned.[95]

Who, then, *was* put to death? The precise identification of all who were sentenced to die could be determined only if the complete records of the Court of Assistants were available, for that court had jurisdiction over all criminal trials "extending to *Life*, Member or Banishment." But clerks who were neither infallible nor immortal, plus the ravages of fire, decay, and time itself have been the despair of those seeking a continuous and complete report of judicial proceedings. Nevertheless, it is surprising how many of the legal documents of seventeenth century Massachusetts have been preserved, transcribed by diligent scholars from almost illegible handscript and made available to later generations.

The decisions of the Court of Assistants are believed to be substantially complete from 1630 to 1673. Winthrop's diary covering the period from 1630 to 1649 serves as a supplementary source, for hangings never seemed to have escaped his notice. From 1644 to 1673 the official reports are considered "fragmentary" by the editor of the third volume of the records of that court, but he assures us he has gleaned additional material from the court files of the several counties, particularly of Suffolk County, the records deposited in the State Archives, old manuscripts in possession of the Massachusetts Historical Society, and elsewhere to complete insofar as possible the annals for that period. It is idle to speculate on the extent of the missing reports, if any, of capital trials. Again from 1673 to 1692 the records are believed to be complete transcripts of the court's proceedings, except for a short period from

April 22, 1686, to December 24, 1689. Judge Sewall's Diary, commencing in 1674, is an additional source of information.

With these limitations in mind, a review of the Bay Colony's records from 1630 to 1692 shows that only nine of the twenty-five capital laws were invoked to cut short a human life: witchcraft, murder, bestiality, adultery, rape, arson, defiance by Quakers, piracy, and treason.

To return to the original question: Who, then, was executed? Who of these seventeenth century residents of Massachusetts heard the solemn words of the judge in the stillness of the court room: ". . . and you are to return from hence to the place from whence you came and from thence to the place of execution, there to be hangd til thou beest dead—& the Lord be mercifull to thy soule!" We can identify at least these men and women who paid the supreme price:

For witchcraft: Prior to the famous Salem trials in 1692, there were only a few trials for this crime, with some acquittals, some convictions, and three executions. In 1692 on "Gallows Hill" (as it is now called) in Salem, the executioner "dispatched" nineteen men and women for "familiarity with the Devil" (as reported in Chapter 14).

For murder: John Williams, a ship's carpenter newly arrived from England, escaped from prison where he was confined for theft and murdered and robbed a fellow prisoner who escaped with him in 1637.[96]

William Schooler, reputed to have been "a common adulterer" in London and wanted there for wounding a man in a duel, fled to New England (leaving his wife in England—"a handsome, neat woman") and allegedly killed "a poor maid" from "Newberry." He had served her as a guide for hire on a long trip through the wilderness from Newbury to a town on the other side of the Merrimack and had abandoned her in the woods, near Swampscott, with no means of survival. Six months later an Indian found her body. Schooler was charged with murder. Evidence adduced against him was entirely circumstantial. Although he admitted to many lies in his original story, he denied the charge of murder. His guilt was evidently based on the theory that failure to act when one has a legal duty to do so might constitute murder as much as an overt act of killing—a common-law principle still invoked in Massachusetts. The court held him "worthy of death, in undertaking the charge of a shiftless maid, and leaving her (when he might have done otherwise) in such a place as he knew she must needs perish . . . ." Nevertheless the case was a doubtful one. "Some ministers and others, . . thought the evidence was not sufficient to take away his life." One wonders if the man's reputation and the circumstance that he escaped from prison while awaiting trial had counted against him, for Winthrop said "he had lived a vicious life, and now lived like an atheist. . . . He was very loath to die, and had hope he should be reprieved"; but the court ordered him hanged in Boston in 1637.[97]

In 1638 the hangman dispatched Dorothy Talby for killing her daughter, a child of three with the strange name of "Difficulty." Dorothy had been suffering from "melancholy or spiritual delusions" and had previously attempted the lives of her husband and herself.[98]

We have previously related the execution of Franklin in 1644 for causing the death of his apprentice.

The case of Mrs. Cornish, a resident of Weymouth who moved to Acomenticus (now York, Maine) reported by Winthrop in 1645, cannot be verified because the Court of Assistants records are incomplete for that year and no mention of the case appears in the General Court records. According to Winthrop's meager account, she was executed for the murder of her husband whose body was found in the river. "Strong suspicion" was directed against her. She was "a lewd woman" and had "confessed to have lived in adultery" with several persons, including the mayor. Furthermore, when she came close to the body it "bled abundantly"—a superstition shared by people of that era that if a body bleeds on the approach or touch of the accused there is an immediate presumption of guilt. Although "she persisted in the denial of the murder," she was condemned and executed. She was probably the same woman who in 1638 had been found by the Court of Assistants "suspitious of incontinency, & was seriously admonished to take heede."[99]

Mary Martin, whose grandfather had been mayor of Plimouth, England, a young maid of 22, servant to Mrs. Bourne in Boston, "finding herself to be with child" and not having the courage to face the taunts and infamy of living in a Puritan community where all would know she was an unwed mother, secretly killed the child on birth and hid the body. Upon the discovery of the deed, she confessed and admitted other sins of fornication and so was condemned to die. She aroused no sympathy from the Governor, who coldly reported a bungling job at the execution in 1646:

> After she was turned off [that is, swung free from the gallows ladder] and had hung a space, she spake, and asked what they did mean to do. Then some stepped up, and turned the knot of the rope backward, and then she soon died.[100]

Judge Sewall's diary records the execution of two servants:

> A Scotchman and Frenchman kill their Master, knocking him in the head as he was taking Tobacko. They are taken by Hew and Cry, and condemned: Hanged. Nicholas Feavor, born in the Ile of Jersey, Robert Driver, born in the Ile of Orknye in Scotland, Executed, Mar. 18, 1675.[101]

James Morgan was executed in 1685 for killing a man in a drunken brawl "by running a spitt into his belly a little above the navell."[102]

Hugh Stone of Andover suffered death on the gallows in 1690 for killing his wife.[103]

Samuel Watts was a pirate. His indictment states that in 1689 "upon the high Seas, that is to say in martins vineyard Sound near Tarpolin Cove . . . Watts being under a Red Flagg . . with force and Armes an Assault did make and with Bullets which he out of small Guns feloniously shot; the body of . . . Samuel Pease [master of the sloop Mary of Boston] in severall places did strike and mortally wound. . . ." He was hanged for murder, but could as well have been hanged for piracy.[104]

Elizabeth Emmerson, a single woman living in Haverhill, killed her two bastard children in 1691 and paid for it with her life.[105]

Skirmishes with Indians caused innumerable deaths of both English and Indians. Which killings might have been scored as the inevitable accompaniment of battles sporadically occurring between these two for-the-most-part "friendly enemies" and which were, in a legal sense, "murders," it is difficult to determine. However, the courts tried and condemned to death an Indian named "Little John" in 1675 for murders of Lancaster residents committed during the period of King Philip's War, and the following year took the lives of four Concord Englishmen for killing three Indian women and three Indian children.[106]

Judge Sewall's laconic diary entry for September 13, 1676, with no further elucidation of the event, reads: "The after part of the day very rainy. Note, there were eight Indians shot to death on the Common, upon Wind-mill hill."[107] How many more Indians were legally executed during or immediately after that war due to their part in the hostilities cannot be determined.

For bestiality: A servant by the name of Hackett [or Hatchet] eighteen or twenty years old, was considered "a very stupid, idle, and ill-disposed boy . . . [who] would never regard the means of instruction." In 1641 they accused him of the crime of bestiality and had one witness, but there was "much scruple" among the magistrates for two witnesses were needed, and so the case went to the General Court. There it was agreed that one witness plus the lad's confession were sufficient. Governor Bellingham, moved possibly by the defendant's youth or guilessness refused to pronounce the sentence, but Deputy Governor Endecott did so and ordered him confined. This case excited a great deal of interest. "Divers of the elders and other christians resorting to him, and laboring by the word of God to convince him of his sin, and the present danger of his soul . . . it pleased the Lord so to bless his own ordinances, that his hard heart melted." His execution was postponed one week to give the lad more time for communion with God. His genuine repentance, evidenced by loud and doleful complaints against himself and his sinful course of life, bewailing his disobedience to his parents and their commands, convinced Winthrop that "the Lord hath received his soul to his mercy." And yet, ever mindful of his Puritanism, Winthrop reporting on the lad's last moments of life, had to remind the reader that the Lord "was not pleased to afford him that measure of peace and comfort as he might be able to hold out to others, lest sinful men, in the love of their lusts, should set mercy and repentence at too low a rate. . . ." Prepared for death, the youth "quietly yielded himself, when he was required."[108]

Benjamin Gourd or Goad of Roxbury, a lad of seventeen, the next to be reported for this capital crime, bitterly regretted his act. "The causes he alleged" for his conduct, according to Judge

Sewall, "were, idlenes, not obeying parents, etc." The court in 1674 condemned him to hang and "the mare yow abused before your execution in your sight shall be knockt on the head."[109]

For adultery: Because of the usual jury's resistance to bringing in a verdict of "guilty as indicted" in adultery cases, it is strange that anyone was executed for this crime which was evidently not uncommon. There were only two recorded hangings for adultery in the history of the Bay Colony, (and none in Plymouth) and these occurred rather early in the life of the Colony (1644) when the Puritans still had a strong influence over legislatures and courts. The sinfulness of the defendants' conduct in this case was made vivid by Winthrop—possibly the reason why these two young people above all others should pay the extreme penalty and why the General Court refused James Britton's petition for a pardon. Let Winthrop tell the story with its poignant lesson to "all young maids":

> At this court of assistants one James Britton, a man ill affected both to our church discipline and civil government, and one Mary Latham, a proper young woman about 18 years of age, whose father was a godly man and had brought her up well, were condemned to die for adultery, upon a law formerly made and published in print. It was thus occasioned and discovered. This woman, being rejected by a young man whom she had an affection unto, vowed she would marry the next that came to her, and accordingly, against her friends' minds, she matched with an ancient man who had neither honesty nor ability, and one whom she had no affection unto. Whereupon, soon after she was married, divers young men solicited her chastity, and drawing her into bad company, and giving her wine and other gifts, easily prevailed with her, and among others this Britton. But God smiting him with a deadly palsy and fearful horror of conscience withal, he could not keep secret, but discovered [disclosed] this, and other the like with other women, and was forced to acknowledge the justice of God in that having often called others fools, etc., for confessing against themselves, he was now forced to do the like. The woman dwelt now in Plimouth patent, and one of the magistrates there, hearing she was detected, etc., sent her to us. Upon her examination, she confessed he did attempt the fact, but did not commit it, and witness was produced that testified (which they both confessed) that in the evening of a day of humiliation through the country for England, etc., a company met at Britton's and there continued drinking sack, etc., till late in the night, and then Britton and

the woman were seen upon the ground together, a little from the house. It was reported also that she did frequently abuse her husband, setting a knife to his breast and threatening to kill him, calling him old rogue and cuckold, and said she would make him wear horns as big as a bull. And yet some of the magistrates thought the evidence not sufficient against her, because there were not two direct witnesses; but the jury cast her, and then she confessed the fact, and accused twelve others, whereof two were married men. Five of these were apprehended and committed, (the rest were gone,) but denying it, and there being no other witness against them than the testimony of a condemned person, there could be no proceeding against them. The woman proved very penitent, and had deep apprehension of the foulness of her sin, and at length attained to hope of pardon by the blood of Christ, and was willing to die in satisfaction to justice. The man also was very much cast down for his sins, but was loth to die, and petitioned the general court for his life, but they would not grant it, though some of the magistrates spake much for it, and questioned the letter, whether adultery was death by God's law now. This Britton had been a professor [adherent of the faith] in England, but coming hither he opposed our church government, etc., and grew dissolute, losing both power and profession of godliness.

They were both executed, they both died very penitently, especially the woman, who had some comfortable hope of pardon of her sin, and gave good exhortation to all young maids to be obedient to their parents, and to take heed of evil company, etc.[110]

For rape: Tom, an Indian, for the rape of another Indian's squaw in 1674;[111] Samuel Guile for the rape of Mary Ash, wife of John Ash, in 1675;[112] Basto, a Negro slave, for the rape of a child of his Master, in 1676;[113] and William Cheny, for the rape of his servant, Experience Holdbrooke, in 1681.[114]

For arson: Arson was not usually punished by death, but in 1681, when this crime was considered more serious as the towns grew more populous and several disastrous fires had proved the danger, two Negro servants were executed for two independent acts of arson. Maria, servant of Joshua Lamb of Roxbury, confessed she had set fire to a dwelling house. Jack, servant to Samuel Woolcot of Weathersfield, set fire to Lieutenant Clark's house in Northampton. The hangings took place on the same day in 1681.[115]

For defiance by Quakers: Boston Common was probably the stage where four Quakers, in 1660, paid with their lives for daring to defy orders of banishment and to return to Boston to "test the bloody laws" (see Chapter 10).

For piracy: The "piraticall seizing of ships" seemed to break forth with some virulence in the later years of the Bay Colony. The court condemned to death five pirates in 1675[116] and thirteen in 1689.[117] These culprits were not foreign pirates from the Spanish Main; they were chiefly English who attacked and attempted to steal some of the ships in the Boston Bay area. A convicted pirate from a foreign country would probably have had little chance for survival, but there was evidently some popular distaste for executing Englishmen for this crime. Of the five condemned in 1675, one was allowed to petition for pardon and was probably not executed; the other four may have been. The thirteen rounded up in 1689 were held in the Boston prison where Judge Sewall and other prominent citizens visited them "and prayed with them." A petition for pirate Hawkins was drawn and presented to Sewall, who agreed to sign. He reported:

> He [Hawkins] was ready to be turn'd off before it [the reprieve] took effect, which gave great disgust to the People [who had come to witness the show]: I fear it was ill done. . . . Some in the Council thought Hawkins, because he got out of the Combination before Pease was kill'd, [Pease was master of the sloop they were attacking] might live as well as Coward [who was pardoned]; so I rashly signed, hoping so great an inconvenience would not have followed. Let not God impute sin. . . .[118]

Eventually, probably all but two were spared, for Sewall wrote that "chiefly through Mr. Winthrop's earnestness [grandson of Governor John Winthrop] in Reprieving, only Tho. Johnson dies" We have already reported the hanging of Watts, one of the pirates, for the murder of Pease.

For treason: There is no record of the execution of any peacetime traitors or conspirators, but in the wake of King Philip's War two Indians, Caleb and Columbine, who had evidently been friendly with the English, but turned against them during the war, were hanged in 1676 for treason, being "open and murderous enemies."[119]

In summary, then, we can say that the Bay Colony government from 1630-1692 condemned to death and executed at least twenty-three persons for witchcraft (but nineteen of these *after* the revocation of the Bay Colony charter); eleven for murder (exclusive of those killed for acts relating directly to King Philip's war); two for bestiality; two for adultery; four for rape; two for arson; four for defying orders of banishment (Quakers); five to six (?) for piracy; and two for treason. The total of 56 or 57 here listed must be considered a minimum figure, considering the fragmentary nature of some of the official documents.[120]

A firm belief in the deterrent effect on all who witnessed the agonies of a human being dangling from a noose prompted the authorities to set up the gallows in a conspicuous place. Although under Hebrew law the most common form of execution prescribed was stoning to death—also in public—the Puritans did not follow this practice. They did not wish to believe God had prescribed any one *method* in commanding that men and women convicted of certain crimes be "surely put to death." At any rate, they preferred the practice they were familiar with in England—a hanging by the neck. Timely publication of the event brought people from miles around to make a morbid holiday out of the final act in this drama of justice. Who knows but what this spectacle served to stay the hand of the young would-be burglar, robber, or pirate?

Hanging was almost the exclusive method of execution. Judge Sewall notes that eight Indians were shot to death in Boston, but this incident occurred in 1676 at the conclusion of the war with the Indians and was, probably, a military execution.[121] The only other exception to the use of the noose in carrying out an official execution was the beheading of an Indian (see p. 302).

For some years certain historians maintained that two people were burned to death in Boston for arson. This statement, which has now been discredited, arose probably from ambiguity in the court record, but such an event as a burning to death would have been so striking, so shocking, and so out of keeping with current practice that it would surely have been commented upon by contemporary writers—which was not the case. The court record condemning to death Maria, a Negress, in 1681, for arson stated that she be taken "to the place of Execution & there be burnt" but the record in the case of the Negro servant, Jack, to be executed for arson on the same day, stated that he "be hanged by the neck till he be dead & then taken doune & burnt to Ashes in the fier with Maria, negro." An assumption that both bodies were to be burned *after* hanging seems more reasonable but no definitive statement can be made.[122]

No one, according to Puritan belief, should be launched into eternity without time to prepare himself to meet his Maker. Thus one who killed suddenly might be guilty of two sins: depriving his victim of his right to further earthly existence and condemning his soul to hell by depriving him of a chance to make his peace with God—if that happened to be necessary. The law had, therefore, provided for a period of at least four days between sentence and execution.[123] During this interval, the reverend elders were on hand to minister to the condemned and to pray with him.

The ministers did not overlook an unexampled opportunity to drive home a lesson on idleness, debauchery, drunkenness, Sabbath breaking, or whatever topic seemed most appropriate to the occasion. It became the custom to preach one or more "execution sermons" preceding the hanging in the presence of the condemned and a large throng of the curious. How could one more forcefully point a moral? Where could one find a more appropriate living example of the just rewards of sin than in the poor sinner sitting abjectly before the preacher unable, probably unwilling, to stop the flow of condemnatory and reproachful words heaped upon his head. Sometimes the condemned himself at the end of the sermon, or just before he mounted the ladder, would address the crowd in words of anguish and complete self-abnegation, warning all listeners to shun his evil example, to heed the word of God, and to obey their parents.

Few of these sermons have been preserved, but we do have a vivid report of an eyewitness to the hanging of James Morgan for murder (see p. 289). John Dunton, a young man who had just come from London where he was in the bookselling business, was in Boston in 1686 and attended this grim event which he described in a long letter he sent back to London as, "a Piece of News, for there has not (it seems) been seen an Execution here this seven years. So that some have come 50 miles to see it. . . ."[124]

The condemned had the unenviable honor of being the subject of sermons by three distinguished divines: Cotton Mather and his father, Increase Mather, and Joshua Moodey. With an audience,

Dunton tells us, of almost five thousand, "they went first to the New Church [the Mathers' church, the Second Church in Boston, rebuilt after the fire of 1676], but the Gallery crack'd, and so they were forced to remove to Mr. Williard's [the Third, or Old South Church]. They were all preach'd with so much Awfulness, and so pathetically apply'd to the Poor Condemned Man, that all the Auditory (as well as myself) were very much affected thereat. . . ."

The sermons were lengthy (the idea of short sermons was not known to the Puritans), but a few brief extracts give the flavor. Rev. Cotton Mather was reported to have said in part:

> . . . My request unto you is, That you wou'd at this hour think of an Interest in Christ.—Surely when the Executioner is laying the Cold Cloth of Death over your Eyes, the Look, with the Shriek of your Soul, will then say, "O now a Thousand Worlds for an Interest in Jesus Christ!" Surely a few minutes after that, when your naked Soul shall appear before the Judgment-Seat of the Most High, you will again say, an Interest in Jesus Christ, is worth whole Mountains of Massive Gold!
>
> . . . The sharp Ax of Civil Justice will speedily cut you down; O for a little good Fruit before the Blow! Manifest your penitence for your Iniquities by a due care to excel in Tempers quite contrary to those ill habits and Customs whereby you have heretofore blasphemed the Worthy Name of Christ and Christianity: Especially employ the last minutes of your Life, in giving a Zealous Warning unto others, to take heed of those things which have been destructive unto you. Tell them what wild Gourds of Death they are, by which you have got your Bane; point out before them those Paths of the Destroyer which have led you down So near unto the Congregation of the Dead. . . .

The Rev. Joshua Moodey is reported to have said:

> . . . You seem to bewail your Sin of Sabbath-breaking: Well, know that you shall never have another Sabbath to break.—The Lord help you to keep this as you ought.—It is a very awful thing to us to look on you, a Person in your Youth, Health, and Strength, Brests full of Milk, and Bones moistened with Marrow, and then to think that within so many Days, this Man, tho' in his full strength, must Dye: And methinks it shou'd be much more awful to you.—Consider, You have no time to get Sin pardoned, and Wrath turn'd away, (if it be not done already) but between this and Death, into the very Borders, and under the Sentence of which, you now are. In the Grave there is

no Repentance, no Remission, Eccles. 9:10. Before four Days more pass over your head, (and O how swiftly do they fly away!) you will be entered into an Eternal and Unchangeable state, of Weal or Wo; and of wo it will be, if speedy, thorough Repentance prevent it not.

But yet know, That notwithstanding all that has been spoken, there is yet hope in Israel concerning this thing. There is a way found out, and revealed by GOD for the Turning of his Anger even from such Sinners. Paul was a Murderer, and yet Pardon'd; Manasseh made the streets of Jerusalem to swim with Innocent Blood, and yet was forgiven. . . .

Cotton's father, Increase, standing before the gallows set up about a mile out of Boston, just before the hangman was called to do his duty, made Morgan's sins clear to him—as if that were necessary at that hour:

. . . Consider what a Sinner you have been; The Sin which you are to dye for, is as red as Scarlet; and many other Sins has your wicked Life been filled with. You have been a stranger to me; I never saw you; I never heard of you, until you had committed the Murder, for which you must dye this Day; but I hear by others that have known you, how wicked you have been; and you have your self confessed to the World, That you have been guilty of Drunkenness, guilty of Cursing and Swearing, guilty of Sabbath-breaking, guilty of Lying, guilty of Secret Uncleanness; as Solomon said to Shimei, Thow knowest the Wickedness which thine own heart is privy to; so I say to you: and that which aggravates your guiltiness not a little, is, That since you have been in Prison you have done Wickedly: You have made your self drunk several Times since your Imprisonment; yea, and you have been guilty of Lying since your Condemnation.

Consider what misery you have brought upon your self: on your Body, that must dye an accursed Death; you must hang between Heaven and Earth, as it were forsaking of both, and unworthy to be in either. And what misery have you brought upon your poor Children? You have brought an Everlasting Reproach upon them. How great will their shame be, when it shall be said to them that their Father was hang'd? Not for his Goodness, as many in the World have been; but for his Wickedness: Not as a Martyr, but as a Malefactor: But that which is Ten thousand thousand times worse than all this, is, That you have (without Repentance,) brought undoing Misery upon your poor, yet precious Soul: Not only Death on your Body, but a second Death on your never-dying Soul: O tremble at that! . . .

After Morgan was on the ladder, he addressed the crowd telling them what Cotton Mather had prompted him to say, but speaking with evident sincerity:

> I pray GOD that I may be a Warning to you all, and that I may be the last that ever shall suffer after this manner. In the fear of GOD I warn you to have a Care of the Sin of Drunkenness, for that's a Sin that leads to all manner of Sins and Wickedness: (Mind and have a Care of breaking the Sixth Commandment, where it is said, *Thou shalt do no Murder.)* For when a Man is in drink, he is ready to commit all manner of Sin, till he fill up the Cup of the Wrath of GOD, as I have done, by committing that Sin of Murder. I beg of GOD, as I am a Dying Man, and to appear before the LORD within a few Minutes, that you may take notice of what I say to you: Have a Care of Drunkenness and ill Company, and mind all good Instruction, and don't turn your back upon the Word of GOD, as I have done. When I have been at a Meeting, I have gone out of the Meeting-House to commit sin, and to please the Lust of my flesh: and don't make a mock at any poor Object of Pity, but bless GOD, that he hath not left you, as he hath justly done me, to commit that horrid Sin of Murder. . . ."

The final scene, described by eyewitness Dunton:

> After he had been about an hour at the Gallows, and had prayed again, his Cap was pulled over his Eyes, and then having said, "O Lord, Receive my Spirit; I come unto thee, O Lord; I come, I come, I come"; he was Turned off, and the multitude by degrees dispers'd. I think, during this Mournful Scene, I never saw more serious nor greater Compassion.

The older Colony to the south of Boston, far less populous and accustomed to a more rural existence than the Bay Colony, was not so often bothered by serious crimes, although it had its share of violations of the sex code and of drunkenness. The Pilgrim leaders were probably as profoundly religious as the men of Boston. They were as firm in their belief that "God gave. . .right Judgments and true lawes" to the Israelites,[125] yet they did not adopt those laws with the same literalness.

When they first posted in Plymouth the capital crimes contained in the 1636 edition of the laws (some five years before the draft of the Body of Liberties was submitted to the people in the Bay Colony), they grouped them thus:[126]

1) "Treason or Rebellion against the person of the King

Portrait of Cotton Mather. Courtesy of the Boston Athenaeum.

State or Commonwealth either of England or these Colonies." Their court records show no executions for this crime.

2) "Wilfull Murder." A number of murder trials enlivened the scene, but most of them ended in acquittals. We shall report below the few that demanded the extreme penalty.

3) "Solemn Compaction or conversing with the divell by way of witchcraft, conjuration or the like." Witchcraft was a universal crime at that time, although no one in Plymouth raised any great hue and cry over the Devil and his disciples. A few were accused; one was tried and acquitted, but no one was executed. Plymouth seemed to have escaped the panic that struck at Danvers Village and Salem in 1692. (See Chapter 14.)

4) "Wilfull & purposed burning of ships [or] howses." A few were accused of arson, none executed.

5) "Sodomy, rapes, buggery." Trials for these sex crimes were occasionally noted but there was only one recorded execution.

In contrast to the Bay Colony, the Plymouth fathers refused to make adultery a capital offense. There seemed to have been some sentiment in favor of the extreme penalty, for "adultery" appeared on the original list, but the record was evidently changed to read: "Adultery to be punished" and in later years to: "Adultery shalbee severly punished."[127] It thus remained a serious but non-capital offense.

These same capital crimes were repeated in the 1658 and the 1671 revisions as written in the Book of Laws, without substantial changes. However, beginning in 1671, a few additional laws were enacted carrying a possible death penalty. For example, a) during and after King Philip's War, it was deemed necessary to make the selling of arms or ammunition to the Indians punishable by death, for, under certain circumstances, such acts amounted practically to treason.[128] b) Burglary and robbery on the highway were made capital crimes on third conviction, but the court was given the right to order, in lieu of death, that the offender be "otherwise grievously punished."[129] c) Piracy on the high seas became a capital offense in 1684.[130]

These crimes, then, the Plymotheans considered most serious and "worthy of death." In the later years of its existence, Plymouth Colony may have added to the list—the records are not clear on this point—but the only crimes that actually led to an execution were murder and buggery. The official records, supplemented by Bradford's *History,* report that at least eleven men and one women were executed for murder, and one lad for a sex crime:

1) John Billington (1590–1630), one of the *Mayflower* passengers, was the first to hang in Massachusetts.[131] For many years he had been a thorn in the side of the Old Colony. He seemed to have been a marked man ever since he, his wife, and two little sons set foot on the *Mayflower,* a maverick from the start in the company of the "Saints". "I know not," wrote Governor Bradford, "by what freinds [he was] shufled into their company," for his was "one of the profanest families" on board. When the ship lay at anchor in Cape Cod harbor, Billington was probably one of the "Strangers" who by "discontented & mutinous speeches" revealed "that when they came a shore they would use their owne libertie; for none had power to command them," as they had no original patent for Plymouth. It was such murmurings that prompted the leaders to draw up that solemn "combination," the "Mayflower Compact." Billington was also evidently the first Pilgrim to be punished. He had, shortly after landing, defied an order of Captain Miles Standish "with opprobrious speeches." Bradford had made a prophetic statement about this troublemaker in a letter he wrote to the agent for the Council in London in 1625: "Billington still rails against you, and threatens to arrest you, I know not wherefore; he is a knave, and so will live and die."[132]

The murder charge brought against Billington in 1630 was that he had waylaid a neighbor with whom he had had a quarrel and "shote him with a gune, wherof he dyed." There was no question of fact, the petit jury finding him "guilty of wilfull murder, by plaine & notorious evidence." There was, however, a serious legal question. As the Plymouth Colony had been planted without a charter, did it have the right to take a person's life? A feeling of anxiety spread among the little group of civil and religious leaders. They turned to the Bay Colony for advice. They consulted Governor Winthrop and others—"the ablest gentle-men in the Bay Colony," asking whether Billington "ought to dye, and the land to be purged from blood," as the word of God had commanded.[133] An affirmative answer from Boston finally brought Billington to an ignominious end on the gallows.

2) In the first eighteen years in the life of the Colony, Billington was the only one to die at the hands of the executioner. But in 1638 another case of willful murder was uncovered—"a matter of much sadness to them."[134] Arthur Peach, "a lustie and a desparate yonge man," the "ring leader," and two runaway servants (a third had escaped capture) died on the gallows for the robbery and murder of an Indian youth of the "Narigansett" tribe who was returning from the Bay Colony carrying cloth and beads he had acquired there in a trade. Should three white men forfeit their lives for the murder of one Indian? "Some of the rude & ignorante sorte" among the English, Bradford reported, raised the question whether "*any* English should be put to death for the Indeans." But English justice triumphed. If it had not, there was some concern that the murder would be speedily avenged and "it would raise a warr." The authorities saw to it that some of the "Narigansett" Indians were present at the hanging, "which gave them & all the countrie good satisfaction. . . ."

3) Not for another ten years did the hangman again respond to an order of the court. In 1648, Alice Bishope, a married woman and the only woman executed in Plymouth Colony according to the official records, ended her life "for felonious murther by her commited, uppon Martha Clark, her owne child, the frute of her owne body."[135]

4) No other executions were reported until the provocations of King Philip's War in 1675. In that year the court ordered the execution of three Indians—two by hanging, one by shooting—for the murder of another Indian who had been friendly to the English and had given them timely warning of the sinister plans of that Indian Chief.[136] That the Indian people might observe more closely the administration of English criminal justice "it was judged very expedient by the Court" to give them a share in the deliberations of the jury. The record states:

> . . . together with this English jury . . . some of the most indifferentest, gravest, and sage Indians [were] admitted to be with the said jury, and to healp to consult and advice . . . these fully concurred with the jury [of 12 Englishmen] in theire verdict.

5) In the following year three Indians were hanged for the "horred murder" of an English woman. It was discovered that one

of the Indians had also been involved in three other murders, while a fourth, who had not taken a direct part in the "crewill villanie," had aided in the preparations and so was found "worthy to die, and so received the centance of death, which was, that his head should be severed from his body, which was immediately accordingly executed."[137]

Although hanging was the usual method of legal execution—as it was in England and the Bay Colony at that time—we note this one reported case of beheading—presumably a more "honorable" death—and one incidence of death by shooting.

The records reveal only one execution for a sex offense, that of Thomas Graunger in 1642 for "buggery." He was "servant to an honest man of Duxbery, being about 16 or 17 years of age." Bradford tells us that it was "a very sade spectakle" and one that he was reluctant to report. "Horrible it is to mention, but the truth of the historie requires it. . . . first the mare, and then the cowe, and the rest of the lesser catle, were kild before his face, according to the law, Levit: 20.15. and he him selfe was executed."[138]

That there were no other executions for this crime or for any other sex offenses (although there were a number of trials for these capital crimes) was indicative of that same quality of mercy occasionally found in the Bay Colony when it came to the taking of a human life. In the case of Sam (an Indian), for example, found guilty of the capital crime of rape of an English girl in 1682, the court made this pronouncement:

> . . . although in an ordinary consideration hee deserved death, yett considering hee was but an Indian, and therfore in an incapasity to know the horibleness of the wickednes of this abominable act, with other cercumstances considered, hee was centanced by the Court to be severly whipt att the post and sent out of country.[139]

† † †

Who should hang for his crimes, and who should be spared? was the dismal question facing the first session of the General Court of the Province government meeting in Boston in June 1692. But the legislators were not alone in this decision. The King's Privy Council, according to the terms of the Charter, had a veto power over all laws of the Province, which were to be sent to London "by the first opportunity" following enactment. Only laws not "disallowed" within three years would become the permanent laws of the Province. The first official act of the Province stated that all laws of the Colonies in effect at the time of the changeover of governments, and not repugnant to the laws of England or inconsistent with the Charter, would be continued as laws of the new government. Thus some 23 capital laws were revived.[140] A few years later the Privy Council sent word of its disapproval of this omnibus law. How could English subjects in America know what laws were "repugnant"? Here was "a darkness & snare to the subject who may be ignorant thereof."[141]

In the meantime, and even before the notice of this disallowance reached Boston, the General Court knew that such sweeping legislation as they had attempted was only a temporary expedient to fill a legislative vacuum. The General Court, therefore, commenced the task of setting up a body of criminal law. Early in its first session it packed thirteen capital offenses into one chapter.[142] Again the Privy Council objected, insisting that each new law be "separately expressed & particularly specified." It would have been happier, it was said, if the Province government had taken over the capital laws of England "in toto," leaving no room for doubt as to what was repugnant. It would be "more for the honor of the Crowne. . .to hang all traytors & fellons upon the statutes of England then [than] upon this chapter."[143] For many years English kings had expressed dissatisfaction with the Colony's practice of taking its capital laws from the Old Testament rather than from the Common Law or the statutes of England and of making the General Court the arbiter of what was repugnant. The Charter now gave the King assurance that Province laws would not be too far out of line.

Following the advice of the Council, the General Court submitted the thirteen capital laws separately. Six were not approved. These six laws have never again called for the forfeiture of a life:

1) *Idolatry,* worshipping "any other God but the true God." No one in the Colonies had suffered death for a direct violation of this law.

2) *Witchcraft.* No longer would American legislators take "God's Word" literally in the injunction, "Thou shall not suffer a witch to live."[144]

3) *Blasphemy.* The Privy Council did not think this crime warranted a hanging but did later give its approval to a blasphemy law providing for severe "bodilie punishments" and "punishments of humiliation," a law that—with milder penalties—is still on the statute books of the Commonwealth of Massachusetts.[145]

4) *Manslaughter,* the unlawful killing of another "suddenly, in . . . Anger or Cruelty of passion" was quite different, the Council pointed out, from "wilful murder upon premeditated malice or hatred." Murder had always been a legitimate cause for hanging, but to execute one for killing "upon sudden heat" was not conformable to the laws of England.[146]

5) In view of the statute on murder, *slaying "through guile, either by poysoning or other devillish practice"* could have been punishable by death without being separately listed as a capital crime. Furthermore, like the laws on witchcraft, blasphemy, and incest, the Council found it "conceived in very uncertain and doubtful terms."[147]

6) *Incest.* The Council did not look favorably upon giving "approbation" to this capital law for a crime which had not usually merited death either in England or in America at that time, although a few years later it approved of severe penalties, less than death, for incestuous marriages.[148]

The Province legislature had thus failed in its attempt to revive five of the old Colonial laws: idolatry, witchcraft, blasphemy, manslaughter, and slaying through guile. The legislature had failed also to get approval for the death penalty for incest, which had not been formerly punishable by death. No effort was made to continue into the eighteenth century the supreme penalty for adultery, man-stealing (commonly referring to the stealing of another's servant), false witness in capital trials, or the old Biblical crimes of cursing or smiting parents or being a rebellious son. Wise men knew that juries were not likely to bring in guilty verdicts in trials for these crimes if made capital. From that time until the present, none of these crimes has ever called for the death penalty in Massachusetts.

Yet the General Court managed to get the Council's approval of fourteen capital laws. Although all of these laws were not enforced to the fullest extent, it is reasonable to conclude that in making these crimes punishable by death the governing authorities most strongly expressed their antipathy toward and abhorrence of these kinds of antisocial behavior that most seriously threatened the peace and safety of the Commonwealth in the eighteenth century:

1) *Burglary* (and robbery) were evidently two crimes that became more frequent with increasing urbanization. By 1715 the General Court believed it necessary to make this crime punishable on first conviction since the 1692 law making it capital only on third conviction had not reduced the frequency of this common-law crime.[149] But the penalty was relatively light if the burglar could show that the dwelling house was not inhabited at the time of the breaking and entry. In 1770 the legislature concluded that the law was ineffectual in preventing burglaries in Boston. Lieutenant-Governor Hutchinson wrote:

> There is no room to doubt that bad people frequently come into this Province from other Governments, where the offence is punished with Death, meerly for the sake of committing it here, at the risque only of a small Fine or light corporal punishment.[150]

Thereafter the crime was made capital whether or not the house was inhabited and whether or not the burglar entered by force. And, the law added, "without benefit of clergy," reflecting its stern attitude toward such offenders.[151]

2) *Robbery* "in the field or highway" was in 1711 made a capital offense on second conviction, having first (in 1692) been made capital only on third conviction. By 1761 it was found "insufficient to restrain ill-minded and wicked ruffians from assaulting and robbing his majesty's liege people as they are travelling the common roads, highways or streets," and, like the crime of burglary, it was made a capital offense on first conviction and without "benefit of clergy."[152]

3) *Polygamy,* a crime that did not cause much concern in the seventeenth century, was evidently on the increase in the Province period. Exceptions were made for those whose spouses had been "beyond the seas" for seven years and whose whereabouts were unknown or who had put to sea in a ship that had not been heard from for three years and was presumed lost.[153]

4) *Piracy,* well known to all seventeenth century mariners

and made a capital offense as early as 1673 by the Bay Colony, had by the turn of the century considerably increased. The Province government provided death for all "treasons, felonies, robberies, murders and confederacies" committed at sea to the same extent as though they had been committed on land, but the jurisdiction over crimes committed on the high seas was not clearly defined.[154]

5) *Concealing the death of a bastard child.* It was evident to the General Court that "many lewd women were concealing the death of children born out of wedlock" to avoid the consequent shame and punishment. "It falleth out sometimes (though hardly it is to be proved), that the said child or children were murthered by the said women their lewd mothers, or by their assent or procurement." The presumption of murder could be overcome by the testimony of one witness that the child was dead at birth.[155]

6) *Treason* could be the most serious of all crimes for it could lead to the total destruction of the state. In language very similar to that later adopted by the authors of the Commonwealth and Federal Constitutions, the Province government declared it to be treason "to compass or imagine the death of our soveraign lord the king, or of our lady his queen, or of their heir apparent to the crown. . .or to levy war against our lord the king, or be adherent to the king's enemies, giving them aid and comfort . . . or to counterfeit the kings great or privy seal, or the seal of this province." Eighty years later the tables were turned. Loyalty to King George the Third was made a capital crime (1776–1777). But if the Colonies had lost the war of independence, the leading American "patriots" could have been hanged as traitors.[156]

7) "*Wilful murder,* upon premeditated malice or hatred."[157]

8) *Rape.* Death for this crime, discretionary with the court in the Bay Colony, was made mandatory. The Province government also made "carnal knowledge of any woman child under the age of 10 years" a capital crime.[158]

9) *Sodomy and Bestiality,* acts that were "contrary to the very light of nature."[159]

10) *Jesuits* (See epilogue to Chapter 5, Church and State).

11) *Counterfeiting.* At least a dozen separate statutes in the Province period testified to the great difficulty the government had had in curbing this lucrative crime that by 1720 had become a serious problem as seen by the Royal Governor, Samuel Shute:

The vile Practice of Counterfeiting the Province Bills, is carried on not only in many parts of these Provinces, but also in Great Britain, which if not timely prevented, must prove very fatal to most of the American Settlements; whose Medium of Trade is Bills of Credit; I therefore recommend it to you as one of the best Expedients to prevent the growth of this wicked Practice, to make it a Capital Crime by a Law, and strictly to put it in Execution. . . .[160]

In a series of laws from 1703 to 1779 the General Court had made death the penalty for counterfeiting or debasing the coins of her majesty Queen Anne or counterfeiting the Province bills of credit or those issued by the governments of New Hampshire, Connecticut, and Rhode Island and, later, of the United Colonies of America.[161]

12) *Arson* had always been a terrifying crime, "especially," the Bay Colony concluded in 1652, "where the howses are neere adjoyninge." The Province government quite naturally continued to decree the death penalty for anyone over the age of fifteen who "willingly and maliciously" burned a dwelling house or public building, barn, mill, malt-house, storehouse, shop, or ship.[162]

13) *Dueling* resulting in the loss of life was to be punished by hanging, the body of the executed to be "buried without a coffin, with a stake drove through the body."[163]

14) *Stealing,* the General Court concluded, was not prevented by fines, treble restitution, or whipping. "Even those that have suffered the penalty in such cases have been so bold and hardy as to perpetuate their wickedness a second and even a third time." In 1736, therefore, the law made death the penalty, without benefit of clergy, on third conviction, if the object stolen was valued at three pounds or more.[164]

Capital Laws of the Commonwealth

The Constitution, approved by the people in 1780, declared that:

all the laws which have heretofore been adopted, used and approved in the Province, Colony or State of Massachusetts Bay, and usually practised on in the courts of law, shall still remain and be in full force, until altered or repealed by the legislature; such parts only excepted as are repugnant to the rights and liberties contained in this constitution.[165]

The Constitution had also stated that "no magistrate or court of law, shall . . . inflict cruel or unusual punishments."[166] But "cruel or unusual" were changing concepts as the General Court launched a new era in the government of Massachusetts. Another look at capital punishment was called for. Legislators were sensitive to the increasing unpopularity of the death penalty as a method of dealing with malefactors who, in the course of committing their crimes, had not caused the loss of life. It was clear that when jurors shy away from a *mandatory* death penalty that seems to them disproportionate to the degree of harm occasioned by the offender, prosecutors fail to get convictions.

The Commonwealth had no desire to rely on the automatic reinstatement of all laws of the Province or Colonies that were not repugnant to the Constitution, nor was it in the mood to burden the people with the fourteen capital laws of the Province period, many of which would have been unenforceable. But it did see fit to place upon the statute books of the new government seven laws that called for the penalty of death that seemed to the General Court, at the end of the eighteenth century and at the beginning of the nineteenth century, to constitute the most serious threats to the peace and welfare of the state:

1) *"Wilful murder,* of malice aforethought," would also embrace the crime of dueling if death should ensue. Accessories before the fact would be considered principals.[167]

2) *Sodomy* was removed from the capital list in 1805.[168]

3) *Burglary,* as defined by the Common Law, for both principals and accessories before the fact. After 1805 the death sentence was applicable only if the dwelling house were occupied and the offender were armed with a dangerous weapon or assaulted the occupant.[169]

4) *Robbery,* a felonious assault for the purpose of robbing or stealing.[170]

5) *Arson,* if it occurred in a dwelling house of another "between sun-set and sun-rise," although no life were lost. A later modification made it a capital offense only if the building were occupied at the time.[171]

6) *Rape* of a woman or carnal abuse of a female child under the age of ten.[172]

7) *Treason* against the Commonwealth.[173]

The early nineteenth century was marked by social and political unrest. From pulpit and lecture platform and from legislative halls, pleas were made for a return to basic Christianity and for a firmer control of social evils. One of those evils was slavery, which then seemed inconsistent with the first article of the Declaration of Rights of the Commonwealth Constitution—"all men are born free and equal." In the minds of many, another evil was the public spectacle of men hanging by the neck until they were dead. The movement to abolish the death penalty reached its full strength before the antislavery campaign achieved maturity. Yet many public-spirited men gained prominence in both.

Objections were raised to the taking of a life when no life was lost in the commission of the crime in question. Sodomy was removed from the capital crimes list in 1805, as already noted. In the same year, robbery was likewise removed, but in the ensuing fourteen years that crime, according to a committee of the legislature, had increased "to an alarming extent." Accordingly, the death penalty was restored in cases where it could be proven that the robbery was committed with a dangerous weapon with intent to kill or maim or that the offender had assaulted his victim.[174] For the first, and only, time in the Commonwealth's history–to date–a death penalty had been repealed and later restored. From 1818 to 1839 six capital laws were still in force: for murder, burglary, robbery, arson, rape, and treason. Most abolitionists focused their attacks on the last five; a few fought for complete abolition. Popular resistance to the execution of criminals was gaining strength not only in New England but in most of the other states and in England and Europe as well. A legislative committee commented in 1836:

> For many years past there has been a growing disposition both in the Old and in the New World, to diminish the frequency of capital punishments. This feeling has prevailed so extensively as to produce, in Great Britain, and some other Transatlantic nations, and in several states of our own confederacy, great and desirable meliorations, in this respect, of their criminal codes ... [but they have not] been carried far enough to satisfy the demands of an enlightened public. ... The time has fully come for the total abolition of the punishment of death, and in this sentiment a very large class of our fellow citizens concur.[175]

Ten years later it was noted that, in this reform, Massachusetts had "not kept pace with her sister states."[176] In 1839 robbery was again removed from the list of capital crimes and, at the same time, burglary ceased to be punishable by death.[177] By 1846 it was said that "public sentiment has now reached that point that no execution can take place without a very open demonstration of feeling against this form of punishment."[178] Finally, in 1852, the General Court reduced the penalty for arson, rape, and treason to life imprisonment.[179] From that time until the present, the executioner has been called upon only in cases where a jury has found a man guilty of murder, and the fight for complete abolition goes on.

Let us review the abolition movement in Massachusetts in the nineteenth century. The General Court met the popular demand for repeal by appointing numerous special study committees. Almost every year from 1831 to 1852 committees of the House or Senate or joint committees of the legislature filed their recommendations, most of them favoring the removal of the death penalty for all crimes except murder, a few calling for the abolition of the gallows altogether. Representative Robert Rantoul, Jr., of Gloucester became the leading champion of the abolition movement. An 1826 graduate of Harvard, Rantoul (1805–1852) was a noted lawyer and lecturer and was also active in the antislavery movement. He was prominent in local and national politics as a member of the General Court and later as U.S. District Attorney and U.S. Senator, filling the unexpired term of Daniel Webster. His reports reflected a thorough study of the subject of capital punishment both here and abroad and had considerable impact upon the decisions of the General Court.

By 1839 four-fifths of the states had provided milder punishments for robbery and burglary, a fact noted by a legislative committee of that year: "If we delay much longer, we may be left alone, the last of all the States of the Union in abandoning this relic of the sanguinary code of the land of our forefathers."[180]

Before that time many of the governors in their inaugural addresses had advocated some amelioration of the capital laws—Caleb Strong in 1804, John Brooks in 1819, Edward Everett in 1836, followed by Marcus Morton in 1840 and George N. Briggs in 1846. Governor Everett suggested a moratorium on capital punishment as an experiment. Governor Morton pointed out that "the statistics of crime satisfactorily show that the number of offenses is not increased by the mitigation of punishments; but, on the contrary, that crimes have diminished nearly in proportion to the amelioration of criminal law . . . the severity of criminal law renders their execution difficult, and thereby defeats the object of them." Governor Briggs saw "grave and serious evils" in making punishments too severe. Not only was it difficult to procure convictions but, when convictions took place, too great a strain was placed upon the Governor's pardoning power. "Wise and judicious legislators," he said to the General Court, "should endeavor to avoid both of these consequences." Legislators did not entirely agree. Senator Waldo Flint, for example, was reluctant to change the law "at the present time [1836], when crime is stalking through the land with unwonted boldness."[181]

The killing of a person, whether it be suddenly by murder or after long deliberation by the state, stirs the emotions and makes it difficult for one to place himself cooly and rationally either on the side of abolition or retention. Two tragedies, frequently cited in debates, caused some people to confirm or to shift their views on this question. A legislative committee chaired by Representative Rantoul in 1837 related the story of an execution that had occurred some fifteen years earlier but had not been forgotten:

> Stephen M. Clarke, a lad but little over seventeen years of age, was, for setting fire to a building in Newburyport, put to death in Salem on the 10th of May, 1821. Such was his horror of death, that it was found necessary, amidst his cries and lamentations, actually to force him from his cell, and drag him to the place of execution. It is much to be doubted whether any person of ordinary sensibility and reflection could have viewed, amidst the parade of soldiers and the sound of martial music, the officers of justice, overcoming with difficulty their natural repugnance to such a task, and dragging with violence a fellow-being, a youth, a mere miserable and deluded boy, to the gallows, there to put him to death in obedience to the laws, without in his heart execrating those laws which required the exhibition of such a horrid spectacle.[182]

The second tragedy occurred in 1843. Abner Rogers, an inmate in the State Prison in Charlestown, fatally stabbed Warden

Charles Lincoln, an event that received wide publicity. Before the trial of the offender (who later was found not guilty by reason of insanity), the Rev. William I. Budington, pastor of the First Parish Church of Charlestown raised his voice against abolition:

> The death of your late superintendent . . . will not be in vain. It has opened the eyes of some, and it will open the eyes of many more, to see the impolicy of the present agitation to abolish capital punishment.[183]

Strong voices were raised in support of or in opposition to repeal of the capital laws then in force—robbery, burglary, arson, rape, treason, and murder, and, after the removal of the death penalty for the crimes of robbery and burglary in 1839, of the four that remained. From the many legislative documents filed with the General Court in this period (1831–1852), we find that the most common arguments focused on the following propositions, many of which are still heard in the legislative halls today in the continuing movement to remove the death penalty for the crime of murder:

1) Convictions cannot be assured when popular sentiment opposes the mandatory punishment of death for crimes other than willful murder. A committee of the House in 1849 described the situation as desperate:

> That juries will either disagree, or will generally acquit, in all trials for capital offences, other than downright murder, has latterly become a fact of the greatest notoriety—well calculated to alarm every friend of pure justice—to undermine the foundations of law.[184]

It was reported by an earlier House committee in 1837 that witnesses were "strongly tempted to suppress material circumstances" while prosecutors omitted, "if possible, those particulars in the description of the offense which make it capital."[185] Attorney-General James T. Austin stated in 1842:

> In the present state of society, it is no longer an abstract question whether capital punishment is right, but whether it be practicable, and that there is good reason to believe that punishment for crime would more certainly follow the commission, if the Legislature should further abrogate the penalty of death.[186]

Evidence that juries had balked when the mandatory penalty seemed to them inappropriate to the crime was cited by numerous legislative committees, for example:

> From 1780 to 1846, the whole number of persons convicted capitally of arson in this Commonwealth, was six, of whom four were executed, and two were either pardoned or had their punishment commuted.[187]

> . . . for the last thirty years [prior to 1837] there has been no one executed for the crime of burglary. Yet not a year has passed in which this crime has not often been committed.[188]

> Every year it becomes more and more difficult [in prosecutions for the capital crime of rape] to obtain verdicts against the guilty, chiefly, as it appears to your committee, from the repugnance prevailing in the minds of jurors against Capital Punishment.[189]

Ten years later, in 1846, a Senate committee reported that over a period of 66 years there were only six executions for rape, while between the years 1832 and 1843 there were nine trials for rape but none was executed.[190]

2) The religious and ethical question. Does a Christian commonwealth have a right to demand the sacrifice of a human life? Both abolitionists and retentionists quoted freely from the Bible, the latter favoring the "Word of God" as it appeared in the Old Testament. Members of the clergy were not wholly on the side of abolition.[191] Obviously, the Bible could not be the final yardstick in resolving the question of the right of the state to take a life. One legislative committee in 1843 declared itself

> incompetent to draw inferences from theological dogmas, and points of scriptual criticism, and apply them to the exigencies of legislation, when these propositions are disputed by so many learned theologians, and disagreed upon by so many pious divines.[192]

Nor could it be said, a Senate committee pointed out, that a humanitarian could not advocate capital punishment: "We believe that the enlightened philanthropist will extend his sympathy to the virtuous rather than to the vicious—to the innocent victim rather than to the hardened murderer."[193] Some two hundred years after the General Court of the Bay Colony had taken the Mosaic code as the foundation of its capital laws, we find a committee of the General Court in 1851 making this declaration:

> The Mosaic code, considered as a system of municipal law, was delivered confessedly to the Jewish people. There is nothing indicating that it was designed for universal application or perpetual duration ... nobody, it is presumed, believes that the Jewish code, with its bloody catalogue of more than thirty capital offences, is still in force as law.[194]

And yet, a Senate committee advocating the retention of the death penalty for murder maintained:

> There are those, and they constitute a large part of the people of the State, who believe, that as to this crime, Jehovah himself hath fixed the penalty, and that to abate an iota of its severity, is to violate a law of the Most High.[195]

3) The vexing question of deterrence. Does the retention of the death penalty actually reduce the number of murders in the Commonwealth? Upon this question abolitionists and retentionists were widely split, the former asserting that crimes were not diminished, but on the contrary, were increased by capital punishments.

Representative Rantoul and others cited elaborate statistics on crimes committed in Holland, Belgium, the British Isles, France, and Italy, as well as from Massachusetts and other states of the Union, to show that the number of murders usually declined with the decreasing use of the death penalty.[196] But a skeptical Senate committee could not draw, from these facts, the conclusion favored by the abolitionists: "There may be a thousand causes operating in one community to produce crimes, that do not exist in another. ... Nothing, in the estimation of your committee, can be more delusive than such comparisons."[197]

Over and over again the abolitionists emphasized the deterent effect of certainty rather than severity in the administration of criminal justice. They cited Cesare Beccaria (1738–1794) famous for his treatise *Dei Delitti e delle Pene* (in 1764) condemning capital punishment and torture, which had a powerful influence on penological reform. "The principle advanced by Becarria and now universally conceded to be correct, is, that 'crimes are more effectually prevented by the *certainty* than the *severity* of punishment.' "[198]

Yet, some legislators maintained, there was another serious consideration:

> Monsters, in the shape of men, will still be found in the midst of us, who can be persuaded, only, 'by the *terrors* of the law.' There will always be those, to whose sense of justice, or propriety, or decency, no appeal can be made with effect; there will always be, as now, those who can be controlled only through their *fears*. For such, punishments must be provided, and, 'while in judgment we should remember mercy,' the good of society, nay, the very existence of society demands, that the punishments should be such, as will, most effectually, deter from the commission of crimes.[199]

4) The possibility of executing the innocent. The fear of such a tragic error was reflected in several legislative reports: "It is certain that in a vast number of instances, innocent persons have been executed[200] . . . [and] it is probable, if the same laws are perpetuated, that similar mistakes will occur again."[201] A few years later a report said, "With all our precaution, it has occured in more than one instance in New England. . .and it may occur again."[202] This was not, said a committee of the House in 1851,

> an imaginary or trifling objection, in view of the existing course of judicial procedure; the liability to misconstruction of the law on the part of the courts, and to mistake or perjury on the part of witnesses; the liability to be circumvented and ensnared by a chain of circumstantial evidence, artfully and wickedly woven; and the inability to rebut, by proof, circumstances which seem to have arranged themselves as if to compass the destruction of the accused. So deeply impressed with the danger . . . was the illustrious Lafayette, that he emphatically declared, in the French Chamber of Deputies, in 1830: "Till the infallibility of human judgments shall have been proved to me, I will persist in demanding the abolition of the punishment of death."[203]

5) The possibility of executing the insane. A committee of the House reported in 1851:

> "The plea of insanity [in criminal cases] has always been, and still is, an odious one, often treated with ridicule and scorn. Yet, with the light which the improved though still imperfect knowledge of the

> medical jurisprudence of insanity has thrown upon the subject, there can be no doubt that, in numerous instances, individuals have been put to death as criminals, who were absolved from criminal responsibility by reason of insanity, and were entitled to the remedial care instead of the vengeance of society.[204]

By 1852 the abolitionists had scored a notable victory but had been unable to convince the General Court that murderers should not pay the supreme penalty, the only social offenders then subject to execution. In the ensuing years as the fight for complete abolition continued some important modifications of the one remaining capital law were adopted:

1) In 1858 the legislature voted to divide the crime of murder into two degrees, following the practice in some of the other states and the recommendation of a joint special committee in 1846, thus permitting a jury some latitude if it thought the accused had not committed a crime warranting death.[205] The death penalty was made to apply only to first-degree murder; that is, murder committed with deliberately premeditated malice aforethought or in the course of a crime punishable by life imprisonment or with extreme atrocity or cruelty. Murder that did not appear to the jury to be in the first degree would be considered second-degree murder, punishable by life imprisonment.[206] This is substantially the law today.

2) Under an 1873 law a defendant acquitted by the jury of murder or manslaughter "by reason of insanity" would be committed to a state lunatic hospital for life but could be discharged by the Governor with the consent of the Council if he thought such person were no longer a danger to others.[207] This, too, is substantially the law today.[208]

3) In the late nineteenth century, considerable popular repugnance to hanging as a method of execution was evident, even though public hangings had been abandoned in 1853. Senate bills of 1888 and 1889 proposed that the court be permitted a choice between hanging and electrocution, the latter a novel method adopted by New York.[209] After the defeat of these bills it was proposed in 1893 that convicted murderers be killed "by the administration of choloroform."[210] This unprecedented suggestion was not acceptable to the legislature. But in 1898 the traditional method

of execution by hanging was permanently outlawed in Massachusetts. Henceforth a more "merciful" death would be brought about by "causing to pass through the body of the convict a current of electricity of sufficient intensity to cause death, and the application of such current must be continued until such convict is dead."[211] The first victim was claimed by the electric chair in the state prison at Charlestown on January 4, 1901. Since that time currents of electricity have taken the lives of 64 others.

4) Should there be no room for mercy, where there were mitigating circumstances, although the defendant were found guilty of murder beyond a reasonable doubt? In 1881 Governor John D. Long expressed his views on capital punishment to the General Court: "an outrage on human sensibilities. . .out of accord with the spirit of the age." He proposed that a jury, "the one tribunal which, above all others, reflects the sentiment of the community," be permitted to recommend mercy with its conviction of guilty, in which case the convict would be sentenced to life imprisonment. He thought such an innovation "would tend to put hanging out of fashion, even while it preserved the terror of the death penalty."[212] But the General Court that year was not ready for such an innovation, and for many years thereafter turned down repeated attempts to incorporate this "mercy" provision into the law. In 1907 the Senate voted favorably on such a bill, but the House defeated it by one vote. By 1950 when only three states still clung to the mandatory death penalty for murder, the Senate after a bitter three-hour debate said "no" by a vote of twenty to fifteen, defeating the amendment for the second consecutive year. However, in the following year the bill was enacted into law, providing that the jury may recommend that the death penalty be *not* imposed after a verdict of guilty of first degree murder if the murder had not occurred in the commission of or attempt to commit the crime of rape. Upon such recommendation, the mandatory sentence would be imprisonment for life, without parole.[213]

In his inaugural address on January 5, 1861, Governor John A. Andrews made this prediction: "The infliction of the penalty of death as a punishment for crime will one day be discontinued among civilized men . . . and it will initiate a new era in the progress of Massachusetts when she shall conform her penal legislation to the most enlightened principles of criminal jurisprudence . . "

How many persons were executed in Massachusetts after 1692? Data are not available to supply a complete answer to this question. We know from a few news items, diaries, and unofficial reports that for a period of about fifty years after the establishment of the Province government a number of pirates were brought to justice, the gallows claiming possibly as many as twenty or thirty. We know, too, that there were a few hangings for murder, for burglary, and for rape and that a few women paid the extreme penalty for killing their illegitimate offspring. But we have been unable to find any report or compilation of the total number of persons executed in the Province period (1692–1780).

From a few secondary sources we can offer the following figures, incomplete though they may be, for the Commonwealth government; that is from 1780 to the present time. It was customary in the nineteenth century to hang the condemned in the counties where the case was tried. No central record was kept of the number of hangings and many of the county records have been lost or destroyed by fires.

Executions in the Commonwealth of Massachusetts[214]

Period	*Number executed*	*Period*	*Number executed*
1780–1789	29	1880–1889	5
1790–1799	4	1890–1899	8
1800–1809	7	1900–1909	9
1810–1819	6	1910–1919	13
1820–1829	11	1920–1929	16
1830–1839	3	1930–1939	18
1840–1845	1	1940–1949	9
1846–1859	(no data)	1950–1959	0
1860–1869	6	1960–1965	0
1870–1879	9		

Can one speculate as to the approximate number of persons executed in the period from 1846 to 1859 for which we have no data? The number was probably not large considering the fact that that was a time of considerable popular sentiment against capital punishment and that after 1852 murder was the only crime for which one could be executed. If there were only four executions from 1830 to 1845 and six in the following decade, it is not unreasonable to assume there were about six in the fourteen years under consideration. With this assumption and the further assumption that the data given above are accurate, we conclude that about 160 persons were executed by the Commonwealth from the adoption of the Constitution in 1780 to the present time.

It is beyond the scope of this brief epilogue to describe the perennial fight in the arena of the General Court for well over a century for the complete abolition of the death penalty.[215] Today there is a marked trend toward the repeal of all capital laws, state by state, as each year fewer persons are hanged, electrocuted, shot, or gassed, although the number of serious crimes has not diminished.

In Massachusetts no one has died at the hands of the executioner during the past nineteen years, yet the General Court has seen fit to keep upon the statute books the death penalty for the crime of murder in the first degree provided the jury does not recommend otherwise. Abolitionists are now predicting that the time will soon come, after an incredibly long struggle, when an enlightened civilization will scorn to take the life of an offender in times of peace—a prediction that brings to mind a hope expressed by the writer of a legislative report addressed to the General Court 128 years ago:

> The whipping post and the pillory survived, for a period, the constitutional prohibition of *cruel and unusual punishments*. They have disappeared, and the gallows, which is more unusual than either of those barbarities had been, and infinitely more cruel and revolting, must soon follow in their train. After the reformation shall have been accomplished, mankind will look back with astonishment at its tardy progress. They will be unable to comprehend how or why it was delayed so long.[216]

10. QUAKERS AND THEIR "DAMNABLE HERESIES"

Take heed you break not our Ecclesiastical Laws, for then ye are sure to stretch by a Halter!—*Governor John Endecott's warning to Quakers, 1656.*[1]

THE little sailing vessel *Swallow,* Symon Kempthorne, Master, nudged the dock in Boston Harbor on a warm July eleventh in 1656 after a tedious windward beat from the West Indies. Deputy Governor Richard Bellingham, forewarned of its coming, acted speedily to nip a threatened "invasion" in the bud and thus to "prevent infection." His officers quickly climbed aboard and placed under arrest two English subjects, Mary Fisher and Ann Austin, who had come from England by way of Barbados, a small island colonized by the English in 1625. The constable, without the formality of an indictment, threw them into the crude Boston prison where they were to remain incommunicado for five weeks until a vessel could be found to take them back "from whence they came." The Council ordered their "corrupt books . . . forthwith burnt and destroyed by the common Executioner."[2]

Who were these religious "fanaticks" from England who claimed membership in a strange "Society of Friends"? Were they Popish emissaries in disguise?[3] Were they witches sent by the Devil?[4] An immediate search of their bodies for "witches' marks" failed to disclose any such telltale "signs," but there was little doubt among the good people of Boston, who had already heard disturbing reports from England, that these women were the first of a tribe of "accursed haereticques" to storm the Puritan defenses. Others were soon to follow.

Only a brief nine years before this event, George Fox (1624–

1690), a shoemaker in England, a thoughtful and devout Christian, had begun to preach the doctrine of the "inner light," a way of communing directly with God. A religious fellowship soon developed in that country, taking the name of "The Society of Friends," a society that repudiated the authority of an ordained ministry and saw no need for creed or ritual, prayer book, or baptism. It sought to substitute spirituality for formality in religious observances, plainness of speech and dress for extravagance, peace and love for hostility and hate. Its disciples, conscious of their serious mission, promptly set out for distant ports, many of them going to the West Indies, then a stepping-stone to America.

The world of religious orthodoxy had not yet had time to fathom the new sect. With an impetuosity almost amounting to panic, it proceeded to stamp out this "snake in the grass.[5] "In derision and scorn," it labelled these headstrong noncomformists "Quakers," from the agitated manner in which they were observed to testify in their religious assemblies.

A full month before the coming of the *Swallow,* the General Court, fearing the worst, had proclaimed "a publicke day of humiliation" to be celebrated in Boston on June 11, 1656, its purpose being:

> to seeke the face of God in behalf of our native countrie in referenc to the abounding of errors, especially those of the Raunters and Quakers, that the Protector [Oliver Cromwell was then in power in England] may be preserved from the machinations of evill minded persons. . . .[6]

At that time there was no law in the Colony making it a crime to belong to The Society of Friends. Indeed, an early statute had expressly stated that no one would be "in any wayes punished" unless he had violated some express law or had committed an act forbidden by the word of God and that the same justice would be enjoyed by all whether inhabitants or foreigners "without partialitie."[7] The Colony prided itself on being a government of laws. By what right then had it proceeded against these two women? Pressed later for an explanation of their imprisonment, the General Court maintained that the Quaker ladies

> were only secured to be sent away by the first oppertunity, without censure or punishment, although theire professed tenents, turbulent

> & contemptuous behaviour to authoritie, would have justified a severer annimadversion. . . .[8]

The Quakers' insistence that each individual was equal in the eyes of the Lord, made them *persona non grata* in a society that considered itself "a sort of mixed aristocracy," where due respect to magistrates and ministers was exacted at all times. Furthermore, in emphasizing the personal, direct revelation of spiritual truth without the mediation of a learned profession of clergy, the Quakers were reacting sharply against the stiff formalism of New England churches. This bold and sudden attack on inflexible and pedantic Puritan orthodoxy struck at the very roots of the Bay Colony churches. Here was a call to arms to which the Puritan ministers were eagerly responsive. The "boldness" of the Quakers in asserting that the institution of religion could be maintained without the keystone of the arch—the learned Puritan minister—prompted the Rev. John Norton, teacher of the First Church in Boston and an overseer of Harvard College, who became the Quakers' bitterest enemy, to write:

> The Doctrines of the Quakers (as to the substance of it) is but the opening of that vast and horrid sink (such as makes the Land to stink in the nostrils both of God and man, more than the Frogs that sometime annoyed Egypt).[9]

In the Puritan mind the conflict was no idle theological dispute. That "damnable heresies, abominable idolatrys" were "practiced to the scandell of religion and hazard of souls" was a dreadful fact that could not lightly be dismissed. Here was a frontal assault on the kind of church government the Puritans had risked their lives and fortunes to establish "in this poore, remote wildernes." Such "notorious errors, haeresies, & blasphemies" might well lead to "provokation of divine jealousie against this people." God was a jealous God who might at any moment inflict terrible chastisements upon the Colony for its apostacy—as He had, indeed, in the past.[10]

That the Puritans never intended to set up a government where all could worship as they pleased is evident from the official records of the Colony. They came to America to set up their own church, free from Church of England control. Because they believed their interpretation of the Bible was the only "pure" or true interpretation, they felt bound to defend it against all detractors. And yet no one was compelled to be a believer. Even in the case of heresy, the Rev. Norton insisted, "we do not inflict any Church-censure . . . without doctrinal conviction on the Church's part, and contumacy on the delinquents part, foregoing."[11] But anyone who openly attacked the existing church did so at considerable personal risk.

There were, as the Rev. Norton saw it, two kinds of heresy —one that was "quiet and alone" and one that was "turbulent and incorrigible." As to the first, he insisted, "we subject not any to civil or corporal punishment," but as to the latter, if "accompanied with soliciting the people to apostacy from the Faith of Christ," it was the duty of the government to put a stop to it. Religious tolerance that amounted to indifference in the face of attack was considered in itself a sin. The Rev. Norton believed no one had the right to "blaspheme the blessed Trinity, the Person and Office of Christ, the holy Scripture, . . . howsoever fallaciously transformed into, and misrepresented under the plausible visard of liberty of Conscience, falsely so-called. . . . But Blasphemies immediate, and heresies carried on with an high hand, and persisted in, are to be suppressed with weapons and punishments where reasons and arguments cannot prevail."[12]

Moreover, we must keep in mind that, because of limited media of communication and the newness of this sect "lately risen up in the world," its doctrines were probably unknown or little understood by the average person. Fear fed on ignorance where there was no will to understand. The somewhat mystical tenet of the "inner light" was characterized by the Rev. John Higgison of Salem as "a stinking Vapour from Hell."[13]

Magistrates joined with ministers in their resolve to root out the "foreign heretics." They could not stomach what they termed the Quakers' "turbulent and contemptuous behavior" in refusing to acknowledge superiors in either church or civil government. Never before had they witnessed men appearing in court who habitually kept their hats on their heads until some court officer forcibly removed them, nor had they faced defendants who in spite of threats of dire penalties dared refrain from any words of deference or respect to the presiding judge.[14] The words used by the Quakers in addressing the court seemed to the magistrates insufferably disparaging. The dignity of the General Court was obviously ruffled. Its laws were challenged to a degree almost unknown since the founding of the government in 1630. Having required residents of the Bay Colony to take an "oath of fidelity," the Court saw Quakers proudly refuse to take an oath of any kind, claiming Christ had forbidden that practice. It witnessed the Quakers' refusal to pay taxes to support the government and the churches or to bear arms in defense of the Colony from the always imminent Indian attacks. By 1658 the Quakers had been castigated by the General Court as

> a pernitious sect . . . who have maintayned many daingerous & horrid tennetts, and doe take upon them to chainge and alter the received laudable customes of our nation giving civill respect to equals or reverence to superiors, *whose action tends to undermine the authority of Civill Government,* as also to destroy the order of the churches, by denying all established formes of worship . . . frequenting private meetings of theire owne. . . .[15]

There is considerable evidence that some of the Quakers who came to New England between 1656 and 1660 were of the "turbulent" rather than the "quiet" type. A number of them were accused of disturbing church services by throwing a discordant note into the meeting. It was not unusual in Puritan churches for a member of the congregation to arise and speak at the conclusion of the "lecture" or sermon, but decorum and civility were expected. Quakers Robinson and Stevenson, who came from Rhode Island to Boston "to test theire Bloody Lawes," gave their own description:

> After . . . we had been some houres in the Towne [Boston], wee passed into theire meeting house, and Declared against there unsanctifyed fast and hipocrisie (for that day was a fast with them) but they soone like Beares Laide violent hands upon us, & by force hailed us forth, & hailed us to Prison. . . .[16]

Describing the examination by the authorities in Boston, Robinson wrote:

> [They were] confounded, & did Rage, & were madd, because I reproved them sharply, & laid there folly & wickedness open; For in the Dominion of the Lord God Allmighty I stood over them, & spake over there heads. . . .[17]

The official record reads that they were committed "to close prison" on June 16, 1659, for "endeavoring to make disturbance before the Congregation was dismist." When brought before the court their conduct was described as:

> Rayling & Contemptous Carriage & Speeches against the whole Court & chardging the Gouvernour in the face of the Court to be Guilty of blood & would not be silenced by the Court but Continued Interupting your honors. . . .[18]

Quaker Edward Burrough later argued that no Quaker ever committed an act of violence:

> Did ever these poor People . . . lift up a hand against them, or appear in any Turbulent gesture towards them? Were they ever found with any Carnal Weapon about them? Or, what was their Crime, saving that they warned sinners to Repent, and the ungodly to turn from his way? . . . No Sedition, evil-dealing, Drunkennesse, Lying, nor any of these things could be charged against them. . . .[19]

Although this new religious sect offered no physical violence, its verbal attacks were devastating.[20] Government leaders, sensing a crisis, hoped the Quakers would depart the jurisdiction quietly and without fanfare and gave them ample opportunities to do so. It was a vain hope. The dry tinder of Calvinistic theology met the kindling flame of the "inner light." The ensuing explosion drove the General Court into a frenzy of law making, resulting in the harshest criminal laws and the most severe application of corporal punishment in the Colony's history.

The General Court did not deem the Quakers qualified for protection under an old law that granted "full liberty" to any who were "orthodox in judgement, and not scandalous in life" to "gather themselves into a Church Estate, provided they do it in a Christian way, with the observation of the Rules of Christ revealed in his word."[21] Obviously, Puritan ministers did not concede that Quakers were "orthodox in judgement."

The death penalties for worshipping "any other God but the Lord God" or for "Reproaching the holy religion of God," and the law providing banishment for those who should go about "to subvert and destroy the Christian Faith and Religion, by broaching and maintaining any damnable Heresies," were still in force. Quakers, denounced as "open and *capitall* blasphemers," could have been prosecuted under the blasphemy law which called for the death penalty, but the General Court decided to enact *special* laws aimed solely at Quakers and those who aided or entertained them or attended their meetings.

The General Court at its first session (in the fall of 1656) following the arrival of the *Swallow,* alleging that "there is a cursed sect of haereticks lately risen up in the world, which are commonly called Quakers, who take uppon them to be immediately sent of God, and infallibly assisted by the spirit to speake & write blasphemouth opinions," enacted a law providing:

a) a fine of one hundred pounds (an extremely heavy fine) for any shipmaster knowingly bringing Quakers into the Colony and imprisonment if he did not "carry them backe to the place whence he brought them";

b) a sentence to the House of Correction for the Quakers themselves where they would be "severely Whipt, and by the master thereof be kept constantly to worke, & none suffered to converse or speake with them";

c) a fine for anyone importing, dispersing, or concealing any Quaker books or writings "concerning theire divilish opinions";

d) a fine for anyone defending the opinions of the Quakers and banishment for persistence in such defense;

e) a whipping or fine for anyone who shall "revile the office or person of magistrates or ministers, as is usuall with the Quakers."

"This order," the record tells us, "was published 21:8 mo, 56, [that is, on the 21st of October, 1656] in severall places of Boston, by beate of drumme."[22] No doubt the authorities thought this law would discourage the spread of this "malignant doctrine" before it got a foothold.

The colonies of Plymouth, Connecticut, and New Haven also enacted anti-Quaker laws but prosecuted offenders less vigorously than the Bay Colony leaders "who are become more Bloody and Cruel, Bold and Impudent, in their Wickedness, than the rest of their Brethren."[23] Many Quakers sought refuge in Rhode Island, noted for its tolerant attitude toward religious people who had fled from other jurisdictions. The Commissioners of the United Colonies urged their southern neighbor to take up the prosecution of Quakers in that plantation but Rhode Island pointed to two remarkable facts (quite overlooked by Massachusetts); namely, that *unpunished Quakers caused them no trouble and that punishing Quakers increased the number of converts*:

> We have no law among us, whereby to punish any for only declaring by words, Etc, theire minds and understandings, concerning the things and ways of God ... and we, moreover, finde, ... where ... these people ... are most of all suffered to declare themselves freely, and are only opposed by arguments in discourse, there they least of all desire to come, and we are informed that they begin to loath this place, for that they are not opposed by the civill authority, but with all patience and meeknes are suffered to say over their pretended revelations and admonitions.... Surely we find that they delight to be persecuted by civill powers; and when they are soe, they are like to gain more adherents by the conseyte of their patient suffereings, than by consent to their pernicious sayings. . . .[24]

These words of wisdom made little impression upon the Bay Colony. Rhode Island had long been held in contempt by the Puritans who, according to a Quaker writer, had called their settlement "Rogues Island" for "none but Whores and Rogues went thither."[25]

In spite of this first law, Quakers came into the Colony in increasing numbers. The General Court ordered more stringent penalties, making the fine of one hundred pounds, then applicable to shipmasters, to apply also to anyone who brought Quakers into the jurisdiction and subjecting those who entertained or shielded Quakers to a fine of forty shillings "for every howers entertainment and concealment" and to imprisonment until the fine was paid.

Cutting off an ear was an unusual penalty, reserved for crimes that were highly offensive, such as burglary on the Lord's Day. To discourage Quakers from coming into the Colony after October 14, 1657, "after they have once suffered what the lawe requireth," the General Court ordered that a male Quaker might "for the first offence, have one of his eares cutt off, and be kept at worke in the howse of correction till he cann be sent away at his owne charge." On second conviction, he might lose his other ear, and on a third conviction offenders might have their "tongues bored through with a hot iron, & kept at the house of correction, close to worke, till they be sent away at their owne charge."

A female Quaker would not have lost an ear under this law, but might have been placed in the House of Correction "at worke till she be sent away at hir owne charge." On a third offense she, too, could have had her tongue bored through with a hot iron.

Prior to this time, inhabitants of the Colony who were converted to this new faith were less severely treated but under this new law "all and every Quaker arising from amongst ourselves" was to be subject to "the like punishment as the lawe provides against forreigne Quakers"; that is, those who came from the West Indies or directly from England.[26]

An increasing number of Colonists joined the new movement or objected to the Court's treatment of the Quakers, for the severity of the penalties drove more sympathizers into their ranks. To prevent this mounting threat to civil and church government, a law was enacted in 1658 providing fines for any who attended Quakers' meetings or supported "theire diabolicall doctrine." Persistence in supporting Quakers could have led to banishment, but sympathizers were to have a chance to recant and to promise they would "not any more vent theire hateful errors, nor use theire sinfull practizes."[27]

Courageous Mary Dyer arrived in Plymouth Colony in December 1659 while Quakers William Leddra and Wenlock Christenson lay in close confinement in the local gaol. Later all three were to journey to the town of Boston to meet a far worse fate. Many other Quakers came up from Rhode Island where they had been frustrated because they were ignored. Plymouth and surrounding towns gave them the opposition they were evidently seeking, and they were able to win numerous converts—some from the older and respected families of the Colony.

At Plymouth also, the authorities feared that these "fanaticks" had come to "Subvert Civill State and to pull downe all churches and ordinances."[28] By 1658 it seemed evident to the General Court that "many persons" had been "greatly corrupted with the Quakers doctrines."[29] With the encouragement of their Boston advisors, the legislators immediately passed a number of restrictive laws, forbidding "foreign Quakers" to enter the Colony and punishing those who brought them in or entertained them in their homes or encouraged them or attended their meetings. They directed the marshall to confiscate their "falce, scandalous and pernicious" writings and to take away their horses, for Quakers on horseback

> have not onely the more speedy passage from place to place to the poisoning of the Inhabitants with theire cursed Tenetts; but alsoe therby have escaped the hands of the officers that might otherwise have apprehended them.[30]

The headstrong Quakers violated these laws at the earliest opportunity and took their punishments heroically. Their suffering in Plymouth was relatively light compared to the deadly cruelty imposed by Governor Endecott and his Boston magistrates. The Plymouth courts were loath to punish them without first trying to turn them from "the error of their waies." They requested some of the high officials to attend Quaker meetings that they might "use their best endeavors by argument and discourse to convince or hinder them,"[31] all, of course, to no avail. Small units (what we might today call "cells") of Quakers gathered together in Marshfield, Scituate, and "Duxburrow," and a larger colony settled in Sandwich on the Cape, farther from the seat of government.

They hanged no Quakers in Plymouth Colony, but they banished them, fined them, whipped them, and in one case bound a Quaker by the neck and heels. Some returned to Rhode Island, but a tenacious few endured whatever punishment was meted out to them, giving the authorities little satisfaction. Nothing seemed to deter them from their characteristic verbal attacks on ministers and magistrates. Quaker Humphrey Norton, for example, when facing the Governor in court said to him "Thy clamorouse toungue I regard noe more then dust under my feet; and thou art like a scoulding woman; and thow pratest and deridest mee . . . ."[32]

The General Court witnessed the ineffectiveness of its laws in keeping all Quakers out of the Colony for "notwithstanding which, by a backe doore they forced entrance," referring to those who came to Boston from Rhode Island subsequent to the law providing a heavy fine for shipmasters who brought them into Boston Harbor. They "have not binn deterred," said the court, "from theire impetuous attempts to undermine our peace and hasten our ruine. . . ."[33] Corporal punishment had proved ineffective in the case of the most determined of the new sect for, as the General Court said, "the losse of the eares of those that offended the second time . . . [was] also too weake a defence against theire impetuous & fanaticke fury. . . "

Prison facilities were too meagre to hold the increasing number of offenders. As one observer wrote:

> . . . they threatened to fill our Prisons, and weary us out (as I have heard) they grew high and bold, and all the courses of that kind did no whit hinder them from intruding upon us; and this wild fire began to take no small Impression in the Country, and you know we are but a little body, and soon overrun and shaken with any distemper.[34]

If corporal punishments were of little avail and prisons were inadequate, there seemed to some to be only one available sanction—the dreaded death penalty. Accordingy, in 1658 the General Court made it lawful to apprehend "foreign Quakers" without a warrant. After a trial by a special jury in the Court of Assistants those found to be "of the sect of the Quakers" could be banished on pain of death (if they should return).[35]

Quakers objected to the appellation "foreign." "We are Englishmen, not foreigners," they maintained, "and we are under the protection of the King." As Bishop later complained:

> Are ye Lord's Propriotors of the *Creation?* May not the *Lord* of Heaven and Earth send *His* messengers among *ye,* without *your* leave? May not an *English* Man come into an *English* Jurisdiction? What *Insolency* is *this?* . . .[36]

George Fox directly challenged the right of the Colonists under the charter to limit emigration as they saw fit and to banish whomever they wished and to punish the nonconformers:

> You Professors and Priests of New-England, did the King give you Liberty for your Seditious Conventicle beyond the Seas, and give you a Patent for your Liberty, and that none others whould have their Liberty in New-England but your selves? and doth your Patent say, That you must Imprison, Banish, Whip, Spoil the Goods of all them that will not conform to your Will-Worship, and Blind Zeal, and Self Righteousness and Formalities; and if any do return after that you have banished them, then you are to Hang them . . .?[37]

The death penalty applied not only to the so-called "foreign

Quakers" but to any of the Colonists who defended their "horrid opinions" or who denied "civil respect & reverence to aequalls & superiors" or condemned court proceedings against the Quakers, but always with the condition that they could escape the penalties of the law if they recanted. And there were some who did:

> Whereas Wm. King. late Quaker, and bannished this jurisdiction, on paine of death, returning without leave into it, ... declared how much he, by the rich grace and mercy of God, was brought to loath & abhorr himself for his sinfull & shamfull practises ... the Court judged it meete, for the encouragement of such that shall returne from those principles & wayes of Sathan & Death, to remitt him as to his further triall ... and judgeth it meet to release & disharge him from the sentence of banishment & death ... & set him in *statu quo* with the rest of the inhabitants, to follow his calling for his owne & familys subsistance. ...[38]

We are told by Bishop that the death penalty law, after a long debate, was passed by a one-vote majority (thirteen to twelve) in the House of Deputies.[39] This drastic law might not have come to a vote at all were it not for a petition signed by twenty-five citizens of Boston, initiated, it is believed, by the Rev. John Norton, in October 1658. The petitioners reminded the General Court that the Colony had already been preserved from "many menacing dangers" through "the pious care & faithfulnes of those which have satt att the helme." But Satan had found new ways of "subverting of our civill & religious Polities" and something must be done, though "your servants [the petitioners] are far from prescribing any thing to your wisdomes [the legislators]." Nevertheless, the petitioners urged "some effectuall & speedy expedient, that may crowne you with being the instrumentall Saviour of this people." Making their prescription a little more explicit, they asked if "it be not necessary to punish soe high incorrigibleness ... with *death,* rather than expose religion, this government, & the whole people to both temporall and externall ruine."[40]

The legislators had every intention of enforcing their laws and did not choose to follow the do-nothing example of Rhode Island. But if they assumed that *all* banished Quakers would remain out of the jurisdiction as many other banished people had done up to that date, they were mistaken. When three Quakers returned and told the Court that it had no right to enact laws "repugnant to the laws of England" and hence no crime had been committed by their return, the authority of the Court was definitely challenged. Here was a test case, for the three who had returned had come back for no other purpose than, as they said, "to test the bloody law." (One was in Barbados; two others were in Rhode Island when the law was enacted, and there they could have remained unmolested.) Governor Endecott and some of the magistrates and ministers were adamant. Neither side would yield. The Quakers believed they were called by the Lord to lay down their lives. Quakers Robinson and Stevenson sent a long letter out of "the Common Gaol in the Bloody Town of Boston" where they were awaiting execution, addressed to "all you magistrates and priests" and by their remarks made it virtually certain that the General Court would "loose face" if it then repealed the law or granted a reprieve:

> Oh! thou New-England, who hast made such a Noise among the Nations: Is thy Religion come to no more than Whipping, Imprisoning, Burning in the Hand, and Cutting off Ears, and Banishing upon Death? . . . Is thy Praying, thy Preaching, thy many Sacrifices, and vain Oblations, come to this. . . . Blush and be ashamed . . . thou art running headlong to Destruction . . . Oh ye Hypocrites! How can you Sing, and keep such a Noise concerning Religion, when your Hands are full of Blood . . . thou boasts in thy Wickedness, and thinks thou doest God good Service, to Hang and put to Death the People called Quakers. . . . Oh you Heads and Rulers of this Town of Boston, who are become so Brutish, and so Dark in your Understandings. . . . If you do put us to Death, this Action of yours will proceed from the Devil, who was a Murtherer from the Beginning. . . .[41]

A short time later these two Quakers were hanged, the first to die for the violation of this new law.

From that time forward, the government was on the defensive to show that execution of Quakers was morally justified, and that the proceedings were well grounded in law. Sensitive to mounting popular criticism, the General Court repeatedly declared that the death penalty law was not "repugnant to the laws of England," for it was "according to the example of England in theire provission against Jesuitts." Evidently no objection had been raised to a similar Colonial law made in 1647 against Jesuits who might come into the Colony.

The government believed that if people were fully informed of the dangers to the state its position would be supported:

> Although the justice of our proceedings ... may rather perswade us to expect incouragement & commendation from all prudent & pious men, then [than] convince us of any necessity to apologize for the same, yet, forasmuch as men of weaker parts, out of pitty & commisseration, (a commendable & Christian virtue, yet easily abused, & susceptible of sinister & daingerous impressions,) for want of full information, may be lesse sattisfied, & men of perverse principles may take occasion heereby to calumniate us, & render us as bloody persecutors,—to satisfy the one & stop the mouths of the other, wee thought it requisite to declare ....
>
> The consideration of our graduall proceedings [a reference to the fact that several lesser penalties had been tried before the death penalty was enacted] will vindicate us from the clamorous accusations of severritie, our oune just & necessary defence calling upon us (other means failing) to offer the points [of the swords] which these person have violently & wilfully rushed upon, & thereby are become *felons de se....*

That is, they would not be corporally punished but simply banished, and, if they returned voluntarily, their execution would be tantamount to suicide. The Court hoped the death penalty would be found to be "warrantable & just" and that people would be convinced that the Court would rather banish the Quakers than hang them—"*wee desire theire life absent rather than theire death present.*"[42]

This statement was the formal exculpation of the General Court upon which it would stand. It was immediately sent to London and appeared there on a large broadside or handbill entitled "A Declaration of the General Court of Massachusetts Holden at Boston in New-England, October 18, 1659, concerning the execution of two Quakers."[43] It was the hope of the General Court that this document would put to rest any murmurings in London over the "usurpation" of power by the Colony. Its proceedings would be found by all reasonable men to have been justified.

But its effect was not as intended. It inspired many Quaker replies and in particular the spirited rebuttal of George Bishop. His publication proved to be an effective piece in portraying the many "whippings, and scourgings, bonds and imprisonment, beatings and chainings" endured by Quakers in New England, "these people of God."[44]

Quaker Edward Burroughs was likewise inspired to write a treatise in reply, entitled "A Declaration of the Sad and Grèat Persecution and Martydom of the People of God, called Quakers, in New-England, for the Worshipping of God."[45] Like a legal brief, Burrough answered the General Court point by point, underlining his contention that the Quakers were punished "without the Breach of any Just Law of God or Man; but only for and because of Differences in Judgment and Practice concerning Spiritual things, and without any transgression of the law of God, or their own Laws; Saving that they made Laws against them, on purpose . . . and without any Power truly derived from the lawful Authority of England, contrary to theire Patent. . . ."

The Court was faced with the arduous duty of dealing with a few who simply would not under any conditions submit to the law, though they courted death. Robinson's statement to the Court in 1659 was quite typical:

> The Word of the Lord came expressly to me, which did fill me immediately with Life and Power, and heavenly Love, by which he constrained me, and commanded me to pass to the Town of Boston, my Life to lay down in his Will . . . To which heavenly Voice I presently yielded Obedience . . . and truly I have a great desire, and will to dye herein, knowing that the Lord is with me. . . .[46]

To such words of valor and consecration to a cause, Governor Endecott had a sharp and merciless rejoinder: "We shall be as ready to take away your Lives, as ye shall be to lay them down,"[47] thus leading to a deadly impasse.

The General Court nominated the Rev. John Norton of the First Church of Boston to draw up a document, to be printed at the public charge, for "the prevention of infection" and to prove that the Quakers' practices tended "to the subvertion of religion, of church order, & civill government" and to show that the courts were proceeding according to law.[48]

Spread upon the records of the General Court on October 18, 1659, were Norton's six theological propositions supporting the government's position:

1) The doctrines of the Quakers were "destructive to funda-

mentall trueths of religion," such as "the sacred Trinity," "the person of Christ" and the "holy Scriptures, as a perfect rule of life."[49] Also, he claimed, "one opinion of theires, of being perfectly pure & without sinne, tends to overthrow the whole gospell & the very vitalls of Christianitie, for they that have no sinne have no neede of Christ, or of his sattisfaction, or his blood to cleanse them from theire sinne; no neede of faith to beleive in Christ . . . no need of repentence . . . no neede of growing in grace . . .," etc.

2) "It is the commandment of the blessed God, that Christians should obey magistrates. [Many Old and New Testament verses were cited in support of this statement.] . . . They [the Quakers] despise dominion & are not afraid to speake evill of dignities (2 Pet. 2:10; Jude 8) though the very aingells would not doe so unto the divill (2 Pet. 2:11; Jude 9)."

3) Solomon (as the story is told in 1 Kings 2) put Shimei to death after he had ignored a warning not to go out of Jerusalem.

4) Quakers were likened to an intruder in one's own home; thus the magistrates who were "the publicke keepers and guardians of the commonwealth" had a right to resist such an intruder and, if his death resulted, "blood would be upon his owne head."

5) Quakers were also likened to "the plague of pestilence or other contagious, noysome, & mortell diseases" from which the government must protect its people. "If sheepe and lambes cannot be preserved from the dainger of woolves, but the woolves will breake in amongst them, it is easy to see what the shepherd or keeper of the sheepe may lawfully doe in such a case."

6) Finally, the Quakers did not act like true Christians for "they choose to go contrary to the expresse directions of Jesus Christ, and the approoved examples of his saints." In short, Jesus Christ, they said, had commanded his disciples that if persecuted in one city they should flee to another (Matt. 10:23). Though the Quakers account it *persecution*, "in trueth it is not so, but the due ministration of justice."[50]

For "his great paynes & worthy labors in the tractate" which "fully disproved" the position taken by the Quakers, a grateful General Court on November 4, 1659, granted the Rev. Norton a large tract of land in Worcester on the shores of Quinsigamond Pond.[51]

The Quakers sharply disagreed with Norton's reasoning. As

they saw their mission in America, they were operating under "an indespensible command from Christ, their Lord" with no liberty

> to chuse or refuse coming thither. . . . Then their sufferings and blood will rest on the heads of the Governours of New England, and will stick closer to them, than to be wiped off by such kind of arguments and reasonings. . . . The Quakers came to you in the name of the Lord to . . . [show] the evil of your waies, to convince you by his light, of your departing from that spirit which was persecuted in you in the time of your sufferings in old England; but ye would not meekly hear and consider of what they had to say to you from the Lord, but presently imprisoned and sent them away, and so proceeded further and further against them, till at length ye came to drink their blood. . . . Judg in your own hearts whether this be not *persecution* of a deep dye. . . .[52]

The Quakers defended their position before the Courts on both legal and ecclesiastical grounds. The anti-Quaker laws, they asserted, were illegal for they were "repugnant to the laws of England" and hence contrary to the Charter, or, as we would say today, they were "unconstitutional." To determine this point the Quakers insisted they must appeal to England, but all appeals had been denied. The General Court had always declared itself to be the last court of appeals in the Colony. To the Court's argument that England had similar laws against Jesuits, the Quakers replied, "But we are not Jesuits."

At any rate, the Quakers maintained, the laws were contrary to the teachings of Christ. Christopher Holder, who had been whipped and imprisoned, sent "A Warninge from the Spirit of the Lord to the Governor & Magistrates & People of Masathusets Bay" from "a Friend To all that love the Lord Jesus Christ in Sincerity & Truth," shortly before his friends, Stevenson and Robinson, were hanged:

> . . . come Bringe your Actions to the light . . . that they may be proved whether they are wrought in God yea or nay . . . so whether you walke up answerable to the Scriptures which yow call your Rule . . . compaire your lawes & actions with the law and actions of the Saints in time of old.
>
> What rule have you with presept or presidente [precedent] . . . in the Scriptures for to prison, whipp, cutt Eares & banish upon paine of death if they returne? Have you any Rule from the Prophets,

christ or the Apostles for these things? did they ever doe so? did the Prophets Imprison any or did Christ banish any, or put any man's person to death? . . . did the Apostles whip any . . . ?

From whom then have yow this power, or who is your Example herein if christ neither any of his Servants never did so nor never commaunded any to doe so . . . . Consider this and lay it to hearte before it is too late . . .

I warne yow to beware how yow take away the life of any man or woman that may come amongst you in the name & feare of the Lord. . . . For assueredly if yow proceed to do soe the feirie Indignation of the Lord will breake forth amongst you. . . . woe & misery will come upon you. . . . beware how you proceed any further. . . .[53]

About two weeks later Holder was sentenced to "banishment, on paine of death, in case he be found within this jurisdiction three daies after the next shipp now bound from hence to England be departed from this harbor."[54] He returned to England with the loss of one ear where he served as a visible reminder of New England's treatment of Quakers.

Four Quakers who defied the order of banishment were hanged on Boston common—William Robinson and Marmaduke Stevenson on October 27, 1659, as already stated, and Mary Dyer on June 1, 1660, and William Leddra on March 14, 1661. A few others were condemned to die but execution of the sentence was stayed at the command of Charles the Second. The Order of the General Court on October 18, 1659, was

Wm Robbison, Marmaduke Stephenson, & Mary Dyer, banished this jurisdiction by the last Court of Assistants on paine of death, being committed by order of the Generall Court, were sent for, brought to the barre, acknowledged themselves to be the persons banished. After a full hearing of what the prisoners could say for themselves, it was put to the question, whither Wm Robbinson, Marmaduke Stevenson, & Mary Dyer, the persons now in prison, who have binn convicted for Quakers, & banished this jurisdiction on paine of death, should be putt to death according as the lawe provides in that case. The Court resolved this quaestion on the affirmative; and the Governor in open Court, declared the sentanc to Wm Robbinson, that was brought to the barr: Wm Robbinson, yow shall goe from hence to the place from whence yow came, & from thence to the place of execution, & there hang till yow be dead. The like sentanc the Gover-

> nor, in open Court, pronounced against Marmaduke Steephenson & Mary Dyer, being brought to the barre one after another, in the same words.[55]

Mary Dyer's reputation in the Colony may have weighed heavily against her. Governor Endecott had not forgotten that in 1637 she had been a close friend of Anne Hutchinson whose theological stand led to her banishment from the Bay Colony and was not far removed from that proclaimed by the Quakers two decades later. Both of these women believed that one could receive God's grace without listening to learned discourses by long-winded preachers. Mary and her husband had accompanied the Hutchinsons to Rhode Island and later returned to England. There Mary became a member of The Society of Friends and in 1657 set sail for America, afire with missionary zeal, passing through Connecticut and Plymouth and setting her heart on Boston where in 1659 she visited her Quaker friends who were languishing in the local prison.

Each defendant was asked if he or she had anything to say after sentence was pronounced. Stevenson said, in part, "Assuredly, if you put us to Death, you'll bring Innocent Blood upon your own Heads, and swift Destruction will come upon you." Mary Dyer said: "The Will of the Lord be done. . . . Yea, joyfully I go." Robinson had prepared a paper to read to the Court giving his reasons for defiance and his predictions of dire consequences to come should innocent blood be shed. The paper was handed to the Governor who, after examining it, ruled that it could not be read in Court.[56]

Three months before his death, Robinson in a letter to George Fox (founder of the Society) and others in England, stated his reason for choosing death rather than seeking a safe retreat in Rhode Island:

> My dear Brethren, it would refresh my tender Bowells to receive a few lynes from you, to hear of the work of the Lord in that Island of England, and garden of God, where the Lillies grow, & pleasant smell ascends up unto the Lord . . . .
>
> My life is sacrifyced up, And Laid downe in the Will of God . . . oh! if I never See your faces more in the outward man, the will of God be done, for I am given freely up my Life to Lay downe at this

Towne of Boston for theire Bloody Lawes to Breake. . . . [We came from Rhode Island] in obedience to the Lord, to beare our testimony against there BLOODY LAW.

When he heard than many banished Quakers had fled the jurisdiction and did not dare return to Boston, Robinson made his decision to go back to Boston. Continuing his account, he wrote, "On the same Day that I heard of it, The Lord laid it on me, my Life to give up, *Bostons-Bloody-Lawes* to try. . . ."[57]

The Court issued to the Marshall the necessary orders for their execution and, evidently anticipating trouble from the crowd who were about to witness not an ordinary hanging (hangings were not at all common at that time) but the first executions in the Colony's history of persons who had not been convicted of witchcraft or of any acts of violence, thought it necessary to call out the guard.

Whereas Wm Robbinson, Marmaduke Stephenson, & Mary Dier are sentenced by this Court to death for theire rebellion, & etc., it is ordered, that the secretary issue out his warrant to Edward Michelson, marshall generall, for repairing to the prison on the twenty seventh of this instant October, & take the said William Robbinson, Marmaduke Stephenson, & Mary Dyer into his custody, & them forthwith, by the aide of Captain James Oliver with one hundred souldiers, taken out by his order proportionably out of each company in Boston, compleately armed with pike, & musketters, with powder & bullett, to lead them to the place of execution, & there see them hang till they be dead, and in theire going, being there, & retourne, to see all things be carried peaceably & orderly. Warrants issúed out accordingly.

. . . Itt is ordered, that thirty sixe of the souldiers be ordered by Capt Oliver to remaine in & about the towne as centinells to preserve the peace of the place while the rest goe to the execution . . . October 18, 1659.[58]

It is quite probable that the Court actually feared a violent outbreak similar to the Antinomian uprising in Münster, Germany many years before the Society of Friends was founded, for it expressed the belief that the Quakers' design was to "undermine & ruine" the government—"wee were well assured by our owne experience, as well as by the example of theire predecessors, in *Munster*."[59]

The Court provided religious solace for the condemned in

A DECLARATION OF THE GENERAL COURT OF THE MASSACHUSETS

Holden at *Boſton* in *New-England*, October 18. 1659. Concerning The execution of two Quakers.

Although the juſtice of our proceedings againſt William Robinſon, Marmaduke Stevenſon, *and* Mary Dyer, *Supported by the Authority of this Court, the Lawes of the Country; and the Law of God, may rather perſwade us to expect incouragement and commendation from all prudent and pious men, then convince us of any neceſſity to Apologize for the ſame, yet foraſmuch as men of weaker parts, out of pitty and commiſeration (a commendable and Chriſtian virtue yet eaſily abuſed, and ſuſceptible of ſiniſter and dangerous impreſſions) for want of full information, may be leſs ſatisfied, and men of perverſer principles, may take occaſion hereby to calumniate us, and render us as bloody perſecutors, to ſatisfie the one, and ſtop the mouths of the other, we thought it requiſite to declare.* That about three Years ſince, divers perſons, profeſſing themſelves *Quakers*, (of whoſe pernicious Opinions and Practiſes we had received intelligence from good hands, from *Barbadoes* to *England*, arrived at *Boſton*) whoſe perſons were onely ſecured, to be ſent away by the firſt opportunity, without cenſure or puniſhment, although their profeſſed tenents, turbulent and contemptuous behaviour to Authority would have juſtified a ſeverer animadverſion, yet the prudence of this Court, was exerciſed, onely in making proviſion to ſecure the Peace and Order here eſtabliſhed, againſt their attempts, whoſe deſign (we were well aſſured of by our own experience, as well as by the example of their predeceſſours in *Munſter*) was to undermine and ruine the ſame, And accordingly a Law was made and publiſhed, prohibiting all Maſters of Ships, to bring any *Quakers* into this Juriſdiction, and themſelves from comming in, on penalty of the Houſe of Correction, till they could be ſent away: Notwithſtanding which, by a back Door, they found entrance, and the penalty inflicted on themſelves, proving inſufficient to reſtrain their impudent and inſolent obtruſions, was increaſed by the loſs of the ears of thoſe that offended the ſecond time, which alſo being too weak a defence againſt their impetuous frantick fury, neceſſitated us to endeavour our ſecurity, and upon ſerious conſideration, after the former experiments, by their inceſſant aſſaults, a Law was made, that ſuch perſons ſhould be baniſhed, on pain of Death, according to the example of *England* in their proviſion againſt *Jeſuites*, which ſentence being regularly pronounced at the laſt Court of Aſſiſtants againſt the parties above named, and they either returning, or continuing preſumptuouſly in this Juriſdiction, after the time limited, were apprehended, & owning themſelves to be the perſons baniſhed, were ſentenced (by the Court) to death, according the Law aforeſaid, which hath been executed upon two of them: *Mary Dyer* upon the petition of her Son, and the mercy and clemency of this Court, had liberty to depart within two dayes, which ſhe hath accepted of. The conſideration of our gradual proceeding, will vindicate us from the clamorous accuſations of ſeverity; our own juſt and neceſſary defence, calling upon us (other means fayling) to offer the poynt, which theſe perſons have violently, and wilfully ruſhed upon, and thereby become *felons de ſe*, which might it have been prevented, and the Soveraign Law *Salus populi* been preſerved, our former proceedings, as well as the ſparing of *Mary Dyer*, upon an inconſiderable interceſſion, will manifeſtly evince, we deſire their lives abſent, rather then their death preſent.

Printed by their order in

NEW-ENGLAND.

Edward Rawſon, Secretary.

Reprinted in *London*, 1659

FINIS.

Document written by the General Court of the Massachusetts Bay Colony for distribution in England, to justify the execution of two Quakers in Boston. Courtesy of The British Museum.

their last hours by sending to them—not ministers of their own choice—but two Congregational ministers, one of whom was the Rev. John Norton, who had favored the death penalty.

> It is ordered, that the Reverend Mr. Zackery Simes & Mr. John Norton repaire to the prison, & tender theire endeavors to make the prisoners sencible of theire approaching dainger by the sentence of this Court, & prepare them for theire approaching ends.[60]

On the day of the execution, then, the three Quakers went to the gallows:

> So, being come to the place of Execution, Hand in Hand, all three of them (Robinson, Stevenson and Dyer), as to a Weding-day, with great cheerfulness of Heart; and having taken leave of each other, with the dear Embraces of one another, in the Love of the Lord, your Executioner put William Robinson to Death, and after him Marmaduke Stevenson, who died, both of them, full of the Joy of the Lord, and stedfast in him, and have received a Crown of Life, Sealing their Testimony with their Blood, their Countenances not changing (tho' the Priests thought to have found it otherwise, and some of them had spoken to this purpose, that they should see whether they would change Countenance, when they had a Halter about their Necks) but they remained as fresh (in a manner) even after they were Dead, as before (as was observed by some.)[61]

At the eleventh hour it was decided that Mary Dyer would not be put to death—at least, not on that day. Her son had petitioned the Court for mercy, but the proceedings had not been disclosed to her.

> Whereas Mary Dyer is condemmed by the Generall Court to be executed for hir offences, on the petition of William Dier, hir sonne, it is ordered, that the said Mary Dyer shall have liberty for forty eight howers after this day to depart out of this jurisdiction, after which time being found therein, she is forthwith to be executed, & in the meanetime that she be kept close prisoner till hir sonne or some other be ready to carry hir away within the aforesaid time; and it is further ordered, that she shall be carried to the place of execution, & there to stand upon the gallowes, with a rope about her necke, till the rest be executed, & then to retourne to the prison & remain as aforesaid.[62]

Mary Dyer was prepared to die. As she walked to the gallows, she said:

> It is an Hour of the greatest Joy I can enjoy in this World—No Eye can see, No Ear can hear, no Tongue can speak, no Heart can understand the sweet Incomes and Refreshings of the Spirit of the Lord which now I enjoy. . . .[63]

As she stood on the gallows ladder and "as the Hangman was ready to turn her off," the proceedings were halted, the petition and order of the Court read, and she was asked to come down. Surprised at this report of her reprieve, she said she was ready to suffer as her two Quaker friends had suffered (who in her sight had just been hanged), but she was pulled down and sent off to prison. The next morning she "tendered her Life again," but the authorities escorted her out of the jurisdiction on horseback.

Following the dictates of her conscience, Mary Dyer resolutely made her way back to Boston where again she proudly took her stand before the Magistrates to bear witness against the "wicked laws" of the Colony. Pursuant to the following order of the General Court she was executed on June 1, 1660:

> The whole Court mett together sent for Mary Dyer, who rebelliously, after sentence of death past against hir, returned into this jurisdiction. Being come before the Court, she acknowledged hirself to be Mary Dyer, the person, & was condemned by this Court to death. Being asked what she had to say why the sentence should not be executed, she gave no other answ[r] but that she denied our lawe, came to beare witnes against it, & could not choose but come & doe as formerly. The whole Court mett together voted, that the said Mary Dyer, for hir rebelliously returning into this jurisdiction, (notwithstanding the favor of this Court towards hir,) shall be, by the marshall generall, on the first day of June, about nine of the clocke in the morning, carried to the place of execution, and, according to the sentence of the Generall Court in October last, be put to death; that the secretary issue out warrant accordingly; which sentence the Governor declared to hir in open Court; & warrant issued out accordingly to Edward Michelson, marshall generall, & to Captain James Oliver, & his order, as formerly.[64]

Bishop's comment on this second sentence of death:

> Putting her twice to Dye; a Cruelty beyond once putting to Death (A Comely Grave Woman, and of a goodly Personage, and one of a good Report, having an Husband of an Estate, fearing the Lord, and a Mother of Children) Did ye Pity, Did ye spare? Had ye compassion? Were Bowels in you? Ye Cruel Murtherers![65]

The last Quaker to hang was William Leddra who had been severely dealt with. In Plymouth Colony he had been in jail nearly a year. In Boston, after whipping him, the jailor held him prisoner for almost another year, chained to a log. He was dragged into court, his leg still chained to the log.[66] The record of the Court of Assistants held at Boston, March 5, 1661 states:

William Ledra notwithstanding his being banished this Jurisdiction on pain of Death by the Last Court of Assistants in September last [1660], Returned into this Jurisdiction, was Committed to Prison in Order to his Tryal. The General Court in October last by their Order gave him with Nickolson & the Rest of the Quakers libertie to pass for England or else to go out of this Jurisdiction engaging not to Return, which he & they rejected and would not Accept of, Save the said Nicholson & his Wife: being now brought to the Barr was Indicted by the Name of William Ledra, for not having the fear of God before his Eyes, notwithstanding your being Sentenced by the Last Court of Assistants held at Boston 4th of September 1660 to Banishment on pain of Death, according to the Laws here established, have Returned into this Jurisdiction in a Rebellious and Seditious Manner contrary to the wholesome Laws of this Country, made for the Preservation of the Peace & wellfare of the same: And in Open Court, on the Reading the Last Court of Assistants Jud[gment?] against him he acknowledged in open Court that he was Person in said Judgment so banished.

In answer to what [he] sayd he was tendered in open Court if he could produce a [law] of England Repugnant to our Law here against Quakers . . . he sayd in open Court, he owed no Subjectio[n to the] wicked Laws of his Jurisdiction, sayd he [w]ould not owne [this] Governour to be his Judge and sayd I have Spoken the truth . . . and sayd I know your Ministers are deluders & yourselves Murderers and If ever I turn to Such Murderers as you are let all this Company Say I have turned from the God, which is the Salvation of his People & this I will seale with my blood.

It was told him he might have his life & be at libertie if he would. he Answered I am willing to dy for it, Saying he Spake the truth . . . .

The Indictment being again Read before the Prisoner at the barr, The Jury Considering the Courts Judgment [and] the Prisoners confession brought in their Verdict they found him Guilty.

The Governour in the Name of the Court Pronounced Sentence against him That Is You William Ledra are to goe from hence to the place you came & from thence be carried to the place of Execution and there hang till you be dead.[67]

Leddra, like the others, was a true martyr. In a letter to friends, written some three months before his execution on March 14, 1661, he wrote:

> . . . And I further Testifie, in the Fear of the Lord God, and witness, with a Pen of Trembling, That the Noise of the Whip on my Back, all the Imprisonments, and Banishing upon pain of Death, and after returning, the loud threatning sound of an Halter, . . . did no more affright me . . . than if they had threatned to have bound a Spider's Web to my Finger. . . .[68]

A jury trial in capital cases had always been the defendant's right, but in the case of the Quakers who had returned after Banishment there seemed to be no questions of fact to be tried. The Quakers readily, and indeed proudly, admitted that they were Quakers, that they had been banished, and that they had knowingly returned "to test the law." Nevertheless they had complained that they had been denied proper legal procedure. That no one should be executed without trial by jury was the rule in England. Lest the Colony be accused of laws repugnant to the laws of England, it ordered in 1660 that no Quaker would be executed without "a legall triall by a jury of twelve men" in the Court of Assistants.[69] Sometimes the cases were heard before the General Court (which also had the right to try capital cases). One of the most dramatic of such cases was the trial of Wenlock Christison, a Quaker who appeared defiantly before the Court after two of his friends, Robinson and Stevenson, had been hanged. An earlier colloquy as reported by Bishop, between Magistrate Thomas Danforth, treasurer of Harvard College and prominent member of the General Court, which took place in the Governor's house in Boston, reveals deep feelings of self-righteousness on both sides. Danforth, laying his hand on Christison's shoulder said:

> Wenlock, I am a mortal Man, and dye I must, and that ere long, and I must appear at the Tribunal-Seat of Christ, and must give an Account for my Deeds done in the Body; and I believe it will be my greatest Glory in that Day, that I have given my Vote for thee to be soundly whipped at this time.

To which Christison made reply:

Oh wicked Man! if thou hast nothing to Glory in, in that Day, but in drawing the Blood of the Innocent, and laying Stripes upon the Servants of the living God, thy Glory will be turned into Shame, and Wo will be thy Portion![70]

At the General Court, Wenlock Christison was "brought before the Judgment-Seat." The trial, as told by Bishop to the "Governours of New-England":

Your Governour [Endecott] asked him, What he had to say for himself, why he should not dye?

Wenlock: I have done nothing worthy of Death; if I had, I refuse not to die.

A Member of the Court: Thou art come in amongst us in Rebellion, which is as the Sin of Witchcraft, and ought to be punished.

Wenlock: I came not in among you in Rebellion, but in Obedience to the God of Heaven; not in Contempt to any of you, but in Love to your Souls and Bodies; and that you shall know one Day, when you and all Men must give an Account of your Deeds done in the Body. Take heed, for you cannot escape the Righteous Judgments of God.

Major-General Adderton: You pronounce Woes and Judgments, and those that are gone before you pronounced Woes and Judgments; but the Judgments of the Lord God are not come upon us yet.

Wenlock: Be not Proud, neither let your Spirits be lifted up; God doth but wait, till the measure of your Iniquity be filled up, and that you have run your ungodly Race, then will the Wrath of God come upon you to the uttermost: And as for thy part, it hangs over thy Head, and is near to be poured down upon thee; and shall come as a Thief in the Night suddenly, when thou thinkest not of it. By what Law will ye put me to Death?

Court: We have a Law, and by our Law you are to Dye.

Wenlock: So said the Jews of Christ, We have a Law, and by our Law he ought to Dye. Who impowered you to make that Law?

Court: We have a Patent, and are the Patentees, judge whether we have not Power to make Laws.

Wenlock: How have you Power to make Laws repugnant to the Laws of England?

Governour: Nay.

Wenlock: Then you are gone beyond your Bounds, and have forfeited your Patent; and this is more than you can answer. Are you Subjects to the King, yea, or nay?

Secretary Rawson: What good will that do you? What will you infer from that?

Wenlock: If you are, say so, for in your Petition to the King, you desire that he would protect you, and that you may be worthy to kneel amongst his Royal Subjects.

Court: Yea.

Wenlock: So am I; and for any thing I know, am as good as you, if not better; for if the King did but know your Hearts, as God knows them, he would see that your Hearts are as rotten towards him, as they are towards God. Therefore seeing that you and I are Subjects to the King, I demand to be tried by the Laws of my own Nation.

Court: You shall be tried by a Bench and a Jury.

Wenlock: That is not the Law, but the manner of it; for if you will be as good as your word, you must set me at Liberty; for I never heard, nor read, of any Law that was in England to Hang Quakers.

Governour: There was a Law to Hang Jesuits.

Wenlock: If you put me to Death, it is not because I go under the Name of a Jesuit, but a Quaker; therefore I do Appeal to the Laws of my own Nation.

Then one of you [a member of the Court] said, That he was in your Hands, and had broken your Law, and you would try him. Wenlock deny'd to be tried by your Law; yet the Jury you caused to be called over, and you told him, He had liberty to object against them, or any of them. Wenlock still appealed to the Law of his own Nation; but still you cryed out, That you would try him; and so deny'd his Appeal.

Wenlock: Your Will is your Law, and what you have Power to do, that you will do: And seeing that the Jury must go forth on my Life, this I have to say to you, in the Fear of the Living God, Jury, take heed what you do, for you Swear by the Living God, That you will true Tryal make, and just Verdict give, according to the Evidence. Jury, look for your Evidence, what have I done worthy of Death? Keep your Hands out of innocent Blood.

A Juryman: It is good Counsel.

So away they [the Jury] went, but having received Their Lesson from you [the Court] and being of the same Spirit, quickly brought him in Guilty.

Secretary: Wenlock Christison, Hold up your Hand.

Wenlock: I will not, I am here, and can hear thee.

Secretary: Guilty or not Guilty.

Wenlock: I deny all Guilt for my Conscience is clear in the sight of God.

Governour: The Jury hath condemned thee.

Wenlock: The Lord doth justifie me, who art thou that condemnest?

Then you [the Court] voted as to the Sentence of Death, and were in a manner confounded; for several could not Vote him Guilty of Death, and to Death Sentence him, so far the Witness of God of the Innocency of the Man prevailed. Then said your Governour, after they had voted once, and some of them would not Consent, "I could find in my Heart (such a Thirst had he after the Blood of the Innocent) to go Home," [to England] being in a great Rage; and so misbehaved himself on the Seat of Judgment, that he furiously flung something on the Table.

Wenlock: It were better for thee to be at Home, than here, for thou art about a bloody piece of Work.

[The Governor then asked for another vote; some would not consent] which inflamed your Governour, and filled him with Wrath, so that he stood up.

Governour: You that will not consent, Record it.

Governour: (Like a Man drunk): "I thank God, I am not afraid to give Judgment. . . . Wenlock Christison, hearken to your Sentence, You must return unto the place from whence you came, and from thence to the place of Execution, and there you must be hanged until you be dead, dead, dead, upon the Thirteenth Day of June, being the fifth Day of the Week . . . .

Wenlock: The Will of the Lord be done, in whose Will I came amongst you, and in his Counsel I stand, feeling his eternal Power, that will uphold me unto the last Gasp, I do not Question it. Known be it unto you all, That if you have Power to take my Life from me, my Soul shall enter into Everlasting Rest and Peace with God, where you your selves shall never come: And if you have Power to take my Life from me, the which I do question, I believe you shall never more take Quakers Lives from them (note my words) do not think to weary out the Living God, by taking away the Lives of his Servants! What do you gain by it? For the last Man that you put to Death, here are Five come in his Room: And if you have Power to take my Life from me, God can raise up the same Principle of Life in Ten of his Servants, and send them among you, in my room, that you may have Torment upon Torment, which is your Portion: For there is no Peace to the Wicked, saith my God.

Governour: Take him away.

So to Prison he was sent.[71]

The next year (1661) saw no abatement in the bitterness of feeling on both sides. At its May session the General Court acknowledged its failure to stem the tide, and reiterated its desire "to try all meanes, with as much lenity as may consist with our safety, to prevent the intrusions of the Quakers," for, after the fourth execution, popular clamor for repeal of the death penalty was heard on all sides. The Court ordered further severe corporal punishments for future offenders, probably in the hope that physical suffering might deter them from further "intrusion" upon the government and thus avoid the necessity of resorting again to the death penalty.

Ordered, that every such vagabond Quaker found within any part of this jurisdiction shall be apprehended by any person or persons, or by the connstable of the towne wherein he or she is taken . . . [and if legally adjudged] to be a wandering Quaker, viz, one that hath not any dwelling or orderly allowance as an inhabitant of this jurisdiction, & not giving civil respect by the usuall gestures thereof, or by any other way or meanes manifesting himself to be a Quaker, shall . . . be stripped naked from the midle upwards, & tied to a carts tayle, & whipped through the towne, & from thence immediately conveyed to the connstable of the next towne towards the borders of our jurisdiction, as theire warrant shall direct, & so from connstable to connstable till they be conveyed through any the outward most townes of our jurisdiction. And if such vagabond Quaker shall returne againe, then to be in like manner apprehended & conveyed as often as they shall be found within the limitts of our jurisdiction, provided every such wandering Quaker, having beene thrice convicted & sent away as abovesaid, & returning againe to this jurisdiction, shall be apprehended & committed by any magistrate or commissioner as abovesaid unto the house of correction ... where, if the Court judge not meete to release them, they shall be branded with the letter R on theire left shoulder, & be severly whipt & sent away in manner as before; and if after this he or shee shall returne againe, then to be proceeded against as incorrigible rogues & ennemys to the common peace, & shall immediately be apprehended & committed to the common jayle of the country, and at the next Court of Asistants shallbe brought to theire tryall, & proceeded against according to the lawe made anno 1658, page 36, for theire banishment on payne of death.[72]

This law also applied to Quakers who "shall arise amongst ourselves." The law was never enforced to the limit; that is, no other Quakers were executed for defying the order of banishment, though a number were severely whipped, and one was branded.

After all the imprisoned Quakers had been made "acquainted with the new lawe made against them," they were released from the prison, told to leave the jurisdiction, and informed that if they should return they would be tried in the Court of Assistants as capital offenders.[73]

The General Court ordered that two Quakers who stood mute before the court:

... be forthwith taken out of the prison, & stript from the girdle upwards by the executioner, & tied to the carts tayle & whipt through the towne with twenty stripes, & then carried to Roxbury, and delivered to the connstable there, who is also to tye them, or cause them, in like manner, to be tied to a carts tayle, & againe whip them through the towne with tenn stripes, & then carried to Dedham, & delivered to the connstable there, who is againe in like manner to cause them to be tied to the carts tayle & whipt with tenn stripes through the towne, & from thenc they are immediately to depart this jurisdiction at theire perrill.[74]

There seems to be little doubt that the whippings were severe. Bishop gives this account of the whipping of Sarah Gibbens and Dorothy Waugh for speaking in the Meeting House after the lecture:

... with a three-fold-corded-knotted Whip, with which ye gave them Ten Lashes a-piece, tearing off their Flesh, and beating it to pieces, and then shut them up, and stop'd the Windows [of the prison], to prevent Air and other Refreshment for eight Days together . . . , [the whip used] not of Whipcord, as in England, but of dryed Guts, such as the Base of Viols, and with three knots at the end, which many times the Hangman lays on with both his Hands, and must needs be of most violent Torture and exercise to the Body.[75]

Probably not all Quakers were dealt with in the brutal manner described by Bishop. Quaker Thomas Newhouse describes his experience:

Upon a Lecture-day at *Boston* in *New England,* I was much pressed in Spirit to go into their Worshiphouse among them, where I stood silent until the Man had done Preaching, then my mouth was opened to the People with a word of Exhortation, but through the violence of some of the People was haled to Prison, from whence, about three hours after, they fetched me out to the Court, where I was examined, and so returned to Prison again until the Morning: and into the Court I was brought again, where they had drawn up a Paper against me, as they thought, of what I had said the day before; and they said, *Come thou Vagabond, and hear this Paper read with two Witnesses, their Hands to it, for we will handle thee:* and I said, *Read on;* Where I stood until they had done: And they asked me, *Whether I owned it, or no:* And I said, *Yea, every Word and would make it good by sound Proof if I might have Liberty to speak.* But they cried, *Away with him;* and some took me by the Throat, and would not suffer me to answer to it, but hurried me down Stairs, to the Carriage of a great Gun, which stood in the Market-Place, where I was stripped, and tied to the Wheel and whipped with Ten Stripes, and then loosed, and tied to a Cart's-tail; and whipped with Ten more to the Town's End; and at *Roxbury,* at a Cart's-tail, with other Ten; and at *Dedham,* at a Cart's-tail, with Ten more, and then sent into the Woods.[76]

By 1660 (before the execution of Dyer and Leddra) the tide had begun to turn. Oliver Cromwell, who had sought to advance the cause of Puritanism by the sword, had died in 1658. The monarchy was to be restored. King Charles, the Second, who was to be crowned in April 1661, inclined toward a greater degree of religious toleration. There was no doubt he had been impressed by first-hand accounts of the sufferings of the Quakers who had returned from New England. Would the Royal Charter of the Bay Colony be at last revoked? Could the King be brought to see the conflict as the Puritans saw it? Governor Endecott, in the name of the General Court, at its December 1660 session ordered that a letter be sent at once to "the high and mighty Prince Charles the Second," setting forth its position:

> Our humble request only is, that ... your majesty would permitt nothing to make an impression upon your royall heart against us, untill wee have both oppertunity & licence to answere for ourselves.

We who prize religious liberty, the General Court maintained, brought the Quakers to trial *not* because of their religion but because they came to destroy our form of government:

> Our libertie to walke in the faith of the gospell with all good conscience according to the order of the gospell ... was the cause of our transporting ourselves, with our wives, our litle ones, & our substance, from that pleasant land over the Atlanticke Ocean into the vast & wast wildernes, choosing rather the pure Scripture worship, with a good conscienc, in this poore, remote wildernes, amongst the heathens, then the pleasures of England, with submission to the impositions of the then so disposed & so farre prevayling hierarchie, which wee could not doe without an evill conscience. ... Wee were not permitted the use of publicke worship [in England] without such a yoake of subscription & conformity as wee could not consent unto without Sinne. ... [We left England] that wee might therefore enjoy divine worship without the humaine [human] mixtures, without offence either to God, man, or our owne consciences ...
>
> ... Concerning the Quakers, open & capitall blasphemers, open seducers from the glorious Trinity, the Lords Christ ... open ennemies to government itself as established in the hands of any but men of theire oune principles, malignant & assiduous promoters of doctrines directly tending to *subvert both* our churches & state, after all other meanes for a long time used in vaine, wee were at last constreined, for our oune safety, to passe a sentence of bannishment against them, upon pain of death. ... the Quakers died, not because of theire other crimes, how capitoll soever, but upon theire superadded presumptuous & incorrigible contempt of authority; breaking in upon us, notwithstanding theire sentence of banishment made knowne to them. Had they not binn restreined, so farr as appeared, there was too much cause to feare that wee ourselves must quickly have died, or worse; and such was theire insolency, that they would not be restreined but by death; nay, had they at last but promised to depart the jurisdiction, & not to returne without leave from the authority, wee should have binn glad to such an oppertunity to have sayd they should not dye.[77]

At the same time the general court urged parliament not to grant appeals. A petition to "this most noble Senate" implored them: "Wee have this hope, that your honnour will be very tender of admitting of appeales in particular cases, as not only prejudicall, but even destructive to us."[78] The General Court feared that if any offender convicted in the Colonial Courts could appeal to England the result would be disastrous to the sovereignty of the Colony. The Quakers, on the other hand, believed that without right of appeal they had no protection against laws that were "repugnant to the laws of England" and thus contrary to the Charter. Captain John Leverett, representative of the Colony in London, was instructed in December 1660 to urge Parliament that:

> no appeales maybe permitted from hence in any case, civill or criminal, which would be such an intollerable & unsupportable burthen as this poore place (at this distance) are not able to undergoe, but would render authority & gov't vaine & uneffectuall, & bring us into contempt with all sorts of people . . . .
>
> Concerning our proceedings against the Quakers . . . if there should be any designe to incourage theire coming hither, or his majesty induced to permitt them theire liberty here (which God forbid) wee entreate you above all things else to use your utmost interest to prevent, as being destructive to our being here, & so contrary to our consciences to permitt, & no lesse oppression of us then the destroying of us and ours by the sword. . . .[79]

The following June (1661) "to begett unity amongst ourselves" in the face of increased opposition to the anti-Quaker laws, the General Court appointed a committee of twelve prominent citizens (including the Rev. Increase Mather and the Rev. John Norton) to draw up a document "touching the pattent, lawes, priviledges, & duty to his majesty."

The report submitted by the committee was a masterly document, broadly conceived and clearly delineating the prerogatives of the Colony, its right to defend itself from all enemies of the state and its virtual independence from English rule.[80]

The King, in a letter dated Sept. 9, 1661, taken across the Atlantic and delivered to the Governor by a messenger (Samuel Shattuck) who as a Quaker had formerly been banished from the Colony,[81] ordered that death sentences already passed but not yet executed be stayed, (including that of Wenlock Christison) and that all prisoners be sent to England where they would be proceeded against in accordance with the laws of England, thus denying the Colonists' request that there be no appeals to English courts, but that part of the King's instructions was not complied with.

Responding to the King's letter of September 9, 1661, the General Court on November 27, 1661, made an unusual announcement:

> Although wee hope, & doubt not, but that if his majesty were rightly informed, he would be farre from giving them such favour, or weakening his authority here so long & orderly setled, yet, that wee may not in the least offend his majesty, this Court doth heerby order & declare, that the execution of the lawes in force against Quakers, as such, so farr as they respect corporall punishment or death, be suspended untill this Court take further order.

The Court then proclaimed the second of January (1662):

> to be kept a day of solemne humilliation and supplication to the Lord . . . for the diverting such calamities as are coming upon us & the people of God the Xtian world throughout.

One of the many "great sinns & evill of the country" making such supplication necessary was "the impetuous & restless intrusions of haereticks & ennemies to the wayes, & ordinances of God; the cursed combination of Antichrist & his adherents. . . ."[82]

About a year after the receipt of the King's letter and the suspension of the laws against the Quakers, the Court decided (Oct. 8, 1662) to reinstate the former "Cart & Whip Act."

> This Court heretofore, for some reasons inducing, did judge meete to suspend the execution of the lawes against Quakers, as such, so farre as they respect corporall punishment or death, during the Courts pleasure. Now, forasmuch as new complaints are made to this Court of such persons abounding, especially in the easterne parts, endeavoring to drawe away others to that wicked opinion, it is therefore ordered, that the last lawe, title Vagabond Quakers, May, 1661, be henceforth in force in all respects, provided that theire whipping be but through three townes; & the magistrate or commissioners, signing such warrant shall appoint both the townes & nomber of the stripes in each town to be given.[83]

Wenlock Christison, who had once been condemned to death,

stood before Deputy Governor Bellingham—after the death penalty had been suspended—and said:

> At this Bar, time was, that Sentence of Death was passed on me, yet, by the help of God, I continue unto this Day, standing over the Heads of you all. . . . Some of your Associates are gone, and the Lord hath laid their Glory in the Dust, and yours is a fading Flower. . . .

He was sent to prison and when again brought before the Court one of the Magistrates said: "If thou hadst been Hang'd, it had been well!"

Christison replied, "You had not Power to take away my Life from me; but my Blood is upon you, for you murthered me in your Hearts." He was then stripped to the waist, made fast to a cart and, with two Quaker women, whipped through Boston, Roxbury, and Dedham, receiving ten stripes in each town. The authorities then drove him "into the wilderness."[84]

In another long and friendly letter to the Colony dated June 28, 1662, King Charles the Second had urged the Colony to adopt a policy of freedom and liberty in matters of conscience *but he did not favor indulgence to Quakers*:

> . . . that freedome & liberty be duely admitted & allowed, so that such as desire to use the Booke of Common Prayer, & perform their devotions in that manner as is established here [in England], be not debarred the exercise thereof, or undergoe any prejudice or disadvantage thereby, they using their liberty without disturbance to others, & that all persons of good & honest lives & conversations be admitted to the sacrement of the Lords supper, according to the Booke of Common Prayer & their children to baptisme. Wee cannot be understood hereby to direct or wish that any indulgence should be granted to those persons commonly called Quakers, whose being [is] inconsistent with any kind of government. Wee have found it necessary by the advice of our Parliament here, to make sharpe lawes against them, and are well contented that yow doe the like there.[85]

The King also expressed his satisfaction with the Colony's "expressions of loyalty, duty, & good affection" and assured them he would preserve the Charter "heretofore granted unto them by our royall father."

The General Court, having the King's assurance that "indulgence" need not be extended to Quakers, ordered in October 1663 that: "Quakers or others, which refuse to attend upon the publick worship of God established here [shall be made] uncapable of voting in all civil assemblyes . . . untill certificate be given of theire reformation."[86]

For a period of about twelve years (1663-1675) no new anti-Quaker laws were enacted. Quakers were less harshly punished; they were, in fact, treated with a degree of toleration. Suddenly tragedy struck the Colony. The Indians went on the warpath. The powerful sachem, Metacomet, (called "King Philip" by the English) led his tribes in 1675-1676 in a massacre of the New England Colonists, pillaging and burning villages and slaughtering hundreds of men, women, and children. It was customary to attribute sudden good fortune to the beneficence of a loving God who rewarded men for their piety and good works. Bad fortune, on the other hand, whether it came in the form of a stroke of lightning, a long summer drought, a shipwreck, or an Indian attack was believed to follow upon a course of conduct displeasing to God. The General Court assembled on November 3, 1675 and made the following declaration:

> Whereas the most wise & holy God, for severall yeares past, hath not only warned us by his word, but chastized us with his rods, inflicting upon us many generall (though lesser) judgments, but we have neither heard the word nor rod as wee ought, so as to be effectually humbled for our sinns to repent of them, reforme, and amend our wayes; hence it is the righteous God hath heightened our calamity, and given commission to the barbarous heathen to rise up against us, and to become a smart rod and severe scourge to us, in burning & depopulating severall hopefull plantations, murdering many of our people of all sorts, and seeming as it were to cast us off, and putting us to shame, and not going forth with our armies, heereby speaking aloud to us to search and try our wayes, and turne againe unto the Lord our God, from whom wee have departed with a great backsliding.[87]

The Court listed the "evils" that had so provoked God's wrath, and thereupon proclaimed a "day of humiliation." Penalties were prescribed for each of the "provoking evils,"[88] one of which was the existence of Quakers in their midst.

> . . . mens thresholds are sett up by Gods thresholds, and mans posts besides Gods posts, especially in the open meetings of Quakers . . . to the scandall of religion, hazard of souls, and provocation of *divine jealousie* against this people. . . .[89]

Both the Quakers and the officials who had prosecuted them attributed the savage Indian uprising to God's wrath. The Quakers saw the fulfillment of their prophesies (made fifteen years earlier) that God would punish those who had committed "violence and outrage upon the innocent." On the other hand, the government believed that God had been sorely provoked because of many sins committed in the Colony—not the least of which was the toleration of "cursed heretics" in their midst.

A lessening in the prosecution of violators of anti-Quaker laws had lent encouragement to those who wished to hold regular Quaker services. The General Court decided that all Quaker meetings must cease lest God be further provoked. In November 1675 it was ordered that any one found at a Quaker meeting would be committed to the House of Correction for three days where he would have "the discipline of the house" (that is, ten stripes on entrance) and there to be placed at hard work on a bread and water diet for three days. A fine of five pounds might be an alternative penalty.[90]

Thomas Hutchinson (Province Governor, 1770–1774), commenting on the effect of this law, wrote in his History in 1765:

> I know of nothing which can be urged, in any wise tending to excuse the severity of this law, unless it be human infirmity, and the many instances in history of persons, of every religion, being fully persuaded that the indulgence of any other was a toleration of impiety, and brought down the judgments of heaven, and therefore justified persecution. This law lost the Colony many friends.[91]

To strengthen the law forbidding Quaker meetings, the General Court ordered that the Constables of each town institute a Sunday search, without a warrant, for the secret meetings of the Quakers and to "break open any door where peaceable entrance is denied them." Those who absented themselves from the "publicke allowed" worship of God on the Lord's Day would be punished unless they could show that they were "necessarily absent by the providence of God."[92]

In 1677 Margaret Brewster, mindful of the people of Nineveh in the days of Jonah who covered themselves with sackcloth and ashes in a ceremony of contrition and repentence and were thus saved from the wrath of the Lord,[93] adopted this same symbolism "as a sign" to bring the Puritans to their knees in repentence over their bloody dealings with the Quakers. Her action shocked the congregation of the Old South Church. She described the event:

> I came into Priest Thatcher's House of Worship with my Hair about my Shoulders, Ashes upon my Head, my Face coloured black and Sackcloth upon my upper Garments ... with nothing but Love in my heart.[94]

Judge Sewall described the scene in his diary:

> In Sermon time there came in a female Quaker, in a canvas Frock, her hair disshevelled and loose like a Periwigg, her face black as ink, led by two other Quakers and two other followed. It occasioned the greatest and most amazing uproar that I ever saw. . . .[95]

The constable said she appeared "in the shape of a Devil." Later she appeared in court where the magistrate said to her:

> you are led by the Spirit of the Devil, to ramble up and down the country, like Whores and Rogues a Cater-wawling. . . . There is but one God, and you do not worship that God which we worship. . . .[96]

The court sentenced her

> . . . to bee stripped unto the waste and to bee tied to a cart's tayle and whip't out of the Town with twenty Stripes, begining at the said meeting house, this to bee done upon the next Lecture day in Boston, and the Marshall is ordered to see the Execution thereof Shee standing committed &c. . . .[97]

Margaret Brewster replied; "The Will of the Lord be done: I am contented."[98]

Seventeen years after the last Quaker was executed, the General Court's letter to the King, approved at its October 1678 session, tried to clear itself from the lingering charge of "persecution":

> The Quakers, at their first coming hither, carried themselves so insolently and contemptuously against authority, rayling at and revilling the Governor, magistrates, & ministers, denouncing fearefull curses in the name of the Lord, . . . publickely disseminating and insinuating their damnable opinions & haethrodoxies, to the great endaingering the true Christian religion, & raysing a divition [division], amongst your majesties good subjects, after the triall of severall other milder meanes used, which prooved ineffectuall to restreine their pressing in amongst us, this Court was forced, for the preservation

of the peace & welfare of this your majesties colony, to make a law for banishment, on paine of death, for all such contemptuous and obstinate intruders, which lawe they presumptuously and willingly transgressed, upon which some of them suffered death; yet, so that till the very last it was offered them, that if they would quietly depart the jurisdiction, and promise not to returne againe, they should be dismissed, which they refused; *nor can it be affirmed with trueth that they were put to death for religion,* nor more then it can be affirmed with trueth that the Jessuites and seminary preists put to death in the time of Queene Elisabeth & King James, of blessed memory, was for religion, who wee know suffered death justly for their breach and contempt of his majesties lawes. [Italics added.][99]

Again, a few years later (1680), Governor Simon Bradstreet "in the name of his majestys Generall Court" wrote a letter to the King, attempting to show that the government's attitude toward Quakers was not inconsistent with the idea of "liberty of Conscience":

Concerning liberty of conscience, the denyall or streightning whereof to others is the great complaint of some against us, & that those who differ from us are, by lawe, subjected to fines & forfeitures for the same, wee must acknowledge that a cheife designe of our fathers & predecessors, in their coming over hither, was to enjoy a freedome in the matters of religious worship, accounting all the losses, hazards, difficulties, & great labours of so vast a transportation, & of their first planting a wildernesse, not to deare a price for the same; but that, after all, a multitude of notorious errors, haeresies, & blasphemies should, with impunity, be openly broached, nourished, & proppogated amongst us, as by the Quakers, & etc., wee presume his majesty doeth not intend; and as for other Prottestant dissentors, that carry it peaceably & soberly, we trust there shall be no cause of just complaint against us on their behalfe. . . .[100]

On May 27, 1681, the Secretary of the General Court made a brief but significant entry in the records: "Title Haeresy, section 9, to put to death bannished Quakers upon the returne, repealed."[101] Thus in a formal sense the serious prosecution of the Quakers came to an end, almost two decades after the last Quaker had ascended the ladder. Thereafter, for a time, the scaffold was used only for those who committed crimes of violence—the rapist, the arsonist, the murderer, and the pirate. But soon the authorities turned their attention to witches, and the hangman was busy again.

We shall not here attempt to resolve an important issue bearing upon the moral justification for the prosecution of the Quakers, which was: Were they in fact disturbers of the peace, interferers with public worship, and a danger to the security of the Colony? The official records tell us that at least in a few instances they upset the religious services in the established churches; they jeered at magistrates; they treated court proceedings scornfully, withholding the respect commonly given and expected; and that some of them wandered about shouting "woes and judgments," earning for themselves the sobriquet "Vagabond Quakers and Ranters." According to the Rev. Norton, Quakers

> affected a grave countenance and posture, wore plain apparel, used few words; cryed in the streets, *Repent, Repent* . . . they lifted up themselves above others, and gloried to be called spirituales, men of the Spirit. . . .[102]

Some of them predicted the downfall of the government and may have increased the feeling of insecurity concerning the political future of the Colony; some predicted the people would be overwhelmed by an "irresistible flood"; others that "a famine and a plague" would end their days. One made the sweeping prophecy that "the name of your General Court, and the appointments and ordinances thereof, will be crowned with infamy and reproach from generation to generation."[103] Another said, "The House of Governour Endicot, a greater Persecutor, should be left Desolate, and become a Dunghill;"—"as did accordingly come to pass," according to Quaker Whiting.[104]

It is quite possible that the majority of Quakers—of whom the court records are silent—were more restrained in their behavior, voicing their protests against the laws but not threatening the security of the government or committing any acts of vilification or disrespect toward ministers and magistrates. There is, however, positive evidence that the "turbulent" Quakers—and there were a goodly number—disturbed the worship in the established meetinghouses. No matter what position we take as to the justification for proceeding against them, we should bear in mind that no Quaker—or anybody else—would be immune from prosecution today were he to disturb the worship of others. Our constitutional guarantees of religious liberty would offer him no protection in such event.[105]

Some ardent Quakers sought to show the errors in Puritan theology by the use of Biblical symbols. Sometimes the methods chosen were the most shocking they could devise. Deborah Wilson walked naked through the town of Salem in 1662. The following year Lydia Wardel, "a young and tender chaste woman," whose husband had been cruelly dealt with because of his Quaker sympathies, appeared stark naked in the congregation at Newbury, symbolizing the "nakedness" of Puritan religious thinking. Her mission failed. A severe whipping was her reward.[106]

Information is not available as to the precise number of Quakers or Quaker sympathizers punished by the courts. We know that four Quakers were hanged. The General Court records contain the names of some thirty to thirty-five others whom the magistrates admonished or fined or ordered whipped, imprisoned, disfranchised, or banished. Records of the Court of Assistants and of the Suffolk and Essex County Courts do not add greatly to this number.

Bishop's narrative covering the period from the arrival of the first Quakers in 1656 down to 1660 (just prior to the execution of the fourth Quaker) was written for the purpose of demonstrating "persecution"; hence there is little reason to believe he underestimated the number punished. He reported forty to fifty banished in that period (the majority of whom evidently never returned), thirty-one whipped (one almost to the point of death), seventy-five to one hundred imprisoned (some for as long as ten months, some, of course, punished more than once). The crowded Boston prison probably fitted Quaker Whiting's description as a "wet, dirty, nasty, stinking Dungeon." In addition, the right ears of three Quakers were cut off, and one Quaker was burned in the hand with the letter H (for Heretic). Five appeals to the English courts were denied, he asserted.[107]

From the very outset, the Quakers had predicted all manner of dreadful happenings, of death , and of sudden catastrophies that would befall the "persecutors" and destroy the Colony itself:

> The Day will come, yes, already is, wherein Men will be as much ashamed of your cruelty, as you are past Shame. . . . this shall be an

> everlasting Monument, a Line of Darkness and Blood, which shall incircle your Name for ever and ever. . . .[108]

A report written by Quakers and published in 1703 in London showed "the Eminent Hand and Judgments of the Lord upon some of the Rulers, Priests, and People of New-England, who had a Hand in persecuting the People of the Lord, called Quakers, there."[109]

Bishop gave some examples of the catastrophes which had occurred to the "persecutors." There was, for instance, the time when great crowds of people were returning from the popular spectacle of the hanging of Robinson and Stevenson,

> passing over a great Draw-bridge, it suddenly brake down in pieces with them, and divers of them were wounded and bruised with the weighty fall thereof; and one or two of them, who seemed to joy in the Death of the Innocent, it's said, That the Bones of their Armes, with Thighs and other parts of their Bodies, were broken in pieces, and after a few Days Torment of Body, and Rotting alive, died; and in this also was the Word of the Lord fulfilled, spoken to the Bench, by the Mouth of that faithful Martyr [Stevenson], who said, Take heed, ye Rulers, what ye do, and be warned before it is too late; and know, that in that Day you put us to Death, shall the Judgments of God come upon this place. . . .

Bishop spoke also of "John Endicot, . . . that Nero-like, unjust Judge of the Innocent . . . . the Hand of the Lord struck him off, he stunk alive, and his Name doth rot . . . ." As a result of his "persecutions," . . . "the Lord cut down Endicot, Root and Branch, and his Hangman its said died in great Horror of Mind, and Torment of Body . . . ."

The Hand of the Lord "with Crack of Thunder, and a Flash of Lightning" killed Captain John Danforth as he lay on his bed; John Webb, who led Mary Dyer to the gallows, was suddenly "after a strange manner" drowned "as he was busie in killing a Whale, or great Fish. . ."; Captain Johnson, who led the soldiers in their march to the gallows with William Leddra, was stricken by the Lord and "is as a Man unmann'd, and bereaft of his wonted Understanding; and so Sottish, that his brethren . . . have degraded him"; as to James Oliver, captain of the militia, "that beastly and bloody spirited Creature . . . without Bowels of common natural

Affection, . . . the blasting Hand of the Lord is [in 1669] risen up, against and over him."

The Rev. John Norton, "Chief-Priest in Boston . . . sunk down and died suddenly . . . as he was walking in his House after Sermon." The Rev. Edward Norris, "Priest in Salem" who had said "what was done to the Quakers, was not Persecution but Prosecution," was "smitten Dumb in his Pulpit, and after a while died." Timothy Dalton, "Priest of Hampton, who call'd it Blasphemy, to say, The Light within was the Light of Christ" was killed by the fall of a tree. "Three also of Priest Wilson's Grand-Children died within a short time after ye had put these two Servants of the Lord to Death [Robinson and Stevenson] . . . the Judgment of the Lord . . . is to be taken Notice of."

Major-General Adderton who, at the trial of Wenlock Christison scorned the woes and judgments of the Quakers, saying "The Judgments of the Lord God are not come upon us yet," fell off his horse "which threw him so, that he dyed, his Eyes being started out of his Head like Sawcers, his Brains out of his Nose, his Tongue out of his Mouth, and his Blood out of his Ears . . . dreadful Example to all that dare to Persecute and make Sport at the shedding of Innocent Blood . . . ."

In addition to these personal tragedies that befell the chief actors in the prosecution, the Quakers believed the Lord inflicted his vengeance upon the entire Colony. In the three or four decades following the period of intense hostility toward the Quakers, the corn was "blasted in the Fields," wheat was smitten at the roots so that not even the cattle would eat it. We know that Indians with tomahawk and arrow inflicted horrible tortures and death upon men, women, and children; an epidemic of smallpox brought many others to their graves; the very Charter of the Bay Colony was taken away by the King in 1684; and finally "a plague of witches" afflicted the people in 1692 and almost brought the Colony to complete ruin.

Quaker Whiting, in his "Short Summary" written for the King in 1669, sings a lament for "fallen" New England:

> Oh! *New England, New England,* how can the tender-hearted (whom thou has most cruelly persecuted and despightfully used) in the sense of thy sad State, forbear to take up a Lamentation for thee,

who seemed beautiful in thy beginning, and lovely wast thou whilst in thy Integrity, which was but for a Moment . . . thy Wickedness is as *Scarlet,* and thy Iniquities as *Crimson,* before the Lord . . . How art thou fallen, oh thou untimely Daughter of *Babylon!* . . . *Wo unto* you, ye Rulers and Hireling-Priests of *New-England* . . . who have drunk the Blood of Martyrs and Saints. . . .[110]

† † †

Under the protection of the Charter of 1692 with its assurance of "liberty of conscience" to all Protestants, the Quakers, whose "damnable heresies" and "subversive doctrines" were no longer such a threat to the government, were permitted to worship unmolested in their own meetinghouses. And yet they were heartily loathed by Episcopalians and Congregationalists alike. The Rev. Cotton Mather who was not born until three years after the last Quaker was hanged in Boston, had expressed some years later his genuine disapproval of the severe treatment they had received at the hands of the Bay Colony officials. He would have advised a lesser penalty—"to have their Heads shaven," for, in his view, they were "mad" rather than criminal.[111] But in the year 1706 when they were sending to England reports of their "sufferings" for non-payment of taxes for the support of the Congregational churches, Mather expressed his feelings, and probably those of other Puritan ministers, toward "the wicked Spirit of Quakerism" when he said, ". . .their Light within is a dark, feeble, sinful Creature, and that to sett it up for Christ and God, which is done in Quakerism, is a very horrible Idolatry."[112]

Puritan ministers of the early eighteenth century saw nothing inconsistent in granting a Quaker immunity from prosecution while holding in utter contempt his Quaker tenets and form of worship. Even Roger Williams, as we have seen, thought Quakerism was an abomination, yet deplored the government's heavy hand in denying their right to follow the dictates of their own consciences so long as they did not disturb the peace. The Province government made its position clear in a preamble to a law enacted in 1702, characterizing them as "irreligious persons averse and opposite to the publick worship of God, and to a learned orthodox ministry," while their refusal to pay the legally required taxes for the support of the established church led to "the encouragement of irreligion and prophaneness."[113] However by 1731—seventy-five years after the first Quaker had "invaded" the Bay Colony—this religious group had acquired a different reputation. Governor Jonathan Belcher, in addressing the House of Representatives, said: "They are generally a Sett of vertuous inoffensive People, and good Members of the Common Wealth."[114]

The Quakers in the Province began to decline in strength and numbers from about 1725 to 1740.[115] We have already briefly traced the major victory won by them and the other "dissenters" in forcing the passage of the "exemption laws," first enacted by the General Court in 1728-1729 which permitted the diversion of their tax contributions to the support of their own churches.[116] But they presented to the Province government, as they had to the Bay Colony, two other major problems: refusal to take part in war and their determination not to take an oath.

They never gave up their resolute opposition to taking part in military activities. The government eventually conceded that, because they "profess to be conscientiously scrupulous of attending in arms at military musters," at the onset of the French and Indian War in 1755 penalties assessed against them were remitted, but for each individual refusal to attend, a certain sum was to be assessed against the town in which they lived and apportioned among them.[117] In 1759 when the Governor called for an enlistment of five thousand men between the ages of sixteen and sixty to support an expedition to Canada, Quakers were again exempted from military duties.[118] A like immunity was granted during the War of Independence, which posed difficult choices for these "people of God," who spurned violence yet found that their sympathies lay largely with the revolutionaries. Some lent their support indirectly to the cause of independence; some remained aloof from the conflict and some found themselves once again labelled "subversive."[119]

Quakers had always refused to disobey the mandate of Christ who, in the Sermon on the Mount, had said "Swear not at all." They were thus unable to take the usual oath of fidelity or of allegience to the King or to testify as a witness or serve on the jury in a court of law. It was not until 1719 that they were allowed to "declare," rather than to swear, in taking an oath of "faith and true allegiance to his majesty King George [the first]." Later laws allowed them, in all cases where an oath was required, to "solemnly and sincerely affirm and declare under the pains and penalties of perjury."[120] These laws were carried down to the present, the statute now reading: "A Friend or Quaker when called upon to take an oath may solemnly and sincerely affirm under the penalties of perjury."[121]

During the eighteenth century, Quakers began to drift into other Colonies, many going to Delaware and West New Jersey and finally to Pennsylvania where William Penn (1644-1718), who had suffered imprisonment in England for espousing Quaker doctrines, founded that new Colony in 1682 as "a holy experiment." In the latter part of the eighteenth and in the early nineteenth century, Pennsylvania Quakers became leaders in prison reform. This erstwhile "pernitious sect . . . who have maintained many daingerous & horrid tennetts . . . to the scandell of religion and hazard of souls" won, in later years, an honored place for themselves in their devotion to works of charity, in their support of the antislavery movement, their campaigns for temperance and for world peace, and by their founding of numerous schools and colleges.

Just 299 years after the Massachusetts Bay Colony had taken the life on Boston Common of devoted Quaker, Mary Dyer, the Commonwealth of Massachusetts unveiled a bronze statue of her,[122] placed on the lawn in front of the east wing of the State House, with this inscription:

MARY DYER
QUAKER
Witness for Religious Freedom
Hanged on Boston Common 1660
"My Life Not Availeth Me
in Comparison to the Liberty
of the Truth."

11. THE COLONIAL DRUNKARD

Drink is in it self a good creature of God, and to be received with thankfulness, but the abuse of drink is from Satan; the wine is from God, but the Drunkard is from the Devil. . . .—*Rev. Increase Mather, 1673.*[1]

DR. MATHER, in his characteristically graphic style, here draws a significant line of demarcation between moderation and excess in the use of alcoholic beverages. Social drinking in its milder forms was neither a sin nor a crime in Colonial Massachusetts. There was nothing in the moral code of the Congregational churches, nor in the book of laws, to put a damper on the practice of social drinking in the tradition of old England. Formidable quantities of beer and wine and even "strong waters" were consumed by all classes of Colonial society from the gentlemen holding the reins of government down to the humblest servant, when he could get it. But when one forsook the company of sober men and was seen in public to "drinck druncken," he was obviously "dishonouring God" and his act became at once a sin and a crime, subjecting him to church censure, if he happened to be a member, and to the displeasure of a Magistrate in a court of law.

Here, then, was a sharp challenge to the orderly administration of government. Drinking, if held within the bounds of respectability, was one thing. Beyond that point it created a near crisis and threatened the safety of the entire community, for as the Bay Colony General Court warned, an excess of drinking ". . . if not speedily prevented . . . will bring some stroake of Gods heavy hand upon us. . . ."

The fear that God would be so provoked that he would inflict some frightful chastisement on the entire population for the sins of the few was ever present in the minds of the Puritans and served the ministers well. Dr. Mather in the sermon above quoted, a quarter of a century after the General Court expressed anxiety about "Gods heavy hand upon us," showed how drunkenness had *in fact* brought on "woful Judgements" which "have ever followed this sin." From the pulpit of the Second Church in Boston in 1673 he said:

> What sad Harvests have we in *New-England* had of late years? and doubtless, the prevailing of this iniquity [drunkeness] hath been one cause of it. The good creatures of God have been greatly abused by many amongst us, unto much Sensuality and Intemperancy, therefore doth the Lord take away creature comforts from us. This last Summer [1673] what excessive Rains have there been? Since that Drunkards are to be seen up and down in almost every Town, no wonder that the Lord in Judgement maketh the Earth drunk. Nay, come yet nearer home, and look upon this great Town. How hath God threatned us for this, as well as other sins? Remember the sad Fire that was here in this part of the Town about three years ago: And where did that Fire break forth? Began it not at the ale house? As if the Lord should from Heaven point with the finger, and say Behold, I am displeased with you because of your excessive drinking. Boston, Boston! take heed of this sin, lest I lay thee even with the ground, and thou become desolate.[2]

The machinery of legislation and the whole armament of criminal justice had to be brought into play to keep people reasonably sober. And yet no voice was heard even suggesting complete prohibition.

The Bay Colony took a stand tinged with deep religious feeling, with which the Plymouth Colony was, of course, in perfect accord. "Drunkennes," said the General Court, "is a vice to be abhored of all nations, especially of those who hold out & profess the gospell of Christ Jesus. . . ."[3] Thus when William Renolds imbibed more than he could hold at Stephen Hopkin's tavern in Plymouth, no one was surprised to see him taken to court "for being drunck . . . that he lay under the table, vomitting in a beastly manner. . . ."[4]

There must have been hundreds of William Renoldses in the Plymouth and Bay Colonies. If the court records are a fair measure, drunkenness was one of the two crimes (the other being fornication) that brought more offenders before the lower courts than any other.[5] At first blush this fact may seem incongruous in governments founded and administered by devoutly religious people. The chief offenders, however, were presumably not the "Saints" who, very soon after the foundations of the government were laid, were greatly outnumbered by men and women who were not even church members. Who, then, were those who defiled the art of gracious tippling so long practiced in England?

Governor William Bradford of Plymouth Plantation was the first to raise this question, fully realizing that future generations would raise it also:

> But it may be demanded how came it to pass that so many wicked persons and profane people should so quickly come over into this land, & mixe them selves amongst them? seeing it was religious men that begane the work, and they came for religions sake. I confess this may be marveilled at, at least in time to come, when the reasons therof should not be knowne. . . .[6]

The *Mayflower,* he said, had picked up "a mixed multitud"[7] in London who, like John Billington, the first of the Colonists to be charged with murder, had "shufled into their company."[8] Later ships carried across the Atlantic to Boston and Plymouth thousands of adventurers, laborers, servants, and not a few who found it convenient to leave London in a hurry. "And by this means," wrote Bradford, "the cuntrie became pestered with many unworthy persons, who, being come over, crept into one place or other. . . ."[9]

Hence, for the first time, unrestricted immigration was deemed a potent factor in the criminal behavior of early Americans.[10]

Beer, the common drink of Londoners, soon became the popular Colony beverage. It was not long before cider, wines, and headier stuff afforded the tavern drinker a wider choice. Enterprising brewers were soon ready for the local trade. A few years later, distillers were setting up their equipment, and importers were offering Spanish and French wines, brandy, and rum.[11]

Indeed, the *Mayflower* on her long pioneer voyage was stocked with "sixe-shilling beere" which served to relieve the rigors and monotony of the trip.[12] But when she dropped anchor off the tip of Cape Cod, the supply had almost run out, a near calamity for Captain Jones and his crew who faced the prospects of a dismal homeward journey with empty beer kegs. And so, Bradford, who was an on-the-spot observer, tells us, the passengers were hasted a shore and made to drinke water, that the sea-men might have the more bear, and one (which was this auther him selfe) in his sicknes desiring but a small cann of beere, it was answered, that if he were their owne father he should have none. . . .[13]

But the captain was more sympathetic, for many of his officers "and lustyest men" were desperately sick, evidently with scurvey. He told the Governor "he should send for beer for them that had need of it, though *he* drunke water homward bound."[14]

Even in their extremity men preferred beer, though the supply of water was unlimited. When the Pilgrims first set foot on American soil, the cool, pure spring water on the Cape did not dispel their thoughts of good English beer and wine. Bradford tells us that the first exploring party sent ashore, catching sight of some Indians, started off in pursuit, over the dunes and through the bush,

hopeing to find their dwellings; but they soone lost both them & them selves, falling into shuch thickets as were ready to tear their cloaths and armore in peeces, but were most distressed for wante of drinke. But at length they found water and refreshed themselves, being the first New-England water they drunke of, and was now in thir great thirste *as pleasante unto them as wine or bear had been in for-times.*[15]

Long before man's first acquaintance with the bacterial content of water, it was generally believed—on the basis, no doubt, of sad experience—that there were substantial health hazards in drinking this harmless appearing liquid. Beer and wine, on the contrary, they held to be not only more "wholesome" but to have some medicinal properties, especially for the alleviation of scurvy, that deficiency disease that so commonly and in many cases fatally struck down ocean travellers.

When certain dissatisfied adventurers, who had forsaken Plymouth and returned to London, complained that the water in the Colony was "not wholsome," Bradford replied:

If they mean, not so wholsome as the good beere and wine in London (which they so dearly love), we will not dispute with them; but els, for water, it is as good as any in the world, (for ought we knowe,) and it is wholsome enough to us that can be contente therewith. . . .[16]

In spite of restrictive liquor laws, an exception was always made for the sale of wine and "strong waters" to "relieve the weake and sicke," provided advance approval of a Magistrate were obtained. Even sales to Indians, strictly prohibited in the middle and later years of the Colonies, were legal if made for the relief of:

> any Indian Bona fide, in any suddain exigent of sickness, faintness, &c not exceeding one dram or two, or by the prescription and direction of some Physitian, under the hand of a Magistrate first obtain. . . .[17]

Again, the legislators made an exception in the law prohibiting the sale of liquor on the Lord's day, a day of strict conformity to sober behavior, "in the case of nessesitie for the releife of those that are sicke or faint or the like for theire refreshing. . . ."[18]

Governor Bradford shared the popular distrust of plain water. As a student of the Scriptures, he was perhaps mindful of what the Apostle Paul had said in his first Epistle to Timothy: "Drink no longer water, but use a little wine for thy stomach's sake and thine oft infirmities. . . ."[19] In commenting on the surprising fact that so many men in the Plymouth Colony had lived "to 60 years of age, and to 65, diverse to 70 and above, and some nere 80," he wrote:

> It must needs be more than ordinarie, and above naturall reason, that so it should be; for it is found in experience, that chaing of aeir, famine, or unholsome foode, *much drinking of water,* sorrows & troubls, etc., all of them are enimies to health, causes of many diseaces, consumers of naturall vigoure and the bodys of men, and shorters of life. . . ."[20]

With the common aversion to "much drinking of water," combined with the tradition of the English tavern, the pleasant custom of "drinking healths" to new arrivals and the lack of any other social drink such as tea or coffee, the consumption of alcoholic beverages increased as the years went by and as people from all walks of life emigrated to the new plantations. In a society where it was common to serve intoxicating drinks at religious ceremonies, at funerals and christenings, at the opening of the legislature, and, in fact, on almost any public occasion where large numbers of people gathered, it might be expected that out of such "a mixed multitude" there would be at least a few town drunkards who lacked that exemplary control demanded of godly persons.

Only seven years after the establishment of the Bay Colony, official recognition was given to the fact

> upon many sad complaints, that much drunkennes, wast of the good creatures of God, mispence of precious time, & other disorders have frequently fallen out in the inns; & common victualing houses within this jurisdiction, whereby God is much dishonoured, the profession of religion reproached, & the welfare of this commonwelth greatly impaired, & the true use of such houses (being the necessary releefe of travellers) subverted. . . .[21]

Eleven years later conditions had evidently not improved. The legislators conceded that "notwithstanding all the hoalsome lawes provided & published" there was an "excesse of drinking & unto drunkennes it selfe . . . to the dishonour of God, the discredit of the gospell, to the shame of the country. . . ."[22]

The Plymouth Colony at a later date joined in the lamentation over "the Intollarable abuse in divers ptes of this Jurisdiction by the bringing in of such great quantities of wine and stronge waters by which greate excesse is occationed both amongst Indians and English. . . ."[23] By 1671 it was noted in Plymouth that "the sin of Drunkeness, doth greatly abound, to the dishonour of God, impoverishing of such as fall into it, and grief of such as are sober minded,"[24] for by that time drunkenness was referred to as "that great and raging sin. . .a growing and prevailing evil. . . ."[25] Legislation had proved ineffective to stop this evil, for in spite of "all the care and endeavours of this Court. . .yet many goe on in it. . . ."[26]

It is easy for twentieth century critics to misjudge the part excessive drinking played in the social life of the Colonies and its place in the total penological picture. On the one hand, the government's insistence that liquor laws be obeyed, lest God wreak his vengeance upon the whole Colony, resulted in a large number of arrests and court appearances. This fact may lead the historian to overemphasize the incidence of excessive drinking in the general population. On the other hand, the lack of complete court records, particularly in the lower courts and in hearings before magistrates, may cause him to underestimate the degree to which excessive drinking had taken hold of the average inhabitant. And yet one is constrained to conclude, from the wording of the many legislative preambles, the variety and number of restrictive laws, and the relative frequency of recorded prosecutions, that the excessive use of intoxicating beverages created a real social problem, particularly among the middle and lower classes.

In trying to keep social drinking within respectable limits to prevent one of the pleasant amenities of Colonial life from inducing idleness or, in its excesses, "dishonoring God" (the bountiful giver of these pleasures), the legislators were constantly concerned lest the legal restraints they imposed would be insufficient to put an end to this "growing evil." The result was a changing body of regulatory laws and orders to curb, without completely prohibiting, the sale and consumption of intoxicating beverages. It would be a mistake to assume that these restrictive laws grew solely out of the imaginative brains of the Pilgrims and Puritans or that they alone considered excessive drinking immoral. In England too, while drinking in moderation was socially approved, drinking in excess was an immoral act and a crime punished by the secular courts. Massachusetts lawmakers were, of course, familiar with these laws and adapted many of them to their own uses, without the necessity of obtaining approval from Parliament. Liquor control was, therefore, by no means the exclusive concern of these God-fearing people in Massachusetts, but there is no denying the fact they added a religious touch to the whole business. Other New England colonies had also sought to control the manufacture, sale, and consumption of intoxicating beverages by laws somewhat similar to those enacted by the Plymouth and the Bay Colonies.[27]

The English practice of requiring retailers to apply for a license was carried over to the Colonies:[28] Stephen Hopkins, one of the original *Mayflower* passengers, at one time Assistant Governor in Plymouth Colony and a prominent citizen there, was on more than one occasion hailed before the courts for some irregularity as a tavern keeper. For example, in 1639, "Mr. Steephen Hopkins, for selling strong water without lycence, proved & confessed in Court, is fyned 3 pounds. . . ."[29]

Brewers and distillers were also under careful scrutiny. In 1637 the Bay Colony decided that all brewers must first obtain authorization from the General Court or the Court of Assistants.[30] Captain Robert Sedgwick's brewery, however, was at that time already a going concern. A resident of Charlestown, and a prominent official of the government, Sedgwick was one of the original members of "The Millitary Company," later called "The Artilerie Company" and, one hundred years later, the "Ancient and Honorable Artillery Company." He was also elected Major Generall of the Colony. The Court legalized the first brewery in the Bay Colony when it said:

> Whereas Captaine Sedgwick hath before this time set up a brew house at his greate charge, & very commodious for this part of the countrey, hee is freely licensed to brewe beare to sell according to the size before licensed dureing the pleasure of the Courte. . . .[31]

The lawmakers overlooked no detail in the beverage business. The *quality* of the brew naturally was of great importance to the public. In the Bay Colony: "Every person Licensed to keep an Ordinary alwayes shall be provided of Strong wholsome Beer, of four Bushels of Malt to a Hogshead. . . ."[32]

Later it was decided that if beer was to be sold for three pence a quart it must contain six bushels of "good barly mault" per hogshead. At the price of two pence a quart, it might contain four bushels of malt, while penny beer need contain only two.[33] It was found necessary to bolster this law subsequently with another that warned that no beer or ale could be sold to the public if: "not made altogether of good barley mault, without any mixture of molasses, course sugar, or other materials insteed of mault. . . ."[34]

Plymouth Colony also was concerned with the quality of the brew: "All ordinary keepers be ordered to keep good beer in theire houses to sell by retaile and that some one in every towne bee appointed to see that the beer they sell be suitable to the prise they sell it for. . . ."[35]

To insure a good brew, some attention had to be paid to skill. The Bay Colony decided:

> to the end that no other but good & wholesome beere be brewed, . . no person whatsoever . . . shall undertake the callinge or worke of brewinge beere for sale but only such as are knowne to have sufficyent skill and knowledge in the art or mistery of a brewer. . . .[36]

Brewers were subject to what we might call an "income tax." Because of "the advantage of their arts and trades" brewers were among those who were "more enabled to help bear the publick charge than common labourers and Workmen" and hence were taxed "on gaines" from their business.[37]

Government control of trade was not uncommon either in the Colonies or in England. Ceiling prices on retail sales of beer, wines, and strong liquors showed considerable variation from time to time.[38] All innkeepers were supposed to know their limitations and were put on notice that those guilty of "excessive prices" for food or drink served in the Bay Colony "shalbee deepeley fined."[39] And many of them were. In Plymouth, too, we find the law enacting its penalty: "Mr. Stephen Hopkins is presented for selling beere for 2 pence the quart, not worth 1 pence a quart. Witness, Kenelme Winslow. Fined. . . ."[40]

Beer, a relatively cheap drink, rather than wine, was made available in all taverns by a law requiring keepers to provide "good and wholesome beare, for the enterteinment of straingers, who, for want thereof, are necessitated to too much needless expence in wine. . . ."[41]

Taverners were looked upon as public servants who followed a respectable calling and could scarcely expect to make exorbitant profits without running afoul of the law on many counts. The Colony taxed all intoxicating beverages, whether locally manufactured or imported.[42] As difficulties arose in the enforcement of these laws, new laws were enacted to prevent secret hideouts and evasions. In the Bay Colony the "auditor gennerall" had the power to search "into all the howses or cellars he knows or suspects any wyne to be. . . ."[43] The collection of taxes and imposts was an onerous job, sometimes "farmed out" to individuals for a consideration under specific contracts with the government.[44]

A tavern keeper was thus burdened with a multiplicity of regulations, all entailing substantial penalties for the delinquent. The first regulatory law for taverns had in fact put the responsibility for drunkenness squarely up to him, for it warned that "The person in whose howse any were found or suffered to drinke drunck be left to the arbitrary fine & punishment of the Governor & Cowncell. . . ."

Furthermore, he had to keep in mind that the Colonial authorities, following the English practice, had permitted taverns in the first place only for the necessary rest and refreshment of travelers, not for local residents of the town. It was not long, however, before they became a haven of sociability for local characters who spent "much precious time" there in affable company over a pot of beer, sack, or rum. Plymouth Colony tried early in its history, without much success, to discourage this practice, ordering that "none shall diett in Inns and Alehouses nor haunt them which are in the townes they live in nor make them the ordinary place of theire abode. . . ."[45] A later enactment forbade any tavern keeper to allow "any townsmen to stay drinking in his house above an houre att one time. . . ."[46]

Thus the license granted to William Bassett, Jr., to sell wine and strong waters in his Sandwich tavern on the Cape expressly denied him the right to "permitt any of the towne to stay drinkeing att his house. . . ."[47] Gyles Rickerd, Jr., of Plymouth was also warned as his father had been before him, when receiving his license, to:

> suffer none of the towne of Plymouth to buy either wine or strong liquors of him of any kind, but such as they will make use of att their owne homes, as the said Rickard will answare it att his perill. . . .[48]

Finally, in 1677, all local residents were barred from Plymouth taverns "except incase of manifest sickness or Nessesitie in that kind. . . ."[49]

The Bay Colony, too, struggled with this obviously unpopular restriction, at first permitting local residents to obtain refreshment provided they did not "remain longer then [than] for their necessary occations."[50] Later laws charged the tavern keeper with seeing that no one "continue tipling above the space of halfe an hour. . . [or]. . .at unseasonable times. . .[or]. . .any time after nyne of the clock. . . ."[51]

The Plymouth tavern keeper, required to keep an eagle eye on all who might be inclined to "unrullynes or rebaldry,"[52] had to be particularly alert to see that there was no "immoderate" or "excessive" drinking in his establishment lest he lose his license for a period of three years. The word "excessive" was a key word, for it marked the distinction between drinking that was socially approved and drinking that was sinful. Puritans did not doubt that "excessive" drinking was to be deplored. Had not the Apostle Paul said in his letter to the Ephesians (5:18) "And be not drunk with wine, wherein is *excess*. . ."? The General Court decided it was necessary to set up a standard for wine drinkers: "It was declared to be excessive drinking of wine when above halfe a pint of wine is allowed at one time to one person to drinke. . . ."[53]

Another fine could be exacted of a tavern keeper if he attempted to hide a drunkard from the prowling constable (who could search a tavern without a warrant) or if he failed to summon a constable when necessary or to hold a drunkard until the law officer arrived on the scene.[54]

Further responsibility was placed on the seller if he continued to offer drinks to those officially declared "common drunkards" whose names had been "set up in some publick place."[55] Indeed, the many burdens placed on a tavern keeper made him virtually a deputy constable, always in danger of losing his business altogether if he tolerated customers who "tarry long at the wine." He had to report also to the authorities any troublesome guests who "doe not attend order, but carry themselves uncivilly, by being importunately desirous of drink when deneyed, and doe not leave the house when required. . . ."[56]

Taverners must have been well acquainted with those local citizens who were most likely to jeopardize their licenses. Sometimes the government issued a specific warning. Plymouth authorities, for example, let it be known that John Barnes, a notorious offender, must be denied the opportunity to offend again: "The ordinary [tavern] keepers of the towne of Plymouth are heerby prohibited to lett John Barnes have any liquors, wine, or strong drinke, att any time, within dores or without, on the penaltie of being fined fifty shillings. . . ."[57]

In Scituate, tavern keepers were required to keep a close tab on three habitual drinkers:

> Whereas Daniell Turner, Joseph Studley, and Peter Worthylake, are complained of for theire abusive frequenting the ordinaryes in Scittuate, spending theire time there, and expending theire estates, soe as they are become very poor, these [orders] are therefore to require all such ordinary keepers as are in Scittuate to take effectuall course that the said persons be not entertained soe frequently and unnessesarily, contrary to the lawes of this government, in theire houses, nor any other like them, as such ordinary keepers will answare it att theire perill. . . .[58]

In Boston, too, it was clear that the taverns and ale houses were not to cater to men who liked to spend "theire time & estate by drincking & tipling."

Not all drinking, of course, was done in the inns. One could have liquor in his own home. A householder could import liquor, if he wished, for "his own pticular use," which in Plymouth in 1668 was limited in amount to "six gallons in the yeare." This law reflected, as many of the criminal laws did, a class distinction:

> if it appeer that any man of quallitie whose condition calleth for further expence in his family that then this law shall not reach them; onely this is to be understood that under pretence of this hee shall not give or sell to be carryed abroad except it be soe that the ordinary keepers have none to supply the necessities of them that are sicke. . . .[59]

Usually inkeepers, too, could keep a little liquor in their own homes "for their owne private & necessary use. . . ."[60] Purchasers did not always consume their drinks on the premises. What we might today call a "package store" was opened in 1686:

> The Court hath granted liberty to Margeret Muffee, of Scituate, to retaile strong liquores in the towne of Scituate, aforesd, to such as buy itt & carry itt out of door, or from her house, & nott drinke itt there, & likewise that she shall not sell such liquores by less quantities than one gallond, & be carefull whome she sells itt too. . . .[61]

Thirsty Indians presented the taverns with one of their most vexatious problems. In the early days of the settlement, friendly negotiations with the Indians were usually consummated with an offering of beer, wine, or cider. The natives soon acquired a liking for the white man's beverages, especially his "strong waters." Tavern keepers discovered that an intoxicated savage was a more obstreperous customer to handle than a muddled Englishman.

New legislation to keep Indians sober was soon placed on the books. The Bay Colony had already been specifically cautioned on this point, even before the first settlers left England. "The Governor and Deputy of the New England Company for a Plantation in Massachusetts Bay" had sent a directive to "Capt. John Endecott et al," but more for morality's sake than for self protection. Dated June 3, 1629, Gravesend, England, the letter said in part:

> Wee pray yow endeavour, though there bee much strong waters sent for sale, yett soe to order it as that the salvages [Indians] may not for our lucre sake bee induced to the excessive use, or rather abuse of it, and at any hand take care our people give noe ill example; and if any shall exceede in that inordinate kinde of drinking as to become

> drunck, wee hope yow will take care his punishment bee made exemplary for all others. . . .[62]

In one of the first recorded laws of the Bay Colony, the General Court in 1633 forbade anyone to "sell, or (being in the course of tradeing,) give any stronge water to any Indean. . . ."[63]

But the pleasure of wine drinking that seemed to have some warrant in Scripture, was a different matter:

> The Court, apprehending that it is not fit to deprive the Indians of any lawfull comfort which God aloweth to all men by the use of wine, do order, that it shalbe lawfull for all such as are or shalbe alowed licence to retaile wines to sell also to the Indians so much as may be fit for their needful use or refreshing. . . .[64]

However, as it turned out, the Indians had a craving for beverages of higher alcoholic content. Ten years after the legislators' liberality as to wine, it had become evident that the Indians "through the excessive and abusive drinking of wine and strong licquors, are frequently overcome, and thereby guilty of swynish drunckennes. . . ." The General Court in 1654 decided it was high time to clamp a tight prohibition on sales to Indians by decreeing a relatively heavy fine of forty shillings for each pint that anyone might "sell, trucke, barter or give. . .to Indians. . .whether known by the name of Rum, strong-waters, Wines, strong Beer, Brandy, Cyder, Perry, or any other strong Liquors. . . ." The usual exceptions were noted in this law, permitting the Indian to have his liquor "in case of suddain extremity, by sickness or fainting, which calls for such help, not exceeding one dram. . .[or]. . .when any Physitian shall prescribe in the way of Physick. . . ."[65]

"Informers" against those who sold to Indians in violation of law were to receive one-third of the fine collected. This provision for rewarding informers (still found in some of our modern statutes) was quite common in Colonial criminal laws. In respect to the law prohibiting sales of liquor without a license, for example, an informer was entitled to "halfe of the fine for his incuragement."[66]

Plymouth Colony too, after some years of sad experience, forbade the sale of both wine and "strong waters" to Indians, except for those who were sick and in need.[67]

By 1657 many of the English believed they were in real peril from intoxicated savages for "excessive drinckinge & drunckeness amongst the Indians" had led to "murder & other outrages," and notwithstanding prohibitory laws "there is litle or no reformation in that kinde. . . ."[68] Nine years later the General Court again noted that "the sinn of drunkenes amongst the Indians doth much increase. . . ."[69]

In the latter years of the Colonies, the authorities tried new controls. An Englishman was then given the right to seize an Indian found drunk and to take him and any liquor he might have with him to the constable. Liquor found in the Indian's possession was to be declared "stollen goods," unless he could prove otherwise. Informers were to receive one-half of the liquor confiscated or its value in money. Indians found guilty of drunkenness who could not pay the rather heavy fine of ten shillings were subject to a whipping "by laying on ten stripes." If they would not divulge the source of their illicit supply, they were subject to imprisonment until they did so. Indians who continued to shield the culprits were subject to a commitment to the house of correction.[70]

Sailors, too, were at times a threat to sobriety. Disembarking from ships putting into Boston Harbor after a long sea voyage, they followed the universal custom of heading for the nearest tavern. The General Court remarked: "many & great miscariages are committed by saylors, in resept [respect] of theire immoderate drinkinge of wine, beere, & stronge liquors. . . ." This custom not only redounded "to the great dishonour of God & reproach of religion & government" but proved to be an economic loss to ship owners, for sailors drinking more than they could pay for were seized and held by the innkeeper until the debt could be satisfied. Many a sailor thus missed his ship as it sailed out of the harbor. The General Court cautioned taverners to provide sailors with only what drinks they could pay for. A new law forbade recovery for their indebtedness, unless guaranteed by the shipmasters.[71]

As early as 1636 it was found necessary to charge Plymouth Colony "victuallers" with a misdemeanor if they permitted children (or servants) to drink and spend their time in the local tavern, but a later law granted an exception to those who had "libertie from theire parents or masters."[72] As time went on, some children must have outwitted the law, for in 1677 the authorities expressly decreed that no wine, strong liquors, or cider could be sold "to any boyes Gerles or single persons tho pretending to come in the name of any sicke person without a note under the hand of some sober person in whose Name they come. . . ."[73]

Even before that time, in the year 1658, much concern was expressed over youths who set out on a Saturday night in a spirit of levity fortified by a little too much of "the good creature." At this time in the life of the Colonies most of the original planters had passed on. A new generation had grown up somewhat less devout and less willing to conform to the strict Sabbath code of their fathers, a Sabbath that commenced at sundown on Saturday. The General Court sitting in Boston in that year said:

> by too sad experience it is observed, the sunn being sett, both every Saturday & on the Lords day, young people & others take liberty to walke & sporte themselves in the streets or feilds in the severall tounes of this jurisdiction, to the dishonor of God and the disturbance of others in theire religious exercises, and too frequently repaire to publicque houses of entertainement, & there sitt drincking, all which tends, not only to the hindering of due preparation for the Saboath, but asmuch as in them lies renders the ordinances of God altogether unprofitable, & threatnes rooting out of the power of godlines, and procuring the wrath & judgmente of God upon us and our posteritie. . . .[74]

Those found guilty of this kind of behavior were subject to a five shilling fine or corporal punishment.

One of the old English traditions, said to have had its origin in antiquity, was the drinking to one another's health. This custom had grown to such proportions in England that Governor Winthrop, probably one of the most abstemious of any of the high officials, thought he might put an end to it before it took firm root in the Bay Colony, by setting a good example in his private life. He wrote hopefully in 1630:

> The governor, upon consideration of the inconveniences which had grown in England by drinking one to another, restrained it at his own table, and wished others to do the like, so as it grew, by little and little, into disuse.[75]

Nine years later the Governor sadly took note of the continued practice which then called for an order of the General Court.

> At the general court an order was made to abolish that vain custom of drinking to one another, and that upon these grounds:

1. It was a thing of no good use.
2. It was an inducement to drunkenness, and occasion of quarrelling and bloodshed.
3. It occasioned much waste of wine and beer.
4. It was very troublesome to many, especially the masters and mistresses of the feast, who were forced thereby to drink more oft than they would, etc.

Yet diverse (even godly persons) were very loath to part with this idle ceremony, though (when disputation was tendered) they had no list nor, indeed, could find arguments, to maintain it. Such power hath custom, etc.

Although drinking healths at that time was not considered one of the more serious crimes, the law (probably drafted by Governor Winthrop himself) stated that drunkenness, quarrelling, and bloodshed induced by this custom ought to be prevented in *all* places and times but

> especialy in plantations, of churches, & common weales, wherin the least knowne evills are not to be tollerated, by such as are bound by soleme covenant to walke by the rule of Gods word in all their conversation. . . .[76]

It would have taken more than the example set by the Governor or the order of the General Court to root out this tradition honored for many centuries and destined to continue for many more. The authorities found themselves powerless to prohibit what the public so ardently embraced. So long as drinking was permitted, friends and strangers too were going to offer drinks to one another's health—"such power hath custom." Six years after this restraining order, there appeared in the record in 1646—without apology or preamble—this simple statement: "The order against drinking one to another is hereby repealed."[77]

Thus the secular authorities acknowledged defeat, but the fight was continued from the pulpit. Many years later the Rev. Increase Mather reproached those Puritans who followed Christ but bowed down to a custom that compelled men to drink more than they wished, "an Heathenish, nay an Idolatrous Rite." In his famous sermon "Wo to Drunkards," he said:

> . . . Papists indeed plead for the lawfulness of it, yet Protestants generally condemn it. . . . [It is] A Shoing-horn to draw on Drunkenness; it is a Bacchean Artifice, which Satan hath devised for that end. . . .

Toward the end of the Bay Colony period, the authorities deemed it necessary to curb drinking on military training days for young men and on "public conventions of people on civil occasions" when it was customary for convivial spirits to get together in the taverns or in the marketplace to share with each other a little of "the creature." But, the General Court observed, this practice led to "drunkeness, fighting, neglect of duty, etc.," and had to be stopped. Accordingly, a law enacted in 1679 forbade the sale of "wine, strong liquors, cider & other inebriating drincks on such occasions . . . ."[78] Earlier days in the life of the Bay Colony had seen more orderly crowds. In 1641 Governor John Winthrop himself reported:

> A great training at Boston two days. About 1200 men were exercised in most sorts of land service; yet it was observed that there was no man drunk, though there was plenty of wine and strong beer in the town, not an oath sworn, no quarrel, nor any hurt done. . . .[79]

The Rev. Increase Mather in 1673 deplored the increasing number of taverns and ale houses in Boston. "I know," he said, "that in such a great Town as this, there is need of such Houses, and no sober minister will speak against the Licensing of them; but I wish there be not more of them then [than] there is any need of."[80] He was sure that God shared this view. By 1681 the General Court was convinced that taverns and other licensed shops were multiplying at too fast a rate. It limited the number of such establishments in the towns of Boston, Salem, Charlestown, Ipswich, Gloucester, Lynn, Hingham, and Newbury. In Boston, for example, there could be but six "wine taverns," ten "inholders," and eight "retaylors for wine & strong licquors out of doores" and in the other towns, of course, a lesser number. In the smaller Bay Colony towns, no more than one public house or "retailor" could be licensed.[81] Three years later it was found that the number of licensed houses in Boston was "not sufficient for the accomodation of the Inhabitants and Trade of the Town, by reason whereof sundry inconveniencies do accrew. . . ." Thereupon the County Court of Suffolk was authorized to license "five or six more Publick Houses in Boston."[82]

Another custom that seemed to have encouraged drinking was brought to the General Court's attention through "sundry & frequent complaints" relating to the workingman's desire for higher wages, or as the Court phrased it, to "oppression by excessive wages of worke men & labourers." The Puritans had long been accustomed to regulating trade by fixing top prices for necessary articles sold at retail and by setting maximum wages for workmen, in contrast to the modern practice of setting *minimum* wages. These complaints concerned an evasive device that not only was considered by their employers an "oppression" but carried with it a threat to sobriety. In its preamble to a new prohibitory law passed in 1672, the Court claimed that, notwithstanding its attempt to combat a trend toward "excess" in wages:

> such oppressions continue & further increase, by a dangerous imposition of such persons on those they worke & labour for, by demanding an allowance of licquors or wine every day, over & aboue their wages, without which it is found, by too sad experience, many refuse to worke. Now, forasmuch as such practize of drincking licquors & wine tends much to the rooting young persons in an evill practice, & by degrees to trayne them up to an habitt of excesse. . . .[83]

The Court warned that any person giving wine or strong liquors to workmen "or boyes that work with them, except in cases of necessity" would be fined twenty shillings for each offense.

The courts did not always have a clear understanding of just what degree of intoxication should be punished, nor could they always distinguish drunkenness from organic diseases or infirmities. The first case of this nature was that of William Busbey who appeared at a Court of Assistants in Cambridge in 1638, "being presented for drunkenness, it was found the falling sicknes."[84]

James Cole, Sr., was another puzzling case. He appeared before a magistrate "on suspision of being drunke." He was an elderly man at the time (and possibly the same person who many years before had opened the first tavern in Plymouth and had in his youthful years been before the courts for drunkenness). He denied the charge, pleading "infeirmitie of body, which may make some think sometimes hee is drunke when hee is not. . . ." The magistrate, evidently not quite convinced, "pased it by" but noted that this incident should be kept in mind "if hee bee found for the future apparently to transgresse againe in the like kind. . . ."[85]

Bay Colony magistrates were given no clear definition or test to guide them. The law simply said, after the word "Drunken," "viz. so as he be thereby bereaved or disabled in the use of his understanding, appearing in his speech or gesture. . . ."[86]

Plymouth legislators wrote into the law an operational definition that was colorful at least, although of doubtful practicality:

> By Drunkenesse is understood a person that either lisps or faulters in his speech by reason of overmuch drink, or that staggers in his going or that vomitts by reason of excessive drinking, or cannot follow his calling. . . .[87]

Drunkenness was a crime—a deliberate, willful crime—just as it is in Massachusetts today, and offenders had to suffer not only rebuke by the clergy but the usual punishments for criminal offenders. Magistrates, as a rule, in dealing with a first offender appearing on a charge of drunkenness, simply fined him and sent him on his way. But they soon found they were dealing with a crime that seemed to be more repetitious than any other, for the drunkards then, as now, were the greatest recidivists known to the courts. In accordance with the usual practice in the criminal courts, one who stubbornly persisted in choosing the path of sin, in spite of legal penalties, suffered a harsher penalty for each subsequent offense until he had learned his lesson.

It seemed to have been generally recognized that continued drinking could become a real addiction, and that few of the "common drunkards" could be reclaimed, but there was little understanding of the nature of compulsive drinking and there was, of course, no notion, such as there is today, that the heavy drinker might be responding to some unconscious need or that "alcoholism was a disease that could be cured." Increase Mather believed there was hope for the addict by salvation through Christ. Surely he was aware of the strong hold alcoholic addiction had on a man when he said. "It [drunkenness] doth so bewitch and besot the committers of it, as that though they know it hath, and will prove hurtful to them, yet they cannot be perswaded to leave it."

In Plymouth Colony a first offender might be fined five shillings, while a second offender would pay ten or, if he could not pay it, be required to sit in the stocks for two hours. On his third appearance before the court, he might be required to put up a bond for his good behavior. Should he continue in spite of ample warnings, he might be asked to pay a fine of five pounds—a relatively heavy fine for a heavy drinker—failing which he would be given a public whipping "and so from time to time as often as they shall be found transgressors in that kinde."[88]

The Bay Colony established a somewhat similar pattern. Third offenders might have to suffer a public whipping (ten stripes), if they could not pay a fine. Indulgence in liquors beyond that point subjected the offender to a possible prison sentence where he would remain for an indefinite term, until he was able to persuade friends to put up a bond for his good behavior. One found guilty of "excessive or long drinking" might find himself in the stocks for a period of three hours "when the weather is seasonable."

Liquor laws were continually changed during the lifetime of the Colonies to meet what seemed to be an increasingly bothersome problem. Judges tried, at one time or another, all of the sanctions legally available to them. Faced with the baffling behavior of men who became drunk time and again in spite of increasing penalties and promises of reform, the authorities displayed commendable patience and leniency. From all available reports, drunkenness was more frequently encountered in the second half of the seventeenth century than in the early years of the new governments. Moralists, in highlighting the evils of today, are often tempted to picture the past as a much less sinful period than it actually was. Perhaps Increase Mather succumbed to this temptation, and yet other evidence corroborated the fact that, since the founding of the Colonies, drunkenness had in fact been "a growing evil." He said in 1676, with a rebuke that—except for the seventeenth century phraseology—might very well have come from a twentieth century pulpit:

> When as our Fathers were *Patterns of Sobriety,* they would not drink a cup of wine nor strong drink, more than should suffice nature, and conduce to their health, men of latter time could transact no business, nor hardly ingage in any discourses, but it must be over a pint of wine or a pot of beer, yea so that Drunkenness in the sight of man is become a common Sin, but how much more that which is Drunkenness in the sight of God.[89]

As stated, the most common penalty was a fine. Judges resorted to the stocks and the whipping post only for the persistent transgressor or for the offender who combined drunkenness with some other crime. Occasionally they saw fit to bar a man from all public drinking places in the town where he lived, as they did in the case of the notorious John Barnes of Plymouth. Only a few were imprisoned for drunkenness, but the law authorized the constable to arrest a drunken person on the spot and to lock him up for "safe keeping . . . till he be sober" and then to take him before a magistrate for legal disposition, a practice common today. A magistrate could, of course, commit a "common drunkard" to a House of Correction, according to a law of 1646, for these houses were established for "idle persons, stubborn persons, runawaies, *common drunkards,* pilferers, common nightwalkers and wanton persons as tending to uncleanes in speech or actions."[90]

On rare occasions a person was "disfranchised of his freedome." The humiliation of wearing on one's person a conspicuous letter D was also a relatively uncommon penalty. Evidently William Perkins and Robert Coles in the Bay Colony were special cases. We note that Perkins' offense was not drunkenness alone and that Cole was a rogue well known to the courts:

> Ordered that William Perkins shall (for drunkenes & other misdemeanors by him comitted) stand att the nexte generall Court one houre in publique vewe, with a white sheete of paper on his brest, haveing a greate D made upon it, & shall attend the pleasure of the Court till hee be dismissed. . . .[91]

Robert Coles, one of the least sober citizens of the Bay Colony, appeared so frequently before the courts that most of the common penalties had been exhausted. The Court of Assistants ordered:

> . . . for drunkenes by him committed att Rocksbury, shalbe disfranchized, weare aboute his necke, & soe to hange upon his outward garment, a D, made of redd cloath, & sett upon white; to contynue this for a yeare, & not to leave it off att any tyme when hee comes amongst company, under the penalty of 40 shillings for the first offence, & 5 pounds for the second, & after to be punished by the court as they thinke meete; also hee is to weare the D outwards, & is enjoyned to appeare att the nexte General Court, & to contynue there till the Court be ended. . . .[92]

The Court was no doubt provoked to this severe penalty because Cole's drinking habits did not yield to ordinary penalties. Only a few months previously he had been sentenced to wear a white sheet of paper on his back "wherein a drunkard shalbe written in greate lettres." On that occasion, however, in addition to drunkenness he was accused of "intiseing John Shotswell['s] wife to incontinency, & other misdemeanor[s]. . . ." Shotswell was also in court at the same time "for distempering himselfe with drinke. . . ."[93]

The humiliation of wearing a large red letter D wherever he went was evidently too much for Cole. He remained sober for the next two months. The General Court then relented, saying that the sentence: "is nowe reversed, upon his submission, & testimoney being given of his good behavior. . . ."[94]

Official records cannot provide us with even an approximation of the number of compulsive drinkers or "alcoholics" in the Colonies. Indeed, the word "acoholic" was not current at that time and, as we have already observed, there was little or no understanding of the nature of alcoholic addiction. We surely cannot assume that all of the "common drunkards" were addicted to alcoholic beverages. It is quite probable, however, that a considerable number of those who were repeatedly before the courts, and repeatedly punished, were, if not addicts, at least on their bibulous way to becoming such. The General Court recognized, at least, the drunkard's overwhelming desire for drink, when it observed in 1654 that in spite of numerous laws made "to suppresse that swinish sinne of drunkennes . . . persons addicted to that vice finde out waies to deceave the lawes. . . ."[95] John Barnes of Plymouth, previously mentioned, seemed to be one whose drinking habits persisted in spite of all manner of punishments endured. Admonitions and fines were of little avail. The Court said in 1658:

> John Barnes, for his frequent abusing himselfe in drunkenes, after former punishment and admonition, is fined five pounds; and in case any shall entertaine him in theire house in a way of drinkeing, shalbee fined the summe of twenty shillings; and if any of the towne of Plymouth shalbee found drinking in his companie, every such to pay two shillings & sixpence.[96]

Opportunities for Barnes to find any further source of supply, or even drinking companions, seemed to have been completely cut off so long as he remained in Plymouth, but evidently he "found out waies to deceave the lawes," for the very next year (1659) he was again charged with drunkenness. The Court then applied a humiliating but totally ineffective penalty—disfranchisement, "for his frequent and abominable drunkenes."[97] In 1661 the legislature increased the fine from twenty to fifty shillings for anyone letting Barnes have any "liquors, wine or strong drinke."[98]

This measure, too, proved ineffective, for in 1665 Barnes was "detected of being twise drunke."[99] The record is silent as to subsequent developments until 1672, when old Barnes came to a sad ending—fatally gored by a bull on his own farm in Plymouth.[100]

Thomas Lucas of Plymouth was undoubtedly a compulsive drinker and, like Barnes, would probably be labelled today an "alcoholic." His criminal case history over a period of 21 years, collected from the official records, shows his futile struggle with the persistent habit of excessive drinking, a habit that was clearly beyond the reach of any penalty the ingenious legislature could devise. Aside from his criminal record, Lucas made no claim to eminence. He is not mentioned by any of his contemporaries in their diaries or "relations." Presumably he was not an educated man, for among the signatures to a coroner's jury report in 1660 a sign with the designation "his marke" stood opposite his name.[101] The records tell us that the court ordered him in 1656 to pay "widdow Dotey" three shillings to settle some "reconings betwixt them."[102] We learn from the records of births that Lucas had four sons and one daughter born between 1656 and 1662, during which time he made a number of appearances before the court.[103] His criminal record collated from the official reports follows:[104]

YEAR	THE OFFENSE	DISPOSITION
1658	"presented for being taken in drinke, it being the 2cond time hee hath bine convict of this crime . . . and for his retailing of strong liquors, himselfe confessing it."	Fine of 15 shillings.
1659	"for being drunke."	Fine of 10 shillings.
1660	(reason not given.)	Fine of 1 pound, 10 shillings.
1660	"for his abusive and threatening speeches and turbulent carriages towards the wife of James Cole, Senior, and the child of James Cole, Junior."	Fine of 30 shillings.
1660	"for refusing to take the oath of fidelitie."	Fine of 10 shillings.
1660	"for being drunke twise."	Fine of 10 shillings.

1661	(reason not given.)	Fine of 2 pounds.
1661	"for being drunke the third time."	To post sureties for his good behavior and a bond of 20 pounds.
1661	"for his presenting himselfe in the Court distempered with drinke, and for his unbeseeming behavior both in words and jesturs before the Court and towards some of the magestrates."	Fine of 40 shillings and imprisonment.
1661	He was found at the home of "Ann, the wife of Thomas Savory . . . on the Lords Day . . . at unseasonable time, viz, in the time of publicke exercise in the worshipe of God, and for being found drunke att the same time under an hedge, in uncivell and beastly manor."	"Refered to the next court for further consideration." (Ann, for accompanying Lucas, was sentenced to sit in the stocks, and for being drunk, fined 5 shillings, and for prophaning the Lord's Day, fined 10 shillings.)
1661	"forfeited his bonds for his good behavior" (posted for his earlier offense of being drunk the third time); evidently drunk again.	Loss of 20 pounds on the bond, but the court remitted 10 pounds.
1663	"for being drunke, it being the third time hee hath ben convicted and sentanced in the Court for being drunke."	"To bee publickely whipt," but the sentence was deferred "until he shalbee taken drunke the next time."
1664	"fownd drunke againe."	Whipt.
1664	"for his abusing of his wife to her danger and hazard, as alsoe for his railing and reviling others, to the desturbance of the Kings peace."	To post a bond for his good behavior for 3 months.
1664	"for swearing."	To sit in the stock "during the pleasure of the Court."
1665	"for swearing by the wounds of God."	Imprisoned 24 hours.
1665	(reason not given.)	Fined 10 shillings.

1669	"for abusing his wife and children, hee appeering in Court and promising reformation, and his wife alsoe appeered att the Court, and testifyed that . . . hee hath not abused them as aforesaid."	Was cleared and released "with admonition."
1670	"for breaking the Kings peace" by "striking of Samuell Jenney."	Fine of "3 shillings and foure pence."
1673	"for being drunke."	"released with admonition."
1675	"for being distempered with drinke, it being soe oftens, and that hee hath borne severall particular punishments gradually, and can not be reclaimed."	"All that sell drinke be strictly ordered and prohibited to lett him have none."
1675	"For reviling some deceased majestrates, and for being drunke."	"whipt att the post."

For almost four years the records are silent as to Thomas Lucas. In January 1679 the final grim entry:

> The sixt day of January, 1678 [1679 by our calendar], being warned upon a jury to view the body of Thomas Lucase, of Plymouth, deceased, and to make inquiry how hee came by his end, wee, whose names are under written, find it as followeth: hee being very ancient & decriped in his limbes, and it being very cold, and haveing drunk some drinke, gott a violent fall into a ditch, in a very dangerous place, could not recover himselfe, but bruised his body, and lying all night in the cold, soe hee came by his end.

† † †

Thomas Lucas of Plymouth had died a drunkard's death in 1679, but hundreds of thousands of other Thomas Lucases staggered down through the ensuing centuries. "That great and raging sin" that vexed the governors and magistrates of the Plymouth and the Bay Colonies and threatened "if not speedily prevented" to "bring some stroake of Gods Heavy hand" upon them was never ultimately prevented but continues with increasing virulence to constitute one of the great social problems of the present era. Preaching, education, a continuous succession of legislative enactments, and the example of the Puritan forefathers notwithstanding, the addiction to alcohol grew to serious proportions until it had become America's fourth most serious health problem. Stern warnings from the pulpit by Increase Mather and his brilliant son, Cotton, had been unavailing.

In the early days of the Royal Province Government, Cotton Mather had expressed his profound moral indignation over the detestable vices, corruptions, and profanities abounding in the year 1696. In his long list of such abominations he called attention to the "Flood of Excessive Drinking" that "hath begun to overwhelm Good order in some Towns, & even to Drown civilitie itself."[105] Time proved the "flood" to be out of control.

After the powerful preaching of both Mathers had been stilled by death, Royal Governor Jonathan Belcher, who served from 1730 to 1741, expressed his deep concern over "the great consumption of Strong Liquors among the People of this Province, more especially of Rhum, to the debauching and ruining of themselves and their Families." Over a period of several years (1730 to 1737) he urged the General Court to increase the excise tax on rum and all distilled liquors, asserting that "Gaming and excessive Drinking" threatened "the Ruin of this People now more than ever." He pleaded with the legislature to take care of its people "least they be delug'd in spirituous Liquors."[106] The General Court responded by enacting new excise laws and by ordering careful and regular inspections of all taverns and public houses of entertainment. Nevertheless, great quantities of alcohlic beverages from foreign countries continued to pour into the Province to supplement those that were locally brewed and distilled. Available to the people in the eighteenth century were beer, ale, cider, rum, brandy, mead, perry, metheglin, other distilled spirits, and "mixed drinks" and a variety of wines listed in the laws as Passado, Madera, Canary, Malaga, Sherry, Port, Fyal, Malmsey, Sack, Muscadell, Tent, and Allicant.[107]

Drunkards were not harshly treated. During the early Province period a man or woman brought into court charged with drunkenness could have been certain of release by the payment of a small fine, provided it was a first offence. Sitting in the stocks for a period of no more than three hours was ordered for those who could not pay. Second offenders might find themselves lodged in jail until they found sureties for their good behavior. Such was the law in 1692–1693.[108] The following year the penalty was increased. Justices of the Peace were given authority to place those who failed to pay their fines in the stocks or in the cage for no more than three hours or in prison for twenty-four hours, or, if the Justices saw fit, they could order the offender whipped by not more than ten stripes.[109] Indians, who would not be particularly humiliated by sitting in the stocks or cage, were simply to be whipped if they failed to pay the fine. As the savages were known to become violent under the influence of the white man's "strong waters," the law permitted anyone to take from them any alcoholic beverage found in their possession and to escort them to court.[110]

In its 1733–1734 session, the General Court found that a fine of five shillings decreed by the first law of 1692–1693 had "in a great measure, proved ineffectual to restrain persons from drunkeness" or from "prophane swearing and cursing" and decided to increase the fine to ten shillings.[111]

But other measures were found necessary. Following the Colonial custom, the General Court ordered that the names of "all persons reputed drunkards or common tiplers" be posted by the selectmen in all public houses. Anyone serving drinks to such persons was liable to a fine of twenty shillings, half of the fine to be awarded to the informer.[112] The courts could also commit a "common drunkard" to a house of correction if one were available in the county.[113]

By 1711 it was declared that taverns, inns, and alehouses were becoming "nurseries of intemperance and debauchery" in spite of the fact that they were licensed and carefully inspected and controlled. People living in a town in which such houses were located were forbidden to consume their wines and liquors there after nine o'clock in the evening. After all, as the Colonial and Province governments frequently reminded them, the true function of a tavern was to provide refreshment for the traveler, not the town drunk.[114]

In order that people might keep these laws constantly in

mind, town clerks were ordered to read at each annual town meeting in March all Province laws on drunkenness, profaness, and other immoralities.[115]

It was the experience of the Province courts, as it had been of the Colonial courts, that a man or woman addicted to alcohol will continue to drink in spite of small fines, whippings, imprisonment, or punishments of humiliation so long as he has access to it—and it was very difficult to deprive him of his source of supply.

Thus the Commonwealth government (1780 to the present) inherited all the problems that accompanied this "atrocious vice." The General Court in 1781 succinctly exposed its evil effects in a statement that would be quite applicable today:

> [Drunkenness] enfeebles the bodies and enervates the minds of men —shortens life—lessens the quantity of labour in the Commonwealth —tends to promote every other vice—extinguishes the moral sense, and is in the most striking manner disgraceful to human nature.[116]

The most common penalty resorted to by the courts then—and now—is a fine, but fines, as Governor Winthrop had discovered in the previous century, do not fall with even justice on the rich and the poor. Nor did they prove to be effective in curbing this common crime. As the use of the stocks, the cage, and the lash were going out of fashion (although not yet outlawed) toward the end of the eighteenth century, other measures had to be devised. The General Court in 1784 gave authority to the probate courts, on the recommendation of the selectmen, to appoint a guardian over a man who, by excessive drink, had wasted his estate and exposed himself or family to want or suffering.[117] Or the courts could send to a workhouse (if there were one in the town) those who spent their time and estate in public taverns "to the neglect of their proper business."[118]

As time went on and the problem increased in seriousness, more reliance was placed on confinement in institutions. By 1836 a sentence to a house of correction for not more than three months was deemed an appropriate penalty for one who failed to pay the fine of $5 for a first offender or $10 for a repeater.[119] When the Reformatory Prison for Women (now known as the Massachusetts Correctional Institution, Framingham) was opened in 1877, another facility was available for the commitment of female drunkards. In 1879 the law permitted the commitment there of second offenders for a period of not less than four months nor more than two years, with the possibility of transfer to the state workhouse at Bridgewater or the almshouse at Tewskbury to complete their sentences.[120]

That repeaters should be more severely punished than first offenders was a penological policy common to the administration of criminal justice from the Colonial period to the present, its purpose being, as explained by the Supreme Judicial Court in an 1882 case: "to prevent the repeated commission of similar offences by imposing severer penalties for each successive violation of law, and thus to save persons from becoming old and hardened offenders."[121]

An 1881 law that was the occasion for this judicial pronouncement established for first offenders a fine of only $1 and costs or a commitment for no more than ten days to a jail or house of correction or a workhouse or, if in Boston, to the House of Industry. But for two convictions of drunkenness within the period of a year the fine was increased to $5 and costs or commitment for a period of not more than two months, while three convictions within the year would entail a fine of $10 and costs or confinement for a period of not more than twelve months. Female drunkards, if not paying the fine on the third offence, were subject to commitment to the Reformatory Prison for Women for a term of twelve to twenty-four months or to any place provided for common drunkards up to twelve months.[122] This nicely worked-out scale of culpability evidently did not prevent the "common drunkard" from demonstrating his fondness for the bottle. Perhaps, it was thought, the penalties were too lenient. Four years later, therefore, the $1 fine and ten-day period of confinement for first offenders was changed to $5 and confinement up to thirty days, while men who were brought into court as third offenders could be sent to the Massachusetts Reformatory (now known as the Massachusetts Correctional Institution, Concord) which was opened in 1884, for a period of one to two years.[123]

The latter half of the nineteenth century proved to be a particularly frustrating period for those who sought to curb this growing social evil. There was hardly a session of the legislature during this period that did not give some attention to this problem. Governor John D. Long in 1881 spoke of "the terrible evil of intemperance, and its devastation of crime, insanity and pauperism" and reported that of the 16,897 criminal cases in the nine criminal courts of Suffolk County, more than seventy-two percent were drunkenness cases, while almost half of the remainder were crimes committed under the influence of alcohol, leaving only about fifteen percent of the cases unrelated to intoxication. Governor George D. Robinson reported in 1886 that forty-seven persons, on the average, were arrested in Boston each day for drunkenness—a higher rate than exists today. Saloons were doing a thriving business, in spite of the many laws regulating the sale and distribution of liquor. In 1888 Governor Oliver Ames reported that "in some of the cities there is a saloon to nearly every hundred of the population."[124] The General Court in 1888 and 1889 adopted a proposed amendment to the state constitution prohibiting the manufacture and sale of intoxicating liquor as a beverage, but the proposal was defeated by popular vote in 1889. In a report of a committee appointed by mayor Josiah Quincy of Boston in 1899 it was stated that in the previous year the total arrests for drunkenness in Boston amounted to 26,157, a higher figure than one would find today in spite of the increase in the city's population: "It is well known," the report stated, "that Boston has always borne an enviable reputation for its high rate of arrests for drunkenness, which far exceeds that of cities like Chicago, New York and Philadelphia."[125]

After long years of failure to reduce the frequency of this crime by any known penological method, the question, still unresolved, was raised and continuously debated in the latter half of the nineteenth century: Is dipsomania (or alcoholism, to use the modern term) a disease, and, if so, should not treatment rather than punishment be prescribed? Numerous state and private institutions came into being during this period to treat as patients those who had become addicted to the intemperate use of alcohol and had lost the power of self-control—institutions with unambiguous names, such as The Appleton Home for Inebriates, The Home for the Fallen (out of which developed the Washingtonian Hospital), the Massachusetts Home for Dipsomaniacs and The New England Home for Intemperate Women.[126] New laws made civil, rather than criminal, procedures available to the courts on the theory that the alcoholic was a sick person in need of treatment, resulting in the commitment of hundreds of men and women to such institutions or to the "insane asylums" of that period. The results were far from encouraging. Nevertheless, those laws, with some modifications, are still operative to provide those who are addicted to alcohol the opportunity of hospital care.[127]

It would not be appropriate in this brief review to examine the very great number of laws, and amendments to them, enacted in the past one hundred years designed to control the liquor industry and to hold the drunkard in restraint.[128] In spite of our abundant hospital facilities and alcoholic clinics that have given the public greater insight into the complex problem of addiction to alcohol, thousands of alcoholics each year appear before our District and Municipal Courts and listen to the official complaint, simply and bluntly worded: "That A.B. was, by voluntary use of intoxicating liquor, drunk."[129]

Not only is drunkenness a crime in Massachusetts, it is the most frequent crime for which men and women are deprived of their liberty. More than half of the inmates of our jails today have been sentenced for drunkenness only. More than half of the inmates of our state correctional institutions who were committed for more serious crimes would probably claim alcohol was an important factor in their criminal behavior. More than half of all arrests in the Commonwealth (with the exception of motor-vehicle violations) are made for the crime of drunkenness, the total annual arrests for this crime usually exceeding 63,000. In terms of alcoholism, the Department of Public Health finds Massachusetts, compared to all other states, exceeded by only three.

In 1956 the General Court launched a new attack on the problem, placing greater emphasis on the need for treatment of the alcoholic, less on punishment of the drunkard. It stressed the wisdom of educating youth on facts relating to alcoholic beverages.[130] And in 1959 it authorized the Commissioner of the Department of Public Health to appoint, with approval of the Public Health Council, a Director of the Alcoholism Program who may work in conjunction with any foundation or scientific organization in developing information on this subject. The Department is required to make a continuous study of treatment methods, and establish diagnostic, treatment, and rehabilitative programs; it must develop and promote preventive and educational programs and seek to coordinate all state agencies working toward the same ends; and, with the aid of the Department of Education, it must prepare materials for use in the public schools and teachers' colleges on the study of alcohol as a beverage.

In spite of the valued contributions during recent years of medical doctors and behavioral scientists to the problem of compulsive drinking and the extensive educational programs keyed to a rational, rather than an emotional or religious appeal, the courts can not overlook the fact that public drunkenness in this Commonwealth is a crime just as in Colonial days. When a person arrested for that crime appears before it, the court may place the case on file or it may fine him (not more than $15) or it may place him on probation (one of the terms of which may be that he voluntarily seek treatment in a state institution or clinic) or commit him to an institution. Under the present law, the one-year or two-year commitments have been abolished, the term being limited to a maximum of thirty days if the drunkard is sent to a jail or house of correction. If committed for a longer period, he must be sent to the Prison Department of the Massachusetts Correctional Institution, Bridgewater, (for many years known as "The State Farm") for a period of no longer than six months. Females convicted of drunkenness must be sent to the Massachusetts Correctional Institution, Framingham, for a like period, if not sent to a jail or house of correction for a period of no more than 30 days. Each of these two correctional institutions is required to provide an alcoholic clinic for the treatment of these offenders. The Commissioner of Correction has power to discharge such men and women on the recommendation of the doctors in charge of the clinics in each of these two institutions and with the approval of their superintendents, but at least sixty days of the sentence must have been served before discharge. Such releases are not conditional, as formerly, and the person is not on parole and cannot be made to return without another court commitment.[131]

Drunkards today are the greatest recidivists in the penological picture. Many individuals have been recommitted to an institution more than one hundred times.

Thus the problem of drunkenness that beset the judges and legislators in the seventeenth century is still with us. In short, one might say, as the General Court sitting in Boston more than three hundred years ago declared, there has been "an excesse of drinking & unto drunkennes it selfe . . . to the dishonour of God, the discredit of the gospell, to the shame of the country."[132]

12. THE MOST COMMON CRIMES AND PENALTIES

> And yet all this [the severity of punishment] could not suppress the breaking out of sundrie notorious sins, (as this year, besides other, gives us too many sad presidents [precedents] and instances,) espetially drunkennes and unclainnes; not only incontinencie betweene persons unmaried, for which many both men & women have been punished sharply enough, but some maried persons allso. . . .—*Governor William Bradford on the increase in crime in Plymouth Colony in 1642.*[1]

ONE cannot accurately judge from a perusal of *selected* cases which crimes were most frequently entered on the court dockets or which penalties were thought most suitable to the occasion. Was the charge of drunkenness the most frequent complaint against Colonial citizens or were the courts mainly concerned with those who violated the sex mores of that day? Was the magistrate's chief weapon in the fight against crime the admonishing finger or was he usually satisfied with nothing less than the stocks, a whipping, or the gallows? To recapture the spirit of Colonial justice, quite thoroughly distorted by writers of historical fiction, we must find our answer in the official documents of court proceedings. Ideally, a definitive determination resides only in a complete tabulation of all criminal cases coming before the public tribunals during the entire period under study. A deliberate selection of cases to "prove" a preconceived notion is all too tempting. And yet the ideal is impossible. A complete record of judicial decisions is not available to the modern student of Colonial criminal justice. Let us be content therefore with an analysis of the relative, rather than the absolute, incidences of the most common crimes and penalties. Such an analysis can be made from adequate samples taken from those court records that have been faithfully preserved.

We have selected for our study certain busy Colonial courts, noting for brief but consecutive periods of time, every case where a finding of guilty was recorded. Tables based on such an analysis should provide us with reasonably satisfactory data from which certain conclusions might be fairly drawn. The courts chosen are:

The Suffolk County Court, which met in the town of Boston. We have chosen a three-year period, 1671 to 1674, where the records (published by the Colonial Society of Massachusetts in 1933, covering the years 1671 to 1680) are believed to be complete for the purpose of our analysis. This court, described in Chapter 3, was one of the "quarterly courts" with original jurisdiction over all criminal matters excepting the most serious crimes punishable by death, dismembering, or banishment, which were tried by the Court of Assistants.[2] Like Massachusetts' Superior Court of today which assigns justices to sit in the various counties, this Colonial court was a busy tribunal dealing with both civil and criminal business. By 1670 Suffolk was a fairly populous county, comprising ten towns. Although census figures for this period are conjectural, Chaffee estimated that the population count a few years later (in 1680) was between seven and ten thousand.[3] (See Table 1.)

The Essex County Court, which usually sat in Salem and Ipswich and occasionally in Salisbury and Hampton. Again we have taken a three-year sample, covering the same period of time. The records of this court (published by The Essex Institute in 1914) presumably report all of the court's criminal business in that county, where the population was considerably less than that of Suffolk. (See Table 2.)

The Plymouth Courts, sitting in the town of Plymouth for the entire Colony. No records are available for the years prior to 1633. We have selected our sample from the first ten years of consecutive reporting, commencing on April 1, 1633. In the Commonwealth publication (Shurtleff edition) in 1855, appear reports of the decisions of the General Court as well as of the Court of Assistants, showing a wide variety of criminal cases, from the trivial to the most serious. There were, of course, far fewer people in

Plymouth Colony than in its younger neighbor to the north, and by 1640 the population was diminishing as the Bay Colony was increasing. The patterns of criminality, however, did not greatly differ in the two colonies. (See Table 3.)

The Court of Assistants, holding sessions for the entire Bay Colony, sitting first in Charlestown, later in Boston, Watertown, and Newetowne (Cambridge). We have taken samples from two periods of this court's existence: a) A ten-year consecutive period of judicial administration commencing with its first session held in Charlestown in August 1630. During this period, before the county courts ("quarterly courts") took over most of the criminal business, the Court of Assistants processed a wide variety of cases. Its records (published in vol. 2 of a compilation printed by the County of Suffolk in 1904) also contained the reported cases taken from the records of the Massachusetts Bay Colony (referred to in our footnotes as MCR). b) A later period in its history comprising a ten-year span commencing on March 3, 1673 (taken from vol. 1 of a compilation printed by the County of Suffolk in 1901). By 1673 this court had for about a quarter of a century tried only the most serious cases, those punishable by death, dismembering, or banishment, or cases on appeal from the lower courts. (See Tables 4 and 5.)

In selecting samples of court records somewhat arbitrarily we omitted the midyears of the Bay Colony because its records were spotty or totally missing for part of the period between 1643 and 1671. We failed to include, therefore, the prosecutions of the Quakers, who were frequently in court, but we have dealt with this important episode in Colonial history in a separate chapter. Likewise by carrying our accounting no further than 1683 we did not note the great number of witchcraft cases coming into the courts in 1692. These also have been considered in a separate chapter. The Massachusetts Colonial Records (published by the Commonwealth in 1853, Shurtleff edition) which report both legislative and judicial proceedings we also omitted from our tabulations because most of the criminal business, except in the early years, was handled by the "quarterly courts" while much of the early reporting (at least up to 1641) was duplicated in the records of the Court of Assistants which we have included.

We have not included the records of single magistrates or

cases of a minor nature heard before the Commissioners Court of Boston where the fine did not exceed forty shillings, for records of these proceedings were not available to us. Nor have we included the records of the Springfield court (1639-1702) where the criminal cases did not differ significantly from those in Suffolk County.[4]

We have, therefore, made no attempt to hazard a guess at the total number of crimes or to arrive at any sort of a "crime rate." Our concern here is merely to determine in a rough way the *relative* frequencies of occurrence of different crimes and penalties during the periods selected for analysis.

TABLE 1

CRIMES AND PENALTIES IN THE SUFFOLK COUNTY COURT

For a three-year period, 1671-1674

PENALTIES

CRIMES	*Number of cases*	*Fine*	*Whipping*	*Bond for good behavior*	*Fine or whipping*	*Restitution*	*Admonition*	*Public acknowledgment*	*Prison*	*Stocks, pillory*	*Leave town*	*Wear placard*	*House of Correction*	*Brand*	*Other**
1. Fornication	46	5	12	3	25		1	4							
2. Stealing	38	5	17	1	3	27	4			2					
3. Liquor law violations	28	19		8			3								1
4. Lord's Day violations	26	11		5			12								1
5. Assault and battery	26	21	4	4	5	1	3				1	2			1
6. Villifying authorities	25	6	7	7	2		1	1	3		1				1
7. Lewd, lascivious, wanton behavior	22	6	9	7	1	1				1	1				2
8. Burglary	16	1	9	4		5	1		1		1			3	3
9. Drunkenness	14	7	5	2											1
10. Attending Quaker meeting	13	7					6								
11. Breach of peace	9	7		3											
12. Abusing constable	6	2	1		1		1								1
13. Aiding prisoners to escape	6	3	1		1		1								
14. Swearing	5	2		2	1		1								
15. Avoiding jury duty, etc.	5	5													
16. Runaway servants	5	1	3							1					
17. Idleness	5			1			1						2		
18. Miscellaneous†	48	14	4	7	4	8	6			1		1	4		8
Totals	343	122	72	54	43	42	41	5	4	5	4	3	6	3	19

* Tabulations in the Other column refer to penalties less often used, such as dispose of into service, support a bastard child, sell into slavery, disfranchise, "disinable" from continuing as "a publique Cryer," sit on the gallows with a rope around one's neck, return to wife in England, cut off hair (two males).

† Under Miscellaneous we have included various crimes less frequently dealt with by the courts: card playing, abusing a servant, wounding accidentally, being disorderly, nonsupport, calling wife "whore," school vandalism, etc.

TABLE 2

CRIMES AND PENALTIES IN THE ESSEX COUNTY COURT

For a three-year period, 1671-1674

CRIMES	*Number of cases*	PENALTIES *Fine*	*Whipping*	*Bond for good behavior*	*Fine* or *whipping*	*Restitution*	*Admonition*	*Public acknowledgment*	*Prison*	*Stocks, pillory*	*Leave town*	*Wear placard*	*House of Correction*	*Brand*	*Other**
1. Fornication	48	7	1		40										
2. Stealing	36	22	1		5	10	1								
3. Breach of peace	32	32													
4. Drunkenness	23	21			1		1								
5. Assault and battery	22	15	3	1	4										
6. Lord's Day violations	15	6					8					1			
7. Lewd, lascivious, wanton behavior	11	7	2	2								3			
8. Swearing	9	7		1	1										
9. Abusing constable	7	7		1											
10. Disorderly living	5														5
11. Avoiding jury duty, etc.	4	4													
12. Liquor law violations	4	4													
13. Miscellaneous†	41	24	2		2	1	7	1	1						3
Totals	257	156	9	5	53	11	17	1	1	0	0	4	0	0	8

* The column headed Other refers to less frequent penalties: to return to spouse (if living apart); to wear lock on leg (runaway servant); to lose license to sell liquor; to serve additional time (runaway servant).

† Under Miscellaneous are those rare occasions in which the following offences brought men and women to court: runaway servants (3); burglary and stealing (1); malicious gossip (1); allowing shuffleboard in tavern (1); pushing wife (1); non-support (1); breaking prison (1); aiding same (1).

TABLE 3

CRIMES AND PENALTIES IN THE PLYMOUTH COURTS

For a ten-year period, 1633-1643

CRIMES	*Number of cases*	PENALTIES *Fine*	*Whipping*	*Bond for good behavior*	*Restitution*	*Admonition*	*Stocks, pillory*	*Prison*	*Banishment*	*Burn on shoulder*	*Death*	*Other**
1. Fornication	19	2	9	1			9					
2. Drunkenness	18	11	2				2					1
3. Lewd, lascivious, wanton behavior	16		10				2		2	2		2
4. Liquor law violations	13	13										
5. Villifying authorities	12	8		2			1		1			
6. Assault and battery	9	9										
7. Tobacco smoking	8	6										
8. Stealing	7		4	1	1					2		
9. Swearing	6					2	1	2				
10. Extortion	6	3			2							
11. Lord's Day violations	6	2	2	1			1		1			
12. Murder	3										3	
13. Miscellaneous†	68	46	5	0	3	1	3	1	2		1	3
Totals	191	100	32	5	6	3	19	3	6	4	4	6

* Other penalties: to be whipt and to wear an AD (adultery) (1); to give an account of his way of living (1); to be banished (1).

† Miscellaneous infrequent crimes: cruelty to servant (1); living alone (1); runaway servant (1); keeping unringed swine (21); selling powder to Indians (1); scoffing at religion (1); sodomy (death penalty); adultery (1); neglecting duty about the ferry (1); calling a man a "rogue" (1).

TABLE 4

CRIMES AND PENALTIES IN THE COURT OF ASSISTANTS

For a ten-year period, 1630-1640

	CRIMES		PENALTIES												
		Number of cases	*Fine*	*Whipping*	*Stocks, pillory*	*Banishment*	*Bond for good behavior*	*Prison*	*Admonition*	*Restitution*	*Disfranchisement*	*Whipping or fine*	*Wear placard*	*Public acknowledgement*	*Other**
1.	Drunkenness	62	33	8	9			1	1		1		2	1	2
2.	Villifying authorities	33	19	8	4	5	3	3	1		2				2
3.	Lewd, lascivious, wanton behavior	20	2	8		1	3		2						6
4.	Stealing	19	2	13	1	3		2		4					5
5.	Fornication	16	4	10	2	1	1	3							3
6.	Liquor law violations	16	15												1
7.	Avoiding jury duty, etc.	13	13												
8.	Swearing	11	6	1	2										2
9.	Runaway servants	8		8											2
10.	Extortion	5	5												
11.	Assault and battery	5		4			2								1
12.	Adultery	4		1											
13.	Murder	3													3
14.	Miscellaneous†	62	32	15	6	5	2	1	4	2		2			6
	Totals	277	131	76	24	15	11	10	8	6	3	2	2	1	33

* Other, less frequent, penalties were : wear a letter D (for drunkenness); wear a T (for thief); wear a V (for lewdness); brand with a T (for thief); wear iron collar; brand on hand. For malicious and scandalous speeches, one person's penalty was to loose his ears, to be fined, whipped, and banished. Still other penalties were: support bastard child or marry the girl; wear cleft stick on tongue (for swearing); serve master longer time; go home to wife (in England); be debarred from pleading other men's causes in court; slavery; lose liquor license, etc. The penalty for the three murders was death.

† Miscellaneous charges appearing less frequently in this court were: travelling on Sunday, gambling, idleness, selling guns to Indians, lending gun to an Indian, taking canoe without authority, idle and disorderly living, disturbing church services, etc.

TABLE 5

CRIMES AND PENALTIES IN THE COURT OF ASSISTANTS

For a ten-year period, 1673-1683

	PENALTIES													
CRIMES	*Number of cases*	*Death*	*Whipping*	*Fine*	*Restitution*	*Gallows sitting*	*Banishment*	*Bond for good behavior*	*Fine or whipping*	*Prison*	*Pillory, stocks*	*Admonition*	*Branding*	*Other**
1. Murder	9	9												
2. Manslaughter	7		1	4	6	1								
3. Lewd, lascivious, wanton behavior	7		7			5	2			1				
4. Villifying authorities	6		1	4					1		1			1
5. Stealing	6		3		3							1		1
6. Piracy	5	5												
7. Rape	4	4												
8. Arson	2	2												
9. Adultery	2		2			2								
10. Attempted rape	1													1
11. Sodomy	1	1												
12. Witchcraft	1													1
13. Miscellaneous†	30		6	3	2		6	4	2	2		10	1	5
Totals	81	21	20	11	11	8	8	4	3	3	1	11	1	9

* Other Penalties: It should be noted that not all who were condemned to die were executed (see Chapter 9). Penalties less often used: to be sold and banished if restitution for stealing not paid; to run the "gantlett" (for treasonable conduct in the war of 1675); to have both ears cut off (for clipping coins, etc.); to forfeit lands, etc.

† Miscellaneous less frequent criminal charges: Disturbing church services; living apart from husband for four years; being an insolent scoffer at religion; aiding pirates; aiding prisoners to escape; lying; making false oath; committing burglary on the Lord's Day (for which a servant was branded with a letter B, whipped, charged with treble damages, and ordered to be sold); uttering blasphemy, etc. Also at one session of the 1673 court ten Quakers appeared for attending a meeting but were simply admonished by the court—a mild penalty compared to the treatment of this sect ten years previously (see Chapter 10). Also in this court (in 1679) Elizabeth Morse was condemned for witchcraft but later reprieved and ordered to stay close at home.

Penalties listed in the Tables have been described in previous chapters. A word should be said about the number of penalties appearing in the Tables for any single crime. There were sometimes multiple penalties for a crime; at other times there was a conviction not followed by a recorded penalty; and in a few cases the record presented some ambiguity. One will not find, therefore, a one-to-one correspondence between the number of cases and the number of penalties in all categories. In any event we believe our analysis of the available data is adequate for our purposes.

We shall comment briefly on the crimes listed in the Tables: *Fornication.* Sex relations between consenting partners not married to each other was—and still is—a punishable offense in Massachusetts. The unique feature of the Colonial laws was that such behavior between couples who were about to be married or who later did marry each other was severely condemned and frequently punished long after the event. More than sixty percent of the defendants in fornication cases in Suffolk and Essex Counties during the periods studied intended marriage or had already been married for some time when brought into court on charges of "fornication before marriage." In our chapter on "Bodilie Punishments" we described the Colonies' attempts to curb this crime by public whippings. Less severe "censures" were also used by the courts, such as a fine or "legal admonition."

If any offender was thought to be the father of a bastard child, the court usually ordered him to give financial support to the mother and child. If he denied his paternity, the court's practice was to call in the attending midwives to testify as to whether or not the mother "in her travail" had named this man as the true father. As she faced a possible death in childbirth in view of the low state of medical knowledge at that time, her statement was similar in a way to a "dying declaration" in Common Law which had some probative value when the declarer knowingly faced the immediate prospect of death.

Our tabulation of fornication cases includes a few cases of "suspicion of fornication" which, in spite of the implied doubt as to the facts, was followed by a court "censure" of some kind. Sammuel Judkin's case in the Suffolk County Court was probably of this sort. The court ordered him whipped "on Suspicion of being naught with Sarah an indian Squaw."[5] (The word "naught" in

Biblical accounts meant "bad" but not necessarily morally bad. It probably gave rise to our word "naughty.")[6]

Stealing on the streets of London at that time was a very serious crime, but the Colonists took a much more lenient attitude toward this fairly common offense. Articles stolen were clothing, food, or trinkets of little value, for there was no great concentration of wealth to tempt any habitual followers of the art of pilferage. The thief was usually a servant who had easy access to his master's goods, and he could have anticipated a good whipping, for of all classes the servant class bore the brunt of that form of penalty. At any rate he was required to make restitution, sometimes threefold, sometimes double. The law left the matter largely to the judge but provided specifically for a treble restitution for stealing from a person's yard or "orchid."[7] Servants could not always meet the restitution requirement in which cases they might have their term of service extended. A completely destitute thief faced the possibility of being sold into slavery, for the Bible had set the precedent for dealing with this type: "if he have nothing, then he shall be sold for theft."[8]

Grand and petty larceny distinctions were not so labelled, but the law provided that a theft of goods worth ten shillings or more was to be more severely treated than "smaller thefts."[9]

Liquor law violations. We have dealt with the legal control of intoxicants earlier. We have included in this category in our tabulations retailing without a license, selling over the legally established price, and selling to Indians. Drunkenness itself we have placed in a separate category.

Lord's Day violations. Any behavior on the Sabbath (commencing at sundown at Saturday evening) that might be construed as "mispending that precious time, which thing tends much to the Dishonour of God, the Reproach of Religion, Grieving the Souls of Gods Servants," etc., might have meant trouble for one who could be so insensitive to or defiant of the Puritan's and the Pilgrim's high reverence for that day.[10] Thus drying one's mildewed sails or hoeing one's garden or taking an unnecessary trip on that day brought men and women into court to answer for their conduct. The Biblical commandment had warned that on that day "thou shalt not do any work," an injunction that applied to anyone in the household, to one's cattle, and to any strangers "within they gates."[11]

The Bay Colony law of 1668 was more specific, making it clear that "no servile worke shall be donn on that day, namely, such as are not workes of piety, of charity, or of necessity."[12] How these terms were to be applied in any particular case was left to the discretion of the magistrates. Plymouth Colony had similar laws regulating the Sabbath.

We have included in this category a few cases of disturbing church worship and of not attending church services. Both Colonies had legislated against frequent neglect of attending public worship on the Lord's Day but had been lax in enforcing the law. Many did not attend church services. Obviously the little meeting-houses could not have accommodated the entire population at one time excepting in the smaller settlements. The General Court in Boston declared in 1635 that "complainte hath bene made to this Court that dyvers persons. . .doe usually absent themselves from church meeteings upon the Lords day."[13] Such absence was probably more marked as time went on. And yet we do find both men and women occasionally given a sharp reminder by the magistrate who sometimes warned them, sometimes fined them, but usually refrained from harsher penalties unless the offense was aggravated by other conduct. The Bay Colony law urging people to attend all public assemblies not only on the Lord's Day but "upon such publike fast dayes & dayes of Thanksgiving as are to be generally held by the appointment of authority" provided fines only for those who failed to attend "without just & necessary cause" and "after due meanes of conviction used."[14] The Plymouth Colony law was also rather mild, punishing only one who "in any lazey slothfull or prophane way doth neglect to come to the publicke worship."[15]

Assault and Battery. Personal encounters, usually between masters and servants, are included here as well as assaults arising out of domestic disputes. In the Suffolk Court in 1672, for example, Mary Thorne was charged with "Abusing and Striking her husband," but as proof was lacking the court "sentanced her to bee cautioned," while Ursula Edwards was ordered whipt or fined for "striking her husband & abusive Carriage & Language."[16]

Villifying authorities. The nature of the Colonial governments and the spirit of the times demanded that citizens revere the exalted position of a governor, magistrate, or minister. Villification by "rash speeches" or "railing and wicked expressions" or contempt of court in any way promptly brought the culprit to the bar of justice. The Bible decreed: "Thou shalt not revile the gods, nor curse the ruler of thy people."[17] Both Colonies felt justified in suppressing any open criticism of the government. The Bay Colony law stated that anyone who "shall openly or willingly defame any Court of Justice, or the Sentences and Proceedings of the same, or any of the Magistrates, or other Judges. . .shall be punished. . . by Whipping, fine, imprisonment, disfranchisment, or banishment, as the quality or measure of the offence shall deserve."[18] A companion act, added after the Quakers had begun their attacks on the ministers, stated that anyone "who shall revile the Office or person of Magistrates or Ministers" was subject to a whipping or a fine.[19]

Lewd, lascivious, wanton behavior. In this category we have included behavior characterized as "unclean," "very filthy," "light," or "unchaste" that might have brought a person under severe condemnation by both church and government. These words had no precise meaning. There was an evident reluctance to call a spade a spade or even to use the word "sex." The word "uncleanness," taken from the Bible, served to cover a variety of sex irregularities. We have also included here a few cases of "dalliance," "whoredom," abduction, and one of bigamy and one of "Suspicion of adultery." Edward Peggy was charged with an unusual crime that properly falls within this general category. He was convicted in the Suffolk County Court in 1674 of "useing indirect meanes by powders or other ways unlawfull to Engage the affections or desires of women kinde to him and for begetting Ruth Henningway of Roxbury with Childe."[20]

Burglary. This crime was almost unknown in the early years. Evidently it was not severely dealt with, although in the later years the General Court made it a capital offense on third conviction. Most of the charges under the heading of "burglary" were for breaking into a warehouse or shop rather than into a dwelling house.

Drunkenness. Here we have listed all charges of being drunk or encouraging others to drink to excess or, in a few cases, being in the company of drunkards.

Quaker meeting. Although by 1671, the date of the beginning of our tabulations of Suffolk County Court entries, the intense prosecution of the Quakers had almost completely subsided, the authorities still abhorred the idea that Quakers should hold their own religious services. A few of these brave "subversives" were brought into court but lightly dealt with. The day was not far distant when Quakers would be given their religious freedom.

Breach of peace. This crime usually involved a public fight or brawl or other public disturbance. The prescribed penalty for fighting was a mere fine, but the law gave the judge considerable latitude. "Several circumstances," the law read, "may alter the degree of offence, as who do smite, who is smitten, with what Instrument, the danger of the wound, more or less, time, place, and provocation, and other the like. . . ."[21]

Those who disturbed the quiet serenity of the night did so at their peril. Three women in Suffolk County, for example, were brought to court "for keeping riotous Company at unseasonable times of night & disturbing theire Neighbours."[22] John Chandler was fined for "suffering people [in his house] to bee singing & fidlin at midnight. . . ."[23]

Abusing constable. In performance of their unpopular duties, constables not infrequently met with insults, defiance, or physical abuse.

Aiding prisoners to escape. Those who aided a prisoner to escape—a crime that seems to appear with surprising frequency in court records—were held to account but usually not severely punished.

Swearing. Profane swearing or cursing in public by any one over the age of discretion was a punishable offense occasionally enforced in the seventeenth century.

Avoiding jury duty, etc. Those who failed to report for jury duty when called or otherwise failed to obey an order of the court were required to pay a small fine.

Runaway servants. Hired servants or persons under indentures living under "family government" seemed to account for much of the petty crime—drunkenness, "uncleanness," fighting, and pilfering. The few runaway servants who attempted to escape from the restricted life they were forced to lead found avoidance of capture difficult. Very early in its history, the Bay Colony tried to discourage escapes of this sort by an enactment that provided that "if any boy (that hath bene whipt for running from his maister) be taken in any other plantation, not haveing a note from his maister to testify his business there, it sh[all be] lawfull for the constable of the said plantation to whip him a[nd] send him home."[24]

Idleness. In a paternalistic society such as the Bay Colony where everyone's conduct was under close scrutiny, any marked deviation from conduct unbecoming a Puritan was not to be tolerated. Those who did not heed the many sermons on this topic had the law to deal with. As early as 1633 the legislature warned that "no person, House-holder or other, shall spend his time Idely or unprofitably, under pain of such punishment, as the County Court shall think meet to inflict."[25] The law asked the constables of each town to take special notice of "common Coasters" (those who wandered up and down the coast), "unprofitable Fowlers" (those who hunted wildfowl but without serious purpose), and "Tobacco takers." Those who neglected or failed to support their families were also to be accounted as idlers and fit subjects for Houses of Correction. A later law authorized an inspection of families in order to get the names for presentation to the court of those who were idle, for that "Sin of Idleness (which is a Sin of Sodom) doth greatly increase."[26]

Disorderly living. Youths who lived alone, not under "family government," or men and women whose spouses were still in England were warned that they could not lead that kind of single life, with all its temptations to sin, and, if they persisted, would be charged with "disorderly living." The court sentenced the youths to live with some family willing to take them and the others were to "repair to their wives or husbands."[27]

Tobacco taking. Smoking tobacco (called "taking" or "drinking tobacco") was not a pleasure on the approved list, and yet it was not absolutely prohibited. It was associated in the mind of the Puritan with idleness, for how could a person smoke and at the same time follow his calling? Its chief danger, however, was not that it led to slothful habits but that it presented a fire hazard in a fire-conscious community. Hence the law that forbade smoking "within twenty Poles of any House, or so near as may indanger the same, or near the Barn, Corn, or Hay cock, as may occasion the firing thereof . . . nor in any Inne or common Victual House, except in a private Room there, so as neither the Master of the said House, nor any other Guest there shall take offence thereat, which if any do, then such person shall forthwith forbear...." Fines collected under this law were to be distributed one-half to the informer, the other half to the poor.[28]

Extortion. Colonists who came from England were quite used to the close regulation of their economic life. Every detail of one's trade or business in the Colonies was governed by some restrictive law. What we might call a "ceiling price" was placed on the sale of beer, wines, liquors, grain, bread, and other commodities. One who sold or bargained at a price above the legal limit could have been charged with "extortion."

The most prominent citizen brought before the courts for this crime was Robert Keayne, a well-to-do merchant and founder of the Ancient and Honorable Artillery Company. He had been in the habit of selling above the current price, which was a crime in itself. It was said that he bought cheaply and sold dearly—in a community that gave no quarter to sharp horse traders. "The cry of the country was so great against oppression," as Governor Winthrop put it, that the General Court in 1639 decided to censure him with an extraordinary fine, two hundred pounds (later reduced to eighty pounds). His church censured him, too, and might have thrown him out had he not been its generous benefactor and loyal supporter and a man of stature in the community. The Rev. John Cotton seized upon this opportunity for a timely sermon on objectionable business practices which, incidentally, would be quite acceptable in today's highly competitive marketplace.[29]

The tabulation of crimes and penalties in the periods under analysis reveals the following facts concerning the penalties:

1) In all courts studied, except the Court of Assistants in its later period, the preponderant penalty was a fine.

2) In the Suffolk County Court, the Plymouth Courts, and the Court of Assistants in its early period the second most frequently imposed penalty was a whipping; in the Essex County Court, a choice between a whipping and a fine.

3) The pattern of punishments differed from one court to another. The County Courts in Suffolk and Essex rarely used the stocks or the pillory. All courts used sparingly sentences to prison or house of correction, branding, and the wearing of placards or

letters. The Essex County Court, having the most limited repertoire of penalties, relied heavily on fines and/or whippings.

4) If we can assume that the sentences calling for a fine or a mere legal admonition or the posting of a bond were less harsh—they were certainly less painful or humiliating—then we can make a rough judgment as to the relative harshness of these courts. We find that these three penalties (sometimes in combination with others) constituted 23% of all penalties in the Court of Assistants in its later period when it was hearing the most serious cases; 46% in that court in its earlier period; 54% in the Suffolk County Court; 57% in the Plymouth courts; and 66% in the Essex County Court.

As far as the crimes themselves are concerned, the tabulation reveals the following facts:

1) In the two county courts and in the Plymouth Courts magistrates had to deal most frequently with those convicted of the crime of fornication; in the Court of Assistants, early period, with drunkenness and, in its later period, with murder.

2) The second most frequent offense in the county courts was stealing; in the Plymouth courts, drunkenness; in the Court of Assistants, early period, villifying authorities and, in its later period, manslaughter and lewd, lascivious, and wanton behavior.

3) Relatively few men and women were found guilty of the more serious crimes such as murder, manslaughter, piracy, rape, arson, witchcraft, sodomy, or adultery.

4) All in all, sex crimes and drunkenness played a most prominent part in the criminological picture.

† † †

Great social and economic advances in the centuries following the Puritan governments wrought natural changes in the pattern of criminal behavior. Some of the offenses that most troubled the magistrates in the seventeenth century gradually passed from the scene:

Witchcraft was no longer a punishable offense a few months after the last witch was hanged in 1692.

Piracy was not a real threat to Massachusetts in the seventeenth century, but it struck with force on the high seas in the early eighteenth century and cost many a pirate his life. It had been made a capital offense in the Bay Colony as early as 1673. Pirates are now but legendary figures not without glamour, not looked upon in retrospect as our Colonial forebears saw them—"evil men . . . bold and notorious Transgressors" in their "wicked and unrighteous practices."[30] The Commonwealth today has no law against piracy, as such, but could prosecute a piratical act within its jurisdiction as murder or robbery or larceny.

Duelling, that aristocratic custom of agreeing to a fight to the death to avenge one's honor, had long been outlawed in England and France before the founding of the Colonies, but it had persisted in spite of strict penalties and was not unheard of in the Province Government. It was not until social approval gradually cooled that this old tradition passed into history.[31] Today in Massachusetts a duelist causing the death of his adversary would be charged with murder. In a nonfatal duel both parties on conviction, until the law was repealed in 1962, could suffer imprisonment up to twenty years with the added disgrace of being unable for that length of time to hold public office.[32]

Counterfeiting is still a serious crime but infrequently engaged in because few people have the necessary skill to make this crime pay. Counterfeiting federal currency is a federal crime, but in Massachusetts today a person who counterfeits a bank bill or promissory note issued by any incorporated banking company risks imprisonment for life.[33]

Scoffing at religion, criticizing a sermon, being a malicious gossip, allowing shuffleboards in one's tavern, playing cards, making "opprobrious speeches" about the Governor, smoking a pipe near a dwelling house, wearing long hair "like womens hair" if a man, or, if a woman, "cutting, curling, and immodest laying out" her hair ("an ill custome" for sober Christians and one that manifests pride), galloping on horseback through the streets of Boston, dancing in taverns, selling gunpowder to Indians, and many other petty vices of the Puritans have long since been removed from the code of criminal laws in Massachusetts.

On the other hand, a surprising number of early Colonial crimes are crimes of modern times in Massachusetts:

Strict sabbath regulations have only recently been removed from the statutes. (See epilogue to Chapter 5.)

"Profane cursing and swearing," a crime derived from the Bay Colony code of laws, was carried over into the Commonwealth government and was not repealed until 1962.[34]

"Blasphemy," a capital crime in the Bay Colony, is still a crime in the Commonwealth, the law following substantially the same wording as that used by the Puritans.

Our laws today regulating sexual conduct have a distinct Puritan flavor. "Lewd and lascivious," an old Puritan term, is well known to our present Municipal and District Court judges. Adultery, a misdemeanor in most American jurisdictions, is a felony in the Commonwealth, having been a capital law under the Puritans, although prosecutions for this crime today are rare, particularly in the case of men. The number of men and women in our penal and correctional institutions today convicted of some sex offense is relatively high compared to other states of the Union, a fact that can reasonably be attributed to the influence of our traditions on the matter of sex which prescribe punishment for the slightest deviation.

A sample of indictment forms in use today shows how, in many instances, the phraseology of the Puritans has survived for more than three hundred years:[35]

> Lewdness. That A.B., during the three months next before the finding of this indictment, was a lewd, wanton and lascivious person in speech and behavior.
>
> Idle and disorderly person. That A.B., during the three months next before the making of this complaint, was an idle and disorderly person, and neglected all lawful business and habitually misspent his time by frequenting houses of ill fame, gaming houses or tippling shops.
>
> Stubborn child. That A.B., during the three months next before the making of this complaint, was a stubborn child, and stubbornly refused to submit to the lawful and reasonable commands of C.D., whose commands said A.B. was bound to obey.
>
> Vagabond. That A.B., for three months next before the making of this complaint, was a vagabond, and wandered about from place to place, neglecting all lawful calling and employment, and not having any home or means of support.

The statute dealing with rogues and vagabonds, until it was amended in 1943, used the language of the Bay Colony law of

1672 and of the Province Government Law of 1699-1700 which survived for about two and a half centuries.[36] It provided (and still does, but with some modifications) for imprisonment up to six months for:

> rogues and vagabonds,
> persons who use any juggling or unlawful games or plays,
> common pipers and fiddlers,
> stubborn children,
> runaways,
> common drunkards,
> common nightwalkers, both male and female,
> persons who with offensive or disorderly act or language accost or annoy in public places persons of the opposite sex,
> pilferers,
> lewd, wanton, and lascivious persons in speech or behavior,
> common railers and brawlers,
> persons who neglect their calling or employment or who misspend what they earn and do not provide for themselves,
> all other idle and disorderly persons. . .who neglect all lawful business and habitually misspend their time by frequenting houses of ill fame, gaming houses, or tippling shops. . . .

Crimes of violence—murder, manslaughter, robbery, assault, and rape—have increased in relative frequency since Puritan days. In a materialistic society where wealth is constantly on display, it is not surprising that robbery (armed and unarmed) has become the crime for which more men are sentenced to the Massachusetts State Prison than for any other, but we cannot account for the fact that this priority is not found in most other states.

The crime that occupied number one or number two position in Colonial days and has never lost its standing is drunkenness. Today, it is by far the most frequent offense (other than minor motor vehicle law violations) that brings men and women before our courts of justice.

The accompanying tables will shed some light on the "most common crimes" in the Commonwealth of Massachusetts 342 years after the founding of the Colony of New Plymouth.[37] All data are from the Statistical Reports of the Commissioner of Correction, Public Document 115.

TABLE 6

CONVICTED MALE OFFENDERS SENTENCED TO THE MASSACHUSETTS STATE PRISON

in a Two-Year Period, 1961 and 1962 *

	THE CRIME	*Number*	*Per cent*
1.	Robbery (armed and unarmed)†	239	25.0
2.	Breaking, entering, and larceny (burglary)	226	23.6
3.	Rape‡	81	8.5
4.	Assault with dangerous weapon and assault to murder	65	6.8
5.	Larceny (including from the person, receiving stolen goods, and being a common and notorious thief)	60	6.3
6.	Carnal abuse and indecent assault	49	5.1
7.	Manslaughter	45	4.7
8.	Forgery and fraud	35	3.7
9.	Violation of narcotic laws	35	3.7
10.	Larceny of auto and operating without authority	27	2.8
11.	Murder, first and second degree	21	2.2
12.	Arson	14	1.5
13.	Incest	12	1.3
14.	Sodomy and unnatural act	9	0.9
15.	Escape	8	0.8
16.	Kidnapping	7	0.7
17.	Motor vehicle violation	5	0.5
18.	Conspiracy	4	0.4
19.	Other	14	1.5
	Total	956	100.0

* We have taken a two-year, rather than a one-year, period to give a larger representative sample.

† It is most unusual for any state prison in the United States to report robbery as the number one offense, but this trend has been observable in Massachusetts for some time.

‡ Massachusetts also has a relatively high rate for sex crimes (as it had in the Puritan government of the seventeenth century). Sex crimes listed as numbers 3, 6, 13, and 14 in the table total 151 or 15.8% of the total. (Those who are adjudicated "sexually dangerous persons" in civil procedures, usually as a result of serious sex crimes, are not included in these figures.)

TABLE 7

CONVICTED FEMALE OFFENDERS SENTENCED TO THE MASSACHUSETTS CORRECTIONAL INSTITUTION, FRAMINGHAM

*in a Two-Year Period, 1961 and 1962**

THE CRIME	*Number*	*Per cent*
1. Drunkenness	282	52.7
2. Lewdness (including lewd cohabitation)	34	6.4
3. Nonsupport	30	5.6
4. Larceny (including from the person and being a common and notorious thief)	24	4.5
5. Idle and disorderly conduct	22	4.1
6. Stubbornness and being a runaway	22	4.1
7. Prostitution	17	3.2
8. Robbery (armed and unarmed)	15	2.8
9. Adultery	14	2.6
10. Narcotic drug law violations	11	2.1
11. Assault and assault with dangerous weapon	11	2.1
12. Vagrancy	9	1.7
13. Forgery	6	1.1
14. Fornication	6	1.1
15. Manslaughter	5	0.9
16. Escape	5	0.9
17. Breaking, entering, and larceny (burglary)	4	0.7
18. Other	18	3.4
Total	535	100.0

* We have taken a two-year, rather than a one-year, period to give a larger representative sample.

TABLE 8

CONVICTED MALE AND FEMALE OFFENDERS SENTENCED TO THE JAILS AND HOUSES OF CORRECTION

*in Massachusetts in 1962***

THE CRIME	*Number*	*Per cent*
1. Drunkenness	6,158	49.2
2. Nonsupport	1,070	8.6
3. Motor vehicle law violations	990	7.9
4. Larceny (including from the person and receiving stolen goods)	893	7.1
5. Assault and battery (including assault with dangerous weapon and with attempt to murder)	489	3.9
6. Breaking, entering, and larceny	451	3.6
7. Tramps, vagrants, and vagabonds	443	3.5
8. Violations of laws against chastity, morality, decency, and good order	407	3.3
9. Disturbing the peace	227	1.8
10. Contempt of court	223	1.8
11. Trespassing	172	1.4
12. Larceny of auto (including operating without authority)	158	1.3
13. Operating auto without licence	150	1.2
14. Forgery and fraud	109	*
15. Carrying weapons	75	*
16. Violations of narcotic drug laws	62	*
17. Carnal abuse and indecent assault	59	*
18. Malicious mischief	54	*
19. Gaming and lottery	48	*
20. Violations of liquor laws	27	*
21. Rape	22	*
22. Escape	14	*
23. Robbery	12	*
24. Manslaughter	8	*
25. Arson	7	*
26. Other	185	1.5
Total	12,513	100.0

* Less than 1%.

** Only 515 (4.1%) of these offenders were female.

TABLE 9

ARRESTS OF MALES AND FEMALES

*in Massachusetts in 1962***

OFFENSE CHARGED	*Number*	*Per cent*
1. Drunkenness†	58,558	47.5
2. Larceny (including attempt and receiving stolen goods)	7,846	6.4
3. Driving while intoxicated	5,920	4.8
4. Assault and battery (including felonious assault)	5,661	4.6
5. Nonsupport	5,117	4.2
6. Delinquency (including stubbornness)	4,600	3.7
7. Driving to endanger	4,188	3.4
8. Breaking, entering, and larceny (burglary)	4,063	3.3
9. Disorderly conduct	3,734	3.0
10. Sex offenses (other than rape but including abuse of a female child and indecent assault)	3,617	2.9
11. Larceny of auto	3,018	2.4
12. Gaming and lottery	1,406	1.1
13. Forgery and fraud	1,314	1.0
14. Destroying property	1,178	*
15. Tramps, vagrants, and vagabonds	1,048	*
16. Trespassing	623	*
17. Robbery (including attempt)‡	622	*
18. Carrying weapons	539	*
19. Violations of liquor laws	535	*
20. Violations of narcotic drug laws	520	*
21. Rape (and attempts)‡	373	*
22. Prostitution	273	*
23. Arson	123	*
24. Manslaughter‡	95	*
25. Murder‡	80	*
26. Other	8,147	6.6
Total	123,198	100.0

* Less than one per cent.

** We are omitting from this table the report of 146,420 minor motor vehicle violations, such as arrests or tickets for illegal parking, disregarding traffic regulations, and the like. Of the total arrests in this table of 123,198, only 9,303 (7.6%) were arrests of females.

† The combined figure of arrests for drunkenness and for driving while intoxicated is 64,478 (52.3%), which is more than the total of arrests for all other charges.

‡ The combined figure of arrests for the serious crimes of rape, robbery, manslaughter and murder constitute less than 1% of the total of arrests.

13. CRIMINAL JUSTICE IN OPERATION

Arbitrary Government is, where a people have men sett over them without their choyce, or allowance: who have power, to Governe them, and Judge their Causes without a Rule. God onely hathe this prerogative whose Sovereintye is absolute, and whose will is a perfect Rule, and Reason it selfe: so as for man, to usurpe such Autye [Authority] is Tiranye, and impietye.

Where the people have Libertye to admitt, or reject their Governors; and to require the Rule, by which they shalbe governed and Judged, this is *not* an Arbitrarye Government.

That the Government of the Massachusetts is such [that is, not arbitrary], will appeare 1: by the foundation of it: 2: by the positive Lawes thereof: 3: by the constant practice, which proves a Custome, then [than] which (when it is for common good) there is no Lawe of man more inviolable.—*Winthrop's Discourse on Arbitrary Government, 1644.*[1]

WE shall deal here with some of the machinery of the administration of criminal justice not directly described in other chapters: the colonial policeman; colonial lawyers; responsibility for crime; judicial discretion; and fugitives from justice. We shall review here only the records of the Bay Colony. There was no substantial difference (in procedure and in legal institutions) in the administration of criminal justice in the smaller and more law-abiding plantation to the south, the original Plymouth Colony.

The Colonial Policeman. The General Court lost no time in installing the traditional English police officer, the constable, for "the preservation of the peace, the discovery & preventing all attempts against the same," whose oath cautioned him to "dealle seriously & faithfully while you shalbee in office, without any synister respect of favor or displeasure."[2] In the first year of the Colony "John Woodbury is chosen constable of Salem, & Thomas Stoughton constable of Dorchester, to contynue in that office for a yeare & after, till newe be chosen."[3] In the same year constables were chosen by the General Court for Charlestown, "Rocksbury," and Watertown to hold office for one year.[4] As the population increased, each town was authorized to choose annually out of the "settled inhabitants and Home-holders" a man suitable for the task. Like jurors and selectmen, he must have taken the oath of fidelity to qualify for the appointment and had to be at least 24 years old "and of honest and good conversations" and with an estate assessed at twenty pounds (later changed to eighty).[5] His duties were so arduous that the General Court in 1636 authorized each town "where there was neede" to appoint two constables "soe their office may not be a burthen unto them, & they may attend more carefully upon the discharge of their office. . . ."[6]

The broad powers and duties of the constable were set forth in detail in a law of 1646 and incorporated in all subsequent Colonial codes:[7]

> . . . every cunstable within our jurisdiction hath, by virtue of his office, full power to make, signe, & put forth pursuites, or hues & cries, after murtherers, manslayers, peace breakers, theeves, robers, burglarers, where no magistrate is at hand; also, to apprehend without warrant such as are overtaken with drinke, swearing, breaking the Saboth, lying, vagrant persons, night walkers, or any other that shall breake our lawes, in any of these; provided, they be taken in the manner, either by the sight of the cunstables themselves, or by present information from others; as also to make search for all such persons, either on the Saboth dayes, or at any other time, when there shalbe occasion, in all houses licensed to sell either beare or wine, or in any other suspected or disordered places, & those to apprehend, & keepe in safe custody, till oportunity serve to bring them before the next magistrate for further examination; provided, when any cunstable is implied [employed], by any of the magistrates, for apprehending of any, he shall not do it without warrant in writing.

Thus we note his authority to arrest, without a warrant, major as well as minor offenders, provided the crimes were committed in his sight or in the sight of those who immediately informed him of it.

The constable's burdens steadily mounted. By 1658 the General Court decided it was time that someone "collected out of the severall lawes" a list of his obligations so that "each connstable may understand his duty." The Court ordered this compilation printed and made available—probably the first peace officer's manual printed in the country.[8] On perusing this list of 26 items, a constable could plainly see that he was not only the town's police officer—and in smaller towns, the *only* police officer—but that, in addition to his general duties set forth in the law of 1646, he must also levy attachments and fines, gather taxes, assist custom men in searching wine cellars, keep a list of lost goods or strayed animals and "cry the same at three generall toune meetings or lectures," provide standard weights and measures, inform the magistrates of "new comers," summon coroner's juries, take charge of the watch and ward, notify freemen of town elections, summon to court men and women not living with their spouses to give an account of their actions, and pursue runaway servants "by sea or land, & bring them backe by force of armes."

He was also to tally the votes for deputies to the General Court[9], to see that jurymen reported for duty[10], to hang dogs that killed sheep if the owners of the dogs refused to do so,[11] and to see that those who killed wolves for ransom were paid ten shillings by the treasurer.[12]

The search for and arrest of drunkards—his principal quarry—must have taken up a good deal of a constable's time. If a tavern keeper found that one of his customers was drunk, it was his duty to summon the constable "to carry such Drunken person before some Magistrate or Commissioner." Evidently this was not always an easy task for we note the law provided that if any one "in his drunkenness offer any abuse to the Constable or others, either by striking, or reviling him or them, or using any endeavours, by himselfe or others to make an escape" the constable had authority to put him in prison pending judicial determination of the charge.[13]

It was his duty to "take notice of . . . common Coasters, unprofitable fowlers [those presumably who could not earn a living by shooting fowl], & other idle persons, & tobacco takers, & present them to the next two Assistants . . . and of such as shall harbor any young people, children, servants, apprentices, students, or schollers, & not hasten them to theire respective imploiments. . . ."[14]

When he or the watchman were on night duty they were required to "secure, by commitment or otherwise, any inhabitant or strainger after tenne of the clocke at night, behaving themselves deboist [debauched], or that giveth not a reasonable ground to the connstable or watchman, or shallbe in drincke, till the lawe be sattisfied. . .& the connstable is to carry them before a magistrate next morning. . . ."[15]

As time went on additional burdens were placed on the constable's shoulders:

to see that taverners and victualers did not permit children, servants, apprentices or "schollars belonging to the Colledg [Harvard], or any Latine schoole, to spend all of their time or estate" in such establishments;[16]

to arrest persons who failed to report for military training;[17]

to report all single women, or wives whose husbands were away, who "entertain or lodge any In-mate or Sojourner" who had not been approved by the officials, the purpose of this law being "to prevent appearance of sin and wickedness in any kinde";[18]

during the anti-Quaker period (1656-1675) to pursue and apprehend Quakers who violated the laws, with the right to commandeer carts and oxen in doing so;[19]

to arrest anyone found at a Quaker meeting and to seek out such meetings, with power to "break open the doore where they are denyed peaceable entrance":[20]

to present to the Magistrates names of those who placed money on horse races. This law was enacted in 1677 when it was believed that men were practicing "that vanity of Horse racing, for mony, or monyes worth, thereby occasioning much misspence of pretious time, and the drawing of many persons from the duty of their particular Callings, with the hazard of their Limbs and Lives." This was a crucial period in the life of the Colony when the Lord had presumably chastened them for lack of Godliness by a crippling Indian war. Horse racing was deemed one of the "Evils that are prevailing among us, in this day of our Calamity."[21]

to make, every three months, a house-to-house canvass, aided by the selectmen and tithingmen in each town, to ferret out those who had not taken the oath of fidelity to the country and "allegience to our King." This law was enacted in 1677 after it was believed that "evil-minded persons" had attempted "to set fire in the town of Boston, and other places" presumably by those who were strangers or disloyal to the government.[22]

to see that no one brought onto the field on military training days any "wines, strong liquor, Cider, or other inebriating Drink (excepting Beer of a peny a quart)," for experience showed that the people and the Indians who came out for these festive occasions, as well as the soldiers, "commit many disorders of Drunkenness, Fighting, neglect of duty, etc." Drinks could be sold, however, if one obtained a license from two magistrates or the Officers in charge.[23]

to read once a year publicly on the Lord's Day all laws relating to the observance of the Sabbath, a task formerly (prior to 1679) performed by the ministers. The constable shared this duty with the town clerk.[24]

In addition to these duties set forth in the law, constables were at the beck and call of the town selectmen. For example, in the town of Boston the constable was ordered to build a saltpeter house in the prison yard, to fence in the burying ground, to see that men working for the town were paid, and to attend to countless other chores. In 1642 the selectmen requested the constable to "give speedy notice to Robt. Nash, Butcher, that with all speed he remove the Stinking garbage out of his yard, nere the street. . . ."[25]

One of the constable's more rugged duties, not already referred to, was his obligation to: "whip or punish any to bee punished where there is not another officer appointed to do it within his owne towne, unlesse hee can get another to do it."[26] Because he had to keep such close watch over his neighbors' morals and frequently had to have a hand in their chastisement, the constable was not destined to be a popular figure in the community. The court records bear witness time and again to charges for "abuseing and striking of the Constable" for "affronting the Constable in the Execution of his Office,"[27] and the like. For neglecting any of his onerous duties, he was subject to the court's censure or forced to pay a fine. For not doing "their best endeavour," for example, "in raysing and prosecuting Hues & cryes by foot, and if need be by horse, after such as have committed Capital crimes," constables were subject to a fine of forty shillings,[28] and there were many smaller fines for dereliction of duty.

It is not surprising that the average citizen did not relish this assignment. By 1653 the General Court found that it was becoming increasingly common for a man chosen constable by his town to refuse the "honor" and to pay willingly the small fine imposed for such refusal. The fine was thereupon increased from twenty shillings to five pounds, except in Boston where evasion was most common and where the fine was increased to ten pounds.[29] Salem also met with special difficulty in inducing men to take over this task and in 1676 was permitted to levy a similar fine of ten pounds.[30]

To keep the peace, pursue "hues and cries," and perform some three dozen miscellaneous duties, a constable desperately needed help if he were to avoid numerous fines for his neglect. Following the time-honored custom of English towns, all able-bodied citizens were required, on the constable's call, to come to his assistance. Refusal to do so subjected the offender to a fine of ten shillings but, "if it shall appear by good testimony, that any shall willfully, obstinately, or contemptuously refuse or neglect" to give assistance, that fine could be increased to forty shillings.[31]

> And that no man may plead ignorance for such neglect or refusall; It is Ordered, that every Constable shall have a *Black staff,* of five foot long, Tipped at the upper end about *five inches* with brass, as a Badge of his Office, which he shall take with him when he goeth to discharge any part of his Office. . . .[32]

In later years (after 1675) constables, like today's "plainclothesmen," were permitted, when acting by virtue of a warrant, to travel about if they wished without the telltale staff, for it was found that the very sight of the staff "in some cases proves inconvenient by giving opportunity to Delinquents to escape."[33]

Because of the real danger of sudden Indian attack, the General Court had at the very outset established a military watch, pressing young men into service and training them in the use of musket and pike. Compulsory military training soon became a Colonial institution:

Every person above the age of Sixteen yeares, shall duely attend all Military exercise and service, as training, watching, warding, under the penalty of five shillings for every fault, except Magistrates, Deputies [to the General Court], & Officers of Court, Elders, & Deacons, the President, Fellows, Students & Officers of Harvard Colledg, & professed school-masters Physitians & Chirurgeons allowed by two Magistrates, Treasurers, Surveyer General, Publick notary, Masters of Ships and other Vessels above twenty tuns, fishermen constantly imployd at all fishing seasons, constant heardsmen, and such other, as for bodily infirmity or other just Cause shall by any County Court or Court of Assistance . . . be discharged, also one servant of every Magistrate & teaching Elder, and the sons & servants of the Major General . . . also such as dwell at remote farmes or have a ferry to pass, shall be exempt from watching in the town, but shall watch and ward, as their Cheife Officer shall direct otherwise, and all farmes distant above four miles, from the place of exercising the Company, or have a ferry to pass over, that have above twenty acres of land in tillage, and twenty head of great Cattle upon such farme, shall upon Reasonable allowance to the Company have one man exempted from ordinary trainings.[34]

The watch was to be set each night, one-half hour after sunset and all suspicious persons questioned by those serving in these military watches under a highly organized militia.

But the Devil was no less real than the Indians. He, too, needed watching. Accordingly, a peacetime watch under the direct supervision of the local constable was set up in 1640 to curb growing "sinfulness," a practice that was continued during the life of the Colony. Its duties, as set forth in a law of 1652 were

". . . to examine all night walkers after tenne of the clocke in the night unlesse they be knoune peaceable inhabitants, to enquire whether [whither] they are going, and what theire buisenes is, and in case of not giving rationall sattisfaction to the watchmen or counstable, then the counstable forthwith to secure them till the morning, and then the counstable to carry such person or persons before the next magistrate or commissioner, or three men (who shall have power as the commissioners have,) to give sattisfaction for theire being abroad at that time of night, and if the said watchmen shall finde any inhabitant or straunger, after tenne of the clocke at night, behaving themselves any way deboist, or that giveth not a reasonable ground to the counstable or watchmen, or shallbe in drincke, to secure them by committment or otherwise, or till the lawe be sattisfied; and further,

> the counstable is to give the watchmen in charge to see all noises in the streetes still, and lights put out, (except upon necessarie occations,) that fiers, as much as maybe, be prevented, any lawe, custome, or usage to the contrary notwithstanding.[35]

Was the Devil believed to be less active in the colder months? The watch (or, as it was sometimes called "the watch and ward") was operative only from May first to the end of September, although in the larger towns of Boston, Charlestown, and Salem the selectmen could extend the period as they saw fit.[36] It was the constable's duty to notify those who were to serve as watch and ward and to supervise their activities. The watch was not to consist of a majority of youths, for the law stated that "able men be joyned with them, that the Watch may be a sufficient Watch." Men were chosen for this service by the selectmen but if a person were "of estate sufficient to huire another" he might do so—a privilege that eventually gave rise to a professional police force.[37]

As in the case of the military watch, the law granted many exemptions: Members of the General Court, officials of church and state, officers in the military, and those who were personally excused by order of the General Court. At the outset, schoolmasters and "such other that have bene brought up in learning" could by excused by any two Magistrates, as though the task were too rough, requiring brawn rather than brain, but in 1661 the General Court declared that this discrimination led to "much inaequallity" and repealed this exemption.[38]

Under English law an officer called the "Beadle" had served English courts for many years as a messenger or court announcer. James Penn, the first Beadle in the Colony, was "to attend upon the Governor, and alwaies to be ready to execute his commands in publique businesses."[39] It was his duty also to "serve summons in civill actions,"[40] to warn jurors to report for duty,[41] and to attend all court and other public meetings.[42] His importance declined both in England and in the Colony, and no further mention is made of the Beadle after 1634.[43] His functions were taken over by the Marshall. Penn himself was appointed the Marshall of the court in 1634.[44]

Thus the Marshall became the first court officer. He was warned that he was not to enter the meeting room when the conversation was private.[45] It was his duty to levy and collect fines, make returns on warrants and attachments, levy court executions, etc., for which he was given stated fees.[46] He was allowed reimbursement for necessary travel—sixpence per mile, later changed to twelve pence, and five shillings for each person committed to prison (to be collected from the prisoner).[47] In serving attachments on "unruly and disobedient persons," the Marshall, like the constable, could call on citizens for assistance.[48] On all executions levied where money was collected and on all fines he turned in to the treasurers of the towns, he was allowed to retain for his services stated proportions, twelve pence per pound and proportionately more for larger amounts.[49] On the other hand he was liable for full restitution for any injury done to anyone in the performance of his duties.[50] In levying fines he could not take away any person's "necessary Bedding, Apparel, Tools, or Arms" or "Implements of Household, which are for the necessary upholding of his life."[51]

Although the Sheriff, a word derived from *shire* (county) and *reeve* (administrative officer), was an important and highly respected appointive officer of old England, we hear nothing at all of him in the Colony records. When the General Court in 1643 divided the "whole plantation within this jurisdiction" into "four sheires, to wit, Essex, Middlesex, Suffolk and Norfolk" it failed to appoint sheriffs to serve as administrative officers of each county.[52] Evidently the necessary duties were performed by the constable, the marshall, and the prison keeper, and no need was felt for a sheriff. The first appointment of a sheriff did not come until early in the Province government.[53]

In the latter part of the colonial period, neither the constable nor the constable's watch and ward could cope with the increasing difficulty of preventing people from profaning the Sabbath. A new weapon to fight the Devil was needed and the unique system of "Tithingmen" came into being. The tithingmen were appointed by the selectmen of each town to inspect and to hold to account ten families in their own neighborhoods. In the absence of the constable, the tithingman had power to apprehend all Sabbath breakers, to carry them before a magistrate, or to commit them to prison.[54]

Colonial Lawyers. Many men who came to New England with Governor Winthrop, or who followed in the next few years, were graduates of Cambridge and Oxford Universities and were familiar with English Common Law. The Governor himself had been admitted to the Inner Temple in London. Although he had not engaged in legal practice, he must have gained considerable practical education in the law as Justice of the Peace where he presided over many criminal cases. Orders of the General Court and decisions of the judiciary attest to a substantial degree of legal learning among Colonial leaders. And yet, during the early years of the Colony, the sight of a practicing lawyer was a rarity.

Almost anyone who had some familiarity with English law could act as another's attorney in drawing legal documents. No license was necessary to practice law since the profession had not yet attained official recognition. Practicing law was hardly deemed a respectable "calling."[55] There were no law schools and few, if any, lawbooks to induce the younger generation to burn the midnight oil on the road to fame and fortune at the bar or to guide the courts in their deliberations. But by 1647 the General Court recognized the need for the basic tools of English practice:

> It is agreed by this Courte, to the end we may have the better light for making & proceeding about laws, that there shalbe these books following procured for the use of the Courte from time to time:
>
> Two of Sir Edward Cooke upon Littleton;
> Two of the Books of Entryes;
> Two of Sir Edward Cooke upon Magna Charta;
> Two of the Newe Tearmes of the Lawe;
> Two Daltons Justice of Peace;
> Two of Sir Edward Cooks Reports.[56]

The "Cooke" referred to was Sir Edward Coke (1552-1634), the illustrious English jurist, the greatest living authority on the Common Law of England at the time of the founding of the Colony. His "Reports" and his "Coke upon Littleton" have been studied by many generations of English and American law students.

Litigants in civil cases or defendants in criminal trials were usually on their own. "The parties in all causes, speake themselves for the most part, and some of the Magistrates where they thinke cause requireth, doe the part of Advocates without fee or reward," wrote a contemporary observer.[57] The dearth of trial counsel might be explained in part by the prohibition against payment of fees. The Body of Liberties stated:

> Every man that findeth himselfe unfit to plead his owne cause in any Court shall have Libertie to imploy any man against whom the Court doth not except, to helpe him, Provided he give him noe fee or reward for his paines. This shall not exempt the partie him selfe from Answering Questions in person as the Court shall thinke meete to demand of him. [58]

Fortunately this damper on the development of a professional bar was not carried over into the subsequent codifications of the laws, and hence was not in effect after 1648.

Lacking court counsel, it was not unusual for a party to seek advice of a Magistrate before trial in a sort of *ex parte* proceeding. This practice was frowned upon, and the Rev. Nathaniel Ward called attention to it in a sermon and advised "that magistrates should not give private advice, and take knowledge of any man's cause before it came to public hearing." The matter was then debated in the General Court, the Deputies approving of Ward's advice, but the Magistrates saw no great harm in this practice and asserted that, if Ward's view prevailed, "we must then provide lawyers to direct men in their causes." Furthermore, they argued, "by this occasion the magistrate hath opportunity to end many differences in a friendly way, without charge to the parties, or trouble to the court," and "it prevents many difficulties and tediousness to the court to understand the cause aright (no advocate being allowed, and the parties being not able, for the most part, to open the cause fully and clearly, especially in public)."[59] However, after the prohibition against fee-taking was dropped (sometime before 1648) and a few lawyers (or at least men of some legal training) were available, the General Court capitulated and prohibited the party at law to seek advice from a Magistrate before trial, finding it "inconvenient and very burdensome to the magistrates, that many persons have recourse to them for advice and counsell in cases which are afterwards like to come to their cognizance in a legall way."[60] From that time on (1649) there was an ever increasing need for lawyers in the Colony, but still a great scarcity of lawyers themselves.

As the General Court served as a Court of Appeals and as a lawyer-member of the House of Deputies might have a stake in a case coming before it for final adjudication, the Court decided to avoid a conflict-of-interest situation by ordering in 1663 that "No person who is a usuall & common atturney in any inferiour Court shall be admitted to sitt as a deputy in this Court."[61]

The low state of the practice of law in the early days of the Colony was exemplified by the frustrating experience of Boston's first practicing lawyer. Thomas Lechford, "a Student or Practiser at Law," as he called himself[62], or "an ordinary solicitor in England," as the General Court characterized him,[63] for he was not a member of the English bar, arrived from London in 1638 for the express purpose of practicing law in the rapidly growing town of Boston, but he stayed only three years and one month. He evidently possessed considerable knowledge and skill and must have looked forward to a flourishing practice with little or no competition. But the fact that he was a member of the Church of England and liked to talk about it put a damper on his professional advancement. Officials at that time looked with a jaundiced eye on all attorneys but were especially inhospitable toward any newcomer as outspoken as he on matters of ecclesiastical and governmental policy. He could not concede the wisdom of church government on the congregational plan without a ruling bishop and did not hesitate to express his unsolicited views to anyone who would listen. "Our chiefe difference," he wrote on his return to England, "was about the foundation of the Church and Ministery, and what rigid separations may tend unto, what is to [be] feared, in case the most of the people here should remaine unbaptized; considerations which may trouble the wisest among us."[64] Furthermore, he did not feel at ease under a republican form of government. In his view, "a Monarchy is the best government for Englishmen; better to suffer some pressures under that kind of government, then [than] to spoile one another with popular elections."[65]

Lechford applied in vain for a humble position with the government, as court clerk or notary, although his *"Note-Book"* testifies he did not lack for clients.[66] But, he discovered, "they could not doe it, for feare of offending the Churches, because of my opinions."[67] Authorities became so annoyed with his discordant views on church government that they summoned him to appear before the General Court:

> Mr. Thomas Lechford, acknowledging hee had overshot himselfe, & is sorry for it, promising to attend his calling, & not meddle with controversies, was dismised.[68]

On the Court's rebuke and dismissal without penalty, he later commented, "giving a quiet and peaceable answer, I was dismissed with favour, and respect promised me by some of the chiefe [officials] for the future."[69]

Once before Lechford had run afoul of the law when he overstepped the bounds of legal ethics. In the first recorded "disbarment" in American jurisprudence, the General Court ruled:

> Mr. Thomas Lechford, for going to the jewry & pleading with them out of Court, is debarred from pleading any mans cause hereafter, unlesse his owne, & admonished not to presume to meddle beyond what hee shalbee called to by the Courts.[70]

In a humble petition to the General Court, Lechford "acknowledging he did offend in speaking to the Jury without leave," admitted that "he knew it was not done by the law of England. Yet he conceived it was not Embracery [unlawfully attempting to influence a jury] for that he had no reward so to doe." By way of extenuation he stated that he had observed the same done by others with "seeming approbations." "Notwithstanding," he confessed, "he is heartily sorry for his offence."[71] His petition was probably acceptable to the court for he evidently continued to practice law.

His writings reveal a frank and honest individual. "I speak according to my light," he wrote, "and dare do no otherwise."[72] Had he shown more tact and understanding of the theological position the Colony was determined to preserve, he might have become a leader in the development of the Massachusetts bar. But the story turned out quite differently:

> I am kept from the Sacrament, and all place of preferment in the Common-wealth, and forced to get my living by writing petty things, which scarce finds me bread; and therefore sometimes I look to planting of corne, but have not yet here an house of my owne to put my head in, or any stock going.[73]

And yet he did perform a number of valuable services as a humble scrivener. He transcribed (and probably edited) the famous Body of Liberties of 1641 and produced a manuscript copy of the earliest records of the General Court.[74] Especially noteworthy was his insistence on the value of preserving a permanent record of legal decisions upon which a body of precedents could be built. Giving sage advice as a firm defender of the principal of *stare decisis,* he proposed to the General Court that all verdicts, judicial commands or writs, and all court proceedings be recorded for posterity:

> Hereby shall the Law of God and Justice be duly administered to the people, according to more certaine and unchangeable rules, so that they might know what is the Law, and what right they may look for at the mouthes of all their Judges. Hereby the Subjects have a great part of their evidences and assurances for their proprieties, both of lands and goods. . . . I feare it is not a little degree of pride and dangerous improvidence to slight all former lawes of the Church or State, cases of experience and precedents, to go hammer out new, according to severall exigencies; upon pretence that the Word of God is sufficient to rule us: It is true, it is sufficient, if well understood. But take heede my brethren, despise not learning, nor the worthy Lawyers of either gown, [law and chancery] lest you repent too late.[75]

About this time, the General Court determined to record all legal proceedings so as to make possible a body of precedents. It is highly probable that Lechford's suggestions appealed to those members of the General Court who had had legal training:

> Whereas many judgments have bene given in our Courts, whereof no records are kept of the evidence & reasons whereupon the verdit & judgment did passe, the records wherof being duely entered & kept would bee of good use for president [precedent] to posterity, & a releife to such as shall have just cause to have their causes reheard & reviewed, it is therefore by this Court ordered & decreed that thenceforward every judgment, with all the evidence, bee recorded in a booke, to bee kept to posterity.[76]

New Englanders at that time were a litigious people. The records are replete with trivial and vexatious suits for libel and slander, for titles to land, for property left by an intestate, for actions for assault and battery, actions for replevin, and so on. Perhaps the readiness with which one could file a suit without incurring lawyers' fees or appeal a case without elaborate briefs, encouraged barratry. As early as 1641 the Body of Liberties sought to discourage incitement to litigation, and subsequent law codes carried forward this warning:

> If any man shall be proved and Judged a common Barrator vexing others with unjust frequent and endlesse suites, It shall be in the power of Courts both to denie him the benefit of the law, and to punish him for his Barratry.[77]

Other sections of the Body of Liberties permitted the courts to fine those who "falsely pretend great debts or damages to vex his Adversary" or presented any "false complaint or clamor" in prosecuting his suit and subsequent laws provided for heavy fines for vexatious suits.[78] As lawsuits multiplied, lawyers became a necessity. By the middle of the seventeenth century lawyers were beginning to assume a more prominent part in litigation, as evidenced by the rule restricting legal oratory. Because of the "many and tedious discourses and pleadings in court," the General Court ordered that

> . . . when any plaintiff or defendant shall plead, by himself or his Attorney, for a longer time than one hour, the party that is sentenced or condemned shall pay 20 shillings for every hour so pleading.[79]

As time went on, names of attorneys began to appear in the official records. In 1669 Daniell Ela, an attorney, was ordered whipped or fined for charging excessive fees. Peter Goulding, in the same court a few years later, was "disenabled for pleading in any court as an attorney (excepting on his own behalf)" after a conviction for "antedating writings" and stirring up lawsuits.[80]

A law of 1673 permitted lawyers for the first time to sue in the name of their clients, rather than in their own names, a departure from the English practice at that time.[81] Toward the end of the seventeenth century the law had gained some recognition as a profession, although defendants in criminal cases were usually not represented by counsel. In the witchcraft trials of 1692 none of the defendants had the benefit of a lawyer, and every accused witch who was tried was found guilty. Perhaps a competent lawyer could have attacked the jurisdiction of the special tribunal set up for the purpose of trying witches or, at the least, could have prevented the introduction of damaging "specter evidence."[82] In later years it was probably not uncommon for a judge in his discretion to assign a lawyer to an indigent defendant. For example, in the trial of the notorious pirate John Quelch and company, June 13,

1704, "the Prisoners moved for Council [counsel] and His Ecellency [Governor Dudley] assigned them Mr. James Meinzes."[83] But the legal *right* of an indigent or unpopular defendant to the protection of counsel in a criminal case at any stage of the proceedings and in any court of the Commonwealth was not to come until many years had gone by.

Finally, official recognition of a professional bar came about in 1686 when the court admitted several attorneys to practice and required them to take the attorney's oath, thus establishing a permanent tradition.[84]

Responsibility for Crime. Who should be punished for wrongful acts against constituted authority, and who should be excused from such penalties—a matter of life and death for some, of the granting or withholding of precious liberty for others? Heated debates over this crucial question in administering justice echo down through the centuries and continue to this day on Boston's Beacon Hill.

Generally speaking, the law is reluctant to punish anyone whom it cannot blame for his antisocial conduct. It reserves its penalties for those it fears or hates. The rationale of the criminal law today is that those who have free will (and under the Common Law this meant anyone over the age of seven unless he could show his own incompetency) and deliberately decide to cast their lot on the side of society's enemies must answer for the consequences of their own acts. On the other hand, those who are mentally ill or defective to such an extent that they do not understand the nature of their acts or do not know that what they do is wrong are to be pitied, not hated. The law cannot in good conscience punish such persons but it will punish those who with a freedom of choice deliberately choose to do evil. The law in effect will censure the "guilty mind" (or, in the old Latin phrase, the *mens rea*) but will not condemn a person too young to form a criminal intent nor one whose free will is obviously lacking or impaired by some form of mental illness or deficiency.

The Bay Colony had not adopted any "test" of criminal responsibility. The M'Naghten rule, the so-called "right-and-wrong test" prevailing in most of the states today, was not laid down until two centuries later.[85] The General Court in 1641 had set down in its Body of Liberties a broad general rule as a guide when the mental condition of the defendant raised doubts in the minds of the magistrates and carried this rule throughout the life of the Bay Colony:

> Children, Idiots, Distracted persons, and all that are strangers or new commers to our plantation, shall have such allowances and dispensations in any Cause whether Criminall or other as religion and reason require.[86]

How many "idiots" or "distracted persons" (a term that must have covered a variety of mental illnesses) came before the courts cannot be determined, for certainly there must have been many cases where the mental condition of the defendant in criminal cases was not known or understood. At that time there was little knowledge of the nature of mental illness. In telling the story of the mental illness or "infirmity" of the wife of Hartford's Governor, Winthrop reveals his understanding of such things:

> Mr. Hopkins, the governor of Hartford upon Connecticut, came to Boston, and brought his wife with him, (a godly young woman, and of special parts,) who was fallen into a sad infirmity, the loss of her understanding and reason, which had been growing upon her divers years, by occasion of her giving herself wholly to reading and writing, and had written many books. Her husband, being very loving and tender of her, was loath to grieve her; but he saw his error, when it was too late. For if she had attended her household affairs, and such things as belong to women, and not gone out of her way and calling to meddle in such things as are proper for men, whose minds are stronger, etc., she had kept her wits, and might have improved [used] them usefully and honorably in the place God had set her. He brought her to Boston, and left her with her brother, one Mr. Yale,[87] a merchant, to try what means might be had here for her. But no help could be had.[88]

When it was quite clear to the magistrates that a person was mentally ill or "distracted," some allowance was made, as illustrated by the case of Sarah Stevens:

> Sarah Stevens committed to prizon upon her saying that she had lyen [lain] with Christopher Lawson; which was fully evidenced against her; but shee denying in Court that shee had soe done The Court judging by her carriages & testimonies concerning her that shee was a distempered crazy woman discharged her.[89]

On the other hand, there was the baffling case of Dorothy Talbie whose crime was much more serious—the killing of her own little daughter, baptized in Salem in 1635 as "Difficult Talbie."[90] Dorothy had no lawyer when her case came to trial in 1638, to raise the issue of insanity or to adduce evidence that she was "distracted" and entitled to special "allowances and dispensations." At that time defendants in criminal cases were not represented by lawyers. At any rate, the general rule of responsibility was not adopted by the General Court until 1641 but even if it had been in effect at that time it would probably not have mitigated the penalty for murder. The Governor recorded the sad story in his diary:

> Dorothy Talbye was hanged at Boston for murdering her own daughter, a child of three years old. She had been a member of the church of Salem, and of good esteem for godliness, etc.; but falling at difference with her husband, through melancholy or spiritual delusions, she sometimes attempted to kill him, and her children, and herself, by refusing meat, saying it was so revealed to her, etc. After much patience, and divers admonitions not prevailing, the church cast her out. Whereupon she grew worse; so as the magistrate caused her to be whipped. Whereupon she was reformed for a time, and carried herself more dutifully to her husband, etc.; but soon after she was so possessed with Satan, that he persuaded her (by his delusions, which she listened to as revelations from God) to break the neck of her own child, that she might free it from future misery. This she confessed upon her apprehension; yet, at her arraignment, she stood mute a good space, till the governour [Winthrop himself] told her she should be pressed to death [the rarely used penalty for those who refused to plead], and then she confessed the indictment. When she was to receive judgment, she would not uncover her face, nor stand up, but as she was forced, nor give any testimony of her repentence, either then or at her execution. The cloth, which should have covered her face [as she stood on the scaffold], she plucked off and put between the rope and her neck. She desired to have been beheaded, giving this reason, that it was less painfull and less shameful. After a swing or two, she catched at the ladder. Mr. [Hugh] Peter, her late pastor, and Mr. [John] Wilson, went with her to the place of execution, but could do no good with her. Mr. Peter gave an exhortation to the people to take heed of revelations, etc., and of despising the ordinance of excommunication as she had done; for when it was to have been de-

nounced against her, she turned her back, and would have gone forth, if she had not been stayed by force.[91]

A few years later another person was hanged who today might have been considered a mental defective who would have been shown special "dispensations." Hackett was a servant "about 18 or 20 years of age" indicted for sodomy, a capital offense. In Winthrop's view the boy "was noted always to have been a very stupid, idle and ill-disposed boy and would never regard the means of instruction, either in the church or family."[92]

There was no age limitation on criminal responsibility excepting as specifically set forth in the laws. There is no evidence that the common-law rule exempting children under seven from punishment by the courts was ever adopted by the Bay Colony. We have mentioned the rule that children would receive "such allowances and dispensations . . . as religion and reason require," and our examination of available court records reveals no case where young children were harshly treated by the courts. In 1668 the General Court ordered that "in all criminall cases every person, younger as well as elders, shall be liable to answer to their owne persons, for such misdemeanours as they shall be accused of," although in civil cases all under 21 years of age had to be represented by parents, masters, or guardians.[93] We have also previously referred to the rule that all children had to be taught the capital laws.[94] But as for the violation of certain specific criminal laws the General Court preferred to set a minimum age of responsibility in each case.

For example, for sodomy, a capital crime, children under fourteen were to be "severely punished" but not executed;[95] for cursing and smiting parents, a capital crime, only those "above sixteen years old, and of sufficient understanding" could be put to death;[96] for being stubborn or rebellious sons, a capital crime likewise, only those "of sufficient years and understanding (viz.) sixteen years of age" were liable;[97] for arson, a capital crime, the law also applied only to those "of the age of sixteen years and upward";[98] for "denying the Scriptures to be the infallible word of God," again the minimum age was sixteen for those who were liable to the death penalty.[99]

For all other capital laws, it might be reasonably assumed that there was no intent to hold young children criminally responsible. Although children under fifteen or sixteen might be accused of such crimes (as indeed some were accused of witchcraft), there is no evidence that anyone under the age of fifteen was executed in the Bay Colony.

No child under the age of discretion, which in this case was fourteen, could be punished by the constable for telling lies that were "pernicious to the Publick-weal," but their parents or masters were directed to "give them due correction. . .in the presence of some officer."[100]

For profaning the Sabbath, the law applied only to those over the age of fourteen.[101] Great responsibility was placed upon parents to see that their children conformed to the rigid Puritan code of conduct on the Sabbath. For example, if a child "above seaven years old, (not that we approve younger Children in evil)" violated the Sabbath laws by playing or "uncivily walking in the Streets and Fields, travelling from Town to Town, going on Ship-board, frequenting Common Houses and other places to Drink, Sport or otherwise to mispend that precious time," the parents were liable to admonishment for the first offense, a fine for the second, and for the third the County Court could "augment punishment according to the merit of the Fact."[102]

There were other laws too, designed to keep children's behavior in line with Puritan standards, that did not set down any age limitation but presumably in such cases the intent was to govern all who were under the age of 21.

Children and servants who became "rude, stubborn, and unruly" could be taken from their parents, after due warning, and placed for some years with Masters who would "force them to submit unto Government" until they were 21, if boys; 18, if girls.[103]

Magistrates could order that children and servants who behaved "disobediently and disorderly towards their Parents, Masters and Governours" be whipped but not by more than ten stripes for each offense, or they could bind them over to the next County Court.[104]

The child or servant who stole fruit from another's orchard or took wood, clothes, or other objects from one's yard could be openly whipped if his parents or guardians would not pay the owners treble damages.[105] Public whipping of children under the age of fourteen was probably rare or possibly never occurred. Usually in the case of small children the parents were ordered to whip them privately in the home but in the presence of a court officer. A law of 1668 provided for the commitment of stubborn children or servants to a House of Correction.[106]

Children born in New England, sons and daughters of the original planters and settlers, were frequently found lacking in those sterling qualities of godliness and devotion so characteristic of their parents. And when they were found remiss in their duties or delinquent in behavior, the blame usually could be attributed to the lack of proper religious training in the home. When the Indians struck in 1675 and devastated the Colony in the series of attacks, religious leaders immediately sought for reasons for God's anger.[107]

What were these evils that provoked the Lord to such length? The General Court set down twelve "provoking evils" and provided appropriate remedies in each case.[108] Only three of the "evils" specifically concerned children and youths.

1) Many young people evidently found it difficult to sit quietly through the long, tedious Sabbath service, the General Court reporting that there was "much Disorder and Rudeness in Youth in many Congregations in time of the worship of God, whereby Sin and Prophaneness is greatly increased." It was thereupon ordered that children and youth must sit together "in publick view" and that "some Grave and Sober Purson" be appointed to watch them and present the names of those found "Delinquent" to the next Magistrate or Court. For the first offense an admonition was in order, for the second a fine of five shillings, to be paid by their parents or governours or a whipping by them or, if found "Incorrigible," they were to be whipt with ten stripes or sent to the House of Correction for three days.

2) There was existing at that time "a woful Breach of the Fifth Commandment . . . in Contempt of Authority, Civil, Ecclesiastical, and Domestical," an evil attributed chiefly to youths and servants who went out at night without permission "meeting with Corrupt Company," a practice "of a very perilous Nature, and the Root of much Disorder." First offenders were to be subject only to an admonition, but for all subsequent convictions one could

have been fined (up to ten shillings) or whipped (not exceeding five stripes).

3) A practice had grown up, "a loose and sinful Custom" among the youths who, like youths today, wished to get away from the dull routine of family life and ride out into the country for a few drinks and a little fun now and then. The General Court found that "oft times Men and Women together" would ride from town to town "upon pretence of going to Lectures" but would instead "Drink and Revil in Ordinaries and Taverns, which is in it self Scandalous, and it is to be feared a notable means to debauch our Youth, and hazard the Chastity of such as are drawn forth thereunto." Unmarried persons who took such journeys "merely for their pleasure" would be considered "Riotous and Unsober persons, and of ill Behavior." Upon conviction they would be required to give sureties for good behavior in the sum of twenty pounds. Upon refusal to do so, they faced a prison sentence of ten days or a fine of forty shillings.

In the seventeenth century there was, of course, no delinquency-prevention program, but the authorities kept a vigilant eye on youth and placed heavy responsibilities on parents. They were required at least once a week to "Catechise their children and servants in the Grounds and Principles of Religion" and if they were unable to do so they were to teach them "some short Orthodox Catechisme without book" so that they would be able to pass a test to be given by the parents or any of the Selectmen.[109] Parents were also charged with the responsibility for bringing up their children "in some lawfull Calling, Labour or imployment, either in husbandry or some other trade, profitable for themselves and the Common-wealth, if they will not or cannot train them up in learning, to fit them to higher imployments."[110]

Parents could chastise their children for disobedience but a child "shall have free libertie to complaine to Authoritie for redresse" if parents "wilfullie and unreasonably deny any childe timely or convenient mariage, or shall exercise any unnaturall severitie towards them."[111] Parents could not with impunity neglect their children, for "neglectors of their families" were deemed to be "idle persons" by a 1668 law and were thus subject to commitment to the House of Correction.[112] Although the term "babysitter" is of modern origin, it was probably not customary to leave children alone at night, as the Urselton family of Ipswich discovered:

> Frances Urselton and his wife were admonished for leaving their children alone in the night in a lonely house, far from neighbors, after having been warned of it. He was to be punished, if any danger came from it.[113]

Judicial Discretion. A penological question—never satisfactorily answered even to this day—was hotly debated in the Bay Colony General Court as early as 1641, shortly after the Body of Liberties had established for the duration of the Colony certain basic civil and religious rights and liberties but without fixing definite penalties, except for crimes where the only penalty was death. In meting out punishment for violations of laws then on the books and subsequently to be enacted, the magistrates had in fact broad discretionary powers. In most cases the law provided for a fine or a whipping or some punishment of humiliation or not infrequently for "imprisonment at pleasure of the Court." Deputies to the General Court were jealous of the prerogatives of the magistrates who were both legislators and judges and, according to Governor Winthrop, were chosen from the wiser and more able among them. Would they use their power fairly and objectively? Would it not be safer if penalties were fixed rather than indeterminate? William Hathorn [or Hawthorne, the first man to be elected speaker of the House in Massachusetts, an ancestor of Nathaniel Hawthorne] raised this question in 1641. He and some of the other deputies

> were very earnest to have some certain penalty set upon lying, swearing, etc., which the deputy [that is, the Deputy Governor, John Endecott] and some other of the magistrates opposed . . . whereupon Mr. Hathorn charged him with seeking to have the government arbitrary, etc., and the matter grew to some heat, for the deputy was a wise and stout gentleman, and knew Mr. Hathorn his neighbor well [they had both come from Salem], but the strife soon fell, and there was no more spoken of it that court.[114]

Winthrop deeply resented any implication that the government over which he presided and for which he was so largely responsible could justly be called "arbitrary." He was prompted a few years later (1644) to write a lengthy and logical essay "vindicating" the Bay Colony from that "aspersion," from which we have taken the quotation at the head of this chapter. There he argued that a "prescript" sentence to be followed blindly by a judge denied the wisdom of God and the authority of the Judges who were, he said, "Gods upon earthe." Two examples given by Winthrop make his position clear: 1) Should two liars be equally punished by a forty shilling fine if one had never told a lie previously and the lie that he was accused of telling was of a harmless sort, while the other was "an olde notorious lyer" and had told a "pernicious lie"? 2) Should the fine be the same for the rich as for the poor? "If the same penalty hitts a Riche man, it paines him not, it is no Affliction to him, but if it lights upon a poore man, it breakes his backe."[115]

The debate between Hathorn and Endecott "gave occasion to some of the magistrates [probably led by Winthrop himself] to prepare some arguments against the course intended," that is, against making all penalties fixed and certain. The magistrates' proposition was that "all punishments, *except* such as are made certain in the law of God [presumably such as those made punishable by death in the Mosaic code], or are not subject to variation by merit of circumstances, ought to be left arbitrary to the wisdom of the judges."[116] The eight arguments adduced constituted the first formal defense of judicial discretion in American criminal courts and thus deserve a prominent place in the history of the administration of criminal justice. They are:[117]

> 1) God hath left a pattern hereof in his word, where so few penalties are prescribed [as fixed penalties], and so many referred to the judges [as discretionary]; and God himself [meaning the lawmakers of Israel several centuries before the founding of Boston] varieth the punishments of the same offences, as the offences vary in their circumstances; as in manslaughter, in the case of a riotous son proving incorrigible, in the same sin aggravated by presumption, theft, etc., which are not only rules in these particular cases, but to guide the judges by proportion in all other cases: as upon the law of adultery [a capital offence], it may be a question whether Bathsheba ought to die by that law, in regard to the great temptation, and the command and power of the kings of Israel. So that which was capital in the men of Jabesh Gilead, Judges (xxi:10) in not coming up to the

princes upon proclamation, was but confiscation of goods, etc., in Ezra 10:8. [See 2 Sam. 14:6, 11.]

2) All punishments ought to be just, and, offences varying so much in their merit by occasion of circumstances, it would be unjust to inflict the same punishment upon the least as upon the greatest.

3) Justice requireth that every cause should be heard before it be judged, which cannot be when the sentence and punishment is determined before hand.

4) Such parts and gifts, as the word of God requires in a judge, were not so necessary, if all punishments were determined beforehand.

5) God hath not confined all wisdom, etc., to any one generation, that they should set rules for all others to walk by.

6) It is against reason that some men should better judge of the merit of a cause in the bare theory thereof, than others (as wise and godly) should be able to discern of it *pro re nata*. [That is, the courts should meet the particular situations as they arise and thus develop a body of law as England had developed its Common Law.]

7) Differences of times, places, etc., may aggravate or extenuate some offences.

8) We must trust God, who can and will provide as wise and righteous judgment for his people in times to come, as in the present or forepassed times; and we should not attempt the limiting of his providence, and frustrating the gifts of others, by determining [predetermining] all punishments, etc.

The magistrates admitted that God had prescribed a definite punishment in capital cases, which was death—"the highest degree of punishment which man's justice can reach"; likewise theft might entail a definite penalty (multiple damages) regardless of the circumstances. Accepting these facts, they wrote, we are not advocating that we should "leave *all* laws arbitrary at the discretion of the judge." To the objection that "the statutes in England set down a certain penalty for most offences," they replied with that spirit of independence reflected so often in Colonial writings that "we are not bound to make such examples ourselves."[118] At any rate, as Winthrop pointed out later, for all great offences and misdemeanors, English law had not demanded fixed penalties.[119] He conceded that he did "not condemn *all* prescript penalties . . . but only so far as they cross with the rules of justice, and prudence, and mercy."[120]

Is the lawmaker better able than the judge to determine the most wise and just penalty in a given case? Winthrop answered this question:

> So if all penaltyes were prescribed, the Jurye should state the case, & the booke holde forthe the sentence, & any Schoolboye might pronounce it: then what need were there of any speciall wisdome, learninge, Courage, zeal or faithfulnesse in a Judge?[121]

By the end of the eighteenth century, Winthrop's able defense of judicial discretion had been lost sight of. Reformers of the criminal law, Cesare Beccaria and Jeremy Bentham and their followers, reacting against the gross *abuse* of discretion and the infliction of harsh penalties, preferred a justice that would be "equal" for all and believed that this noble aspiration could be achieved if the legislature would predetermine the penalty for each crime. Beccaria's view was in sharp contrast to that of Winthrop. Beccaria, in his *Treatise on Crimes and Punishments* (1764) held:

> The legislators, not judges, should make the laws; the duties of judges are solely to determine whether a crime as defined by the legislators has been committed and to pronounce the sentence determined by law.

Thus punishment, the classical school of criminology maintained, should fit the crime, not the criminal. In more recent times we have seen the return to the judicial discretion advocated by Winthrop in the wide use of the semi and the completely indeterminate sentences.

As it was customary to refer disputed political issues to the clergy, particularly where the officials deemed it appropriate to seek the will of God, two questions were propounded to them: 1) "Whether we may warrantably prescribe certain penalties to offences, which may probably admit variable degrees of guilt," and 2) "Whether a judge be bound to pronounce such sentence as a positive law prescribs, in case it be apparently above or beneath the meritt of the offence."[122]

On the whole, the ministers sustained the position of the magistrates, who believed judges should have broad discretionary powers. The ministers' report, which was written into the records of the General Court, made these points:[123]

1) Even though there may be mitigating circumstances in

the crimes that were listed as capital crimes and in theft, it is proper to establish definite penalties, for the laws of Moses (in Numbers 35:16,17,18,20,21 and Exod. 22:1) made this clear.

2) On the other hand, there are some crimes where the "variable circumstances" must be taken into consideration. For example, "the striking of a neighbor may be punished with some pecuniary mulct, where the striking of a father may be punished with death" [presumably because it was a violation of the fifth Commandment and a capital offence both in Israel and, under certain circumstances, in Boston]; or to gather sticks on the Sabbath "with an high hand" [a Biblical expression, meaning presumptuously] could be punished with death but to do so "privily, & in some neede" would merit a lesser penalty.

3) A judge could take into consideration whether the crime committed was the offender's "first offence or customary; whether he was enticed thereto, or the enticer; whether hee were principall or accessary; whether unadvised or witting, & willing, etc." In such cases the judge should have some latitude to choose between certain minimum and maximum sentences, such as five to forty shillings fine or five to forty stripes on his bare back, etc. But judges should avoid unfair disparity of sentences:

> care would be taken that a magistrate attend in his sentence as much as may be to a certeine rule in those circumstances, lest some person, whose sinns be alike circumstantiated with another, if his punishment be not equall the one with the other, one may thinke himselfe more unequally dealt withall than another.

In speaking of that kind of judicial discretion in sentencing that might cause one to "thinke himselfe more unequally dealt withall than another," Winthrop put his finger on a problem that has persisted to this day and has been a topic of bitter complaint in our prisons since the opening of the "penitentiary prison" at Charlestown in 1805.

4) If the judge is "perswaded in conscience" that a crime deserves a greater punishment than the law allows he nevertheless has no power to go higher; but if the law seems to be more severe "than the offence deserveth, it is his part to suspend his sentence till, by conference with the lawgivers, hee find liberty either to inflict the sentence or to mittigate it."

5) The General Court, too, should be able to mitigate the penalty in the case of good public servants, "out of respect to the publick good service which the delinquent hath done to the state in former times. So Solomon mittigated the punishment of Abiathar, for his service done to his father formerly (1 Kings, 2:26, 27)."

Magistrates and ministers were thus in general agreement that courts should not surrender their right to make discretionary judgments. Even in the case of violations of some of the capital laws, the death penalty was seldom invoked when mitigating circumstances could be found, though the supreme penalty was the only penalty stated in the law.

They had written into the record "That no magistrate hath power to vary from the poenalty expressed in any lawes, either to mittigate or exceede the same, without consulting with the General Court" and "that certaine poenalties may, & ought to be, prescribed in diverse cases, though the offences admit of variable degrees of guilt."[124] And yet it is doubtful that the General Court was consulted in the numerous cases where mitigation was considered. The rule in practice seemed to have been to make the penalty fit the individual case. It would have been contrary to the spirit of Puritan equity to limit to any automatic dispensation of justice magistrates who were deemed to be God's agents.

In 1668 when physical assaults were evidently becoming more frequent, the General Court allowed judges a free hand in punishing any person who "shall beate, hurt, or strike any other person." The reason given was that

> in this case, severall circumstances may alter the degree of the offence, as who do smite, who is smitten, with what instrument, the danger of the wound, more or less, time, place, & provocation, & other the like, it is left to the discretion of the judges aforesaid, upon hearing & consideration, to impose such poenalty or poenalties as in their discretion shall seeme just, aequall, & proportionable to the merrit of the offence.[125]

Fugitives From Justice. Criminals, escaping prisoners, and runaway servants who fled the jurisdiction of the Massachusetts Bay Colony to the independent colonies of Plymouth, New Haven, or Connecticut were subject to arrest and return, pursuant to an intercolonial agreement, the forerunner of modern interstate compacts.

"The United Colonies of New England" came into being on May 19, 1643, when Articles of Confederation were concluded in Boston between these four colonial governments.[126] The fugitive-from-justice clause was incidental to the basic purposes of the federation, which were declared to be:

> . . . a firm and perpetual league of friendship and amity, for offence and defence, mutual advice and succor upon all just occasions, both for preserving and propagating the truth and liberties of the gospel, & for this our mutual safety and welfare.[127]

The urgent need for mutual defence against threatened assaults by Indians (particularly the "Nariganset" and "Pequott" tribes) who, it was rumored at that time, were intent on driving the English into the sea, was probably the mainspring of the confederacy, but the joining of hands in "propagating the truth and liberties of the gospel" widened the gap between English Episcopacy and Congregationalism and was not looked upon with composure by the English government. A royal commission that King Charles the Second sent to the colonies some years later (1665) pronounced the union illegal:

> There is no power in the Charter to incorporate with other colonies, nor to exercise any power by that association: both belongs to the kings prerogative.[128]

To this attack, the General Court, in the habit of taking an independent attitude toward royal commissions, replied with a strong rebuttal, reasserting the desperate need for mutual assistance in the case of Indian attack.[129] No further protest from the King was heard.

Two commissioners from each of the four colonies met annually until 1670, after which meetings were held every third year in Boston or Plymouth or Hartford. By 1669 the General Court conceded that the union was "greatly weakened, and at present useless"[130] and suggested that new articles be drawn between Massachusetts, Plymouth, and Connecticut, New Haven having been absorbed by the latter in 1662. The newly organized federation (1670) continued until the loss of the Charter in 1684, but the need for it was less urgent, and it diminished in prestige and usefulness, although it retained its fugitive-from-justice clause that provided:

> ... that if any servant run away from his master into any of these confederate jurisdictions, that in such case, upon certificate of one magistrate in the jurisdiction out of which the said servant fled, or upon other due proof, the said servant shall be delivered either to his master or any other that pursues and brings such certificate or proof: And that upon the escape of any prisoner or fugitive for any criminal cause, whether breaking prison or getting from the officer, or otherwise escaping, upon the certificate of two magistrates of the jurisdiction out of which the escape is made, that he was a prisoner or such an offender at the time of the escape, the magistrate, or some of them of the jurisdiction where for the present the said prisoner or fugitive abideth, shall forthwith grant such a warrant as the case will bear, for the apprehending of any such person and the delivery of him into the hand of the officer or other person who pursueth him; and if there be help required for the safe returning of any such offender, then it shall be granted unto him that craves the same, he paying the charges thereof.[131]

Although the records do not tell us how many, if any, fugitives were returned to the colony from which they had fled, the Confederation during its four decades had fulfilled its main purpose of presenting a united front against hostile Indian tribes. Furthermore, it served as an inspiration and, in a sense as a model, for future articles of confederation.

The General Court in 1661, to demonstrate its allegience to the King, declared, "In case (for the future) any [person] legally obnoxious & flying from the civil justice of the state of England, shall come over to these partes, they may not heer expect shelter."[132]

About a hundred years later, the Colonies again felt the need for a pact of mutual assistance. Articles of Confederation were drawn in 1776 and ratified a few years later by thirteen Colonies. Again Rhode Island was not a party. The English Colonies, breaking away from their mother country, considered themselves virtually independent "states." "The United States of America" was a natural sequel to the "United Colonies of New England." Those who drew up the Articles of Confederation were probably familiar with the earlier document. A comparison of the wording of the two documents makes it evident, according to some historians, that the Articles of Confederation (which was superseded by the Constitution of The United States in 1787) was a lineal descendant of the original "United Colonies of New England."[133]

14. "THOU SHALT NOT SUFFER A WITCH TO LIVE"

I am abundantly satisfied that there have been, and are still most cursed Witches in the Land. More than one or two of those now in Prison, have freely and credibly acknowledged their Communion and Familiarity with the Spirits of Darkness; and have also declared unto me the Time and Occasion, with the particular Circumstances of their Hellish Obligations and Abominations—*The President of Harvard College, the Rev. Increase Mather, 1692.*[1]

UNDER the law, in the Bay Colony and in Plymouth a witch was a person who had a "familiar spirit," or consulted with one, and was thus in direct communion with the Devil and bound by a solemn oath to carry out his evil designs. As every child knew (for the law directed that no child should be ignorant of the capital laws) the surrender of one's soul to the Devil made one liable to the penalty of death.[2] No lighter punishment seemed appropriate in view of the clear command of God: "Thou shalt not suffer a witch to live."[3]

The humblest servant in the colonies shared with the most learned a belief in the reality of witches and the Devil. A common social heritage bound all men to worship God and to loathe evil, evil personified by a real Devil who resided in a real Hell and who could make life miserable on earth. Under such overwhelming social pressures, who would presume to explain the "providences of God" or the "powers of Darkness" or the "preternatural" events of "the invisible World" in terms of natural law?

The idea that man could form an intimate and evil partnership with the Devil was not original with our seventeenth century forebears but was virtually a universal belief that had its roots deep in the past, even before the Christian era.[4] In the fifteenth, sixteenth, and seventeenth centuries, a compelling fear of these evil spirits swept over the continent of Europe from Scandinavia to the Mediterranean, and the study of "demonology" implanted this fear in the hearts of men in every little town and parish. Thousands of witches, including many children, were hanged or burned to death, the latter a penalty never exacted in New England. Kittredge asserted that at least 3,400 witches were executed in Scotland, while, for the continent of Europe, "half a million is thought to be a moderate estimate." In Alsace, 134 witches were burned at the stake within a two-week period.[5]

Thus the belief in witchcraft was not peculiar to Puritanism. Protestants of all shades of theological persuasion, as well as Catholics, Hebrews, and pagans fell under its spell. Mackay made the observation that, although every Christian theological creed or dogma had been in dispute at one time or another, the belief in witchcraft in the fifteenth, sixteenth, and seventeenth centuries was "as well established as the authenticity of the Scriptures or the existence of a God." The "witch mania," as he called it, was said to have commenced in earnest with the papal bull issued by Pope Innocent VIII in 1488, providing for "inquisitors in every country, armed with the apostolic power to convict and punish." One inquisitor alone, he reported, was responsible for the conviction and burning of nine hundred witches in a fifteen year period of service to his church. In the early days of witch burning, Catholics seemed to have taken the lead, but "in after times we also find that the Lutherans and Calvinists became greater witch-burners than ever the Romanists had been."[6]

Seventeenth century New Englanders fell heir to centuries of thinking on the nature of mysterious natural phenomena for which scientific explanations would have been totally inadequate and, at best, an intrusion into the domain of the priesthood where explanations were readily available for whatever seemed to emanate from either God or the Devil. The prosecution of witches in the colonies came after the "mania" had reached its peak in Europe. The number of executions in New England was relatively insignificant, yet the story of the Salem trials attracted an extraordinary number of writers and dramatists down to the present time and constitutes a relevant part of the story of the administration of criminal justice in Massachusetts.

With this background of uncritical belief and the prestige of Scripture and of history, the stage had been set for a major outbreak of the "mania" in this part of the world. The conflagration began in Salem Village (now Danvers) in the winter of 1691-1692 in the home of the Rev. Samuel Parris, but we are not warranted in saying that were it not for the behavior of the irresponsible and "afflicted" little girls in his home the tragic scenes on "gallows hill" would never have taken place. Almost anyone could have provided the spark. The dry logs of a potential fire were there.

The belief in a Devil as a living personality led many to conjure up in their own minds a picture of his physical appearance. Cotton Mather, conceding that he had never actually laid eyes on him, described him, from reports he had heard, as "a short and a Black Man. . .no taller than an ordinary Walking-Staff; hee was not of a Negro, but of a Tawney, or an Indian colour; hee wore a High-Crowned Hat, with strait Hair; and had one Cloven-Foot."[7] Actually there was not one Devil, but many. "When we speak of, The Devil, 'tis, A name of Multitude," he said. "It means not One Individual Devil. . .but it means a Kind, which a Multitude belongs unto. Alas, the Devils, they swarm about us, like the Frogs of Egypt. . . ." And yet, there is one who is "the General of those Hellish Armies; Our Lord, that Conquered him, has told us the Name of him; 'tis Belzebub; 'tis he that is *the Devil,* and the rest are his Angels, or his Souldiers."[8]

Most of the intellectuals in the Bay Colony were competent theologians and to them people looked for explanations of the "preternatural." According to Morison, "It was the people who composed what one might call the Harvard scientific group of that day—Morton, Willard, Stoughton, and the Mathers—who took the keenest interest in witchcraft."[9] Of those, all but Stoughton were ministers. Stoughton, however, was a Puritan through and through and had been a preacher before he turned to the law. He was certain in his own mind that New England was infested with witches and that upon due conviction they deserved no better fate than death. It was common at that time for the ministers to attribute any strange, unexplained natural phenomena to "remarkable providences of God" or to divine retribution. A sudden stroke of lightning, an earthquake, a drought, a fire, or an Indian attack might all have a common cause, the direct intervention of God —or of the Devil.

Probably no one was greatly surprised, therefore, when Captain John How testified on June 30, 1692, in the special court in Salem that

> . . . some of his Cattle were Bewitched to Death, leaping three or four foot high, turning about, speaking, falling, and dying at once; and going to cut off an Ear, for an use, that might as well perhaps have been omitted, the Hand wherein he held his Knife was taken very numb, and so it remained, and full of Pain, for several Days, not being well at this very Time. . . .[10]

He placed the blame on his sister-in-law Elizabeth How who, it was said, "had been baptized by the Devil in the River, at Newbury-Falls."

The "combustion and confusion" associated with Salem in 1692 was not New England's first skirmish with the Devil. The antiwitchcraft law had been on the books from the outset in both Colonies. In the smaller and more tranquil Colony to the south, relatively little was heard about those who were suspected of "Solemn Compaction or conversing with the Devil by way of witchcraft conjuration or the like," and no one charged with that offense had to forfeit his or her life. The Plymouth Court Records report the case of only one defendant standing trial before a jury "of life and death" for having some familiarity with the Devil. Mary Ingham of Scituate was indicted in 1677 for having "malliciously procured much hurt, mischeiffe, and paine unto the body of Mehittable Woodworth . . . causing her . . . to fall into violent fitts," until she was "almost bereaved of her sences." The jury found Mary Ingham not guilty.[11]

Prior to the outbreak in Salem in 1692, the sinister word "witch" was heard at relatively infrequent intervals in the Court of Assistants, the usual tribunal for the trial of capital cases. More often it became an issue in one of the county courts where a man sued his neighbor for defamation of character at a time when calling one a "witch" was clearly actionable. In such cases juries usually brought in a verdict for the plaintiff. The suit for defamation brought by Jane James, a 64-year-old widow, was representative of that type of civil action that was fairly common in Bay Colony courts. It clearly illustrates how accusations of witchcraft could —and often did—arise out of the mystic and turbid anxiety of a nightmare. The record of the Salem court on June 25, 1667, showed:

> Writ: Jane James; widow v. Richard Rowland; defamation; for saying that plaintiff came in at a hole in the window in Rowland's house, took him by the throat and almost choked him as he lay in his bed and called her old hag; dated June 17, 1667. . . .

Usually defendants could produce other testimony to support their accusations. In this case, Jane was fortunate in having witnesses on her side:

> Capt. James Smith, aged about forty-three years, deposed that he, Samuell Aborne, sr., and Richard Rowland were in bed together when suddenly the latter screeched, started up and said he was almost choked with the old hag, Goody James, who, he said had come in through a hole in the window and had him fast by the throat, etc. Deponent saw nothing although the room was very bright with the light of the moon. Sworn in court.

Samuell Aborne "aged about fifty-six," also testified, presumably to the same effect. Another witness, John Furbush, testified that "he had often heard Richard Rowland and his wife call Jane James, Jesable [Jezebel] and devil." Verdict for plaintiff.[12]

There were, in this period, probably less than a dozen prosecutions for witchcraft in the Courts of Assistants or the General Court. In all but four cases, the Court dismissed the charges or, if the accused were put on trial "by God and Countrey" (i.e., by a jury) a verdict of "not guilty" was returned. In some cases juries brought in special verdicts of "guilty of *suspicion* of witchcraft," thus sparing the defendant's life.

In one of the four cases, the Court of Assistants in 1681 reprieved the guilty woman on the petition of her husband. Elizabeth Morse of Newbury, a midwife long suspected of witchcraft, spent a miserable year in prison before she was allowed to go home to live out her life, continuously professing her innocence and "praying to and resting upon God in Christ for Salvation."[13]

Three women who were not so fortunate as Mary Ingham or

Elizabeth Morse in this pre-Salem period were Margaret Jones, Anne Hibbins, and Goody Glover.[14]

Margaret Jones, executed in Boston on June 15, 1648, was the first to die in Massachusetts for this crime, but possibly not the first in New England, for there is an unconfirmed report of an execution in 1646 or 1647 in Hartford. Very little of the specific charges have been preserved, but the account given by Governor Winthrop describes so well the kind of evidence admitted by the court in the face of a strong plea of innocence that we shall quote his diary entry in its entirety:

> At this court one Margaret Jones of Charlestown was indicted and found guilty of witchcraft, and hanged for it. The evidence against her was, 1. that she was found to have such a malignant touch, as many persons, (men, women, and children,) whom she stroked or touched with any affection or displeasure, or, etc., were taken with deafness, or vomiting, or other violent pains or sickness, 2, she practising physic [medicine], and her medicines being such things as (by her own confession) were harmless, as aniseed, liquors, etc., yet had extraordinary violent effects, 3, she would use to tell such as would not make use of her physic, that they would never be healed, and accordingly their diseases and hurts continued, with relapse against the ordinary course, and beyond the apprehension of all physicians and surgeons, 4. some things which she foretold came to pass accordingly; other things she could tell of (as secret speeches, etc.) which she had no ordinary means to come to the knowledge of, 5, she had (upon search) an apparent teat in her secret parts as fresh as if it had been newly sucked, and after it had been scanned, upon a forced search, that was withered, and another began on the opposite side, 6. in the prison, in the clear day-light, there was seen in her arms, she sitting on the floor, and her clothes up, etc., a little child [the so-called witch's imp], which ran from her into another room, and the officer following it, it was vanished. The like child was seen in two other places, to which she had relation; and one maid that saw it, fell sick upon it, and was cured by the said Margaret, who used means to be employed to that end. Her behavior at her trial was very intemperate, lying notoriously, and railing upon the jury and witnesses, etc., and in the like distemper she died. The same day and hour she was executed, there was a very great tempest at Connecticut, which blew down many trees, etc.[15]

Even a woman of high social position could not escape the

charge of witchcraft. Anne Hibbins was the wife of William Hibbins, one of the Assistants, a prominent citizen of the town of Boston and a man of considerable wealth. Two years after his death and eight years after the hanging of Margaret Jones, the accusations of her neighbors led to a bill of indictment that sealed her fate. Presumably the evidence against her was overwhelming; otherwise the Deputy Governor, Richard Bellingham who was her own brother (or so it was reported) would have come to her defense. Although the specific evidence does not appear in the record, Hutchinson wrote that her husband had been a merchant in Boston:

> but losses in the latter part of his life had reduced his estate, and increased the natural crabbedness of his wife's temper, which made her turbulent and quarrelsome, and brought her under church censures, and at length rendered her so odious to her neighbours as to cause some of them to accuse her of witchcraft.[16]

The verdict of the jury finding her guilty in 1655 was not entirely satisfactory to the magistrates, and they asked the General Court to hear the case. The whole Court found her guilty, and Governor Endecott pronounced the sentence of death, ordering "the marshall gennerall" to take a sufficient guard with him and see that she "hang till she was dead" on "the 5th day next come fortnight, presently after the lecture at Boston, being the 19th of June next [1656]."[17] On that day Increase Mather, age seventeen, graduated from Harvard College, destined to play a prominent part in later witchcraft prosecutions.

Thirty-two years went by before the populace witnessed another hanging for witchcraft. The widow Goody Glover, "one of the wild Irish, of bad character" was the mother of the laundress for John Goodwin, "a grave man and a good liver at the north part of Boston."[18] He was convinced that four of his children, ranging in age from five to thirteen, were bewitched, and there seemed to be evidence that could not be impugned that that "ignorant and scandalous old woman" who "own'd her self a Roman Catholick" and "spoke Irish" at her trial (necessitating the calling in of interpreters) had thrown his children into strange fits "beyond those that attend an Epilepsy, or a Catalepsy, or those that they call The Diseases of Astonishment." It is idle to assume that the court was unduly prejudiced against her because of her religious faith—or the lack of it.[19] When the Rev. Cotton Mather asked her if she believed in God, he reported that "her Answer was too blasphemous and horrible for any Pen of mine to mention." Her diabolic afflictions alone were enough to convict her. The "Cries, the Shrieks, the Tortures of these poor Children" furnished conclusive evidence that the Devil was at work in the home of this God-fearing mason, John Goodwin, and that this "miserable old woman," Goody Glover, was the self-confessed Devil's confederate. Goodwin's children fell into grotesque fits and "frolicks," suffered temporary paralysis of their limbs, cried out "of dismal Blowes with great cudgels laid upon them" (invisible to others present who claimed, nevertheless, they could see the red marks where the cudgels had struck), became at one time speechless, at another totally deaf. "They would fly like Geese; and be carried with an incredible Swiftness thro the air, having just their Toes now and then upon the ground, and their Arms waved like the Wings of a Bird. One of them . . . flew the length of the Room, about 20 foot . . . none seeing her feet all the way touch the floor." Sometimes they would bark like dogs, again they would purr like cats. One of the little girls, taken by Cotton Mather into his home as an act of kindness and to furnish him "with Evidence and Argument as a Critical Eye-Witness to confute the Saducism of this debauched Age" (for there were those who doubted the existence of angels and devils), was unable to listen to the Word of God without being cast into "very terrible Agonies." But she could, with complete relaxation and contentment read a Quaker book, a book of jests, a book expressing disbelief in witches or a "popish Book"—writings that the Devil would surely approve. Any book authored by Increase or Cotton Mather, or the latter's grandfather, John Cotton, "would bring hideous Convulsions."

Cotton Mather's report of this case and his interpretation of these "Mysteries of Darkness" had the strong support of the Rev. Charles Morton of Charlestown, the Reverends James Allen and Joshua Moody of the First Church in Boston, and the Rev. Samuel Willard of the Old South Church of Boston, the latter taking a most cautious and critical stand on the admissibility of evidence in witchcraft proceedings. The Rev. Joshua Moody was so impressed with what he saw at the home of John Goodwin that he wrote a letter to the Rev. Increase Mather who was at that time (October 1688) in London. He said, in part:

> Wee have a very strange thing among us, which we know not what to make of, except it bee Witchcraft, as we think it must needs be. 3 or 4 children of one Goodwin, a Mason, that have been for some weeks grievously tormented, crying out [complaining] of head, eies, tongue, teeth; breaking theyr neck, back, thighs, knees, leggs, feet, toes, etc.; & then they roar out, Oh my head, Oh my neck, & from one part to another the pain runs almost as fast as I write it. The pain is (doubtles) very exquisite, & the cries most dolorous & affecting, & this is noteable that two or more of them cry out of the same pain in the same part, at the same time, & as the pain shifts to another place in one, so in the other, & thus it holds them for an hour together & more: when the pain is over they eat, drink, walk, play, laugh, as at other times. . . . Wee cannot but think the devill has an hand in it by some instrument.[20]

The Glover case was the forerunner of the outbreak of witchcraft in Salem Village about three and a half years later. The children there were similarly "bewitched" and behaved in a very similar manner. Mather had published his report of the Glover case, not omitting a single fascinating detail, and it is quite likely that the people of that little settlement north of Boston were thoroughly familiar with it. In this respect we may be justified in saying that Cotton Mather's influential writings and sermons played a significant part in the outbreak of witchcraft accusations in Salem and environs.

This twenty-six-year-old preacher in the North Church, a precocious student and scholarly pastor, could not understand how any intelligent person with some acquaintance with history and some familiarity with Scripture stories replete with references to witches, sorcerers, and wizards could for a moment doubt their reality. The historical evidence, confirmed by God's Word, was, to Mather, reasonable and conclusive. But, "last of all," he wrote, "personal Experience has made it impossible for mee to bee of any other Belief. . . .'Seeing is Believing.' . . .one that hath Seen, and known, what I have must have been the greatest Sot in the World, if hee did not Beleeve as I do":

> Not *I* only, but my whole Countrey, saw a most Illustrious Conviction of *Witchcraft,* when *Glover* was convicted. Her *Magical Images*

> [her "poppets," as they were called] were found, and shee actually showed the whole Court by what *Caeremonies* used unto *them,* shee Directed her *Familiar Spirits,* how and where to torment the Objects of her malice. The *Experiments* were made over and over again before the whole Court; . . . Shee also made a punctual Confession of her Witchcraft.[21]

A unique aspect of this case that had such an important bearing on the Salem cases, was that Glover herself never denied the accusations but showed some pride in her "profession." When a search of her house revealed little "poppets" made of rags, stuffed with goat's hair, she not only acknowledged ownership but demonstrated that "her way to torment the Objects of her malice, was by wetting of her Finger with her Spittle, and stroaking of those little Images." When she held an image in her hand, "one of the Children fell into sad Fits, before the whole Assembly." As Mather said, this demonstration was repeated with the same results.[22] Obviously, it left no room for doubt.

Glover's actions were so unusual—"the night after, she was heard expostulating with a Devil" whom she addressed as her "Prince"—that some thought she might be "craz'd in her Intellectuals" and had brought upon herself "by Folly and Madness the Reputation of a Witch." The court proceeded with caution, for probably few, if any, in authority at that time had ever taken part in the legal condemnation of a witch. Six physicians were called in "to examine her very strictly" (similar to the current practice of calling for an examination by two psychiatrists in capital cases), but they "returned her Compos Mentis; and Sentence of Death was pass'd upon her."

Without an understanding of the rationale of the Puritan ministers, who took such an active part in the proceedings, in accounting for the strange "preternatural" phenomena, we cannot fairly judge the tragic events of those days.

One could take the role of an objective reporter, tracing the origin of demonology to its source in folklore and mythology, treading the path of misery and bloodshed down to the present time, showing how sorcery and witchcraft in some parts of the world today still have their practitioners.[23] Or one could focus on the power of suggestion and the psychology of hysteria that might explain how the complaints of a few young girls in Salem Village set off a chain reaction of fateful consequences. Or, looking back over the centuries with a psychoanalyst, one might see how witchcraft was "an exteriorization of the repressed sexual conflicts of women" and how "excessive sexual repression" (and certainly New England under the influence of Puritan preachers was not noted for liberalism in the expression of one's sexual drives) was what "made the Witch craft epidemic possible in the first place." Or one might prefer to look upon the Devil's "pranks" in terms of the modern researcher in psychic phenomena, being akin to levitation, telepathy, clairvoyance, or poltergeists, all of which, he might claim, have been demonstrated in modern times—but without the aid of the Devil. Or one might take the position that witchcraft gained support in New England at this particular time because of the profound social and political changes then taking place, leading to a feeling of uncertainty and insecurity.[24]

We are interested, in this brief account of witchcraft prosecutions, only in showing how the belief in the Devil incarnate, which long antedated the Protestant movement, was perfectly rationalized by seventeenth century New England theologians and how it harmonized so well with the fabric of Puritanism, leading inevitably to indictments, trials, and executions. Witchcraft, in addition to the physical and mental suffering it caused, was a kind of heresy, a blasphemy worse than atheism. Religious leaders for more than two centuries had drawn upon the frightening folklore of witchcraft and woven it skillfully into their definitions of heresy, for it was easier to condemn a heretic if it could be shown that he was a witch. Such doctrines as the witch's mock Sabbath, his unholy sacraments, his intimate and sensuous relations with the Devil, could be regarded as attempts to overthrow orthodox beliefs. In New England, witches were not indicted for heresy—it was much easier to indict them for witchcraft—but their sacrilege was notorious. The Devil in New England adapted well to New England customs:

> The Witches do say, that they form themselves much after the manner of Congregational Churches; and that they have a Baptism and a Supper, and Officers among them, abominably Resembling those of our Lord.[25]

From the many contemporary writings on witchcraft we have selected as representative of clerical opinion at the time of the

Salem trials a small portion of the voluminous material produced by Increase and Cotton Mather, father and son, who were the most ardent spokesmen for the prosecution although, as we shall observe later, they were among those who urged extreme caution in the admission of evidence before the special tribunal. It matters little to which Mather one turns for opinion on this subject, for they were in complete agreement. Increase said of his son's exposition *The Wonders of the Invisible World,* "I perused and approved of that Book before it was printed; and nothing but my Relation to him hindred me from recommending it to the World."[26] A few excerpts from Cotton Mather's *Wonders* make clear the logic of their position:[27]

> If any are Scandalized, that New-England, a place of as serious Piety, as any I can hear of, under Heaven, should be troubled so much with Witches; I think, 'tis no wonder: Where will the Devil show most Malice, but where he is hated, and hateth most.[28]
>
> The first Planters of these Colonies were a chosen Generation of Men. ... *New-England* was a true *Utopia.* But, alas, the Children and Servants of those old Planters must needs afford [furnish] many, degenerate Plants, and there is now risen up a Number of People, otherwise inclined than our *Joshua's.*

Mather reviewed the Colony's difficulties: "A variety of Calamity has long follow'd this Plantation; and we have all the Reason imaginable to ascribe it to the Rebuke of Heaven upon us for our manifold *Apostasies.* . . ." He mentioned "a continual *blast* upon some of our principal Grain". . ., "wasting *Sicknesses,* especially Burning and Mortal Agues," the Indian attacks, "desolating *Fires* . . ., *Losses by Sea,*" and "now at last the Devils are . . . in *Person* come down upon us. . . ." Cotton Mather was alarmed over "the declining state of the *Power* of *Godliness* in our Churches" toward the end of the seventeenth century when the influence of the Puritan clergy had noticeably diminished.

> That there is a *Devil,* is a thing Doubted by none but such as are under the Influences of the *Devil.* For any to deny the Being of a *Devil* must be from an Ignorance or Prophaneness, worse than *Diabolical* . . . the *Experience* of Mankind as well as the *Testimony* of Scripture, does abundantly prove the Existence of such a Devil.
>
> [The Devil had special cause to be angry with New-Englanders, for

they] "are a People of God settled in those, which were once the *Devil's* Territories; and it might easily be supposed that the *Devil* was exceedingly disturbed, when he perceived such a People here accomplishing the Promise of old made unto our Blessed Jesus, *That He should have the Utmost parts of the Earth for his Possession.*

"It was a rousing alarm to the *Devil* when a great Company of English Protestants and Puritans, came to erect Evangelical Churches, in a corner of the world, where he had reign'd without any controul for many ages; and it is a vexing eye-sore to the *Devil,* that our Lord Christ should be known, and envied and preached in this howling Wilderness, wherefore he [the Devil] has left no stone unturned, that so he might undermine his Plantation, and force us out of our Country. . . . [The Devil] sees men lying in the Bosom of God, but himself damned in the bottom of Hell; and this enrages him exceedingly.

As God is omnipotent, the Devil was permitted "to make a descent upon the children of men" as he was permitted formerly to visit the earth with earthquakes caused by subterranean fires.[29]

The Devil surely, was a party in the *Earthquake,* whereby the Vengeance of God, in one black Night sunk Twelve considerable Cities of *Asia,* in the Reign of *Tiberious.* . . . I suspect, That we shall now be visited with more Usual and yet more Fatal *Earthquakes,* than were our Ancestors . . . . there will again be an unusual Range of the Devil among us, a little before the *Second Coming* of our Lord. . . .

The Devil thus Irritated, immediately try'd all sorts of Methods to overturn this poor Plantation. . . . But, All those Attempts of Hell have hitherto been Abortive.

The Devil is now making one Attempt more upon us; an Attempt more Difficult, more Surprizing, more snarl'd with unintelligible Circumstances than any we hath hitherto Encountered; an attempt so *Critical,* that if we get well through, we shall soon enjoy *Halcyon* Days, with all the *Vultures* of Hell *Trodden under our Feet.*

An Army of *Devils* is horribly broke in upon the place which is the Center, and after a sort, the *First-born* of our *English* Settlements [referring to Salem]; and the Houses of the Good People there are fill'd with the doleful Shrieks of their Children and Servants, Tormented by Invisible Hands, with Tortures altogether preternatural.

[And thus Cotton Mather saw] *"An Horrible Plot against the Country by Witchcraft, and a Foundation of Witchcraft then laid* [referring to a discovery of witchcraft forty years earlier] *which if it were not seasonably discovered, would probably Blow up, and pull down all the Churches in the Country.*

The "Tortures, Outcries, and Havocks which Devils confessedly Commissioned by Witches, make among their Neighbours" were quite obvious to any casual observer in Salem Village in the late winter and spring of the year 1692. The story of the diabolical mischief perpetrated in that little village (now called Danvers, some seven miles from the center of the town of Salem) has been told and retold in great detail many times.[30] The essential facts are these:

The Rev. Samuel Parris, the minister of the little parish in the village, had returned from the West Indies with several slaves to serve the parsonage as household servants. Tituba, an Indian woman, said to be part Negro, was well versed in some of the black arts of voodooism acquired in her native land. The minister's nine-year-old daughter, Elizabeth, her eleven-year-old cousin Abigail Williams, with Anne Putnam, a twelve-year-old and several other girl friends of Elizabeth who were slightly older, soon learned some of the fascinating little tricks of magic that any God-fearing person of the older generation might consider trafficing with the devil. Evidently Tituba was a good teacher, but her informal classes had to be kept from the eyes of her master and mistress. It was not long before the younger girls began to act as though they were "possessed," running around the house on all fours, barking, and falling into screaming and horrifying convulsions. The contagion spread until all the girls seemed to have been similarly "afflicted," acting very much like the Goodwin children whose conduct we have already described. It is not unlikely that they were familiar with that story from the published report of Cotton Mather. When local physicians, called in by Parris, were unable to diagnose the girls' suffering in terms of any disease known at that time, the only conclusion open to them was "demoniac possession"—a matter for ministers, not physicians, to deal with.[31] Prayers, soothing words, Bible reading, or fasting were of no avail, the girls screaming at the very sound of every holy word. Finally they were induced to name their tormentors. Elizabeth who had been most "afflicted" named Tituba as the witch in her life. Soon two other names were called out—Sarah Good and Sarah Osburne. All three unfortunate women were immediately arrested on warrants and confined in the prison at Ipswich to await a hearing before a magistrate. But the matter did not end there. Other women in the community were soon "cried out upon." The "witch mania" of Salem Village and surrounding towns had begun, and the little "afflicted" girls became the chief witnesses for the prosecution in the judicial hearings that followed.

Those charged with witchcraft were quite promptly brought before one or two magistrates for a hearing to determine whether the accused should be dismissed or held for trial by a court competent to try capital cases. Once the hearing commenced, the fate of the helpless defendant was usually sealed. It was said that not more than one out of one hundred was dismissed at that stage in the proceedings.[32] These hearings attracted large and curious crowds, served to spread the news of the assault on Salem by the Devil and his "Diabolick Aids," aroused fears and suspicions that rapidly led to more accusations of witchcraft, pitted neighbor against neighbor and sometimes husbands against wives, and initiated a slow panic that could not be stopped until the lives of twenty men and women had been snuffed out.

As an illustration of the kind of evidence introduced at these preliminary hearings, let us take the case of Elizabeth Procter and her husband John. A matronly woman, held in high esteem in the community, Elizabeth was astonished that such base charges should have been leveled at her. She probably shared the common belief in the Devil and in witches but she *knew* that she had made no covenant with the little black man with the cloven foot. This report is taken from Hutchinson's *History*.[33] Although he was not born until after the turn of the century, he claimed that "many of the original examinations have fallen into my hands." This pretrial hearing conducted by Thomas Danforth, Deputy Governor, with the Rev. Samuel Parris as recorder, was held on April 11, 1692 in the meetinghouse in Salem and attended by Samuel Sewall as an observer. Sarah Cloyce, sister of Rebecca Nurse, was first examined. Attention was then directed to Elizabeth Procter and later to her husband John, who had been drawn into this legal dead-end street in a noble attempt to clear his wife.

Q. Elizabeth Procter! you understand whereof you are charged, viz.

to be guilty of sundry acts of witchcraft; what say you to it? Speak the truth, and so you that are afflicted [addressing the complaining witnesses], you must speak the truth, as you will answer it before God another day.

Q. Mary Walcot! [a 16-year-old accuser] doth this woman hurt you?

A. I never saw her so as to be hurt by her.

Q. Mary Lewis! [a 19-year-old servant in the Putnam household, usually called Mercy Lewis] does she hurt you?

A. (Her mouth was stopped).

Q. Ann Putnam [a 12-year-old child, frequently "afflicted," who took a leading part in bringing many a suspect before the magistrates], does she hurt you?

A. (She could not speak).

Q. Abigail Williams! [Elizabeth Parris' eleven-year-old cousin, one of the little girls in the Parris home who started all of Salem Village talking about witches] does she hurt you?

A. (Her hand was thrust in her own mouth).

[Up to this point no positive evidence had been adduced against Elizabeth Procter, but it must have been obvious that the Devil did not want his secrets revealed and had been able to shut the mouths of these little girls.]

Q. John! [John Indian, one of Parris's slaves and husband of Tituba] does she hurt you?

A. This is the woman that came in her shift and choaked me. [Meaning that she had come to him in a dream or as an apparition or as a "specter."]

Q. Did she ever bring the book? [The Devil's black book which carried the signatures of all those he had induced to make a covenant with him.]

A. Yes Sir.

Q. What to do?

A. To write.

Q. What, this woman? [It must have been surprising to the court that a woman of her bearing and character and reputation in the community could have stooped so low.]

A. Yes Sir.

Q. Are you sure of it?

A. Yes Sir.

(Again, Abigail Williams and Ann Putnam were spoke to by the court, but neither of them could make any answer, by reason of dumbness or other fits.)

Q. What do you say Goody Procter to these things?

A. I take God in heaven to be my witness, that I know nothing of it, no more than the child unborn. [A strong denial but everyone knew that one who had signed a covenant with the Devil does not dare reveal that fact, hence an accused is deprived of that defense.]

Q. Ann Putnam! doth this woman hurt you?

A. Yes Sir, a great many times.

(Then the accused looked upon them and they fell into fits.) [To the court this "demonstration" right before the eyes of everyone present was positive evidence that would be hard for any accused to refute or explain.]

Q. She does not bring the book to you, does she?

A. Yes Sir, often, and saith she hath made her maid set her hand to it.

Q. Abigail Williams! does this woman hurt you?

A. Yes Sir, often.

Q. Does she bring the book to you?

A. Yes.

Q. What would she have you do with it?

A. To write in it and I shall be well. Did not you, said Abigail [to the accused], tell me, that your maid had written [in the book]?

A. [Procter] Dear Child, it is not so. There is another judgment, dear child.

(Then Abigail and Ann had fits. By-and-by they cried out, Look you, there is Goody Procter upon the beam. [That is, they "saw" what no one else could see, the apparition of Elizabeth Procter sitting on one of the ceiling beams of the meeting house.] By-and-by, both of them cried out of Goodman Procter [the accused's husband who was standing beside her in court] himself, and said he was a wizard. [Male witches were often referred to as wizards.] Immediately, many, if not all of the bewitched had grievous fits.)

Q. Ann Putnam! who hurt you? [Ann was evidently writhing on the floor in assumed or genuine agony.]

A. Goodman Procter and his wife too.

(Afterwards, some of the afflicted cried out, There is [Goodman] Procter going to take up Mrs. Pope's feet; and her feet were immediately taken up.)

Q. What do you say, Goodman Procter, to these things?

A. I know not, I am innocent. [What else could he say?]

(Abigail Williams cried out, There is Goodman Procter going to Mrs. Pope, and immediately, said Pope fell into a fit.)

[The Court:] You see the devil will deceive you; the children could see what you was going to do before the woman was hurt. I would advise you to repentence, for the devil is bringing you out. [The court found these experiments with Mrs. Pope most convincing and damaging to Procter who stood motionless while his invisible spirit played havoc with this young and respectable matron.]

(Abigail Williams cried out again, There is Goodman Procter going to hurt Goody Bibber; and immediately Goody Bibber fell into a fit. There was the like of Mary Walcot, and divers others.)

(Benjamin Gould gave in his testimony, that he had seen Goodman Corey and his wife [Giles and Martha Corey who were later both condemned and executed], Procter and his wife, Goody Cloyse, Goody Nurse, and Goody Griggs in his chamber [bedroom] last thursday night.)

(Elizabeth Hubbard, [a 17-year-old friend of the accusing girls] was in a trance during the whole examination.)

(During the examination of Elizabeth Procter, Abigail Williams and Ann Putnam, both made offer to strike at said Procter; but when Abigail's hand came near, it opened, whereas it was made up into a fist before, and came down exceeding lightly, as it drew near to said Procter, and at length with open and extended fingers, touched Procter's hood very lightly. Immediately Abigail cried out, her fingers, her fingers, her fingers burned, and Ann Putnam took on most grievously, of her head, and sunk down.)

Thus ended the testimony, leaving no doubt in the mind of the court and the observers that the Procters were active agents of the Devil, their unequivocal denials constituting one more bit of incriminating evidence. Surely here was ample evidence for holding them for trial—a trial that would not do much more than repeat the same kind of testimony. And so they were hustled off to prison.

When Samuel Sewall (who, with a number of other Magistrates and ministers, had observed the proceedings) returned home he entered in his diary:

> April 11th, 1692. Went to Salem, where, in the Meeting-House, the persons accused of Witchcraft were examined; was a very great Assembly; 'twas awful to see how the afflicted persons were agitated. Mr. Noyes [the Rev. Nicholas Noyes, Jr., pastor of the First Church in Boston] pray'd at the beginning, and Mr. Higginson [the Rev. John Higginson, pastor of the same church] concluded.[34]

On August 5 of that year the Procters were to stand before Judge Sewall and the other judges of the trial court and the jury to hear themselves and four other witches condemned to death.

When the pretrial hearings were at their height, the affairs of state were in a most anomalous condition. The Colony was struggling through what was later called "an inter-charter period" between the revocation of the Charter in 1684 and the establishment of a new Province Government under the watchful eye of a Governor appointed by the King, rather than one elected by the people, and administered in accordance with the new Charter of 1691. At the suggestion of Increase Mather who was then acting as the Colony's agent in London, the Crown appointed Sir William Phips the first Royal Governor of the Province Government. In many respects Phips was an excellent choice, for he was a native New Englander, having been born and brought up in a little settlement near the Kennebec river (in territory now in the state of Maine), one of twenty-six children. From humble surroundings he rose to ship captain, won high honors as an adventurer, and was knighted by King James II in 1687 for recovering for England a fortune in lost treasure from a sunken Spanish galleon in the West Indies.

He returned to New England after the ceremony of knighthood with the title of "High Sheriff of New England," but he was more interested in leading a naval expedition against the French in Canada which proved quite successful, although a later expedition (after he assumed the office of governor) was a dismal failure. In the meantime he became a member of the Mathers' church and was baptized in 1690 by Cotton, who hailed him as "one of my dearest Friends."

On May 14, 1692, the new Royal Governor arrived in Boston. His most pressing problem was the judicial handling of well over one hundred charges of witchcraft. Phips was no lawyer. He was a man of action who had not learned to read or write until he was twenty-one. He was advised to set up a trial court at once as the General Court of the new government had not yet met and new courts had not yet been established for the trial of capital cases. He readily accepted this advice and promptly went off on a military venture to Nova Scotia and later to Quebec to fight real Indians and Frenchmen, leaving it to those at home to deal with Spirits from the Invisible World. He explained his actions in these words:

> When I first arrived I found this Province miserably harrassed with a most Horrible witchcraft or Possession of Devills which had broke in upon severall Townes, some scores of poor people were taken with preternaturall torments some scalded with brimstone some had pins stuck in their flesh others hurried into the fire and water and some dragged out of their houses and carried over the tops of trees and hills for many Miles together; it hath been represented to mee much like that of Sweden thirty years agoe, and there were many committed to prison upon suspicion of Witchcraft before my arrivall. The loud cries and clamours of the friends of the afflicted people with the advice of the Deputy Governor [William Stoughton] and many others prevailed with mee to give a Commission of Oyer and Terminer [literally, a court "to hear and determine," well known to English lawyers] for discovering what witchcraft might be at the bottome or whether it were not a possession. . . . . I was almost the whole time of the proceeding abroad in the service of Their Majesties [King William and Queen Mary who reigned from 1689 to 1694] in the Eastern part of the Country and depended upon the Judgement of the Court as to a right method of proceeding in cases of Witchcraft. . . .[35]

Portrait of Samuel Sewall, one of the "witchcraft judges" of Salem. Courtesy of the Essex Institute, Salem, Massachusetts.

Although Sir William had appointed to this Court of Oyer and Terminer his trusted Deputy Governor Stoughton as Chief Justice and others who were "persons of the best prudence and figure that could then be pitched upon,"[36] legal scholars have seriously questioned the legality of the court itself which was set up without a vote of the General Court or specific authorization under the new charter.[37]

On June 2, 1692, the court convened in Salem, giving a ray of hope (soon to be extinguished) to those who lay chained in the foul quarters of the prisons in Salem and surrounding towns, some for as long as three months, many of them with expectations of acquittal from a court comprised of men of intelligence and high standing in the Colony.

On the bench was Chief Justice Stoughton (1631–1701), Lieutenant Governor, a graduate of Harvard, one of the most able men in Massachusetts. A former preacher, though not called to any church, he had turned his attention to the law and in later years was the first Chief Justice of the Superior Court of the Province government, the forerunner of the present Supreme Judicial Court of the Commonwealth. Unfortunately for the accused, he was a firm believer in witches and thought death was a just penalty on conviction.

Also serving on the bench was Samuel Sewall (1652–1730), Harvard graduate, merchant, and later judge, Overseer of Harvard College, member of the Artillery Company (later the Ancient and Honorable Artillery Company), author, scholar, and well-respected citizen.

Others appointed to the court were: John Hathorne, a Salem magistrate (an ancestor of the nineteenth century author Nathaniel Hawthorne, who changed the spelling of the name); Major John Richards, a Dorchester merchant; Wait Still Winthrop, a physician and grandson of Governor John Winthrop; Peter Sergeant, a wealthy merchant and later the husband of Governor Phip's widow; Major Bartholomew Gedney, a physician in Salem; and Nathaniel Saltonstall of Haverhill. Saltonstall was grandson of Sir Richard, one of the founders of the Bay Colony, and ancestor of Richard Saltonstall, a Superior Court judge in the Province government from 1736–1756, and of Leverett Saltonstall, Governor of the Commonwealth from 1939 to 1945 and United States

Senator from Massachusetts from 1945 to the present time. This Nathaniel Saltonstall of Haverhill was, it was reported, "very much dissatisfied with the proceddings" and resigned from the court after its first conviction. He was replaced by Jonathan Corwin, a Salem magistrate who had had an active part in pretrial hearings. Thomas Newton was appointed attorney for the crown but was succeeded on July 26 by Andrew Checkley, an apothecary, to prosecute the cases as the "King's Attorney General."[38]

Although the court sat in Salem, it was commissioned to hear all witchcraft crimes committed in Suffolk, Essex, and Middlesex Counties. Because of the acute frenzy in the town of Salem and the known sympathy on the part of some of the judges for the poor "afflicted" girls, one of the accused while awaiting trial wrote a letter from the Salem prison to five of the ministers asking them to intercede for him in getting a change of venue to Boston or, if that were not possible, then to ask for the removal of the appointed judges and their replacement by others. The court had already sent six women to their deaths. To John Procter, the accused, prospects for acquittal seemed very dim—as indeed they were. "We know," he wrote, "in our own Consciences, we are all Innocent Persons" and yet he was sure that his accusers, the judges and jury, had "condemned us already before our Tryals."[39] But there was no help forthcoming. In four weeks' time Procter's life was taken away.

None of the defendants had counsel to object to the admission of hearsay evidence or the much disputed "spectral evidence" or to raise any question of the legality of the procedure or the proper jurisdiction of the court. A public defense of a witch would have rendered a defender immediately suspect. Furthermore, few of the judges had had legal training, and no one showed any fastidiousness about any fine points of law. Consequently almost any kind of damaging evidence was well received and was all the more convincing because it was not rebutted. The defendants themselves brought in no witnesses and had little to say on their own behalf. Most of the evidence, by its very nature, was not rebuttable.

A dispute arose over the crucial question of "spectral evidence." When, for example, an "afflicted" person testified in court that one night while in bed an apparition appeared to him "in the shape of" or likeness of Goody X and threatened him or grieviously injured him, although it could be shown that Goody X herself was at that moment in her own bed some miles distant, that testimony was known as "spectral evidence." The theory to account for this experience that was frightening and seemed very real to the "afflicted" was that, once Goody X had formed a covenant with the Devil, he could appear in her likeness at any place or time he chose—and he usually chose to appear at night in some man's bedchamber! Such testimony had real probative value in showing that Goody X was guilty of witchcraft. The question at issue: Could the Devil "afflict" someone by appearing "in the shape of" an innocent person; that is, a person who had not covenanted with him? The Mathers, and some of the other ministers, were certain that the Devil had this power, and they could quote scripture and cite history to prove it. Hence they urged caution in admitting "spectral evidence" concerning a person of unblemished reputation on the uncorroborated testimony of the person who experienced the "specter." Chief Justice Stoughton and some of the other judges took the opposite view—at least until after many of the accused had been condemned. Testimony of a witness that the apparition was "in the shape of" Goody X created a very strong suspicion of her guilt because (in Stoughton's view) the Devil would be powerless to represent her if she were innocent. Had the Mathers' view prevailed at the outset, a few lives, at least, might have been saved.

The jury was usually of like mind with the judges but played a somewhat subordinate role. It had been the practice in Colonial courts for judges to express dissatisfaction with jury verdicts when they thought the verdicts were against the weight of evidence, or for any other reason unsatisfactory. In such cases juries could be sent out for a reconsideration of the evidence. For example, in the trial of Rebecca Nurse the jury had probably carefully pondered the dangerous testimony of "spectral evidence" which was scarcely credible in the case of this fine woman, a devoted mother and a virtuous citizen, and they were no doubt familiar with the warning issued by the Mathers. At any rate, their verdict was "Not guilty." That this was an unpopular verdict was soon apparent:

> ... immediately all the accusers in the Court, and suddenly after, all the afflicted, out of Court, made an hideous out-cry, to the amazement, not only of the Spectators, but the Court also seemed strangely surprized; one of the Judges exprest himself not satisfied, another of

them as he was going off the Bench, said they would have her Indicted anew. . . .[40]

The Chief Justice said "he would not Impose upon the Jury" but thought they should reconsider one statement the defendant had made in her testimony that the jury may have overlooked. When a witness (who had confessed that she was a witch) had been brought into court to testify for the prosecution, the defendant had remarked, "What, do you bring her? *she is one of us.*" By this Rebecca Nurse later said she meant, "One of us *prisoners,*" but the Court took her to mean "one of us *witches.*" Upon the court's expression of dissatisfaction with the verdict, the foreman of the jury asked for an opportunity of repeating the statement to the defendant and asking for her interpretation. When he did so she made no reply. The jury thereupon changed its verdict to "Guilty." Rebecca later submitted a declaration in writing to the court indicating that she did not understand "how the Court took up [interpreted] my words," adding that she was "something hard of hearing, and full of grief." But it was too late.

Not everyone in the Bay Colony shared Judge Stoughton's confidence in the justice of the proceedings. There were those who were skeptical of the sincerety of the "afflicted" adolescents whose hysterical behavior seemed too contrived to be genuine. There were those who, although believing that there was a Devil and that Witches were his disciples, had a feeling of unreality upon the indictment of suspects well known in the community for their piety and good works. And yet there was only one dissenting judge on the Court of Oyer and Terminer. We have already noted how Nathaniel Saltonstall walked out after the first conviction "very much dissatisfied with the proceddings of it," an act that naturally brought him under suspicion but he never elaborated publicly on his reasons and escaped harassment by withdrawing to his home in Haverhill and keeping a discreet silence.

There were two men in Boston who were critical of the whole sorry business—Thomas Brattle and Robert Calef—but neither expressed himself in writing publicly until the storm in Salem had abated. Calef's "More Wonders of the Invisible World" was not published until 1700. It was a bitter attack on Cotton Mather's "The Wonders of the Invisible World: Being an Account of the Tryals of Several Witches, Lately Executed in New-England."

Calef was certain innocent blood had been shed, and he placed a large share of the blame on Cotton Mather, who was infuriated by his charges. To Calef, the accusing girls were simply "a parcel of possessed, distracted [a term usually meaning mentally ill], or lying Wenches, accusing their Innocent Neighbours, pretending they see their Spectres (i.e.) Devils in their likeness Afflicting of them . . . [causing] Brother to Accuse and Prosecute Brother, Children their Parents, Pastors and Teachers their immediate Flock unto death . . . all which Tragedies, tho begun in one Town [Salem Village], or rather one Parish [that of the Rev. Samuel Parris], has Plaguelike spread more than through that Country. And by its Eccho giving a brand of Infamy to this whole Country, throughout the World. . . ." Calef did not commence his writings until five years after the last execution. "We cannot recall those to Life again that have suffered, supposing it were unjustly. . .[but] I presume I need make no Apology for my Endeavours to prevent, as far as in my power, any more such bloody Victims or Sacrifices." If Calef had let his views be known in that fateful spring of 1692, the "brand of Infamy to this whole Country, throughout the World" might have been avoided; but who could tell, Calef himself might then have been one of the "bloody Victims or Sacrifices."[41]

Calef's friend, Thomas Brattle, was also a skeptic, or, as Cotton Mather would have said, "a Sadducee," but his publication likewise came to light too late to save the nineteen condemned witches. A Boston merchant, then only 24 years old, Brattle was a graduate of Harvard College and later treasurer of that institution for twenty years. He had achieved some distinction as a mathematician and astronomer. With a mind trained in science rather than in theology (although no graduate of Harvard in that era could be a stranger to theology), he presented a critical analysis (more objective than that of Calef's) of the kind of evidence that led to convictions of witchcraft. His analysis, in the form of a letter dated October 8, 1692, addressed simply to "Reverend Sir" was probably privately circulated a few days before the convening of the General Court on October 12. What were his criticisms of "the Salem proceedings"?[42]

> I cannot but condemn this method of the Justices, of making this touch of the hand a rule to discover witchcraft. . . . I know a man

> that will venture two to one with any Salemite whatever, that let the matter be duly managed, and the afflicted person shall come out of her fitt upon the touch of the most religious hand in Salem.[43]

Another point raised by Brattle was why, if a witch "by a look of the eye" cast the afflicted into fits, do they not cast others into fits? A very pertinent question—one actually raised by John Alden when he was examined by the magistrates at a pretrial hearing at Salem Village on May 31, 1692:

> They [the Magistrates] bid Aldin look upon the Accusers, which he did, and then they fell down. Aldin asked Mr. Gidney [Bartholomew Gedney, one of the magistrates soon thereafter to be appointed to the Court of Oyer and Terminer] what Reason there could be given, why Aldin's looking upon *him* did not strike *him* down as well; but no reason was given that I heard.[44]

"This Salem philosophy," wrote Brattle (apropos of "the look of the eye"), some men may call the new philosophy; but I think it rather deserves the name of Salem superstition and sorcery, and it is not fitt to be named in a land of such light as New-England is." As for the look-and-touch demonstration, "the reasonable part of the world. . .will laugh. . .and conclude that the said S.G. [Salem Gentlemen] are actually possessed, at least, with ignorance and folly."

Brattle wondered how judges could be so impressed with the confessions of witches (who make accusations against the accused) when the judges themselves claimed that confessors "are under the influence of the Devill?" Let us be thankful that "all men are not bereft of their senses. . .that considerate and thinking men. . . will not thus be imposed upon."

Brattle further felt that judges should advise the jury that there is a difference between saying that one is afflicted by the prisoner at the bar and saying that one is afflicted by the appearance and shape of such a person, an obvious criticism of "spectral evidence."

As for "witches marks" being offered as incriminating evidence, Brattle comments: "I wonder what person there is, whether man or woman, of whom it cannot be said but that, in some part of their body or other, there is a preternatural excrescence. The term is a very general and inclusive term." In witchcraft lore a witch can shed no tears, a bit of superstition not overlooked by the Salem judges. But, said Brattle, such belief betrays "great ignorance in the nature of passion. . . . Some there are who never shed tears; others there are that ordinarily shed tears upon light occasions, and yet for their lives cannot shed a tear when the deepest sorrow is upon their hearts. . . . Who knows not that an ecstasye of Joy will sometimes fetch teares, when as the quite contrary passion will shutt them close up?"

The protestations of innocence by the condemned when about to die was most impressive to Brattle, who may have been present at the execution of some of them. They forgave their accusers, "they spake without reflection on Jury and Judges . . . they seemed very sincere, upright, and sensible of their circumstances. . .[their] management of themselves, from the Gaol to the Gallows, and whilst at the Gallows, was very affecting and melting to the hearts of some considerable Spectatours. . . ."

Certain influential people, Brattle pointed out, were allowed to go free or to escape from prison ". . .certainly distributive Justice should have its course, without respect to persons. . . ." When warrants are issued merely on the information given by afflicted children to whom the Devil supplied the names of persons who did not even know the children, then liberty, "the great priviledge of an Englishman," vanishes.

Brattle did not believe he was alone in his criticism. "There are several about the Bay, men for understanding, Judgment, and Piety, inferiour to few, (if any,) in New England that do utterly condemn the said proceedings, and do freely deliver their Judgment in the case to be this, viz. that these methods will utterly ruine and undoe poor New England." He named Simon Bradstreet and Thomas Danforth and two ministers, Increase Mather and Samuel Willard, as distinguished men who were "dissatisfyed" with the Salem trials. He included also Nathaniel Saltonstall and "the Rev'd Elders, almost throughout the whole Country" with the *exception* of the Rev. John Hale (who subsequently changed his views on witchcraft), the Rev. Nicholas Noyes (pastor at Beverly, who also changed his views after his wife had been accused but who, prior to that, had been an active supporter of the prosecution), and the Rev. Samuel Parris (in whose home in Salem Village the conflagration started, as we have seen). He adds the names of three judges who were "dissatisfyed" but took no active part and said of some of "the Boston Justices" (whom he did not name) that they were "resolved rather to throw up their commissions than be active in disturbing the liberty of their Majesties' subjects, merely on the accusations of these afflicted, possessed children."

"The Devill's book," said Brattle, had "no reality"..."the witches' meeting, the Devill's Baptism, and mock sacraments, which they oft speak of, are nothing else but the effect of their fancye, depraved and deluded by the Devill, and not a Reality to be regarded or minded by any wise man."

He concluded: "What will be the issue of these troubles, God only knows; I am afraid that ages will not wear off that reproach and those stains which these things will leave behind them upon our land. I pray God pity us, Humble us, Forgive us, and appear mercifully for us in this our mount of distress."

In this contemporary and remarkably insightful condemnation of the proceedings, we find an ample supply of legal arguments that, in the hands of some seventeenth century Clarence Darrow, might have prevented "that reproach and those stains" that the Salem witch trials have, in truth, "left behind them upon our land."

By tradition and training Puritan ministers were believers in devils and witches. Nevertheless they suspected something might be wrong with an administration of justice that could as readily find the devil's cohorts among pious churchgoers as among notorious old hags. They were therefore constantly reminding the judges that great care must be used in detecting witches. The Rev. Cotton Mather expressed his concern:

> If a drop of Innocent Blood be shed, in the Prosecution of the Witchcrafts among us, how unhappy are we! ... But on the other side, if the storm of Justice do now fall only on the Heads of those guilty Witches and Wretches which have defiled our Land, How Happy![45]

His father, Increase, too, was most eager to see that no innocent person was convicted and took a leading part in setting forth rules of "sufficient conviction." Fourteen ministers called upon Increase to propound in writing his views on some of the "unjustifiable ways of discovering Witchcrafts" in order to "prevent the taking any wrong steps in this dark way." His report entitled "Cases of Conscience Concerning Witchcrafts" appeared a little too late (October 1692) to be effective as a guide to the judges, but it was not known at that time that the last execution had already taken place. Both Increase and Cotton Mather had, however, been in early communication with the judges to urge them to treat cautiously the "spectral testimony." Cotton had written a letter to Major John Richards before the convening of the Court of Oyer and Terminer begging him not to "lay more stresse upon pure Spectre testimony then [than] it will bear."[46] Increase reported, after nineteen witches had been executed, that "the Judges affirm, that they have not convicted any one *meerly* on the account of what Spectres have said, or of what has been presented to the Eyes or Imaginations of the sick bewitched Persons."[47]

After the first witch had been hanged, the Governor, who was in town for a short while, sought the advice of the ministers as to how the prosecution should be managed, for ministers, rather than judges, were believed to be experts in the matter of witchcraft. Twelve Boston ministers signed their names to a statement presumably drawn by Cotton Mather, dated June 15, 1692, recommending: "the speedy and vigorous Prosecution of such as have rendered themselves obnoxious, according to the Direction given in the Laws of God, and the wholesome Statutes of the English Nation, for the Detection of Witchcrafts" but at the same time pointing to the "need of a very critical and exquisite Caution, lest by too much Credulity for things received only upon the Devil's Authority, there be a Door opened for a long Train of miserable Consequences. . ." and urging that no one be condemned merely because the accused was represented by a Specter, for "a Daemon may, by God's Permission appear. . .in the Shape of an innocent, yea, and a vertuous Man." Evidence of suffering claimed to be caused merely "by a Look or Touch of the Accused" was, they said, not to be considered "an infallible Evidence of Guilt."[48]

It was Increase Mather's opinion that "It were better that ten suspected Witches should escape, than that one innocent Person should be Condemned."[49] How far the ministers' advice was heeded we cannot say. It was Brattle's belief that, had a certain Boston minister's "notions and proposals been harkened to, and followed, when these troubles were in their birth, in an ordinary way, they would not have grown unto that height which now they have. . . ."[50] He did not name this minister who was, quite possibly, the Rev. Samuel Willard of the Old South Church whose courage in speaking out won him "unkindness, abuse, and reproach from many men."[51]

At the request of the Governor and the Council, Cotton Mather wrote an account of the trials of George Burroughs, Bridget Bishop, Susanna Martin, Elizabeth How, and Martha Carrier, "not as an Advocate but as an Historian." His report is not a transcript of the record, nor is it an eyewitness account since he was not present at any of the trials, although he attended some of the executions. Procuring his material from the clerk of the court, Stephen Sewall, brother of Judge Samuel Sewall, he made a summary and abridgement that evidently was an accurate representation of the evidence upon which a verdict of guilty was obtained. Chief Justice Stoughton and Judge Samuel Sewall, after perusing the reports, found "the Matters of Fact and Evidence, Truly reported."[52] We have selected, both for its brevity and its interest, the case of Martha Carrier, who seemed to have conformed more faithfully to the popular stereotype of a witch than some of the others.[53]

The Trial of Martha Carrier,
at the Court of Oyer and Terminer,
Held by Adjournment at Salem, August 2, 1692.

Martha Carrier was Indicted for the bewitching certain Persons, according to the Form usual in such Cases, pleading *Not Guilty,* to her Indictment; there were first brought in a considerable number of the bewitched Persons; who not only made the Court sensible of an horrid Witchcraft committed upon them, but also deposed, That it was *Martha Carrier,* or her Shape [or Specter], that grievously tormented them, by Biting, Pricking, Pinching and Choaking of them. It was further deposed, That while this *Carrier* was on her Examination, before the Magistrates, the Poor People were so tortured that every one expected their Death upon the very spot, but that upon the binding of *Carrier* they were eased. Moreover the Look of *Carrier* [her glance] then laid the Afflicted People for dead; and her Touch, if her Eye at the same time were off them, raised them again: Which Things were also now seen upon her Tryal. And it was testified, That upon the mention of some having their Necks twisted almost round, by the Shape of this *Carrier,* she replyed, *Its no matter though their Necks had been twisted quite off.*

Before the Trial of this Prisoner, several of her own Children had frankly and fully confessed, not only that they were Witches themselves, but that this their Mother had made them so. This Confession they made with great Shews of Repentance, and with much Demonstration of Truth. They related Place, Time, Occasion; they gave an account of Journeys, Meetings and Mischiefs by them performed, and were very credible in what they said. Nevertheless, this Evidence was not produced against the Prisoner at the Bar, inasmuch as there was other Evidence enough to proceed upon.

Benjamin Abbot gave his Testimony, That last March was a twelvemonth, this Carrier was very angry with him, upon laying out some Land, near her Husband's: Her Expressions in this Anger, were, *That she would stick as close to Abbot as the Bark stuck to the Tree; and that he should repent of it afore seven Years came to an End, so as Doctor Prescot should never cure him.* These Words were heard by others besides *Abbot* himself; who also heard her say, *She would hold his Nose as close to the Grindstone as ever it was held since his name was* Abbot. Presently after this, he was taken with a Swelling in his Foot, and then with a Pain in his Side, and exceedingly tormented. It bred into a Sore, which was launced by Doctor *Prescot,* and several Gallons of Corruption ran out of it. For six Weeks it continued very bad, and then another Sore bred in the Groin, which was also lanced by Doctor *Prescot.* Another Sore then bred in his Groin, which was likewise cut, and put him to very great Misery: He was brought unto Death's Door, and so remained until *Carrier* was taken, and carried away by the Constable, from which very Day he began to mend, and so grew better every Day, and is well ever since.

Sarah Abbot also, his Wife, testified, That her Husband was not only all this while Afflicted in his Body, but also that strange extraordinary and unaccountable Calamities befel his Cattle; their Death being such as they could guess at no Natural Reason for.

Allin Toothaker testify'd, That *Richard,* the son of Martha *Carrier,* having some difference with him, pull'd him down by the Hair of the Head. When he Rose again, he was going to strike at *Richard Carrier;* but fell down flat on his Back to the ground, and had not power to stir hand or foot, until he told *Carrier* he yielded; and then he saw the shape of *Martha Carrier,* go off his breast.

This *Toothaker,* had Received a wound in the *Wars;* and he now testify'd, that *Martha Carrier* told him, *He should never be Cured.* Just afore the Apprehending of *Carrier,* he could thrust a knitting

Needle into his wound, four inches deep; but presently after her being siezed, he was thoroughly healed.

He further testify'd, that when *Carrier* and he sometimes were at variance, she would clap her hands at him, and say, *He should get nothing by it;* whereupon he several times lost his Cattle, by strange Deaths, whereof no natural causes could be given.

John Rogger also testifyed, That upon the threatning words of this malicious *Carrier,* his Cattle would be strangely bewitched; as was more particularly then described.

Samuel Preston testify'd, that about two years ago, having some difference with *Martha Carrier,* he lost a *Cow* in a strange Preternatural unusual manner; and about a month after this, the said *Carrier,* having again some difference with him, she told him; *He had lately lost a Cow, and it should not be long before he lost another;* which accordingly came to pass; for he had a thriving and well-kept *Cow,* which without any known cause quickly fell down and dy'd.

Phebe Chandler testify'd, that about a Fortnight before the apprehension of *Martha Carrier,* on a Lordsday, while the Psalm was singing in the *Church,* this *Carrier* then took her by the shoulder and shaking her, asked her, *where she lived*: she made her no Answer, although as *Carrier,* who lived next door to her Fathers House, could not in reason but know who she was. Quickly after this, as she was at several times crossing the Fields, she heard a voice, that she took to be *Martha Carriers,* and it seem'd as if it was over her head. The voice told her, *she should within two or three days be poisoned.* Accordingly, within such a little time, one half of her right hand, became greatly swollen, and very painful; as also part of her Face; whereof she can give no account how it came. It continued very bad for some dayes; and several times since, she has had a great pain in her breast; and been so siezed on her leggs, that she has hardly been able to go. She added, that lately, going well to the House of God, *Richard,* the son of *Martha Carrier,* look'd very earnestly upon her, and immediately her hand, which had formerly been poisoned, as is abovesaid, began to pain her greatly, and she had a strange Burning at her stomach; but was then struck deaf, so that she could not hear any of the prayer, or singing, till the two or three last words of the Psalm.

One *Foster,* who confessed her own share in the Witchcraft for which the Prisoner stood indicted [Ann Foster, a confessing witch, died in prison before trial], affirm'd, that she had seen the prisoner at some of their *Witch-meetings,* and that it was this *Carrier,* who perswaded her to be a Witch. She confessed, that the Devil carry'd them on a pole, to a Witch-meeting; but the pole broke, and she hanging about *Carriers* neck, they both fell down, and she then received an hurt by the Fall, whereof she was not at this time recovered.

One *Lac*y [Mary Lacy was the daughter of Ann Foster], who likewise confessed her share in this Witchcraft, now testify'd, that she and the prisoner were once Bodily present at a *Witch-meeting in Salem Village;* and that she knew the prisoner to be a Witch, and to have been at a Diabolical sacrament, and that the prisoner was the undoing of her, and her Children, by enticing them into the snare of the Devil.

Another *Lacy* [who may have been the daughter of Mary], who also confessed her share in this Witchcraft, now testify'd, that the prisoner was at the *Witch-meeting, in Salem Village,* where they had Bread and Wine administered unto them.

In the time of this prisoners Trial, one *Susanna Sheldon* [one of the "afflicted" girls, aged about 18], in open Court had her hands Unaccountably ty'd together with a Wheel-band, so fast that without cutting, it could not be loosed: It was done by a *Spectre;* and the Sufferer affirm'd, it was the *Prisoners.*

Memorandum. This Rampant Hag, *Martha Carrier,* was the person, of whom the Confessions of the Witches, and of her own Children among the rest, agreed, That the Devil had promised her, she should be *Queen of Heb.* [Seventeen days later the "Queen" died on the gallows.]

The nineteen men and women who bravely climbed the ladder to die the ignoble death of a witch steadfastly denied their guilt with their last breaths and with a faith in God that never faltered. But there were others less brave or less sure of their own innocence.

Formal confessions were obtained from: 1) Those who, thoroughly convinced of the reality of witches, were led to believe, in the course of time and after repeated stories of their "specters" mischievously flitting about, that they were indeed witches as charged in the indictments, and that the Devil had, in some way, taken possession of their souls and had obtained assent to afflict others in their "shapes."[54]

Very young children were naturally particularly susceptible to this kind of thinking. Dorothy Faulkener, age ten; Abigail Faulkener, age eight; and Sarah Carrier (whose mother was one of the condemned), age seven or eight were among the confessed witches.[55] The youngest child to be thrown into the prison, where she was held in chains, was Dorcus, the five-year-old child of the notorious witch, Sarah Good.[56] Possibly her mother had taught her something about the folklore of witchcraft. The Rev. Deodat Lawson who had been pastor in Salem Village a few years before Satan spun his fine "Thred of Spiritual Wickedness" in that community, in his "Brief and True Narrative" reported that he had been informed by the magistrates and ministers that "the afflicted complained, they had often been Bitten by this child, and produced the marks of a small set of teeth." On examination "at the Prison-Keepers House" the child confessed that:

> it had a little Snake that used to Suck on the lowest Joynt of it[s] Fore-Finger [a typical witch "imp"]; and when they inquired where, pointing to other places, it told them, not there, but *there,* pointing on the Lowest point of Fore-Finger; where they Observed a deep Red Spot, about the Bigness of a *Flea-bite,* they asked who gave it that *Snake?* whether the great Black man? It said no, its Mother gave it.[57]

2) Formal confessions were obtained also from those who falsely confessed to save their own lives. At the outset it may have been feared that a confession meant certain death but it soon became evident that no confessed witch went to the gallows. Those who publicly admitted that they were—or had been—under the Devil's control aroused pity, rather than condemnation, for, in a sense, they had by their admission renounced their covenant and had returned to the society of good people. Such confessions confirmed the Court's belief in witchcraft and must have eased the consciences of the magistrates and aided the prosecution. But in their confessions they usually implicated nonconfessing suspects, thus giving the authorities more suspects to deal with. When it was realized that a confession might be a passport to freedom or at least an escape from the gallows, the pressure was almost irresistible:

> That which did mightily further such Confessions, was their nearest and dearest Relations urging them to it. These [the accused] seeing no other way of escape for them, thought it the best advice that could be given; hence it was that the Husbands of some, by counsel often urging, and utmost earnestness, and Children upon their Knees intreating, have at length prevailed with them, to say they were guilty.[58]

A plausible confession contained the usual legends associated with witchcraft—a cat, a black man who was the Devil who offered his black book, a transportation through the air on a pole (sometimes as many as four on one pole), a rendevous with the Devil who baptized the confessor and made her renounce her former baptism, the "affliction" of several people and finally the anger of the Devil at her confession.

Calef reported that "about Fifty having confest themselves to be Witches, of which not one Executed."[59] A number renounced their confessions at a later date—a dangerous decision, as Samuel Wardwell discovered when he was brought to trial after recanting, for he was condemned and executed. But after the last execution there were many who repudiated their confessions.

3) There were also those who confessed under duress or torture.

> It may be here further added concerning those that did Confess, that besides that powerful Argument, of Life (and freedom from hardships and Irons not only promised, but also performed to all who owned their guilt), There are numerous Instances, . . . of the tedious Examinations before private persons, many hours together; they all that time urging them to Confess (and taking turns to perswade them) till the accused were wearied out by being forced to stand so long, or for want of Sleep, etc. and so brought to give an Assent to what they said; they then asking them, Were you at such a Witch-meeting, or have you signed the Devil's Book, etc. upon their replying, yes, the whole was drawn into form as their Confession.[60]

A torture to extract a confession *prior* to conviction "by clear and sufficient evidence" or by the use of "such Tortures as are Barbarous and Inhumane" was unlawful in the Bay Colony.[61] And yet such means were sometimes used, just as unlawful "third-degree" methods are sometimes used today by law-enforcement authorities. John Procter, writing from the Salem prison on July 23, 1692, where he was awaiting trial, reported that several witches had confessed and implicated him because they were subjected to torture. Even his own son was so treated:

> My son William Procter, when he was examin'd, because he would not confess that he was Guilty, when he was Innocent, they tied him Neck and Heels till the Blood gushed out at his Nose, and would have kept him so 24 Hours, if one more Merciful than the rest, had not

Death warrant of Bridget Bishop, endorsed by the sheriff charged with her execution for witchcraft in 1692. Courtesy of the Essex Institute, Salem, Massachusetts.

taken pity on him, and caused him to be unbound. These actions are very like the Popish Cruelties.[62]

In totaling the final score when the Salem "mania" had run its course, Calef reported:

> And now Nineteen persons having been hang'd, and one prest to death, and Eight more condemned, in all Twenty and Eight, of which above a third part were Members of some of the Churches in N. England, and more than half of them of a good Conversation in general, and not one clear'd; About Fifty having confest themselves to be Witches, of which not one Executed; above an Hundred and Fifty in Prison, and above two Hundred more accused. . . .[63]

Of the total who were accused as witches, all but the nineteen escaped the final penalty.[64] Abigail Faulkener and Elizabeth Procter, pleading pregnancy, evaded the hangman. Mary Bradbury of Salisbury contrived to get out of the jurisdiction through the intercession of some friends. Dorcus Hoar just escaped the noose at the eleventh hour by confessing. A confession was not a guarantee of immunity, but, as it turned out, no confessing witch was hanged in Salem. We find this entry in Judge Sewall's diary:

> Sept. 21. A petition is sent to Town in behalf of Dorcus Hoar, who now confesses: Accordingly an order is sent to the Sheriff to forbear her Execution, notwithstanding her Warrant to die to-morrow. This is the first condemned person who has confess'd.[65]

Who were those fourteen women and six men offered as human sacrifices to the "witch mania" that "horribly broke in upon . . . the first born of our English Settlements" in 1692? Who were those who chose death rather than to confess to that which they knew to be a lie?

Hanged on June 10, was *Bridget Bishop* ["Alias Bridget Oliver," after the name of her first husband], the first witch to be tried by the Court of Oyer and Terminer (June 2) and the first to be hanged, had little chance of escaping the extreme penalty. She had been suspected of witchcraft over a period of twenty years and had been a tavern keeper of unsavory reputation where she had permitted the playing of "shovel board" (or "shuffle board") which had been prohibited in public since 1647.[66] She faced a courtroom full of men and women willing to testify against her. Witnesses swooned upon the touch of her hand and "at the shaking of her Head, or the Turning of her Eyes, they presently and painfully fell into like postures." Few doubted she was a witch. Even her husband failed to come to her defense. Prejudices were running high. "There was little occasion," said Cotton Mather, "to prove the Witchcraft, it being Evident and Notorious to all Beholders."[67] A parade of witnesses testified to every kind of evil thing a witch was supposed to do, from afflicting young children by the glance of her eye to murder by some invisible means.

Hanged on July 19, was *Rebecca Nurse,* an intelligent, courageous, pious Puritan of 71. She came from a Salem family of decent people and was a devoted mother of eight children and the eldest of three sisters, all accused of "horrible afflictions" visited upon their accusers. How the jury's verdict of "not guilty" after a long trial, featuring much "spectral evidence," was changed to "guilty" has already been related. In spite of a petition submitted on her behalf by forty of her neighbors at some risk to themselves[68] and a reprieve by Governor Phips who was impressed by her character (but who later cancelled the reprieve out of sympathy for the "afflicted"), she was excommunicated by her church and two weeks later taken to Gallows hill with four other witches.

Also hanged on July 19, was *Sarah Good* who, in sharp contrast to the saintly Nurse, was a shrewish, idle, slovenly woman who probably looked the part of a witch. There was little pity for this pipe-smoking "hag." She was one of the first to be "cried out upon" by the little girls in the home of the Rev. Samuel Parris and was the mother of the youngest witch, little five-year-old Dorcus. She, like many other accused witches, was believed to be the cause of children falling ill and cattle suddenly dropping dead. She had a gruff and surly manner and a caustic tongue. As she was about to hang, the Rev. Nicholas Noyes urged her to repent and confess, to which she replied: "You are a lyer; I am no more a Witch than you are a Wizard, and if you take away my Life, God will give you Blood to drink."[69]

Elizabeth How, a Topsfield matron whose two daughters and blind husband stood by her in her travail, was also hanged on July 19. She was a woman of good reputation in the community, yet it was said her "specter" had been giving people trouble for nine or ten years. Witnesses testified that ghosts had appeared to them, saying "that this How had Murdered them; Which things were fear'd but not proved." Testimony was given, however, that she had directed many "preternatural Mischiefs" toward people who had displeased her. She had a special knack of causing other people's cows to die unaccountably. There is little doubt that the jury was impressed by statements of witches who had confessed and had implicated her in diabolical plots.

Susanna Martin, another who was hanged on July 19, in the opinion of Cotton Mather:

> was one of the most impudent, scurrilous, wicked Creatures in the World; and she did now throughout her whole Tryal, discover [reveal] her self to be such an one. Yet when she was asked, what she had to say for her self? Her chief Plea was, That she had lead a most virtuous and holy Life.[70]

She had an unusual power to afflict people by "the Cast of her Eye," and her "specter" was the most destructive and mischievous of any of the witches. It would appear to men at night while they were in bed and lie on them; it would sometimes appear in the likeness of a cat; it would drive cattle madly into the sea where they drowned; and when her spirit shape was struck at with a stick in the hands of John Pressy who "gave it near forty blows," it was discovered on the next day she "was in a miserable condition by pains and hurts that were upon her." She had been seen—a most incriminating bit of evidence—"at several of those hellish Randevouzes" as testified to by a man who had been carried through the air "from one Witch-meeting to another, for near two years together."[71]

Another woman hanged on July 19 was *Sarah Wild* [or Wildes] of Topsfield, who was accused, along with several other citizens of that town, of "sundry acts of witchcraft" on the "afflicted" children of Salem Village—Ann Putnam, Mercy Lewis, and Abigail Williams—the same children who had been the cause of bringing many others to their trials.

George Burroughs was a most unusual witch who was hanged on August 19. A graduate of Harvard in the class of 1670, he had been the Salem pastor from 1680 to 1682 but had later gone to Wells (now encompassed within the state of Maine) where he settled with his third wife and seven children. "He was a very Puny Man," wrote Cotton Mather, "yet he had often done things beyond the strength of a Giant" and obviously could have accomplished these feats only with the aid of the Devil. For example, he could take up his gun "of about seven foot Barrel" and could hold it out with one hand as one holds a pistol, yet strong men could not hold it with both hands. Or he could take up "whole Barrels fill'd with Malasses or Cider, in very disadvantageous Postures, and Carrying of them through the difficultest Places out of a Canoo to the Shore." But there was ample evidence of a different nature to convince a jury. Ghosts of his former wives hovered around, claiming that he had murdered them; witnesses who testified that every day they were "Tortured by Invisible Hands" were sure that Burroughs' specter was responsible. One witness testified that "a little black Hair'd Man came to her" with the Devil's book and bragged that "he was a Conjurer, above the ordinary Rank of Witches." This "conjurer" was obviously Burroughs, whose hair was black. Other Puritan ministers, horrified that one of their calling might be a witch, would not come to his defense. The Rev. Increase Mather, who wrote that "it becomes those of my Profession to be very tender in Cases of Blood," said that he had attended Burroughs' trial and "had I been one of his Judges, I could not have acquitted him," impressed with the testimony of those who said "they saw him do such things as no Man that has not a Devil to be his Familiar could perform."[72] On the day of his execution, as reported by Robert Calef:

> "Mr. Burroughs was carried in a Cart with the others, through the streets of Salem to Execution; when he was upon the Ladder, he made a Speech for the clearing of his Innocency, with such Solemn and Serious Expressions, as were to the Admiration of all present; his Prayer (which he concluded by repeating the Lord's Prayer,) was so well worded, and uttered with such composedness, and such (at least seeming) fervency of Spirit, as was very affecting, and drew Tears from many (so that it seemed to some, that the Spectators would hinder the Execution). . . . as soon as he was turned off [hanged], Mr. Cotton Mather, being mounted upon a Horse, addressed himself to the People, partly to declare, that he [Burroughs] was no ordained Minister, and partly to possess [assure] the People of his guilt; saying That the Devil has often been transformed into an Angel of Light; and this did somewhat appease the People, and the Executions went on. . . .[73]

Judge Sewall was also present on this occasion and noted that all of the condemned "said they were innocent, Carrier and all.

Mr. [Cotton] Mather says they all died by a Righteous Sentence." Sewall also commented that Burroughs' prayer and speech to the crowd as he was about to die "did much move unthinking persons, which occasions their speaking hardly concerning his being executed."[74]

George Jacobs, Sr., an elderly Salem citizen, outspoken and defiant, was also hanged on August 19. He was accused not only by the "afflicted" children and his own maidservant, but by his own twenty-year-old granddaughter, Margaret Jacobs who had confessed her own guilt as a witch, definitely implicating him. The day before his execution she admitted her confession was false and begged his forgiveness. He "not only forgave her, but also Prayed with and for her." She sent a petition to the special court that illustrates how some confessions were obtained:

> . . . they told me, if I would not confess, I should be put down into the dungeon and would be hanged, but if I would confess I should have my life; the which did so affright me, with my own vile wicked heart, to save my life made me make the like confession I did, which confession, may it please the honoured court, is altogether false and untrue. . . .[75]

Having renounced her confession, she was scheduled for trial as a witch (for it was certainly not the court that had promised her immunity) but at the appointed time she had an "Imposthume [an abscess] in her head" and her trial was never rescheduled. It was not until many months later, after the last execution, that she was released from the "loathsome Dungeon" (Salem prison) and given her freedom. Her eleventh-hour withdrawal of her confession did not, however, save her grandfather's life. Evidently there was sufficient "spectral evidence" and other testimony to satisfy the authorities of his guilt.

Martha Carrier of Andover was hanged on August 19. We have already recounted the trial of this "Rampant Hag."

Also hanged on August 19 was *John Proctor* of Salem, an outspoken critic of the whole business. After coming to the defense of his wife, Elizabeth, he suddenly found himself "cried out upon" by the "afflicted" children and heard himself denounced as "a most dreadful wizard." His good reputation, his courage, and his forthright denials could not prevail against the testimony of little girls given "with so much earnestness" that the magistrates at the pretrial hearing committed him to the prison with his wife. They were tried together on August 5 and condemned to death in spite of the pleading of many of their friends. Elizabeth's life was spared, as she pleaded pregnancy, but John went to his death two weeks after his trial, with four other witches who "protested their innocency as in the presence of the great God, whom forthwith they were to appear before" declaring that it was their wish "that their blood might be the last innocent blood shed upon that account."[76] He asked for the prayers of the Rev. Nicholas Noyes, "but it was wholly denied, because he would not own himself to be a Witch."[77]

While the Proctors were in prison, the Sheriff seized their "Goods, Provisions and Cattle . . . threw out the Beer out of a Barrel, and carried away the Barrel; emptied a Pot of Broath, and took away the Pot, and left nothing in the House for the support of the Children."[78]

John Willard also was hanged on August 19. A constable of Salem whose duty it was to serve warrants on the accused, he finally sickened of the job. When he refused to "fetch up some that he had better thoughts of, he declined the Service, and presently after he himself was accused of the same Crime."[79] He made his escape as far as "Nashawag" (now Lancaster), but it was not far enough to outreach the arm of the law. He was charged with "spectral" murders.

Giles Cory was pressed to death on September 19. The oldest of the condemned, then in his 75th year, he defied the court by denying his guilt and refused to "put himself upon Tryal by the Jury (they having cleared none upon Tryal) and knowing there would be the same Witnesses against him [as at the pretrial hearing], rather chose to undergo what Death they would put him to."[80] They chose the penalty of pressing to death, the old *peine forte et dure,* the common-law method of dealing with those who refused to be tried by a jury in felony cases, a penalty never before (or since) used in Massachusetts.[81] By this action, Giles made it possible for his heirs to inherit his property—a right denied in the case of those who died by hanging, and we might assume that that was the reason for this grim choice. The penalty consisted in the placing of weights on a prone body, gradually increasing the weights until the accused changed his mind or was able to breathe no longer. Evidently this form of punishment was not relished by the court, and attempts were made up to the last to dislodge him from his determination, as Judge Sewall's diary indicates:

> Monday, Sept. 19, 1692. About noon, at Salem, Giles Corey was press'd to death for standing Mute; much pains was used with him for two days, one after another, by the Court & Capt. Gardner of Nantucket who had been of his acquaintance but all in vain. . . .[82]

On September 22, *Martha Corey* was hanged. She was the third wife of Giles, some twenty years his junior, a kindly and pious church member who dared say quite openly that she did not believe there were any witches in the land. She seemed to be the most unlikely person to be called one. And yet when she was in the meetinghouse "in Sermon time," little eleven-year-old Abigail Williams (who had led so many down the path of death) called aloud "Look where Goodw. C [Goodwife Corey] sits on the Beam suckling her Yellow bird [her 'imp'] betwixt her fingers!"[83] At the pretrial hearing, Abigail and her nine-year-old cousin Elizabeth Parris and their friend, twelve-year-old Ann Putnam "did vehemently accuse her . . . of afflicting them, by Biting, Pinching, Strangling, etc. And that they did in their Fit see her Likeness coming to them, and bringing a Book to them." As for the little "Yellow bird," all Martha could do was to say "She had no familiarity with any such thing. She was a Gospel Woman: which Title she called her self by; and the Afflicted Persons told her, ah! She was, A Gospel Witch."[84] To the magistrates Martha said "they [the "afflicted"] were poor, distracted Children, and no heed to be given to what they said," but Martha soon learned that "no heed" was given to her protests. "She denied all that was charged upon her, and said, They could not prove [her] a Witch; she was that Afternoon Committed to Salem-Prison; and after she was in Custody, she did not so appear to them [the children], and afflict them as before."[85] After almost six months in prison, during which time her church excommunicated her, the trial court, without much difficulty did "prove" she was a witch. Protesting her innocence to the last, she "concluded her Life with an Eminent Prayer upon the Ladder."[86] Giles and Martha Corey were the only married couple to be executed as witches.

On September 22, *Mary Esty* (or Easty) was hanged. She was the sister of Rebecca Nurse and Sarah Cloyce, all accused of witchcraft. She was a gentle, Christian woman of fifty-six, living in Topsfield and of such a sweet disposition that even the magistrates had some doubts about her guilt. After she had been in prison awhile, she was released for a short time but returned when the "afflicted" Mercy Lewis again went into a horrible fit. On September 9, after a great deal of "evidence" was brought in against her, including the finding of "an Excrescence [on her body], which they called a Tet" (a teat, one of the indications that she had a "familiar" and hence was surely a witch), she was condemned.[87] While in prison, probably a few days before her execution, she sent a petition to "the Honorable Judge and Bench" and the "Reverend Ministers":

> The Lord above knows my Innocency . . . as at the great day will be known to Men and Angels. I Petition to your Honours not for my own Life, for I know I must die, and my appointed time is set. . . . I question not, but your Honours do to the utmost of your powers, in the discovery and detecting of Witchcraft and Witches, and would not be guilty of Innocent Blood for the World; but *by my own Innocency I know you are in the wrong way.* . . . I would humbly beg of you, that your Honours would be pleased to Examine some of those confessing Witches, I being confident there are several of them have belyed themselves and others, as will appear, if not in this World, I am sure in the World to come, whither I am going. . . . the Lord alone, who is the searcher of all hearts, knows that as I shall answer it at the Tribunal Seat, that I know not the least thing of Witchcraft, therefore I cannot, I durst not belye my own Soul. . . .[88]

Only thirteen days elapsed between Mary's sentence and her execution. This moving appeal was probably not seen by the judges and ministers until close to the eleventh hour; it was probably too late—much too late—to deflect the inexorable course of events. But she was obviously sincere in her appeal to spare innocent blood and in her plea to examine incriminating confessions more carefully. Coming as it did from a woman certain of death (Puritans placed great credence in dying declarations) and from a woman formerly of spotless character, the appeal may have had a subtle effect on subsequent events. At any rate, there were no more executions after that day when she "took her last farewill of her Husband, Children and Friends" and when, it was reported, she was "as Serious, Religious, Distinct, and Affectionate as could well be exprest, drawing Tears from the Eyes of almost all present."[89]

Samuel Wardwell of Andover, possibly really thought he was a witch. He also was hanged on September 22. He confessed, but, on further knowledge of the whole business acquired from others in the prison, he repudiated his story of the covenant with the Devil and was therefore:

> soon brought upon his Tryal; his former Confession and Spectre Testimony was all that appeared against him. At Execution while he was speaking to the People, protesting his Innocency, the Executioner being at the same time smoaking Tobacco, the smoak coming in his [Wardwell's] Face, interrupted his Discourse, those Accusers said, the Devil hindred him with smoak.[90]

Alice Parker of Salem, *Mary Parker* of Andover, *Ann Pudeater* of Salem, *Wilmot Redd* (or Reid) of Marblehead and *Margaret Scott* of Rowley also gave up their lives on the scaffold on September 22—the day that marked the termination of executions for "wickedly and feloniously" entering into a "covenant with the Evil Spirit, the Devil."

After the sheriff had completed his official duties, the Reverend Nicholas Noyes, who had demonstrated such zeal in ridding the land of the Devil: ". . . turning him[self] to the Bodies, said, what a sad thing it is to see Eight Firebrands of Hell hanging there."[91]

The dramatic tragedy enacted on Gallows Hill on that September day when "Eight Firebrands of Hell" played leading roles, marked the beginning of the end of the "witch mania" in New England. Never again in the Colonies did anyone pay with his life for "having or consulting with a familiar Spirit." At that time, however, more executions were expected. That fall of 1692 there were still about one hundred fifty in prison "and above two Hundred more accused."[92] In those crowded and foul prisons in Salem and Boston, many lay in shackles for eight or nine months before they were released in the fall and winter following. The Court of Oyer and Terminer had adjourned in September. The Chief Justice, and perhaps some of the other members, and some of the unyielding members of the new General Court that convened on October 12 expected the special trial court to take up again its solemn duty of ridding the country of Devils. But it never reconvened. Judge Samuel Sewall, who (as we have related) was a prominent member of that court, entered in his diary on October 26, 1692, this item:

> A Bill is sent in about calling a Fast, and Convocation of Ministers, that may be led in the right way as to the Witchcrafts. The season and manner of doing it, is such, that the Court of Oyer and Terminer count themselves thereby dismissed. 29 Nos. and 33 Yeas to the Bill. . . .[93]

On October 29 appears this note: "Mr. Russel asked whether the Court of Oyer and Terminer should sit, expressing some fear of inconvenience by its fall. Governour said it must fall."[94]

Governor Phips returned from the wars to find that his political enemies were "seeking to turn it all upon me." In his letter to the English government (part of which was quoted on p. 474), he sought to clear himself and to explain his position:

> . . . when I came home I found many persons in a strange ferment of dissatisfaction . . . but on enquiring into the matter I found that the Devill had taken upon him the name and shape of severall persons who were doubtless inocent and to my certain knowledge of good reputation for which cause I have now forbidden the committing of any more that shall be accused without unavoydable necessity, and those that have been committed I would shelter from any Proceedings against them wherein there may be the least suspition of any wrong to be done unto the Innocent. . . . I hereby declare that as soon as I came from fighting against their Majesties Enemyes and understood what danger some of their innocent subjects might be exposed to, if the evidence of the afflicted persons only did prevaile . . . I did before any application was made unto me about it put a stop to the proceedings of the Court and they are now stopt till their Majesties pleasure be known. . . .[95]

Although the special Court of Oyer and Terminer had expired, a new court for the regular trial of felonies was available but:

> Henceforth . . . the Juries generally acquitted such as were Tried, fearing they had gone too far before. And Sir William Phips, Governour, Reprieved all that were Condemned, even the Confessors, as well as others. And the Confessors generally fell off from their Confessions; some saying, they remembred nothing of what they said; others said they had belied themselves and others. Some brake Prison and ran away, and were not strictly searched after, some acquitted,

> some dismissed and one way or other all that had been accused were set or left at liberty . . . it was thought safer to under do than over do, especially in matters Capital, where what is once compleated cannot be retrieved: but what is left at one time, may be corrected at another, upon a review and clearer discovery of the state of the Case. Thus the matter issued somewhat abruptly.[96]

One execution in June, five in July, five in August, and eight in September (with one man pressed to death in September for standing mute) must have seemed to the intelligent leaders of the Bay Colony and Province more than an adequate compliance with the word of God: "Thou shalt not suffer a witch to live." When that frightful summer of 1692 was over, sober reflection began to replace the inexorable demand for the forfeiture of human lives. Powerful forces were at work to bring the grim business to an end.

In the first place, the terrifying scenes on Gallows Hill in Salem were unprecedented, for the Colony had not been a "hanging" government. Prior to 1692 executions in Massachusetts were not a common sight. Probably many in those great crowds of spectators who turned out to witness the sheriff in the performance of his stern duties had never before seen an execution. It was only a question of time before curiosity would be replaced by abhorrence and disgust. Even in midsummer small groups of citizens were protesting to the extent that they dared risk condemnation themselves.

Secondly, the determined insistence of the ministers—Samuel Willard, Increase Mather, and his son Cotton—and a few thoughtful citizens that the Devil could, and probably did, appear to some of the accusers in the "shape of" an innocent person finally prevailed and won the support of the Governor over the objections of Chief Justice Stoughton. To place so much credence in "spectral testimony" was to disregard the warning of the ministers that the court should use "a very critical and exquisite caution" lest "innocent blood be shed." The terrible realization was coming to some of those who were vitally concerned with the proceedings that "innocent blood" probably had, in fact, been shed because the court had put too much reliance on "spectral evidence" and on the accusations of those who confessed only to save their own lives.

Finally, the accusations grew beyond all reasonable bounds until so many people were accused that the charges became a *reductio ad absurdum*:

> ... experience shewed that the more there were apprehended, the more were still Afflicted by Satan, and the number of Confessors increasing, did but increase the number of the Accused, and the Executing some, made for the apprehending of others; for still the Afflicted complained of being tormented by new objects as the former were removed. So that those that were concerned, grew amazed at the numbers and quality of the persons accused and feared that Satan by his wiles had inwrapped innocent persons under the imputation of that Crime. ... *it cannot be imagined that in a place of so much knowledge, so many in so small a compass of Land should so abominably leap into the Devils lap at once.*[97]

When accusers "cried out upon" such fine Christian characters as the wife of the Rev. John Hale, pastor at Beverly, and the Rev. Samuel Willard, the eminent minister of the Old South Church who had been critical of the proceedings of the court, and finally Lady Phips, the Governor's wife (because in her husband's absence she had issued a warrant for the discharge of an accused who she did not believe was guilty), it became evident that no one was safe and that eventually every prominent person in the Colony would be involved if he dared raise a finger of protest. Naturally Governor Phips put an end to the proceedings that "threatened this Province with destruccion."[98] Thereafter, no witches were executed in Massachusetts.

† † †

On September 22, 1692, Massachusetts for the last time took the life of a person accused of being a witch. After the final session of the special trial Court of Oyer and Terminer on September 17, the prosecution of suspected witches continued in desultory fashion throughout the fall and winter, but juries in the newly created Superior Court of Judicature had no heart for the task of sending more victims to the gallows when the discredited "spectral testimony" no longer had much weight in a court of law. Out of more than thirty untried indictments remaining, not more than three or four guilty verdicts were reached. In May 1693, Governor Phips took a firm stand and refused to allow the grim business to continue. He ordered released upon the payment of their prison fees, those already condemned, who had spent many long weeks shackled in the prisons, and those still awaiting trial. This release was much to the chagrin of the once Presiding Justice of the witch-trial court, William Stoughton, who had just assumed the duties of the Chief Justice of the new court and who, to his dying day in 1701, never admitted that he had acted wrongfully in ridding the country of those poor, "devil-possessed" souls.

The General Court had reconvened in the fall of 1692. In its 1692-1693 session, it made two attempts to place witchcraft again on the capital crimes list, probably in the belief that under the new Charter the jurisdiction of the court might be challenged if the prosecutions were to continue. Both attempts failed because the King's Privy Council would not give its approval, although notification of its decision did not reach the Province in time to prevent the continuation of the trials into the spring of 1693.[99]

In the next few years there was evident a restless body of public opinion inclined to the view that, because of the Devil's "horrible plot against the country," innocent blood had, in fact, been shed. A sense of guilt lay heavily upon the hearts of those who had had a share in the proceedings as well as those who had not dared to raise a finger of protest. Now one could speak out with impunity. The clergy and some of the leading citizens of Boston had for some time desired that a day be set aside for fasting and prayer, but the sensitivities of the judges of the late Court of Oyer and Terminer who had acted according to their best lights had to be taken into consideration. By 1696, however, the time seemed appropriate to seek God's grace and forgiveness for whatever errors had been made during that direful year, 1692. The unsuccessful expedition against Port Royal in Nova Scotia, the loss to the French and Indians of the fort at Pemaquid (now in the state of Maine), the failure of harvests, the increase in piracy, the spread of contagious diseases for which there was no cure, and, finally, a depleted treasury were clear evidence that "the Anger of God is not yet turned away; but his Hand is still stretched out against his people, in manifold judgments." The authorities were willing to listen to the Rev. Samuel Willard of the Old South Church who, with some of the other Boston ministers, had urged "exquisite caution" in the witchcraft proceedings. Accordingly, an official proclamation, probably drawn up by his friend and parishioner, Samuel Sewall, on December 17, 1696, called for a day of fasting and prayer to be held on January 14, 1697. The proclamation pointed out, among other calamities that had befallen the Province, "the late Tragedie raised amongst us by Satan and his Instruments" which called for prayers to the Lord that he "would humble us . . . and pardon all the Errors of his Servants."[100]

Sewall, who had played a prominent part as one of the judges of the trial court, was deeply troubled in spirit. Eight days after the Proclamation he had buried his young daughter, Sarah, having already lost five other children through illness in their early years. Sensitive and devout, he wondered whether these domestic tragedies had not been visited upon him by a reproving God. If so, only a public and humble acknowledgement of his errors in the witchcraft affair would suffice to allay his anguished soul. And so, on the fast day, he stood up in the meetinghouse while his friend, the Rev. Samuel Willard read to the congregation his confession:

> Samuel Sewall, sensible of the reiterated strokes of God upon himself and family; and being sensible, that as to the Guilt contracted upon the opening of the late Commission of Oyer and Terminer at Salem (to which the order for this Day relates) he is, upon many accounts, more concerned than any that he knows of. Desires to take the Blame and shame of it. Asking pardon of men. And especially desiring prayers that God, who has an Unlimited Authority, would pardon that sin and all other his sins; personal and Relative; And according to his infinite Benignity, and Sovereignty, Not Visit the sin of him, or of any other, upon himself or any of his, nor upon the land; But that He would powerfully defend him against all Temptations to Sin, for the future; and vouchsafe him the efficacious, saving Conduct of his Word and Spirit.[101]

About the same time twelve members of the witch-trial jury signed and issued a remarkable document frankly admitting that they had not been able "to withstand the mysterious delusions of the Powers of Darkness, and Prince of the Air." They doubted whether they had followed God's command that there must be at least two witnesses to justify a verdict of death (citing Deut. 17:6 upon which Article 47 of the Body of Liberties had been based) and feared that they had "ignorantly and unwittingly" brought upon themselves and others "the Guilt of Innocent Blood" which God may not pardon (citing 2 Kings 24:4). "Sadly deluded and mistaken, for which we are much disquieted and distressed in our minds; and do therefore humbly beg forgiveness," they explained that they had acted "under the power of a strong and general Delusion" and were "utterly unacquainted with and not experienced in matters of that Nature." They concluded with a promise that they would not "do such things again on such grounds for the whole World."[102]

Thus the fast day did much to bring men to God, humbly seeking forgiveness. Probably most thoughtful people in the Province, less than four years after Governor Phips had put an end to the trial of witches, were in sympathetic agreement with the jury —that in 1692 they were "under the power of a strong and general Delusion." The Rev. Cotton Mather of the Second Church, on that day of the general fast presented to his congregation twenty articles of confession listing the sins of that period, among them:

> Wicked Sorceries have been practiced in the Land, and yett in the Troubles from the Divels, thereby brought in among us, those Errors, on both Hands, were committed, which wee have cause to bewayl with much Abasement of Soul before the Lord.[103]

The following night Mather was afflicted "with discouraging Thoughts" and feared that "the Divine Displeasure must overtake my Family, for my not appearing with Vigor enough to stop the proceedings of the Judges, when the Inextricable Storm from the Invisible World assaulted the Countrey."[104]

The Rev. John Hale, pastor of Beverly, who, according to Calef, had "been very forward in these Prosecutions" but who had changed his views after his wife had been accused, also decided at this time to sit down and write out a thoughtful and straightforward account of the whole tragic affair, admitting that "among Satans Mysteries of iniquity, this of Witchcraft is one of the most difficult to be searched out by the Sons of men," concluding that there was some ground to fear "that there hath been a great deal of innocent blood shed in the Christian World, by proceeding upon unsafe principles, in condemning persons for Malefick Witchcraft." His little book, *A Modest Inquiry Into the Nature of Witchcraft,* was completed in 1698 but not published until 1702. In the book, he wrote, "We have cause to be humbled for the mistakes and errors which have been in these Colonies, in their Proceedings against persons for this crime. . .but such was the darkness of that day. . . we walked in the clouds, and could not see our way."[105]

Even Ann Putnam, who as a child had given such damaging testimony of her personal "afflictions" in Salem Village in the winter of 1692, made her humble apologies fourteen years later in 1706 in the village meetinghouse in Salem. She acknowledged sadly her part in bringing the guilt of innocent blood upon the country, but she declared that:

> ... what was said or done by me against any person, I can truly and uprightly say before God and man, I did it not out of any anger, malice, or ill-will to any person, for I had no such thing against one of them, but what I did was ignorantly, being deluded of Satan. And particularly as I was a chief instrument of accusing Goodwife Nurse and her two sisters, I desire to lie in the dust and to be humbled for it, in that I was a cause, with others, of so sad a calamity to them and their families.[106]

By 1703 it had been generally acknowledged that errors had been made in the admission of evidence and that innocent men and women had been convicted and executed. And there were others who had been condemned but released from prison after the governor had stopped all hangings. Three of these, Abigail Faulkner, Sarah Wardel (Wardwell) and Elizabeth Proctor (the latter two being widows of men who had been hanged) petitioned the court for the setting aside of the attainders of felony. On July 27, 1703, the General Court declared their convictions, judgments, and attainders repealed, reversed, and made null and void and that no corruption of blood or forfeitures of goods and chattels be incurred and that they be "reinstated in their just Credit and reputation."[107]

Six years later (eight years after the death of the presiding judge of the witch-trial court) some of the heirs of those who had been executed petitioned the General Court for a reversal of the judgments, removal of attainders, and remuneration for "what they have been Damnified in their Estates." After almost two years of discussion and delay the General Court on November 2, 1711, reversed and made null and void the judgments and attainders of some of the executed witches and of some who had been condemned but not executed—22 in all.[108]

A committee was appointed to assess the damages each petitioner should receive. After it had arrived at an agreed figure, the committee reported to the General Court which, by another special act in that year, awarded damages to each one, varying from 150 pounds to the heirs of John Procter to 7 pounds, 6 shillings to the heirs of Martha Carrier, that "rampant hag." Eight women who were condemned but not executed also received compensation. Six of the executed were omitted from these special Acts (probably because no heirs joined in the petition).[109] Philip English, who had been imprisoned as a suspected witch but, being a man of some means had been granted bail, fled the country. He was never brought to trial but had lost a large part of his estate. He had asked for an indemnification of 1500 pounds but was denied. However, in 1718, he was granted 200 pounds.[110] Thomas Rich, son of Martha Corey by a former husband, had been overlooked but was awarded 50 pounds in 1724.[111]

For the next two centuries the General Court of Massachusetts was concerned with more pressing business than removing attainders of felony arising out of the proceedings of the Court of Oyer and Terminer. But in 1957 the heirs of Ann Pudeator of Salem, one of the witches hanged on September 22, 1692, but who was one of the six omitted from the special Acts of 1711, claimed that they were "still distressed by the record" in 1692. The General Court thereupon passed a Resolve, approved by Governor Foster Furcolo on August 28, 1957, stating that "Ann Pudeator and certain other persons [not naming them]" who were executed for "Witchcraft" *"may have been* illegally tried, convicted and sentenced by a *possibly illegal* court." The General Court resolved:

> That in order to alleviate such distress and although the facts of such proceedings cannot be obliterated, the General Court of Massachusetts declares its belief that such proceedings, even if lawful under the Province Charter and the law of Massachusetts as it then was, were and are shocking, and the result of a wave of popular hysterical fear of the Devil in the community, and further declares that, as all the laws under which said proceedings, even if then legally conducted, have been long since abandoned and superseded by our more civilized laws no disgrace or cause for distress attaches to the said descendants or any of them by reason of said proceedings. . . .[112]

That Resolve, one might assume, should have ended the matter. But John B. Hatch of Salem now maintains that the Resolve is illegal, for the 1692 trials were held under the aegis of the British crown over which the Commonwealth of Massachusetts has no authority. He has therefore petitioned the General Court in recent years to take "all necessary and possible legislative steps . . . to liberate the state's 'witch' dead from their illegal limbo." His proposal would require the General Court to memorialize the Congress of the United States to forward a resolution to the present Queen Elizabeth and to the United Nations, to the end that the Salem "witches" might be tried *in absentia* in the British House of Lords and there have their court convictions quashed.[113]

And that should be the last stage in the legal proceedings that commenced in Salem Village 273 years ago.

15. "THE LIGHT HERE KINDLED"

> Thus out of smalle beginnings greater things have been prodused by his hand that made all things of nothing, and gives being to all things that are; and as one small candle may light a thousand, so the light here kindled hath shone to many, yea in some sorte to our whole nation; let the glorious name of Jehova have all the praise.—*Gov. William Bradford, 1631*[1]

IN December 1620 the "first beginners," as Bradford called them, laid "the foundation of all the Plantations and Colonies in New-England."[2] Neglected by historians for almost two centuries, Plymouth Colony has once again regained its historical significance. The world will not soon forget those men of sturdy courage and devotion to an ideal and their gallant struggle to return to the "anciente puritie" of worship with its "primitive order, libertie, & bewtie."

Their deep faith in God—a God who they reverently believed held a special place in his heart for the "Saints"—profoundly affected all aspects of the administration of criminal justice in the ensuing years and left its imprint on the laws now directing the wheels of justice in the Commonwealth of Massachusetts.[3]

Ten years later they were joined by a few English Puritans who were fired with a zeal for greater liberty in the worship of God than they could hope for in old England. These devout men engaged themselves and their families "in a hazardous and awfull undertaking" by braving the great Atlantic to seek new homes and a new life in the "wilderness" of New England. Submitting themselves to the "providence of God," they set sail for America in the spring of 1630 in a fleet of eleven ships. On the flagship

Arbella, forty-two-year-old John Winthrop had personal possession of the Royal Charter granted the year before by King Charles I, a document that was to serve as the legal basis for the government of the Massachusetts Bay Colony for more than half a century.

In the next decade, some ten thousand men and women, children, and servants sought a new existence in the Bay Colony, most of them motivated more by a desire for economic betterment or by the love of adventure than by a yearning for religious freedom. The leaders of the Colony, however, were Puritans through and through. By and large they were men of exceptional ability, many of them trained in theology or law in English universities. No one could doubt that they were dedicated to the creation of a new plantation where they could follow God's word to the extent that God gave them grace to understand it. It was natural, therefore, that the criminal law of early Massachusetts—and, in fact, for many years to come—would draw heavily on the Bible for its inspiration and that the Puritan ministers would play a key role in the interpretation of God's word as it applied to the social offender.

Not all the early settlements in America were able to survive the hazards of the wilderness, but the Colony of New-Plymouth and the Massachusetts Bay Colony, through the industriousness and ingenuity of those early pioneers, did, growing into political adulthood from Colony, to Royal Province, to the Commonwealth of Massachusetts. Plymouth developed an orderly and formal structure of representative government without benefit of a Royal Charter. But it always remained small. After the founding of the Bay Colony, its population declined. When in the 1660s it could count three thousand souls within its boundaries, it was still only one-fourth or one-third the size of the Bay Colony. In 1691 it was merged with the larger colony by a charter granted by William and Mary, narrowly escaping a merger with the Province of New York.

The Bay Colony, on the other hand, had derived its powers from the Royal Charter of 1629, a surprisingly liberal document, authorizing its General Court to admit freemen, to elect its own officers, to make laws, to establish courts and, in effect, to develop from a trading company to a political entity with an increasing degree of independence from the mother country.

It had a "Greate and Generall Courte" that could not be dissolved without a majority vote of its own members—unlike Parliament which was frequently dissolved at the whim of the ruling monarch. Comprised of men elected annually by the people, it was "the chief civil power of this Commonwealth" with extensive administrative, legislative, and judicial functions. As time went on, it relinquished most of its judicial business to the County Courts and to the powerful Courts of Assistants, reserving to itself the right to hear appeals. Its power lay in its rights to investigate and to make laws and orders for the governing of the country. The independent Colony of New Plymouth established similar legislative and judicial institutions.

One of the most noted deliberative bodies in the world, the General Court of the Bay Colony, now in continuous existence for more than three and one-third centuries,[4] derived its authority from the Charter of 1629, a document so broad and flexible it did not hinder the Colonists in shaping their political institutions to suit their own ends by drawing heavily on the doctrine of implied powers. The Charter was only in a very broad sense their constitution. The General Court proved to be the final court of appeal in interpreting its own laws, allowing no appeal to the courts of England from its own decisions. The King, during this early period, was too busy with his own affairs to become greatly concerned whether laws made in Boston might be repugnant to those of the Realm but what Governor Winthrop said was probably true: "In those things wherein we had varied from our patent [Charter] we did not touch the foundation of government."

Questions of legal interpretation were frequently propounded not to a body of law-trained men (there were few such in the Colony) but to the reverend elders who, particularly in the earlier years, occupied a respected niche in the halls of government and whose long "opinions" cited "leading cases" from Scripture rather than from the Common Law. Such advisory opinions, although not binding on the General Court, carried great weight in a Colony founded on a deep faith in God's will and word.

During the first two decades of Bay Colony government, a struggle for power between the Magistrates and freemen took place, each concession to the freemen marking one step further toward a more democratic form of government. As an aristocracy was considered to be rule by the best, so democracy was considered to be the most inferior form of government because it did not assure a necessary relationship between political power and political wisdom. The Colonial government was not deemed a "pure aristocracy" but rather one "mixt of an aristocracy & democracy in respect of the General Court" (where both Magistrates and Deputies sat). Even in the Court of Assistants where only Magistrates sat on the bench, there was "some place for a democraticall dispensation in respect of the jurors."

Yet, although the word "democratic" was not then a word held in high esteem, the Colony gradually assumed a far more democratic form than one could have found in England at that time. The people annually elected all governmental officers; there were to be no kings, no hereditary right to office, no dictators. Representative government was established by the decision to send Deputies to the General Court to represent each town and by the declaration that only the General Court could decide who could be given the franchise or what laws for the country should be enacted or what taxes levied. A bicameral legislature was set up, each house to have a negative vote on the other—a system still in use in the General Court today. The town meeting was introduced, democracy at the grass roots, where townspeople chose selectmen to assure an orderly disposal of town business. Everyone, voter or nonvoter, citizen or foreigner, was granted the right to present his grievances in petitions to the General Court. And a comprehensive system of courts was set up for the administration of civil and criminal justice.

A violator of one of the many criminal laws of the Colony would have found—unless religious bigotry or human passion intervened—that no one could be punished without a trial and a right to appeal to the higher court, and no sentence could be passed:

> . . . unlesse it be by vertue or equitie of some expresse law of the Country waranting the same, established by a generall Court and sufficiently published, or in case of the defect of a law in any partecular case by the word of god. . . .[5]

To establish a government of laws, rather than of men, the legislature recognized the need for a systematic compilation of laws. In a few years both colonies began the publication of a book of laws arranged in alphabetical sequence which, after many spirited discussions and numerous delays, they brought to completion and made available to the citizens of each town. They republished these codes—governing both civil and criminal affairs—at various times as the need arose for an up-to-date and convenient compilation.

The "civil rights and liberties" of a seventeenth century Massachusetts citizen were set forth under the heading of "Generall Fundamentals" in both Colonies, assuring him of a relatively high degree of fair and just treatment if he should run afoul of the many "orders" of the General Courts. They were drawn partly from the Common Law of England and, in the early days of the Colonies, from the Mosaic code. For example, in the Bay Colony, a man (or woman) brought before the bar of justice was entitled to due process of law and was to enjoy the "same justice and law" that was available to all residents of the colony, whether he was an "inhabitant or forreiner." He could not (with one minor exception) be compelled by torture to testify against himself. He had a right to bail, with certain exceptions; to freedom from double jeopardy; to a speedy trial by a jury of his peers with an opportunity of challenging his jurymen. He could not be convicted of a capital crime by the testimony of only one witness; he could not be imprisoned for debt if the law could find satisfaction in some other way. He was not to be subject to punishments that were deemed "inhumane, barbarous or cruell." A condemned man could petition the General Court for a pardon and could not be executed without a waiting period of at least four days.

Not everyone was to be held wholly responsible for his criminal behavior, as special consideration was to be granted to "children, idiots or distracted [insane] persons" or to "new comers" who might have been unfamiliar with the laws and customs. Servants had a right to fair treatment and no one could be held in bond slavery or as a serf under a feudal system. Later the Bay Colony established the right to self-defence, the presumption of innocence, and the right to go free if not prosecuted within a year (the so-called statute of limitations) except for certain capital and other serious offenses. Plymouth Colony also established somewhat similar "civil rights and liberties" although its system of administration of criminal justice was less comprehensive than that of its neighbor to the north.

Yet several striking factors militated against the perfecting of a system that would be agreeable to the orthodox and the unorthodox, the conformist and the rebel; that would, in short, be truly a government of laws administered without human bias. In the first place, although all government officials had to stand for annual elections and could therefore be readily repudiated for arbitrary conduct, the franchise (outside of town meetings) was limited for many years to those who would be most likely to defend the kind of government the Puritans came to America to establish; namely, those who were members of the Congregational churches. Secondly, a spirit of religious intolerance, common throughout Christendom at that time, led to the enactment of strict laws, and a rigid enforcement of them, against the "heretic." Finally, since the small group of leaders "at the helm" were dedicated to defend a particular form of government and church discipline, their zeal led to the banishment of those who, it was believed, might endanger the whole enterprise and make it impossible for the Colony to carry out its covenant with God.

In both colonies the state was closely bound to the church by ties of mutual respect and defense, as well as by common theological sympathies—a normal state of affairs for that era. Yet functionally there was such a clear demarcation of legal rights and obligations that the evidence does not warrant our characterizing the government as a theocracy. Legally, church and state were separate institutions; psychologically, they had learned that it was to their mutual advantage to render reciprocal support, for they had grown up, as the Secretary of the General Court put it, "like two twinnes."

The Puritans disclaimed any attempt "to bind all men to the same tenets and practise," but "damnable heresies" simply could not be tolerated. It was clear they led to "the subversion of the Christian faith, and destruction of the Souls of men." The state therefore felt compelled to come to the aid of the church. Ordinary or occasional offenders could be dealt with by fines or whippings, but the articulate dissenters who stirred multitudes to sedition and civil disobedience had to be ordered to leave the jurisdiction.

Thus they were charged with "the forcing of men in matters of conscience towards God to believe as others believe and to practice and worship as others do." Under fire from their friends in England and bitterly rebuked by local dissenters such as Roger Williams, Anne Hutchinson, the Anabaptists, and the Quakers, the Puritan leaders held their ground and justified their stand. John Cotton and John Winthrop, chief representatives of church and state in the first two decades of the Bay Colony's life, in all honesty and sincerity believed they acted only as Christ would have acted had he lived in Boston. To their critics they offered a logical and unusually lengthy defense, so sure were they of the justice of their decisions. If one has found the Truth, is it not one's duty to defend it against all detractors? No doubt these leaders agreed with Nathaniel Ward who asserted that to be tolerant of *all* religions, one must be "either an atheist, or an Heretique or an Hypocrite, or at best a captive to some lust: Polypiety is the greatest impiety in the world."[6]

The law did not demand that one's religious beliefs need ever be against one's own conscience, for "no Humane [human] power be Lord over the Faith and Consciences of men"; and yet one must be punished if his beliefs, openly expressed, tended to subvert the church or state or were incompatible with the *peaceful* operation of those institutions. "Tender consciences seeking light" were to be respected, but the sword of justice must be drawn in defense of the church against those who "bring in & cry up unwarrantable Revelations, inventions of men, or any carnall liberty, under a deceitfull colloure of liberty of consciance," just as today one might promote subversive acts under color of freedom of speech. Cotton defended his position:

> Wee believe there is a vast difference betweene mens inventions and God's institutions; wee fled from mens inventions [in the "corrupt" Church of England], to which we else should have beene compelled; wee compell none to mens inventions. . . . I tell you the truth, wee have tolerated in our church some Anabaptists, some Antinomians, and some Seekers, and do so still at this day [written between 1645 and 1653]. [Those who] carry their dissent more privately and inoffensively . . . are borne withall in much meekenesse. . . .[7]

When differences of opinion arose as to the meaning of Christ's message, the Puritan minister was the final court of appeal. Cotton felt it necessary to reply to charges of infallibility:

> Wee are farr from arrogating infallibility of judgement to ourselves

or affecting uniformity; uniformity God never required, infallibility he never granted us. Wee content ourselves with unity in the foundation of religion and of church order; Superstructures wee suffer to varie; wee have here presbyterian churches as well as congregationall, and have learned (through grace) to keepe the unity of spirit in the bond of peace; only *wee are loth to be blowne up and down (like chaff) by every winde of new notions. . . .*[8].

The tragedy of the story was that both prosecuted and prosecutor were Christians, believers in the divinity of Christ and, for the most part, in the Bible as "the written and infallible Word of God." Their diversity of opinion rested in the *interpretation* of the Christian message—and such interpretation often marked the dividing line between freedom and punishment.

The basic theories of Colonial jurists seemed to have been that the infliction of physical suffering on the violator of public law served to 1) propitiate a watchful God who needed constant reassurance that the solemn Covenant under which they labored would be strictly honored and sin closely checked; 2) permit the sinner to atone for his ungodliness, and 3) deter the public offender from further transgressions, warning all who might witness his suffering that such "uncivill behaviour" would not be tolerated.

The forms of corporal punishment were not distinguished by originality. They were copies or adaptations of penalties long practiced in old England. Whipping on the bare back, the most common form, was swift and economical to administer. That it was painful also can be taken for granted, although in many cases the stripes were not "heavily laid on." The administration of this penalty, as well as of all "bodilie punishments" was carefully controlled by numerous restrictive laws. Almost any lawbreaker could be whipped, judicial discretion being what it was, but men and women most likely to suffer at the whipping post proved to be those who violated the sex mores. Branding with a hot iron, cutting off an ear or two, burning in the hand or shoulder, or boring the tongue were less frequently used. The ducking stool seems to have been a rarity, few reports of its use being found in the court records available.

Corporal punishments were administered with less harshness than in old England. The Colonies had outlawed cruelty. Although one today might look upon the whipping post as a cruel instrument of torture, it was not generally so regarded in that day and age. Aside from the Quaker episode, there were few instances of purely vindictive retaliation. Some of the Hebrew laws were woven into the fabric of Colonial law, yet the eye-for-an-eye doctrine was not in evidence; nor did the Colonial people adopt the harsher penalties mentioned in the Pentateuch, such as stoning to death, drowning, burning to death, or serious mutilation.

Long delays between arrest and punishment were practically unknown. The criterion for the sound administration of criminal justice laid down by eighteenth and nineteenth century criminologists and reformers that punishments should be swift and certain were fairly well exemplified in the Colonies. "Bodilie punishment" did not always follow conviction where it was authorized by law, for judges frequently considered the mitigating circumstances or the penitence or social rank of the offender. Furthermore, courts were usually responsive to pleas of mercy and stood ready to accept a fine instead of a whipping unless the crime was considered "very shamefull" or the life of the offender "vitious and profligate."

As one reviews case after case of moral dereliction in the Colonies, one might gain the impression that Massachusetts' seventeenth century citizens were weak willed and of little virtue. But one should bear in mind that we have assembled here the "sins" of the people, not their good deeds; that crime was easily detected in a compact community where everyone seemed to be the keeper of his neighbor's morals; and that these plantations, particularly the Bay Colony, were being constantly supplied with new settlers, many of whom cared little about keeping a Covenant with God. Governor Winthrop summed it up when he said in 1641, "As people increased, so sin abounded."

In addition to bodily punishments, there were the punishments of humiliation. The government's emphasis on the feeling of shame was striking. Great care was taken to see that an offender suffered in public and that his friends and neighbors were visibly acquainted with his degradation. One wore a placard, for example, with his crime spelled out in capital letters "that others may hear and be ashamed of breaking out into like wickedness." This sort of treatment, it was believed, would be as great a deterrent to some as "bodilie punishment" to others. And it probably was.

Most of these penalties were not inventions of the Puritans or

Pilgrims but were carried over from old England. And yet the Colonists administered the penalties in a very different manner. Running throughout the records, one notes a personal touch in the decisions of the magistrates. The men and women who stood before them were no doubt known to them, for the towns were compact and harbored few strangers. Magistrates could thus select the most appropriate penalties out of a wide variety of possible choices.

Moral standards of the communities were high, and those who wandered off the narrow path were hailed into court for offenses that, in many cases, we would consider trivial today. Most of those who gave expression to their natural appetites and were punished for it were servants. They necessarily led a restricted life with many pleasures denied them, and they were the first to kick over the traces. A strict sex code forbade consensual sex relations before marriage, cautioned against too great familiarity with the opposite sex outside of marriage, and attempted to curb "ribald speeches" or any sort of lewd or lascivious behavior. Profane cursing or swearing, lying (if it were a "pernicious" lie), drunkenness, idleness, "disorderly living" or living away from one's spouse, family quarreling, merrymaking late at night, disobeying strict Sabbath laws, and many other deviations led straight to court if seen by the constable or reported by some prying neighbor. Open verbal attacks on the government or reviling magistrate or minister particularly aroused the hostility of the justices, and usually called for more severe measures.

Nathaniel Hawthorne, in his American classic *The Scarlet Letter* depicted the poignant suffering of a young lady in the town of Boston in midseventeenth century who confessed to adultery and bastardy. The stern Puritanical court, so the story goes, totally insensitive to her contrite spirit and fine character, sentenced her to wear for the rest of her life a scarlet letter A sewn on her upper garment, unless she would reveal the identity of her lover. This sort of historical fiction has served to strengthen the distorted image that the average American has of the Puritan character. Actually, there was no law in the government established by Puritans, and in its early years dominated by them, that authorized this kind of sentence. Nor has any case come to light where a Bay Colony court meted out such treatment or required the wearing of a letter for life. Nor did Plymouth courts ever sentence a person to wear such a letter for life. The legal penalty for adultery in Boston was death, the usual penalty a fine or whipping or a choice between the two. Perhaps the author's confusion was due to the fact that Plymouth Colony, refusing to make adultery a capital offense, enacted a law in 1658 providing that a convicted adulterer, in addition to a whipping, would be required to wear "two Capitall letters viz: A D cut out in cloth and sowed on theire upermost Garments on theire arme or backe."[9] But the Bay Colony Puritans did not follow Plymouth's example. Many years later, (1694) the Province government passed a law requiring the adulterer to wear a "capital A, of two inches long and proportionate bigness, cut out in cloth of a contrary colour to their cloaths, and sewed upon their upper garments, on the outside of their arm, or on their back, in open view."[10] But by 1694 the Puritans had long since ceased to play a dominant role in legislative halls. The case of Hester Prynne, therefore, as a fictional character is hardly symbolic of Puritan justice.

In spite of the fact that seventeenth century England was not known for its leniency toward criminal offenders, we find relatively few cases in these two Colonies (with the possible exception of the Quaker and witchcraft episodes) where the penalties seemed particularly overbearing or merciless. Puritan magistrates, it is true, expressed deep-seated moral indignation when confronted with blatant sin condemned by both statute and the word of God, but they also had a heart.

At the very outset the Massachusetts penal system drew heavily upon English tradition. Justice could not have been administered in the English manner without the familiar local gaol or prison. Used chiefly as a place for the temporary holding of those whose sentences had not yet been carried out at the whipping post or stocks or for those who could not pay their fines or were awaiting their appearance in court, the first prisons served also as places of confinement for those who were made to suffer "in durance vile" for offending the King's peace. Contrary to opinions frequently expressed by modern writers of criminology texts, the courts sentenced men and women to prison *as* punishment—just as they do today, although for a more indeterminate and shorter period of time. This practice of using the local prison or jail as a form of punishment grew increasingly common and persisted down through the eighteenth century until a state prison for those sentenced to hard labor was set up in 1785. Colonial offenders, in fact, not infrequently spent many months in seventeenth century prisons.

No one enjoyed his enforced stay in the local gaol. Nor did any member of the General Court cry "coddling," for the coarse food (for which the prisoner had to pay), the poorly heated rooms with no sanitary facilities, and the enforced idleness must have been hard for one to endure even though he were used to rugged and primitive existence. Escapes, consequently, were frequently attempted and were surprisingly successful. Obviously, the frail wooden structures were temptations for the agile and resourceful individual unless he were known as a dangerous criminal, in which case he might have been shackled and kept "in close confinement."

To a modern criminologist the most striking feature of these early prisons was their lack of security and their poor surveillance. But time was to cure these defects. At any rate, there was always the "Castle," that harbor fortress where the difficult prisoner could be carefully guarded if necessary. In the course of time, succeeding generations spent considerable thought and money on devising greater security until they had developed in the nineteenth century a kind of fortress type of prison which they bequeathed to the present generation of criminals.

Another noteworthy development in Colonial penology was the emergence in the middle of the seventeenth century of the idea of "correction," also borrowed from old England. Houses of Correction entered the picture as institutions designed to afford the vagrant and the petty thief an opportunity to improve his time in manual labor and to learn a useful trade. Punishment was not to be completely abandoned, for each inmate was whipped on entrance as a sort of reminder of his wickedness and whipped again if he did not obey instructions within, but the inmate's welfare was for the first time given some consideration. But time wrought changes. It might be only a slight oversimplification to say that the Colonial House of Correction was designed to correct, the Colonial prison was designed to punish; on the other hand, the modern prison has developed an extensive industrial and correctional program, while many a modern house of correction has been allowed to become a house of idleness and punishment.

Neither the Pilgrims nor the Puritans experienced a need to offer a *rationale* for capital punishment by which they might be judged by future generations. Executing a man or woman convicted of a serious crime was an accepted practice in England and, in fact, in all civilized countries at that time. There existed no lobby for the abolition of that practice.

But Colonial leaders did not follow the English tradition blindly. They worked out their own body of laws in terms they believed would please God, and they achieved a remarkably humane and reasonable administration of criminal justice for the times in which they lived. Theirs was a very personal God, mightily interested in every detail of their existence, alert to every transgression of His commands. The "infallible and whole will of God, which he purposed to make knoune to mankinde" was made manifest in the inspired writings of the prophets and holy men of Israel. There New Englanders could find a Rule "to guide all their Affaires." And there they could find ample "warrant" for the taking of a human life to balance the scales of justice, to right a heinous wrong, or, in the case of murder, "to purge the land from blood." It was natural that the first capital laws of the Bay Colony were derived almost verbatim from the Pentateuch. It was natural, too, that Colonial leaders trained in the law later modified and added to these early enactments to suit their special conditions or to allow for recognized principles of the English Common Law.

Hanging an offender, then, was not done with the joy of vindictiveness. (It was only in their dealings with Quakers and witches that their Christian compassion seemed to have deserted them.) To Governors Bradford and Winthrop, a hanging was a very sad spectacle, but there were times when they saw no alternative to this grim penalty, for they were mindful of their "Covenant" with God who guided and protected them in all their afflictions and tribulations but whose "heavy hand" was ever ready to strike down both the godly and the sinner if a guilty person should escape when "he ought to die."

They did not enter into lengthy discussions of the deterrent effect of capital punishment. But surely they must have believed that the lesson learned by a public hanging before hundreds of spectators would be taken to heart—and it probably was. They capitalized on the grim event by long, moralizing sermons preached to the condemned a few days before or at the time of his dispatch to the next world. They showed grave concern over the saving of his soul at the eleventh hour and were usually successful in causing him to repent, to condemn himself, to acknowledge the justice of his penalty, and to warn others to fear God and to shun the kind of life that led him to his sad end.

The Colonial records reveal (insofar as they are complete) that the supreme penalty was exacted only for witchcraft, murder, bestiality, adultery, rape, arson, defying orders of banishment (Quakers), piracy, and treason. Most of the capital laws, then, exemplified that kind of behavior which was particularly abhorrent to the Pilgrims and Puritans, but these were not such abominations in the eyes of their Lord God that there was no alternative to the forfeiture of a life.

The Quakers were something else again. The "People of God" who came rushing headlong into Massachusetts to tell everyone about the direct and invisible fellowship with God were frightfully impatient. George Fox and his devoted followers were deeply convinced that the Puritans had not gone far enough in breaking free from the beliefs and practices of the Roman Catholic Church. Although they had given up the forms of worship retained by the Church of England, the Puritans practiced a religion, as the Quakers saw it, of empty form without power, preaching without light, human fellowship without the spirit of God or the grace that comes through Jesus Christ. They must be told about the "Inner Light" that makes communication with God a personal and direct experience. They must be shown that there was no need of ritual or ceremony or sermons and hence no need of a "hireling priesthood." They must prepare to give up their "false God and false worship" and to accept not only a new way of life in its relationship to God but a radical change in their social institutions.

The Quakers must have known that they could not accomplish so drastic a change in religious and social thinking without a struggle that would call for personal courage of the highest order. And the best of the Quaker missionaries were ready to "freely give their lives" for the cause. They were in no mood for a quiet and peaceful discussion of ecclesiastical matters; nor were the Puritans in any mood to listen to these strange preachings. Both sides showed bad manners, uncontrolled tempers, and complete intolerance.

The "cursed heretics" had come into the Colony at a very bad time. Puritans had been losing ground; heresy was increasing. The generation who had been born in New England and who were then growing into adulthood were being accused of profaning the Sabbath. Drunkenness was more prevalent; fornication and other sins more frequently committed. These perilous times were a season for strengthening, not diluting, religious affiliations. Then came the "Quaker invasion" that threatened like a flood to wash away the Puritan foundations and to rebuild on the foundations of "notorious errors, haeresies and blasphemies."

Their "damnable heresies" were harder to bear than those of Anne Hutchinson or Roger Williams for they not only attacked current theological beliefs but, when rebuked and brought into court, they predicted the imminent downfall of the government. Thus they were condemned as "open enemies of government itself" and "subversive of church and state." But they were "subversives" completely lacking in subtlety, never "going underground" or flying false colors, but diligently seeking opposition wherever they could find it. They did not attempt to teach the overthrow of government by force, for they were pacifists. They fought an ideological war with tongues sharper than any man's sword.

When the Quakers said they could not "bow down to your God, nor your worship" because it was "false," the Puritans replied "There is but one God," and "you do not worship that God which *we* worship!"

When the Quakers refused to show deference to magistrates or ministers, for all men were equal before God in the Quaker way of life, they violated one of the fundamental practices of the Colonists. One's adoration, the Quakers maintained, should be shown only to God—"he that kneeleth or prostrates himself to man, what doeth he more to God? He that boweth and uncovereth his head to the creature, what hath he reserved to the Creator?" Therefore one could not expect a Quaker to remove his hat in a court of law, nor could one expect the local constable to show sympathetic understanding of this new sect that had just come into the Colony evidently to destroy it.

When the Puritans charged the Quakers with tending to "overthrow the whole gospell & the very vitalls of Christianitie" and accused them of promoting doctrines that were "destructive to fundamentall trueths of religion" they found little comfort in the Quaker's comment: "You be a stifnecked people goten up high in your owne wisdome, as the scribes and pharisees were, who put Christ to death. . . ."

While the Colonists believed that if Quaker heresies were publicly shouted on the streets without interference by the authorities Divine jealousies would be provoked against all the people, hence prosecution must follow, the Quakers insisted that such punishment was "persecution" and reminded New Englanders that Christ "never persecuted any, neither taught he any such doctrine, as to imprison any, or whip, or stock, or banish, or put to death for conscience sake, as the Rulers of New-England have done."[11]

Although the General Court in the Bay Colony had previously declared that "the well ordereing of the Militia is a matter of great concernment to the safety and welfare of the Common-wealth" and ordered that every male over sixteen (with certain exemptions) attend military exercise and training, the Quakers refused to obey the law, saying that Christ had taught them to denounce all wars and never to bear arms against their fellow men, not even against the "savages."

When the Bay Colony required an "oath of fidelity" of all residents and all strangers of two-months' residence, the Quakers insisted that taking an oath would be unlawful, for Christ had said, "Swear not at all."

Punishment followed punishment, ever increasing in severity until four Quakers paid the extreme penalty. What might have been the outcome had not King Charles put a stop to the hangings? The fury of the storm subsided then flared up again and finally blew itself out.

Quakers were a temporary plague, but drunkards were always with them. That there should be in the Bay and Plymouth Colonies, founded by men devoted to the keeping of a covenant with God, an "excess of drinking & unto drunkennes it selfe" and that by 1671 drunkenness should have become "a great, and raging sin . . . a growing and prevailing evil" was a matter of long concern to the Great and General Court and a development that aroused the moral indignation of the ministers and teachers of the Congregational churches.

Drinking was an acceptable social custom that permeated all classes of Colonial society, but drunking to excess was a "vice to be abhored of all nations, especially of those who held out & profess the gospell of Christ Jesus." Drunkenness was also a crime, as it is today, punishable by a small fine or, in aggravated cases, by a whipping or placing in the stocks or imprisonment or by "punishments of humiliation." It was one of the most frequent crimes that brought men into the courts in spite of a multiplicity of laws and constant watchfulness on the part of the constable. Heavy responsibilities were placed upon tavern keepers, not only to see that they served wholesome beer at a fair price, but that they denied service of beer, wine, or "strong waters" to the town drunkards whose names were posted in some public place.

Indians, who had a special liking for the white man's beverages, created a special problem, for they were prone to become violent and even homicidal when drinking to excess. Laws were finally enacted to prohibit the sale of liquor to Indians unless it could be shown that they were sick and in need, for wine, beer, and other alcoholic drinks were believed to have some medicinal value.

Colonial legislators were well aware of the fact that there were many compulsive drinkers in Massachusetts who, even after repeated punishments, could not be "reclaimed." In spite of carefully drawn laws designed "to suppress that swinish sinne of drunkennes . . . persons addicted to that vice finde out waies to deceave the lawes." And yet there was no other way to deal with such sinners but to warn, to admonish, and to punish.

Governor Bradford was puzzled as to why crimes of drunkenness and "unclainess" were so prevalent in colonies devoted to the worship of God and the keeping of His Covenant. With a perceptive feeling for history—later generations would surely want to know why—he commented:

> Marvilous it may be to see and consider how some kind of wickednes did grow & breake forth here, in a land wher the same was so much witnessed against, and so narrowly looked unto, & severly punished when it was knowne; as in no place more, or so much, that I have known or heard of. . . .[12]

He then proceeded to expound on the prevalence of "sundrie notorious sins" in Plymouth Colony, from three aspects:

> 1) [*The theological.*] . . . one reason may be, that the Divell may carrie a greater spite against the churches of Christ and the gospell hear, by how much the more they indea[v]our to preserve holynes

and puritie amongst them, and strictly punisheth the contrary when it ariseth either in church or comone wealth; that he might cast a blemishe & staine upon them in the eyes of [the] world. . . . I would rather thinke thus, then that Satane hath more power in these heathen lands, as som have thought, then [than] in more Christian nations, espetially over Gods servants in them.

2) [*The psychological.*] An other reason may be, that it may be in this case as it is with waters when their streames are stopped or dammed up, when they gett passage they flow with more violence, and make more noys and disturbance, then when they are suffered to rune quietly in their owne chanels. So wikednes being here more stopped by strict laws, and the same more nerly looked unto, so as it cannot rune in a comone road of liberty as it would, and is inclined, it searches every wher, and at last breaks out wher it getts vente.

3) [*The statistical.*] A third reason may be, hear [here] (as I am verily perswaded) is not more evills in this kind, nor nothing nere so many by proportion, as in other places; but they are here more discovered and seen, and made publick by due serch, inquisition, and due punishment; for the churches looke narrowly to their members, and the magistrats over all, more strictly then [than] in other places. Besids, here the people are but few in comparison of other places, which are full & populous, and lye hid, as it were, in a wood or thickett, and many horrible evills by that means are never seen nor knowne; wheras hear [here], they are, as it were, brought into the light, and set in the plaine feeld, or rather on a hill, made conspicuous to the view of all.

Bradford's analysis was penetrating, and court statistics must be cautiously interpreted. We can hardly conclude from our data that the moral tone of the Colonies was fainthearted or that most of its citizens were dabbling in sin. For one thing, there were simply too many eyes watching the offender. To begin with, there was the constable. The Bay Colony constable, chosen by his town for a one-year term and subject to a fine if he refused the position, was the chief law enforcement officer. His duties were manifold, his burdens so onerous and exacting that few men sought the office while many were willing to pay the fine exacted of those who refused to accept the appointment. He went about unarmed with a black staff as his badge of office, ferreting out crime and arresting drunks and Sabbath breakers, occasionally in hot pursuit of "mertherers, manslayers, peace breakers, theeves, robers, burglarers." Like the modern police officer he could call on the citizenry for aid in the pursuit and arrest of an offender and could arrest without a warrant anyone committing a crime in his presence or in the sight of those who immediately informed him of it. He also had the unpleasant task of whipping convicted offenders, unless he could get others to do it.

The marshall was the court officer, whose duty it was to serve warrants and attachments and other court papers and to give support to the constable in maintaining an orderly community.

Although the General Court divided the Bay Colony into four counties as early as 1643, no sheriffs were appointed until after the revocation of the Charter.

Boston's first practicing lawyer, coming into the Bay Colony in 1638, soon learned that at that early period the Colony was not receptive to men of his profession, particularly those who held religious and political views at variance with those of church and government leaders. Even though Governor Winthrop and some others who held high positions in the government had had legal training in the English Inns of Court, they looked with some suspicion upon those who sought to earn a living by pleading other men's cases, but finally permitting them to do so if they charged no fee. For the first few decades the law was hardly a respectable "calling," and no facilities were provided to encourage the training of prospective lawyers. It was at the outset common practice for every man to be his own lawyer in pleading his case in court. New Englanders were a litigious people and a flood of lawsuits surged into the courts. It was natural for a layman to turn to a learned magistrate *before* trial for legal advice, quite possibly the same magistrate who later would preside at the man's trial. The General Court had to put an end to this practice because it had become "inconvenient and very burdensome" to the magistrates, but the magistrates themselves realized that it would then be necessary for them to provide lawyers. As the population grew and living together gave rise to complex problems of legal rights, it became inevitable that a legal profession would emerge, as it had in England. Official recognition of a legal bar might be dated from 1686 when the courts admitted attorneys to practice and required of them an attorney's oath, very similar to the oath required today.

The Bay Colony did not adopt any crucial "test" of criminal

responsibility, such as the so-called "right-and-wrong" test of modern times. It did, however, suggest "special allowances and dispensations" to children, idiots, and the mentally disturbed (or the "distracted persons" as they were called). It did not follow the common-law rule of excusing all children from criminal liability under the age of seven, nor did it propose any definition of "idiot." Nevertheless, in dealing with children, the courts exhibited a surprising degree of humane and kindly treatment toward the very young, usually referring the willfull, unruly, or disobedient child to his parents for correction. Young children were not publicly whipped and, so far as available records reveal the judgments of the courts, probably no child under fifteen was executed. Great care was taken to see that children were properly brought up, knew the capital laws, learned their catechism, received an education and some vocational training, and did not "mispend" their time and their money in taverns where liquor was sold or violate the Sabbath laws in traveling about or engaging in sports or frivolous activities. Many of the criminal laws set a minimum age limit, usually fourteen or sixteen, excusing from punishment offenders below such limits.

Because so little was known in those days about mental illness and because the official records seldom gave an adequate description of the offenders appearing before the courts, it is idle to speculate on the number who were excused from criminal responsibility or under what circumstances "special allowances and dispensations" were actually granted by the courts.

The Deputies feared that, if magistrates were permitted broad discretion in sentencing offenders, they might abuse this discretion and that a government of men rather than of laws might result, thus bringing the Colony under attack as "arbitrary." As an able advocate for the magistrates, Winthrop argued vigorously for judicial discretion, discounting any possibility that an arbitrary government would result if magistrates used the wisdom God had given them. After all, were not magistrates "Gods upon earthe"? The General Court consulted the ministers who, in a long opinion, gave substantial support to the theory of judicial discretion. The magistrates did not ask that *all* laws be made arbitrary; they conceded that certain penalties should be fixed (as they were in the Old Testament) but they condemned fixed penalties that, as Winthrop said, "cross with the rules of justice, and prudence, and mercy." The magistrates did not win a clear-cut victory. Nevertheless, in *practice* judges were permitted wide discretion in dealing with men and women who appeared before them.

The accused men and women could not easily expect to escape justice by fleeing to a neighboring colony, for the colonies of Plymouth, New Haven, and Connecticut were joined with the Bay Colony in an intercolonial compact called "The United Colonies of New England," the chief purposes of which were religious and military. But one of the provisions of this confederation was that escaped prisoners or other fugitives from justice who fled from one colony to another, could be apprehended and turned over to the pursuer. This document was the forerunner of numerous compacts now in existence in New England, making it difficult for such persons to achieve immunity from prosecution by fleeing from one jurisdiction to another.

Even witches could not escape the constable. Their fabled broomsticks could not carry them to safety once the long arm of the Puritan law reached out for them. In this age of scientific skepticism, we look back with horror at the dreadful record of executions in the Massachusetts Bay Colony in the years 1648 to 1692 when twenty-two "witches," charged with "covenanting with the Devil," were hanged, while one was pressed to death, two died while awaiting trial in a "stinking dungeon," and many others were condemned by a court of justice but spared only because the "witch mania" came to an abrupt end in the fall of that fateful year 1692. It is easy for us some three centuries later to pass harsh judgment on the "unreasonable," "sadistic," and "credulous" Puritans who brought this "storm of Justice . . . on the Heads of those guilty Witches and Wretches which have defiled our Land." But a more objective and dispassionate reflection compels us to turn our attention to the context in which these tragic events were nurtured.

The belief in a personified Devil engaged in a perpetual war against mankind was virtually universal in the seventeenth century and earlier, a belief that has not entirely disappeared to this day. Theologians of different faiths had skillfully woven the old demonological folklore into their own theories of the role of the Devil in their scheme of things, closely identifying witchcraft with heresy. The result was the commencement of legal prosecutions with fatal consequences for most of the accused. It is not surprising, therefore, to hear the Rev. Cotton Mather warn the community of "an Horrible Plot against the Country by Witchcraft" and to incite the people to rid the land of witches, lest the Devil in his great wrath "Blow up, and pull down all the Churches in the Country." Puritan ministers provided the rationale, based on the Scriptures, upon which the government might rightfully proceed, and they advised a vigorous prosecution, yet they strongly urged "a very critical and exquisite Caution" in the admission of "spectral evidence" and in the prosecution of persons of good reputation, advice that, had it been heeded sooner, might have considerably reduced the number whose lives were cut short on Gallows Hill in Salem.

We should also remember that it was as common for an educated person in seventeenth century New England to believe that witches were real persons who, in the toils of the Devil, were commissioned to carry out his evil designs in some "preternatural" manner as it is for us today to believe in radio waves which are a prominent part of our own "invisible world." The evidence produced at witches' trials was so abundant, so "palpable" (to use Cotton Mather's term), and so dramatic that no jury could for long have any reasonable doubts of the guilt of the accused. Even the accused themselves, for the most part, believed in witchcraft while denying their own participation in the Devil's plot.

Those who governed the Bay Colony knew from the lessons of history the sad consequences of tolerating that "most Horrible witchcraft or Possession of Devills which had broke in upon severall Townes" in 1692. War had to be declared against the Devil. Although the belief in witchcraft was not indigenous to Puritanism any more than to any other faith of that day, it was the authority of the Bible that had the strongest appeal to Puritans. It was the greatest weakness of the Puritan position that the words spoken by religious leaders reflecting another culture and another era and recorded in a book known as the Holy Bible were taken literally to be "the word of God." Hence the admonition contained in the Book of Exodus, "Thou shalt not suffer a witch to live," was warrant enough to send many good men and women to their deaths, even though they may have been members of a Puritan church and persons of unblemished reputation in the community. And yet, after 1692, this command strangely lost its compelling force or through some rationalization was differently interpreted. At least today, Massachusetts witches, if there are any, are suffered to live in peace.

The citizen of the Commonwealth today still has his life shaped and guided by the laws and the concepts of justice of these "first beginners." And because the Massachusetts experience was so crucial and so central to the whole settlement of the English on these shores, the knowledge here gained, so slowly and so painfully, has reached out, touching first the laws of the thirteen colonies, and finally leaving its imprint to a significant degree on the statutes of the fifty states and the federal constitution itself. The "one small candle" that Bradford wrote of has indeed lit its thousands and "shone to many," and of the "smalle beginings" which we have here traced, "greater things have been prodused."

APPENDIX A

THE BODY OF LIBERTIES OF 1641

The Liberties of the Massachusets Collonie in New England, 1641.

THE free fruition of such liberties Immunities and priveledges as humanitie, Civilitie, and Christianitie call for as due to every man in his place and proportion without impeachment and Infringement hath ever bene and ever will be the tranquillitie and Stabilitie of Churches and Commonwealths. And the deniall or deprivall thereof, the disturbance if not the ruine of both.

We hould it therefore our dutie and safetie whilst we are about the further establishing of this Government to collect and expresse all such freedomes as for present we foresee may concerne us, and our posteritie after us, And to ratify them with our sollemne consent.

Wee doe therefore this day religiously and unanimously decree and confirme these following Rites, liberties and priveledges concerneing our Churches, and Civill State to be respectively impartiallie and inviolably enjoyed and observed throughout our Jurisdiction for ever.

1. No mans life shall be taken away, no mans honour or good name shall be stayned, no mans person shall be arested, restrayned, banished, dismembred, nor any wayes punished, no man shall be deprived of his wife or children, no mans goods or estaite shall be taken away from him, nor any way indammaged under colour of law or Countenance of Authoritie, unlesse it be by vertue or equitie of some expresse law of the Country waranting the same, established by a generall Court and sufficiently published, or in case of the defect of a law in any parteculer case by the word of god. And in Capitall cases, or in cases concerning dismembring or banishment according to that word to be judged by the Generall Court.

2. Every person within this Jurisdiction, whether Inhabitant or forreiner shall enjoy the same justice and law, that is generall for the plantation, which we constitute and execute one towards another without partialitie or delay.

3. No man shall be urged to take any oath or subscribe any articles, covenants or remonstrance, of a publique and Civill nature, but such as the Generall Court hath considered, allowed and required.

4. No man shall be punished for not appearing at or before any Civill Assembly, Court, Councell, Magistrate, or Officer, nor for the omission of any office or service, if he shall be necessarily hindred by any apparent Act or providence of God, which he could neither foresee nor avoid.

Provided that this law shall not prejudice any person of his just cost or damage, in any civill action.

5. No man shall be compelled to any publique worke or service unlesse the presse be grounded upon some act of the generall Court, and have reasonable allowance therefore.

6. No man shall be pressed in person to any office, worke, warres or other publique service, that is necessarily and suffitiently exempted by any naturall or personall impediment, as by want of yeares, greatnes of age, defect of minde, fayling of sences, or impotencie of Lymbes.

7. No man shall be compelled to goe out of the limits of this plantation upon any offensive warres which this Commonwealth or any of our freinds or confederats shall volentarily undertake. But onely upon such vindictive and defensive warres in our owne behalfe or the behalfe of our freinds, and confederats as shall be enterprized by the Counsell and consent of a Court generall, or by authority derived from the same.

8. No mans Cattel or goods of what kinde soever shall be pressed or taken for any publique use or service, unlesse it be by warrant grounded upon some act of the generall Court, nor without such reasonable prices and hire as the ordinarie rates of the Countrie do afford. And if his Cattle or goods shall perish or suffer damage in such service, the owner shall be suffitiently recompenced.

9. No monopolies shall be granted or allowed amongst us, but of such new Inventions that are profitable to the Countrie, and that for a short time.

10. All our lands and heritages shall be free from all fines and licenses upon Alienations, and from all hariotts, wardships, Liveries, Primer-seisins, yeare day and wast, Escheates, and forfeitures, upon the deaths of parents or Ancestors, be they naturall, casuall or Juditiall.

11. All persons which are of the age of 21 yeares, and of right understanding and meamories, whether excommunicate or condemned shall have full power and libertie to make there wills and testaments, and other lawfull alienations of theire lands and estates.

12. Every man whether Inhabitant or fforreiner, free or not free shall have libertie to come to any publique Court, Councel, or Towne meeting, and either by speech or writeing to move any lawfull, seasonable, and materiall question, or to present any necessary motion, complaint, petition, Bill or information, whereof that meeting hath proper cognizance, so it be done in convenient time, due order, and respective manner.

13. No man shall be rated here for any estaite or revenue he hath in England, or in any forreine partes till it be transported hither.

14. Any Conveyance or Alienation of land or other estaite what so

ever, made by any woman that is married, any childe under age, Ideott or distracted person, shall be good if it be passed and ratified by the consent of a generall Court.

15. All Covenous or fraudulent Alienations of Conveyances of lands, tenements, or any heriditaments, shall be of no validitie to defeate any man from due debts or legacies, or from any just title, clame or possession, of that which is so fraudulently conveyed.

16. Every Inhabitant that is an howse holder shall have free fishing and fowling in any great ponds and Bayes, Coves and Rivers, so farre as the sea ebbes and flowes within the presincts of the towne where they dwell, unlesse the free men of the same Towne or the Generall Court have otherwise appropriated them, provided that this shall not be extended to give leave to any man to come upon others proprietie without there leave.

17. Every man of or within this Jurisdiction shall have free libertie, notwithstanding any Civill power to remove both himselfe, and his familie at their pleasure out of the same, provided there be no legall impediment to the contrarie.

Rites Rules and Liberties concerning Juditiall proceedings.

18. No mans person shall be restrained or imprisoned by any authority whatsoever, before the law hath sentenced him thereto, if he can put in sufficient securitie, bayle or mainprise, for his appearance, and good behaviour in the meane time, unlesse it be in Crimes Capitall and Contempts in open Court, and in such cases where some expresse act of Court doth allow it.

19. If in a general Court any miscariage shall be amongst the Assistants when they are by themselves that may deserve an Admonition or fine under 20 sh. it shall be examined and sentenced amongst themselves, If amongst the Deputies when they are by themselves, it shall be examined and sentenced amongst themselves, If it be when the whole Court is togeather, it shall be judged by the whole Court, and not severallie as before.

20. If any which are to sit as Judges in any other Court shall demeane themselves offensively in the Court, The rest of the Judges present shall have power to censure him for it, if the cause be of a high nature it shall be presented to and censured at the next superior Court.

21. In all cases where the first summons are not served six dayes before the Court, and the cause briefly specified in the warrant, where appearance is to be made by the partie summoned, it shall be at his libertie whether he will appeare or no, except all cases that are to be handled in Courts suddainly called, upon extraordinary occasions, In all

cases where there appeares present and urgent cause Any Assistant or officer apointed shal have power to make out Attaichments for the first summons.

22. No man in any suit or action against an other shall falsely pretend great debts or damages to vex his Adversary, if it shall appeare any doth so, The Court shall have power to set a reasonable fine on his head.

23. No man shall be adjudged to pay for detaining any debt from any Crediter above eight pounds in the hundred for one yeare, And not above that rate proportionable for all somes what so ever, neither shall this be a coulour or countenance to allow any usurie amongst us contrarie to the law of god.

24. In all Trespasses or damages done to any man or men, If it can be proved to be done by the meere default of him or them to whome, the trespasse is done, It shall be judged no trespasse, nor any damage given for it.

25. No Summons pleading Judgement, or any kinde of proceeding in Court or course of Justice shall be abated, arested or reversed upon any kinde of cercumstantiall errors or mistakes, If the person and cause be rightly understood and intended by the Court.

26. Every man that findeth himselfe unfit to plead his owne cause in any Court shall have Libertie to imploy any man against whom the Court doth not except, to helpe him, Provided he give him noe fee or reward for his paines. This shall not exempt the partie him selfe from Answering such Questions in person as the Court shall thinke meete to demand of him.

27. If any plantife shall give into any Court a declaration of his cause in writeing, The defendant shall also have libertie and time to give in his answer in writeing, And so in all further proceedings betwene partie and partie, So it doth not further hinder the dispach of Justice then the Court shall be willing unto.

28. The plantife in all Actions brought in any Court shall have libertie to withdraw his Action, or to be nonsuited before the Jurie hath given in their verdict, in which case he shall alwaies pay full cost and chardges to the defendant, and may afterwards renew his suite at an other Court if he please.

29. In all actions at law it shall be the libertie of the plantife and defendant by mutual consent to choose whether they will be tryed by the Bench or by a Jurie, unlesse it be where the law upon just reason hath otherwise determined. The like libertie shall be granted to all persons in Criminall cases.

30. It shall be in the libertie both of plantife and defendant, and

likewise every delinquent (to be judged by a Jurie) to challenge any of the Jurors. And if his challenge be found just and reasonable by the Bench, or the rest of the Jurie, as the challenger shall choose it shall be allowed him, and tales de cercumstantibus impaneled in their room.

31. In all cases where evidences is so obscure or defective that the Jurie cannot clearely and safely give a positive verdict, whether it be a grand or petit Jurie, It shall have libertie to give a non Liquit, or a spetiall verdict, in which last, that is in a spetiall verdict, the Judgement of the cause shall be left to the Court, And all Jurors shall have libertie in matters of fact if they cannot finde the maine issue, yet to finde and present in their verdict so much as they can, If the Bench and Jurors shall so suffer at any time about their verdict that either of them cannot proceede with peace of conscience the case shall be referred to the Generall Court, who shall take the question from both and determine it.

32. Every man shall have libertie to replevy his Cattell or goods impounded, distreined, seised, or extended, unlesse it be upon execution after Judgement, and in paiment of fines. Provided he puts in good securitie to prosecute his replevin, And to satisfie such demands as his Adversary shall recover against him in Law.

33. No mans person shall be Arrested, or imprisoned upon execution or judgment for any debt or fine, If the law can finde competent meanes of satisfaction otherwise from his estaite, and if not his person may be arrested and imprisoned where he shall be kept at his owne charge, not the plantife's till satisfaction be made, unlesse the Court that had cognizance of the cause or some superior Court shall otherwise provide.

34. If any man shall be proved and Judged a commen Barrator vexing others with unjust frequent and endless suites, It shall be in the power of Courts both to denie him the benefit of the law, and to punish him for his Barratry.

35. No mans Corne nor hay that is in the feild or upon the Cart, nor his garden stuffe, nor any thing subject to present decay, shall be taken in any distresse, unles he that takes it doth presently bestow it where it may not be imbesled nor suffer spoile or decay, or give securitie to satisfie the worth thereof if it comes to any harme.

36. It shall be in the libertie of every man cast condemned or sentenced in any cause in any Inferior Court, to make their Appeale to the Court of Assistants, provided they tender their appeale and put in securitie to prosecute it, before the Court be ended wherein they were condemned, And within six dayes next ensuing put in good securitie before some Assistant to satisfie what his Adversarie shall recover

against him; And if the cause be of a Criminall nature for his good behaviour, and appearance, And everie man shall have libertie to complaine to the Generall Court of any Injustice done him in any Court of Assistants or other.

37. In all cases where it appears to the Court that the plantife hath wilingly and witingly done wronge to the defendant in commenceing and prosecuting an action or complaint against him, They shall have power to impose upon him a proportionable fine to the use of the defendant or accused person, for his false complaint or clamor.

38. Everie man shall have libertie to Record in the publique Rolles of any Court any Testimony given upon oath in the same Court, or before two Assistants, or any deede or evidence legally confirmed there to remaine in perpetuam rei memoriam, that is for perpetuall memoriall or evidence upon occasion.

39. In all actions both reall and personall betweene partie and partie, the Court shall have power to respite execution for a convenient time, when in their prudence they see just cause so to doe.

40. No Conveyance, Deede, or promise whatsoever shall be of validitie, If it be gotten by Illegal violence, imprisonment, threatenings, or any kinde of forcible compulsion called Dures.

41. Everie man that is to Answere for any Criminall cause, whether he be in prison or under bayle, his cause shall be heard and determined at the next Court that hath proper Cognizance thereof, And may be done without prejudice of Justice.

42. No man shall be twise sentenced by Civill Justice for one and the same Crime, offence, or Trespasse.

43. No man shall be beaten with above 40 stripes, nor shall any true gentleman, nor any man equall to a gentleman be punished with whipping, unles his crime be very shamefull, and his course of life vitious and profligate.

44. No man condemned to dye shall be put to death within fower dayes next after his condemnation, unles the Court see spetiall cause to the contrary, or in case of martiall law, nor shall the body of any man so put to death be unburied 12 howers unlesse it be in case of Anatomie.

45. No man shall be forced by Torture to confesse any Crime against himselfe nor any other unlesse it be in some Capitall case, where he is first fullie convicted by cleare and suffitient evidence to be guilty, After which if the cause be of that nature, That it is very apparent there be other conspiratours, or confederates with him, Then he may be tortured, yet not with such Tortures as be Barbarous and inhumane.

46. For bodilie punishments we allow amongst us none that are inhumane, Barbarous or cruell.

47. No man shall be put to death without the testimony of two or three witnesses, or that which is equivalent thereunto.

48. Every Inhabitant of the Countrie shall have free libertie to search and veewe any Rooles, Records, or Regesters of any Court or office except the Councell, And to have a transcript or exemplification thereof written examined, and signed by the hand of the officer of the office paying the appointed fees therefore.

49. No free man shall be compelled to serve upon Juries above two Courts in a yeare, except grand Jurie men, who shall hould two Courts together at the least.

50. All Jurors shall be chosen continuallie by the freemen of the Towne where they dwell.

51. All Associates selected at any time to Assist the Assistants in Inferior Courts, shall be nominated by the Townes belonging to that Court, by orderly agreement amonge themselves.

52. Children, Idiots, Distracted persons, and all that are strangers, or new commers to our plantation, shall have such allowances and dispensations in any Cause whether Criminall or other as religion and reason require.

53. The age of discretion for passing away of lands or such kinde of herediments, or for giveing, of votes, verdicts or Sentence in any Civill Courts or causes, shall be one and twentie yeares.

54. When so ever any thing is to be put to vote, any sentence to be pronounced, or any other matter to be proposed, or read in any Court or Assembly, If the president or moderator thereof shall refuse to performe it, the Major parte of the members of that Court or Assembly shall have power to appoint any other meete man of them to do it, And if there be just cause to punish him that should and would not.

55. In all suites or Actions in any Court, the plaintife shall have libertie to make all the titles and claims to that he sues for he can. And the Defendant shall have libertie to plead all the pleas he can in answere to them, and the Court shall judge according to the intire evidence of all.

56. If any man shall behave himselfe offensively at any Towne meeting, the rest of the freemen then present, shall have power to sentence him for his offence. So be it the mulct or penaltie exceede not twentie shilings.

57. When so ever any person shall come to any very suddaine untimely and unnaturall death, Some Assistant or the Constables of that

Towne shall forthwith sumon a Jury of twelve free men to inquire of the cause and manner of their death, and shall present a true verdict thereof to some neere Assistant, or the next Court to be helde for that Towne upon their oath.

Liberties more peculiarlie concerning the free men.

58. Civill Authoritie hath power and libertie to see the peace, ordinances and Rules of Christ observed in every church according to his word. so it be done in a Civill and not in an Ecclesiastical way.

59. Civill Authoritie hath power and libertie to deale with any Church member in a way of Civill Justice, notwithstanding any Church relation, office or interest.

60. No church censure shall degrade or depose any man from any Civill dignitie, office, or Authoritie he shall have in the Commonwealth.

61. No Magestrate, Juror, Officer, or other man shall be bound to informe present or reveale any private crim or offence, wherein there is no perill or danger to this plantation or any member thereof, when any necessarie tye of conscience binds him to secresie grounded upon the word of god, unlesse it be in case of testimony lawfully required.

62. Any Shire or Towne shall have libertie to choose their Deputies whom and where they please for the Generall Court. So be it they be free men, and have taken there oath of fealtie, and Inhabiting in this Jurisdiction.

63. No Governor, Deputy Governor, Assistant, Associate, or grand Jury man at any Court, nor any Deputie for the Generall Court, shall at any time beare his owne chardges at any Court, but their necessary expences shall be defrayed either by the Towne or Shire on whose service they are, or by the Country in generall.

64. Everie Action betweene partie and partie, and proceedings against delinquents in Criminall causes shall be briefly and destinctly entered on the Rolles of every Court by the Recorder thereof. That such actions be not afterwards brought againe to the vexation of any man.

65. No custome or prescription shall ever prevaile amongst us in any morall cause, our meaneing is [not to] maintaine anythinge that can be proved to be morallie sinfull by the word of god.

66. The Freemen of every Towneship shall have power to make such by laws and constitutions as may concerne the welfare of their Towne, provided they be not of a Criminall, but onely of a prudential nature, And that their penalties exceede not 20 sh. for one offence. And that they be not repugnant to the publique laws and orders of the Countrie.

And if any Inhabitant shall neglect or refuse to observe them, they shall have power to levy the appointed penalties by distresse.

67. It is the constant libertie of the free men of this plantation to choose yearly at the Court of Election out of the freemen all the General officers of this Jurisdiction. If they please to dischardge them at the day of Election by way of vote. They may do it without shewing cause. But if at any other generall Court, we hould it due justice, that the reasons thereof be alleadged and proved. By Generall officers we meane, our Governor, Deputy Governor, Assistants, Treasurer, Generall of our warres. And our Admirall at Sea, and such as are or hereafter may be of the like generall nature.

68. It is the libertie of the freemen to choose such deputies for the Generall Court out of themselves, either in their owne Townes or elsewhere as they judge fitest. And because we cannot foresee what varietie and weight of occasions may fall into future consideration, And what counsells we may stand in neede of, we decree. That the Deputies (to attend the Generall Court in the behalfe of the Countrie) shall not any time be stated or inacted, but from Court to Court, or at the most but for one yeare, that the Countrie may have an Annuall libertie to do in that case what is most behoofefull for the best welfaire thereof.

69. No Generall Court shall be desolved or adjourned without the consent of the Major parte thereof.

70. All Freemen called to give any advise, vote, verdict, or sentence in any Court, Counsell, or Civill Assembly, shall have full freedome to doe it according to their true Judgements and Consciences, So it be done orderly and inofensively for the manner.

71. The Governor shall have a casting voice whensoever an Equi vote shall fall out in the Court of Assistants, or generall assembly, So shall the presedent or moderator have in all Civill Courts or Assemblies.

72. The Governor and Deputy Governor Joyntly consenting or any three Assistants concurring in consent shall have power out of Court to reprive a condemned malefactour, till the next quarter or generall Court. The generall Court onely shall have power to pardon a condemned malefactor.

73. The Generall Court hath libertie and Authoritie to send out any member of this Comanwealth of what qualitie, condition or office whatsoever into forreine parts about any publique message or Negotiation. Provided the partie sent be acquainted with the affaire he goeth about, and be willing to undertake the service.

74. The freemen of every Towne or Towneship, shall have full power to choose yearly or for lesse time out of themselves a convenient num-

ber to fitt men to order the planting or prudentiall occasions of that Towne, according to Instructions given them in writeing, Provided nothing be done by them contrary to the publique laws and orders of the Countrie, provided also the number of such select persons be not above nine.

75. It is and shall be the libertie of any member or members of any Court, Councell or Civill Assembly in cases of makeing or executing any order or law, that properlie concerne religion, or any cause capitall, or warres, or Subscription to any publique Articles or Remonstrance, in case they cannot in Judgement and conscience consent to that way the Major vote or suffrage goes, to make their contra Remonstrance or protestation in speech or writeing, and upon request to have their dissent recorded in the Rolles of that Court. So it be done Christianlie and respectively for the manner. And there dissent onely be entered without the reasons thereof, for the avoiding of tediousnes.

76. Whensoever any Jurie of trialls or Jurours are not cleare in their Judgements or consciences censerneing any cause wherein they are to give their verdict, They shall have libertie in open Court to advise with any man they thinke fitt to resolve or direct them, before they give in their verdict.

77. In all cases wherein any freeman is to give his vote, be it in point of Election, makeing constitutions and orders, or passing sentence in any case of Judicature or the like, if he cannot see reason to give it positively one way or an other, he shall have libertie to be silent, and not pressed to a determined vote.

78. The Generall or publique Treasure or any parte thereof shall never be exspended but by the appointment of a Generall Court, nor any Shire Treasure, but by the appointment of the freemen thereof, nor any Towne Treasurie but by the freemen of that Towneship.

Liberties of Women.

79. If any man at his death shall not leave his wife a competent portion of his estate, upon just complaint made to the Generall Court she shall be relieved.

80. Everie marryed woeman shall be free from bodilie correction or stripes by her husband, unlesse it be in his owne defence upon her assalt. If there be any just cause of correction complaint shall be made to Authoritie assembled in some Court, from which onely she shall receive it.

Liberties of Children.

81. When parents dye intestate, the Elder sonne shall have a doble

portion of his whole estate reall and personall, unlesse the General Court upon just cause alleadged shall judge otherwise.

82. When parents dye intestate haveing noe heires males of their bodies their Daughters shall inherit as Copartners, unles the Generall Court upon just reason shall judge otherwise.

83. If any parents shall wilfullie and unreasonably deny any childe timely or convenient mariage, or shall exercise any unnaturall severitie towards them, such childeren shall have free libertie to complaine to Authoritie for redresse.

84. No Orphan dureing their minoritie which was not committed to tuition or service by the parents in their life time, shall afterwards be absolutely disposed of by any kindred, freind, Executor, Towneship, or Church, nor by themselves without the consent of some Court, wherein two Assistants at least shall be present.

Liberties of Servants.

85. If any servants shall flee from the Tiranny and crueltie of their masters to the howse of any freeman of the same Towne, they shall be there protected and susteyned till due order be taken for their relife. Provided due notice thereof be speedily given to their maisters from whom they fled. And the next Assistant or Constable where the partie flying is harboured.

86. No servant shall be put of for above a yeare to any other neither in the life time of their maister nor after their death by their Executors or Administrators unlesse it be by consent of Authoritie assembled in some Court or two Assistants.

87. If any man smite out the eye or tooth of his man servant, or maid servant, or otherwise mayme or much disfigure him, unlesse it be by meere casualtie, he shall let them goe free from his service. And shall have such further recompense as the Court shall allow him.

88. Servants that have served deligentlie and faithfully to the benefitt of their maisters seaven yeares, shall not be sent away emptie. And if any have bene unfaithfull, negligent or unprofitable in their service, notwithstanding the good usage of their maisters, they shall not be dismissed till they have made satisfaction according to the Judgement of Authoritie.

Liberties of Forreiners and Strangers.

89. If any people of other Nations professing the true Christian Religion shall flee to us from the Tiranny or oppression of their persecutors, or from famyne, warres, or the like necessary and compulsarie

cause, They shall be entertayned and succoured amongst us, according to that power and prudence, god shall give us.

90. If any ships or other vessels, be it freind or enemy, shall suffer shipwrack upon our Coast, there shall be no violence or wrong offerred to their persons or goods. But their persons shall be harboured, and relieved, and their goods preserved in safety till Authoritie may be certified thereof, and shall take further order therein.

91. There shall never be any bond slaverie, villinage or Captivitie amongst us unles it be lawfull Captives taken in just warres, and such strangers as willingly selle themselves or are sold to us. And these shall have all the liberties and Christian usages which the law of god established in Israell concerning such persons doeth morally require. This exempts none from servitude who shall be Judged thereto by Authoritie.

Off the Bruite Creature.

92. No man shall exercise any Tirranny or Crueltie towards any bruite Creature which are usuallie kept for man's use.

93. If any man shall have occasion to leade or drive Cattel from place to place that is far of, so that they be weary, or hungry, or fall sick, or lambe, It shall be lawful to rest or refresh them, for a competant time, in any open place that is not Corne, meadow, or inclosed for some peculiar use.

94. *Capitall Laws.*

1.

Deut. 13. 6, 10.
Deut. 17. 2, 6.
Ex. 22. 20.

If any man after legall conviction shall have or worship any other god, but the lord god, he shall be put to death.

2.

Ex. 22. 18.
Lev. 20. 27.
Dut. 18. 10.

If any man or woeman be a witch, (that is hath or consulteth with a familiar spirit,) They shall be put to death.

3.

Lev. 24. 15, 16.

If any person shall Blaspheme the name of god, the father, Sonne or Holie Ghost, with direct, expresse, presumptuous or high handed blasphemie, or shall curse god in the like manner, he shall be put to death.

4.

Ex. 21. 12. Numb. 35. 13, 14, 30, 31. If any person committ any wilfull murther, which is manslaughter, committed upon premeditated malice, hatred, or Crueltie, not in a mans necessarie and just defence, nor by meere casualtie against his will, he shall be put to death.

5.

Numb. 25, 20, 21. Lev. 24. 17. If any person slayeth an other suddaienly in his anger or Crueltie of passion, he shall be put to death.

6.

Ex. 21. 14. If any person shall slay an other through guile, either by poysoning or other such divelish practice, he shall be put to death.

7.

Lev. 20. 15, 16. If any man or woeman shall lye with any beaste or bruite creature by Carnall Copulation, They shall surely be put to death. And the beast shall be slaine, and buried and not eaten.

8.

Lev. 20. 13. If any man lyeth with mankinde as he lyeth with a woeman, both of them have committed abhomination, they both shall surely be put to death.

9.

Lev. 20. 19 and 18, 20. Dut. 22. 23, 24. If any person committeth Adultery with a maried or espoused wife, the Adulterer and Adulteresse shall surely be put to death.

10.

Ex. 21. 16. If any man stealeth a man or mankinde, he shall surely be put to death.

11.

Deut. 19. 16, 18, 19. If any man rise up by false witnes, wittingly and of purpose to take away any mans life, he shall be put to death.

12.

If any man shall conspire and attempt any invasion, insurrection, or publique rebellion against our common wealth, or shall indeavour to surprize any Towne or Townes, fort or forts therein, or shall treacherously and perfediouslie attempt the alteration and subversion of our frame of politie or Government fundamentallie, he shall be put to death. [Later publications of this law added the citation, "Numb. 16, 2 Sam. 3, 18, 20."]

95. *A Declaration of the Liberties the Lord Jesus hath given to the Churches.*

1.

All the people of god within this Jurisdiction who are not in a church way, and be orthodox in Judgement, and not scandalous in life, shall have full libertie to gather themselves into a Church Estaite. Provided they doe it in a Christian way, with due observation of the rules of Christ revealed in his word.

2.

Every Church hath full libertie to exercise all the ordinances of god according to the rules of scripture.

3.

Every Church hath free libertie of Election and ordination of all their officers from time to time, provided they be able, pious and orthodox.

4.

Every Church hath free libertie of Admission, Recommendation, Dismission, and Expulsion, or deposall of their officers, and members, upon due cause, with free exercise of the Discipline and Censures of Christ according to the rules of his word.

5.

No Injunctions are to be put upon any Church, Church officers or member in point of Doctrine, worship or Discipline, whether for substance or cercumstance besides the Institutions of the lord.

6.

Every Church of Christ hath freedome to celebrate dayes of fasting and prayer, and of thanksgiveing according to the word of god.

7.

The Elders of Churches have free libertie to meete monthly, Quarterly, or otherwise, in convenient numbers and places, for conferences, and consultations about Christian and Church questions and occasions.

8.

All Churches have libertie to deale with any of their members in a church way that are in the hand of Justice. So it be not to retard or hinder the course thereof.

9.

Every Church hath libertie to deale with any magestrate, Deputie of Court or other officer what soe ever that is a member in a church way in case of apparent and just offence given in their places, so it be done with due observance and respect.

10.

Wee allowe private meetings for edification in religion amongst Christians of all sortes of people. So it be without just offence for number, time, place, and other cercumstances.

11.

For the preventing and removeing of errour and offence that may grow and spread in any of the Churches in this Jurisdiction, And for the preserveing of trueith and peace in the severall churches within themselves, and for the maintenance and exercise of brotherly communion, amongst all the churches in the Countrie, It is allowed and ratified, by the Authoritie of this Generall Court as a lawfull libertie of the Churches of Christ. That once in every month of the yeare (when the season will beare it) It shall be lawfull for the minesters and Elders, of the Churches neere adjoyneing together, with any other of the breetheren with the consent of the churches to assemble by course in each severall Church one after an other. To the intent after the preaching of the word by such a minister as shall be requested thereto by the Elders of the church where the Assembly is held, The rest of the day may be spent in publique Christian Conference about the discussing and resolveing of any such doubts and cases of conscience concerning matter of doctrine or worship or government of the church as shall be propounded by any of the Breetheren of that church, will leave also to any other Brother to propound his objections or answeres for further satisfaction according to the word of god. Provided that the whole action be guided and moderated by the Elders of the Church where the Assemblie is helde, or by such others as they shall appoint. And that no thing be concluded and imposed by way of Authoritie from one or more churches upon an other, but onely by way of Brotherly conference and consultations. That the trueth may be searched out to the satisfying of every mans conscience in the sight of god according his worde. And because such an Assembly and the worke theirof can not be duely attended to if other lectures be held in the same weeke. It is therefore agreed with the consent of the Churches. That in that weeke when such an Assembly is held, All the lectures in all the neighbouring Churches for that weeke shall be forborne. That so the publique service of Christ in this more solemne Assembly may be transacted with greater deligence and attention.

96. Howsoever these above specified rites, freedomes Immunities, Authorites and priveledges, both Civill and Ecclesiastical are expressed onely under the name and title of Liberties, and not in the exact forme of Laws or Statutes, yet we do with one consent fullie Authorise, and earnestly intreate all that are and shall be in Authoritie to consider them as laws, and not to faile to inflict condigne and proportionable punishments upon every man impartiallie, that shall infringe or violate any of them.

97. Wee likewise give full power and libertie to any person that shall at any time be denyed or deprived of any of them, to commence and prosecute their suite, Complaint or action against any man that shall so doe in any Court that hath proper Cognizance or judicature thereof.

98. Lastly because our dutie and desire is to do nothing suddainlie which fundamentally concerne us, we decree that these rites and liberties, shall be Audably read and deliberately weighed at every Generall Court that shall be held, within three yeares next insueing, And such of them as shall not be altered or repealed they shall stand so ratified, That no man shall infringe them without due punishment.

And if any Generall Court within these next thre yeares shall faile or forget to reade and consider them as abovesaid. The Governor and Deputy Governor for the time being, and every Assistant present at such Courts, shall forfeite 20sh. a man, and everie Deputie 10sh. a man for each neglect, which shall be paid out of their proper estate, and not by the Country or the Townes which choose them, and whensoever there shall arise any question in any Court amonge the Assistants and Associates thereof about the explanation of these Rites and liberties, The Generall Court onely shall have power to interprett them.

APPENDIX B

THE ATTORNEY'S OATH

THE long arm of tradition in the administration of justice is exemplified in the form of the oath required of attorneys who practiced in the courts. Compare, for example, the wording of the oaths of the earlier centuries with that in use today.

a) The first known attorney's oath, Benton[1] maintained, was in existence as early as 1246 and was doubtless in use from the time of the Act of Henry IV in 1402:

> You shall doe noe Falshood nor consent to anie to be done in the office of Pleas of this Courte wherein you are admitted Attorney. And if you shall knowe of anie to be done you shall give Knowledge thereof to the Lord Chiefe Baron or other his Brethren that it may be reformed You shall delay noe man for Lucre Gaine or Malice you shall increase noe Fee but you shall be contented with the old Fee accustomed. And further you shall use your selfe in the office of Attorney in the said office of Pleas in this Courte according to your best Learninge and Discretion. So helpe you God.

b) The first known attorney's oath in Massachusetts. During the intercharter period (1684–1691) in the administration of Joseph Dudley, the record of proceedings on July 26, 1686, states:

> *Ordered* That the Oath following be administered to the Attourneyes before they be admitted Attourneyes in Court:
>
> You shall do no falshood nor deceit nor consent to any to be done in this Court, and if you know of any to be done, you shall give knowledge thereof to the Judge of this Court for the time being or some other of his Majesties Councill or Assistants of this Court, that it may be reformed; you shall delay no Man for lucre or malice; you shall encrease no Fees but be contented with such Fees as are by order of Councill or the Judge of this Court allowed you, or that may be allowed you in time to come. You shall plead no Plea, nor sue any Suits unlawfully to hurt any Man, but such as shall stand with Order of the Law and your Conscience, you shall not wittingly or willingly sue, nor procure to be sued any falce Suite, nor give aid, or consent to the same on paine of being expulsed from the Court for ever, and further you shall use and demean you selfe in your Office of an Attorny within the Court according to your Learning and discretion. *So help you God.*[2]

c) The second form of the attorney's oath was drawn by the General Court of the Province of Massachusetts Bay (1702):

> You shall do no falsehood nor consent to any to be done in the court, and if you know of any to be done you shall give knowledge thereof to the justices of the court, or some of them, that it may be reformed. You shall not wittingly and willingly promote, sue or procure to be sued any false or unlawful suit, nor give aid or consent to the same, You shall delay no man for lucre or malice, but you shall use yourselfe in the office of an attorney within the court according to the best of your learning and discretion, and with all good fidelity as well to the court as to your clients. So help you God.[3]

d) The attorney's oath in the Commonwealth of Massachusetts today:

> I, (repeat the name) solemnly swear that I will do no falsehood, nor consent to the doing of any in court; I will not wittingly or willingly promote or sue any false, groundless or unlawful suit, nor give aid or consent to the same; I will delay no man for lucre or malice; but I will conduct myself in the office of an attorney within the courts according to the best of my knowledge and discretion, and with all good fidelity as well to the courts as my clients. So help me God.[4]

APPENDIX C

A COMPARISON OF THE CIVIL RIGHTS AND LIBERTIES OF THE MASSACHUSETTS BAY COLONY WITH THOSE OF THE COMMONWEALTH OF MASSACHUSETTS TODAY

Civil Rights and Liberties in the Massachusetts Bay Colony	*Civil Rights and Liberties Today*
The Purpose of Government	
"The free fruition of such liberties Immunities and priveledges as humanitie, Civilitie, and Christianite call for as due to every man in his place and proportion without impeachment and Infringement hath ever bene and ever will be the *tranquillitie* and Stabilitie of Churches and Commonwealths. And the deniall or deprivall thereof, the disturbance if not the ruine of both."—*Preamble to the Body of Liberties.*	"We the people of the United States, in order to form a more perfect union, establish justice, insure domestic *tranquility,* provide for the common defence, promote the general welfare, and secure the blessings of liberty to ourselves and our posterity, do ordain and establish this Constitution for the United States of America."—*Preamble to the Federal Constitution.* "The end of the institution, maintenance and administration of government, is to secure the existence of the body-politic, to protect it, and to furnish the individuals who compose it, with the power of enjoying in safety and *tranquility,* their natural rights, and the blessings of life."—*Preamble to Commonwealth Constitution.*
Due Process	
No one was to be punished except in accordance with the "expresse law of the Country" (which, in effect, was to say without "due process of law"), or, if no law had been enacted on a given case, then by	No one is to be punished "without due process of law."—*Federal Constitution, 5th Amendment.* No *state* shall "deprive any person of life, liberty or property, with-

"the word of God."—*Body of Liberties, Art. 1.*

out due process of law."—*Federal Constitution, 14th Amendment.*[1]

Equal Protection of the Laws

Every resident of the Bay Colony (freemen, nonfreemen, and foreigners) was to "enjoy the same justice and law . . . without partialitie or delay."—*Body of Liberties, Art. 2.*

No *state* shall "deny to any person within its jurisdiction the equal protection of the laws."—*Federal Constitution, 14th Amendment.*

"All men are born free and equal, and have certain natural, essential, and unalienable rights. . . ." —*Commonwealth Constitution, Part 1, Art. 1*

No Torture, nor Cruel and Inhumane Punishment

No torture to extract a confession except in capital cases after conviction where there were confederates, but, in any case, no tortures that were "barbarous and inhumane."—*Body of Liberties, Art.* 45.

No "cruel and unusual punishments [shall be] inflicted."—*Federal Constitution, 8th Amendment*

"No magistrate or court of law, shall . . . inflict cruel or unusual punishments." — *Commonwealth Constitution, Part 1, Art 26.*

A Right to Bail

With certain expressed exceptions, no one was to be imprisoned before sentence if he could furnish bail.—*Body of Liberties, Art. 18.*

"Excessive bail [which would, in effect, be the denial of bail] shall not be required."—*Federal Constitution, 8th Amendment.*

"No magistrate or court of law shall demand excessive bail or sureties."—*Commonwealth Constitution, Part 1, Art 26.*

Double Jeopardy

No one was to be twice sentenced for the same crime.—*Body of Liberties, Art. 42.*

No one "for the same offence to be twice put in jeopardy of life or limb. . . ."—*Federal Constitution, 5th Amendment.*

As the federal amendment applied only in federal courts and as the Massachusetts Constitution was silent on this point, the General Court in 1836 enacted this law (still in effect): "A person shall not be held to answer on a second indictment or complaint for a crime of which he has been acquitted upon the facts and merits. . . ."—*Massachusetts General Laws (tercentenary edition) ch. 263, sec. 7.*

Speedy Trials

Criminal cases were, if possible, to be heard "at the next Court."—*Body of Liberties, Art. 41.*

"In all criminal prosecutions, the accused shall enjoy the right to a speedy and public trial. . . ."—*Federal Constitution, 6th Amendment.*

Recognizing the principle that justice delayed is justice denied, the General Court has enacted laws to assure speedy indictments and trials. —*Massachusetts General Laws, ch. 277, sec. 15, sec. 72; ch. 212, sec. 24.*

Right to Jury Trial

In criminal trials, one could choose whether he were to be tried by the bench or by the jury.—*Body of Liberties, Art. 29.*

"In all criminal prosecutions," the accused shall have a right to be tried "by an impartial jury of the state and district wherein the crime shall have been committed. . . ."—*Federal Constitution, 6th Amendment.*[2]

". . . the legislature shall not make any law, that shall subject any person to a capital or infamous punishment, excepting for the government of the army and navy, without trial by jury."—*Commonwealth Constitution, Part 1, Art. 12.* The accused may waive his right to a jury trial, except in capital cases, if he chooses to do so.—*Jones* v. *Robbins,* 8 Gray 329 (1857).[3]

Right to Challenge Jurymen

Challenges of individual jurymen were permitted in criminal cases if the judge found the challenges to be "just and reasonable."—*Body of Liberties, Art. 30.*

Any number of challenges are permitted in our federal and state courts "for cause" (such as having some relationship to the accused, an interest in the case, expressed bias, etc.) but the defendant is also allowed a certain number of "peremptory" challenges without disclosing his reasons—three in Massachusetts in criminal trials (except in murder trials where the number allowed is twelve). In federal courts, the allowance is slightly more liberal.—*Rule 24 of the Rules of Criminal Procedure for U.S. District Courts; Massachusetts General Laws, ch. 234, sec. 28 and 29.*

Two Witnesses Required in Certain Cases

In capital cases, at least two witnesses, or that which might be considered equivalent thereto, were required for conviction, a rule taken from the Bible.—*Body of Liberties, Art. 47.*

"No persons shall be convicted of Treason unless on the Testimony of two Witnesses to the same overt Act, or on Confession in open Court."—*Federal Constitution, Art. 3, sec. 3.*

"No person shall be convicted of treason except by the testimony of two witnesses to the same overt act . . . unless he confesses the same in open court."—*Massachusetts General Laws, ch. 264, sec. 4.*

No Hasty Executions

No one could be executed within four days after sentence, with certain exceptions.—*Body of Liberties, Art. 44.*

There is no specific constitutional provision on this point, but Massachusetts law provides that no execution can take place earlier than twenty days after notification of the sentence is sent to the Superintendent of the State Prison. Usually appeals consume at least a year's time and frequently much more. — *Massachusetts General Laws, ch. 279, sec. 45.*[4]

Imprisonment for Debt or Fine

The Bay Colony law, liberal in nature (far more so than contemporary laws in England regulating creditor-debtor relationships), did not demand imprisonment for debt or fine if other means of satisfaction could be found (such as a property levy or satisfaction by labor for the creditor or payment in corn or other produce). The Bay Colony law was humanely administered in civil proceedings but, more frequently than English laws, called for imprisonment in criminal prosecutions.—*Body of Liberties, Art 33.*

Probably few problems in the administration of criminal justice in eighteenth and nineteenth century Massachusetts prompted so much legislation as that of imprisonment for debt. Laws of the Province and of the early Commonwealth governments were designed to prevent undue hardship for debtors, as well as fraud upon creditors; to keep debtors in the prisons segregated from criminals;[5] and to allow debtors' release upon taking a debtor's oath (claiming inability to pay).

The common practice of throwing debtors into jail because they could not pay their creditors continued down to the middle of the nineteenth century. Modern laws have dispensed with the debtor's oath in civil cases and now provide for a careful examination into his ability to pay, in the nature of an equity proceeding by the courts.[6] —*Massachusetts General Laws, ch. 224.*

Nevertheless, one may be imprisoned for nonpayment of a fine or a tax and credited with one dollar for each day of confinement.—*Massachusetts General Laws, ch. 127, sec. 144–146; ch. 224, sec. 28.*

Right to a Pardon

Only the General Court could grant a pardon but, if the Court was not in session the Governor, with the consent of the Deputy Governor or any three Assistants, could grant a reprieve until the next session of the General Court. —*Body of Liberties, Art. 72.*

In the federal administration of criminal justice, the President of the United States alone may grant an absolute or conditional pardon or a commutation of sentence for all offenses against the United States (except in cases of impeachment).

The Commonwealth Constitution places the pardoning power in the hands of the Governor who, with the consent of the Executive Council, can pardon any prisoner in any penal or correctional institution at any time, upon the written petition of the prisoner. This authority extends to pardons after conviction but before sentence, to commutations of sentences, and to absolute or conditional releases.—*Commonwealth Constitution, Art. 73 of the Amendments; Massachusetts General Laws, ch. 127, sec. 152–154.*

Right to Appeal

Appeals from the lower to the higher courts and eventually to the

Appeals can be made on constitutional grounds from any inferior

General Court were common, but no appeals to the courts of England or to Parliament were allowed.—*Body of Liberties, Art. 36.*

court in the federal judiciary to the one Supreme Court of the United States in accordance with procedures determined by Congress.—*Federal Constitution, Art. 3, sec. 2 and federal statutes.*

Persons convicted in Massachusetts courts (the District and Municipal courts and the Boston Juvenile Court) have a right of appeal to the Superior Court and thence to the Supreme Judicial Court and in certain cases (where an interpretation of the United States Constitution is required for a correct decision), to the United States Supreme Court.

Right to Counsel

In the early days of Colonial government one could be represented in court by counsel provided the counsel charged no fee. When in the course of time professional lawyers acquired some status, this condition was removed, but an indigent defendant had no right to demand legal representation.—*Body of Liberties, Art. 26.*

In all criminal prosecutions in the federal courts, the accused shall "have the assistance of counsel for his defence."—*Federal Constitution, 6th Amendment.*

In Massachusetts courts, the accused shall be "fully heard in his defence by himself, or his counsel, at his election."—*Commonwealth Constitution, Part 1, Art. 12.*

Neither of the above constitutional provisions made clear the right of an indigent defendant to demand the appointment of an attorney for his defense to be paid out of public funds, although federal courts have liberally construed the 6th Amendment in his favor. However, since the case of *Gideon* v. *Wainwright* (1963) it is evident that the 14th Amendment of the Federal Constitution guaranteeing "due process of law" to "any person," combined with the 6th Amendment, applies also to state trials. Hence in any criminal case (with some vagueness as to the application of the principle to minor misdemeanors) tried in federal or state courts, a defendant must be allowed counsel, if not at his own expense, then at the expense of the government.—*Gideon* v. *Wainwright, 372 U.S. 335 and Rule 10 of the Supreme Judicial Court of Massachusetts.*

Lapse of Time as a Defense

The Colonial rule required that, if one were to be prosecuted for a minor crime, proceedings would have to be commenced within one year. There was no time limitation, however, on capital or other serious crimes. — *Massachusetts Bay Colony Law of 1652.*

Federal criminal law and the statutes of the Commonwealth of Massachusetts also permit no restrictions of time on prosecutions for murder or other capital crimes. In federal proceedings, there is a five-year limitation on noncapital crimes and in the Commonwealth a six-year limitation for most serious crimes, but a ten-year limitation on crimes involving armed robbery, armed assault with intent to rob or murder, and the like, and a twelve- or eighteen-month limitation on certain specified minor crimes.—*U.S. Code, Title 18, sec. 3281-3282; Massachusetts General Laws, ch. 277, sec. 63; ch. 272; sec. 11; ch. 271, sec. 1.*

Some of the civil rights and liberties enumerated in Chapter 4 have not been specifically mentioned in this Appendix: 1) In Chapter 13 appears further discussion of the subject of criminal responsibility. 2) Slavery and involuntary servitude, not extensive in Colonial Massachusetts and yet not uncommon, were abolished in Massachusetts in 1788 and in the nation by the 13th Amendment to the Federal Constitution, ratified in 1865. 3) Cruel and abusive treatment of servants that the Colonial authorities sought to prevent would be punishable today in the same manner as such treatment of any person by another, since class distinctions ceased to be recognized by law upon the adoption of the Commonwealth Constitution. 4) The fundamental principles of the right of self defense and the presumption of innocence were and are still characteristic of English and American law.

APPENDIX D

THE FORM OF INDICTMENTS

IN the Massachusetts Bay Colony, indictments were usually concise, direct, and specific (in constrast to the verbose forms used in the nineteenth century) and brought in the Devil as a sort of codefendant. The indictment of Abigaile was typical:

> Abigaile Johnson now resident in Boston being presented by the Grand Jury & was Indicted by the name of Abigaile Johnson for that she not having the feare of God before hir eyes & being Instigated by the Divill did in or upon the one & thirtieth day of January last in the night being found in bed with Darby Bryan comitt the act of Adultery with him Contrary to the peace of our Soveraigne Lord the King his Crowne & dignity the lawes of God & of this Jurisdiction. . . .[1]

A typical witchcraft indictment was that of George Burroughs in 1692:

> The Jurors for our sovereign Lord and Lady the King and Queen, present, that George Burroughs, late of Falmouth in the Province of Massachusets bay, clerk, the ninth day of May, in the fourth year of the reign of our sovereign Lord and Lady William and Mary, by the grace of God of England, Scotland, France and Ireland, King and Queen, defenders of the faith, etc. and divers other days and times, as well before as after, certain detestable arts called withcrafts and sorceries, wickedly and feloniously hath used, practised and exercised, at and within the town of Salem, in the county of Essex aforesaid, in, upon and against one Mary Walcot of Salem village in the county of Essex, single woman; by which said wicked arts, the said Mary Walcot, the ninth day of May, in the fourth year above said, and divers other days and times as well before as after, was and is tortured, afflicted, pined, consumed, wasted and tormented, against the peace of our sovereign Lord and Lady the King and Queen, and against the form of the statute in that case made and provided. Endorsed *Billa vera*.[2]

Indictments in the nineteenth century lost their Puritan simplicity. When appellate courts were reversing convictions because of some technical fault in the indictment those who drafted those documents were careful to omit no detail, in utter disregard of redundancy or syntax. The indictment in Comm. v. Costley (118 Mass. 1, [1875]) for example, took 324 words to say that Costley intentionally "with malice aforethought" shot and killed Julia Hawks. James H. Costley was indicted for murder, in one count, as follows:

> The jurors for the Commonwealth of Massachusetts on their oath present, that James H. Costley, late of Hanover in the county of Plymouth, on the thirteenth day of May in the year of our Lord one thousand eight hundred and seventy-four, at Braintree in the county of Norfolk aforesaid, with force and arms in and upon one Julia Hawks, feloniously, wilfully, and of his malice aforethought, did make an assault; and that the said James H. Costley a certain pistol, then and there charged with gunpowder and one leaden bullet, then and there feloniously, wilfully, and of his malice aforethought, did discharge and shoot off to, against and upon the said Julia Hawks; and that the said James H. Costley, with the leaden bullet aforesaid, out of the pistol aforesaid, then and there by the force of the gunpowder aforesaid, by the said James H. Costley discharged and shot off as aforesaid, then and there feloniously, wilfully, and of his malice aforethought, did strike, penetrate and wound the said Julia Hawks in and upon the left side of the head of the said Julia Hawks; giving to the said Julia Hawks then and there, with the leaden bullet aforesaid, so as aforesaid discharged and shot off out of the pistol aforesaid, by the said James H. Costley, in and upon the left side of the head of the said Julia Hawks, one mortal wound of the depth of six inches and of the breadth of half an inch; of which said mortal wound the said Julia Hawks then and there instantly died. And so the jurors aforesaid, on their oath aforesaid, do say that the said James H. Costley, her, the said Julia Hawks, in the manner and by the means aforesaid, feloniously, wilfully, and of his malice aforethought, did kill and murder; against the peace of said Commonwealth, and contrary to the form of the statute in such case made and provided.

Costley's lawyer appealed his conviction. One ground of the appeal was that the indictment was defective as it had not stated that the pistol that Costley "did discharge and shoot off" was held in his hand. The brief cited English precedents, going back to the time of Queen Elizabeth. The Chief Justice of the Supreme Judicial Court held, nevertheless, that the omission was not material.

About twenty–five years later the General Court decided to return to the simple, straightforward style of Colonial times. It enacted a law that is still in operation, providing that indictments will not be considered defective merely because of some technical omission so long as the defendant is able to "understand the charge and to prepare his defense."[3] An indictment for murder by shooting is sufficient today if it merely states that "A.B. did assault C.D. with a gun, with intent to murder him by shooting him in the head and by such assault did kill and murder C.D."[4]

APPENDIX E

OATH OF A JURYMAN

Oath of a juryman in a noncapital case

In the Massachusetts Bay Colony[1]

You swear by the Living God, that in the Cause or Causes now legally to be committed to you by this Court; You will true Tryal make, and just Verdict give therein, according to the Evidence given you, and the Laws of this Jurisdiction: So help you God, etc.

In the Commonwealth Today[2]

You shall well and truly try the issue between the commonwealth and the defendant, (or the defendants, as the case may be,) according to your evidence; so help you God.

Oath of a juryman in a capital case

You Do Swear by the Great Name of Almighty God; that you will well and truely try, and true deliverance make of such Prisoners at the Bar, as you shall have in charge, according to your Evidence: So help you God, etc.

You shall well and truly try, and true deliverance make, between the commonwealth and the prisoner at the bar, whom you shall have in charge, according to your evidence; so help you God.

NOTES

LIST OF ABBREVIATIONS USED IN NOTES

Bradford's *History*

Governor William Bradford's *Of Plimoth Plantation,* printed under the direction of the Secretary of the Commonwealth by order of the General Court, with a report of the proceedings incident to the return of the manuscript to Massachusetts (Wright & Potter Printing Co., Boston, 1898).

Col. Laws (1648)

The Book of the General Lawes and Libertyes Concerning the Inhabitants of the Massachusets, printed according to order of the General Court, Cambridge, 1648, reprinted from the copy in the Henry E. Huntington Library, with an Introduction by Max Farrand, (Harvard University Press, Cambridge, 1929).

Col. Laws (1660)

The Book of the General Lawes and Libertyes Concerning the Inhabitants of the Massachusets, printed according to order of the General Court, Cambridge, 1660, reprinted, with supplements to 1672 and with the Body of Liberties of 1641, with introduction by William H. Whitmore, by order of the City Council (Boston, 1889).

Col. Laws (1672)

The General Laws and Liberties of the Massachusets Colony, printed by order of the General Court, Cambridge, 1672, reprinted with supplements through 1686 with an introduction by William H. Whitmore, by order of the City Council (Boston, 1887).

Court of Assistants

Records of the Court of Assistants of the Colony of the Massachusetts Bay, 1630–1692, published by the County of Suffolk; v. 1 and v. 2 edited by John Noble, clerk of the Supreme Judicial Court, in 1901 and 1904; v. 3 edited by John F. Cronin, clerk of the Supreme Judicial Court, 1928.

Essex County Court

Records and Files of the Quarterly Courts of Essex County, Massachusetts (1636–1683) (published by The Essex Institute, Salem, Mass., 1911–1921, 8 volumes, George F. Dow, editor).

Hutchinson's *History*

The History of the Colony of Massachusetts Bay, from 1628 to 1691, by William Hutchinson, Lieutenant Governor of the Massachusetts Province (and later Chief Justice and Governor), v. 1, ed. 2, (London, 1765) v. 2 and v. 3, entitled *The History of the Province of Massachusetts Bay from 1691 to 1774* (published in London in 1768 and 1828).

Hutchinson Papers

The Hutchinson Papers, 2 volumes, edited by William H. Whitmore and William S. Appleton (published by The Prince Society, Munsell, Albany, New York, 1865).

MCR

Massachusetts Colonial Records. *Records of the Governor and Company of the Massachusetts Bay in New England,* 6 volumes, (1628–1686), Dr. Nathaniel B. Shurtleff, editor (published by order of the General Court; from the Press of William White, Printer to the Commonwealth, Boston, 1853–1854).

PCR

Plymouth Colonial Records. *Records of the Colony of New Plymouth in New England, 1633–1691.* Dr. Nathaniel B. Shurtleff edited v. 1 through v. 6 (Court Orders, 1633–1691); v. 7 (Judicial Acts, 1636–1692); and v. 8 (Miscellaneous Records, 1633–1689). David Pulsifer edited v. 9 and v. 10 (Acts of the Commissioners of the United Colonies of New England, 1643–1679); v. 11 (Laws, 1623–1682) and v. 12 (Deeds, etc., 1620–1651). (Published by order of the General Court, William White, Printer to the Commonwealth, 1855–1861).

Plym. Laws

The Compact with the Charter and Laws of the Colony of New Plymouth, published, with other documents relating to Plymouth Colony, by order of the General Court, under the supervision of William Brigham (Dutton and Wentworth, Printers to the State, Boston, 1836).

Prov. Laws

Acts and Resolves of the Province of Massachusetts Bay, v. 1 through v. 5 (1692–1780). Volumes 6 through 21 constitute an Appendix, containing both public and private acts for the same period. (Published by order of the General Court, Wright and Potter, Printers to the State, Boston, 1869–1922).

Sewall's *Diary*

The Diary of Samuel Sewall, 1674–1729 (published as v. 5, 6, and 7 of the 5th series of the *Collections of the Massachusetts Historical Society,* Boston, 1878).

Suffolk County Court

Records of the Suffolk County Court, 1671–1680 (published as v. 29 and v. 30 of the *Collections of the Colonial Society of Massachusetts)* with an introduction by Zechariah Chafee, Jr. (Boston, 1933).

Winthrop's *History*

James Savage, President of the Massachusetts Historical Society, edited the manuscript "Journal" (1630–1644) of John Winthrop, calling it *The History of New England from 1630 to 1649 by John Winthrop, Esq., the first Governour of the Colony of Massachusetts Bay* (Little Brown and Company, Boston, 1853).

Winthrop Papers

Winthrop Papers, v. 1 to v. 5 (1498–1649) (published by the Massachusetts Historical Society, Boston, 1929–1947).

NOTES

PROLOGUE

1. "Silly" had a different connotation in the sixteenth and seventeenth centuries than it has today. From the German *selig* (blessed), it came to mean "happy" or "innocent." "Silly sheep" was a not uncommon expression. A "silly bee" was a creature without learning or sophistication, yet capable of great accomplishments for his "commonwealth."

This work by Captain John Smith (1579–1631) was published in London in 1616. Other books by Captain Smith were: *A True Relation of such occurrences and accidents of noate as hath hapned in Virginia . . .* (London, 1608); *A Map of Virginia with a Description of the Countrey, the Commodities, People, Government and Religion . . .* (Oxford, 1612); *New England Trials Declaring the successe of 26. Ships employed thither within these sixe yeares . . .* (London, 1620); *The Generall Historie of Virginia, New England, & the Summer Isles* in 6 parts (London, 1624); *An Accidence or the Path-Way to Experience, Necessary for all Young Seamen . . .*—the first book published in England on seamanship, navigation, and naval gunnery (London, 1626); *The True Travels, Adventures, and Observations of Captaine John Smith, in Europe, Asia, Africke, and America, beginning about the yeere 1593 and continued to this present 1629 . . .* (London, 1630); and *Advertisements For the unexperienced Planters of* New England, *or any where. Or the Pathway to experience to erect a Plantation . . .* (London, 1631). Edward Arber has included reprintings of most of Smith's writings in *The English Scholar's Library* (No. 16), London, 1878-1884.

2. From Book 4 of *The Generall Historie.* (See note 1.)

3. Smith had been a soldier from the early age of fifteen or sixteen and had visited many foreign countries. At the age of twenty-three, he was Captain of Cavalry in the service of the Duke of Transylvania, Wallachia, and Moldavia in the wars of Hungary. He claimed that in single combat he had cut off with his sword the heads of three Turks. Henceforth he adopted the "Three Turks' Heads" on his shield, which appears on some of his books and maps. For a well documented biography of Smith and a defense of his claims see Philip L. Barbour, *The Three Worlds of Captain John Smith,* Houghton Mifflin Co., Boston, 1964.

4. From *Advertisements.* (See note 1.)

5. From *A Description.* (See note 1.)

6. See Smith's map of New England published in his *Advertisements.* (See note 1.)

7. From *An Accidence.* (See note 1.)

8. Smith narrates the story of this exploration in *A Description.* (See note 1.)

9. From *Advertisements.* (See note 1.) The first to call the land "New England," Smith placed it in relation to lands already explored:

New England is that part of *America* in the Ocean Sea [the Atlantic], opposite to Nova Albion [Albion was the ancient and poetical name for Great Britain and Nova Albion the name given to what is now California] in the South Sea [the Pacific], discovered by the most memorable Sir *Francis Drake* in his Voyage about the world, in regard whereof this is stiled *New England,* being in the same latitude. *New France* of it is Northwards, South-wards is *Virginia,* and all the adjoyning continent with new *Granado, new Spaine,* new *Andolosia* [Andalusia was an old province of Spain] and the *West-Indies.*—From *A Description,* (see note 1).

10. See p. 10.

11. From *A Description.* (See note 1.)

12. From *A Description.* (See note 1.)
13. From *A Description.* (See note 1.)
14. From *New England Trials.* (See note 1.)
15. From *Advertisements.* (See note 1.)
16. From *Advertisements.* (See note 1.)
17. From *New England Trials.* (See note 1.)
18. From *Advertisements.* (See note 1.)
19. From *A Description.* (See note 1.)
20. From *A Description.* (See note 1.)
21. From *The Generall Historie,* Book 5. (See note 1.)
22. From *A Description.* (See note 1.)
23. From *A Description.* (See note 1.)
24. From *Advertisements.* (See note 1.)
25. From *Advertisements.* (See note 1.)
26. From *Advertisements.* (See note 1.)
27. From *Advertisements.* (See note 1.)
28. From *The True Travels.* (See note 1.)
29. Published in London, 1589. Hakluyt (c. 1553-1616), a gifted scholar, at the age of thirty was acquainted with "the chiefest captaines at sea, the greatest merchants, and the best mariners" of England at that time. His first work *Divers Voyages touching the Discoverie of America* was published in 1582 when he was twenty-nine. During his lifetime he was considered an authority on the explorations and discoveries made by English mariners.
30. From *The Generall Historie,* Book 1 (See note 1). Gosnold (?–1607) also gave the name "Martha's Vineyard" to an island off the southern shore of Cape Cod. See *Mass. Hist. Soc. Proc.* v. 36, (1902), p. 247 f.
31. From *Advertisements.* (See note 1.)
32. From *Advertisements.* (See note 1.)
33. From *Advertisements.* (See note 1.)
34. For an analysis of the promotional literature of that period, see "The Colonial Impulse," by Howard Mumford Jones in *Proc. of the Amer. Philos. Soc.,* v. 90 (1946) pp. 131–161.

CHAPTER 1

1. From the Massachusetts General Court edition, published in 1898, of William Bradford's manuscript *Of Plimoth Plantation*—not only a delightfully frank revelation of the Pilgrim achievement, but the most authentic history of their settlement in New England, covering the narrative of their life in England, their journey to Holland, their Atlantic crossing, and the story of the Colony of New Plymouth down to 1647. Early historians (such as Prince, Hubbard, Cotton Mather, Hutchinson, and others) were familiar with this document, which was written between the years 1630 and 1650, but no complete copy had been made when it disappeared from sight after 1767. For nearly a century it was believed forever lost. In 1855 it turned up in the library of the Bishop of London in Fulham, England, where it had evidently been resting incognito. Upon its discovery, Charles Deane, realizing its great historical value, edited the first American publication of this document for the Massachusetts Historical Society—See *Mass. Hist. Soc. Coll.,* 4th ser., v. 3 (1856) pp. 19–23. In 1897 the Lord Bishop of London delivered it to the American ambassador, Thomas F. Bayard. In an impressive ceremony before the Senate and House of the Massachusetts General Court on May 26, 1897, it was returned to the Commonwealth and accepted by Governor Roger Wolcott. It can now be seen in the Massachusetts Archives museum. A number of other reprintings have been made from the original. The most recent and most completely annotated is that by Samuel Eliot Morison, *Of Plymouth Plantation, 1620–1647 by William*

Bradford, Sometime Governor thereof (Alfred A. Knopf, New York, 1952). Prior to the Morison edition, citations from Bradford were usually taken either from the Commonwealth edition used here or the later Mass. Hist. Soc. publication of 1912 in 2 volumes, edited by Worthington C. Ford, entitled *History of Plymouth Plantation, 1620-1647*.

2. The Pilgrims would have suffered fewer casualties if they had set sail in the month when the mayflower makes its appearance, rather than in September, but they were victims of circumstance, rather than of poor judgment. Three centuries later the Massachusetts General Court designated the mayflower (*Epigaea repens*) "the state flower or floral emblem of the Commonwealth" (ch. 181, Acts of 1918).

3. When the *Mayflower* left England, there were on board 102 passengers. Bradford did not report the number of men in the crew. Banks estimated that "the full roster of officers and crew numbered fifty"—Charles E. Banks in "The Officers and Crew of the Mayflower, 1620–1621," in *Mass. Hist. Soc. Proc.*, v. 60 (1926–1927), pp. 210–221. One passenger and one crew member died at sea. A son was born at sea to Steven and Elizabeth Hopkins and appropriately named "Oceanus." A son named "Peregrine" (meaning "pilgrim") was born to William and Susanna White, as the ship lay in Cape Cod Harbor (now Provincetown). Peregrine outlived all of the Pilgrims, dying in Marshfield at the age of 83. Four Pilgrims died as the ship lay in the harbor, including Dorothy, Bradford's wife, who fell overboard and drowned.

4. All of the passages quoted from William Bradford (1590–1657) in this chapter were taken from the Commonwealth edition of the Bradford manuscript referred to in note 1 above, unless otherwise stated. Bradford used the then current Julian or Old Style calendar, but his dates can be converted into the Gregorian or New Style by the addition of ten days.

5. Bradford's reference to the Scriptures was probably to Paul's Epistle to the Corinthians in I Cor. 12:28.

6. Samuel Eliot Morison in "The Pilgrim Fathers, their Significance in History" in *Col. Soc. of Amer. Trans.*, v. 38 (1947–1951) pp. 387–413.

7. Reports had been circulated in England of the near disaster in Virginia and of the dangers of travelling on the high seas where French or Spanish privateers might put a sudden end to a long voyage. The Pilgrims were not pioneers in the sense of travellers to a new and unexplored country. There was no doubt that many explorers with high hopes met with "lamentable misseries," as Bradford put it. Anyone undertaking the transatlantic voyage took a calculated risk.

8. This patent, called the first Peirce patent, has been lost; hence the territorial limits of what might have been the new colony in the vicinity of what is now New York City are unknown. A second Peirce patent was issued by the "Council established [in November, 1620] at Plymouth [England] in the County of Devon for the planting, ruling, ordering and governing of New England in America," the Council when first organized not knowing the Pilgrims had failed to reach "northern Virginia." When Peirce, in whose name the patent was issued in June 1621, heard that the Pilgrims were "hopefully seated" in New England, he managed to substitute another, making himself "cheefe Lord" over that territory. This scheme might have had tragic consequences for the Pilgrims, but "the Lord Marvelously crost him." An "extraime tempest" beset him, Bradford tells us, when he was halfway across the Atlantic and ended his aspirations, causing him to return to England. He surrendered his rights, and the original patent was restored. This patent which did not set out any specific boundaries (for the Council had little knowledge of the geography of the country) is in the Registry of Deeds in Plymouth, Massachusetts. It has been printed, with comments by Charles Deane, in *Mass. Hist. Soc. Coll.* v. 2 (1854) 4th ser., pp. 158–163. In 1630 the Council issued another patent, signed by the Earl of Warwick (now known as the Warwick patent) to William Bradford who thereupon could have become "cheefe Lord," but in 1640 he chose to assign it to the freemen of the Colony. It granted rights to

all of Cape Cod, some land on the Kennebec River (now in the state of Maine) and all of the land around the town of Plymouth extending as far north as the Cohasset River and south to the Narragansett River. Although the Colony did not receive a grant under the royal seal (as did the Massachusetts Bay Colony) an orderly government would probably have survived the claims of various entrepreneurs without any charter or patent at all. However, as stated in a letter from England, the purpose of the Warwick patent was "to make you a corporation, and so to inable you to make & execute lawes," thus setting a legal basis for this self-governing Colony. This patent may be seen in Massachusetts Archives museum. Although the Pilgrims were the first to establish a government seated at Plymouth, there had been at least forty recorded voyages to New England prior to the sailing of the *Mayflower*—see *Prologue to New England* by Henry F. Howe (Farrar & Rinehart, New York, 1943) .

9. Most historians do not credit Nathaniel Morton's story as told in his "New England's Memoriall," published in Cambridge, Mass. (1669). Although the selection of Plymouth for a settlement was unplanned, once it became a reality, it seemed to have been taken for granted. Here, certainly, was a place they knew something about from Captain Smith's writings. After they dropped anchor in the snug harbor of Cape Cod [Provincetown] no one suggested they try to make Hudson's River that winter. The London adventurers must have assumed for many months that the Pilgrims were at their planned destination *if* they had crossed the ocean successfully. Williston states: "When word came at length of the Pilgrims' whereabouts, far from their announced destination, Weston and his partners evinced no slightest surprise. Nor did the Pilgrims ever offer them an explanation"—George F. Williston in *Saints and Strangers* (Reynal & Hitchcock, New York, 1945) p. 146.

10. The original document has been lost, but the copy in Bradford's history is probably an accurate transcription of the "combination."

11. Governors were elected annually. Bradford was Governor almost continuously until his death in 1657, having served thirty terms. "To no one among the original Pilgrims," writes Morison, "did the Colony owe so much as to Bradford; and of America's colonial founders, only John Winthrop, William Penn, Captain John Smith, and Lord Baltimore can be mentioned in the same breath"—Samuel Eliot Morison, *The Story of the "Old Colony" of New Plymouth, 1620–1692* (Alfred A. Knopf, New York, 1960) .

CHAPTER 2

1. From "A Modell of Christian Charity" written by Governor John Winthrop on board the *Arbella* in 1630. Published in *Winthrop Papers,* v. 2, pp. 282-295.

2. In October 1629 John Winthrop (1588–1649) succeeded Mathew Cradock who was the first Governor of the Massachusetts Bay Company in England, having been elected in March of that year. Cradock chose to remain in England; hence when Winthrop arrived in America in June 1630 with the Charter in his personal possession, he became the first Governor of the Massachusetts Bay Colony.

3. Unless otherwise stated, quotations from Winthrop's writings in this chapter were taken from the first year of his *Journal* (1630–1649) as published by the Mass. Hist. Soc. in *The Founding of Massachusetts,* (Boston, 1930) . Quotations from Winthrop's subsequent entries in his *Journal* were taken from the James Savage edition.

4. *Winthrop Papers,* v. 2, p. 278 (See note 1.)

5. Although Sir Richard Saltonstall lost out on the governorship, a direct descendant of this illustrious gentleman was elected Governor of the Commonwealth of Massachusetts in 1938. Leverett Saltonstall went on from the Governor's office (1939-1944) to represent his state in the United States Senate (1944-1966).

6. See *The Winthrop Fleet of 1630; An Account of the Vessels, the Voyage,*

the Passengers and their English Homes from Original Authorities by Charles E. Banks (Houghton Mifflin Company, Boston, 1930).

7. See *Governor Winthrop's Course Across the Atlantic* by Horace E. Ware (University Press, Cambridge, 1909).

8. *Winthrop Papers,* v. 2, p. 302.

9. The "Dorchester [England] Adventurers" had set up a little trading and fishing post in 1623 near what is now Gloucester. In 1625 Roger Conant and John Leyford had come from Plymouth to join them. In 1626 some of them moved to Naumkeag (Salem) where Captain John Endecott (1589–1665) joined them in 1628. They were barely able to exist during the severe winter of 1628–1629, but they had the assistance of Samuel Fuller, a physician, who had come up from Plymouth. Taking time out from his medical duties, the good doctor took advantage of the opportunity to persuade some of the Anglicans to adopt the congregational form of church discipline. Endecott was made Governor by a vote of the General Court in London on April 30, 1629, (MCR, v. 1, p. 361), but Winthrop on his arrival on June 12, 1630, took over the command. However, Endecott was later elected Governor of the Bay Colony many times and became one of its most prominent citizens. See "John Endecott and John Winthrop" by William C. Endicott in *Mass. Hist. Soc. Proc.,* v. 64 (1930–1932) pp. 3–26. The Indian name Naumkeag or Nahum Keike was replaced by "Salem," from the Hebrew "Shalom," meaning "peaceful."

10. From Winthrop's first letter to his wife after his arrival in New England, dated July 16, 1630.—*Winthrop Papers,* v. 2, p. 302.

11. *Winthrop Papers,* v. 2, p. 313.

12. Charles E. Banks is not entirely in agreement with this opinion. See his *The Planters of the Commonwealth* (Houghton Mifflin Company, Boston, 1930) and the review of his book by G. Andrews Moriarty in *New Eng. Q.,* v. 4 (1931) pp. 346–347.

13. MCR, v. 1, p. 91 (1631).

14. Rev. Francis Higgeson's (1617–1670) *New-Englands Plantation, or a Short and True Description of the Commodities and Discommodities of that Countrey* (London, 1630).

15. Robert C. Winthrop's chapter: "Boston Founded" in v. 1 of *The Memorial History of Boston,* Justin Winsor, editor (Ticknor & Co., Boston, 1880).

16. Edward Johnson's (1598–1672) *Wonder-Working Providence of Sions Saviour in New England* (London, 1658).

17. From the early records of Charlestown as quoted by Robert C. Winthrop in *Boston Founded.* (See note 15.)

18. MCR, v. 1, p. 75 (1630).

19. MCR, v. 1, p. 101 (1632).

20. See Winthrop's discourse on reformation without the necessity for complete separation: "Reasons to prove a necessitye of reformation from the Corruptions of Antechrist which hath defiled the Christian Churches, and yet without absolute separation from them, as if they were no Churches of Christ"—*Winthrop Papers,* v. 3, pp. 10–14.

21. Winthrop's "Modell of Christian Charity." (See note 1.)

22. From the constitution of the New England Confederation, May 19, 1643, Bradford's *History,* p. 496.

23. See "'Persecution' as a Factor in Emigration to New England, 1630–1640," by Charles E. Banks in *Mass. Hist. Soc. Proc.,* v. 63 (1929–1930) pp. 136–154, with comments by Samuel E. Morison. For the Puritans' ideas on reform of the Church of England see chapter one of Edmund S. Morgan *Visible Saints,* (New York University Press, New York, 1963).

24. Nellis M. Crouse, "The Causes of the Great Migration, 1630–1640" in *New Eng. Q.,* v. 5 (1932) pp. 3–36.

25. *The Planters Plea: or the Grounds of Plantations Examined and usuall Objections Answered,* (London, 1630).

26. See Prologue.

27. Higgeson's "New-Englands Plantation." (See note 14.)

28. MCR, v. 1, p. 10 (1629) .

29. MCR, v. 4, pt. 2, p. 25 (1661) .

30. Winthrop's *History,* v. 1, p. 364.

31. See "The Massachusetts and New Hampshire Boundary Line Controversy, 1693–1740" by Jonathan Smith, in *Mass. Hist. Soc. Proc.,* v. 43 (1909–1910) , pp. 77–88.

32. Smith's *Advertisements.* (See note 1, Prologue) .

33. See "The Royal Charter, or Patent, of the Colony of the Massachusetts Bay" in *The Founding of Massachusetts* (Mass. Hist. Soc., Boston, 1930) .

34. MCR, v. 1, p. 49 (1629) .

35. MCR, v. 1, pp. 50–51 (1629) .

36. Winthrop himself commented some fourteen years later on this unusual proceeding that it was the custom to keep the "chiefe Government" in the hands of those who resided in England, that this custom was followed in the granting of patents for Virginia, the Bermudas, and the West Indies, and that "this was intended" in the case of the New England Charter, but "with much difficulty we gott it abscinded." How this provision was "abscinded" has never been completely explained.—*Winthrop Papers,* v. 4, p. 470.

37. MCR, v. 1, p. 59 (1629) .

38. Winthrop's *History,* Appendix, vol. 1, p. 476. With his accustomed modesty Winthrop, by letter on that same day, informs his wife parenthetically of his election as Governor, "So it is that [it] hath pleased the Lorde to call me to a further trust in this businesse of the plantation, then [than] either I expected or finde my selfe fitt for [being chosen by the Company to be their Gouvenor] the onely thinge that I have comforte of in it is, that heerby I have assurance that my charge is of the Lorde and that he hath called me to this worke: O: that he would give me an heart now to answeare his goodnesse to me, and the expectation of his people! I never had more need of prayers. . . . "—*Winthrop Papers,* v. 2, p. 161, (1629) .

39. From Francis Higgeson's *Journal* of his voyage to New England in 1629 as reprinted in *The Founding of Massachusetts* (Mass. Hist. Soc., Boston, 1930) .

40. MCR, v. 1, pp. 398–407 (1629) .

41. See Chapter 4.

42. Much has been written on this era of American history. Aside from the references noted above, we shall mention only three secondary sources that have been of especial value in compiling material for this chapter: *Builders of the Bay Colony* by Samuel Eliot Morison (Houghton Mifflin Company, Boston, 1930) ; *The Puritans* by Perry Miller and Thomas H. Johnson (American Book Co., New York, 1938) ; and *The Puritan Dilemma: The Story of John Winthrop* by Edmund S. Morgan (Little, Brown & Co., Boston, 1958) . The original Charter has been preserved and can now be seen under glass in the Archives Museum of the State Department at the State House, Boston.

CHAPTER 3

1. Body of Liberties, No. 1 (1641). From a reprinting in the Colonial Laws of 1660, p. 33. See Appendix A.

2. From a letter written by the Governor and Deputy of the New England Company for a Plantation in Massachusetts Bay to Captain John Endecott in Salem in 1629. MCR, v. 1, p. 393.

3. Ibid; MCR, v. 1, pp. 386–407 (1629) .

4. Legislative and judicial institutions in the Colony of New Plymouth were so

similar to those of the Bay Colony that we have omitted a description of them here. Plymouth, however, did not decide that a freeman must be a member of a local church if he wished to vote, but they came close to it, saying that, in addition to being 21 years of age and "of sober and peaceable conversation," he had to be "Orthodox in the Fundamentals of Religion." He could be disfranchised if found to be "notoriously vitious or scandalous, as common Lyars, Drunkards, Swearers, Apostates from the Fundamentals of Religion . . . or doth manifestly appear to be disaffected to this Government"—Laws of 1671. As in the Bay Colony, he could also lose his right to vote if he were a "Quaker Rantor"—PCR, v. 11, p. 177 (1658).

5. From the Royal Charter of 1629, MCR, v. 1, pp. 16–17. This grant in almost identical words was carried over to the Province Charter and written into the Constitution of the Commonwealth of Massachusetts, Part 2, ch. 1, Sec. 1, Art. 4.

6. MCR, v. 1, p. 11 (1629).

7. Winthrop's *History* v. 1, pp. 98–103 (1632). Neither the Charter nor the General Court had given the Governor any special administrative powers or the right to veto legislation or appoint judges.

8. Although frequently referred to by today's press as "The Great and General Court," the official title of the present Massachusetts legislature is "The General Court of Massachusetts"—Massachusetts Constitution, Part 2, ch. 1, Sec. 1, Art. 1.

9. MCR, v. 1, pp. 169–170 (1636).

10. MCR, v. 1, p. 118 (1634); also in the Body of Liberties (1641) no. 69, with the added words "or adjourned" and included in the Col. Laws of (1660) p. 143; (1672) p. 35. Colonial citizens were aware of the fact that in 1629, the year the King granted the Charter, he had dissolved Parliament (which turned out to be his last).

11. MCR, v. 1, pp. 3-20 (1629). Although eighteen Assistants were called for, seven could constitute a quorum.

12. In the first two years of the Bay Colony government those who most frequently sat in the General Court or on the bench of the Court of Assistants and thus controlled the affairs of state were: John Winthrop (Governor), Thomas Dudley (a later Governor), Roger Ludlowe (a later Deputy Governor), Increase Nowell (Secretary), William Pinchion, or Pynchon (elected a Magistrate in Springfield), Simon Bradstreet (a later Governor and at the time of his death in 1697 the last survivor of those who came over in 1630), and John Endecott (a later Governor of the Colony and former Governor at Salem). Those whose names appeared as Assistants less frequently, but more than once in this period, were: Richard Saltonstall (son of Sir Richard who had returned to England), Edward Rossiter, Thomas Sharpe, William Coddington (a later Treasurer), and John Winthrop, Jr. (Son of the Governor and noted in his own right as Colonial leader and later Governor of the Colony of Connecticut).

13. MCR, v. 4, pt. 2, p. 166 (1665). King Charles the Second confirmed the Charter of 1629.

14. MCR, v. 1, p. 89 (1631). Governors, Deputy Governors, and Assistants were Magistrates.

15. Winthrop's *History* v. 1, pp. 213–214 (1635). "Open notice" of a judge's entrance into the courtroom is the practice today in Massachusetts courts.

16. Winthrop's *History* v. 1, p. 213 (1635).

17. MCR, v. 1, p. 79 (1630).

18. Body of Liberties (1641) no. 67. Also in Col. Laws (1648) p. 21; (1660) p. 150; (1672) p. 48, which added Commissioners for the United Colonies and Secretary of the General Court.

19. MCR, v. 1, p. 87 (1631). Also in Col. Laws (1660) p. 153; (1672) p. 55.

20. *Plain Dealing: or, Newes from New-England* by Thomas Lechford (London, 1642). At the time this law was enacted, there was evidently no popular resentment; it was clearly within the scope of the Colony's fundamental philosophy.

21. *Builders of the Bay Colony* by Samuel E. Morison (Houghton Mifflin Company, Boston, 1930) pp. 340–341.

22. MCR, v. 4, pt. 2, p. 166 (1665).

23. MCR, v. 4, pt. 2, pp. 117-118 (1664), p. 167 (1665). Also in Col. Laws (1672) pp. 55-56. To be admitted as a freeman one also had to be 24 years of age, a householder, and a settled inhabitant.

24. Hutchinson's *History,* v. 1, pp. 25–26.

25. MCR, v. 1, p. 213 (1637). Also in Col. Laws (1660) p. 143; (1672) p. 36.

26. MCR, v. 4, pt. 2, p. 88 (1663). Also in Col. Laws (1672) p. 48.

27. MCR, v. 4, pt. 2, p. 143 (1665). Also in Col. Laws (1672) pp. 54–55.

28. MCR, v. 1, pp. 116-121 (1634). This was the first popular legislative assembly in New England. (In Virginia a House of Burgesses had been established as early as 1619.)

29. Winthrop's *History* v. 1, p. 153 (1634).

30. Winthrop's *History* v. 1, p. 157 (1634). The following year Ipswich (formerly Aggawam) and Weymouth (formerly Wessaguscus) sent representatives; Newbury (formerly Wessacumcon) sent representatives in 1636, and in the following years many other towns were represented.

31. MCR, v. 1, pp. 116–121 (1634).

32. Winthrop's *History* v. 1, p. 84 (1631).

33. MCR, v. 1, p. 178 (1636); p. 254 (1639). Also in Col. Laws (1648) p. 16; (1660) p. 145; (1672) p. 40. Later (1653) towns of no more than thirty freemen were not required to send a Deputy—MCR, v. 4, pt. 1, p. 154. Boston, because of its relatively large population in 1681, was permitted to send three Deputies—MCR, v. 5, p. 305 (1681). At the Courts of Election (as the May Court was called) every freemen cast his own vote. If he lived at a distance, he could vote by proxy.

34. MCR, v. 4, pt. 1, p. 206 (1654). Also in Col. Laws (1660) p. 145; (1672) p. 41.

35. MCR, v. 4, pt. 2, p. 87 (1663); Col. Laws (1672) p. 41.

36. Col. Laws (1648) p. 17; (1660) p. 145; (1672) p. 40.

37. Body of Liberties (1641) no. 12. Also in Col. Laws (1648) p. 35; (1660) p. 170; (1672) p. 90.

38. Constitution of the Commonwealth of Massachusetts, Part 1, art. 19.

39. *Winthrop Papers,* v. 4, p. 388 (1643).

40. *Winthrop Papers,* v. 4, p. 387 (1643).

41. *Winthrop Papers,* v. 4, pp. 382–383 (1643).

42. "A Modell of Christian Charity," *Winthrop Papers,* v. 2, pp. 282-295.

43. Hutchinson's *History,* v. 1, p. 497.

44. *Winthrop Papers,* v. 4, pp. 349–352, 380–391. See also Winthrop's *History* v. 2, pp. 83, 86, 139–144 (1642–1643). For discussions of the case of *Sherman* vs. *Keayne* see "The Supreme Judicial Power in the Colony of Massachusetts" by Mark Howe and L. F. Eaton, Jr., in *New Eng. Q.,* v. 20, pp. 291–316 (1947); "The Negative Vote in Massachusetts," *Mass. Hist. Soc. Proc.,* v. 46 (1912–1913) pp. 276–285.

45. MCR, v. 1, p. 170 (1636). Col. Laws (1648) p. 16; (1660) p. 142; (1672) p. 35. Thus the negative vote was mutual, as it is today.

46. MCR, v. 2, pp. 58–59 (1644). Also in Col. Laws (1648) p. 16; (1660) p. 142; (1672) p. 34–35. The first meeting of the Deputies sitting by themselves was on May 29, 1644. Twenty four towns were represented. MCR, v. 3, p. 1 (1644). The courts usually met in the church meetinghouses in Boston until the first Town House was built about 1658, financed largely from a legacy left by Capt. Keayne (the noted defendant in the *Sherman* vs. *Keayne* case reported in this chapter). After half a century's use, the original Town House was destroyed by fire. A new State House, an elegant brick building which still stands, was built in 1712, and there the legislature and the courts held their sessions until the present State House on Beacon Hill was ready for occupancy in 1798. See *Re-Dedication of the Old*

State House, Boston, July 11, 1882, 6th ed., (official publication of the City of Boston, 1893).

47. General Laws of Massachusetts, ch. 3, sec. 23.

48. Winthrop's *History* v. 2, p. 193 (1644).

49. MCR, v. 2, p. 58 (1644); v. 3, pp. 179–180 (1644).

50. MCR, v. 2, p. 285 (1649).

51. Hutchinson's *History,* v. 1, p. 37.

52. MCR, v. 2, p. 91 (1644). Also in Col. Laws (1660) p. 141; (1672) p. 34.

53. MCR, v. 4, pt. 2, p. 493 (1671).

54. See Chapter 4, pp. 85-99.

55. Body of Liberties, no. 36 (1641). Also in Col. Laws (1660) p. 122; (1672) p. 3.

56. MCR, v. 1, pp. 78, 79, 81 (1630).

57. Col. Laws (1648) p. 2; (1660) 122; (1672) p. 3.

58. Body of Liberties (1641) no. 72. Also in Col. Laws (1660) p. 142; (1672) p. 35.

59. MCR, v. 3, pp. 2, 10, 62, 122, 183, 210, 422 (1644–1657); v. 4, pt. 1, p. 286, (1657); p. 449 (1660). Although the General Court said in 1671 "free debates are the indubitable right of the said Court," a limitation was placed on long-winded speakers by a law of 1640 which declared that no man in the General Court shall speak "above three times to any cause without leave from the Governor or Court upon paine of 12 pence a time"—MCR, v. 1, p. 304 (1640); v. 4, pt. 2, p. 493 (1671).

60. Art. XXI and LXXI of the Amendments to the Constitution of Massachusetts.

61. Winthrop's *History* v. 2, pp. 262–263 (1645). The Magistrates were willing to relinquish the negative vote if the number of Deputies would be reduced to the number of Magistrates, but the freemen would not agree—MCR, v. 2, p. 88 (1644).

62. MCR, v. 2, p. 91 (1644).

63. MCR, v. 1, pp. 167, 174, 195 (1636–1637). Winthrop's *History,* v. 1, pp. 219–220 (1636), 363–364 (1639); v. 2, pp. 77–78, 108, 204 (1642–1644).

64. MCR, v. 1, p. 264 (1639).

65. MCR, v. 2, p. 5 (1642); pp. 90–96 (1644). See "The Massachusetts Council of the Magistrates" by Ellen E. Brennan, *New Eng. Q.,* v. 4, pp. 54–93 (1931).

66. MCR, v. 2, pp. 285-286 (1649). Also in Col. Laws (1660) pp. 143-144; (1672) p. 36.

67. MCR, v. 2, p. 279 (1649). Also in Col. Laws (1660) p. 143; (1672) p. 36.

68. Body of Liberties, no. 36 (1641). Also in Col. Laws (1648) p. 2; (1660) p. 122; (1672) p. 3.

69. MCR, v. 1, p. 239 (1638); v. 2, p. 279 (1649). Also in Col. Laws (1648) p. 32; (1660) pp. 167-168; (1672) p. 87.

70. MCR, v. 1, p. 169 (1636).

71. MCR, v. 2, p. 38 (1643). Mass. Archives, v. 6, no. 123.

72. MCR, v. 1, p. 175 (1636). Also in Col. Laws (1648) pp. 14–15; (1660) p. 143; (1672) p. 36.

73. MCR, v. 2, p. 84 (1644).

74. MCR, v. 2, pp. 287–288 (1649). Also in Col. Laws (1660) p. 200; (1672) p. 157.

75. Col. Laws (1660) p. 182; (1672) p. 210.

76. Col. Laws (1648) p. 43; (1660) p. 183; (1672) p. 105.

77. Col. Laws (1648) p. 30; (1660) p. 163; (1672) pp. 79, 84.

78. Col. Laws (1660) pp. 148–149; (1672) p. 46.

79. See Chapters six and seven.

80. MCR, v. 4, pt. 1, pp. 60–61 (1651). Attempts to regulate dress occurred as early as 1634—MCR, v. 1, p. 126 (1634); p. 183 (1636); p. 274–275 (1639); repealed in (1644) v. 2, p. 84. Col. Laws (1660) p. 123; (1672) p. 5.

81. MCR, v. 3, pp. 13-14 (1646); p. 125 (1648); p. 357 (1654). Also in Col. Laws (1648) p. 10; (1660) p. 134; (1672) p. 23. Magistrates were required to pay a tax to support the ministry but were given a tax-free estate in 1645. After repeal of this provision in 1654, they were granted a salary of 35 pounds per year. They were allowed their food and expenses and free ferry trips during sessions of the courts.

82. MCR, v. 3, p. 67 (1646). Also in Col. Laws (1648) p. 22; (1660) p. 151; (1672) p. 50. Deputies were also allowed free passage by ferry.

83. Col. Laws (1648) p. 42; (1660) p. 177; (1672) p. 109.

84. MCR, v. 1, p. 210 (1637). Also in Col. Laws (1648) p. 41; (1660) p. 177; (1672) p. 109.

85. MCR, v. 4, pt. 2, p. 4 (1661). Also in Col. Laws (1672) p. 155. Magistrates, however, were not immune from penalties if they should "transgresse the limits of their liberty & authority . . . or use reproachful or unbeseeming speaches"—MCR, v. 1, p. 213 (1637).

86. Col. Laws (1648) p. 38; (1660) p. 172; (1672) p. 102.

87. MCR, v. 3, p. 263 (1652). Also in Col. Laws (1660) p. 182; (1672) p. 120.

88. MCR, v. 2, p. 30 (1642). Also in Col. Laws (1648) p. 12; (1660) p. 138; (1672) p. 29. Also in the company of Overseers of Harvard College were the Governor, the Deputy Governor, the teaching Elders of Cambridge, Watertown, Charlestown, Boston, Roxbury, and Dorchester, and the President of the College.

89. MCR, v. 2, p. 207 (1647). Also in Col. Laws (1648) p. 37; (1660) p. 172; (1672) p. 101.

90. Col. Laws (1648) p. 2; (1660) p. 122; (1672) p. 3.

91. MCR, v. 1, p. 239 (1638); v. 3, p. 111 (1647). Also in Col. Laws (1648) pp. 5, 8; (1660) pp. 127, 132; (1672) pp. 13, 20.

92. MCR, v. 3, pp. 111-112 (1647). Also in Col. Laws (1648) p. 5; (1660) p. 127; (1672) p. 13.

93. MCR, v. 3, p. 355 (1654). Also in Col. Laws (1660) pp. 136–137; (1672) p. 27.

94. MCR, v. 4, pt. 2, p. 450 (1670). Also in Col. Laws (1672) p. 54.

95. Col. Laws (1648) p. 24; (1660) p. 153; (1672) p. 58.

96. Col. Laws (1660) p. 187; (1672) p. 127. Such persons could be committed to the House of Correction.

97. MCR, v. 4, pt. 2, pp. 19, 59 (1661–1662). Also in Col. Laws (1660) p. 156; (1672) p. 62.

98. Col. Laws (1672) p. 324 (1684).

99. MCR, v. 3, p. 94 (1646). Also in Col. Laws (1648), p. 20; (1660) p. 148; (1672) p. 45.

100. MCR, v. 4, pt. 2, pp. 59–60 (1662). Also in Col. Laws (1660) p. 222 (1662); (1672) p. 57.

101. MCR, v. 3, p. 114 (1647). Also in Col. Laws (1648) p. 24; (1660) p. 153; (1672) p. 57.

102. Ibid.

103. Col. Laws (1660) p. 158; (1672) p. 66.

104. MCR, v. 2, pp. 104-105 (1645). Also in Col. Laws (1648) p. 35; (1660) p. 171; (1672) pp. 91–92.

105. MCR, v. 3, pp. 114-115 (1647). Also in Col. Laws (1648) p. 7; (1660) pp. 130–131; (1672) p. 19.

106. MCR, v. 2, p. 178 (1646). Also in Col. Laws (1660) p. 194; (1672) p. 145.

107. MCR, v. 4, pt. 2, pp. 100–101 (1664).

108. Col. Laws (1672) p. 216 (1674).

109. MCR, v. 4, pt. 1, pp. 59-60 (1651). Also in Col. Laws (1660) p. 137; (1672) p. 27. In 1685 a criminal prosecution was begun in the County Court and carried to the Court of Assistants—Court of Assistants, v. 2. pp, 192-193 (1685). A man 41 years of age, evidently considered "a vain and loose" person, had been entertaining Harvard students in one of the student's rooms where they were allegedly feasting on stolen

turkeys. No other charge was brought, but this affair in itself seemed serious enough to the authorities. See "A Trial; in 1685, for 'Frequenting the College Contrary to Law,'" by John Nobel, in *Col. Soc. of Mass. Pub.*, v. 3, (1895-1897) pp. 448-470.

110. For a detailed description of the judicial system in the Bay Colony, with particular reference to Springfield, see *Colonial Justice in Western Massachusetts, 1639-1702: The Pynchon Court Record,* Joseph H. Smith, editor. (Harvard Univ. Press, Cambridge, 1961). As to "Strangers Courts," see MCR, v. 1, p. 264 (1639). Also in Col. Laws (1648) p. 15; (1660) p. 144; (1672) pp. 37–38.

111. MCR, v. 5, p. 477 (1685).

112. Body of Liberties, no. 66 and no. 74 (1641). Also in Col. Laws (1648) p. 51; (1660) pp. 49, 196; (1672) p. 148. Selectmen who were chosen but refused to serve were subject to payment of a fine. They were the chief officers of town government. By 1647 there were 33 towns in the Bay Colony, MCR, v. 2, p. 225 (1647). Town meetings where anyone might speak his piece were characteristic of local government in New England.

113. Col. Laws (1660) pp. 156, 164; (1672) p. 61.

114. MCR, v. 1, p. 239 (1638); v. 2, pp. 208–209 (1647); v. 4, pt. 1, p. 103, (1652); p. 202 (1654); pp. 321–322 (1658). Also in Col. Laws (1660) p. 133; (1672) p. 22.

115. MCR, v. 5, p. 139 (1677). In towns where there was no Magistrate, they could punish offenders by fines of less than forty shillings or corporal punishment not exceeding ten stripes.

116. MCR, v. 4, pt. 1, pp. 61–63 (1651). Also in Col. Laws (1660) p. 133; (1672) p. 21.

117. Col. Laws (1672) p. 217.

118. For a thoroughly documented analysis of the civil and criminal law of the Bay Colony from 1630 to 1650 showing the "extent to which English institutions and customary modes of action were carried into the New World," see *Law and Authority in Early Massachusetts* by George L. Haskins (The Macmillan Company, New York, 1960).

119. *Winthrop Papers,* v. 4, pp. 468–488 (1644).

120. See "The Dudley Records" in *Mass Hist. Soc. Proc.,* v. 33 (1899-1900) pp. 222-286, and "Dudley's Speeches," ibid., v. 7 (1863–1864), pp. 487–490; *The Andros Tracts,* William H. Whitmore, ed., 3 v., pub. of the Prince Soc., Boston, 1868; the Mass. Archives, v. 36 (1690–1691).

121. "Increase Mather's Brief Account of the Agents, 1691," in *Narratives of the Insurrections, 1675-1690,* Charles M. Andrews, ed., (Charles Scribner's Sons, N. Y., 1915).

122. For an account of the administrations of the Royal Governors in the Province period see chap. 2 of vol. 2 of *The Memorial History of Boston,* note 15 chap. 2 and Leonard W. Labaree's *Royal Government in America: A Study of the British Colonial System before 1783,* (Yale Univ. Press, 1930).

123. *Three Hundred Years of the General Court of Massachusetts, 1630–1930,* official publication of the Commonwealth of Massachusetts, 1931.

124. A description of the courts of that period can be found in Emory Washburn's *Sketches of the Judicial History of Massachusetts from 1630 to the Revolution in 1775,* (Little and Brown, Boston, 1840); and William T. Davis' *History of the Judiciary in Massachusetts—Colonial, Province and Commonwealth,* (Boston Book Co., Boston, 1900). For later developments see Mass. Gen. Laws, Chap. 119, 211, and 218; and also Alan J. Diamond's *The Superior Court of Massachusetts: Its Origin and Development,* (Little, Brown and Co., Boston, 1960).

CHAPTER 4

1. Body of Liberties, 1641. From "A Coppie of the Liberties of the Massachusetts Colonie in New England" as it appears in a lithograph reproduction in Col. Laws,

1660. As it is one of the important documents in American legal history, it is reprinted in its entirety in Appendix A of this book.

2. Body of Liberties, no. 1 (1641), quoted at the beginning of Chapter 3.

3. William Blackstone, whose famous *Commentaries* appeared a century and a quarter later (the first American edition appearing in 1771–1772), expressed the view of the Common Law of England on this point: "For a mistake in point of law, which every person of discretion not only may, but is bound and presumed to know, is in criminal cases no sort of defence. *Ignorantia juris, quod quisque tenetur scire, neminem excusat,* is as well the maximum of our law, as it was of the Roman."—*Commentaries on the Laws of England; Book the Fourth on Public Wrongs* (paperback edition, published by Beacon Press, Boston, 1962) Chap. 2, p. 27.

4. Winthrop's *History,* v. 1, p. 309 (1637); see also MCR, v. 1, p. 91 (1631); p. 92 (1631); p. 225 (1638); p. 301 (1640).

5. Winthrop's *History,* v. 1, p. 388 (1639).

6. Winthrop's *History,* v. 1, p. 191 (1635).

7. MCR, v. 1, p. 137 (1635).

8. MCR, v. 1, pp. 174–175 (1636).

9. MCR, v. 1, p. 222 (1638).

10. Winthrop's *History,* v. 1, pp. 388–389 (1639).

11. Winthrop's *History,* v. 1, p. 388 (1639). It was Winthrop's thought that it might be wiser to "raise up laws by practice and custom," as the English Common Law had developed, rather than to depend on a system of statutory enactments some of which might be judged to be repugnant to those of England (p. 389).

12. Cotton (1584–1652) achieved fame also as one who was influential in the establishment of the Boston Latin School in 1635, now the oldest educational institution in the United States with continuous existence, antedating Harvard College by one year. Cotton was the father-in-law of Increase Mather and grandfather of Cotton Mather.

13. George L. Haskins, *Law and Authority in Early Massachusetts* (The Macmillan Company, New York, 1960) p. 125.

14. Samuel E. Morison, *Builders of the Bay Colony* (Houghton Mifflin Company, Boston, 1930) pp. 228–229.

15. A reprint of Cotton's code appears in *The Hutchinson Papers,* v. 1, pp. 181–205 and in an "Abstract" of the laws in *Mass. Hist. Soc. Coll.,* 1st series, v. 5, pp. 173–187 (1798). See also Worthington C. Ford, "Cotton's 'Moses His Judicials'" in *Mass. Hist. Soc. Proc.,* v. 36 (1902) pp. 274–284.

16. The Reverend Nathaniel Ward (1578–1652) wrote *The Simple Cobler of Aggawam,* printed in London in 1647 for "Stephen Bowtell at the signe of the Bible in Popes-Head Alley."

17. Art. 98 of the Body of Liberties.

18. Art. 96 of the Body of Liberties.

19. MCR, v. 1, pp. 292–293 (1640).

20. MCR, v. 1, p. 346 (1641). See also F. C. Gray, "Remarks on the Early Laws of Massachusetts Bay, with the Code adopted in 1641, and called the Body of Liberties, now first printed" in *Mass. Hist. Soc. Coll.,* 3rd series, v. 8, pp. 191–237 (1843).

21. Nowel's introduction to Col. Laws of 1648.

22. Winthrop's *History,* v. 2, p. 66 (1641). There were 98 Articles but, if we add the preamble and the concluding section, we can see why Winthrop called them 100 laws.

23. Col. Laws (1660) pp. 21-24. See also Charles J. Hilkey, "Legal Development in Colonial Massachusetts, 1630–1686," Columbia University, *Studies in Hist., Econ. and Public Law,* v. 37, no. 2 (1910).

24. MCR, v. 1, p. 16 (1629).

25. For a comprehensive research study of this case see p. 18 of George L. Kittredge, "Dr. Robert Child the Remonstrant," in *Col. Soc. Mass. Pub.,* v. 21

(1919) pp. 1–146. Morison's account of this important episode in the Bay Colony's history is more sympathetic with Child (Chapter 8 of the volume cited in note 14 to this chapter).

26. The full text of the "Remonstrance" is in *Hutchinson Papers,* v. 1, pp. 214–223.

27. MCR, v. 3, pp. 90–91 (1646).

28. MCR, v. 3, p. 94 (1646) and p. 113 (1647). See also Winthrop's *History,* v. 2, p. 356 (1646).

29. MCR, v. 3, p. 94 (1646). For a summary of the "Remonstrance" as seen by the government and its refutation, see Winthrop's *History* v. 2, pp. 348–356 (1646). For the Court's twelve specifications finding Child's "falce & scandalous passages . . . tending to sedition," see MCR, v. 3, pp. 90–91 (1646).

30. Winthrop's *History,* v. 2, p. 352 (1646). At this time, King Charles I was preoccupied with a civil war that eventually cost him his head. He had little time to be concerned with the growing independence of the Colonies. A century later the laws of Parliament did indeed reach beyond the shores of England and the King's writs became painful realities. The "writs of assistance," for example, that enabled British officers to search homes without warrants in their attempts to locate smuggled goods were one of the many irritants that brought forth another and *final* "declaration of independence" in 1776 and led to the drawing of the fourth article of the Bill of Rights of the Federal Constitution providing that the people would be "secure in their persons, houses, papers and effects, against unreasonable searches and seizures."

31. Winthrop's *History,* v. 2, p. 352 (1646).

32. Winthrop's *History,* v. 2, p. 348 (1646). The denial of the franchise to non-church members was modified by a law prepared just prior to the "Remonstrance" affair, but not enacted until 1647, permitting nonchurch members to vote in town meetings. The town meeting form of government, a distinct contribution to political science, had been established in Boston in 1636 (MCR, v.1, p. 172) but it was not until 1647 that any citizen of the town was permitted to vote for selectmen and on matters of taxation and town government, provided he was 24 years of age and had not been convicted of any "evill carriage" against the government, commonwealth, or churches—MCR, v. 2, p. 197 (1647).

33. MCR, v. 2, p. 162 (1646). The "Declaration" is in the *Mass. Arch.,* v. 10, pp. 321–337. See Richard B. Morris, "Massachusetts and the Common Law: The Declaration of 1646," *Amer. Hist. Rev.,* v. 31 (1926) pp. 443–453.

34. Winthrop's *History,* v. 2, p. 30 (1640).

35. MCR, v. 5, p. 200 (1678).

36. MCR, v. 2, pp. 168–169 (1646). See also Winthrop's *History,* v. 2, p. 352 (1646).

37. MCR, v. 2, p. 196 (1647); p. 262 (1648). "Printed in Cambridge, 1648" but not available until 1649. Historians for a period of about 250 years believed that all copies of this code had been lost, but in 1906 one of the originals turned up in England and, after a long delay, was shipped to America where it was reprinted by the Harvard University Press in 1929 with an introduction by Max Farrand. The original is now in the Henry E. Huntington Library, San Marino, California.

38. George L. Haskins, *Law and Authority in Early Massachusetts* (The Macmillan Company, New York, 1960) p. 2.

39. Col. Laws (1660) with supplements to 1672.

40. Col. Laws (1672) with supplements to 1686.

41. Richard L. Perry (ed.) *Sources of Our Liberties: Documentary Origins of Individual Liberties in the U. S. Constitution & Bill of Rights* (Amer. Bar Foundation, Chicago, 1959) p. 17. See also Massachusetts Constitution, Part 1, Art. XII; U.S. Constitution, 14th Amendment.

42. See Chapter 10 on Quakers.

43. See p. 17 of the book by Perry cited in note 41.

44. Art 2, Body of Liberties. Also in Col. Laws (1648) p. 32; Col. Laws (1660) p. 193; Col. Laws (1672) p. 143.

45. MCR, v. 3, pp. 243–244 (1651) ; also in Col. Laws (1660) p. 123; Col. Laws (1672) p. 5. In the early days of the Bay Colony "noe person, either man or woman," was permitted to wear "newe and immodest fashions" with lace, or with silver or gold threads, etc.—MCR, v. 1, p. 126, (1634) .

46. Art. 43, Body of Liberties.

47. Art. 89, Body of Liberties; also in Col. Laws (1660) p. 193; Col. Laws (1672) p. 143.

48. Art. 45, Body of Liberties; also in Col. Laws (1648) p. 50; Col. Laws (1660) p. 187; Col. Laws (1672) p. 129.

49. Art. 18, Body of Liberties; also in Col. Laws (1648) p. 28; Col. Laws (1660) p. 160; Col. Laws (1672) p. 74.

50. Col. Laws (1660) pp. 140-141, 152, 154, 156; Col. Laws (1672) pp. 33, 52, 59, 61.

51. Art. 42, Body of Liberties; also in Col. Laws (1648) p. 46; Col. Laws (1660) p. 187; Col. Laws (1672) p. 129.

52. Art. 41, Body of Liberties; also in Col. Laws (1648) p. 16; Col. Laws (1660) p. 144; Col. Laws (1672) p. 38.

53. MCR, v. 4, pt. 2, p. 89 (1663) ; also in Col. Laws (1672) p. 128.

54. Art. 29, Body of Liberties; also in Col. Laws (1648) p. 51; Col. Laws (1660) p. 197; Col. Laws (1672) p. 152.

55. Court of Assistants, v. 1, pp. 114–115 (1677) . The Court inflicted the same sentence on Abigail.

56. MCR, v. 1, p. 118 (1634) . The trial might have been held by the General Court, in which case there would have been no jury. Also in Col. Laws (1648) p. 32; Col. Laws (1660) p. 167; Col. Laws (1672) p. 86.

57. Art. 30, Body of Liberties; also in Col. Laws (1648) p. 51; Col. Laws (1660) pp. 197–198; Col. Laws (1672) p. 152.

58. James F. Stephen, *A General View of the Criminal Law of England* (2nd ed., The Macmillan Company, New York, 1890) p. 18.

59. Art. 31, Body of Liberties; also in Col. Laws (1648) p. 32; Col. Laws (1660) p. 167; Col. Laws (1672) p. 87.

60. Art. 76, Body of Liberties; also in Col. Laws (1648) p. 32; Col. Laws (1660) p. 168; Col. Laws (1672) p. 87.

61. Art. 49, Body of Liberties; also in Col. Laws (1648) p. 32; Col. Laws (1660) p. 168; Col. Laws (1672) p. 87. In the mid and later years of the Colony, the requirement was changed to one court a year, although a juryman was subject to call for a special jury "of life and death or banishment."

62. Art. 77, Body of Liberties; also in Col. Laws (1648) p. 52; Col. Laws (1660) p. 198; Col. Laws (1672) p. 153.

63. Art. 63, Body of Liberties; also in Col. Laws (1660) p. 167; Col. Laws (1672) p. 86.

64. Art. 47, Body of Liberties; MCR, v. 2, p. 182 (1646) . Also in Col. Laws (1648) p. 54; Col. Laws (1660) p. 201; Col. Laws (1672) p. 158.

65. MCR, v. 2, p. 182 (1646) .

66. Court of Assistants, v. 1, pp. 10–11 (1673) .

67. Winthrop's *History,* v. 2, pp. 56-57. Most of the elders agreed, said Winthrop, that "where the fact itself speaks, or the offender freely confesseth, there needs no other witness. . . . " Thus the two-witness rule was broadly interpreted.

68. Art. 33, Body of Liberties; also in Col. Laws (1648) pp. 2–3; Col. Laws (1660) pp. 123–124; Col. Laws (1672) p. 6.

69. Art. 46, Body of Liberties; also in Col. Laws (1648) pp. 48–50; Col. Laws (1660) p. 187; Col. Laws (1672) p. 129.

70. See Chapter 6 of this book.

71. Art. 44, Body of Liberties; also in Col. Laws (1648) pp. 12–13; Col. Laws (1660) p. 139; Col. Laws (1672) p. 30.

72. Art. 72, Body of Liberties; also in Col. Laws (1660) p. 142; Col. Laws (1672) p. 35.

73. MCR, v. 1, p. 94 (1632).

74. See this chapter, pp. 83 ff.

75. MCR, v. 4, part 2, p. 196 (1665). See also MCR, v. 5, pp. 198–203 (1678) and v. 4, pt. 2, p. 25 (1661).

76. Art. 26, Body of Liberties. (Not incorporated in subsequent codes.) See chapter 13.

77. Art. 52, Body of Liberties; also in Col. Laws (1648) p. 52; Col. Laws (1660) p. 198; Col. Laws (1672) p. 152.

78. Art. 91, Body of Liberties; also in Col. Laws (1648) p. 4; Col. Laws (1660) p. 125; Col. Laws (1672) p. 10. For a note on slavery in Massachusetts in the seventeenth century, see "Judge Tucker's Queries Respecting Slavery," in *Mass. Hist. Soc. Coll.*, 1st ser., v. 4, pp. 191–211, (1795).

79. Ibid.

80. Art. 87, Body of Liberties; also in Col. Laws (1648) p. 39; Col. Laws (1660) p. 175; Col. Laws (1672) p. 105.

81. See case of Franklin, p. 278 this book. See also comments pp. 154–157 of Haskins (op. cit, note 13 above).

82. MCR, v. 2, p. 212 (1647) (derived from Exodus, 22:2); also in Col. Laws (1660) p. 171; Col. Laws (1672) p. 92.

83. MCR, v. 3, pp. 424–425 (1657); v. 4, part 1, pp. 290–291 (1657).

84. MCR, v. 3, pp. 266–267 (1652); Col. Laws (1660) p. 163; Col. Laws (1672) p. 79.

85. For a discussion of the common-law adoptions in the Colonies, see Paul S. Reinsch, "The English Common Law in the Early American Colonies," *University of Wisconsin Bull.*, v. 2 (1897–1900) pp. 397–455; Richard B. Morris (note 33 above); George L. Haskins, "A Problem in the Reception of the Common Law in the Colonial Period," *University of Pennsylvania Law Rev.*, v. 97 (1949) pp. 842–853; and George A. Billias (ed.), *Law and Authority in Colonial America*, (Barre Publishers, Barre, Mass. 1965).

86. MCR, v. 2, p. 212 (1647).

87. PCR, v. 1, p. 43 (1636).

88. PCR, v. 2, p. 62 (1643).

89. PCR, v. 11.

90. PCR, v. 11.

91. PCR, v. 11, p. 3 (1623).

92. The "General Fundamentals" appears in the 1672 code.

93. See S. A. Riesenfeld, "Law-Making and Legislative Precedent in American Legal History," *Minn. Law Rev.* v. 33 (1949), pp. 103-144. See also Haskins (note 13 supra), chap. 11 and 12.

CHAPTER 5

1. *The Simple Cobbler of Aggawam* [Ipswich] *in America*, by Nathaniel Ward, under the pseudonym Theodore de la Guard, (London, 1647). See p. 85 of the D. Pulsifer edition, Boston 1843.

2. For an exposition of Puritanism in the seventeenth century, see Perry Miller's essay on "The Puritan Way of Life" in *The Puritans*, by Perry Miller and Thomas H. Johnson (American Book Co., New York, 1938).

3. U.S. Constitution. Art. 1 of the Bill of Rights.

4. "A Modell of Christian Charity," a sermon or address delivered by Governor

John Winthrop on board the *Arbella* in 1630, *Winthrop Papers* v. 2, pp. 282–295.

5. Increase Nowell (1590-1655) in the introduction to Col. Laws (1648).

6. MCR, v. 2, p. 177, (1646) .

7. A manuscript poem by Governor William Bradford of Plymouth, published in *Mass. Hist. Soc. Coll.,* 1st ser., v. 3, pp. 79–80 (1810) .

8. MCR, v. 4, pt. 2, pp. 221–222, (1665) . From a reply of the General Court to the report of the Royal Commissioners.

9. *The Emancipation of Massachusetts* by Brooks Adams (1848–1927) , a grandson of the sixth president of the United States, a lawyer and social essayist (Houghton Mifflin Company, Boston, 1887) .

10. MCR, v. 1, pp. 174–175, (1636) .

11. MCR, v. 4, pt. 2, p. 314, (1666) .

12. MCR, v. 4, pt. 1, p. 328, (1658) ; Col. Laws, (1660) p. 147; Col. Laws, (1672) p. 44.

13. Body of Liberties (1641) , no. 58; Col. Laws, (1648) p. 20; Col. Laws (1660) p. 147; Col. Laws, (1672) p. 44.

14. Plym. Laws p. 107.

15. MCR, v. 1, p. 73, (1630) v. 4, pt. 1, pp. 314–315, (1657) . The General Court, through the County Courts, assumed the responsibility for supplying funds for ministers for towns that were "wholly destitute of ministers."

16. Col. Laws, (1648) p. 20; Col. Laws, (1660) pp. 148–149; Col. Laws, (1672) p. 45.

17. Winthrop's *History,* v. 1, p. 355, (1639) . (The term "New England" was often used by early writers to apply only to the Massachusetts Bay Colony. Winthrop was sometimes addressed by friends writing from England as "Governor of New England." Winthrop mentions the colonies of Plymouth, Rhode Island, and Connecticut only as their affairs bear upon that of the Bay Colony, his history dealing almost exclusively with the latter.) Plymouth Colony had decreed that oil from whales cast up on the shore within a township should belong to the town but a barrel of merchantable oil had to be delivered to the central government. In 1662, however, its General Court recommended that the towns "sett apart some parte of every such fish or oyle for the Incouragement of an able Godly Minnester amongst them." Plym. Laws, p. 135.

18. MCR, v. 1, p. 168 (1636); Col. Laws (1648) p. 18; Col. Laws (1660) p. 47; Col. Laws (1672) p. 43.

19. MCR, v. 4, pt. 1, p. 417 (1660) .

20. "A Modell of Christian Charity" (see note 4 above) .

21. Col. Laws (1648) p. 23; Col. Laws (1660) p. 153; Col. Laws (1672) p. 55.

22. Winthrop's *History,* v. 2, pp. 307–308, (1645) .

23. Winthrop's *History,* v. 2, p. 323 (1646) . Puritans saw magistrates as God's agents, commonly putting it this way: "The office of Civill Magistrate is an office appointed by God for the administration of justice, and preservation of peace, *both* in church and Common-wealth." (Daniel Featley, D.D., in *The Dippers dipt, or the Anabaptists Duck'd and Plung'd Over Head and Eares,* etc. London, 1645, at p. 143.)

24. Winthrop's *History,* v. 1, p. 97 (1632). Later Winthrop told the people "the church could not inquire into the justice and proceedings of the court" as Christ had disclaimed this power in his practice. Ibid, v. 1, p. 300 (1637) . See also Winthrop's "Essay Against the Power of the Church to sit in Judgment on the Civil Magistrates," *Winthrop Papers,* v. 3, pp. 505–507 (1637) .

25. *The Creeds and Platforms of Congregationalism* by Williston Walker (Scribner's, New York, 1892) pp. 235–236. The Cambridge Platform of 1648 declared it was the "duty of the magistrate, to take care of matters of religion." His goal was "not only the quiet & peaceable life of the subject, in matters of righteousness & honesty, but also in matters of godliness, yea of all godliness." See also "Church and State in the Early Years of the Massachusetts Bay Colony" by Aaron B. Seidman, *New England Q.,* v. 18 (1945) pp. 211–233; and "The Significance and

Influence of the Cambridge Platform of 1648" by Henry W. Foote, *Mass. Hist. Soc. Proc.,* v. 69 (1947–1950) pp. 81–101.

26. A letter written by the Rev. John Cotton in 1636 to Lord Say and Seal in England, Hutchinson's *History,* v. 1, appendix 3.

27. Body of Liberties (1641) no. 59; Col. Laws (1648) p. 20; Col. Laws (1660) p. 147; Col. Laws (1672) p. 44.

28. Body of Liberties, no. 60. Col. Laws (1648) p. 20; Col. Laws (1660) p. 147; Col. Laws (1672) p. 44.

29. Body of Liberties, no. 95, sec. 1–5. Col. Laws (1648) p. 18; Col. Laws (1660) p. 147; Col. Laws (1672) p. 44.

30. MCR, v. 4, pt. 1, p. 366 (1659). The King in 1665 declared this law to be "directly against the lawe of England" and hence contrary to the Charter, MCR, v. 4, pt. 2, p. 212 (1665). It was accordingly repealed, but not until 1681, MCR, v. 5, p. 322 (1681).

31. Winthrop's *History,* v. 2, p. 31 (1641).

32. Hutchinson's *History,* v. 2, p. 486 (1637), the transcript of the trial of Anne Hutchinson.

33. MCR, v. 4, pt. 2, p. 165 (1665).

34. MCR, v. 4, pt. 2, p. 221 (1665).

35. MCR, v. 4, pt. 2, pp. 25–26 (1661).

36. The Rev. John Cotton's answer to a letter from Sir Richard Saltonstall was written from London, probably between 1645 and 1653. *Hutchinson Papers,* v. 2, pp. 131-132.

37. The exact date of Williams' birth is unknown. It is variously reported as in the years 1599 to 1606 and was probably 1602 or 1603; his death was in 1683. See note in *Mass. Hist. Soc. Proc.,* v. 23 (1886–1887) pp. 253–254. Several biographies and innumerable essays on the life of Williams are available. For a critical evaluation of his accomplishments by a student of Puritanism see *Roger Williams: His Contribution to the American Tradition* by Perry Miller (Bobbs-Merrill, New York, 1953; Atheneum paperback, 1962).

38. A statement of the Rev. Francis Higginson (1586–1630) who came to New England with the Salem settlers in 1629, as quoted by Henry W. Foote in "The Significance and Influence of the Cambridge Platform of 1648," *Mass. Hist. Soc. Proc.,* v. 69 (1947-1950) pp. 82-101.

39. John Winthrop's essay on "Reformation without Separation," *Winthrop Papers,* v. 3 p. 12.

40. Bradford's *History* pp. 369–370 (1633).

41. Winthrop's *History,* v. 1, p. 204 (1635).

42. *The Bloody Tenent yet more Bloody: By Mr. Cottons endevour to wash it white in the Blood of the Lambe,* by Roger Williams of Providence in New-England, (London, 1652). In his preface "to the Merciful and Compassionate Reader," Williams calls himself "the unworthiest of all the followers of Jesus." To settle a controversy in the seventeenth century, antagonists did not use the public platform for a spectacular debate (as they might today) but seized their pens and produced countless pages of closely reasoned argument. In a reply to a letter of John Cotton, Roger Williams produced his *Bloudy Tenent of persecution, for cause of conscience* (1644), bitterly attacking the Bay Colony's determination to use the courts to keep men within theological bounds. Cotton replied (1647) with *The Bloudy Tenent, washed and made white in the bloud of the Lambe,* which was followed by Williams' rebuttal (1652), *The Bloody Tenent yet more bloody: by Mr. Cottons endevour to wash it white in the blood of the Lambe.* (Dates are publication dates, for each of these writings appeared in book form.)

43. *The Bloody Tenent yet more Bloody. . . .*

44. *The Covenant of Grace: Discovering the Great Work of a Sinners Reconciliation to God* by John Cotton (London, 1655).

45. Epistle of Paul to Titus (3:10, 11).

46. *The Bloody Tenent yet more Bloody,* etc.; note 42 above.

47. *The Covenant of Grace,* etc.; note 44 above. The Proverbs (26:3).

48. *Letters of Roger Williams,* John R. Bartlett, ed. 1st ser., v. 6, pp. 278-279, (Narragansett Club, Providence, R. I., 1874).

49. *The Bloody Tenent yet more Bloody,* etc, note 42 above.

50. Ibid.

51. MCR, v. 1, p. 394 (1629). See the long and scholarly opinion of Chief Justice John Marshall in *Johnson and Graham's Lessee* v. *M'Intosh,* 21 U.S. Supreme Court 543 (1823), upholding the legality of land titles in America granted by English charters based on discovery and subsequently consolidated by purchase or conquest; and "Communication" by Mr. Charles Deane in *Mass. Hist. Soc. Proc.,* v. 12, pp. 341–353 (1873).

52. Winthrop's *History,* v. 1, pp. 145–146 (1633).

53. "For declaring such opinions as these on the continent of Europe, anywhere except in Holland," wrote historian John Fiske, "a man like Williams would in that age have run great risk of being burned at the stake. In England, under the energetic misgovernment of [Archbishop] Laud, he would very likely have had to stand in the pillory with his ears cropped, or perhaps, like Bunyan and Baxter, would have been sent to jail"—*The Beginnings of New England* (Houghton Mifflin Company, Boston, 1889).

54. MCR, v. 1, pp. 160–161 (1635).

55. Winthrop's *History,* v. 1, p. 204 (1635).

56. *A Letter of Mr. John Cotton, Teacher of the Church of Boston in New-England, to Mr Williams, a Preacher there* (London, 1643).

57. MCR, v. 1, p. 18 (1629). The Governor of the Commonwealth was granted this authority (almost verbatim) by the Constitution of 1780 (pt. 2, ch. 2, Art. 7). It was not repealed until 1918.

58. In a letter to the General Court in 1651, Williams claimed that "in the Pequt troubles . . . I hazarded my life into extreme dangers, by labouring to prevent the Leauge between the Pequts & the Narigansets & to worck a Leauge between the English & the Narigansetts . . . the fruit whereof (as our much honoured Mr Winthrop deceased wrote to me) hath bene Peace to the English ever since." "Petition of Roger Williams," in *Mass. Hist. Soc. Coll.,* v. 4, ser. 4, p. 472.

59. *Mass. Archives,* v. 10, p. 233, reprinted in "Why was Roger Williams Banished?" by Henry S. Burrage in *The Amer. J. of Theology,* v. 5, no. 1 (1901) pp. 1–17.

60. See Burrage, note 59 above; also *J. of the House of Representatives* (1876) pp. 61–62. See also "As to Roger Williams, and his 'Banishment' from the Massachusetts Plantation" by Henry M. Dexter (Congregational Pub. Soc., Boston, 1876). who defended the Puritans and earnestly justified the expulsion of Williams.

61. *J. of the House of Representatives* (1899) p. 765; (1900) pp. 48, 113, 135. *House Doc.* 112–1900.

62. *J. of the House of Representatives* (1901) p. 659; (1902) p. 177; (1903) pp. 167, 370, 388, 686; (1904) pp. 146, 608, 625; (1905) pp. 184, 283, 294. *House Doc.* 504–1903.

63. *J. of the House of Representatives* (1906) pp. 174, 252, 261.

64. Chap. 11 of the Resolves of 1936.

65. The Rev. John Cotton's reasons for leaving England were set forth in a letter reprinted in the *Hutchinson Papers,* v. 1, pp. 60–65.

66. Winthrop's *History,* v. 1, p. 239 (1636).

67. Ibid, v. 1, p. 356 (1639).

68. Anne Hutchinson (1591–1643) lived at the corner of School and Washington Streets. Her residence is now marked by a tablet placed on the building later erected there and occupied for many years by The Old Corner Book Store.

69. Hutchinson's *History,* v. 1, p. 55.

70. *A Short Story of the Rise, reign, and ruine of the Antinomians, Familists*

& Libertines, that infected the churches of New-England, by "an eye and eare-witnesse of the carriage of matters there." The author's name is not given, but historians attribute authorship to the Rev. Thomas Weld of Roxbury (London, 1644).

71. Hutchinson's *History,* v. 2, p. 482.

72. Of the many secondary sources on the story of the antinomian controversy, one of the most complete is *Three Episodes of Massachusetts History* by Charles Francis Adams (Boston, 1892). See also Adams' *Antinomianism in the Colony of Massachusetts Bay: 1636–1638* (Prince Society, Boston, 1894). For a broader coverage, see *Orthodoxy in Massachusetts, 1630–1650* by Perry Miller (Harvard University Press, Cambridge, 1933).

73. The Puritan's position on the question of divine revelation has been reversed by his Congregational and Unitarian successors, as we see in the hymn "Light of Ages and of Nations" by Samuel Longfellow, sung in present-day church services. The third verse: "Lord, that word abideth ever;/ Revelation is not sealed;/ Answering now to our endeavor,/ Truth and right are *still revealed.*" (Italics added.)

74. *Wonder-Working Providence of Sions Saviour; Being a Relation of the First Planting in New England in the Yeare, 1628* (London, 1654) by Edward Johnson (1598–1672).

75. Winthrop's *History,* v. 1, p. 294 (1637).

76. Winthrop's *History,* v. 1, p. 255 (1636).

77. *A Short Story,* etc.; see note 70. Battis, writing in 1962, believes that her views were most appealing to those merchants whose economic interests were in conflict with those who held the power in Boston. From an analysis of citizens of that day who could be identified with the Hutchinson cause, he concluded that they were, for the most part, the wealthier and more influential—*Saints and Sectaries* by Emery Battis (University of North Carolina Press, Chapel Hill, 1963).

78. *A Short Story,* etc.; see note 70.

79. Ibid.

80. Winthrop's *History,* v. 1, p. 254 (1636); italics added.

81. MCR, v. 1, pp. 189, 196, 207 (1637). Correspondence from Wheelwright (1592–1679) to the General Court after his banishment can be found in *Winthrop Papers,* v. 4, pp. 414–415, 449–450 (1643). Wheelwright's sermon has been reprinted in *Mass. Hist. Soc. Proc.,* v. 9 (1866-1867) pp. 256-274.

82. "A Remonstrance and Petition," defending Mr. Wheelwright is reprinted in *Hutchinson Papers,* v. 1, p. 72–74.

83. MCR, v. 1, pp. 207–208 (1637).

84. MCR, v. 1, p. 189 (1637).

85. Winthrop's *History,* v. 1, pp. 265 and 294 (1637).

86. "A Brief Answer to a Certain Declaration," *Hutchinson Papers,* v. 1, pp. 93–94.

87. *Winthrop's History,* v. 2, p. 198 (1644).

88. MCR, v. 1, p. 196 (1637).

89. Edward Rawson's letter to Governor Winthrop, *Winthrop Papers,* v. 4, p. 97.

90. Winthrop's "Defence of an Order of Court made in the Year 1637" and Henry Vane's "A Brief Answer" with a further reply by Winthrop, in *Hutchinson Papers,* v. 1, pp. 79–113.

91. *Hutchinson Papers,* v. 1, p. 81.

92. Winthrop's *History,* v. 1, p. 294 (1637).

93. Hutchinson's *History* contains a transcript, presumably complete, of the "trial" of Anne Hutchinson, v. 2, pp. 482–520. See also "The Case Against Anne Hutchinson" by Edward S. Morgan in *New Eng. Q.,* v. 10 (1937) p. 635 or the colorful narrative of the Hutchinson affair as told by Winnifred K. Rugg in *Unafraid, A Life of Anne Hutchinson* (Houghton Mifflin Company, Boston, 1930)

or the sociological study by Emery Battis, *Saints and Sectaries* (University of North Carolina Press, Chapel Hill, 1963).

94. Winthrop's *History,* v. 1, p. 294 (1637).

95. Hutchinson's *History;* see note 93.

96. Ibid.

97. MCR, v. 1, p. 207 (1637).

98. *A Short Story,* etc; see note 70.

99. Winthrop's *History,* v. 1, p. 310 (1638).

100. *Mass. Hist. Soc. Proc.,* v. 24 (1887-1889), pp. 159-191.

101. Ibid.

102. Ibid.

103. Winthrop's *History,* v. 1, p. 310 (1638).

104. MCR, v. 1, p. 211 (1637).

105. MCR, v. 1, p. 278 (1639).

106. MCR, v. 1, pp. 212–213 (1637).

107. *Anne Hutchinson's Refuge in the Wilderness* by Otto Hufeland (privately published, 1929).

108. *A Short Story,* etc. See note 70.

109. Winthrop's *History,* v. 1, p. 313 (1638).

110. Winthrop's *History,* v. 1, p. 314 (1638).

111. Ibid. v. 1, p. 317 (1638). Italics added.

112. As the local physician had reported that the peculiar "monster" consisted of some thirty separate parts, the ministers were quick to conclude that it symbolized her "Thirty Monstrous & Heretical Opinions." (Preface to *A Short Story,* etc., note 70.) Battis (note 77) states that Anne at the time was 46 years old and had already given birth to 15 children; that the "monster" was "a menopausal baby" or more technically "a hydatidiform mole," not well understood at that time.

113. *A Short Story,* etc (note 70).

114. William Bradford's letter to Winthrop, April 11, 1638, in *Winthrop Papers,* v. 4, p. 23. Edward Howse, writing from England to John Winthrop, Jr., in 1639, referring to the reports he had received of the Dyer and Hutchinson "monsters," said "it cannot be deneyed but we have conceived many monstrous imaginations of Christ Jesus," *Winthrop Papers,* v. 4, p. 115.

115. *A Short Story,* etc (note 70).

116. Ibid.

117. See note 1.

118. This chapter, pages 121-123.

119. MCR, v. 4, pt. 2, p. 374 (1668).

120. MCR, v. 2, p. 85 (1644).

121. *Mass. Hist. Soc. Coll.,* 5th ser., v. 8, p. 200.

122. *Mass. Hist. Soc. Coll.,* 4th ser., v. 6, pp. 536–540.

123. MCR, v. 2, p. 141 (1645).

124. Winthrop's *History,* v. 2, p. 307 (1645).

125. Col. Laws (1660) p. 154; (1672) p. 59.

126. Winthrop's *History,* v. 2, pp. 213–214 (1644).

127. MCR, v. 2, p. 141 (1645); v. 3, p. 51 (1645).

128. MCR, v. 2, p. 149 (1646); v. 3, p. 64 (1646).

129. MCR, v. 3, p. 174 (1649).

130. Essex County Court, v. 1, p. 92; MCR, v. 3, pp. 67–68 (1646). Winter (or Witter) was in trouble with the authorities a few years later for calling infant baptism "a badge of the whore"—*The Memorial History of Boston,* Justin Winsor, editor (Ticknor & Company, Boston, 1880) v. 1, p. 178.

131. Essex County Court, v. 1, p. 52 (1643).

132. Essex County Court, v. 1, p. 52 (1643).

133. Essex County Court, v. 1, p. 70 (1644).

134. *Hutchinson Papers,* v. 1, pp. 173–174 (1645).

135. *Ne Sutor ultra crepidam: or brief Animadversions upon the New-England Anabaptists,* by Samuel Willard (1640–1707), Teacher of a Church in New-England (London, 1681, pub. by S. Green upon assignment of S. Sewall).

136. *Ill Newes from New-England: or A Narrative of New-Englands Persecution,* by John Clark, Physician of Rode Island in America (London, 1652). Reprinted in *Coll. of the Mass. Hist. Soc.,* v. 2, ser. 4 (1854).

137. Ibid, p. 47.

138. MCR, v. 4, pt. 2, p. 291 (1665); Court of Assistants, v. 3, pp. 171–175.

139. MCR, v. 4, pt. 2, pp. 373–375 (1668).

140. MCR, v. 4, pt. 2, p. 413 (1668).

141. A letter from Sir Richard Saltonstall to Mr. Cotton and Mr. Wilson, presumably after Gold's sentence; reprinted in the *Hutchinson Papers,* v. 2, pp. 127–129.

142. Cotton's answer to the letter from Saltonstall; reprinted in the *Hutchinson Papers,* v. 2, pp. 129–134.

143. From Willard's *Ne Sutor* (note 135).

144. In 1642 La Tour, a Roman Catholic, "came in a French shallop with some 14 men. . . . They staid here about a week, and were kindly entertained, and though they were papists, yet they came to our church meeting"—Winthrop's *History,* v. 2, p. 106 (1642).

145. Letter from Edward Howes to John Winthrop, Jr., Nov. 23, 1632, *Winthrop Papers,* v. 1, p. 94.

146. Winthrop's *History,* v. 1, pp. 117–118 (1632).

147. See *Catholicism in New England to 1788* by Rev. Arthur J. Riley, Catholic University of America, (Washington, D. C., 1936).

148. MCR, v. 2, p. 193 (1647); Col. Laws (1648) p. 26; (1660) p. 158; (1672) p. 67.

149. Essex County Court, v. 8, p. 225 (1681).

150. Winthrop's *History,* v. 1, p. 189 (1635); MCR, v. 1, pp. 137, 145, 146 (1635).

151. MCR, v. 4, pt. 1, p. 78 (1652); also in Col. Laws (1660) p. 154; (1672) pp. 59–60.

152. MCR, v. 2, p. 179 (1646). On the first enactment the law was to read A WANTON GOSPELLER. Also in Col. Laws (1648) pp. 19–20; (1660) p. 148; (1672) pp. 44–45.

153. MCR, v. 2, p. 178 (1646); also in Col. Laws (1660) p. 148; (1672) p. 45.

154. Exodus 22:28; MCR, v. 1, pp. 212–213 (1637); also in Col. Laws (1648) p. 36.

155. Col. Laws (1660) p. 156; (1672) p. 61.

156. MCR, v. 1, p. 240 (1638); also in Col. Laws (1648) p. 20; (1660) p. 148; (1672) p. 45.

157. MCR, v. 1, p. 140 (1635).

158. MCR, v. 2, pp. 177–178 (1646); also in Col. Laws (1648) p. 20; (1660) p. 148; (1672) p. 45.

159. MCR, v. 4, pt. 2, p. 395 (1668); also in Col. Laws (1672) p. 134.

160. MCR, v. 5, p. 133 (1677). In 1679 the law requiring the ministers to read the Sabbath laws from the pulpit was amended. From that time on, this duty was transferred to the constable or the town clerk at some public meeting—MCR, v. 5, p. 243 (1679).

161. Essex County Court, v. 7, p. 251 (1679).

162. Col. Laws (1672) p. 270 (1679).

163. MCR, v. 4, pt. 1, p. 150 (1653); also in Col. Laws (1660) p. 189; (1672) pp. 132–133.

164. MCR, v. 4, pt. 1, p. 347 (1658); also in Col. Laws (1660) p. 190; (1672) p. 133.

165. MCR, v. 5, p. 239 (1679) ; also in Col. Laws (1672) p. 269 (1679) .

166. MCR, v. 2, p. 177 (1646) ; also in Col. Laws (1660) pp. 154–156; (1672) pp. 58–59.

167. MCR, v. 2, p. 178; v. 3, p. 100 (1646) pp. 201, 205 (1650) ; also in Col. Laws (1660) p. 194; (1672) p. 145.

168. MCR, v. 2, p. 177 (1646) ; also in Col. Laws (1648) p. 29; (1660) p. 163; (1672) p. 77.

169. See *The Compact with the Charter and Laws of the Colony of New Plymouth,* William Brigham, editor (published by order of the General Court, Boston, 1836) .

170. MCR, v. 1, p. 99 (1632) .

171. MCR, v. 1, p. 244 (1639).

172. Court of Assistants, v. 2, p. 101.

173. MCR, v. 1, p. 312 (1640); Winthrop's *History,* v. 2, p. 22 (1640). To deny the doctrine of original sin was to undermine Puritan orthodoxy. Banishment as a penalty for this serious offense was deemed fitting.

174. MCR, v. 1, p. 316 (1641) .

175. Essex County Court, v. 1, p. 51 (1642) .

176. Ibid, v. 1, p. 69 (1644) .

177. Ibid, v. 1, p. 99 (1646) .

178. Ibid, v. 1, p. 59 (1643) .

179. Ibid, v. 2, p. 168 (1659) .

180. Ibid, v. 3, p. 111 (1663) .

181. Ibid, v. 3, p. 269 (1665) .

182. Suffolk County Court, v. 1, p. 307 (1673) .

183. Court of Assistants, v. 1, p. 197 (1681) .

184. See Chapter 10.

185. John Locke (1632–1704), in his four letters on toleration raised no objection to an established church, provided it conformed to the simplicity of the Gospels. Convinced of the demonstrable certainty of God, he could not be fully tolerant toward atheists, and yet his views on the understanding of man and the nature of God and his broad tolerance of those who disagreed with him on subtleties of theological doctrine had a powerful influence, not only on contemporary thought, but on the political philosophy of the eighteenth and nineteenth centuries.

186. The Province Charter has been reprinted in Province Laws, v. 1, pp. 1–20. Italics added.

187. Queen Anne (Queen of Great Britain, 1702–1714) , in her instructions to Governor Joseph Dudley as he took command of the Province government in 1702, reminded him that he was "to permitt a Liberty of Conscience to all Persons (*except Papists*) so [long as] they be contented with a Quiet and Peacable Enjoyment of the same, not giving offence or Scandall to the Government" (italics added) —*Mass. Hist. Soc. Coll.*, v. 9, p. 108 (Charles C. Little and James Brown, Boston, 1846) .

188. Prov. Laws, v. 1, ch. 1 (1700) .

189. For a frank and thoroughly documented report of anti-Catholic prejudice see *Catholicism in New England to 1788* by Arthur J. Riley, (Catholic University of America Press, Washington, D. C., 1936) .

190. According to Riley (see note 189 above) the Confession of Faith, the standard Protestant catechism in use in New England in the eighteenth century, revealed to young and impressionable minds this bit of information: the Pope was "that Antichrist, that Man of Sin and Son of Perdition, that exalteth himself in the Church against Christ and all that is called God." Paul Dudley, (1665–1751) Chief Justice of the Province (a son of Governor Joseph Dudley) established by will a foundation at Harvard to provide for a series of lectures, eight of which given by prominent professors or divines, dealt with "the idolatry, errors, and

superstitions of the Romish Church" and had a far-reaching influence (Riley, pp. 21–24).

191. Riley (note 189 above, p. 207).

192. General Laws, ch. 127, sec. 88, enacted by ch. 126 of the Acts of 1875. The Protestant chaplain, who alone was responsible for the religious education of all prisoners, strongly objected to the passage of this law, predicting that if it became law (as it did) the state prison would be required to furnish special facilities for worship by Jews, High Church Episcopalians, and Chinese.

193. Prov. Laws, v. 7, note p. 537 (1694) taken from *Mass. Archives,* v. 11, p. 79.

194. *Church and State in Massachusetts from 1740 to 1833,* by Jacob C. Meyer (Western Reserve University Press, Cleveland, 1930).

195. *The Boston Gazette* No. 565 (Sept. 28–October 5, 1730) published the "Proclamation" of Jonathan Belcher, "Capt. General and Governor in Chief," dated September 22, 1730.

196. The expression "damnable heresies," so frequently used by Puritan writers, was probably taken from the Second Epistle General of Peter, 2:1 (King James Version).

197. The cornerstone of the present King's Chapel, replacing the original church built in 1687–1689, was laid in 1749. This Episcopal church became Unitarian in 1785–1787. See *The Commemoration By King's Chapel, Boston, of the Completion of Two Hundred Years Since its Foundation*—on Wednesday, December 15, 1886—(Little, Brown and Co., Boston, 1887).

198. *Church and State in Massachusetts, 1691–1740* by Susan M. Reed (University of Illinois Press, Urbana, 1914).

199. Prov. Laws, Ch. 26 and 46 (1692–1693). See also further enactments in support of the ministry: ch. 8 (1695–1696); ch. 21 (1750–1751); ch. 7 (1756–1757); ch. 24 (1759–1760); ch. 9, (1767–1768); ch. 17 (1771–1772); ch. 14 (1775–1776); ch. 18 (1779–1780).

200. Prov. Laws, ch. 10 (1702); ch. 9 (1706–1707); ch. 17 (1715–1716); ch. 14 (1723–1724).

201. Prov. Laws, ch. 7 (1727–1728); ch. 4 (1728–1729); ch. 6 (1729–1730); ch. 11 (1731–1732); ch. 6 (1734–1735); with further amendments down to the Commonwealth period.

202. The most complete history is that of Anson Phelps Stokes in *Church and State in the United States,* 3 vol. (Harper & Row, Publishers, New York, 1950). In addition to Meyer (note 194 above) and Reed (note 198 above), see also *The Story of Religion in America* by William W. Sweet (Harper & Row, Publishers, New York, 1930).

203. Meyer (note 194 above) stated that in 1820 the religious denominations in Massachusetts were distributed approximately as follows: Congregationalists, 373; Baptists, 153; Methodists, 67; Quakers, 39; Episcopalians, 22; Universalists, 21; others, 23. It was reported in a 1962 United States Supreme Court decision that there were in the United States 83 separate religious bodies each with memberships exceeding 50,000 (*Abington* v. *Schempp,* 374 U.S. 203). It has been estimated that if all religious sects of whatever size were considered the total number would be in the vicinity of 230.

204. Massachusetts did not ratify these amendments until March 2, 1939.

205. See Chapter 9.

206. Prov. Laws, ch. 20 (1697).

207. *Commonwealth* v. *Kneeland,* 37 Mass. 206 (1838). See "The Blasphemy of Abner Kneeland" by Henry Steele Commager in *New Eng. Q.,* v. 8 (1935) pp. 29–41.

208. Prov. Laws, ch. 22 (1692–1693); also ch. 9 (1693–1694) and ch. 6 (1711–1712).

209. Prov. Laws, ch. 20 (1760–1761) and ch. 29 (1760–1761).

210. Under a law enacted by the General Court in 1962 (now chapter 136 of the General Laws), the term "Lord's Day" was for the first time displaced by the term "Sunday," and the "Lord's Day Laws" are now officially known as "Common Day of Rest Laws," their purpose being civil rather than sectarian. The new law prohibits Sunday opening of shops and businesses but specifically allows 43 exceptions. This law has been upheld by the Supreme Court decision in the case of *Gallagher* v. *Crown Kosher Super Market,* 366 U.S. 617. See discussion of this decision in "Notes," *Bos. Univ. Law Rev.,* v. 43 (1963) pp. 386-395.

211. *Zorach* v. *Clauson,* 343 U.S. 306, 313 (1952).

212. Art. 11 of the Amendments to the Massachusetts Constitution.

213. Art. 2 of the Declaration of Rights of the Massachusetts Constitution.

214. Part 2, ch. 6, art. 1 of the Massachusetts Constitution. As in the early English common law the word of an avowed atheist was worthless; hence such a person could not be a witness in a court trial. In Massachusetts no atheist could testify in a court of law until 1859. See James B. Thayer, "A Chapter of Legal History in Massachusetts," *Harvard Law Review,* v. 9, (1895-1896), pp. 1–11.

215. From the opinion of Justice Samuel F. Miller in the case of *Watson* v. *Jones,* 80 U.S. 679 (1871).

CHAPTER 6

1. Winthrop's *History,* v. 1, p. 212 (1635). Winthrop had stood for more leniency toward offenders "in the infancy of the plantation," but after discussion with others agreed "to take a more strict course" on the advice of the ministers.

2. Suffolk County Court, p. 185 (1672).

3. Suffolk County Court, p. 154 (1672).

4. See Chapter 14.

5. Suffolk County Court, p. 125 (1672).

6. Suffolk County Court, p. 340 (1673).

7. MCR, v. 3, p. 417; v. 4, pt. 1, pp. 278–279 (1656).

8. Body of Liberties (1641) no. 1; Bay Col. Laws (1648) p. 1; (1660) p. 121; (1672) p. 1.

9. MCR, v. 1, p. 74 (1630); Court of Assistants, v. 2, p. 3 (1630).

10. MCR, v. 1, p. 82 (1630); Court of Assistants, v. 2, p. 9 (1630).

11. MCR, v. 1, p. 243 (1638).

12. Body of Liberties (1641) no. 46; Bay Col. Laws (1648) p. 46; (1660) p. 187; (1672) p. 129. The Constitution of the Commonwealth of Massachusetts likewise forbids any magistrate or court of law to "inflict cruel or unusual punishments"—Art. 26 of the Declaration of Rights. A similar provision can be found in the United States Constitution, Amendment 8 of the Bill of Rights.

13. Note, for example, the case of Franklin who was hanged for his cruel treatment of his servant that resulted in the servant's death, Chapter 9, p. 278.

14. Body of Liberties (1641) no. 87; Bay Col. Laws (1648) p. 39; (1660) p. 175; (1672) p. 105. This law was similar to that of the Hebrews as found in Exodus 21:26–27.

15. Body of Liberties (1641) no. 85; Bay Col. Laws (1648) p. 39; (1660) p. 175; (1672) p. 105.

16. Body of Liberties (1641) no. 83; Bay Col. Laws (1648) p. 12; (1660) p. 137; (1672) p. 28.

17. Body of Liberties (1641) no. 92; Bay Col. Laws (1648) p. 16; (1660) p. 144; (1672) p. 39.

18. Body of Liberties (1641) no. 80; Bay Col. Laws (1660) p. 171; (1672) p. 101.

19. Ibid.

20. MCR, v. 1, p. 339 (1641).
21. Deuteronomy 25:2, 3.
22. Body of Liberties (1641) no. 43; Bay Col. Laws (1648) p. 50; (1660) p. 187; (1672) p. 129.
23. Second Epistle to the Corinthians 11:24.
24. Bay Col. Laws (1648) p. 50; (1660) p. 187; (1672) p. 129.
25. Suffolk County Court, p. 558 (1675).
26. Suffolk County Court, p. 518 (1674).
27. Suffolk County Court, p. 558 (1675).
28. Body of Liberties (1641) no. 43. The original was changed later to read: " . . . nor shall any Man be punished with Whipping, except he have not otherwise to answer the Law [as for example, by the payment of a fine], unless his Crime be very shameful, and his course of life vicious and profligate"—Col. Laws (1648) p. 50; (1660) p. 187; (1672) p. 129.
29. Leviticus 24:22.
30. Body of Liberties (1641) no. 2; Bay Col. Laws (1660) p. 193; (1672) p. 143.
31. Bay Colony Laws (1648) p. 4; (1660) p. 127; (1672) pp. 12–13.
32. Bay Colony Laws (1648) p. 5; (1660) p. 127; (1672) p. 13.
33. Bay Colony Laws (1648) p. 7; (1660) p. 131; (1672) p. 19.
34. Bay Colony Laws (1648) p. 11; (1660) pp. 136–7; (1672) p. 27.
35. Bay Colony Laws (1660) p. 143; (1672) p. 36.
36. Bay Colony Laws (1660) p. 156; (1672) p. 61.
37. Bay Colony Laws (1648) pp. 22–23; (1660) p. 151; (1672) p. 51.
38. Bay Col. Laws (1648) p. 24; (1660) p. 153; (1672) p. 58.
39. Bay Col. Laws (1660) p. 154; (1672) p. 59.
40. Bay Col. Laws (1660) p. 156; (1672) p. 62.
41. Bay Col. Laws (1648) p. 23; (1660) p. 153; (1672) p. 54.
42. Bay Col. Laws (1648) p. 35; (1660) p. 171; (1672) p. 91.
43. Bay Col. Laws (1660) p. 255 (1668); (1672) p. 98.
44. Bay Col. Laws (1660) p. 171; (1672) p. 101.
45. Bay Col. Laws (1672) p. 133.
46. Bay Col. Laws (1660) p. 189; (1672) p. 133.
47. Bay Col. Laws (1660) pp. 189–190; (1672) pp. 132–133.
48. Bay Col. Laws (1660) p. 194; (1672) pp. 144–145.
49. Bay Col. Laws (1672) p. 235.
50. Bay Col. Laws (1672) pp. 152–153.
51. Bay Col. Laws (1672) p. 208 (1673).
52. Bay Col. Laws (1672) p. 234 (1675).
53. Bay Col. Laws (1672) pp. 235–236 (1675).
54. From the records of the Suffolk County Court only.
55. Col. Laws (1648) p. 23; (1660) p. 153; (1672) pp. 54–55.
56. Exodus 22:16; MCR, v. 2, pp. 21–22 (1642).
57. The law did not specify the numbers of weeks. In the Essex County Court in 1658 a woman was held on suspicion of "uncleanness," having borne a child about 32 weeks after marriage, but she was discharged by the court—Essex County Court, v. 2, p. 101.
58. Suffolk County Court, p. 780 (1677).
59. Essex County Court, v. 5, p. 231 (1673).
60. MCR, v. 1, p. 287 (1640).
61. MCR, v. 1, p. 246 (1638).
62. Court of Assistants, v. 2, p. 86 (1639).
63. PCR, v. 1, p. 127 (1639). For a dramatic account of the whipping of Dorothy Temple, the first woman whipped in Plymouth Colony, according to Carl Sandburg, see his novel *Remembrance Rock* (Harcourt, Brace & World, New York, 1948) pp. 305–311. Public whipping of a woman for being the mother of a bastard child was the traditional penalty, but it was extremely improbable, especially in

Plymouth Colony where whippings were relatively mild, that she should be whipt with such brutality (as described by Sandburg) that her back "was a mass of flesh with the look of raw beef to be hung over a fire and broiled."

64. MCR, v. 1, p. 287 (1640).
65. County Court, Springfield, p. 209 (1641)—from *Colonial Justice in Western Massachusetts, 1639–1702—The Pynchon Court Record,* Joseph Smith, editor (Harvard University Press, Cambridge, 1961).
66. Essex County Court, v. 1, p. 44 (1642).
67. Essex County Court, v. 1, p. 380 (1654).
68. PCR, v. 4, p. 22 (1662).
69. Suffolk County Court, pp. 1023–1024 (1679).
70. Suffolk County Court, p. 1161 (1680).
71. PCR, v. 6, pp. 63–64 (1681).
72. Essex County Court, v. 8, pp. 285–287 (1682).
73. Court of Assistants, v. 2, p. 9 (1630).
74. MCR, v. 1, p. 99 (1632).
75. Court of Assistants, v. 2, p. 43 (1634).
76. Court of Assistants, v. 2, p. 49 (1634).
77. Court of Assistants, v. 2, p. 59; MCR, v. 1, p. 155 (1635).
78. Court of Assistants, v. 2, p. 62 (1636).
79. Essex County Court, v. 1, p. 6 (1637).
80. Court of Assistants, v. 2, p. 70 (1637).
81. Essex County Court, v. 1, p. 6 (1637).
82. Essex County Court, v. 1, p. 9 (1638).
83. See report of this case in Chapters 9 and 13.
84. PCR, v. 1, p. 132 (1639).
85. MCR, v. 1, p. 270 (1639).
86. MCR, v. 1, p. 297 (1639).
87. MCR, v. 1, p. 334 (1641).
88. Essex County Court, v. 1, p. 25 (1641).
89. PCR, v. 2, p. 73 (1644).
90. Suffolk County Court, p. 116 (1672).
91. Suffolk County Court, p. 1098 (1679).
92. Court of Assistants, v. 1, p. 189 (1680).
93. Essex County Court, v. 8, pp. 90–91 (1681).
94. Suffolk County Court, pp. 478–479 (1674).
95. Suffolk County Court, p. 521 (1674). Hudson was the son of Governor John Leverett.
96. PCR, v. 4, p. 106 (1665).
97. Suffolk County Court, v. 29, pp. 82–83 (1672).
98. Bay Col. Laws (1672) p. 208 (1672).
99. Bay Col. Laws (1672) pp. 12–13 (1642).
100. Bay Col. Laws (1672) pp. 62–63 (1661).
101. Essex County Court, v. 5, p. 382 (1674).
102. PCR, v. 11, pp. 48, 98, 175.
103. MCR, v. 1, pp. 99–100 (1632).
104. MCR, v. 1, p. 163; Court of Assistants, v. 2, p. 60 (1635).
105. MCR, v. 1, p. 183 (1636).
106. PCR, v. 1, p. 74 (1638).
107. Essex County Court, v. 4, p. 234 (1670).
108. Suffolk County Court, p. 88 (1672).
109. Suffolk County Court, p. 235 (1672).
110. Essex County Court, v. 6, p. 253 (1677).
111. Court of Assistants, v. 2, p. 200 (1681).
112. Winthrop's *History,* v. 1, pp. 67–68 (1631).
113. MCR, v. 1, p. 88; Court of Assistants, v. 2, p. 16 (1631).

114. Winthrop's *History,* v. 1, pp. 119, 122 (1632, 1633); v. 2, pp. 233-5 (1644).
115. MCR, v. 1, p. 295 (1640).
116. MCR, v. 1, p. 283 (1639).
117. Essex County Court, v. 2, p. 48 (1657).
118. Court of Assistants, v. 1, p. 51 (1675).
119. Court of Assistants, v. 1, pp. 56–57 (1675).
120. Court of Assistants, v. 1, p. 57 (1675).
121. Court of Assistants, v. 1, p. 57 (1675).
122. Court of Assistants, v. 1, pp. 145–146 (1679).
123. Court of Assistants, v. 1, pp. 283–284 (1685).
124. See pp. 265-266.
125. Bay Col. Laws (1672) pp. 229–231 (1675).
126. Court of Assistants, v. 1, p. 254 (1684).
127. Essex County Court, v. 1, p. 15 (1639).
128. MCR, v. 1, p. 177 (1636).
129. Essex County Court, v. 1, p. 99 (1646).
130. Bay Col. Laws (1672) p. 206; MCR, v. 4, pt. 2, pp. 513–514 (1672).
131. Essex County Court, v. 6, pp. 386–387 (1678).
132. U.S. Bureau of the Census, *Historical Statistics of the United States, Colonial Times to 1957* (Washington, D.C., 1960) p. 756. At the beginning of the Commonwealth period (1780) the Massachusetts population had grown to 268,627.
133. Prov. Laws, ch. 5 (1694–1695). By the same law, polygamy was made a capital offense.
134. Ibid.
135. Prov. Laws, ch. 29 (1762–1763).
136. Prov. Laws, ch. 2, (1695–1696).
137. Ibid.
138. Prov. Laws, ch. 18 (1692–1693).
139. Prov. Laws, ch. 10 (1705–1706).
140. Prov. Laws, ch. 2 (1711–1712).
141. Prov. Laws, ch. 6 (1711–1712).
142. Prov. Laws, ch. 20 (1697).
143. Prov. Laws, ch. 18 (1692–1693).
144. Prov. Laws, ch. 6 (1711–1712); ch. 17 (1693–1694).
145. Prov. Laws, ch. 22 (1694–1695).
146. Prov. Laws, ch. 18 (1692–1693).
147. Prov. Laws, ch. 8 (1704–1705).
148. Prov. Laws ch. 2 (1702–1703).
149. Prov. Laws, ch. 18 (1775–1776).
150. Prov. Laws, ch. 44 (1776–1777).
151. Prov. Laws, ch. 5 (1778–1779).
152. Prov. Laws, ch. 25 (1778–1779).
153. Prov. Laws, ch. 18 (1692–1693).
154. Prov. Laws, ch. 7 (1749–1750).
155. Prov. Laws, ch. 18 (1692–1693).
156. Prov. Laws, ch. 18 (1736–1737).
157. Prov. Laws, ch. 18 (1692–1693).
158. Prov. Laws, ch. 16 (1769–1770).
159. Prov. Laws, ch. 18 (1692–1693).
160. Prov. Laws, ch. 2, (1711–1712).
161. Prov. Laws, ch. 20 (1761–1762).
162. Prov. Laws, ch. 1 (1719–1720).
163. Prov. Laws, ch. 15 (1728–1729).
164. Prov. Laws, ch. 19 (1769–1770).
165. Prov. Laws, ch. 6 (1711–1712); ch. 5 (1727–1728); ch. 20 (1760–1761).
166. Prov. Laws, ch. 9 (1693); ch. 18 (1692–1693).

167. Commonwealth Laws: ch. 4, 40, 44, 52, of the Acts of 1784; ch. 21 of the Acts of 1785 and ch. 38 of the Acts of 1786.

168. Governor John Hancock's address to a joint session of the Legislature on January 31, 1793. Acts and Laws of the Commonwealth (1792–1793) p. 694.

169. Commonwealth Law: ch. 134 of the Acts of 1812.

170. Governor John Brooks' address to a joint session of the legislature on June 1, 1819. Resolves of the General Court of the Commonwealth, 1819–1824, p. 30.

171. Answer of the Senate to the address of Governor Brooks (see note 170).

172. Commonwealth Law: ch. 105 of the Acts of 1825, approved Feb. 28, 1826. In its first "Act for the punishment of certain crimes against the United States," approved on April 30, 1790, Congress prescribed the following penalties for a variety of crimes: fines, imprisonment, death, whipping (no more than 39 stripes) and standing in the pillory. A half century later Congress abolished the punishment of whipping and standing in the pillory for violations of federal laws: ch. 36, sec. 5, Laws of 1839. With the exception of the state of Delaware, all states in this country have abolished these penalties. Delaware still provides for whipping for certain crimes. A person convicted on several indictments may receive as many as sixty lashes, "strokes on the bare back well laid on." Title 11 of the Del. Code, sec. 3907-3908.

CHAPTER 7

1. From Governor Winthrop's "Arbitrary Government Described: & the Government of the Massachusetts Vindicated From that Aspersion," an essay in which this quotation is found, taken from Proverbs 17:10. *Winthrop Papers,* v. 4, pp. 468-488 (1644).

2. Col. Laws (1648) p. 23; (1660) pp. 153, 189; (1672) p. 91, 131.

3. PCR, v. 1, p. 12 (1633).

4. MCR, v. 1, p. 269 (1639).

5. Court of Assistants, v. 2, p. 85 (1639).

6. MCR, v. 1, p. 260 (1639); v. 1, p. 291 (1640).

7. PCR, v. 4, p. 51 (1664).

8. PCR, v. 3, pp. 28, 36 (1653).

9. PCR, v. 3, p. 75 (1654).

10. PCR, v. 3, p. 82 (1655).

11. Essex County Court, v. 1, p. 115 (1647).

12. Essex County Court, v. 1, p. 244 (1651).

13. Essex County Court, v. 1, p. 378 (1654).

14. Essex County Court, v. 1, p. 414 (1656).

15. Essex County Court, v. 4, p. 416 (1671).

16. Essex County Court, v. 3, p. 111 (1663).

17. PCR, v. 5, p. 81 (1671).

18. Suffolk County Court, v. 29, p. 443 (1674).

19. Suffolk County Court, v. 30, p. 782 (1677).

20. Suffolk County Court, v. 30, p. 886 (1678).

21. MCR, v. 1, p. 112 (1633).

22. MCR, v. 1, p. 268 (1639); Court of Assistants, v. 2, p. 86 (1639).

23. MCR, v. 1, p. 248, 269 (1639); Court of Assistants, v. 2, p. 81, 87.

24. PCR, v. 3, pp. 111–112 (1657).

25. PCR, v. 2, p. 28 (1641).

26. Col. Laws (1648) pp. 19–20; (1660) p. 148; (1672) pp. 44–45. The original law enacted in 1646 (MCR, v. 2, p. 179) ordered this inscription on the paper: "A WANTON GOSPELLER."

27. Court of Assistants, v. 2, p. 124 (1642).

28. Essex County Court, v. 1. p. 380 (1654).

29. Essex County Court, v. 6, p. 265 (1677).
30. Suffolk County Court, v. 29, p. 302 (1673).
31. Essex County Court, v. 5, p. 291 (1674).
32. Suffolk County Court, v. 29, p. 231 (1673).
33. Essex County Court, v. 5, pp. 239–240 (1675).
34. Suffolk County Court, v. 30, p. 697 (1676).
35. MCR, v. 1, p. 335 (1641).
36. Court of Assistants, v. 1, pp. 56–57 (1675).
37. Court of Assistants, v. 1, pp. 114–115 (1677).
38. Court of Assistants, v. 1, p. 252 (1683).
39. PCR, v. 2, p. 163 (1650).
40. Essex County Court, v. 1, pp. 286–287 (1653).
41. Essex County Court, v. 1, p. 360 (1654).
42. Essex County Court, v. 1, pp. 51–53 (1643).
43. Essex County Court, v. 1, p. 59 (1643).
44. Suffolk County Court, v. 29, pp. 90–91 (1672).
45. Essex County Court, v. 5, p. 35 (1672).—The vulgar reference to the dog was an old Biblical expression (Proverbs 26:11; 2 Peter 2:22).
46. MCR, v. 1, p. 108 (1633); p. 244 (1638); Winthrop's *History,* v. 1, pp. 124, 132, 146 (1633).
47. MCR, v. 1, p. 252 (1639).
48. Essex County Court, v. 1, p. 70 (1644).
49. Essex County Court, v. 1, p. 99 (1646). To the citizens of today, this crime may seem to have been a very trivial one not deserving punishment, but the authorities of the Bay Colony may have been acquainted with the story in the fourth book of Moses (Numbers 15:32–36). There God commanded Moses to have a man stoned to death who had gathered sticks on the Sabbath.
50. Essex County Court, v. 1, p. 157 (1648).
51. Essex County Court, v. 2, p. 50 (1657).
52. PCR, v. 4, p. 10 (1662).
53. PCR, v. 11, p. 173 (1655).
54. PCR, v. 4, p. 47 (1663).
55. Suffolk County Court, v. 29, pp. 89–90 (1672).
56. Essex County Court, v. 7, p. 314 (1679).
57. Suffolk County Court, v. 30, p. 867 (1677).
58. PCR, v. 1, p. 35 (1635).
59. MCR, v. 1, p. 252 (1639).
60. PCR, v. 2, p. 174 (1651).
61. Essex County Court, v. 1, p. 159 (1649).
62. PCR, v. 2, p. 174 (1651).
63. PCR, v. 3, p. 37 (1653).
64. PCR, v. 4, p. 117 (1666).
65. PCR, v. 2, p. 147 (1649).
66. PCR, v. 1, pp. 60–61 (1637); v. 2, p. 47 (1642); v. 2, p. 138 (1649); v. 2, p. 168 (1651).
67. Suffolk County Court, v. 29, p. 89 (1672).
68. Suffolk County Court, v. 29, p. 116 (1672).
69. Suffolk County Court, v. 29, p. 259 (1673).
70. Suffolk County Court, v. 29, p. 443 (1674).
71. Suffolk County Court, v. 30, p. 645 (1675).
72. Suffolk County Court, v. 30, p. 675 (1675).
73. Suffolk County Court, v. 30, p. 868 (1677).
74. Suffolk County Court, v. 30, p. 943 (1678).
75. Col. Laws (1660) p. 143; (1672) p. 36.
76. MCR, v. 1, p. 267 (1639).
77. PCR, v. 6, p. 153 (1685).

78. PCR, v. 6, p. 160 (1685). For other cases of sentencing for slavery see Court of Assistants, v. 2, pp. 78, 79 (1638) and p. 89 (1639).
79. PCR, v. 3, p. 73 (1655).
80. PCR, v. 3, p. 75 (1655).
81. PCR, v. 1, p. 68 (1637).
82. Suffolk County Court, v. 30, pp. 646–647 (1675).
83. Suffolk County Court, v. 29, p. 147 (1672).
84. Essex County Court, v. 4, p. 132 (1669).
85. Suffolk County Court, v. 30, p. 600 (1675).
86. Suffolk County Court, v. 29, p. 151 (1672).
87. Essex County Court, v. 3, p. 254 (1665).
88. PCR, v. 3, p. 91 (1655).

CHAPTER 8

1. From John Dunton's *Letters From New-England,* written in 1686. See note 124 of Chapter 9.
2. MCR, v. 1, p. 74 (1630).
3. MCR, v. 1, p. 83 (1631).
4. MCR, v. 1, p. 100 (1632).
5. MCR, v. 1, p. 129 (1634); p. 158 (1635).
6. MCR, v. 1, p. 337 (1641).
7. Winthrop's *History,* v. 2, p. 59 (1641).
8. MCR, v. 2, p. 230 (1648).
9. Ibid.
10. MCR, v. 3, p. 168 (1648).
11. MCR, v. 3, pp. 180–181 (1649).
12. MCR, v. 3, p. 218 (1650); pp. 232–233 (1651); v. 4, pt. 1, pp. 9, 34 (1650); p. 51 (1651); v. 4, pt. 2, p. 120 (1669); p. 435 (1669); v. 5, p. 237 (1679); p. 275 (1680).
13. MCR, v. 2, p. 230 (1648).
14. MCR, v. 4, pt. 1, p. 390 (1659).
15. Suffolk County Court, p. 595 (1675).
16. MCR, v. 5, p. 275 (1680).
17. MCR, v. 3, p. 260 (1652); v. 4, pt. 1, p. 85 (1652).
18. Essex County Court, v. 1, p. 12 (1639).
19. The Ipswich prison was said to be a wooden building three stories high, twenty feet long and sixteen feet wide, partitioned within and having a shingled exterior.
20. Essex County Court, v. 1, p. 348 (1654).
21. Essex County Court, v. 2, p. 180 (1659).
22. MCR, v. 4, pt. 1, pp. 124–125 (1653).
23. MCR, v. 3, p. 361; v. 4, pt. 1, p. 214 (1654).
24. This old prison is now maintained by the Old York Historical and Improvement Society, Inc., of York, Maine.
25. MCR, v. 4, pt. 1, p. 434 (1660).
26. MCR, v. 4, pt. 2, p. 22 (1661).
27. See Joseph B. Felt, *Annals of Salem* (James Munroe & Co., Boston, 1849).
28. Essex County Court, v. 4, p. 164 (1669).
29. Essex County Court, v. 8, p. 335 (1682).
30. Essex County Court, v. 8, pp. 336–337 (1682).
31. PCR, v. 11, p. 11 (1636).
32. PCR, v. 11, pp. 120 (1658).
33. PCR, v. 11, pp. 125–126 (1660).
34. PCR, v. 1, p. 75 (1638).

35. PCR, v. 1, p. 115 (1639).
36. PCR, v. 2, p. 24 (1641).
37. MCR, v. 5, p. 57 (1675). According to the Rev. John Eliot in a letter dated January 17, 1676, there were about 350 souls "put upon a bleak, bare island, the fittest we have, where they suffer hunger and cold." [Quoted in *Mass. Hist. Soc. Proc.,* v. 47 (1879–1880) p. 252.]
38. MCR, v. 5, p. 64 (1675).
39. See "The Indians of Eastern Massachusetts," ch. 6, v. 1 of *The Memorial History of Boston* Justin Winsor, editor (Ticknor & Co., Boston, 1880). See also *Mass. Archives,* v. 61, p. 119.
40. MCR, v. 5, p. 84 (1676).
41. MCR, v. 5, p. 228 (1679).
42. MCR, v. 1, p. 113 (1634).
43. MCR, v. 2, pp. 155, 158, 251 (1646–1648).
44. MCR, v. 1, pp. 123, 124, 136 (1634–1635).
45. Winthrop's *History,* v. 1, p. 271 (1637).
46. Winthrop's *History,* v. 2, pp. 184, 187–188 (1643). MCR, v. 2, p. 36 (1643). The name of the fortress was changed in 1705 to "Castle William," in honor of the new King, William the Third, and in 1799 changed again to "Fort Independence" when ceded to the United States.
47. MCR, v. 1, p. 181 (1636).
48. MCR, v. 1, p. 198 (1637).
49. MCR, v. 4, pt. 1, pp. 279–280 (1656). See also *Mass Archives* v. 10, pp. 239 and 282.
50. MCR, v. 4, pt. 2, p. 21 (1661).
51. See memorial to Nicholas Upsall in *New Eng. Hist. & Genealogical Reg.,* v. 34 (1880) pp. 21–31.
52. MCR, v. 4, pt. 2, p. 21 (1661).
53. MCR, v. 4, pt. 2, p. 27 (1661).
54. MCR, v. 4, pt. 2, p. 50 (1662).
55. Act 18, Eliz., c. 3, s. 5 (1575–1576). This act was repealed in 1597 and replaced by Act 39, Eliz., c. 4, for "The punyshment of Rogues Vagabonds and Sturdy Beggars."
56. See "Elizabethan Houses of Correction" by Austin Van der Slice in *J. of Crim. Law and Criminol.,* v. 27 (1936) pp. 45–67.
57. See "Pioneering in Penology" by Thorsten Sellin (University of Pennsylvania Press, Philadelphia, 1950). Dr. Sellin describes the establishment by Amsterdam burghers of two houses of correction, one for men and one for women, which were the first of such houses on the continent and the models for other countries.
58. "Bridewell" became a sort of generic name for workhouses or houses of correction. Calling a person "a Bridewell-bird" was tantamount to calling a person a "jailbird" today.
59. MCR, v. 1, p. 401 (1629). We cannot be sure that the corporation had in mind a house of correction as distinct from a prison, for, at that time, the Colonial people did not always use these terms with the precise connotation they later acquired.
60. MCR, v. 4, pt. 1, p. 222 (1655); Col. Laws (1660) p. 186; (1672) p. 127.
61. MCR, v. 4, pt. 1, p. 257 (1656); Col. Laws (1660) p. 187; *Mass. Archives* v. 38b, pp. 245–246 (1656).
62. See Chapter 10.
63. PCR, v. 3, p. 137 (1658).
64. PCR, v. 11, p. 120 (1658).
65. PCR, v. 11, p. 204 (1660).
66. Ibid.
67. MCR, v. 5, p. 237 (1679).
68. MCR, v. 4, pt. 1, p. 257 (1656).

69. MCR, v. 4, pt. 1, p. 257, 305 (1656–1657). Col. Laws (1660) p. 187; *Mass. Archives,* v. 38b, pp. 245–246 (1656). The amount earned by the prisoner was increased to six pence out of the shilling in later years. Col. Laws (1672) p. 127.

70. See Chapter 10.

71. MCR, v. 4, pt. 2, p. 43 (1662); Col. Laws (1672) pp. 152-153.

72. Col. Laws (1672) p. 208 (1673).

73. Col. Laws (1672) p. 234 (1675).

74. Col. Laws (1672) p. 236 (1675).

75. Col. Laws (1672) p. 262–263 (1678).

76. Col. Laws (1672) p. 289 (1681).

77. MCR, v. 1, p. 217 (1637).

78. MCR, v. 4, pt. 2, p. 137 (1644); Suffolk County Court, v. 30, p. 844 (1677).

79. MCR, v. 2, pp. 195–196 (1647).

80. MCR, v. 1, p. 217 (1637).

81. MCR, v. 1, p. 260 (1639). The purchasing power of twenty pounds at that time is difficult to assess. We know that the Governor's annual salary was usually one hundred pounds (MCR, v. 1, p. 127 (1634) p. 215 (1637) v. 2, p. 194 (1647) v. 4, pt. 1, p. 147 (1653), although the government sometimes found it difficult to make these payments and for a year or more paid only fifty pounds—MCR, v. 2, p. 53 (1643).

82. Suffolk County Court, p. 912 (1678).

83. Essex County Court, v. 5, p. 249 (1673).

84. MCR, v. 4, pt. 2, p. 89 (1663); Col. Laws (1672) p. 128; Mass. Gen. Laws (tercentenary edition) c. 125, s. 14; c. 127, s. 2.

85. MCR, v. 2, p. 182 (1646); Col. Laws (1648) p. 45; (1660) p. 186; (1672) p. 126.

86. MCR, v. 4, pt. 2, p. 89 (1663); Col. Laws (1672) p. 128.

87. PCR, v. 11, p. 52 (1646). Plymouth changed the allowance from two pence a day to three pence in 1646 and to four pence in 1660 PCR, v. 11, pp. 94, 171).

88. Suffolk County Court, pp. 310–311, 435.

89. Essex County Court, v. 2, p. 39 (1657).

90. MCR, v. 4, pt. 2, p. 423 (1669); Col. Laws (1672) pp. 127–128.

91. The law today in the Commonwealth of Massachusetts reads: "A jailor or officer who, except as provided in the following section, *voluntarily* suffers a prisoner in his custody upon conviction or upon a charge of crime to escape *shall suffer the punishment and penalties to which the prisoner whom he suffered to escape was sentenced* or would be liable to suffer upon conviction . . . —Gen. Laws (c. 268, s. 18). A jailor voluntarily permitting an escape is subject to twenty years' imprisonment, but if the escape is through his own *negligence* he may be fined or imprisoned up to two years—Gen. Laws (c. 268, s. 19 and 20).

92. Suffolk County Court, p. 912 (1678).

93. Essex County Court, v. 8, pp. 32–33 (1680).

94. Essex County Court, v. 8, p. 31 (1680).

95. Essex County Court, v. 6, p. 103 (1675).

96. Essex County Court, v. 5, p. 84 (1672).

97. Court of Assistants, v. 1, p. 21 (1674).

98. Suffolk County Court, p. 844 (1677).

99. Suffolk County Court, p. 126 (1672).

100. The practice of letting jail inmates work during the day in outside employment, returning to the jail at night, is found today in a number of jurisdictions. The so-called "Huber Law" in Wisconsin (1913) pioneered this practice; in Massachusetts the so-called "Day Work Program" for women in the Massachusetts Correctional Institution, Framingham, has superseded the old "Indenture" law enacted in 1879, permitting release of certain inmates for domestic service for indefinite periods of time, ch. 127, sec. 85 of the Gen. Laws.

101. Suffolk County Court, pp. 82–83 (1672).

102. Col. Laws (1672) p. 208 (1673).
103. *Mass. Archives,* v. 38b, p. 249a.
104. MCR, v. 4, pt. 2, p. 423 (1669).
105. Suffolk County Court, p. 88 (1672).
106. Court of Assistants, v. 1, pp. 115–116 (1677).
107. Essex County Court, v. 5, p. 249 (1673).
108. Essex County Court, v. 3, p. 153 (1664).
109. Suffolk County Court, p. 484 (1674); p. 520 (1674).
110. MCR, v. 2, p. 153 (1646); Col. Laws (1648) p. 22; (1660) p. 31; (1672) p. 51.
111. Body of Liberties no. 41; Col. Laws (1648) p. 16; (1660) p. 144; (1672) p. 38.
112. Body of Liberties no 18. Col. Laws (1648) p. 28; (1660) p. 160; (1672) p. 74.
113. MCR, v. 4, pt. 1, p. 346 (1658); Col. Laws (1660) p. 156; (1672) p. 61.
114. C. 167 of the Acts of 1834 abolished imprisonment for debt.
115. MCR, v. 4, pt. 2, p. 89 (1663); Col. Laws (1672) p. 128.
116. Body of Liberties no. 33; Col. Laws (1648) p. 2; (1660) p. 123; (1672) p. 6.
117. MCR, v. 4, pt. 2, p. 42 (1662).
118. MCR, v. 4, pt. 2, p. 58 (1662); Col. Laws (1660) p. 222; Col. Laws (1672) p. 7.
119. MCR. v. 4, pt. 2, pp. 107, 121, 138, 333-334, 349, 405, 430 (1664–1669).
120. PCR, v. 11, pp. 46, 95 (1645).
121. PCR, v. 11, p. 48 (1645); p. 57 (1650); p. 98 (1658); pp. 175–176 (1658).
122. PCR, v. 2, p. 98 (1646).
123. MCR, v. 1, p. 249 (1639); p. 198 (1637); Suffolk County Court p. 411 (1674); Essex County Court, v. 3, p. 412 (1667).
124. MCR, v. 1, p. 177 (1636).
125. MCR, v. 1, p. 193 (1637).
126. MCR, v. 1, p. 176 (1636).
127. MCR, v. 1, p. 178 (1636).
128. PCR, v. 2, p. 36 (1642).
129. PCR, v. 2, pp. 37, 42 (1642).
130. Court of Assistants, v. 2, p. 120 (1642).
131. PCR, v. 4, p. 76 (1664).
132. PCR, v. 4, p. 101 (1665).
133. Essex County Court, v. 3, p. 431 (1667).
134. Essex County Court, v. 5, p. 376 (1674).
135. Suffolk County Court, pp. 101–102 (1679). See Chafee's comments pp. lxxix-lxxx.
136. Essex County Court, v. 7, pp. 224, 227 (1679).
137. Essex County Court, v. 7, p. 406 (1680).
138. Essex County Court, v. 7, p. 266 (1679).
139. The Province government in 1699 reenacted the old Colonial law of 1655 based on a sixteenth century law of England that had ordered the building of a house of correction in each county at the county's charge. That law had never been fully implemented. Its purpose, as restated by the Province law, was "for the keeping, *correcting* and setting to work of rogues, vagabonds, common beggars, and other leud, idle and disorderly persons." It permitted the use of the common prison in any county where no house of correction had been built (ch. 8, Acts of 1699–1700, italics added). At that same time the sheriff was placed in charge of all of "the king's common goals [gaols], prisons and prisoners" in his county (ch. 9, Acts of 1699–1700). The Commonwealth government also reenacted this law in virtually the same language (ch. 54, Acts of 1787), which has been carried down to the present time. The law now reads: "The County Commissioners in each county, except Dukes, shall at the expense of the county provide a house or houses of correction . . . for the safe keeping, *correction,* government and employment of

offenders." (Gen. Laws, ch. 126, sec. 8, italics added). For a brief account of the county penal institutions in Massachusetts today see *The Basic Structure of the Administration of Criminal Justice in Massachusetts,* pp. 61–63, 4th ed., 1964, prepared by the author for the Department of Correction of Massachusetts.

140. Castle Island (called Castle William in the early eighteenth century, after King William the Third, and Fort Independence when it was under federal jurisdiction from 1799 to 1879, but always known to Bostonians as "Castle Island") was made the State Prison by the Commonwealth by chap. 63 of the Acts of 1784 "to provide some place, other than the common goals, for the reception and confinement to hard labour of persons convicted of larcenies, and other infamous crimes." The prisoners were placed in the custody of the officers of the garrison but later special guards were provided. Prisoners' clothing was to be of two distinct colors "as a badge of infamy."

The General Court appointed a committee in 1799 (ch. 68 of the Resolves) to select land in Charlestown and to build thereon a prison not to cost more than $30,000. In 1803, by ch. 51 of the Resolves, Charles Bullfinch, noted architect of the State House and other public buildings, was appointed to superintend the building of a prison, to be enclosed by a stone wall, with a capacity of 100 prisoners but with room for expansion (ch. 54 of the Resolves of 1802).

In 1953, the new maximum-security correctional institution at Walpole was declared by the General Court to be "the general penitentiary and prison of the Commonwealth" and authorization was given for the removal of prisoners from the Charlestown institution when Walpole was ready for occupancy (ch. 591, Acts of 1953). It was officially opened in February 1956, although a few prisoners, as a working crew, were transferred there from Charlestown the previous year.

For a brief description of the present correctional institutions of the Commonwealth, see *The Basic Structure of the Administration of Criminal Justice,* referred to above, note 139.

141. Chapter 62, Acts of 1878 authorized the removal of prisoners from the Charlestown prison and their transfer to Concord where a new state prison had been built. It was evidently the intent of the authorities at that time to abandon permanently the old prison, for ch. 36 of the Resolves of 1878 authorized the Governor and Council to lease, sell, or otherwise dispose of the land when the prison was completely vacated.

142. Chapter 255 of the Acts of 1884 authorized the officials to prepare the old prison at Charlestown for use once more and to return some of the prisoners there from Concord when that institution was made into a Reformatory.

143. Chapter 385 of the Acts of 1874 authorized the building of a Reformatory Prison for Women with a capacity of five hundred.

144. Chapter 165 of the Acts of 1847 established the State Reform School for boys under the age of sixteen (excepting those serving a life sentence), but the age was lowered in subsequent years to exclude boys over fourteen (ch. 202 of the Acts of 1864). The Nautical School was established by ch. 285 of the Acts of 1859 for boys fifteen to eighteen (later changed to from twelve to eighteen) as a branch of the State Reform School to give instruction in navigation and seamanship. It was abolished in 1872 (ch. 68 of the Acts of that year). The Industrial School for Girls was established by ch. 442 of the Acts of 1855 for girls from seven to twelve years of age, with a provision that they could be held until eighteen. The Industrial School for Boys was intended for boys between the ages of fifteen and eighteen (ch. 639 of the Acts of 1908). The institutions for delinquent and wayward youth now in operation are briefly described in *The Basic Structure,* etc., pp. 102–106, referred to in note 139 above.

145. Chapter 275 of the Acts of 1852 authorized the building of an almshouse in Bridgewater. Chapter 45 of the Acts of 1872 changed the almshouse into the State Workhouse and Primary School, the inmates of the almshouse having been sent to Tewksbury. The name of the institution was changed to the State Farm by

ch. 264 of the Acts of 1887 and changed again by ch. 770 of the Acts of 1955 to Massachusetts Correctional Institution, Bridgewater. It is now the largest of the Commonwealth's correctional institutions.

146. Chapter 225 of the Revised Laws authorized the establishment of an industrial camp for prisoners which was opened in Rutland in April 1904. A hospital for tubercular prisoners was authorized by ch. 355 of the Acts of 1905 and united with the prison camp under the title "The Prison Camp and Hospital" by ch. 243 of the Acts of 1906.

147. Established by ch. 289 of the Acts of 1927. For a history of that institution see *The Development of Penological Treatment at Norfolk Prison Colony in Massachusetts* by Walter H. Commons, Thomas Yahkub, and Edwin Powers (Bur. of Soc. Hygiene, New York, 1940).

148. Authorized by ch. 755, Acts of 1951.

149. See almost any modern textbook on criminology that has a chapter on the history of prisons.

150. Prov. Laws, ch. 22 (1694–1695).

151. Prov. Laws, ch. 2 (1711–1712).

152. Prov. Laws, ch. 7 (1698).

153. Prov. Laws, ch. 30 (1764–1765).

154. Prov. Laws, ch. 2 (1702–1703).

155. Prov. Laws, ch. 18 (1692–1693).

156. Prov. Laws, ch. 1 (1719) and ch. 15 (1728–1729).

157. Prov. Laws, ch. 1 (1702–1703).

158. Prov. Laws, ch. 17 (1700–1701).

159. Prov. Laws, ch. 2 (1711–1712).

160. Prov. Laws, ch. 29 (1762–1763).

161. Prov. Laws, ch. 18 (1692–1693).

162. Prov. Laws, ch. 22 (1749–1750).

163. Prov. Laws, ch. 7 (1749–1750).

164. Prov. Laws, ch. 22 (1749–1750).

165. Prov. Laws, ch. 1 (1700).

166. See Negley K. Teeters, *The Cradle of the Penitentiary: the Walnut Street Jail at Philadelphia, 1773–1835,* sponsored by the Penn. Prison Soc. (1955); and Negley K. Teeters and John D. Shearer, *The Prison at Philadelphia: Cherry Hill* (Columbia University Press, New York, 1957), p. 10.

167. Chapter 63, Acts of 1784; see also ch. 170, Acts of 1790 and ch. 171, Acts of 1791. The first prisoners were received on October 24, 1785.

168. Chapter 39 of Resolves of 1785.

169. Message of Governor Samuel Adams to the General Court on June 4, 1794.

170. Message of Governor Increase Sumner to the General Court on January 11, 1799.

171. William Roscoe (1753–1831), eminent English historian, attorney, and prison reformer, declared that the keynote of a prison should be "benevolence." After a study of prisons in England and on the Continent and in Massachusetts, New York, and Pennsylvania about 1818, it was his opinion that the Charlestown institution was a "benevolent" prison. "The reformation of the criminal," he wrote, "should be the *motive,* the *object,* and the *measure* of all our exertions." To punish without attempting to reform, was, in his view, "a mere act of retribution or revenge." His opinions reflected the great reform movement in the administration of criminal justice of the latter part of the eighteenth century and early nineteenth, both abroad and in the United States. *Observations on Penal Jurisprudence, and the Reformation of Criminals* (London, 1819.)

172. Governor John Brooks' inaugural address to the General Court on June 6, 1820.

173. Connecticut opened its Old Newgate state prison in 1790 in an abandoned

copper mine in Simsbury, compared by some historians to the Black Hole of Calcutta. New York followed with its State Prison in New York City, also called Newgate, in 1797, and its famous Auburn Prison in 1816–1817 and opened a new prison at Sing Sing in 1828–1829. Virginia established a state prison in 1797; New Jersey in 1798; Vermont in 1809; Maryland in 1811; New Hampshire in 1812; Ohio in 1815; Maine in 1823; Pennsylvania in 1826 (the Western Penitentiary in Pittsburg). The separate system of prison discipline called the "Pennsylvania system" was launched in 1829 at the Eastern State Penitentiary in Philadelphia, locally referred to as "Cherry Hill" because it was built on the site of a cherry orchard. See Orlando F. Lewis, *The Development of American Prisons and Prison Customs: 1776–1895* (Prison Association of New York, 1922); Teeters and Shearer (note 166 above); Charles R. Henderson, editor, *Penal and Reformatory Institutions* (The Russell Sage Foundation, New York, 1910); Negley K. Teeters, *They Were in Prison: A History of the Pennsylvania Prison Society* (John C. Winston Co., Philadelphia, 1937). See the *Reports of the Prison Discipline Society,* compiled by the Rev. Mr. Louis Dwight, in three volumes, covering the period from 1826 to 1854, from the Press of T. R. Marvin, Boston, 1855. Here one will find reports of prison conditions from many American and European prisons, recommended standards for prisons of that era and some harsh words concerning the Pennsylvania system of prison discipline.

174. From Gideon Haynes, *Pictures from Prison Life: An Historical Sketch of the Massachusetts State Prison* (Lee and Shepard, Boston, 1869). Warden Haynes' interesting account is the only published history of that prison, but it covers only the first 63 years of its 150-year life.

175. Ibid.

176. Chapter 176, Acts of 1818; repealed in part by ch. 118, Acts of 1828.

177. Haynes (note 174 above).

178. Ibid.

179. Rules of the Board in 1812, as quoted by Haynes (note 174 above).

180. Legislative Document, Senate, no. 6 (1827).

181. Legislative Document, House, no. 1 (1817).

182. Answer of the House of Representatives on June 6, 1820, to the speech of Governor John Brooks.

183. Governor Levi Lincoln in his message to the General Court on January 4, 1826.

184. Governor Levi Lincoln in his message to the General Court on January 2, 1828.

185. Chapter 134 of the Acts of 1826.

186. Description of "the new prison" by Haynes (note 174 above).

187. Governor Levi Lincoln in his address to the General Court on January 5, 1831.

188. Governor Levi Lincoln in his message to the General Court on June 2, 1828.

189. Governor Levi Lincoln in his address to the General Court on January 9, 1832.

190. Governor John Davis in his address to the General Court on January 13, 1835.

191. Governor George N. Briggs in his address to the General Court on January 13, 1846.

192. Governor George N. Briggs in his address to the General Court on January 11, 1848.

193. Haynes (note 174 above).

194. Report of the State Prison, Public Document no. 25 (1860).

195. Haynes (note 174 above).

196. Report of the state prison, Public Document no. 15 (1864).

197. Special Report on Prisons and Prison Discipline (State Board of Charities 1865).

198. Report of the state prison, Public Document no. 25 (1860).

199. Report of the state prison, Public Document no. 13 (1869).

200. Report of the state prison, Public Document no. 13 (1867).

201. Report of the state prison, Public Document no. 13 (1871).

CHAPTER 9

1. *The Wicked Mans Portion, or A Sermon preached at the Lecture in Boston in New-England the 18th day of the 1 moneth* [March] *1674 when two men were executed, who murthered their master.* by Increase Mather (Printed by John Foster, Boston, 1675).

2. The Royal Charter of the Governour and Company of the Massachusetts Bay in New England, dated March 4, 1629.

3. The number of capital laws in the Pentateuch has been variously computed, differences depending on interpretations and methods of classification. Speare accounts for 33. See *Essays on the Punishment of Death,* 4th ed., by Rev. Charles Spear (published by the Author, Boston, 1844).

4. MCR, v. 4, pt. 1, p. 78 (1652).

5. From John Winthrop's "Discourse on Arbitrary Government," *Winthrop Papers,* v. 4, pp. 468–488, p. 473.

6. *Laws of Moses and the Code of Hammurabi* by S.A. Cook (London, 1903). *A Dictionary of the Bible,* James Hastings, editor, extra vol. (Charles Scribner's Sons, New York, 1904). *Babylonian and Assyrian Laws, Contracts and Letters* by C.H.W. Johns (Charles Scribner's Sons, New York, 1904). The Code of Hammurabi is compared with the laws of the Pentateuch in Chapter 14 of *Sources of Ancient and Primitive Law,* compiled by Albert Kocourek and John H. Wigmore (Little, Brown and Company, Boston, 1915).

7. Writers like Fluegel, for example, claim that the Hebrews drew up an original body of laws quite independent of the Code of Hammurabi. See *The Humanity, Benevolence and Charity Legislation of the Pentateuch and the Talmud* by Maurice Fluegel (H. Fluegel & Co., Baltimore, 1908). All Hebrew scholars claim that the eye-for-an-eye doctrine was humane, for it assured the offender that his punishment would not be out of proportion to his offense—an eye for an eye, rather than a life for an eye, and so on.

8. Thomas Hutchinson, the eighteenth century Governor of the Province Government just before the revolution, Chief Justice of the Superior Court and historian of Massachusetts, commented on this point: "Perhaps a roman catholic, for the adoration of the host, might have come within this law." Hutchinson's *History,* v. 1, p. 440.

9. MCR, v. 2, p. 177 (1646); also in Col. Laws (1648) p. 29; (1660) p. 163; (1672) p. 77.

10. The Rev. John Eliot wrote *The Day-Breaking if not the Sun-Rising of the Gospell with the Indians in New-England* (London, 1647) reprinted in *Mass. Hist. Coll.,* 3rd series, v. 4. See also Winthrop's account of Eliot's work in his *History* v. 2, pp. 370–371.

11. Code of Hammurabi, Laws no. 1 and 2.

12. MCR, v. 2, pp. 176–177 (1646); v. 3, p. 98 (1646).

13. Mass. Gen. Laws, c. 272, s. 36. See epilogue to Chapter 5.

14. MCR, v. 2, p. 212 (1647); Col. Laws (1648) p. 37; (1660) p. 171; (1672) p. 92.

15. Code of Hammurabi, Laws no. 206–208.

16. Mass. Gen. Laws, ch. 265, sec. 2.

17. Mass. Gen. Laws, ch. 265, sec. 28 and 16. Poisoning is still a serious crime in Massachusetts. An attempt to murder by poisoning is punishable by twenty years confinement and by life imprisonment if poison is mixed with food, drink, or medicine with intent to kill.

18. Today's statute, derived from the Body of Liberties, makes these crimes punishable by imprisonment up to twenty years—Mass. Gen. Laws, ch. 272, sec. 34.

19. Code of Hammurabi, Law no. 129.

20. Massachusetts is one of the few states making adultery a felony. It is now punishable by imprisonment in the state prison up to three years. Gen. Laws, ch. 272, sec. 14. Under this law, derived from the Body of Liberties, an unmarried woman cannot be charged with adultery for sexual intercourse with a married man.

21. "Adultery: A Review," Winfred E. Ohlson, *Boston University Law Review,* v. 17 (1937) pp. 328–368, 533–622. *The Law of Adultery and Ignominious Punishments,* Andrew McF. Davis (Press of Charles Hamilton, Worcester, Mass., 1895).

22. MCR, v. 1, p. 91 (1631); Court of Assistants, v. 2, p. 19 (1631).

23. Ibid.

24. Court of Assistants, v. 2, pp. 66–70 (1637); Winthrop's *History,* v. 1, p. 309.

25. MCR, v. 1, p. 225 (1638).

26. Today kidnapping is a capital crime in the federal government and in some states. In Massachusetts the maximum penalty for kidnapping when combined with extortion is imprisonment for life—Gen. Laws, ch. 265, sec. 26.

27. Deut. 24:7; see also Exod. 21:16.

28. Code of Hammurabi, Law no. 3.

29. Perjury on the trial of an indictment for a capital crime is now punishable in Massachusetts by imprisonment for life or for any term of years—Gen. Laws, ch. 268, sec. 1.

30. MCR, v. 5, p. 339 (1682); Col. Laws (1672) p. 291 (1682).

31. MCR, v. 2, p. 6 (1642); Col. Laws (1648) p. 11; (1660) pp. 136, 260; (1672) pp. 26, 149.

32. Under Jewish law an offender was required to marry the damsel and to pay her father fifty shekels of silver—Duet. 22:28–29.

33. Winthrop's *History,* v. 2, p. 58 (1641).

34. Winthrop's *History,* v. 2, pp. 54–58 (1641).

35. Winthrop's *History,* v. 2, p. 57 (1641).

36. Winthrop's *History,* v. 2, p. 58 (1641).

37. MCR, v. 2, p. 61 (1644).

38. MCR, v. 4, pt. 1, p. 91 (1652).

39. MCR, v. 4, pt. 1, p. 283 (1656).

40. MCR, v. 2, p. 21 (1642).

41. Ibid.

42. Col. Laws (1648) p. 6; (1660) p. 129; (1672) p. 15.

43. MCR, v. 4, pt. 1, pp. 218–219 (1654).

44. Court of Assistants, v. 3, pp. 199–200 (1669).

45. MCR, v. 4, pt. 2, pp. 437–438 (1669); Court of Assistants, v. 3, p. 200 (1669).

46. MCR, v. 2, p. 179 (1646); Col. Laws (1648) p. 6; (1660) p. 129; (1672) p. 15.

47. MCR, v. 2, pp. 179–180 (1646); Col. Laws (1648) p. 6; (1660) p. 129; (1672) p. 15.

48. MCR, v. 5, p. 339 (1682).

49. The application of the term "stubborn child" is now limited to those under 21—Mass. Gen. Laws, ch. 272, sec. 53. The indictment now may read: "That A. B., a minor . . . was a stubborn child, and stubbornly refused to submit to the lawful and reasonable commands of C.D., whose commands said A.B. was bound to obey"—Mass. Gen. Laws, ch. 277, sec. 79.

50. MCR, v. 2, p. 22 (1644).
51. Identity of these two young men is revealed in the editor's footnote to Winthrop's *History*, v. 2, p. 203 (1644).
52. Winthrop's *History*, v. 2, pp. 203–204 (1644).
53. Col. Laws (1648) p. 4–5; (1660) p. 127; (1672) pp. 12–13.
54. MCR, v. 4, pt. 2, pp. 511–512 (1672); Col. Laws (1672) p. 204.
55. Ibid.
56. See pp. 143–144 and 152–153.
57. MCR, v. 4, pt. 1, p. 78 (1652); Col. Laws (1660) p. 154; (1672) pp. 59–60.
58. MCR, v. 2, pp. 176-177 (1646); Col. Laws (1648) p. 24; (1660) pp. 154-156; (1672) pp. 58–63.
59. Col. Laws (1648) p. 24; (1660) p. 154; (1672) pp. 58–59.
60. MCR, v. 4, pt. 1, p. 78 (1652); Col. Laws (1660) p. 154; (1672) pp. 59–60.
61. MCR, v. 4, pt. 1, p. 83 (1652); Col. Laws (1660) p. 152; (1672) p. 51.
62. MCR, v. 5, pp. 49–50 (1675); Col. Laws (1672) p. 229–231 (1675).
63. MCR, v. 4, pt. 2, p. 563 (1673); v. 5, pp. 447–448 (1684); Col. Laws (1672) p. 211 (1673).
64. MCR, v. 5, p. 194 (1678).
65. MCR, v. 5, p. 447 (1684); Col. Laws (1672) pp. 315–316 (1684).
66. *Winthrop Papers*, v. 4, p. 476 ff.
67. *The Spirit of Jewish Law*, George Horowitz (Central Book Co., New York, 1953).
68. MCR, v. 4, pt. 1, p. 213 (1654); Court of Assistants, v. 3, pp. 34–35 (1654).
69. Court of Assistants, v. 3, pp. 36–37 (1654).
70. MCR, v. 4, pt. 1, p. 213 (1654).
71. Samuel Sewall's *Diary*, June 15, 1674. See also the case of Richard Nason, accused of blasphemy but found "not so guilty of that fact as that by our law he ought to dye"—MCR, v. 4, pt. 1, pp. 244–245 (1655).
72. Court of Assistants, v. 1, pp. 29–30 (1674).
73. Court of Assistants, v. 1, pp. 306–307, 321 (1688).
74. Court of Assistants, v. 3, pp. 24-25 (1653); MCR, v. 4, pt. 1, p. 145 (1653.
75. Court of Assistants, v. 1, pp. 242–243 (1683).
76. Winthrop's *History*, v. 2, pp. 225–227 (1644). When Winthrop argues that, if a person kills another while committing an act that is evil in itself he should be condemned as a murderer, his reasoning is similar in principle to the modern doctrine of "felony murder" held in Massachusetts today; that is, if a person kills another in the course of the commission of a crime punishable by life imprisonment or death, his crime is deemed to be murder in the first degree although he had no intention of killing—Mass. Gen. Laws, ch. 265, sec. 1.
77. Court of Assistants, v. 1, p. 252 (1683).
78. Court of Assistants, v. 2, p. 108 (1641).
79. Court of Assistants, v. 1, p. 70 (1676).
80. Court of Assistants, v. 1, pp. 70–71 (1676).
81. See p. 91.
82. Court of Assistants, v. 3, p. 192 (1667).
83. Winthrop's *History*, v. 2, pp. 305–306 (1645).
84. MCR, v. 2, pp. 211–212 (1647).
85. Court of Assistants, v. 3, p. 67 (1657); Essex County Court, v. 2, p. 60 (1657).
86. Court of Assistants, v. 3, pp. 216–217 (1672).
87. Court of Assistants, v. 2, p. 121 (1643).
88. MCR, v. 4, pt. 1, p. 49 (1654).
89. Essex County Court, v. 8, p. 15 (1680).
90. Court of Assistants, v. 3, pp. 144-145 (1664).
91. MCR, v. 4, pt. 2, pp. 217–218 (1665); Court of Assistants, v. 3, pp. 138–139 (1663); Essex County Court, v. 3, pp. 111, 117 (1663); p. 227 (1664).

92. MCR, v. 4, pt. 2, pp. 158–161, 184–186 (1665).

93. MCR, v. 4, pt. 2, p. 218 (1665).

94. MCR, v. 4, pt. 2, p. 218 (1665). See also MCR, v. 4, pt. 2, pp. 195–197 (1665).

95. Court of Assistants, v. 1, p. 102 (1677).

96. Winthrop's *History,* v. 1, p. 288; Court of Assistants, v. 2, p. 69 (1637).

97. Winthrop's *History,* v. 1, pp. 288–290, 387; Court of Assistants, v. 2, p. 69 (1637).

98. Winthrop's *History,* v. 1, pp. 335–336; Court of Assistants, v. 2, p. 78 (1638); MCR, v. 1, p. 246 (1638).

99. Winthrop's *History,* v. 2, pp. 257–258 (1645); Court of Assistants, v. 2, p. 74 (1638).

100. Winthrop's *History,* v. 2, pp. 368–370.

101. Sewall's *Diary,* Feb. 13, 1675; Court of Assistants, v. 1, pp. 30, 32, 33 (1674).

102. Court of Assistants, v. 1, pp. 294–295 (1685).

103. Court of Assistants, v. 1, pp. 303–304 (1689–1690). At Stone's request Rev. Cotton Mather preached his execution sermon on Dec. 29, 1689.

104. Court of Assistants, v. 1, pp. 318–320 (1689).

105. Court of Assistants, v. 1, p. 357 (1691).

106. Court of Assistants, v. 1, p. 53 (1675). Court of Assistants, v. 1, p. 71 (1676).

107. Sewall's *Diary,* Sept. 13, 1676.

108. Winthrop's *History,* v. 2, pp. 58–60; MCR, v. 1, p. 344 (1641).

109. Court of Assistants, v. 1, pp. 10–11 (1673); Samuel Sewall's *Diary,* April 2, 1674.

110. Winthrop's *History,* v. 2, pp. 190–191 (1643); Court of Assistants, v. 2, p. 139 (1644). James Britton had been whipped six years earlier, in Governor Winthrop's administration, for some "reproachful" remarks on church government —Winthrop's *History,* v. 1, p. 347 (1638). In 1644 he confessed to the Governor that "he did what he could to commit Adultery with Mary the wife of Mr. Latham but he was not then himself, having been drinking all the night till midnight at his own house with 16 of his neighbors." (*Winthrop Papers,* v. 4, p. 446.) Britton was not the kind of man to whom the Governor was likely to extend mercy.

111. Court of Assistants, v. 1, pp. 21–22 (1674).

112. Court of Assistants, v. 1, p. 50 (1675).

113. Court of Assistants, v. 1, p. 74 (1676); Samuel Sewall's *Diary,* June 22, 1676.

114. Court of Assistants, v. 1, p. 199 (1681).

115. Court of Assistants, v. 1, pp. 198–199 (1681).

116. Court of Assistants, v. 1, pp. 34–39 (1675).

117. Court of Assistants, v. 1, pp. 305–321 (1689).

118. Sewall's *Diary,* Jan. 17, 27, 1689.

119. Court of Assistants, v. 1, p. 76 (1676).

120. The records of the Essex County Court in 1670 (v. 4, p. 314) report that a person (unnamed) who had been imprisoned in Salem "broke prison and was lately executed for theft." (We can find no confirmation of this report in other documents.)

121. Sewall's *Diary,* Sept. 13, 1676.

122. Court of Assistants, v. 1, pp. 198–199 (1681). See "The Case of Maria in the Court of Assistants in 1681," by John Noble, *Pub. of the Col. Soc. of Mass.* (1904) v. 6, pp. 323–336. Abner C. Goodell, Jr. in his *The Trial and Execution for Petit Treason of Mark and Phillis,* (University Press, Cambridge, 1883), reported the execution by burning of one person in Cambridge in 1755, the only known case of a legal execution by this method in the annals of Massachusetts, aside from the case of Maria about which there has been much disagreement. Phillis, a Negro slave, was found guilty of the murder of her master, which under the Common Law, constituted petit treason and called for the punishment of burning at the

stake. Her accomplice Mark, also a Negro slave, was hung. Goodell's report was also published in *Mass. Hist. Soc. Proc.,* v. 20 (1883), pp. 122-157.

123. Body of Liberties, no. 44; Col. Laws (1648) p. 12–13; (1660) p. 139; (1672) p. 30.

124. *Letters Written From New-England, A.D. 1686 by John Dunton—in Which are Described His Voyages by Sea, His travels on Land, and the Characters of His Friends and Acquaintances.* (Printed for the Prince Society, Boston, 1867) pp. 118–136. Reprinted in part in *The Puritans* by Perry Miller and Thomas H. Johnson (American Book Co., New York, 1938) pp. 414–420.

125. From an official statement of Nathaniel Morton, clerk of the General Court, PCR, v. 11, pp. 148–149 (1658) .

126. PCR, v. 11, p. 12 (1636) ; p. 94–95 (1658) ; p. 172 (1671) .

127. For the usual punishment of adultery, see p. 262.

128. PCR, v. 5, p. 173 (1677) .

129. Plymouth Laws, p. 246.

130. PCR, v. 6, pp. 136–139 (1684) .

131. Bradford's *History,* pp. 329–330 and 109.

132. "Governour Bradford's Letter Book," Reprinted in *Mass. Hist. Coll.,* 1st series, v. 3, pp. 27–84, p. 37.

133. Numbers 35:33.

134. PCR, v. 1, pp. 96–97 (1638) ; Bradford's *History,* pp. 432–435 (1638) .

135. PCR, v. 2, p. 134 (1648) .

136. PCR, v. 5, pp. 167–168 (1675) .

137. PCR, v. 5, pp. 205–206 (1676) .

138. PCR, v. 2, p. 44 (1642) ; Bradford's *History,* pp. 474–475 (1642) .

139. PCR, v. 6, p. 98 (1682) .

140. Prov. Laws, ch. 1 and 43 (1692–1693) . Of the 25 capital laws of the Bay Colony, two had already been repealed—the law demanding death for Quakers who returned after banishment, and the stubborn-and-rebellious-son law.

141. Prov. Laws, v. 1, notes on p. 110. From 1692 to 1780 the government enacted 1938 public laws. Only 47, or 2.4% of these laws were "disallowed" by the Privy Council. Thirty-five of the 47 "disallowances" came in the early years (1692–1700) when the Province was struggling to establish its laws, not knowing in every case what might be considered "repugnant." In the eighteenth century the Privy Council rarely interfered with Province legislation, "disallowing" less than 1% of the 1,721 laws enacted in that century.

142. Prov. Laws, ch. 19 (1692–1693) .

143. Prov. Laws, v. 1, notes on p. 110.

144. See Chapter 14.

145. Prov. Laws, ch. 20 (1697). Mass Gen. Laws, ch. 272, sec. 36. See the epilogue to Chapter 5.

146. Prov. Laws, ch. 17 (1697) . See letter from Privy Council in Prov. Laws, v. 1, p. 56. The maximum penalty for manslaughter in Massachusetts today is imprisonment for twenty years—Mass. Gen. Laws, ch. 265, sec. 13.

147. Prov. Laws, ch. 19 (1692–1693) .

148. Prov. Laws, ch. 19 (1692–1693) ; ch. 2 (1695–1696) .

149. Prov. Laws, ch. 1 (1715–1716) .

150. Prov. Laws, v. 5, notes on p. 64.

151. Prov. Laws, ch. 16 (1769–1770) . "Benefit of clergy," a term derived from twelfth century English law, arose out of the claim of ecclesiastical authorities that they should be exempt from punishments inflicted by temporal courts and subject only to those of the spiritual courts. The test to determine whether one was an ecclesiastical person, or "clericus," thus enabling him to escape the penalty of death, was his ability to read a particular verse from the Bible (Psalms 51:1) which became known as the "neck verse." The law was extended to many secular classes but did not apply to the more atrocious crimes, hence the division between

"clergyable" and "non-clergyable" offenses. In order that a layman might not claim the privilege twice after a conviction for a "clergyable" offense, he was branded on the thumb. The gradual extension of this privilege served to modify the harsh penalties of English law. It was not, so far as we can determine, openly invoked in the Bay or Plymouth Colonies, although there were a few instances of its use in the eighteenth century in Massachusetts and some of the other American Colonies where an offender pleaded "benefit of clergy" and was dismissed with a branding on the thumb. Province legislators frequently added to a capital law the phrase "without benefit of clergy" to make sure no one convicted under that law would escape the death penalty by pleading this old Common Law right. A bill to abolish this practice in Massachusetts passed the Senate (then called the Council) in 1730 and reached a third reading in the House but failed of passage. (*Journal of the House of Representatives of Mass.,* v. 10 (1731–1732), p. 43, *Mass. Hist. Soc. Pub.,* 1929). It was finally outlawed in the Commonwealth in 1785, the General Court stating that it was "originally founded in superstition and injustice" and had operated "very inadequately and disproportionately" (Chap. 56, Acts of 1784). An act of Congress put an end to it in the federal courts in 1790 but it was not abolished in England until 1825. See William Blackstone's essay *Of the Benefit of Clergy,* ch. 28, Bk. 4 of his famous *Commentaries on the Laws of England* [1765–1769], (Beacon Press, Boston, 1962). For its history and its application in American courts see "Benefit of Clergy" by Edward J. White in *Amer. Law Rev.* 46 (1912) 78–94.

152. Prov. Laws, ch. 18 (1692–1693); ch. 2 (1711–1712); ch. 21 (1761–1762).

153. Prov. Laws, ch. 5 (1694-1695); ch. 19 (1698).

154. Prov. Laws, ch. 4 (1696). Piracy was not uncommon during the entire seventeenth century but had not become a serious threat until the latter part of that century and the early eighteenth. The Plymouth Colony had been warned in 1657 by the London corporation that "the seas are very dangerous in regard of pyrates which continually enfests the same"—PCR, v. 10, p. 185.

155. Prov. Laws, ch. 11 (1696).

156. Prov. Laws, ch. 12 (1696); ch. 32 (1776–1777). Compare the wording of the Federal Constitution (Art. 3, sec. 3)—"in levying war against them [the United States], or in adhering to their enemies, giving them aid and comfort" and a similar wording in the Commonwealth statute—Gen. Laws., ch. 264, sec. 1. During the Province period there were other capital laws for treasonable conduct by soldiers and mariners, particularly during the period of wars with the French. These laws have not been set forth in this chapter. See Prov. Laws, ch. 4 (1693–1694); ch. 20 and 21 (1699–1700); ch. 7 (1704–1705); ch. 8 (1706–1707); ch. 6 (1744–1745).

157. Prov. Laws, ch. 17 (1697).

158. Prov. Laws, ch. 18 (1697).

159. Prov. Laws, ch. 18 and ch. 19 (1697).

160. *The Boston Gazette,* Oct. 31 to Nov. 7, 1720. Samuel Shute was the Royal Governor of the Province from 1716 to 1722.

161. Prov. Laws, ch. 2 (1702–1703); ch. 6 (1714); ch. 10 (1720–1721); ch. 18 (1735–1736); ch. 44 (1776–1777). There were many other noncapital laws penalizing acts of counterfeiting, a crime that was evidently almost impossible to prevent.

162. MCR, v. 3, p. 264 (1652); Prov. Laws, ch. 9 (1705–1706).

163. Prov. Laws, ch. 1 (1719–1720); ch. 15 (1728–1729).

164. Prov. Laws, ch. 18 (1736–1737).

165. Massachusetts Constitution, Part II, ch. 6, sec. 6.

166. Ibid, Declaration of Rights, art. 26. In the Federal Bill of Rights, art. 8, the wording is similar.

167. Commonwealth Laws, ch. 44 of the Acts of 1784 and ch. 123 of the Acts of 1804. The latter provided that the body of a person executed for murder committed in a duel would be "dissected and anatomized." The Federal Constitution gives

Congress power "to define and punish piracies and felonies committed on the high seas, and offences against the law of nations" (Art. 1, sec. 8) .

168. Commonwealth Laws, ch. 46, Acts of 1784; ch. 133, Acts of 1804. The latter enactment reduced the penalty to imprisonment up to ten years following one year of solitary confinement. The law of 1784 was repealed by ch. 88, Acts of 1805.

169. Commonwealth Laws, ch. 48 and 65 of the Acts of 1784; ch. 101 of the Acts of 1805.

170. Commonwealth Laws, ch. 52, Acts of 1784; ch. 124, Acts of 1819.

171. Commonwealth Laws, ch. 58, Acts of 1784; ch. 72, Acts of 1830.

172. Commonwealth Laws, ch. 68, Acts of 1784; ch. 97, Acts of 1805; ch. 86, Acts of 1816.

173. Treason was evidently one of the laws carried over from the Province government, not specifically placed on the Commonwealth statute books until 1836 (ch. 124 of the Acts of that year) but sixteen years later the penalty was reduced to life imprisonment (ch. 259 of the Acts of 1852) . Since the adoption of the Federal Constitution there was little need for such a law in Massachusetts. "Treason against the Commonwealth can hardly be anticipated under circumstances which would not make it treason also against the general [federal] government, by whose laws and authorities it may be tried and punished"—House Doc. 8, 1836. A case did arise, however, in 1786 when Daniel Shays led a rebellion in the western part of the state, protesting excessive taxation. None of those convicted was executed, although legally guilty of a capital offense. The life imprisonment penalty is still on the statute books of the Commonwealth (Gen. Laws, ch. 264, sec. 2) .

174. Commonwealth Laws, ch. 143 of the Acts of 1804; ch. 124 of the Acts of 1818; Sen. Doc. 73 (1836) p. 14.

175. House Doc. 8 (1836) pp. 5–6. The population of the Commonwealth had grown from 268,627 in 1780 to 610,408 in 1830.

176. Senate Doc. 58 (1846) p. 15. For a report of the nationwide drive for abolition during this period, see "Movements to Abolish the Death Penalty in the United States" by Louis Filler in *The Annals of the Amer. Acad. of Pol. and Soc. Science* (Nov. 1952) pp. 124–136.

177. Commonwealth Laws, ch. 127 of the Acts of 1839.

178. From the first annual report of the Mass. Society for the Abolition of Capital Punishment (1846) .

179. Commonwealth Laws, ch. 259, Acts of 1852.

180. House Doc. 10 (1839) p. 6.

181. Senate Doc. 73 (1836) p. 20.

182. House Doc. 4 (1837) p. 49.

183. From a sermon preached in the meetinghouse of the First Parish in Charlestown by its pastor, entitled "Capital Punishment: A Discourse, occasioned by the Murder of the Late Warden of the Massachusetts State Prison" (printed by T. R. Marvin, 24 Congress St., Boston, 1843) .

184. House Doc. 135 (1849) p. 8. English courts at this time were also having great difficulty in getting convictions in capital cases where hanging seemed completely inappropriate for the crime in question. Sir William Blackstone (1723–1780), English jurist, reported in the 1760's that "no less than 160 [offenses] have been declared by acts of Parliament, to be felonies without benefit of clergy; or, in other words, to be worthy of instant death." In the next 60 years the "no less than 160" was said to have grown to 220. Juries were not willing to bring in a verdict of guilty where the charge was shoplifting or stealing an object worth no more than five shillings, knowing the penalty was death. When convictions were obtained, a reprieve usually followed. Sir Samuel Romilly (1757–1818) , noted English legal reformer, led the fight for amelioration of the English criminal laws, commencing about 1808. See his *Observations on the Criminal Law of England, as it relates to Capital Punishments, and on the Mode in which it is administered,* ed. 3 (London, 1813) . The multiplication of the capital laws had reached an absurdity.

Within a seven-year period (1806–1813), he reported, of the 1872 persons convicted of shoplifting or stealing, only one was executed. From 1830 to about 1860 Parliament was active in repealing most of England's capital laws, finding that "the public mind revolts at capital punishment in cases not atrocious."

185. House Doc. 4 (1837) pp. 53–54.

186. Senate Doc. 20 (1842) p. 5, quoted in House Doc. 149 (1851) pp. 20–21.

187. Senate Doc. 58 (1846) p. 15.

188. House Doc. 4 (1837) p. 53.

189. House Doc. 8 (1836) p. 8.

190. Senate Doc. 58 (1846) pp. 14–15. By 1846 most of the states, and all New England states except Massachusetts, had removed the death penalty for the crime of rape. Yet in 1964, seventeen states, the District of Columbia, and the federal government provided the death penalty as a possible punishment for rape. Can such a penalty be considered, in the light of the trend toward abolition and the decreasing use of capital punishment nationally, as "cruel and unusual punishment?" For a discussion of this question see Herbert L. Packer, "Making the Punishment Fit The Crime," *Harvard Law Review,* v. 77, pp. 1071-1082 (1964).

191. See *Punishment by Death: Its Authority and Expediency* by Rev. George B. Cheever (John Wiley, New York, 1855). The author (1807-1890), noted preacher and antislavery campaigner, based his closely reasoned treatise advocating the death penalty for murderers on the assumption that the Hebrew laws of the Old Testament were not the laws of Moses but the laws of God, universal and immutable. The command in Genesis (9:6) "Whoso sheddeth man's blood, by man shall his blood be shed" (given to the people long before Moses' time) was not abrogated by Christ who said, "Think not that I am come to destroy the law, or the prophets: I am not come to destroy, but to fulfil" (Matt. 5:17).

192. House Doc. 73 (1843) p. 6.

193. Senate Doc. 69 (1837) p. 5.

194. House Doc. 149 (1851) p. 6.

195. Senate Doc. 58 (1846) p. 22.

196. House Doc. 196 (1848) Appendix A.

197. Senate Doc. 69 (1837) p. 35.

198. House Doc. 149 (1851) p. 19.

199. House Doc. 4 (1837) pp. 133–134.

200. Perhaps the author of this statement had in mind the trial, conviction, and execution of two Irishmen in 1806. Associate Justice Robert Sullivan of the Massachusetts Superior Court, in an article entitled "The Murder Trial of Halligan and Daley; Northampton, Massachusetts, 1806," published in the *Mass. Law Quarterly,* v. 49 (1964) pp. 211–224, showed how strong prejudices against Roman Catholics made a fair trial impossible for these two defendants who maintained their innocence until the last. Years later, it was said, the actual murderer, on his deathbed, confessed that he was the sole actor in the crime, thus clearing Halligan and Daley who had been convicted on very tenuous circumstantial evidence.

201. House Doc. 8 (1836) p. 17.

202. House Doc. 10 (1839) p. 8.

203. House Doc. 149 (1851) p. 25.

204. House Doc. 149 (1851) p. 26.

205. Sen. Doc. 58 (1846) pp. 12–13.

206. Commonwealth Laws, ch. 154 of the Acts of 1858.

207. Commonwealth Laws, ch. 227 of the Acts of 1873.

208. Mass. Gen. Laws, ch. 123, sec. 101.

209. Sen. Doc. 293 (1888); Sen. Doc. 323 (1889). New York was the first state to enact a law providing for the electrocution of the condemned. The law was enacted in 1888. At Auburn Prison on August 6, 1890, the "electric chair" claimed its first victim.

210. House Doc. 370 (1893).

211. Commonwealth Laws, ch. 326 of the Acts of 1898.

212. Governor Long's address to the General Court in 1881; Sen. Doc. 239 (1881). See also House Doc. 382 (1900) and House Doc. 164 (1901).

213. Commonwealth Laws, ch. 203 of the Acts of 1951; ch. 770 of the Acts of 1955 and ch. 731 of the Acts of 1956. "Lifers" can be made eligible for parole by a commutation by the Governor with the consent of the Council—a not infrequent occurrence. During the abolition movement of 1831–1852 abolitionists offered, as a substitute penalty, solitary confinement for life in the state prison with no possibility of escape or pardon (parole had not as yet come into the penological picture) where the convict would be "cut off from the world but compelled to live . . . a distressing silence in solitude"—House Doc. 15 (1831). A House committee favoring the death penalty argued that this substitute offered by the "professed advocates for mercy" would be worse than death (a view with which modern penologists would agree). "Against the exercise of *such mercy,* your committee beg leave to enter their solemn protest. . . . Leave refinements in cruelty to slumber among the ruins of the Inquisition . . ."—House Doc. 4 (1837) pp. 123-124; Sen. Doc. 73 (1836) pp. 7-8.

214. Source of Data: For the period 1780 to 1846, Senate Document 58 (1846), p. 14, and House Doc. 196, Appendix A; for the period 1860 to 1889, *The Boston Herald* for May 25, 1890; for the period 1890 to 1899, a research report by Raymond T. Bye entitled *Capital Punishment in the United States,* published in 1919 by the Committee on Philanthropic Labor of Philadelphia; for the period 1900 to the present, official records of the Department of Correction, Commonwealth of Massachusetts, which show that no women were executed in this period and that there has been no execution to date since May 9, 1947.

215. For a sketch of the legislative history of capital punishment in Massachusetts listing the most important official documents, see the scholarly report and recommendations of *The Special Commission Established for the Purpose of Investigating and Studying the Abolition of the Death Penalty in Capital Cases,* House Doc. 2575 (1958), printed in 1959. A majority of the Commission recommended complete abolition.

216. House Doc. 4 (1837) p. 41. Sixty-one years later the gallows did, in fact, disappear, only to be followed by the electric chair.

CHAPTER 10

1. George Bishop (?–1668), an ardent Quaker with a fiery pen, wrote a comprehensive denunciation of the "wretched hypocrites" and "cruel murtherers" of the Bay Colony—"Rulers of Sodom, and inhabitants of Gomorrah." He called his book: *New-England Judged, Not by Man's, but the Spirit of the Lord and the Sum Sealed up of New-England's Persecutions.* Part 1 narrates events from 1656 to 1660. It was published in London in 1661. Part 2 covers the period from 1660 to 1665 and was first published in London in 1667. In 1703 Joseph Gore of London bound the two parts together and published them in one volume, with Part 1 "somewhat abbreviated" and the whole supplemented by some personal documents by John Whiting and other Quakers. Quotations from Bishop in this chapter are from the 1703 edition, "printed and sold by T. Sowle, in White-Hart-Court in Gracious-Street." The statement (from p. 19, Part 1) here attributed to Endecott (1589–1663), Governor of the Bay Colony, may have been hearsay, so far as Bishop was concerned, but it is consistent with the official statements of the 67-year-old Governor who led the attack against the Quakers. The term "damnable heresies" is from Second Peter 2:1.

2. *Mass. Arch.,* v. 10, no. 234.

3. "Quakerism is Popery in a new dress, or rather Popery and worse . . . ," wrote a New Englander to a friend in London about 1660—from a letter in the appendix to *The Brief Tractate* of the Rev. John Norton (see note 9 below). And

yet the Quakers in their theological position were just as anti-Catholic as the Puritans.

4. Although the Salem witch trials were not to take place for another 36 years, Puritans as well as non-Puritans of that age believed in the reality of witches. The Bay Colony had already executed three women for "familiarity with the Devil." Quakers were not infrequently referred to as witches, although never officially charged with the capital crime of witchcraft.

5. *The Snake in the Grass: or, Satan Transform'd into an angel of light, discovering [revealing] the deep and unsuspected subtilty which is couched under the pretended simplicity, of many of the principle leaders of those people call'd Quakers,* Charles Leslie (1650–1722), ed. 2. "Printed for Charles Brome, at the Gun at the West-end of St. Paul's, London, 1697."

6. MCR, v. 4, pt. 1, p. 276 (1656).

7. This liberal law, incorporated in all Colonial Codes—Col. Laws (1648) p. 1 (1660) p. 121; (1672) p. 1 was derived from the Body of Liberties of 1641, Art. 1.

8. MCR, v. 4, pt. 1, p. 385 (1659). It was Bishop's claim that holding these two women in the Boston prison, deprived of visits, books, pen and ink, and even their Bibles, with little food and no beds, was punishment indeed, for which there was no legal justification. Governor Endecott, who was in Salem when the *Swallow* docked in Boston harbor, was reported to have said that "if he had been there he would have had them well Whipp'd"—Bishop, op cit, note 1, pp. 4–10, Part 1.

9. *The Heart of New-England Rent at the Blasphemies of the present Generation; or a brief Tractate, concerning the Doctrine of the Quakers, Demonstrating the destructive nature thereof, to Religion, the Churches, and the State; with consideration of the Remedy against it,* p. 2, by John Norton (1602–1663) Teacher of the Church of Christ at Boston. "Printed by J.H. for John Allen at the Rising Sunne in St. Pauls Church-yard" (London, 1660).

10. MCR, v. 5, p. 60 (1675).

11. Norton, (op cit, note 9) p. 72.

12. Norton, (op. cit, note 9) pp. 71–72. It was almost two centuries after Norton's time before religious freedom for *all* religious sects and denominations was guaranteed by an amendment to the constitution of the Commonwealth of Massachusetts in 1833.

13. Bishop (op. cit, note 1) p. 380, Part 2.

14. Quakers considered flattery or obeisance to fellow men an evil, for all men were equal before the Lord. As for taking an oath, Quakers quoted Matthew 5:33–37 where Christ said "Ye have heard that it hath been said of them of old time, Thou shalt not foreswear thyself, but shall perform unto the Lord thine oaths: But I say unto you, Swear not at all. . . . Let your communication be, Yea, yea; Nay, nay. . . . "

15. MCR, v. 4, pt. 1, pp. 345–346 (1658).

16. From a letter by Quaker William Robinson to George Fox and others in England, published in the *Mass. Hist. Soc. Collections,* 4th ser., v. 9, p. 156. The letter was dated July 12, 1659.

17. Ibid, pp. 156–157.

18. Court of Assistants, v. 3, pp. 68–69 (1659).

19. Edward Burrough in *A Declaration of the Sad and Great Persecution and Martydom of the People of God, called Quakers, in New-England, for the Worshipping of God,* a reply to the 1660 petition of the General Court to the King (R. Wilson, London, 1660).

20. Both Quaker and Puritan took pen in hand and produced an amazing array of letters, tracts, and books defending their views and attacking the opposition. Usually they wrote in deadly earnestness, sometimes with sly humor. When Roger Williams wrote his *George Fox Digged out of his Burrow* (referring to the founder of The Society of Friends and the prominent English Quaker, Edward Burrough), Fox and John Burnyeat published their rejoinder, *A New-England*

Fire-Brand Quenched, Being Something in Answer unto a Lying, Slanderous Book. . . . (London, 1678) .

21. Col. Laws (1648) p. 18; (1660) pp. 146-147; (1672) p. 43, based on the Body of Liberties of 1641, no. 95.

22. MCR, v. 4, pt. 1, pp. 277–278 (1656) .

23. Bishop (op. cit, note 1) p. 235, appendix.

24. Records of the Colony of Rhode Island and Providence Plantations, v. 1, p. 377 (1657) .

25. Samuel Groom in *A Glass for the People of New-England, in which they may see themselves and Spirits, and if not too late, Repent and Turn from their Abominable ways and cursed Contrivances,* p. 13 (London, 1676) .

26. MCR, v. 4, pt. 1, pp. 308–309 (1657) . There is no record of the infliction of tongue boring or the loss of *both* ears. Bishop and other Quaker writers would no doubt have reported these penalties had they occurred.

27. MCR, v. 4, pt. 1, p. 321 (1658) .

28. PCR, v. 11, p. 120 (1657) .

29. PCR, v. 11, pp. 121, 205 (1658) .

30. PCR, v. 11, pp. 126, 205 (1660) .

31. PCR, v. 11, p. 130 (1661) .

32. PCR, v. 3, p. 140 (1658) .

33. MCR, v. 4, pt. 1, p. 385 (1659) .

34. From letter cited in note 3.

35. MCR, v. 4, pt. 1, pp. 346–347 (1658) .

36. Bishop op cit, note 1 p. 43.

37. George Fox in "Queries by another hand for the New-England priests and elders to answer," in p. 31 *A Glass for the People of New-England. . . .* (see note 25) . Quakers contemptuously called Colonial ministers "Priests" or "Professors." Groom in the book cited here explained that the term "professors" meant "such as profess God, Christ and Scriptures, and Ordinances of the Gospel, *but live in another Spirit.*"

38. MCR, v. 4, pt. 2, p. 8 (1661) .

39. Bishop, op cit, note 1, p. 102, Part 1.

40. *Mass. Arch.,* v. 10, no. 246.

41. Bishop, op cit, note 1, pp. 238–244, Part 1.

42. MCR, v. 4, pt. 1, pp. 384–386 (1659) .

43. A reproduction of this Broadside can be found in *Mass. Hist. Soc. Proc.,* v. 42, p. 203, and on p. 341 of this book.

44. Bishop, op cit. note 1, pp. 128–129, Part 1.

45. See note 19.

46. Bishop op cit, note 1, pp. 128–129, Part 1.

47. Bishop, op cit, note 1, p. 95, Part 1.

48. MCR, v. 4, pt. 1, p. 348 (1658) .

49. Quakers charged with denying the "Trinity," challenged the "most refined Professors of the Christian Religion" to find any mention of "Trinity" in the Gospels.

50. MCR, v. 4, pt. 1, pp. 386–390 (1659) .

51. *Mass. Arch.,* v. 10, no. 260a.

52. *An Examination of the Grounds or Causes, which are said to induce the Court of Boston in New-England to make that order or Law of Banishment upon pain of Death against the Quakers . . . ,* pp. 69–70, by "Isaac Penington, the Younger. Printed for L. Lloyd next to the Sign of the Castle in Cornhill" (London, 1660) .

53. Court of Assistants, v. 3, pp. 104–105 (1659) .

54. MCR, v. 4, pt. 1, p. 391 (1659) .

55. MCR, v. 4, pt. 1, p. 383 (1659) .

56. Bishop, op cit, note 1, pp. 121–122, Part 1. Bishop published Robinson's

reply to the court which it would not permit Robinson to read. See Bishop, pp. 127–131.

57. See note 16. "The Trial of Quakers William Robinson, Marmaduke Stevenson and Mary Dyer" has been published in *American State Trials,* John D. Lawson, editor, (F. H. Thomas Law Book Co., St. Louis, 1914) v. 1, pp. 813-824.

58. MCR, v. 4, pt. 1, pp. 383–384 (1659).

59. MCR, v. 4, pt. 1, p. 385 (1659).

60. MCR, v. 4, pt. 1, p. 383 (1659).

61. Bishop, op cit, note 1, p. 125, Part 1.

62. MCR, v. 4, pt. 1, p. 384 (1659).

63. Bishop, op cit, note 1, p. 134, Part 1.

64. MCR, v. 4, pt. 1, p. 419 (1660).

65. Bishop, op cit, note 1, p. 157.

66. See Bishop op cit, note 1. See also *Several Epistles Given forth by Two of the Lords Faithful Servants, whom he sent to New-England, to Bear Witness to his Everlasting Truth* by William Leddra and William Robinson (London, 1669), and Joseph Besse's *A Collection of the Sufferings of the People called Quakers,* in 2 vols. (Luke Hinde, London, 1753).

67. Court of Assistants, v. 3, pp. 93–94; MCR, v. 4, pt. 1, p. 433 (1660).

68. Bishop op cit, note 1, p. 296, Part 1. An account of the hanging of Leddra can be found in *An Addition to the Book, Entitled, The Spirit of the Martyrs Revived* by Ellis Hookes (London, 1682).

69. MCR, v. 4, pt. 1, p. 433 (1660).

70. Bishop, op cit, note 1, pp. 467–468, Part 2.

71. Bishop, op cit, note 1, pp. 336–340, Part 2.

72. MCR, v. 4, pt. 2, p. 3 (1661).

73. MCR, v. 4, pt. 2, p. 19 (1661).

74. MCR, v. 4, pt. 2, p. 20 (1661).

75. Bishop, op cit, note 1, p. 59, Part 1; p. 357, Part 2.

76. Thomas Newhouse in Hookes' volume cited in note 68.

77. MCR, v. 4, pt. 1, pp. 450–452 (1660). A statement probably drafted by Gov. Endecott.

78. MCR, v. 4, pt. 1, p. 453 (1660).

79. MCR, v. 4, pt. 1, pp. 455–456 (1660).

80. This document of June 1661 amounted to a declaration of substantial independence from English rule—MCR, v. 4, pt. 2, pp. 25-26.

81. The poet, John Greenleaf Whittier (1807–1892), a Quaker, in his "The King's Missive" celebrated the dramatic return of a banished Quaker bearing a letter from the King which he presented to the Governor under circumstances that proved humiliating to the proud Endecott. A copy of the King's letter and Samewell Shattock's (his spelling) descriptive of the event has been published in the *Mass. Hist. Soc. Collections,* v. 9, 4th ser., pp. 159–161.

82. MCR, v. 4, pt. 2, pp. 34–35 (1661).

83. MCR, v. 4, pt. 2, p. 59 (1662).

84. Bishop, op cit, note 1, pp. 458-459, Part 2.

85. MCR, v. 4, pt. 2, pp. 165–166 (1665).

86. MCR, v. 4, pt. 2, p. 88 (1663).

87. MCR, v. 5, p. 59 (1675).

88. See p. 624.

89. MCR, v. 5, p. 60 (1675).

90. Ibid.

91. Hutchinson's *History,* v. 1, p. 320.

92. MCR, v. 5, p. 134 (1677).

93. Book of Jonah 3:6–10. Later writers, noting that a smallpox epidemic struck Boston in later years, interpreted Margaret Brewster's blackened face as prophetic, for the smallpox was sometimes called the "black pox."

94. Besse (note 66 supra) v. 2, p. 260.
95. Sewall's *Diary,* July 8, 1677.
96. Besse (note 66, supra) v. 2, p. 264.
97. Suffolk County Court, v. 30, p. 843 (1677) .
98. Besse (note 66, supra) v. 2, p. 264.
99. MCR, v. 5, pp. 198–199 (1678) .
100. MCR, v. 5, p. 287 (1680) .
101. MCR, v. 5, p. 322 (1681) .
102. Norton, op cit, note 9, p. 6.
103. See John Whiting's *Truth and Innocency Defended against Falsehood and Envy,* published with Bishop (note 1, supra) .
104. Bishop, op cit, note 1, p. 492, Part 2. Endecott died in 1665.
105. Mass. General Laws: sec. 38 and 39 of ch. 272; sec. 14 of ch. 136.
106. Bishop, op cit, note 1, pp. 376, 383, Part 2. Bishop interpreted nakedness as a symbol of Boston's "hardheartedness, cruelty and immodesty, in stripping and whipping of women." Thomas Hutchinson (see note 91 above) in 1765 commented, "Deborah Wilson went through the streets of Salem, naked as she came into the world, for which she was well whipped. For these and such like disturbances, they might be deemed proper subjects either of a mad-house or house of correction, and it is to be lamented that any greater severeties were made use of."—v. 1, p. 204. For the case of Deborah Wilson and the judgment of the court, see Essex County Court records, v. 3, p. 17 (1662) . Her mother and sister were also punished for aiding and abetting her. For the case of Lydia Wardel, see Essex County Court, v. 3, p. 64 (1663) . See also in the same volume, page 68, the case of Eloacom Aldrous' wife.
107. Bishop, op cit, note 1, p. 121, Part 2.
108. Bishop, op cit, note 1, pp. 406–407, Part 2.
109. Bishop, op cit, note 1, pp 481-486, 136, 463-464, and 490-493, Part 2.
110. Bishop, op cit, note 1, pp. 487–488, Part 2.
111. Joseph Grove, in a preface to Bishop (see note 1 of this chapter) , quoting from Cotton Mather's *Magnalia Christi Americana.*
112. From "The Diary of Cotton Mather" published in 1911 by the Massachusetts Historical Society in its *Collections,* 7th series, v. 7, p. 571.
113. Prov. Laws, ch. 10 (1702) , supplementing the laws of 1692–1693.
114. Journal of the House of Representatives of Mass., v. 10, p. 300 (Mass. Hist. Soc., Boston, 1929) .
115. See chapter on "The Quakers and their Allies" in *Church and State in Massachusetts, 1691–1740* by Susan M. Reed (University of Illinois Press, Urbana, 1914) .
116. See epilogue to Chapter 5; Prov. Laws, ch. 4 (1728-1729); ch. 6 (1729); ch. 11 (1731) and supplementary enactments down to the end of the Province period.
117. Prov. Laws, ch. 32 (1755–1756) ; ch. 36 (1757–1758) ; ch. 17 (1757–1758) ; ch. 26 (1762–1763) ; ch. 6 (1770–1771) ; ch. 14 (1775–1776) .
118. Prov. Laws, ch. 3, 21, and 31 (1758–1759) .
119. Prov. Laws, ch. 21 (1776-1777). See *A People Among Peoples: Quaker Benevolence in Eighteenth-Century America* by Sydney V. James (Harvard University Press, Cambridge, Mass., 1963) .
120. Prov. Laws, ch. 11 (1719–1720) ; ch. 20 (1743–1744) ; ch. 6 (1747–1748) and supplementary chapters down to the end of the Province period.
121. Mass. Gen. Laws, ch. 233, sec. 17, derived from the Province Laws.
122. Many statues commemorating the careers of male heroes can be found in Massachusetts, but only two have been erected by the Commonwealth in honor of women. The first was that of Anne Hutchinson, placed in 1915 on the west wing lawn of the State House. Anne had been Mary Dyer's mentor and dear friend during the Antinomian crisis in the Bay Colony. After the General Court banished Anne in 1637, Mary went to England where she in later years became devoted to

the cause of the Society of Friends. She returned to New England determined to show the Puritans the error of their ways and suffered a martyr's death. Her statue is the creation of Sylvia Shaw Judson, sculptor, and was made possible through a legacy from the estate of Zenas Ellis of Fairhaven, Vermont, a descendant of this noted Quaker. The Art Commission of the Commonwealth gave its official approval to the erection of this statue in 1959.

CHAPTER 11

1. From a sermon preached in Boston in 1673 by the Rev. Increase Mather, the very personification of Puritanism, entitled "Wo to Drunkards. Two Sermons testifying against the Sin of Drunkenness: Wherein the Wofulness of that Evil, and the Misery of all that are addicted to it, is discovered from the Word of God," (printed by Marmaduke Johnson and sold by Edmund Ranger, Bookbinder, Boston, 1673.) It was customary at that time to refer to wine and spiritous liquors as "the creature of God," or simply as "the creature." Probably Mather's source of inspiration was a passage from the Apostle Paul's First Epistle to Timothy (4:4), "For every creature of God is good, and nothing to be refused, if it be received with thanksgiving."

2. Ibid.

3. MCR, v. 2, p. 171 (1646).

4. PCR, v. 1, p. 75 (1638).

5. See Chap. 12 on the incidence of crimes in the Plymouth and Bay Colonies.

6. Bradford's *History,* p. 476 (1642).

7. Bradford's *History,* p. 477 (1642). The "mixed multitud" expression used by Bradford was another borrowing from the Old Testament. The original planters who felt that they were harshly treated in England likened themselves to the Israelites who were driven out of Egypt and sought refuge in the land of Canaan. The author of the Book of Exodus described the flight of the Israelites under the leadership of Moses and stated that "a mixed multitude went up also with them"—(Exod. 12:38).

8. Bradford's *History,* p. 330 (1630).

9. Bradford's *History,* p. 477 (1642).

10. For Bradford's further explanation of the causes of crime in Plymouth Colony, see in this book, Chap. 15.

11. Regulatory laws most frequently mentioned beer, cider, and "strong waters"; less frequently mentioned were Spanish wine, French wine, brandy, perry, and rum, and occasionally mum (a strong ale) and *aqua vitae* (a general term for distilled liquor, such as gin). Whiskey, as such, does not seem to appear in the records. Alcoholic beverages available to the Colonial people are described in "Puritan Liquor in the Planting of New England" by Dean Albertson in *The New England Quarterly,* v. 23, pp. 477–490 (1950).

12. The *Mayflower* should not be singled out as a carrier of beer. All transatlantic ships of that period carried large stocks of beer and usually a quantity of wine to carry them through the ordeal of long and thirsty passages over the ocean where mariners dared not rely entirely on water.

13. Bradford's *History,* p. 112 (1620).

14. Bradford's *History,* pp. 112–113 (1620).

15. Bradford's *History,* pp. 98–99 (1620). Italics added.

16. Bradford's *History,* pp. 194–195 (1624).

17. Plym. Laws, p. 290 (1671).

18. PCR, v. 11, p. 137 (1662).

19. First Epistle to Timothy (5:23).

20. Bradford's *History,* p. 494 (1643), italics added.

21. MCR, v. 1, pp. 213-214 (1637).

22. MCR, v. 2, p. 257 (1658); also in v. 3, p. 139 (1658).

23. Plym. Laws, p. 135 (1662).
24. Plym. Laws, p. 251 (1671).
25. Plym. Laws, p. 251 (1671).
26. Plym. Laws, p. 251 (1671).
27. See "The Alcohol Problem and the Law" by Edward G. Baird, in *Quart. J. Alcohol,* v. 5, pp. 143ff (1944); v. 3, pp. 335ff (1945); v. 1, pp. 110ff (1946); v. 2, pp. 271ff (1946). Baird quotes an English statue of 1606 regulating taverns in phraseology that very closely resembled that used in the Colonies a few years later—further evidence of the fact that much of the Massachusetts law was derived from English antecedents.
28. MCR, v. 1, p. 106 (1633); also in Colonial Laws (1648) pp. 29-31; (1660) pp. 163-166 and 233; (1672) pp. 79, 83-84.
29. PCR, v. 1, p. 137 (1639).
30. MCR, v. 1, p. 214 (1637).
31. MCR, v. 1, p. 214 (1637). At a General Court held at Boston on March 13, 1639, a license was granted to R. Sedgwick and others to organize the "Millitary Company of the Massachusetts," for "the advancement of the military arte, & exercise of armes"—MCR, v. 1, p. 250-251 (1639).
32. Col. Laws (1660) p. 164; (1672) p. 80.
33. MCR, v. 3, pp. 241–241 (1651); MCR, v. 5, p. 135 (1677); Col. Laws (1672) p. 251 (1677).
34. Col. Laws (1672) p. 80; also in MCR, v. 4, pt. 2, p. 344 (1667).
35. Plym. Laws, p. 155 (1669).
36. MCR, v. 3, p. 241 (1651); Col. Laws (1660) p. 126; (1672) p. 11.
37. Col. Laws (1660) p. 135; (1672) pp. 23–24. Other crafts and trades similarly assessed were: Butchers, bakers, victuallers, smiths, carpenters, tailors, shoemakers, joiners, barbers, millers, masons, "and all other manual persons and Artists."
38. MCR, v. 1, p. 126 (1634); p. 214 (1637); p. 258 (1639); v. 3, p. 317 (1653); v. 4, pt. 1, p. 151 (1653); v. 4, pt. 2, p. 365–366 (1668); PCR, v. 1, p. 38 (1636); v. 5, p. 60 (1671), establishing a price of five shillings a gallon and two pence a gill for rum.
39. MCR, v. 1, p. 280 (1639).
40. PCR, v. 1, p. 87 (1638).
41. MCR, v. 2, p. 286 (1649); also in v. 3, p. 173 (1649).
42. MCR, v. 2, p. 82 (1644); p. 106 (1645); v. 3, p. 51–52 (1645); also in Col. Laws (1648) pp. 26–27; (1660) pp. 159–160; (1672) pp. 67–68 and 253.
43. MCR, v. 3, p. 65 (1646); also in v. 2, p. 148 (1646).
44. PCR, v. 1, p. 13 (1633); Col. Laws (1660) p. 242, (1668).
45. PCR, v. 11, p. 113 (1638).
46. PCR, v. 11, p. 113 (1646).
47. PCR, v. 3, p. 159 (1659).
48. PCR, v. 3, p. 181 (1660); p. 159 (1659).
49. PCR, v. 11, p. 244 (1677).
50. MCR, v. 1, p. 214 (1637).
51. MCR, v. 2, p. 100 (1645); p. 172 (1646); also in Col. Laws (1648) p. 30; (1660) p. 164; and (1672) p. 80.
52. PCR, v. 5, p. 43 (1670).
53. MCR, v. 2, p. 100 (1645); also in Col. Laws (1648) p. 30; (1660) p. 164; and (1672) p. 80.
54. MCR, v. 2, p. 257 (1648); also in Col. Laws (1660) p. 164; (1672) p. 80.
55. Plym. Laws, p. 251 (1671).
56. PCR, v. 5, p. 59 (1671).
57. PCR, v. 3, p. 219 (1661); for law in the Massachusetts Bay Colony barring those who to the "prejudice of theire families," sit "drincking & tipling" in taverns & ale houses, see MCR, v. 4, pt. 2, p. 463 (1670).

58. PCR, v. 6, p. 7 (1679).
59. PCR, v. 11, p. 224 (1668).
60. MCR, v. 1, pp. 213–214 (1637).
61. PCR, v. 6, p. 187 (1686).
62. MCR, v. 1, pp. 406–407 (1629).
63. MCR, v. 1, p. 106 (1633).
64. MCR, v. 2, p. 85 (1644).
65. MCR, v. 4, pt. 1, p. 201, (1654); also in Col. Laws (1660) p. 161; (1672) p. 75-76.
66. MCR, v. 2, p. 171–173 (1646).
67. Plym. Laws, p. 89 (1646); p. 151 (1667); p. 290 (1671).
68. MCR, v. 3, pp. 425–426 (1657); v. 4, pt. 1, p. 289; Rev. Laws (1672) pp. 75–76.
69. MCR, v. 4, pt. 2, p. 297 (1666); also in Col. Laws (1660) p. 236; (1672) p. 77.
70. MCR, v. 4, pt. 2, p. 297 (1666); also in Col. Laws (1672) pp. 77–78.
71. MCR, v. 3, p. 184 (1650).
72. PCR, v. 11, p. 195 (1663); also in Plym. Laws, p. 47 (1636).
73. PCR, v. 11, p. 244 (1677).
74. MCR, v. 4, pt. 1, p. 347 (1658); also in Col. Laws (1660) p. 190; (1672) p. 133.
75. Winthrop's *History,* v. 1, p. 44 (1630).
76. Winthrop's *History,* v. 1, p. 390 (1639); MCR, v. 1, pp. 271–272 (1639). The General Court ordered a fine of twelve shillings for this crime, one-half of the fine collected to be paid to the informer.
77. MCR, v. 2, p. 121 (1645); also in v. 3, p. 30 (1645).
78. MCR, v. 5, p. 211 (1679); also in Col. Laws (1672) p. 265.
79. Winthrop's *History,* v. 2, pp. 49-50 (1641).
80. Increase Mather diary, *Mass. Hist. Soc. Proc.,* v. 33 (1899–1900) p. 402.
81. Col. Laws (1672) p. 351 (1681).
82. Col. Laws (1672) p. 320 (1684).
83. MCR, v. 4, pt. 2, p. 510 (1672); also in Col. Laws (1672) p. 202. This practice survived the seventeenth century. *The Christian Science Monitor,* commenting on the current antialcohol campaign of the present French Government, reported: "The old custom of paying workers in certain industries partly in alcoholic drinks is being forbidden or limited. In some parts of France, agricultural workers receive up to seven quarts of wine a day in hot weather, and in certain types of factories up to six quarts a day. In plants where tiles and cement are produced, the French Government has already succeeded in getting the wine payment reduced to two quarts"—Dec. 2, 1960.
84. MCR, v. 1, p. 233 (1638); Court of Assistants, v. 2, p. 75 (1638).
85. PCR, v. 5, p. 81 (1671).
86. Col. Laws (1600) p. 164; (1672) pp. 80-81. This definition was a little less elaborate but cast in the same general form as that given by Increase Mather who said a man is considered drunk when he is "so overcome with wine [he uses the word "wine" in this context to cover "all other inebriating drinks"] as that he can neither speak nor act like a rational creature, when reason is disturbed thereby, and Sense and Speech and Motion fail, when neither the Head nor Hand can do their offices aright"—from his sermon of 1673, "Wo to Drunkards" (see note 1).
87. PCR, v. 11, p. 50 (1646); also in Plym. Laws, (1645) p. 84; (1671) p. 251.
88. Plym. Laws, p. 251 (1671).
89. From Rev. Increase Mather's sermon entitled: "An Earnest Exhortation to the Inhabitants of New-England, to Hearken to the voice of God in his late and present Dispensations," (printed by John Foster, Boston, 1676).
90. Col. Laws (1660) p. 187; (1672) p. 127.
91. Court of Assistants, v. 2, p. 62 (1636).
92. Court of Assistants, v. 2, p. 41 (1634); MCR, v. 1, p. 112 (1634).
93. Court of Assistants, v. 2, pp. 34–35 (1633); MCR, v. 1, p. 107 (1633).

94. MCR, v. 1, p. 118 (1634).
95. MCR, v. 4, pt. 1, p. 203 (1654).
96. PCR, v. 3, p. 129 (1658).
97. PCR, v. 3, p. 176 (1659).
98. PCR, v. 3, p. 219 (1661).
99. PCR, v. 4, p. 106 (1665).
100. PCR, v. 5, p. 88 (1672).
101. PCR, v. 3, p. 196 (1660).
102. PCR, v. 3, p. 110 (1656).
103. PCR, v. 8, p. 23 (1656–1662).
104. The criminal history of Thomas Lucas is recorded in PCR at the following places: v. 3, pp. 150, 173, 181, 200, 206, 207, 212, 220; v. 4, pp. 33, 51, 55, 66, 101; v. 5, pp. 16-17, 39, 118, 169, 182; v. 6, p. 7; v. 8, pp. 97, 103, 104, 114, 131 (1658-1670).
105. Prov. Laws, v. 7, (v. 2 of Appendix), notes p. 532, concerning ch. 54 (1696–1697), appointing a Day of Prayer and Fasting.
106. *The Boston Gazette,* issues of Dec. 14–21, 1730; Nov. 22–29, 1736; May 23–30, 1737. See also issue of Nov. 28-Dec. 5, 1737.
107. The Dudley Records, reprinted in *Mass. Hist. Soc. Proc.,* v. 33 (1899) p. 241; Prov. Laws, ch. 6 (1711—12).
108. Prov. Laws, ch. 18 (1692–1693).
109. Prov. Laws, ch. 9 (1693).
110. Prov. Laws, ch. 17 (1693–1694).
111. Prov. Laws, ch. 13 (1733–1734).
112. Prov. Laws, ch. 22 (1694–1695).
113. Prov. Laws, ch. 8 (1699–1700).
114. Prov. Laws, ch. 6 (1711–1712). This law also prohibited all "singing, fiddling, piping, or any other musick, dancing or revelling" in the taverns or public houses.
115. Ibid.
116. Chapter 53 of the Acts of 1781.
117. An Act passed March 10, 1784.
118. An Act passed Jan. 1, 1789.
119. Revised Statutes (1836) ch. 130, sec. 18.
120. Chapter 229 of the Acts of 1879.
121. *Comm.* v. *Hughes,* 133 Mass. 496 (1882).
122. Public Statutes (1881) ch. 207, sec. 25 and 26.
123. Chapter 365 and 375 of the Acts of 1885.
124. Governor's addresses to the General Court.
125. Boston City Doc. 158 (1899), Report of the Advisory Committee on the Penal Aspects of Drunkenness.
126. House Doc. No. 2000 (1945). See Special Supplement of over 300 pages, printed with that document, written by Judge Joseph T. Zottoli, late Associate Justice of the Boston Municipal Court and chairman of "The Special Commission to Investigate the Problem of Drunkenness in Massachusetts."
127. Gen. Laws, ch. 123, sec. 62, 80, and 86.
128. Judge Zottoli (see note 126 above) traced the history of legislation relating to alcoholic beverages in great detail and, in a thoroughly documented report, discussed the medical and legal aspects of drunkenness in Massachusetts.
129. Gen. Laws, ch. 277, sec. 79.
130. Gen. Laws, ch. 111, sec. 4A, based on ch. 715 of the Acts of 1956.
131. Gen. Laws, ch. 272, sec. 48; ch. 127, sec. 136A.
132. MCR, v. 2, p. 257 (1658) and v. 3, p. 139 (1658).

CHAPTER 12

1. Bradford's *History,* p. 459.
2. Col. Laws (1648) p. 14; (1660) p. 143; (1672) p. 36.
3. Suffolk County Court, *Introduction* by Zechariah Chafee, Jr., p. xvii.
4. Col. Laws (1648) pp. 8–9; (1660) pp. 132–133; (1672) pp. 21–22. See *The Pynchon Court Record in Colonial Justice in Western Massachusetts (1639-1702),* Joseph H. Smith, editor (Harvard University Press, Cambridge, 1961).
5. Suffolk County Court, p. 183 (1672).
6. Jeremiah 24:2.
7. Col. Laws (1648) p. 5; (1660) p. 127; (1672) p. 13.
8. Exodus 22:3.
9. Col. Laws (1660) pp. 127–128; (1672) p. 13.
10. Col. Laws (1660) p. 189; (1672) p. 132.
11. Exodus 20:10.
12. MCR, v. 4, pt. 2, p. 395 (1668); Col. Laws (1672) p. 19.
13. MCR, v. 1, p. 140 (1635).
14. MCR, v. 2, p. 178 (1646); Col. Laws (1648) p. 20; (1660) p. 148; (1672) p. 45.
15. PCR, v. 11, p. 100 (1651).
16. Suffolk County Court, p. 116 (1672).
17. Exodus 22:28.
18. Col. Laws (1660) p. 143; (1672) p. 36; MCR, v. 1, pp. 212–213 (1637).
19. Col. Laws (1660) p. 156; (1672) p. 61.
20. Suffolk County Court, p. 485 (1674).
21. Col. Laws (1672) p. 11.
22. Suffolk County Court, v. 29, p. 183 (1672).
23. Suffolk County Court, p. 232 (1673).
24. MCR, v. 1, p. 115 (1634).
25. MCR, v. 1, p. 109 (1633); Col. Laws (1648) pp. 25–26; (1660) p. 158; (1672) p. 66.
26. Col. Laws (1672) p. 294 (1682).
27. MCR, v. 1, p. 186 (1636); Col. Laws (1660) p. 172; Col. Laws (1672) pp. 101-102.
28. Col. Laws (1648) p. 50; (1660) p. 195; (1672) p. 146; MCR, v. 1, pp. 241–242 (1638).
29. MCR, v. 1, p. 281 and 290 (1639-1640); Winthrop's *History,* v. 1, pp. 381-382 (1639).
30. Col. Laws (1672) p. 211; MCR, v. 4, pt. 2, p. 563 (1673).
31. The most famous American duel was fought as late as 1804 between a reluctant Alexander Hamilton and Aaron Burr in which Hamilton met death in New Jersey at a place where his eldest son had been killed in a duel three years earlier.
32. Gen. Laws, ch. 265, sec. 6.
33. Gen. Laws, ch. 267, sec. 8.
34. Gen. Laws, ch. 272, sec. 37, repealed by ch. 285, Acts of 1962.
35. Gen. Laws, ch. 277, sec. 79.
36. Gen. Laws, ch. 272, sec. 53.
37. We have not included here a table of sentences to the Massachusetts Correctional Institution, Concord, an institution to which the younger offenders are usually committed, nor a table of sentences to the Massachusetts Correctional Institution, Bridgewater, a highly specialized institution for defective delinquents, criminal insane, "sexually dangerous persons," and drunkards. Sentences to Concord do not differ greatly from sentences to the State Prison with the exception that sentences for robbery (armed and unarmed) rank second in frequency to sentences for breaking, entering, and larceny. The Prison Department at the Bridgewater institution holds men sentenced for drunkenness only. In 1962, there were 3382

men sentenced for this crime, most of them fifty years of age or older. At the time of their sentence that year, 96.5% of these men had served one or more former commitments.

CHAPTER 13

1. John Winthrop's "Discourse on Arbitrary Government" in *Winthrop Papers,* v. 4, pp. 468–488 (1644).

2. MCR, v. 1, p. 252 (1639); Col. Laws (1648) p. 57; (1660) p. 207; (1672) p. 168. For a study of the origin of the word "constable" and of the office of constable in England see "Constables" by Herbert B. Adams in *New England Historical and Genealogical Register,* v. 36 (1882) pp. 174–187; 255–276.

3. MCR, v. 1, p. 76 (1630).

4. MCR, v. 1, p. 79 (1630).

5. Col. Laws (1660) pp. 195–196; (1672) p. 148.

6. MCR, v. 1, p. 172 (1636); Col. Laws (1648) p. 13; (1660) p. 195; (1672) p. 147–148.

7. MCR, v. 2, p. 150 (1646); v. 4, pt. 1, pp. 324–327 (1658); Col. Laws, (1648) p. 13; (1660) pp. 139–140; (1672) pp. 31–32; *Mass. Archives,* v. 5, 38B, no. 17A.

8. MCR, v. 4, pt. 1, pp. 324–327 (1658).

9. Col. Laws (1660) p. 145; (1672) p. 41.

10. Col. Laws (1648) pp. 31–32; (1660) p. 167; (1672) p. 86.

11. Col. Laws (1660) p. 191; (1672) p. 138.

12. MCR, v. 2, p. 252 (1648); Col. Laws (1648) p. 54; (1660) p. 202; (1672) p. 160.

13. Col. Laws (1660) p. 164; (1672) pp. 80–81.

14. MCR, v. 4, pt. 1, p. 325 (1658); Col. Laws (1660) p. 158; (1672) pp. 66, 236 (1675).

15. MCR, v. 4, pt. 1, p. 326 (1658).

16. Col. Laws (1660) p. 137; (1672) p. 27.

17. Col. Laws (1672) p. 204.

18. Col. Laws (1672) p. 216 (1674).

19. Col. Laws (1672) p. 234 (1675); (1661) p. 63.

20. Col. Laws (1672) p. 250 (1677).

21. Col. Laws (1672) p. 347 (1677).

22. MCR, v. 5, pp. 154–155 (1677); Col. Laws (1672) pp. 257–258 (1677).

23. MCR, v. 5, p. 211 (1679); Col. Laws (1672) p. 265 (1679).

24. MCR, v. 5, p. 243 (1679); Col. Laws (1672) p. 272 (1679).

25. Second Report of the Record Commissioners of the City of Boston, containing the "Boston Records, 1634–1660" (Rockwell and Churchill, Boston, 1881).

26. MCR, v. 1, p. 339 (1641); v. 4, pt. 1, p. 324 (1658); Col. Laws (1648) p. 13; (1660) p. 139; (1672) p. 31.

27. Suffolk County Court, p. 884 (1677) and p. 1015 (1679).

28. Col. Laws (1648) p. 13; (1660) p. 140; (1672) p. 31.

29. MCR, v. 3, p. 298 (1653); v. 4, pt. 1, p. 121 (1653); Col. Laws (1648) p. 23; (1660) p. 153; (1672) pp. 55–56.

30. Col. Laws (1660) p. 196; (1672) p. 148, 247 (1676). In addition to the satisfaction derived from his authority over others, the constable was allowed fees for the performance of many of his duties. Constable Georg Keysar, for example, was allowed ten shillings for whipping four persons and two shillings for a "hue and cry" in 1670—Essex County Court, v. 4, p. 314.

31. MCR, v. 2, pp. 150–151 (1646); Col. Laws (1648) p. 13; (1660) p. 140; (1672) p. 31.

32. MCR, v. 2, p. 151 (1646); Col. Laws (1648) p. 13; (1660) p. 140; (1672) p. 31; *Mass. Archives,* v. 38b, no. 17a.

33. MCR, v. 5, p. 29 (1675); Col. Laws (1672) p. 221 (1675).

34. Col. Laws (1648) pp. 42–43; (1660) pp. 177–178; (1672) p. 109.

35. MCR, v. 4, pt. 1, p. 103 (1652); v. 3, p. 282 (1652); Col. Laws (1660) pp. 198–199; (1672) pp. 154–155. In the 1660 laws the word "deboist" of the 1652 law was changed to "debauchedly."

36. MCR, v. 4, pt. 1, p. 83; v. 3, p. 265 (1652).

37. Col. Laws (1648) p. 52; (1660) pp. 198–199; (1672) pp. 154–155.

38. MCR, v. 1, p. 293 (1640); v. 4, pt. 2, p. 4 (1661); Col. Laws (1660) pp. 199, 227; (1672) p. 155.

39. MCR, v. 1, p. 74 (1630); Court of Assistants, v. 2, p. 2 (1630).

40. Court of Assistants, v. 2, p. 2 (1630).

41. Court of Assistants, v. 2, p. 38 (1633).

42. MCR, v. 1, p. 351 (no date).

43. MCR, v. 1, p. 128 (1634).

44. Ibid.

45. MCR, v. 1, p. 189 (1637).

46. MCR, v. 2, p. 199 (1647); Col. Laws (1648) p. 38; (1660) pp. 172–174; (1672) pp. 51, 102–104, 220 (1675).

47. MCR, v. 1, p. 217 (1637); v. 2, p. 171 (1646); v. 3, pp. 94–95 (1646).

48. MCR, v. 4, pt. 1, p. 18 (1650); Col. Laws (1660) p. 173; (1672) p. 103.

49. MCR, v. 1, p. 217 (1637); v. 3, p. 112 (1647); Col. Laws (1660) p. 173; (1672) p. 103.

50. Col. Laws (1660) p. 174; (1672) p. 104.

51. Ibid.

52. MCR, v. 2, p. 38 (1643). The geographical boundaries of Norfolk county were not the same as the present Norfolk county but comprised a more northerly area, including these towns: "Salsberry, Haverill, Excetter, Dover and Strawberry Banck," the last named town later called Portsmouth.

53. The appointment of sheriffs was authorized by the Province Charter of 1691, and they were probably appointed shortly thereafter. Chapter 9 of the Acts of 1699–1700 gave sheriffs custody of all jails, prisons, and prisoners at an annual salary of ten pounds, excepting in Suffolk County where the salary was thirty pounds. Thomas Lechford, Boston's first lawyer, in listing the Colonial officials in Boston between 1638 and 1641, wrote: "There is a Marshall, who is [serves as?] a Sheriffe or Bailiffe, and his Deputy is the Goaler and executioner"—pp. 38–39 of Lechford's book cited in note 57.

54. MCR, v. 5, p. 133 (1677); Col. Laws (1672) pp. 249–250 (1677).

55. Hostility to the legal profession antedated the Puritans. Max Radin traces this hostility back to medieval times in "The Ancient Grudge: A Study in the Public Relations of the Legal Profession," *Virginia Law Rev.,* v. 32 (1946) pp. 734–752.

56. MCR, v. 2, p. 212 (1647).

57. Thomas Lechford of Clements Inne, *Plaine Dealing: or, Newes from New-England* (London, 1642). The Boston edition was published in 1867 by J. K. Wiggin & Wm. Parsons Lunt, with Introduction and Notes by J. Hammond Trumbull.

58. Body of Liberties (1641) Art. 26. One of the few articles not carried over into the compiled laws. In the early Province period, attorneys' fees were prescribed by law for court appearances. In the Superior Court of Judicature, twelve shillings; in the Inferior Court of Common Pleas, ten shillings "and no more." Only attorneys who had taken the oath could receive these fees—*Mass. Archives,* v. 40, pp. 716–717 (1701).

59. Winthrop's *History,* v. 2, p. 43 (1641).

60. MCR, v. 3, p. 168 (1649); Col. Laws (1660) p. 141; (1672) p. 34.

61. MCR, v. 4, pt. 2, p. 87 (1663); Col. Laws (1660) p. 224; (1672) p. 41. Today slightly more than one-fourth of all members of the General Court are members of the bar.

62. P. 4 of Lechford's book cited in note 57.

63. MCR, v. 2, p. 206 (1647) .

64. Pp. 77-78 of Lechford's book cited in note 57.

65. P. 152 of Lechford's book cited in note 57.

66. *Note-Book Kept by Thomas Lechford, Esq., Lawyer, in Boston, Massachusetts Bay, from June 27, 1638, to July 29, 1641.* The American Antiquarian Society published the *Note-Book* in 1885 (John Wilson and Son, University Press, Cambridge, Mass., Edward Everett Hale, Jr., editor) .

67. See the footnote on p. 71 of Lechford's book cited in note 57. Trumbull edition.

68. MCR, v. 1, p. 310 (1640) .

69. See p. 77 of Lechford's book cited in note 57.

70. MCR, v. 1, p. 270 (1639) ; Court of Assistants, v. 2, p. 87 (1639) .

71. P. 182 of Lechford's *Note-Book* cited in note 66.

72. P. xxiii of Lechford's book cited in note 57.

73. P. 69 of Lechford's book cited in note 57.

74. Col. Laws (1660) p. 8; see pp. 237–238 of Lechford's *Note-Book* cited in note 66. A highly prized manuscript copy of the General Court Records up to 1646 (formerly one of Governor Hutchinson's possessions) has been preserved and is now in the Treasure Room of the Boston Public Library. The first 224 pages of this record are in the handwriting of Thomas Lechford.

75. Pp. 28-30 of Lechford's book cited in note 57. *"Stare decisis"* literally means to stand by decisions made. As a general principal of law, it means that when a point of law has been well settled by the courts it becomes a precedent for subsequent decisions. This principle has been important in the development of the Common Law and gives stability to the law which otherwise would be lacking.

76. MCR, v. 1, p. 275 (1639); Col. Laws (1648) p. 46; (1660) pp. 187-188; (1672) pp. 129-130.

77. Body of Liberties (1641) Art 34; Col. Laws (1648) pp. 3–4; (1660) p. 125; (1672) p. 9.

78. Body of Liberties (1641) Art. 22 and 37; Col. Laws (1648) p. 49; (1660) p. 122; (1672) p. 3.

79. Cited in Emory Washburn, *Sketches of the Judicial History of Massachusetts, 1630-1775* (Little and Brown, Boston, 1840) pp. 52-53.

80. Essex County Courts, v. 4, p. 198 (1669) and v. 7, p. 416 (1680) .

81. MCR, v. 4, pt. 2, p. 563 (1673) ; Col. Laws (1672) p. 211.

82. See Nathan Matthews' comments on this point in "The Results of the Prejudice Against Lawyers in Massachusetts in the 17th Century," *Mass. Law Quarterly,* v. 13 (1928) pp. 73–94. See also Chapter 14 of this book.

83. "Boston Newsletter," June 19, 1704, as published in *An Historical Digest of the Provincial Press,* compiled and edited by Lyman H. Weeks (Boston, 1911).

84. This oath appears in the Massachusetts Council Records under Governor Joseph Dudley in 1686, reprinted in the *Massachusetts Historical Society Proceedings,* v. 33 (1899–1900) p. 261. See Appendix B of this book. See also Hollis R. Bailey, *Attorneys and their Admission to the Bar in Massachusetts* (William J. Nagel, Boston, 1907) . See also Frank W. Grinnell, "Bench and Bar in Colony and Province (1630-1776)," Chapter 6 in *Commonwealth History of Massachusetts,* Albert B. Hart, editor (The State History Company, New York, 1928) .

85. M'Naghten, a paranoiac, murdered in 1843 the secretary to the Prime Minister of England, Sir Robert Peel, mistaking him for the latter. A jury found him not guilty by reason of insanity and hence not responsible for his crime. Because of the popular indignation over this highly publicized crime, the High Court Judges were asked for an advisory opinion on the rule of criminal responsibility. The Judges declared that if a person were suffering from some mental defect to such an extent that he did not know the nature of his act or that it was wrong he was not responsible and hence could not be punished as a criminal. This

English rule, subsequently adopted by the courts, became known as "the right-and-wrong" test. For a review of the rules for establishing criminal responsibility in Massachusetts prior to the M'Naghten case, see George T. Bigelow and George Bemis, *Report of the Trial of Abner Rogers, Jr.* (Little & Brown, Boston, 1844).

86. Body of Liberties (1641) Art. 52; Col. Laws (1648) p. 51; (1660) p. 198; (1672) p. 152.

87. Mr. Yale was the uncle of Elihu Yale, patron of The Collegiate School in Saybrook, Connecticut, renamed Yale College in his honor in 1718.

88. Winthrop's *History,* v. 2, pp. 265–266 (1637).

89. Suffolk County Court, v. 1, p. 436 (1674).

90. Winthrop's *History,* v. 1, footnote p. 336 (1638). Dorothy had been "chained to a post" by order of the Essex County Court in 1636 "for frequent laying hands on her husband to the danger of his life" and for contemning authority when brought into court. In 1638 she again appeared before the court "for misdemeanors against her husband" and was ordered whipped—Essex County Court, v. 1, pp. 6 and 9. Perhaps her husband had a part in her "melancholy" condition for he was later excommunicated "for much pride and unnaturalness to his wife."

91. Winthrop's *History,* v. 1, pp. 335–336 (1638); MCR, v. 1, p. 246 (1638).

92. Winthrop's *History,* v. 2, pp. 58–59 (1641).

93. MCR, v. 4, pt. 2, p. 397 (1668); Col. Laws (1672) p. 2.

94. MCR, v. 2, pp. 6 and 9 (1642); Col. Laws (1648) p. 11; (1660) p. 136; (1672) pp. 26 and 149.

95. Col. Laws (1648) pp. 5-6; (1660) pp. 128-129; (1672) pp. 14-15.

96. Ibid.

97. Ibid.

98. Col. Laws (1660) p. 152; (1672) p. 52.

99. Col. Laws (1660) p. 154; (1672) p. 59.

100. MCR, v. 2, pp. 104-105 (1645); Col. Laws (1648) pp. 35-36; (1660) p. 171; (1672) pp. 91–92.

101. Col. Laws (1660) p. 189; (1672) p. 132.

102. Ibid.

103. Col. Laws (1648) p. 11; (1660) p. 136; (1672) p. 26.

104. MCR, v. 3, p. 355 (1654); Col. Laws (1660) pp. 136–137; (1672) p. 27.

105. MCR, v. 2, p. 180 (1646); Col. Laws (1648) p. 5; (1660) p. 127; (1672) p. 13.

106. MCR, v. 4, pt. 2, p. 395 (1668). Houses of Correction were provided for the confinement chiefly of "idle persons, stuborne persons, . . . runawayes, common drunkards, pilferers, common night walkers, & wanton persons, as tending to uncleanes in speeches or actions, & the like"—MCR, v. 3, p. 399 (1656).

107. Called by the Puritans "King Philip's War."

108. MCR, v. 5, pp. 59–63 (1675); Col. Laws (1672) pp. 233–237 (1675). The other nine "provoking evils" were: 1) neglect by the church to catechize the children and to inquire into "their Spiritual States"; 2) the "manifest Pride openly appearing amongst us in that long Hair like Womens Hair is worn by some men either their own, or others Hair made into Perewigs: And by some Women wearing Borders of Hair, and their Cutting, Curling, and Immodest laying out their Hair, which practice doth prevail and increase especially among the younger sort"; 3) "the evil of pride in Apparrel, both for Costliness in the poorer sort, and vain, new strange Fashions both in poor and rich, with naked Breasts and Arms . . . Superfluous Ribbons," etc.; 4) " . . . the open meetings of Quakers, whose Damnable Heresies, Abominable Idolatries, are hereby Promoted, Embraced and Practised to the Scandal of Religion, Hazard of Souls, and Provocation of Divine Jealusie against his People" (including evidently King Philip's war); 5) "much Prophaneness amongst us in persons turning their Backs upon the publick Worship before it is finished, and the Blessing pronounced"; 6) "the shameful and Scandalous Sin of

Excessive drinking Tipling, and Company keeping in Taverns and Ordinaries"; 7) common swearing and cursing "in ordinary Communication, which is a Sin that grows amongst us"; 8) "the sin of Idleness (which is a Sin of Sodom) doth greatly increase"; 9) shopkeepers and merchants charging too much for their goods and "Mechanicks and Day Labourers" also guilty of that evil, a crime the Colonial people called "oppression."

109. Col. Laws (1648) p. 11; (1660) p. 136; (1672) p. 26.

110. Ibid.

111. Body of Liberties (1641), Art. 83; Col. Laws (1648) p. 12; (1660) p. 137; (1672) p. 28.

112. MCR, v. 4, pt. 2, p. 395 (1668).

113. Essex County Court, v. 2, p. 247 (1660).

114. Winthrop's *History,* vol. 2, p. 67 (1641).

115. *Winthrop Papers,* v. 4, pp. 468–488 (1644).

116. Winthrop's *History,* v. 2, p. 67 (1641).

117. Winthrop's *History,* v. 2, pp. 67–68 (1641).

118. Winthrop's *History,* v. 2, pp. 68–69 (1641).

119. *Winthrop Papers,* v. 4, p. 474 (1641).

120. Winthrop's *History,* v. 2, p. 257 (1644); *Winthrop Papers,* v. 4, p. 487 (1644).

121. *Winthrop Papers,* v. 4, p. 473 (1644).

122. MCR, v. 2, p. 93 (1644); Winthrop's *History,* v. 2, pp. 251–252 (1644).

123. MCR, v. 2, pp. 92–95 (1644).

124. MCR, v. 2, p. 96 (1644).

125. MCR, v. 4, pt. 2, p. 397 (1668).

126. MCR, v. 2, p. 31 (1642); p. 36 (1643); p. 69 (1644) and elsewhere. Rhode Island was conspicuously absent. From the beginning this Colony had been a maverick among the English plantations. It had not been imbued with Puritan orthodoxy; on the contrary, it had served as a refuge for those who had been driven out of the Bay Colony "for conscience sake." In a letter to Governor Bradford of Plymouth Colony in 1642, Governor Winthrop made clear his hostility to this new Colony to the south that had defied Bay Colony magistrates and ministers "secretly also sowing the seeds of Familisme and Anabaptistrie. . . . We are not willing to joyne with them in any league or confederacie at all"—Bradford's *History,* p. 461 (1642).

127. The Articles of Confederation can be found in Winthrop's *History,* v. 2, pp. 121–127 (1643) and in Bradford's *History,* pp. 496–504. The "Acts of the Commissioners of the United Colonies of New England" are set forth in detail in PCR, v. 9 and v. 10. For later reflections on the first New England compact see John Quincy Adams' address, "The New England Confederacy of MDCXLIII," given on the two hundredth anniversary of the signing of the Articles of Confederation, *Mass. Hist. Soc. Coll.,* 3rd ser., v. 9, pp. 189–223; and Constance M. Green's article, "The New England Confederation" in v. 1, ch. 9 of the *Commonwealth History of Massachusetts,* Albert B. Hart, editor (The State History Co., New York, 1927).

128. MCR, v. 4, pt. 2, p. 213 (1665).

129. MCR, v. 4, pt. 2, p. 231 (1665).

130. MCR, v. 4, pt. 2, p. 443 (1669).

131. Winthrop's *History,* v. 2, p. 126 (1643); Bradford's *History,* p. 502 (1643); MCR, v. 4, pt. 2, pp 514–515 (1672).

132. MCR, v. 4, pt. 2, p. 26 (1661).

133. See L. K. Mathews, "Benjamin Franklin's Plans for a Colonial Union, 1750–1775" in *American Political Science Review,* v. 8 (1914), pp. 393–412.

CHAPTER 14

1. The Reverend Increase Mather (1639–1723), then president of Harvard College and minister of the North Church (later known as the Old North and still later as The Second Church in Boston), made this definite assertion in a preface to his *Cases of Conscience Concerning Witchcrafts,* a scholarly dissertation on the subject, written at the request of fourteen ministers to "discover the depths of this Hellish Design." It was essentially a protest against improper methods of detecting witches and a warning against "the taking of any wrong steps in this dark way." Evidently it was written in October 1692 but not published until 1693, in Boston, and "Reprinted at London, for John Dunton, at the Raven in the Poultry. 1693." It was republished in London by John Russell Smith in 1862 and bound with Cotton Mather's (1662–1728) *The Wonders of the Invisible World: Being an Account of the Tryals of Several Witches Lately Executed in New-England* and several other discourses by both Increase and his son Cotton. The quotation here reproduced is taken from p. 285 of the 1862 publication.

2. See Chap. 9, "They Shall Surely be Put to Death."

3. Exodus 22:18. See also Leviticus 20:27, "A man also or woman that hath a familiar spirit, or that is a wizard, shall surely be put to death: they shall stone them with stones: their blood shall be upon them"; also I Samuel 28:3; Deuteronomy 18:10–12; and, for a discussion of "The Witch in Holy Writ," see *The History of Witchcraft and Demonology,"* ch. 5, by Montague Summers (Alfred A. Knopf, New York, 1926).

4. Of the many research studies on the history of demonology and witchcraft, too numerous to list in this brief report of New England witchcraft, one has been of special interest to us, "The Witch Mania" chapter in Charles Mackay's volume on *Extraordinary Popular Delusions and the Madness of Crowds,* first published in London in 1841, reprinted in 1852, and republished in 1932 by Farrar, Straus and Cudahy, Inc., New York, with a Foreword by Bernard M. Baruch.

5. Kittredge, George L., *Witchcraft in Old and New England.* (Harvard University Press, Cambridge, 1929) p. 368.

6. Mackay (in the volume cited in note 4 above), pp. 479, 480, 482. The English psychoanalyst Ernest Jones, former president of the International Psychoanalytical Association, stated in his *Nightmare, Witches, and Devils* on p. 214 (W. W. Norton & Co., Inc., New York, 1931) that nineteenth century research on witchcraft pointed to the conclusion that "the essential responsibility for it unquestionably rests on the Roman Catholic Church."

7. It was customary for New Englanders to picture the Devil not as a goat or horse or in some other animal form, as was common in fifteenth and sixteenth century Europe, but as a black man, not unlike the native Indian, but the idea of one or more cloven feet persisted. Mather's description was derived from an interview with Mercy Short, a bewitched seventeen-year old child who was the object of special study by Mather as reported in his "A Brand Pluck'd Out of the Burning," written in 1692 or 1693 and reprinted by George L. Burr in *Narratives of the Witchcraft Cases: 1648–1706* (Charles Scribner's Sons, New York, 1914). Burr's volume is an invaluable collection of narratives by resident observers, reproducing documents not easy for the student of the subject to find in their original form.

8. Cotton Mather's *Wonders of the Invisible World* (note 1 above) pp. 44 and 45. In the Gospel According to St. Matthew (12:24), the "prince of the devils" is spelled "Beelzebub."

9. Morison, Samuel E. in *Harvard College in the Seventeenth Century* (Harvard University Press, Cambridge, 1936) p. 495 of Part 2.

10. Cotton Mather's report of the trial of Elizabeth How in Burr (see note 7 above) pp. 237–240, and in Mather's *The Wonders of the Invisible World* (see note 1 above) p. 151. Burr's reproduction changes the word "speaking" in line two

to "squeaking," which may make more sense.

11. PCR, v. 5, pp. 223–224 (1677).

12. Essex County Court, v. 3, p. 413 (1667).

13. The Rev. John Hale (1636-1700) in "A Modest Enquiry Into the Nature of Witchcraft," p. 412 in Burr (see note 7 above). Hale had been pastor at Beverly, not far from Salem, and took a great interest in the court proceedings, strongly favoring prosecutions at the outset but changing his views after his own wife was accused. His "Modest Inquiry" was published in Boston in 1702.

14. There is an unresolved question here as to how many witches were executed in the Bay Colony prior to 1692. Some eighteenth and nineteenth century writers speak of four, five, or six but evidence now seems to point to three definitely known. One or two executions in Connecticut may have been erroneously included. If there had been any executions in the Bay Colony, other than that of Margaret Jones, prior to 1648, surely Governor Winthrop would have noted them in his Journal (covering the years 1630–1649). Some authors may have included the case of Mary Parsons of Northampton, who, indicted on two counts—witchcraft and murder—was found not guilty of the former and acknowledged she had killed her own child and for this crime was sentenced in 1651 to death, although no statement of her execution appears in the court records–MCR, v. 3, p. 229 (1651); v. 4, pt. 1, pp. 47-48 (1651). At any rate, Mary Parsons evidently died before her execution could be carried out. See Samuel E. Morison in "William Pynchon, The Founder of Springfield" in *Mass. Hist. Soc. Proc.,* v. 64 (1930) pp. 67–108. Her husband, Hugh, had also been tried as a witch on the testimony of Mary. A Court of Assistants on May 12, 1652, found him "guilty," but the judges not consenting to the verdict (presumably because Mary confessed that *she* had killed the child, not her husband through witchcraft), sent the case to the General Court where a "not guilty" verdict was rendered—MCR, v. 4, pt. 1, p. 96 (1652). Thomas Hutchinson, writing in the following century, with many of the original documents in his possession, wrote of Anne Hibbins as the second to die (in 1656) in the Bay Colony. Of the Glover execution in 1688 he commented: "none had suffered for near thirty years in the Massachusetts colony," thus making that case the third, which accords with our findings after an examination of available court records—Thomas Hutchinson (1711–1780), *The History of the Colony and Province of Massachusetts Bay* (Harvard University Press, Cambridge, 1936) v. 2. p. 18. William F. Poole, on the other hand, in Chapter 4, "Witchcraft in Boston," of v. 2 of *The Memorial History of Boston* (Justin Winsor, editor, Ticknor and Co., Boston, 1881) believed there might have been twelve, at the most, who were executed in New England prior to 1692, but the evidence is incomplete.

15. Winthrop's *History,* v. 1, pp. 397–398 (1648).

16. Hutchinson's *History* (see note 14 above) v. 1, p. 187.

17. MCR, v. 4, pt. 1, p. 269 (1656). See also *Mass. Hist. Soc. Proc.,* v. 24 (1889), p. 316 where it was stated that Anne had been excommunicated from the Second Church fifteen years earlier and was probably "unsettled" in her mind.

18. Hutchinson's *History* (see note 14 above) v. 2, p. 19. The narrative following is taken from Cotton Mather's *Memorable Providences, Relating to Witchcrafts and Possessions,* written in 1689 when he was only 27 years old, already a distinguished scholar and preacher. This book was reprinted in London in 1691 and in Edinburgh in 1697 and reproduced in part by Burr (see note 7 above).

19. Taking a different view, George F. O'Dwyer, in "Ann Glover, First Martyr to the Faith in New England," *Hist. Rec. and Studies,* U.S. Cath. Hist. Soc. (1921), pp. 70–79, in an angry attack on Cotton Mather, asserted that Puritan bigotry toward Roman Catholics played a key role in Glover's trial and legal condemnation.

20. *Mass. Hist. Soc. Coll.* (1868), 4th ser. v. 8, pp. 367–368.

21. An undated and untitled manuscript by Cotton Mather, edited by Worthington C. Ford and published as the "Mather-Calef Paper on Witchcraft" in *Mass. Hist. Soc. Proc.,* v. 47 (1914) pp. 260-268.

22. The idea that one could inflict injury on another by sticking pins into a miniature replica of the object of one's malice was centuries old and was the kind of "black magic" employed by some of the "witches." Whether some sort of telepathy was unwittingly employed is, of course, not known. "I know a Woman," wrote Cotton Mather, "whose Brother was tortured with a cruel, pricking, Incurable Pain in the Crown of his Head: which continued until there was found with her a Poppet in Wax, resembling him, with a pin stuck into the Head of it; which being taken out, he Recovered Immediately." See the "Mather-Calef Paper (note 21 above), p. 265.

23. See Gerald B. Gardner's *Witchcraft To-day* (Citadel Press, New York, 1955) for the story of the current practice of witchcraft in the British Isles; M. H. Wilson's "Witch Beliefs and Social Structure" (in South Africa), the *Amer. J. of Sociol.,* v. 56 (1951) pp. 307–313; Clyde K. Kluckhohn's "Navaho Witchcraft," (Harvard University, 1944, *Papers of the Peabody Museum,* v. 22, no. 2); or William B. Seabrook's *Witchcraft, its Power in the World To-day,* (Harcourt Brace & Co., New York, 1940).

24. Some attempts have been made to explain the actions of the "afflicted" girls in terms of hysterical behavior, involuntary, and of unconscious motivation, without any special malice toward the accused. See Edward W. Taylor's "Some Medical Aspects of Witchcraft," (Harvard Medical School, Cambridge, 1927). Dr. Taylor was professor of neurology at Harvard. For an explanation of the sexual basis of witchcraft see Jones (note 6 supra). Abundant evidence of the sexual symbolism of witchcraft rituals can be found in *The Encyclopedia of Witchcraft and Demonology,* by Russell H. Robbins (Crown Publishers, New York, 1960). For the psychic explanation see Josiah P. Quincy in "The Supernormal in New England History" in *Mass. Hist. Soc. Proc.,* v. 40 (1906) pp. 439–453; or Barrett Wendell (1855–1921), professor of English at Harvard University, writing in 1892 when there was a great interest in the occult, in "Were the Salem Witches Guiltless?" *Hist. Coll. of the Essex Institute,* v. 29 (1892); or Allen Putnam's *Witchcraft of New England Explained by Modern Spiritualism* (Colby and Rich, Boston, 1880). Putnam had lectured in Boston on psychic phenomena, in which he was a firm believer. For the social and political explanation see *The Formative Years: 1607–1763,* by Clarence L. Ver Steeg (Hill and Wang, New York, 1964) p. 144.

25. Cotton Mather's *Wonders of the Invisible World* (see note 1 above) pp. 160–161.

26. Increase Mather's "Postscript" to his *Cases of Conscience . . .* (p. 288; see note 1 above).

27. Cotton Mather's *The Wonders of the Invisible World* (see note 1 above). The passages are taken out of their original order but not out of context.

28. Mather is here quoting from "the excellent Baxter" (Matthew Baxter), the renowned English Puritan preacher who had written a preface to one of Mather's books.

29. To those who asked why an omnipotent and loving God "permitted" the Devil to inflict such miseries on Christian communities, the Puritans had a ready answer: " 'T is true, the *Divels* can do *no Evil* without a special permission from our Great God whose *Kingdome Ruleth over all;* but from one end of the *Scripture* to the other wee here are entertained with Terrible Examples of the *Evil,* which the just Vengeance of Heaven has permitted the *Divels,* to do unto men that have hearkened unto the suggestions of those *Wicked ones*"—From the "Mather-Calef Paper," (see note 21 above).

30. The vast amount of historical and creative writing inspired by the drama of the Salem witch trials is a challenge to a bibliographer but we shall not attempt here to do more than point out a few useful sources: the official court records; the original documents on file in the *Massachusetts Archives* (particularly v. 135) now on microfilm; the archives and original papers on file at the Essex Institute and the Essex County Court House in Salem; Burr's volume (see note 7

above) of narratives by those who were on the spot; the Massachusetts Historical Society's *Collections* and *Proceedings;* and the Mathers' writings in particular, already referred to. For secondary sources, Charles W. Upham's *Salem Witchcraft with an Account of Salem Village and a History of Opinions on Witchcraft and Kindred Subjects* (Wiggin and Lunt, Boston, 1867) is considered the standard work on this subject, thorough and well documented but by no means unbiased; *Witchcraft in Salem Village in 1692* by Winfield S. Nevins (Lee and Shepard, Boston, 1892) is also useful. A brief (sixty pages), accurate, and readable account is *Witchcraft in Salem Village* (part of a larger work on *New France and New England*) by the historian John Fiske (Houghton Mifflin Company, Boston, 1904). A more modern treatment in informal narrative style is the work of Marion L. Starkey, *The Devil in Massachusetts: A Modern Inquiry into the Salem Witch Trials* (Alfred A. Knopf, New York, 1950). Starkey's work contains a bibliography of references that are indispensable to the student of the Salem witchcraft episode.

31. "Demoniac possession" has not been an acceptable explanation for historians of the Salem outbreak of witchcraft. Various attempts have been made to explain how restless, sexually repressed, adolescent and preadolescent girls found Puritan theology frightening and exciting—not dull, as we may think of it today. Nevertheless, the hysterical behavior of the young girls, falling into fits with "hideous scrietch and noise" should not be considered a unique episode in American history. Today we hear reports not of a "witch mania," but of a "Beatlemania." Psychiatrist Bernard Saibel, child guidance expert for the Washington State Division of Community Services, reported a meeting in Seattle attended by 14,000 teenagers who came to see and to hear four young Englishmen known as "The Beatles" in a musical performance described as "loud, primitive, insistent, strongly rhythmic." The psychiatrist described his experiences (as reported in *The Boston Globe* of August 26, 1964) as "unbelievable and frightening. . . . it had the impact of an unholy bedlam, the like of which I have never seen. . . . The hysteria and the loss of control go far beyond the impact of the music. Many of those present became frantic, hostile, uncontrolled, screaming, unrecognizable beings . . . *as if possessed by some demonic urge,* defying in emotional ecstacy the restraints which authorities try to place on them." (Italics added.)

32. Hutchinson's *History* (see note 14 above) v. 2, p. 45.

33. Ibid, v. 2, pp. 27–30. We are quoting only that part of the hearing which concerned the Procters. We have made a few changes in format and punctuation and added words in brackets for clarification. We have made no word changes.

34. Sewall's *Diary,* p. 358.

35. Letter of Governor Phips, dated Oct. 12, 1692. From Burr, p. 196; (see note 7 above). For a narrative of his life, see "The Rise of William Phips" by Viola F. Barnes in *New Eng. Q.,* v. 1 (1928) pp. 271–294.

36. Ibid, p. 199, Phips' letter dated February 21, 1693.

37. The legality of the Court of Oyer and Terminer has been frequently debated. Washburn took the stand that, because it was illegally established in the first place, the court perpetrated "a series of judicial murders without a parallel in American History"—Emory Washburn in *Sketches of the Judicial History of Massachusetts, 1630–1775* (Charles C. Little & James Brown, Boston, 1840). But the court has had its defenders, too, although the preponderance of opinion leans towards Washburn's view. Had the law against witchcraft been voided by the cancellation of the Charter in 1684? Had Governor Andros, by proclamation a few years later, revived all existing Colonial laws not inconsistent with those of England? Had Governor Phips the authority to set up a special court without the express vote of the General Court which at that time had not yet convened? Were the court procedures and the rules of evidence any different from those in vogue in English courts? If the court had been legally established by the General Court, would the results have been any different? See "The Results of the Prejudice Against Lawyers in Massachusetts in the 17th Century" by Nathan Matthews, v. 13,

Mass. Law Q., v. 13, no. 5, pp. 73-94 (1928); see also discussions carried on in the *Mass. Hist. Soc. Proc.* v. 20 and 21 (1883–1884) by Abner C. Goodell and Peleg W. Chandler.

38. *Mass. Arch.*, v. 135, p. 101.

39. Robert Calef's *More Wonders of the Invisible World* as reproduced in Burr (see note 7 above) pp. 362–363. Calef, a Boston merchant, was Cotton Mather's severest critic. His book was printed in 1700 in London and was branded by Mather as a volume of "invented and notorious lies."

40. Ibid, pp. 358–359.

41. Ibid, pp. 289–393.

42. William Brattle's lengthy letter is reproduced by Burr pp. 169-190. See note 7 above.

43. Brattle's point was well taken, but the Court did not set up any controlled experiments. Intelligent men were skeptical, but the practice continued. Increase Mather wrote: "Sometimes the Power of Imagination is such, as that the Touch of a Person innocent and not accused shall have the same effect." He cited an English case where the experiment was tried. A person who was *not* accused as a witch touched the "afflicted" maid whose vision was cut off by an apron placed over her eyes, "which produced the same effect."—"Cases of Conscience" (see note 1 above) p. 263.

44. Calef's *More Wonders* in Burr, (see note 7 above) p. 354.

45. *The Wonders of the Invisible World* in Burr (see note 7 above) p. 164.

46. In "Mather Papers," *Mass. Hist. Soc. Coll.*, 4th ser., v. 8, p. 392.

47. Postscript to *Cases of Conscience* p. 286 (see note 1 above).

48. Ibid, pp. 289–291. In his Dairy entry on May 1, 1692, Cotton Mather said he had always testified against "spectral Representation both publickly and privately; and in my Letters to the Judges, I particularly, besought them, that they would by no means admitt it; and when a considerable Assembly of Ministers gave in their Advice about the Matter, I not only concurred with their Advice but it was *I* who drew it up"—Published in *Mass. Hist. Soc. Coll.*, 7th ser. v. 7, pp. 150–151.

49. *Cases of Conscience* p. 283 (see note 1 above).

50. Brattle's letter p. 187. (See note 42 above).

51. Poole (see note 14 above) believed that Brattle was referring to Cotton Mather.

52. *The Wonders of the Invisible World* p. 167 (see note 1 above).

53. Ibid, pp. 154–159.

54. For an account of the reasons given to Increase Mather by some of the witches for their confessions (later repudiated when the danger of hanging was past) see "Recantation of Witchcraft, Oct. 19, 1692" in *Mass. Hist. Soc. Coll.*, v. 3, 2d ser., pp. 221-225.

55. Hutchinson's *History* v. 2, p. 44 (see note 13 above).

56. See p. 493.

57. Increase Mather's *Further Account of the Tryals of the New-England Witches* as reproduced in Burr, pp. 209–210 (see note 7 above). The Rev. Deodat Lawson, former pastor at Salem prior to the outbreak, also reports this case in his *Brief and True Narrative* (Burr, p. 160) evidently getting his report from Mather.

58. Calef's *More Wonders* in Burr, p. 376 (see note 7 above).

59. Ibid, p. 373.

60. Ibid, p. 375–376.

61. Body of Liberties (1641), no. 45; Col. Laws (1648) p. 50; (1660) p. 187; (1672) p. 129.

62. Calef's *More Wonders* in Burr p. 363 (see note 7 above).

63. Ibid, p. 373.

64. Historians of the Salem witchcraft prosecutions almost invariably report twenty executions. On the other hand, those who lived through this period and published their observations always reported nineteen. Technically, the latter

group is correct. Giles Corey was not tried; hence he was not condemned or executed. He was pressed to death for refusing to put himself on trial, his body yielding to the gradual pressures while his indomitable spirit precluded surrender. Counting Corey, and the two who died in prison while awaiting trial, we might say there were 22 "sacrifices" to the "witchcraft mania."

65. Sewall's *Diary,* p. 365.

66. MCR, v. 2, p. 195; v. 3, p. 114 (1647) ; Col. Laws (1648) p. 24; (1660) p. 153; (1672) p. 57.

67. Cotton Mather's *Wonders of the Invisible World* pp. 129–130; see note 1 above. "The Trials of Bridget Bishop and George Burroughs for Witchcraft" can be found in *American State Trials,* John D. Lawson, editor (F. H. Thomas Law Book Co., St. Louis, 1914) v. 1, pp. 514–530.

68. Rebecca's quiet fortitude through this ordeal has added a note of poignancy to that tragic summer in Salem. See Charles S. Tapley's *Rebecca Nurse: Saint but Witch Victim* (Marshall Jones Co., Boston, 1930) . Tapley wrote that it has been estimated that by 1930 Rebecca had 30,000 descendants. And none of them, we presume, was a witch. On July 30, 1892, the Nurse Monument Association held memorial exercises in Danvers Center to "commemorate the noblest feature of the shameful persecution . . . by adding to the monument it erected in 1885 to this most notable of the witch victims a granite tablet inscribed with the names of forty of her townspeople who endeavored, in the face of danger, to save her from her impending doom."—*The New York Times,* July 31, 1892.

69. Calef's *More Wonders* in Burr, p. 358.

70. Cotton Mather's *Wonders of the Invisible World* p. 148; see note 1 above.

71. Ibid, pp. 138–148.

72. Ibid, pp. 120–129. Increase Mather's remarks are from his *Cases of Conscience* p. 286; see note 1 above.

73. Calef's *More Wonders* in Burr, pp. 360–361; see note 7 above. Calef's hostility toward Cotton Mather was so strong we cannot be sure that his portrayal of the minister was always faithful to the truth. Fiske (note 30 above) questions whether Mather could have said that Burroughs himself was an impersonation of the devil.

74. Sewall's *Diary,* p. 363.

75. Calef's *More Wonders* in Burr, pp. 364-365; (note 7 above) ; also in Hutchinson's *History,* v. 2, p. 39.

76. Brattle's letter, p. 177; see note 7 above.

77. Calef's *More Wonders* in Burr, pp. 361-362; see note 7 above.

78. Ibid, p. 361.

79. Ibid, p. 361.

80. Ibid, p. 367. There was no doubt that Cory was then an old man, his age usually stated as about eighty. The records of the Essex County Court, however, show that one Gyles Corey (undoubtedly the same person, the name being variously spelled in the records) was "about 55 years" in 1672, making him about 75 in 1692. The records of that court also show that he was frequently involved in lawsuits with his neighbors, one describing him as "a very quarrellsom and contentious bad neighbor"—Essex County Court, v. 5, p. 54 (1672) ; v. 7, p. 91 (1678) .

81. Englishmen were familiar with this method of forcing a person to plead, but the Colonists had never before resorted to it, although, many years before the Salem trials, Governor Winthrop had threatened to invoke it. In 1638 when Dorothy Talbye stood accused of infanticide and appeared before the court "she stood mute a good space, till the governour [Winthrop] told her she should be pressed to death, and then she confessed the indictment"—Winthrop's *History,* v. 1, p. 336.

82. Sewall's *Diary,* p. 364.

83. "A Brief and True Narrative of Some Remarkable Passages Relating to sundry Persons Afflicted by Witchcraft, at Salem Village . . . " by the Rev. Deodat

Lawson, pastor in Salem Village from 1684 to 1688, as reproduced by Burr, p. 154; see note 7 above.

84. Ibid, p. 155. See also Calef's *More Wonders* in Burr, pp. 343-344 (note 7 above).

85. Lawson, pp. 156–157 (see note 83 above).

86. Calef's *More Wonders* in Burr, p. 367 (see note 7 above).

87. Ibid, p. 368.

88. Ibid, pp. 368–369 (italics added).

89. Ibid, p. 368.

90. Ibid, p. 367.

91. Ibid, p. 369. Again we cannot be sure that these were the exact words of Noyes nor, if they were his words, what connotation he intended.

92. Calef's *More Wonders* in Burr, p. 373.

93. Sewall's *Diary,* p. 367.

94. Ibid, p. 368.

95. Governor Phips' letter, pp. 196–198 (see note 7 above and note 98 below).

96. Hale's "A Modest Inquiry," p. 422 (see note 13 above).

97. Ibid, pp. 421, 423 (italics added).

98. Phips' letter of February 21, 1693, in Burr, p. 201 (see note 7 above). This letter first appeared in print in the *Mass. Hist. Soc. Proc.,* v. 21 (1884) pp. 340-342, copied from the Archives of the Public Record Office in London for Abner C. Goodell.

99. Prov. Laws, ch. 19 and 40 (1692–1693).

100. Prov. Laws, ch. 54 (1696–1697). See notes in Prov. Laws, Appendix (1692–1702) p. 531.

101. Sewall's *Diary,* p. 445.

102. From Calef's *More Wonders* as published in Burr, pp. 387–388 (see note 7 above). Also published in Upham, pp. 474–475 of v. 2 (see note 30 above).

103. "Cotton Mather's Diary," published in *Mass. Hist. Soc. Coll.,* 7th ser., v. 7, p. 215.

104. Ibid, p. 216.

105. From Hale's "Modest Inquiry," pp. 403, 425, 426, 427 (see note 13 above).

106. From Nevins' *Witchcraft in Salem Village in 1692,* p. 250 (see note 30 above).

107. Prov. Laws, Private Act no. 16 (1703) (Vol. 1 of the Appendix); *Mass. Arch.* v. 135, no. 124.

108. Prov. Laws, Private Act, no. 26 (1711) (Vol. 1 of the Appendix); see discussion of the passage of the attainder law in *Mass. Hist. Soc. Proc.* v. 20 and 21 (1883–1884).

109. Prov. Laws, ch. 80 (1711–1712) v. 4 of the Appendix. The six executed witches whose names were omitted in these laws were Bridget Bishop, Susanna Martin, Alice Parker, Ann Pudeator, Wilmot Reed, and Margaret Scott. Their convictions thus remained unreversed.

110. Prov. Laws, ch. 82 (1718) v. 4 of the Appendix.

111. Prov. Laws, ch. 93 (1724) v. 5 of the Appendix.

112. Chapter 145 of the Resolves of 1957.

113. See Senate Bill no. 50 (1959); Senate Bill no. 51 (1959); House Bill no. 91 (1960); House Bill no. 92 (1960). See also letter from Mr. Hatch to the *Record-American,* March 12, 1965. So far, Mr. Hatch's bills have not been passed by the General Court.

CHAPTER 15

1. Bradford's *History,* p. 332 (1631).

2. The term "New England" or "New-England" was used without precise geographical meaning. Captain John Smith thought of it as that region from Penobscot (now part of Maine) to and including Cape Cod, or from 45° of latitude to 41°. On the west its boundaries were undefined, for it reached out to a vague

"South Sea" (Pacific Ocean). "Massachusetts" and "New England" were sometimes used synonymously. See "The Name 'New England' as Applied to Massachusetts," by Albert Mathews, *Col. Soc. of Mass. Pub.*, v. 25 (1922–1924) pp. 382–390.

3. The number of books and articles relating the story of the Pilgrims runs into the thousands. A helpful bibliography can be found in George F. Willison's "Selected Bibliography" in his *Saints and Strangers* (Reynal and Hitchcock, New York, 1945) and in Samuel Eliot Morison's "Reading Suggestions" in his *Story of the "Old Colony" of New Plymouth, 1620–1692,* (Alfred A. Knopf, New York, 1960).

4. *Three Hundred Years of the General Court of Massachusetts, 1630–1930* (official publication of the Commonwealth, 1931).

5. Body of Liberties (1641) no. 1; also in Col. Laws (1648) p. 1; (1660) p. 121; (1672) p. 1.

6. From Nathaniel Ward's *The Simple Cobbler of Aggawam in America,* (London, 1647).

7. *Hutchinson Papers,* v. 2, pp. 132–133.

8. Ibid.

9. PCR, v. 11, pp. 95, 172.

10. Prov. Laws, 1694–1695, ch. 5. See Davis, A.M. in "The Law of Adultery and Ignominious Punishments" in Proceedings of the American Antiquarian Society, 1895.

11. From Joseph Nicholson's *The Standard of the Lord lifted up in New-England, in Opposition to the Man of Sin . . . with a warning from the Lord to the rulers and magistrates, priests and people of New-England; but more especially to the rulers and magistrates of the bloody town of Boston, who have put the servants of the living God to death,* p. 8 (Written in the Boston prison, published in London, 1660).

12. Bradford's *History,* p. 459ff (1642).

APPENDIX B

1. Josiah H. Benton, *The Lawyer's Official Oath and Office* (Boston Book Company, Boston, 1909).

2. As reprinted in the *Mass. Hist. Soc. Proc.*, v. 33 (1899–1900) p. 261.

3. Prov. Laws (1701-1702) ch. 7, effective June 21, 1702; *Mass. Archives,* v. 40, no. 716-717.

4. Massachusetts General Laws, ch. 221, sec. 38, derived from Commonwealth Laws, ch. 23, Acts of 1785.

APPENDIX C

1. See Felix Frankfurter's "Memorandum on 'Incorporation' of the Bill of Rights into the Due Process clause of the Fourteenth Amendment," *Harv. Law Rev.* v. 78 (1965) pp. 747–783; and Louis Henkin's "'Selective Incorporation' in the 14th Amendment," *Yale Law J.*, v. 73 (1963) pp. 74–88, in which he discusses the question whether the whole of the Federal Bill of Rights applies to the states under the Fourteenth Amendment.

2. One of the specific complaints against the King of Great Britain enumerated in the Declaration of Independence of 1776 was "for depriving us in many cases, of the benefits of Trial by Jury."

3. On the right to a jury trial and the right to waive this privilege, see Frank W. Grinnell, "John Winthrop and the Constitutional Thinking of John Adams," in *Mass. Hist. Soc. Proc.*, v. 63 (1929–1930) pp. 91–119; and Massachusetts General Laws, ch. 263, sec. 6.

4. In the celebrated case of Sacco and Vanzetti, who were tried for murder

committed in an armed robbery in Massachusetts, the jury found both defendants guilty of murder in the first degree on July 14, 1921, but their executions did not take place until August 23, 1927.

5. A Province government law of 1705 was written to keep men who were imprisoned solely for debt separated from men committed for crimes—an early step in the classification of prisoners. The law permitted a debtor a separate chamber and "liberty of the yard" if he could pay a small fee and put up a bond. The preamble to this law stated that "in divers counties within the Province, the prisons are so small that when there are any number of prisoners there are not rooms or apartments sufficient for receiving and securing of them, without lodging felons and other criminals, and prisoners for debt, together in one and the same room, *which ought not to be. . . .* "—Prov. Laws, (1705–1706) ch. 1 (italics added). This principle of separation was followed by both Province and Commonwealth governments.

6. See Bernard Ginsburg, "The New Poor Debtor Law," *Boston University Law Rev.*, v. 8 (1928) pp. 23–43.

APPENDIX D

1. Court of Assistants, v. 1, p. 115 (1677).
2. Hutchinson's *History*, v. 2, p. 56 (1692).
3. Gen. Laws, ch. 277, sec. 34.
4. Gen. Laws, ch. 277, sec. 79.

APPENDIX E

1. Col. Laws (1660) p. 206; (1672) p. 167. The final "etc." shortened the original form, which was, "So help you God, in our Lord Jesus Christ." Eventually the portion represented by "etc." was omitted.
2. Massachusetts General Laws, ch. 278, sec. 4.

INDEX